The Scottish Legal System

For Cherry, Toby, Honor and Rebecca

R M W

The Scottish Legal System

Fourth edition

Robin M White LLB, LLM, Cert Soc Anth, AIL, JP
Senior Lecturer in Law, University of Dundee

Ian D Willock MA, LLB, PhD
Emeritus Professor, University of Dundee

Published by
Tottel Publishing Ltd
Maxwelton House
41–43 Boltro Road
Haywards Heath
West Sussex
RH16 1BJ

Tottel Publishing Ltd
9–10 St. Andrew Square
Edinburgh
EH2 2AF

ISBN 978-1-84592-778-3
© Reed Elsevier (UK) 1993, 1999, 2003
First published by LexisNexis Butterworths 1993
Second edition 1999
Third edition 2003
Reprinted with amendments by Tottel Publishing Ltd 2006
© Tottel Publishing Ltd 2007
Fourth edition 2007

British Library Cataloguing-in-Publication Data
A catalogue record for this book is available from the British Library

Typeset by Phoenix Photosetting, Chatham, Kent
Printed and bound in Great Britain by
M & A Thomson Litho Ltd., East Kilbride, Glasgow

Preface

When the first edition of this book was published, devolution was not even a glint in politicians' eyes, while this fourth edition might just conceivably be the last published in the United Kingdom. Thus fast can things happen.

In the intervening years, there have been numerous large changes in the workings of the Scottish legal system to incorporate. Most obvious, of course, have been the introduction of devolution through the Scotland Act 1998 and the embedding of human rights through the Human Rights Act 1998. They were taken account of in the third edition, but since then, quite apart from updating in relation to those changes, other sorts of change have continued apace. These range from considerable alterations to the system of complaints about lawyers (partly incorporated in the revised third edition, though the changes are still uncompleted at the time of publication), to the introduction of a Supreme Court for the United Kingdom (also, as yet, uncompleted), by way of myriad other matters such as the continuing saga of the European Union, changes in the method of appointing judges, the insertion of District Courts into a 'unified' court system with a name change (again, as yet, uncompleted) and so on. (As in other parts of the law, it is clear that there never is a right time to produce a new edition).

However, what is most noticeable in this fourth edition is the splitting of a number of very lengthy chapters into a larger number of shorter ones (with a much fuller Contents page). So the change from eight chapters to 15 does not denote a near-doubling of size (though, by the iron Law of Expanding Editions, it is slightly longer than the last). In addition to this, and less obvious, is the consequential re-location of some material. Thus, for instance, discussion of the European Court of Justice has moved from the section on 'Europe' to the chapter on courts. It is hoped that this re-organisation is helpful.

In the labour of amending, correcting and updating, we have received considerable assistance from Jamie Marshall (entering his final LLB year at the time of publication), who read the whole of the third edition to make suggestions on inclusion, style and comprehensibility from a user point of view; from our colleagues Anne Duncan and David Hart (of Dundee University Law Library) in the sections on the citation and publication of legislation and precedent; from Philip Forte (University of Abertay Dundee) and Colin Munro (University of Edinburgh) who commented on the book from another users' point of view; and from other colleagues (though chiefly Colin Reid) in the Dundee School of Law, who pointed out useful examples and surprising occurrences for inclusion. None bears any responsibility for what appears.

We hope the book will continue to be of use in courses on the Scottish Legal System in Scottish universities and colleges, and of interest to general readers anywhere in the world who wish to learn about its subject matter.

We have endeavoured to state the law as at 1 July 2007.

Robin M White
Ian D Willock
July 2007

Contents

Preface v
Abbreviations xiii
Table of UK statutes xiii
Table of Scottish statutes xxi
Table of UK and Scottish statutory instruments xxiii
Table of European and International legislation xxvii
Table of cases xxxi

1   Introduction   1
    Why have law?   1
    Some kinds of law we all know   1
    So what exactly is law?   2
    The law of a state   3
    Is law a good or a bad thing?   5
    Law is always subject to change   5
    Law and power   7
    Law as a way of getting things done   7

2   Scotland – nation and state   9
    Nation and state   9
    The emergence of Scotland   10
    Early medieval Scotland   11
    The later Middle Ages   15
    The Reformation   21
    The Union of the Crowns   23
    The 17th century: religious feuds   24
    The 18th century   26
    The 19th century   30
    The 20th and 21st centuries   32
    Conclusion   35

3   Institutions   37
    Constitutions and constitutional reform   37
    The United Kingdom   38
    'Europe' – the Council of Europe and the European
        Convention on Human Rights   65

'Europe' – the European Union, including the European
   Community   75

4   Institutions – courts, judges and tribunals   85
   United Kingdom courts, tribunals and related institutions   85
   Court procedure   126
   Tribunals, other related institutions, and principal English and
      Welsh, and Northern Ireland courts   140

5   Sources of Law   157
   The meanings of 'sources of law'   157
   Ranking of sources   159
   The major formal sources of law   161
   The minor formal sources of law   164
   Quasi-sources   171

6   Legislation – European Community law   179
   The institutional background   179
   The meaning, types and styles of Community law   179
   The Community legislative processes   187
   The relationship between Community law and national systems
      in general, and the United Kingdom in particular   190
   Publication and citation of Community law   201

7   Legislation United Kingdom Parliamentary legislation
      (including the Human Rights Act 1998)   207
   The institutional background   207
   The nature and style of United Kingdom Parliamentary
      legislation (including human rights legislation)   207
   The United Kingdom Parliamentary legislative procedure   219
   Publication and citation of Great Britain and United Kingdom
      Parliamentary Legislation   237

8   Legislation – Acts of the Scottish Parliament   243
   The institutional background   243
   The nature and style of Scottish Parliamentary legislation   243
   The Scottish Parliamentary legislative process   250
   Publication and citation of Acts of the Scottish Parliament   257

9   Legislation – United Kingdom delegated legislation   261
   The institutional background   261
   The nature of delegated legislation   261
   Types of United Kingdom delegated legislation and their
      form   268

Ulra vires and judicial control of United Kingdom delegated
     legislation   278
Citation and Publication of United Kingdom delegated
     legislation   280

10 Legislation – Scottish Delegated legislation   283
     The institutional background   283
     The nature of Scottish delegated legislation   283
     Controls over delegated legislation and Scotland   289
     Types of delegated legislation in Scotland and their form   291
     Ultra vires and judicial control of delegated legislation in
         Scotland   292
     Citation and publication of delegated legislation in Scotland   292

11 Legislation - application and interpretation   295
     The application, construction and interpretation of
         legislation   295
     The need for application   296
     Modes of constructing and interpreting legislation   300
     The traditional mode of construction and interpretation of
         legislation in the United Kingdom   301
     Construction and interpretation on legislation by United
         Kingdom courts under the influence of Community law   321
     Modification of construction and interpretation by United
         Kingdom courts through the European Convention on
         Human Rights and the Human Rights Act 1998   329
     Modification of construction and interpretation by United
         Kingdom courts through the Scotland Act 1998   323

12 Judicial precedent – *Ratio decidendi, Obiter dicta* and
         Stare decisis   335
     Precedent as a source of law   335
     Ratio decidendi and *Obiter dicta*   344
     Stare decisis   354
     The system in practice – the civil courts   360
     The system in practice – tribunals   367
     The system in practice – the criminal courts   367
     Precedent and the European Court of Justice   372
     Precedent and the European Court of Human Rights   373

13 Judicial precedent – the law reports   375
     The nature and significance of law reports   375
     Citation of cases   377
     Form and content of law reports   382

Principal series of law reports   386
Electronic reporting and computerised retrieval of law
    reports   396

14 Legal services   399
The need for legal services   399
History of the legal profession   400
Legal professions?   405
Organisation of the legal profession   406
Legal expertise   408
Admission to the legal profession   413
Standards of practice and behaviour   414
New forms of organisation   417
Protection of the public   419
Complaints and discipline   422
Privileges   425
Alternative ways of delivering legal services   426

15 Law reform   441
Why law reform?   441
Pressures for law reform   442
The instruments of law reform   444

Appendix 1   461
A note on the nature of rules   461

Appendix 2   465
Scottish Courts (simplified)   465
    Civil courts   465
    Criminal courts   466
English and Welsh courts (simplified)   468
    Civil courts   468
    Criminal courts   469
Northern Ireland courts (simplified)   471
    Civil courts   471
    Criminal courts   472
Some United Kingdom tribunals   474

Appendix 3   477
'Europe'   477

Index   479

Abbreviations

AC	Law Reports, Appeal Cases (House of Lords and Privy Council) 1890–
All ER	All England Law Reports 1936–
App Cas	Law Reports, Appeal Cases (House of Lords) 1875–90
APS	Acts of the Parliament of Scotland (Record Edition, 12 vols)
Bell App	S S Bell's Scotch Appeals (House of Lords) 1842–50
CMLR	Common Market Law Reports 1962–
Ch	Law Reports, Chancery Division 1890–
Co Rep	Coke's Reports 1572–1616
Cox CC	Cox's Criminal Cases 1843–1941
ECR	European Court of Justice Reports 1954–
EHRR	European Human Rights Reports 1979–
F	Fraser's Session Cases 1898–1906
F(J)	Justiciary cases in Fraser's Session Cases 1898–1906
ICR	Industrial Cases Reports 1972–
IRLR	Industrial Relations Law Reports 1972–
Irv	Irvine's Justiciary Reports 1851–68
JC	Justiciary Cases 1917–
JLSS	Journal of the Law Society of Scotland
JR	Juridical Review
KB	Law Reports, King's Bench Division 1900–52
LJR	Law Journal Reports 1947–49
M	Macpherson's Session Cases 1862–73
Macq	Macqueen's House of Lords Reports 1851–65
Mor	Morison's Dictionary of Decisions (Court of Session) 1540–1808
PD	Law Reports, Probate, Divorce and Admiralty Division 1875–90
Pat	Paton's House of Lords Appeal Cases 1726–1821
QB	Law Reports, Queen's Bench Division 1891–1901, 1951–

QBD	Law Reports, Queens Bench Division 1874–90
R	Rettie's Session Cases 1873–98
R(J)	Justiciary cases in Rettie's Session Cases 1873–98
Rob	Robertson's Scotch Appeals (House of Lords) 1707–27
SC	Session Cases 1907–
SCCR	Scottish Criminal Case Reports 1981–
SCLR	Scottish Civil Law Reports 1987–
Shaw's Appeals	P Shaw's Scotch Appeals (House of Lords) 1821–26
SJ	Scottish Jurist 1829–73
SLT	Scots Law Times 1893–
SLT (Lands Tr)	Lands Tribunal for Scotland Reports in Scots Law Times 1971–
Swin	Swinton's Justiciary Reports 1835–41
TLR	Times Law Reports 1884–1952
WLR	Weekly Law Reports 1953–

Table of UK Statutes

[References are to page number]

	PAGE
Abolition of Domestic Rates (Scotland) Act 1987	220
Abortion Act 1967	235, 444, 453
Act for Securing the Protestant Religion and Presbyterian Church Government (Scotland) 1707	27
Act of Succession 1701	26
Act of Union with Scotland Act 1706	27, 39, 53, 172
Acts of Parliament (Commencement) Act 1793	211, 217
Acts of Parliament Numbering and Citation Act 1962	211
Administration of Justice Act 1956	309
Administration of Justice (Scotland) Act 1933	
s 16	285
Adoption Act 1930	446
Adoption Act 1976	215
Adoption (Scotland) Act 1978	215
Age of Legal Capacity (Scotland) Act 1991	234, 444
s 2 (3)	446
Agricultural Holdings (Scotland) Act 1991	148
Agricultural Wages (Scotland) Act 1949	50
AIDS (Control) Act 1987	442
Aliens Act 1705	26
Animals (Scientific Procedures) Act 1986	49
Anti-Terrorism, Crime and Security Act 2001	220, 225, 229, 331, 379
ss 21–23	69
Appellate Jurisdiction Act 1876	111, 113
Appellate Jurisdiction Act 1887	117
Appellate Jurisdiction Acts 1908	117
Arbitration Act 1971	303
Articles of Union 1707	27
Asylum and Immigration Act 1996	210, 214
Asylum and Immigration Appeals Act 1993	210
Asylum and Immigration (Treatment of Claimants, etc) Act 2004	210
Badgers Act 1991	435

	PAGE
Bankruptcy (Scotland) Act 1985	49
Bills of Exchange Act 1882	233
British Nationality and Status of Aliens Act 1914	210
British Nationality and Status of Aliens Act 1918	210
British Nationality and Status of Aliens Act 1922	210
British Nationality and Status of Aliens Act 1933	210
British Nationality and Status of Aliens Act 1943	210
British Nationality Act 1948	210
s 34(2)	217
British Nationality Act 1958	210, 217
British Nationality (Falkland Islands) Act 1983	210
British Nationality (Hong Kong) Act 1997	210
British Nationality Act 1964	210
s 3(3)	217
British Nationality (No 2) Act 1964	210
British Nationality Act 1965	210
British Nationality Act 1981	39, 187, 210
s 49	217
53	217
(2), (3)	217
(5)	218
Schs 1–9	219
Sch 4	216
Sch 7	216
British Railways Act 1992	212
Burgh Police (Scotland) Act 1892	
s 90	305
Capital Allowances Act 2001	209, 214, 232
Pts 1–12	214
Sch 1, Pt 2	215
Child Abduction and Custody Act 1985	308
Children and Adoption Act 2006	223
Children (Scotland) Act 1995	439
Civic Government (Scotland) Act 1982	270
s 110	276
112	270
ss 114, 115	276
Civil Defence (Grants) Act 2002	209

PAGE

Civil Jurisdiction and Judgments Act
    1982
    Pt II   100
    s 3(3)   325
    Sch 8   100
Climate Change and Sustainable
    Energy Act 2006 ch 19   234
Comhairle nan Eilan Siar (Eriskay
    Causeway) Order Confirmation
    Act 2000 c i   236
Communication Act 2003   232
Companies Act 1949 . . . . 233, 305
Companies Act 1981   232
Companies Act 1985 . . . . 232, 233
Company Directors Disqualification
    Act 1986
    s 25   217
Consolidated Fund and
    Appropriation Acts 212, 229
Consolidation of Enactments
    (Procedure) Act 1949 . . . . . . 211, 458
Constitutional Reform Act 2005 . . 43, 111,
                                        152, 220
    Pts 1-7   112
    Pt 5   218
    ss 1-6   218
    ss 1, 2   44
    s 3 . . . . 44, 89, 91
    5 . . . . 89, 91
    6   218
    ss 7, 8 . . . . 155, 218
    s 9   218
    ss 9–149   218
    s 17   44
    23   115
        (1)   112
    24   115
    25(1), (2)   115
    26(5)–(8)   116
    40(3)   117
    41 . . . . 112, 365, 371
    60   115
        (1)   116
    147   218
        (1)-(3)   218
    149   217
    Sch 8   116
    Sch 11 .112
Constitutional Reform Act 2006
    Pt 3   111
    s 23   116
    ss 26-31   116
Consular Fees Act 1980
    s 1(1)   265
Consumer Credit Act 1974   452
Consumer Protection Act 1987 . . .   198
    Pt I   325
    s 1   325

PAGE

Control of Pollution Act 1974   217
Court of Session Act 1808 . . . . 31, 342
Court of Session Act 1810   342
Court of Session Act 1825   342
Court of Session Act 1830   342
Court of Session Act 1988 . . . . . 104, 127,
                                        457
    s 1(1)   106
    2(6)   109
    5   270
Crime and Punishment (Scotland)
    Act 1997   133
    s 25   138
    49   416
Criminal Defence Service (Advice
    and Assistance) Act 2001   209
Criminal Injuries Compensation Act
    1995   166
Criminal Justice Act 1982   295
Criminal Justice Act 1988 . . . . 34, 166, 305
    ss 108–117   166
Criminal Justice Act 2003 . . . . . . 154, 222
    s 103(1)   312
Criminal Justice (Terrorism and
    Conspiracy) Act 1998
    s 5   218
Criminal Law Act 1977   299
Criminal Law (Consolidation) Act
    1995   232
Criminal Procedure (Scotland) Act
    1975 . . . . 232, 316
    s 289E(2)   299
        (5)(a)   300
    457A(1)(b)   299
Criminal Procedure (Scotland) Act
    1987 c46   241
Criminal Procedure (Scotland) Act
    1995 . . . . 102, 131, 211,
                                    231, 232, 457
    s 3(3)   102
    5 102
    92(3)   131
    150(3)   247
        (3A), (3B)   247
        (4)   247
    194   232
    194A 138, 232
    ss 194B–194I   232
    s 195   232
    196   136
    219(8)   102
    225   96
    234   233
    ss 234A–234K   232
    s 235   233
    245   233
    ss 245A–245H   233
    s 246   233

	PAGE
Criminal Procedure (Scotland) Act 1995 – *contd*	
s 259	459
ss 302, 303	136
s 305	271, 285
Sch 9A	138
Dangerous Dogs Act 1991	220
Dangerous Drugs Act 1965	
s 5	314
Data Protection Act 1998	49
Debtors (Scotland) Act 1987	458
Deregulation and Contracting Out Act 1994	266
Disability Discrimination Act 1975	50
District Courts (Scotland) Act 1975	92
Dundee Gas Order Confirmation Act 1921	231
Easter Act 1928	217
Edinburgh Poor Relief Act 1800	231
Education (No 2) Act 1986	
s 48	71
Education Reform Act 1988	
s 23	265
ss 202–208	270
Education (Scotland) Act 1962	279
Education (Scotland) Act 1980	147
Pt IV	280
s 114(2)	280
Education (Scotland) Act 1981	
Sch 6, para 13	280
Education (Student Loans) Act 1990	265
s 1(1)	265
(2)(a)	265
s 1(2)(b)	265
Sch 2	265
Employment Act 1980	
s 17(8)	306
Employment Act 2002	443
Employment Rights Act 1996	443
s 8(4)(a)	171
Enactments (Procedure) Act 1949	231, 232
English Bill of Rights	25
Enterprise Act 2002	209
Schs 1–36	219
Equal Pay Act 1970	50, 125, 190, 198
s 1(2)(c)	328
Equality Act 2006	75
European Communities Act 1972	3, 54, 157, 160, 196, 198, 199, 288, 325, 326, 327
s 2(1)	196, 198
(2)	198, 265, 272, 274, 287, 324
(4)	198
3	372

	PAGE
European Communities Act 1972 – *contd*	
s 3(1)	196, 326
(2)	196
Sch 2	198
European Parliamentary Elections Act 1999	230
Extradition Act 1870	338
Family Law (Scotland) Act 1985	
s 9(1)(a)	2
Finance Acts	212, 229
Finance Act 1933	314
Finance Act 1976	310
Finance Act 1995	
s 160	232
Finance Act 2000	
Schs 1–40	219
Finance (No 2) Act 1940	279
Financial Services Act 1986	411
Fire Services Act 1947	58
Food and Environmental Protection Act 1985	
s 1(1), (2)	317
(6)	317
Sch 1, para 1(d)	317
Foreign Jurisdiction Act 1890	265
Game Act 1773	305
Gaming Act 1968	317
Gender Recognition Act 2004	
s 19(3)	305
25	304
George Donald Evans and Deborah Jane Evans (Marriage Enabling) Act 1987	235
HBOS Group Reorganisation Act 2006 ch i	236
Heritable Jurisdictions (Scotland) Act 1746 c 43	17, 98
Higher Education Act 1998	230
Highways Act 1959	232
Highways (Scotland) Act 1771	317
House of Lords Act 1999	45
Housing Act 2004	51, 249
Housing (Homeless Persons) Act 1977	449, 453
Human Rights Act 1998	4, 54, 66, 71, 72, 73, 74, 75, 88, 121, 157, 159, 172, 207, 208, 220, 224, 228, 229, 245, 251, 253, 254, 267, 295, 296, 301, 303, 309, 321, 330, 332, 370, 373
s 1	72, 228
2	229, 330, 350, 357, 360, 361, 364, 367, 368, 370, 371, 373
3	229, 330, 333
(1)	330, 333

PAGE

Human Rights Act 1998 – *contd*
s 3(2) 331
ss 4, 5 331
s 6 .... 73, 229
   (3), (4) 73
7 .... 73, 229
   (7) 73
8 .... 73, 229
10 .... 265, 332
19 .... 210, 225, 229
21(1) 244, 284
Sch 1 .... 72, 74, 228
Sch 2 332
Sch 11 74
Human Tissue Act 2004 442
Hunting Act 2004 230
Immigration Acts 210
Immigration Act 1971 210
s 4(3) 273
28 213
ss 28A-28K 213
s 29 213
33 215
Immigration Act 1988 210
Immigration and Asylum Act 1999 .. 210, 277
ss 1–31 214
s 22 214
ss 32–43 214
s 83(1), (2) 263
   (4) 271, 272
85(3) 263
87(3)(e) 213
   (ea) 213
   (f) 213
ss 128–139 213
s 169(2) 216
Sch 5, Pt 1 .... 271, 272
Sch 6 263
Sch 15 216
Immigration, Asylum and Nationality
   Act 2006 .... 210, 220
s 64(2) 210
Income and Corporation Taxes Act
   1988 .... 209, 232
Income Tax (Earnings and Pensions)
   Act 2003 232
Industrial Training Act 1964 141
Insolvency Act 1986 217
s 120(3) 101
Interpretation Act 1978 .... 211, 308
s 3 235
Judicial Committee Act 1833 .... 117, 119
Judicial Committee (Amendment)
   Act 1895 117
Judicial Pensions and Retirement Act
   1993
s 26(4)–(7) 108
Sch 6, para 10 99

PAGE

Land Registration (Scotland) Act 1979
s 30(2) 287
Law Agents (Scotland) Act 1873 .. 404
Law Commissions Act 1965 454
s 2(2) 455
3 .... 455, 457
   (1)(b) 457
Law Reform (Miscellaneous
   Provisions) (Scotland) Act 1966
s 4 446
Law Reform (Miscellaneous
   Provisions) (Scotland) Act
   1990 .... 275, 405, 440, 451
ss 1–75 451
s 16 440
24 426
30 .... 418, 425
31 418
   (3) 418
32 419
34 424
35 107
   (3) 108
36 407
37 404
Schs 1–9 451
Laws of the Marches 1249 10
Legal Aid (Scotland) Act 1986 .. 427, 428
s 17(2B) 432
18 .... 430, 432
19 .... 430, 432
23 430
24 430
   (3) 430
25 430
28A 133
   (9A) 133
Legal Aid and Solicitors (Scotland)
   Act 1949 .... 405, 427
Legislative and Regulatory Reform
   Act 2006 .... 198, 208, 233, 234,
                  266, 264, 274, 279
Part 1 .... 266, 267
s 1 266
   (3) 266
   (6) 267
s 2 266
3 267
4 266
5 267
6 267
8 267
9 267
13 274
ss 14–18 275
Licensing (Scotland) Act 1976 452
Life Peerages Act 1958 45
Limited Partnerships Act 2000 417

PAGE

Local Government (Scotland) Act
1973 .... 222, 275
s 201 .... 236, 270, 288
(1) 272
(2) 275
202 .... 270, 276, 288
(4)–(7) 275
202A 276
203 .... 270, 288
Local Government (Scotland) Act 1994
s 74 303
79 303
Maplin Development Act 1973 c64   236
Marine etc Broadcasting (Offences)
Act 1967 c41 232
Marriage (Scotland) Act 1977 158
Matrimonial Homes (Family
Protection) (Scotland) Act 1981   452
Mental Health (Public Safety and
Appeals) (Scotland) Act 1999 .   73
Mental Health (Scotland) Act 1984 .   428
Mental Health (Scotland) Act 1999 .   211
Mental Health (Amendment)
(Scotland) Act 1999 244
Mercantile Law Amendment Act
1856 32
Merchant Shipping Act 1988 196
Merchants House of Glasgow
(Crematorium) Order
Confirmation Act 1950 14 Geo
6 ch xxvi 231
Military Lands Act 1892
Pt II 279
Misuse of Drugs Act 1971 .... 49, 441
s 5 318
Murder (Abolition of Death Penalty)
Act 1965 215
Mussel Fishery (Cockenzie) Order
Confirmation Act 1894 231
National Health Service (Scotland)
Act 1978 147
Nationality, Immigration and Asylum
Act 2002 210
s 5(b) 213
140(3) 213
Niall Mcpherson Indemnity Act
1954, c 29 236
Northern Ireland Act 1974
s 1(3), (4) 264
Sch 1(1)(b) 264
Northern Ireland Act 1998 264
Northern Ireland Act 2000 264
Northern Ireland Constitution Act
1973
ss 2, 3 264
Occupiers' Liability (Scotland) Act
1960 454
Official Secrets Acts 1911-89 ..... 49, 210

PAGE

Official Secrets Act 1911
s 2 211
Official Secrets Act 1989 ...... 211, 212,
218
s 15 218
16(2) 210
Outer Space Act 1986
s 1 218
14 218
Papal Bull of Paul III 1535 105
Parliamentary Commissioner Act
1967 150
Parliament Acts 212
Parliament Act 1911 ...... 211, 212, 230,
275
Parliament Act 1949 .... 230, 275
Pittenweem Harbour Order
Confirmation Act 1992 236
Planning and Compensation Act
1991 222
Police and Criminal Evidence Act
1984 66
Police (Scotland) Act 1857 30
Police (Scotland) Act 1967
s 4 286
Prescription and Limitation
(Scotland) Act 1973
s 3 171
Prevention of Crimes Act 1871 ... 319
s 7 319
Prevention of Damage By Rabbits
Act 1939 2 & 3 Geo 6 c44 ... 241
Prevention of Terrorism Act 2005 ... 229,
331
Prevention of Terrorism (Temporary
Provisions) Act 1984 69
Prevention of Terrorism (Temporary
Provisions) Act 1989
s 27 215
Price's Patent Candle Co Ltd Act
1992 cxvii 241
Prisons (Scotland) Act 1989 231
Private Legislation Procedure
(Scotland) Act 1936 .... 236, 255
Proceeds of Crime Act 2003 34
Procurators (Scotland) Act 1865 .. 404
Peerage Act 1963 45
Race Relations Act 1968
s 3(1) 304
Race Relations Act 1976 .... 50, 157,
307, 308
s 1(1)(b)(iii) 213
3(1) 300
(3) 304
20 304
(1), (2) 304
Railtrack (Waverley Station) Order
Confirmation Act 2000 ch vi .. 236

PAGE

Railways Act 1993
  s 129   271
    (2)(c)   271
Reformation Act 1560   22
Regulatory Reform Act 2001 . . . 266, 268
Rent Act 1977
  Sch 1, para 4(2)   331
Representation of the People Act
    1983
  s 3(1)   120
Representation of the People
    (Scotland) Act 1832
  s 11   316
Representation of the People
    (Scotland) Act 1868   315
River Humber (Upper Pyewipe
    Outfall) Act 1992   236
Road Safety Act 1967   442
Road Traffic Act 1988 . . . . 49, 264
  ss 6–8   442
  s 38   174
Road Traffic Act 1991   222
Road Traffic Offenders Act 1988
  s 54 . . . .   7, 49
Road Traffic Regulation Act 1984 . .   264
Roads (Scotland) Act 1984
  s 37(1)(b)   278
    (6)   278
  38(1), (2)   278
  143(1)   278
Royal Assent Act 1967   211
Sale of Goods Act 1893   32
Scotland Act 1978 . . . . 211, 244
Scotland Act 1998 c46 . . . . 15, 38, 46, 47,
                    53, 73, 160, 172, 210,
                    211, 220, 226, 236,
                    239, 244, 255, 262,
                    263, 265, 283, 284,
                    285, 286, 289, 295,
                    296, 301, 303, 321,
                    332, 451, 459
  Pt IV   254
  ss 6–8   52
  s 23   452
    (8)   451
  27(1)   56
    (8)   54
  28   52
    (2)   250
    (6)   245
    (7) 51, 209, 244, 248
  29 . . . . 50, 52, 62, 229,
                                        333
    (1)   64
    (2)(c), (d)   64
    (3) 53, 333
    (4) 53, 451
  30 . . . .   50, 64

PAGE

Scotland Act 1998 c46 – *contd*
  s 30(2) 48, 266
  31   251
  32   253
  33 . . . . 42, 253
  35   253
  36   252
    (3) 451, 459
  37   15
  44(1)   55
  45(1)   56
  46   56
  47(1), (2)   56
  48(1)   56
  51   57
  52 . . . .   57, 59
  53 . . . . 57, 59, 64, 98, 198, 275
  54 . . . . 57, 59, 64, 229
  56   57
  57 . . . . 57, 287
    (1)   198
    (2) 57, 64, 333
  58 . . . . 41, 58
  63 . . . . 58, 59
  64(1)   61
  ss 73–75   61
  s 87   42
  ss 88–90   58
  s 89   266
  93   58
  95   109
    (4)   107
    (6)–(11)   109
  100   62
  101 . . . . 332, 333
  104 . . . . 262, 266
  ss 105, 106   266
  s 107 . . . . 248, 266
  108   58
  ss 113, 114   266
  s 115   274
  118   290
  126(4), (5)   53
  127   215
  Sch 3, para 6   451
  Sch 4 . . . . 53, 64, 266
  Sch 5 . . . . 48, 64, 266
  Sch 6   62
  Pt II   42
  Sch 7   274
  Sch 8, para 5   236
Scottish Borders Council (Jim Clark
    Memorial Rally) Order
    Confirmation Act 1996   236
Scottish Enterprise Act 1999   211
Scottish Legal Services Ombudsman
    Etc Act 1997
  s 2   425

PAGE

Senior Court Act 1981   109
Sex Discrimination Act 1975 . . . 6, 50, 307,
                                    328
  s 1   304
  4   304
  6(2)   194
  80(1)   265
    (3)   265
Sex Discrimination Act 1986   190
Sexual Offences (Amendment) Act
  2000   230
Sheriff Courts (Scotland) Act 1907 . .   97,
                                    127
Sheriff Courts (Scotland) Act 1971 .   97
  s 1   98
  4 . . . .   98, 99
  5   99
  6   98
  7 . . . . 98, 100, 101
  9   98
  11   99
  ss 11A–11D   99
  s 12   100
  ss 14–17   98
  ss 24, 25   98
  s 32   271
  ss 35–38   101
  ss 41, 42   101
  s 65A   99
Short Titles Act 1896 . . . . 210, 211
Small Landholders (Scotland) Act
  1911   58
Social Security Act 1980
  ss 9, 10   272
  Sch 3   272
Social Security Act 1986 . . . . 33, 452
  s 20   268
Social Security Act 1989
  Sch 9   216
Social Security Act 1998
  s 4   140
  Sch 1   140
Social Security Administration Act
  1992
  Pt IV   433
Solicitors (Scotland) Act 1933   405
Solicitors (Scotland) Act 1980 . . . 405, 452
  Pt V   404
  s 1(2)   408
  34 . . . . 175, 272
  35   175
  s 39A   421
  ss 42A–42C   421
  s 43   419
  ss 50–54   424
  s 53   175
  53A   421
  Sch 4, Pt I   424

PAGE

Solicitors (Scotland) Act 1988   405
Solicitors (Scotland) Act 1991   234
Special Immigration Appeals
  Commission Act 1997   210
Statute Law (Repeals) Act 2004 c14 .   231
  Sch Pts 1–10   231
Statute Law Revision (Scotland) Act
  1906   231
Statute Law Revision (Scotland) Act
  1964   210
Statutory Instruments Act 1946 . . .   273,
                                    277
  ss 2–7   273
  s 3(2)   273
Statutory Orders (Special Procedure)
  Act 1945 . . . . 236, 256
Summary Procedure (Scotland) Act
  1864   304
Supreme Court Act 1981   109
Supreme Court of Judicature Act
  1873   112
Supreme Court of Judicature Act
  1875   112
Taking of Hostages Act 1982
  s 1   218
Teaching and Higher Education Act
  1998   265
Telecommunications Act 1984   232
Tenants' Rights Etc Act 1980   306
Terrorism Act 2000   69
Terrorism Act 2006   220
Tobacco Advertising and Promotion
  Act 2002 ch 36   223
  s 21   287
  22(1)   287
Trade Union and Labour Relations
  (Consolidation) Act 1992
  s 199   175
  207   175
Transport Act 1962
  s 67 . . . . 271, 275
Transport Act 1982
  s 27   7
Transport Act 1985
  s 125   174
Tribunals and Inquiries Act 1992 . .   144
  Sch 1, Pts I, II   144
Tweed Fishing Act 1859
  s 10   318
Unfair Contract Terms Act 1977 . .   34
United Reformed Church Act 2000 .   236
Universities (Scotland) Act 1889 . .   315
Universities (Scotland) Act 1966 . .   453
Valerie Mary Hill and Alan Monk
  (Marriage Enabling) Act 1985
  cl   241
War Crimes Act 1991 . . . . 230, 315
War Damage Act 1965 . . . . 315, 445

	PAGE		PAGE
Water Act 1989	211,	Wildlife and Countryside Act 1981	
	212	ss 60, 61	216
s 4	218	Wireless Telegraphy Act 1949	232
13	218	Wireless Telegraphy Act 1967	232
23	218	Wireless Telegraphy Act 1998	232
95	218	Wireless Telegraphy Act 2006	232
194(6)–(9)	218	Zambia Independence Act 1964 . . .	264
Sch 2	218	Zetland Masonic Sick and Widows	
Sch 5	218	and Orphans Fund Order	
Welsh Language Act 1967	212	Confirmation Act 1900	231

Table of Scottish Statutes

[References are to page number]

PAGE

Abolition of Feudal Tenure etc
   (Scotland) Act 2000 (asp 5) .. 13, 250
   s 1 459
   72 248
Act of 1424 on Legal Aid for the
   Poor APS II, 8 .... 401, 427
Act of 1455 APS II, 43 401
Act of 1535 Acta Dominorum
   Concilii III, 434, 438 427
Act of 1541 APS II, 371 105
Act of 1567 APS III, 41 401
Act of Security (Scotland) 1703 ... 26
Adults with Incapacity (Scotland) Act
   2000 (asp 4) 250
APS II, 238 21
APS II, 10 20
APS II, 105 20
APS VIII, 80 258
APS IX, 38 25
APS XI, 411 28
APS XI, 446 27
Sch 6 250
Bail, Judicial Appointments, Etc
   (Scotland) Act 2000 (asp 9) .. 74, 92,
                   99, 250
   s 7 99
Black Acts 1541 20
Budget (Scotland) Acts 254
Census (Amendment) (Scotland) Act
   2000 (asp 3) 209
Charter of Queen Mary 1563 398
Charter to the Abbey of Scone 1164 10
Claim of Right 1689 .... 25, 165
College of Justice Act 1532 c 2 105
Commissioner for Children and
   Young People (Scotland) Act
   2003 (asp 17) 255
Convention Rights (Compliance)
   (Scotland) Act 2001 (asp 7) . 244, 250
Council of the Law Society of
   Scotland Act 2003 (asp 14) ..255, 405,
                   452
Criminal Procedure (Amendment)
   (Scotland) Act 2002 (asp 4) .. 257
   s 1(1) 247
Criminal Procedure (Amendment)
   (Scotland) Act 2004 (asp 5) .. 135

PAGE

Criminal Procedure (Amendment)
   (Scotland) Act 2004 – contd
   s 6(5)(b) 135
Criminal Proceedings (etc) (Reform)
   (Scotland) Act 2007 (asp 6) .. 135
   Pt 4 92
   s 50 136
   ss 50–54 137
   ss 59–61 94
   s 62 97
   63 94
   67 95
   (7) 96
Declaration of Arbroath 1320 ...14, 15, 24
Debt Arrangement and Attachment
   (Scotland) Act 2002 (asp 17) .131, 458
   s 2(3)(a)(iii) 247
Dog Fouling (Scotland) Act 2003
   (asp 12) 255, 452,
                   453
Freedom of Information (Scotland)
   Act 2002 (asp 13) 7
Fur Farming (Prohibition) (Scotland)
   Act 2002 (asp 10) 246, 247
Homelessness etc (Scotland) Act
   2003 (asp 10) 453
Housing (Scotland) Act 2001 (asp 10)
   Sch 10 248
International Criminal Court
   (Scotland) Act 2001 (asp 13) . 246
Land Reform (Scotland) Act 2003
   (asp 2) 246, 247
   Pts 1–4 247
   ss 1–100 247
Laws of the Four Burghs. *See Leges et*
   Consuetudines Quatuor Burgorum
Legal Profession and Legal Aid
   (Scotland) Act 2007 (asp 5) . 405, 425,
                   427
Leges et Consuetudines Quatuor
   Burgorum 10
Mental Health (Public Safety and
   Appeals) (Scotland) Act 1999
   (asp 1) 246, 250
National Covenant of Scotland 1638 . 24
Protection from Abuse (Scotland)
   Act 2001 (asp 14) 448

PAGE

Protection of Wild Mammals
(Scotland) Act 2002 (asp 6) ..   73
Public Finance and Accountability
(Scotland) Act 2000 (asp 1) ..   250
Regulation of Care (Scotland) Act
2001 (asp 8)   259
Robin Rigg Offshore Wind Farm
(Navigation and Fishing)
(Scotland) Act 2003 (asp 19) .   256
Royal Mines Act 1424 c 13 .... 243, 258,
302
Salmon and Freshwater Fisheries
(Consolidation) (Scotland) Act
2003 (asp 15)   255
Scottish Commission on Human
Rights Act 2006 (asp 16)   74
ss 1–4   75
Sch 1   75
Scottish Public Services Ombudsman
Act 2002 (asp 11) 151, 246
Scottish Qualifications Authority Act
2002 (asp 14)
s 1(1)–(6)   249
(7)(a)(i)–(iii)   249
(b)   249

PAGE

Scottish Qualifications Authority Act
2002 – contd
(8), (9)   249
ss 2–6   249
Senior Judiciary (Vacancies and
Incapacity) (Scotland) Act 2006
(asp 9)   90
Statute of 1473   20
Statute of 1496   20
Stirling-Alloa-Kincardine Railway
and Linked Improvements Act
2004 (asp 10)   256
Test Act 1681   29
Theft Act 1607   255
Union with England Act 1707 .... 27, 53,
172, 258
Art XIX   15
University of St Andrews
(Postgraduate Medical Degrees)
Act 2002 (asp 15) 246, 453
s 2   249
Water Environment and Water
Services (Scotland) Act 2003
(2003 asp 3)
Schs 1-4   249

Table of UK and Scottish Statutory Instruments, Circulars, Codes of Practice etc

[References are to page number]

PAGE

A34 Trunk Road (Chievely Interchange) (40 Miles Per Hour Speed Limit) Order 2007, SI 2007/233 264

Act of Adjournal (Criminal Procedure Rules) 1996, SI 1996/513 .... 131, 267, 285

Act of Sederunt (Fees of Advocates in Speculative Actions) 1992, SI 1992/1897 407

Act of Sederunt) (Rules of Court) (Consolidation and Amendment) 1965, SI 1965/321 285

Act of Sederunt (Rules of the Court of Session) 1994, SI 1994/1443 .. 127
rule 260B 449

Act of Sederunt (Rules of the Court of Session Amendment No 7) (Miscellaneous) 1999, SSI 1999/109 289

Act of Sederunt (Rules of the Court of Session Amendment) (Witnesses' Fees) 1999, SI 1999/187 (S 9) 270

Act of Sederunt (Sheriff Court Ordinary Cause Rules) 1993, SI 1993/1956 127

Act of Sederunt (Ordinary Cause Rules, Sheriff Court) 1983, SI 1983/747 271

Act of Sederunt (Small Claim Rules) 2002, SSI 2002/133 127

Act of Sederunt (Summary Cause Rules) 2002, SSI 2002/132 ... 127

Admission as a Solicitor with Extended Rights (Scotland) Rules 1992 .... 412, 426

Advice and Assistance (Scotland) (Prospective Cost) (No 3) Regulations 1988, SI 1988/2288 (S 223) 277

Animals and Animal Products (Import and Export) (England) (Amendment) Regulations 2007, SI 2007/3 263

PAGE

British Gas Corporation (Disposal of Wytch Farm Oilfield Interest) Directions 1981, SI 1981/ 1459 269

British Nationality Act 1981 (Commencement) Order 1982, SI 1982/933 217

Cider and Perry and Wine and Made-wine (Amendment) Regulations 2007, SI 2007/4 263

Circular HSC(IS)32 176

City of Dundee District Bylaws for Prohibiting the Consumption of Alcohol in Designated Places 1995 262

Civil Jurisdiction and Judgments Order 2001, SI 2001/2929 Sch 2, para 6 100

Civil Procedure Rules 1998, SI 1998/3132 .... 153, 222

Civil Service Order 1982 165
Civil Service Order 1991 165
Civil Service Order 1995 165

Code of Conduct for Criminal Work 1996 .... 416, 431

Code of Conduct for Public Defence Solicitors in Scotland 133

Code of Conduct of the Bar Councils of the European Community 1988 / Cross-Border Code of Conduct 415

Code of Practice on Picketing under Trade Union and Labour Relations (Consolidation) Act 1992, s 199 175

Consular Fees (Amendment) Order 2006, SI 2006/1912 264

Crown Office Prosecution Code ... 132

Customs and Excise (Personal Reliefs for Special Visitors) (Amendment) Order 2007 SI 2007/5 263

Diplomatic Service Order in Council 1991 165

Diplomatic Service Order in Council (first) 1994 165

PAGE

Diplomatic Service Order in Council
(second) 1994   165
Diplomatic Service Order in Council
1995   165
Diplomatic Service Order in Council
2004   165
Dundee–Aberdeen Trunk Road
(A94) (Stracathro Junction)
(Prohibition of Specified Turn)
Order 1990, SI 1990/1829 . . .   273
Employment Code of Practice issued
under the Race Relations Act
1976   175
Environmental Impact Assessment
(Scotland) Regulations 1999,
SSI 1999/1   287
Equal Pay (Amendment) Regulations
1983, SI 1983/1794 . . . . 190, 198,
297, 311, 328
European Communities
(Designation) Order 2002, SI
2002/248   269
European Communities (Services by
Lawyers) Order 1978, SI
1978/1910   425
Faculty of Advocates Disciplinary
Code 1988   423
Faculty of Advocates Disciplinary
Code 2002   423
Feeding Stuffs (Application of 200
Technical Additives, etc)
(Scotland) Regulations 2005,
SI 2005/3362 (S13)   276
Fixed Penalty Order 2000, SI
2000/2792   136
Food Protection (Emergency
Prohibitions) (Amnesic Shellfish
Poisoning) (East Coast) (No 4)
(Scotland) Order 2003, SSI
2003/393
art 4   317
Food Protection (Emergency
Provisions) (Amnesic Shellfish
Poisoning) (West Coast) (No 12)
(Scotland) Order 2005, SSI
2006/6   292
Foreign Compensation (People's
Republic of China) Rules
Approval Instrument, SI
1988/153   269
Guidance issued under Transport Act
1985, s 125   174
Guide to the Professional Conduct of
Advocates 1988 . . . . 406, 415,
421, 423
5.10   407
9.6   407

PAGE

HMS Forest Moor and Menwith Hill
Station By-laws 1986   279
Highway Code   174
Housing (Grants for Fire Escapes in
Houses of Multiple Occupation)
(Prescribed Percentage)
(Scotland) Order 1990, SI
1990/2242   277
Human Rights Act 1998 (Designated
Derogation) Order 2001, SI
2001/3644 . . . . 69, 229
Immigration and Asylum Act 1999
(Commencement No 1) Order
1999, SI 1999/3190   277
Immigration and Asylum Act 1999
(Commencement No 16) Order
2004, SI 2004/297   277
Immigration and Asylum Appeals
(Procedure) Rules 2000, SI
2000/2333   269
Immigration (Registration with
Police) Regulations 1972, SI
1972/1758   273
Income Support (General) Regulations
1987, SI 1987/1967   268
Injuries in War (Shore Employment)
Compensation (Amendment)
Scheme 1990, SI 1990/1946 . .   269
Justice of the Peace (Scotland) Order
2007, SSI 2007/210 . . . . 95, 96
Law Society of Scotland 1989 Code
of Conduct for Scottish
Solicitors, revised 2002   415
Land Registration (Scotland) Act
1979 (Commencement No 12)
Order 1998, SI 1998/2980 . . .   287
Land Registration (Scotland) Act
1979 (Commencement No 13)
Order 1999, SSI 1999/111 . . .   287
Letters Patent of 14 February 1917 .   165
Maximum Number of Judges (Scotland)
Order 2004, SSI 2004/499
Art 2   106
Merchant Shipping (Registration of
Fishing Vessels) Regulations
1988, SI 1988/1926   196
Milk (Special Designations)
(Scotland) Order 1988, SI
1988/2191 (S 213)   277
Motor Vehicles (Tests) Regulations
1981, SI 1981/1694   264
Motor Vehicle (Variation of Speed
Limits) Regulations 1947,
SR&O 1947/2192   264
Motor Vehicle (Variation of Speed
Limits) Regulations 1986, SI
1986/1175   264

PAGE

Motorway Traffic (Speed Limit)
Regulations 1974, SI 1974/502 .   264
Nationality, Immigration and Asylum
Act 2002 (Commencement (No
1) Order 2002, SI 2003/1   277
Parliamentary Constituencies
(Scotland) Order 2005, SI
2005/250 (S1)   276
Pedal Cycles (Construction and Use)
Regulations 1983, SI 1983/1176 .   264
RAF Alconbury By-laws 1985   279
Regulatory Reform (Forestry) Order
2006, SI 2006/0780   268
Regulatory Reform (Game) Order
2007, SI 2007/2007   268
Requisitioning of Ships Order of 4
April 1982   165
Road Vehicles (Authorisation of
Special Types) General Order
2003, SI 2003/1998   264
Road Vehicles (Construction and
Use) Regulations 1986, SI
1986/1078   264
Royal Instructions of 14 February 1917   165
Scotland Act 1998 (Agency
Arrangements) (Specification)
Order 1999, SI 1999/1512 . . .   58
Scotland Act 1998 (Agency
Arrangements) (Specification)
Order 2002, SI 2002/261 (S 1) . .   285
Scotland Act 1998 (Agency
Arrangements) (Specification)
(No 3) Order 2006, SI
2006/3338   58
Scotland Act 1998 (Commencement)
Order 1998, SI 1998/3178 . . .   264
Scotland Act 1998 (Transfer of
Functions to the Scottish
Ministers, etc) Order 1999,
SI 1999/1750 . . . . 58, 269, 285
Scotland Act 1998 (Transfer of
Functions to the Scottish
Ministers, etc) Order 2006, SI
2006/304 (S 3)   58
Scotland Act 1998 (Transitory and
Transitional Provisions)
(Publication and Interpretation etc
of Acts of the Scottish Parliament)
Order 1999, SI 1999/1379
arts 4, 5   246
Sch 1, paras 11–14   248
Sch 2   248
Scotland Act 1998 (Transitory and
Transitional Provisions)
(Statutory Instruments) Order
1999, SI 1999/1096
art 2(1)   289

PAGE

Scotland Act 1998 (Transitory and
Transitional Provisions)
(Statutory Instruments) Order
1999 – contd
art 4(2)   289
5   291
arts 5–8   290
8, 9   292
Scottish Development Department
Memorandum No 85/1973 . . .   176
Scottish Home and Health
Department Circular 6/1992
(CPF/2/7) 30 April 1992   175
Scottish Legal Aid Board 1998 Code
of Practice affecting those
solicitors who are registered to
provide legal services
remunerated by Criminal Legal
Aid   416
Scottish Parliament (Disqualification)
Order 2002, SI 2003/409
(S 4)   285
Scottish Qualifications Authority Act
2002 (Commencement No 1)
Order 2002, SSI 2002/335
art 3(2)   249
70mph, 60mph and 50mph
(Temporary Speed Limit) Order
1977   264
70mph, 60mph and 50mph
(Temporary Speed Limit)
(Continuation) Order 1978, SI
1978/1548   264
Sheriff (Removal from Office) Order
1992, SI 1992/1677   100
Statutory Maternity Pay
(Compensation of Employers)
Amendment Regulations 2002,
SI 2002/225   269
Solicitors Accounts Rules   175
Solicitors (Scotland) Accounts
Rules   417
Solicitors Code of Conduct   410
Solicitors Practice Rules   175
Southern Rhodesia (United Nations
Sanctions) Order 1968   275
Teachers (Education, Training and
Certification) (Scotland)
Regulations 1967,
SI 1967/1162   275
Temporary Speed Limit
(Continuation) Order 1978, SI
1978/1548   264
Tobacco Advertising and Promotions
Act 2002 (Commencement No
5) (Scotland) Order 2003, SSI
2003/11 (C5)   287

PAGE

Tobacco Advertising (Commencement)
(Scotland) Order 2002, SSI
2002/512 (C26) 287

Tobacco Advertising
(Commencement No 4)
(Scotland) (Amendment and
Transitional Provisions) Order
2003, SSI 2003/80 (C3) 287

Town and Country Planning
(Determination of Appeals by
Appointed Persons)
(Prescribed Classes) (Scotland)
Amendment Regulations 1989,
SI 1989/577 277

Town and Country Planning
(General Development)
(Scotland) Order 1959, SI
1959/1361 316

PAGE

Trading with the Enemy
Proclamation 1914 165

Transfer of Undertakings (Protection
of Employment) Regulations
1981, SI 1981/1794 328
reg 5(3) 310

Travellers Charter (HM Revenue &
Customs) 177

Water Bylaws (Milngavie Waterworks,
Loch Katrine, Loch Arklet, Glen
Finglas) Extension Order 1990,
SI 1990/2250 277

Woodland Grants Scheme Applicants
Charter for England (Forestry
Commission) 177

Zambia Independence Order 1964,
SI 1964/1652
Sch 2 264

Table of European and International Legislation

[References are to page number]

PAGE

Accession Treaties 182
Accession Treaties 1973, 1981, 1986,
    1995, 2007 80
Brussels Convention Relating to the
    Arrest of Seagoing Ships 309
Charter on Fundamental
    Freedoms 79
Commission Regulation (EEC) No
    417/85 of 19 December 1985 on
    the application of Art 85(3) of
    the Treaty to categories of
    specialisation agreements 184
Convention on Jurisdiction and
    Enforcement of Judgments . . . 182
Convention on the Civil Aspects
    of International Child
    Abduction 308
Council Directive of 16 August 1961
    on administrative procedures
    and practices governing the
    entry into and employment and
    residence in a Member State of
    workers and their families from
    other Member States of the
    Community 323
Council Directive 64/221/EEC of 25
    February 1964 on the
    coordination of special measures
    concerning the movement and
    residence of foreign nationals
    which are justified on grounds of
    public policy, public security or
    public health OJ L56 of
    04.04.1964 p 850 (S Edn
    1963-4 p 117) 193, 205,
                                        323
Council Directive 80/987/EEC of 20
    October 1980 on the
    approximation of the laws of the
    Member States relating to the
    protection of employees in the
    event of the insolvency of their
    employer 194,
                                        195
Council Directive 68/151/EEC, First
    Directive on Company Law
    Harmonisation 205

PAGE

Council Directive 77/187/EEC of 14
    February 1977 on the
    approximation of the laws of the
    Member States relating to the
    safeguarding of employees' rights
    in the event of transfers of
    undertakings, businesses or parts
    of businesses 328
Council Directive 77/249/EEC of 22
    March 1977 to facilitate the
    effective exercise by lawyers of
    freedom to provide services . . . 418
Council Directive 86/113/EEC laying
    down minimum standards for
    the protection of laying hens
    kept in battery cages 185
Council Directive 87/328/EEC of 18
    June 1987 on the acceptance for
    breeding purposes of pure-bred
    breeding animals of the bovine
    species (Directive on Animal
    Semen) 205
Council Directive 90/364/EEC of 28
    June 1990 on the right of
    residence (OJ 1990 L180/26) .202, 205
Council Directive 93/104/EC of 23
    November 1993 concerning
    certain aspects of the organization
    of working time 180
Council Regulation No 15 of 16
    August 1961 on initial measures to
    bring about free movement of
    workers within the Community . 323
Council Regulation 1251/70/EEC on
    the right to remain in the
    territory of a Member State after
    having been employed in that
    State, OJ L124, 30.6.70, p 24 (S
    Edn 1970 (II), p 402 205
Directive 84/253/EEC, Eighth
    Council Directive of 10 April
    1984 based on article 54(3)(g) of
    the Treaty on the approval of
    personsresponsible for carrying
    out the statutory audits of
    accounting documents (OJ 1984
    L126/20) 186

PAGE

Directive 85/347/EEC, Products
  Liability Directive (OJ 1985 L
  183/22) 198
EEC Treaty 1957 (Treaty of Rome)
  (now EC Treaty) ... 76, 77, 172, 179,
                  182, 183, 190, 197,
                        203, 205
  preamble 76, 183
  Pts I–III 183
  Pt V 183
  Pt V Titles I-XXI 183
  Pt V Title I Chapter 1, sections 1-5   183
  Pt V Title VII Chapters 1-5 183
  Arts 1-2 76
  Art 2 192
  Arts 3-4 .... 76, 77
  Art 7 (ex Art 4) 325
    10 (ex Art 5) 194
    12 (ex Art 6) 197
    14 (ex Art 7a; ex Art 8a) 183
    18 (ex Art 8a) 183
    25 (ex Art 12) 191, 193
    28 (ex Art 30) 326
  Arts 39-41 (ex Arts 48-50) 193
  Art 39(1) (ex Art 48(1)) 322
    (3)(b) (ex Art 48(3)(b)) .. 184
    40 (ex Art 49) 184
    43 (ex Art 52) 184
    46(2) (ex Art 56(2)) 323
    48 (ex Art 58) 197
    94 (ex Art 100) 180, 187
    137 (ex Art 118) 187
    138 (ex Art 118a) 180
    141 (ex Art 119) 125, 190, 192
    202 EC 81
    205 EC 183
    211 (ex Art 155) 186
    230 (ex Art 173) 180
    231 (ex Art 174) 180
    234 (ex Art 177) 125, 183, 190,
                  191, 192, 193,
                  194, 196, 197,
                  203, 326, 327,
                  357, 372, 373,
                  392, 449
    249 (ex Art 189) 184, 185, 186,
                  190, 193, 195,
                  325
    251 (ex Art 189b) 189
    252 (ex Art 189c) 188
    253 (ex Art 190) 185, 205, 322
    254 (ex Art 191) 185, 205
    272 (ex Art 203) 183
    281 (ex Art 210) 183
    308 (ex Art 235) 180, 187
Second to Fifth Protocols 184
Sixth Protocol (Statute of the
  European Court of Justice) ... 184

PAGE

Equal Pay Directive, Council Directive
  75/117/EEC of 10 February 1975
  on the approximation of the laws
  of the Member States relating to
  the application of the principle of
  equal pay for men and women .   125,
                  190, 198, 328
Equal Treatment Directive, Council
  Directive 76/207/EEC of
  9 February 1976 on the
  implementation of the principle
  of equal treatment for men and
  women as regards access to
  employment, vocational training
  and promotion, and working
  conditions 186, 190, 194, 323
European Convention on Human
  Rights and Fundamental
  Freedoms 3, 37, 40, 41, 54,
             58, 63, 64, 66, 67, 70,
             71, 72, 73, 74, 75, 79,
             87, 121, 159, 160, 163,
             179, 181, 195, 208, 228,
             229, 244, 253, 295, 296,
             301, 309, 324, 329, 330,
             332, 366, 373
  Arts 1–16 68
  Art 1 .... 70, 72, 228
    3 .... 69, 70, 120,
                  373, 379
    5 .... 69, 73, 220,
                  229, 374, 379
    (1)(f) 69
    (3) 69
  Art 6 .... 65, 74, 95, 99,
                  291, 374
    7 .... 181, 338, 370
    8 73
    13 .... 72, 228
    14 73
    15 .... 72, 228
  Arts 17, 18 69
  Art 34 .... 71, 73
    35 122
    43 122
    46 123
  First Protocol 72, 228
    Art 1 .... 69, 73
    2 .... 69, 70
    3 69
  Fourth Protocol 72
    Arts 1-3 67
  Sixth Protocol 72, 228
    Art 1 69
  Seventh Protocol 72
    Arts 1-5 67
  Eleventh Protocol 122
  Thirteenth Protocol, Art 1 69

PAGE

EU Charter of Fundamental Rights . . 66, 79
EU Treaty   172
First Accession Treaty 1972 . . . . . 182, 195,
                                       199, 325
International Convention Against
    Taking Hostages 1979   218
International Covenant on
    Economic, Social and Cultural
    Rights 1966   66
International Covenant on Civil and
    Political Rights 1966   66
Kyoto Protocol on Climate Change   285
Lomé Convention 1976   182
Luxembourg Accord 1966   182
Merger Treaty 1965 . . . . 77, 182
Regulation 170/83 (OJ 1983 L24/1)
    of 25 January 1983 establishing a
    Community system for the
    conservation and management of
    fishery resources   181
Regulation (EC) 3595/85 of 17
    December 1985 applying
    generalized tariff preferences for
    1986 in respect of certain
    industrial products originating in
    developing countries (OJ 1985
    L352/1)   185
Regulation (EEC) No 1408/71 of the
    Council of 14 June 1971 on the
    application of social security
    schemes to employed persons
    and their families moving within
    the Community Regulation
    1408/71   326
Single European Act 1986 . . . . 77, 182,
                                       188, 189,
                                       203, 443

PAGE

Solemn League and Covenant 1643 . .   24
Switzerland/EEA bilateral Agreement
    2002   80
Treaty of Amsterdam 1997 . . . . 78, 83, 84,
                                125, 180, 183, 203
Treaty of Nice 2000 OJ C80/1,
    10.03.01 . . . . 79, 83, 125,
                                   183, 202
Treaty of Peace between James IV
    and Henry VII 1503   16
Treaty of Union 27, 39, 45
    Art II   27
    Art 19   107
    Art XVIII   28
Treaty on European Union 1993
    (Maastricht Treaty) . . . 77, 78, 83, 84,
                                182, 189, 203
    preamble   77
    Art 1   77
    Art 2   78
    Art 33 (ex Art K.5)   183
    Art 49 (ex Art O)   189
    Art A   183
    Art B   183
    Art K.1   183
    Art K.2   183
    Art K.3(2)(c)   183
UK Treaty of Accession 1972   187
Appendix: Declaration by the
    Government of the United
    Kingdom of Great Britain and
    Northern Ireland on the
    definition of the term nationals
    (amended 1982)   187
United Nations Universal
    Declaration of Human Rights
    1948 . . . .   66, 67

Table of Cases

[References are to page number]

PAGE

A

A v Scottish Ministers; sub nom Anderson v Scottish Ministers [2001] UKPC D5, 2002 SC (PC) 63, [2003] 2 AC 602, 2001 SLT 1331 73
A & Others v Secretary of State for the Home Department [2004] UKHL 56, [2005] 2 AC 68, [2005] 2 WLR 87, [2005] 3 All ER 169, [2005] UKHRR 175, HL 69, 220, 229, 332, 349, 379
A & Others v Secretary of State for the Home Department (No 2) [2005] UKHL 71, [2006] 2 AC 221, [2006] 1 All ER 575, HL 349, 379
AIB Finance Ltd v Bank of Scotland 1993 SCLR 851, 1995 SLT 2, 2nd Div 307, 311
AMT, Petitioner. See T, Petitioner
Adams v Scottish Ministers 2003 SC 171, OH; 2004 SC 665, IH 62
Adams v Scottish Ministers 2003 SLT 366, 2002 SCLR 881, OH 73, 245
Agricultural, Horticltural and Forestry Industry Training Board v Aylesbury Mushrooms Ltd [1972] 1 WLR 190, [1972] 1 All ER 280, (1971) 116 SJ 57 . . . 281
Aitken's Trustees v Aitken 1927 SC 374, 1927 SLT 308 378
Alfons Lüttike GmbH v EC Commission (Case 4/69) [1971] ECR 325, ECJ 372
American Express v Royal Bank of Scotland (No 2) 1989 SLT 650, OH 358
Anderson (James McAulay) v HM Advocate 1996 JC 29, 1996 SCCR 115, 1996 SLT 155, HCJ Appeal 330, 409, 413, 422
Anderson v Jenkins Express Removals Ltd (1944) 1 November (unreported) 305
Anderson v McCall (1866) 4 M 765 170
Anderson v Scottish Ministers. See A v Scottish Ministers
Anns v Merton London Borough Council [1978] AC 728, [1977] 2 All ER 492, [1977] 2 WLR 1024, HL 353, 395, 396
Arthur JS Hall & Co v Simons [2002] 1 AC 615, [2000] 3 WLR 543, [2000] 3 All ER 673, HL 422
Assam Railways and Trading Co Ltd v IRC [1935] AC 445, [1934] All ER Rep 646, 18 TC 509, HJC (KBD) 313
Attorney General v de Keyser's Royal Hotel [1920] AC 508, [1920] All ER Rep 80, HL . 165
Attorney General v Prince Ernest Augustus of Hanover [1957] AC 436, [1957] 2 WLR 1, [1957] 1 All ER 49, HL 305
Attorney General for Canada v Attorney General for Ontario [1937] AC 326, PC . . . 195
Attorney General for Jersey v Holley [2005] UKPC 23, [2005] 2 AC 580, [2005] 3 All ER 371, [2005] 2 Cr App Rep 588, PC 119
Ayrshire Employers Mutual Insurance v IRC 1946 SC(HL) 1, 1946 SLT 235, HL . . 318
Azienda Agricola Monte Arosu Srl v Regione Autonoma della Sardegna (Case C-403/98) [2001] ECR I-103, [2002] 2 CMLR 14, ECJ 193

B

B and B 1965 SC 44, 1st Div 446
BBC v Commission (Case T-7089) [1991] ECR II-535, CFI 391
Ballantyne (John) (1859) 3 Irv 352 380
Barras v Aberdeen Steam Trawling and Fishing Co Ltd 1933 SC (HL) 21, 1933 SLT 338 307

PAGE

Barratt Scotland Ltd v Keith 1993 SCLR 120, 1994 SLT 1343, 2nd Div   313
Bartonshill Coal v Reid (1858) 3 Macq 266, 31 LTOS 255   362
Batchelor v Pattison and Mackersy (1876) 3 R 914 . . . . 409, 421
Beglan, Petr 2002 SLT 1175   338
Bell v Bell 1940 SC 229   361
Black v Carmichael; Carmichael v Black 1992 SLT 897, 1992 SCCR 709 . . . . 169, 445
Black-Clawson International Ltd v Papierwerke Waldhof Aschaffenburg AG [1975] AC
    591, [1975] 2 WLR 513, [1975] 1 All ER 810, HL   313
Boaler, Re; Vexatious Actions Act 1896, Re [1915] 1 KB 21, [1914-15] All ER Rep
    1022, CA   305
Boncza-Tomaszewski (aka Fraser) v HM Advocate 2000 SCCR 657, 2000 JC 586,
    2001 SLT 336, HCJ   139
Bott v MacLean 2006 JC 85 . . . . 356, 370
Brasserie du Pecheur SA v Germany (Case C-46/93) [1996] QB 404, [1996] 2 WLR
    505, [1996] All ER (EC) 301, (1996) 1 CMLR 889, ECJ   196
British Airways Board v Laker Airways [1985] AC 58, [1984] 3 WLR 413, [1984] 3 All
    ER 39, HL   195
Brodt v King 1990 SLT (Sh Ct) 17, 1991 SLT 272, 2nd Div 409, 421
Brogan v UK (Series A/145-B) (1988) 11 EHRR 117, (1988) Times, November 30,
    ECtHR   69
Brown v Hamilton District Council 1983 SC (HL) 1, 1983 SLT 397   449
Brown v Rentokil Ltd 1996 SC 415, 1996 SLT 839, [1995] IRLR 211, Ex Div   197
Brown v Rentokil Ltd [1992] IRLR 302, EAT   367
Brown v Stott 2000 SLT 379, 2000 SCCR 314   65
Brown v Stott 2001 SC (PC) 43, [2003] 1 AC 681, [2001] 2 WLR 817, 2001 SLT 59,
    PC   74
Bruce v Smith (1890) 17 R 1000   170
Bryan v UK Series A No 335-A, (1996) 21 EHRR 342, [1996] 1 PLR 47, [1996] 2
    EGLR 123, 22 November 1995, ECHR   393
Bryceland, Petr 2003 SLT 54, 2002 SCLR 995   338
Buchanan (James) & Co Ltd v Babco Forwarding and Shipping (UK) Ltd [1978] AC
    141, [1977] 3 WLR 907, [1977] 3 All ER 1048, HL   309
Bugg v Director of Public Prosecutions; Director of Public Prosecutions v Percy [1993]
    QB 473, [1993] 2 WLR 628, [1993] 2 All ER 815, DC   279
Bulmer (HP) Ltd v Bollinger (J) SA [1974] Ch 401, [1974] 3 WLR 202, [1974] 2 All
    ER 1226, CA   196
Burmah Oil Co Ltd (Burmah Trading) v Lord Advocate 1964 SC(HL) 117, [1965] AC
    75, [1964] 2 WLR 1231, HL   445

C

CILFIT Srl v Ministry of Health (Case 283/81) [1982] ECR 3415, [1983] 1 CMLR
    472, ECJ 323, 372
Caledonian Railway Co v North British Railway Co (1881) 8 R (HL) 23, 6 App Cas
    114   319
Caledonian Railway Co v Greenock Corporation 1917 SC (HL) 56, 1917 2 SLT 67 .   447
Calvin's Case (1608) 7 Co Rep 1a   24
Campbell and Cosans v UK (1982) 4 EHRR 293, ECHR   71
Case of Proclamations (1611) Co Rep 74   165
Church v HM Advocate 1995 SLT 604, 1995 SCCR 194   370
Clancy v Caird 2000 SC 441, IH   74
Clark v Kelly. See Kelly v Clark
Clarke v Chief Adjudication Officer (Case 384/85) [1987] ECR 2865, [1987] 3 CMLR
    277, ECJ   392
Colley v Poland 2005 SLT 436, HCJ 317, 318
Commerzbank AG v Large 1977 SC 375, 1977 SLT 219, IH   359
Commission v Council (the ERTA Case) (Case 22/70) [1971] ECR 263, [1971]
    CMLR 335, ECJ   187

PAGE

Commission v United Kingdom (Case 61/81) [1982] ECR 2601, [1982] 3 CMLR
284, [1982] ICR 578, ECJ 125, 190, 198, 328
Commission v United Kingdom (Case 165/82) [1984] 1 CMLR 44, [1984] ICR 192,
[1984] 1 All ER 353, [1984] IRLR 29, ECJ   190
Commission v United Kingdom (Case C-246/89) [1991] ECR I-4585, ECJ   197
Commissioners of Customs and Excise v Cure and Deeley Ltd [1962] 1 QB 340,
[1961] 3 All ER 641   279
Costa v ENEL (Case 6/64) [1964] ECR 585, [1964] CMLR 425, ECJ   191
Council v Commission (Case 45/86) [1987] ECR 1493, ECJ   185
Court of Session Practice Note No 5 of 2004 - Form Of Opinions And Neutral
Citation   381
Crofter Hand Woven Tweed Co Ltd v Veitch 1942 SC(HL) 1, [1942] AC 435, [1942]
1 All ER 142, HL   387
Cromarty Leasing v Turnbull 1988 SLT (Sh Ct) 62   360
Cullen v Cullen 2000 SC 395, 2000 SLT 540   360
Customs and Excise Comrs v Robert Gordon's College 1995 SLT 1139   311

D

Da Costa en Schaake NV and others v Nederlandse Belastingadministratie (Cases 28-
30/62) [1963] ECR 31, [1963] CMLR 224, ECJ   372
Dalgleish v Glasgow Corporation 1976 SC 32, 1976 SLT 157, IH 302, 307, 362
Darling v Gray & Sons (1892) 19 R (HL) 31; sub nom Wood v Gray & Sons [1892] AC
576, HL 364, 379, 446
Defrenne v Sabena (Case 43/75) [1976] ECR 455, [1976] 2 CMLR 98, ECJ   192
Department for the Environment, Food & Rural Affairs v ASDA Stores Ltd [2003]
UKHL 71, [2004] LLR 439, HL   327
Dick v Burgh of Falkirk 1976 SC(HL) 1, 1976 SLT 21, HL 364, 446
Director of Public Prosecutions v Schildkamp [1971] AC 1, [1970] 2 WLR 279, [1969]
3 All ER 1640, HL   305
Donoghue v Stevenson 1932 SC (HL) 31, 1932 SLT 317; sub nom M'Alister (or
Donoghue v Stevenson [1932] AC 562, HL 128, 171, 343, 348, 352,
353, 362, 379, 447
Dorset Yacht Co v Home Office [1970] AC 1004, [1970] 2 WLR 1140, [1970] 2 All ER
294, HL   353
Doughty v Rolls-Royce plc [1992] IRLR 126, [1992] 1 CMLR 1045, CA   194
Drummond's Judicial Factor v HM Advocate 1944 SC 298, 1944 SLT 399   378
Duguid v Fraser 1942 JC 1   387
Duke v Reliance Ltd [1988] AC 359, (1988) 2 WLR 359, [1988] 1 All ER 626, [1988]
IR 339, HL   328
Duncan (William) v Town of Arbroath (1668) Mor 10075   358
Duncan v Jackson (1905) 8 F 323, 13 SLT 932, IH   316

E

E v T 1949 SLT 411   379
Ealing London Borough Council v Race Relations Board [1972] AC 342, [1971] 2
WLR 71, (1971) 70 LGR 219, HL   304
Edwards v UK (No 13071/87) (1993) 15 EHRR 417, ECHR   330
Elabas v Secretary of State for the Home Department 2004 SLT 1082 (Note) 347, 381
Elliott v HM Advocate 1995 SLT 612, 1995 SCCR 280   370
English v Smith 1981 SCCR 143, 1981 SLT (Notes) 113   380

F

Factortame Ltd v Secretary of State for the Environment, Transport and the Regions
(Costs) (No 2) [2002] EWCA Civ 932, [2003] QB 381, [2002] 3 WLR 1104,
[2002] 4 All ER 97   379
Farqharson v White (1886) 13 R(J) 29   305

PAGE

Farrell v Alexander [1977] AC 59, [1976] 3 WLR 145, [1976] 2 All ER 721, HL;
    [1976] QB 345, [1975] 3 WLR 642, [1976] 1 All ER 129, CA 306
Farrell v Farrell 1990 SCLR 717, Sh Ct 360
Felixstowe Dock and Railway Co v British Transport Docks Board [1976] 2 CMLR
    655, [1976] 2 Lloyd's Rep 656, CA 196
Fortington v Lord Kinnaird 1942 SC 239, 1943 SLT 24 168
Foster v British Gas (Case C-188/89) [1991] QB 405, [1990] 3 CMLR 833, [1990]
    IRLR 353, ECJ 194
Fothergill v Monarch Airlines Ltd [1981] AC 251, [1980] 3 WLR 209, [1980] 2 All ER
    696, HL 309
France v Commission (Case C-59/91) [1992] ECR I-525, ECJ 391
Francovich v Italy (Cases C-6/90 and C-9/90) [1991] ECR I-5357, [1992] IRLR 84,
    ECJ 192, 194
Friend v Lord Advocate 2004 SC 78, OH; 2006 SC 121, IH 62

G

Galbraith v HM Advocate (No 2) 2001 SLT 953 370
Garland v British Rail Engineering Ltd [1983] 2 AC 751, [1982] 2 WLR 918, [1982] 2
    All ER 402, [1982] 2 CMLR 174, HL 197, 328
Gatoil International v Arkwright-Boston Manufacturers Mutual Insurance 1985
    SC(HL) 1, [1985] AC 255, [1985] 2 WLR 74, HL 309
Germany v Commission; Tariff Quota on Wine, Re (Case 24/62) [1963] ECR 63,
    [1963] CMLR 347, ECJ 391
Germany v Commission (Cases 218, 283-285, 287/85) [1988] CMLR 11, (1987)
    Times, September 17, ECJ 187
Ghaidan v Godin-Mendoza [2004] UKHL 30, [2004] 2 AC 557, HL 331
Gillick v West Norfolk and Wisbech Area Health Authority and the DHSS [1986] AC
    112, [1985] 3 WLR 830, [1985] 3 All ER 402, HL 176
Giménez Zaera v Instituto Nacional de la Seguridad Social (Case 126/86) [1987] ECR
    3697, ECJ 192
Glasgow Corporation v Central Land Board 1956 SC(HL) 1, 1956 SLT 41, [1956]
    JPL 442, HL 362
Globe Insurance Co v Mackenzie (1850) 7 Bell App 296, 22 SJ 625 358
Gordon v Murray (1765) Mor 16818 358
Grad (Franz) v Finanzamt Traunstein (Case 9/70) [1970] ECR 825, [1971] CMLR 1,
    ECJ 195, 324
Grant v Duke of Gordon (1781) Mor 12820, 2 Pat 582 359
Gray v St Andrews and Cupar District Committees of Fife County Council 1911 SC
    266, (1910) 2 SLT 354 317
Gray's Trustees v Royal Bank of Scotland (1895) 23 R 199, 3 SLT 168 358
Great Western Railways Co Ltd v Owners of the SS Mostyn [1928] AC 57, [1927] All
    ER Rep 113, 97 LJP 8, HL 351
Greenhuff (1838) 2 Swin 236 338
Greenshields v Magistrates of Edinburgh (1710-11) Rob 12 113
Grieve v Edinburgh and District Water Trustees 1918 SC 700, 1918 SLT 72 165

H

H, Petrs 1997 SLT 3 338
HM Advocate v Al-Megrahi (No 4) 2002 JC 99, 2002 SCCR 1433 370
HM Advocate v Graham 1985 SLT 498 316
HM Advocate v Macgregor (1773) Mor 11146 369
HM Advocate v McLean 2000 JC 140, 2000 SLT 299, 2000 SCCR 112 65
HM Advocate v McNab 2000 JC 80, 2000 SLT 99, 1999 SCCR 930 65
HM Advocate v McPhee 1935 JC 46, 1935 SLT 179 380
HM Advocate v Montgomery and Coulter 2000 JC 111, 2000 SCCR 959 65
HM Advocate v Stallard 1989 SCCR 248, 1989 SLT 469 169

PAGE

Hadmor Productions v Hamilton [1983] 1 AC 191, [1982] 2 WLR 322 [1981] 2 All ER
    724, HL 310
Handyside v United Kingdom (1976) A/24, 1 EHRR 737, ECHR 373
Hanlon v Law Society [1981] AC 124, [1980] 2 WLR 756, [1980] 2 All ER 199, HL .. 307
Hay v UK No 41894/99, ECHR 2000-XI, ECHR 393
Hedley Byme & Co v Heller & Partners [1964] AC 465, [1963] 3 WLR 101, [1963] 2
    All ER 575, HL 353
Heydon's Case (1584) 3 Co Rep 7a, 76 ER 637 317
High Court of Justiciary Practice Note No 2 of 2004 Form Of Opinions And Neutral
    Citation 381
Hill v Orkney Islands Council 1983 SLT (Lands Tr) 2 305
Hoekstra v HM Advocate (No 3) 2000 SCCR 676, 2000 JC 599 418
Humphries, Petr 1982 SLT 481 338
Huntar v Huntar (1573) Mor 16233 376
Hyslops v Gordon (1824) 2 Shaw's App 451, HL 359

I

Inco Europe Ltd and Others v First Choice Distribution and Others [2000] 1 WLR
    586 303
Inglis v British Airports Authority 1978 SLT (Lands Tr) 30 .... 176, 313
Institute of Chartered Accountants in Scotland, Petr 2002 SLT 921 338
Internationale Handelsgesellschaft (Case 11/70) [1970] ECR 1125, [1972] CMLR
    255, ECJ 181, 191
Ireland v UK Series A No 25, (1979-80) 2 EHRR 25, ECtHR 70
Isoglucose Case. *See* Royal Scholter-Honig v Intervention Board

J

Jacksons (Edinburgh) v Constructors John Brown 1965 SLT 37 358
Jacobs v Hart (1900) 2 F(J)33 304
James Kemp (Leslie) Ltd v Robertson 1967 SC 229, 1967 SLT 213, OH 305
Jefford v Gee [1970] 2 QB 130, [1970] 2 WLR 702, [1970] 1 All ER 1202, CA 447
Jessop v Stevenson 1987 SCCR 655, 1988 SLT 223, 1988 SC (JC) 17, HCJ 360, 368
Johnston v Chief Constable of the RUC (Case 222/84) [1987] QB 129, [1986] 3 WLR
    1038, [1986] 3 CMLR 240, ECJ 324
Junior Books Ltd v The Veitchi Company Ltd 1982 SC (HL) 244, [1983] AC 520,
    1982 SLT 492, HL 377

K

K v Craig 1997 SC 327, 1997 SLT 748, 1997 SCLR 566, 1st Div; affd 1999 SC (HL)
    1, 1999 SLT 219, 1999 SCLR 67, HL 319
Kaur v Lord Advocate 1980 SC 319, 1981 SLT 322, OH 330
Keane v Gallagher 1980 SLT 144 318
Kelly v Clark 2003 SC (PC) 77, 2003 SCCR 194, 2003 SLT 308 .... 63, 74, 93
Kelly v MacKinnon 1982 SCCR 205, 1983 SLT 9, HCJ 302, 307
Kelly v Nuttal & Sons Ltd 1965 SC 427, 1965 SLT 418, 2 Div 305
Kerr v Earl of Orkney (1857) 20 D 298 447
Khaliq v HM Advocate 1984 JC 23, 1984 SLT 137, 1983 SCCR 483 ... 135, 169, 338, 380
Kidston v Annan 1984, SLT 279, 1984 SCCR 20 445
Kirkwood v HM Advocate 1939 JC 36, 1939 SLT 209 369

L

L, Petrs (No 1). *See* L v Kennedy
L v Kennedy 1993 SCLR 693; sub nom L, Petrs (No 1) 1993 SLT 1310, 1st Div ... 338
Laker Airways v Department of Trade [1977] 1 QB 643, [1977] 2 WLR 234, [1977] 2
    All ER 182, CA 164

PAGE

Leadbetter v Hutcheson 1934 JC 70, 1934 SLT 319   318
Litster v Forth Dry Dock and Engineering Co Ltd 1989 SLT 540, [1990] AC 546,
    HL 310, 328, 329
'Lockerbie Bomber' Case. *See also* HM Advocate v Al-Megrahi (No 4)   139
London and Clydeside Estates v Aberdeen District Council 1980 SC(HL) 1, 1980
    SLT 81, [1980] 1 WLR 182, HL   316
London Street Tramways v London County Council [1898] AC 375, 78 LT 361, HL ..   363
Lord Advocate v Sprot's Trustees (1901) 3 F 440, (1901) 8 SLT 403, IH   307
Lord Gray's Motion 2000 SC (HL) 46, [2002] 1 AC 124   45

M

MT v DT 2000 SLT 1442, 2000 SCLR 1057   360
M'Alister (or Donoghue) v Stevenson. *See* Donoghue v Stevenson
McAra v Edinburgh Magistrates 1913 SC 1059, 1913 2 SLT 110   170
Macarthys v Smith [1979] ICR 785, [1979] 3 All ER 325, [1979] 3 CMLR 44, 381,
    CA 196, 327
McColl v Strathclyde Regional Council 1983 SLT 616, [1984] JPL 351   434
MacCormick v Lord Advocate 1953 SC 396, 1953 SLT 255   46
McCutcheon v HM Advocate 2002 SLT 27 .... 370, 448
MacDonald (Robert Grant) v HM Advocate 1999 SLT 533, 1999 SCCR 146, 1999
    GWD 6-291, HCJ Appeal 313, 459
Macfarlane v Tayside Health Board 2000 SC (HL) 1, [2000] 2 AC 59, [1999] 3 WLR
    1301, [1999] 4 All ER 691   349
McFadyen v Annan 1992 SLT 163, 1992 JC 53, 1992 SCCR 186   370
McInally v John Wyeth and Brother Ltd 1992 SLT 344   434
McKendrick v Sinclair 1972 SC (HL) 25, 1972 SLT 110, (1972) Times, March 21,
    HL   446
McLachlan, Petitioner 1987 SCCR 195, HCJ   379
McLaughlin v Boyd 1935 JC 19 .... 338, 370
McLeod (Alastair) v HM Advocate (No 2). *See* McLeod, Petitioner
McLeod, Petitioner; sub nom McLeod (Alastair) v HM Advocate (No 2) 1998 JC 67,
    1998 SLT 233, 1998 SCCR 77, HCJ Appeal   330
McTear's Exrx v Imperial Tobacco [2005] CSOH 69, 2005 2 SC 1   389
McWilliams v Lord Advocate 1992 SCLR 954, 1992 SLT 1045, OH   313
Magistrates of Ayr v Lord Advocate 1950 SLT 102   279
Magistrates of Buckie v Dowager Countess of Seafield's Trustees 1928 SC 525, 1928
    SLT 362   305
Magor and St Mellons Rural District Council v Newport Borough Council [1952] AC
    189, [1951] 2 All ER 839, 115 JP 613, HL; [1950] 2 All ER 1226, CA   302
Malloch v Aberdeen Corporation 1973 SC 227, 1974 SLT 253   279
Mandla v Lee [1983] AC 548, [1983] 2 WLR 620, [1983] 1 All ER 1062, HL; [1983]
    QB 1, [1982] 3 WLR 932, [1982] 3 All ER 1108, CA 300, 308
Manuel v Attorney General [1982] 3 WLR 821, [1982] 3 All ER 786, ChD   350
Marleasing SA v La Commercial Internacionale de Alimentacion SA (Case C-106/89)
    [1990] ECR I-1435, [1992] CMLR 305, [1993] BCC 421, ECJ   195
Marshall v Clark 1957 JC 68, 1958 SLT 19, HCJ (full Bench)   279
Marshall v Southampton and South West Area Health Authority (Case 152/84) [1986]
    QB 41, [1986] 2 WLR 780, [1986] 1 CMLR 688, ECJ   194
Mayne & Others v Minister of Agriculture, Fisheries and Food [2001] EHLR 5, [2000]
    All ER (D) 976, (2000) Independent, 9 October, QBD   327
Melluish v Fitzroy Finance [1996] 1 AC 454, [1995] 3 WLR 630, [1995] 4 All 453,
    HL   311
Milne v Tudhope 1981 JC 53, 1981 SLT (Notes) 42, HCJ   445
Mitchell v Mackersy 1905 8 F 198, 13 SLT 570   358
Montrose Peerage Case (1853) 1 Macq 401   302
Moore v Secretary of State for Scotland 1985 SLT 38   330

PAGE

Morgan Guaranty Trust Co of New York v Lothian Regional Council 1995 SC 151,
    1995 SCLR 225, 1995 SLT 299, IH 169, 358, 366, 445
Morrison v HM Advocate 1991 SLT 57, 1990 SCCR 235, 1990 JC 299 .... 370, 448
Mullen v Barr & Co 1929 SC 461, IH 447
Murphy v Brentwood District Council [1990] 1 AC 398, [1990] 3 WLR 414, [1990] 2
    All 908, HL 353
Murray v UK RJD 1996-I, 8 February 1996, (1996) 22 EHRR 29, ECHR 393

N

NV Algemene Transport en Expeditie Onderneming van Gend en Loos v Nederlandse
    Administratie der Belastingen (Case 26/62) [1963] ECR 1, [1963] CMLR 105,
    ECJ 191, 192, 193, 378
Nairn v St Andrews and Edinburgh University Courts 1909 SC(HL) 10, 16 SLT
    619 .... 308, 315
National Panasonic (UK) Ltd v Commission (Case 136/79) [1980] ECR 2033, [1980]
    3 CMLR 169, [1981] 2 All ER 1, ECJ 268, 322, 323
Nicol's Trustees v Sutherland 1951 SC(HL) 21, 1951 SLT 201; sub nom Sutherland v
    Nicol [1951] WN 110, 95 SJ 187, HL 306
Nold (J) v EC Commission (Case 4/73) [1974] ECR 491, [1974] 2 CMLR 338, ECJ .. 181
Nyazi v Ryman Conran [1988] RDLR 85, EAT 300

P

Palmer v Inverness Hospitals Board of Management 1963 SC 311, 1963 SLT 124 ... 176
Parlement Belge, The (1879) 4 PD 129, CA 195
Patmor Ltd v City of Edinburgh District Licensing Board 1988 SLT 850, 1st Div ... 317
Pepper (Inspector of Taxes) v Hart [1993] AC 593, [1992] 3 WLR 1032, [1993] 1 All
    ER 42, HL 310, 311, 312
Perrie, Petr 1992 SLT 655, 1991 SCCR 475 .... 338, 378
Pickstone v Freemans pic [1989] AC 66, [1988] 2 All ER 803, [1988] ICR 697, [1987]
    2 CMLR 572, HL 307, 328, 392
Plaumann & Co v Commission (Case 25/62) [1963] ECR 95, [1964] CMLR 29, ECJ .. 323
Polemis and Another and Furness Withy & Co Ltd, Re [1921] 3 KB 560, [1921] All ER
    Rep 40, 90 LJKB 1353, CA 380
Practice Direction (Judicial Precedent) [1966] 1 WLR 1234, [1966] 2 Lloyd's Rep 151,
    110 SJ 584 .... 363, 364
Practice Direction on the Form of Judgments, Paragraph Marking and Neutral
    Citation of 11 January 2001 [2001] 1 WLR 194, [2001] 1 All ER 193 382
Practice Direction – Neutral Citations of 14 January 2002 [2002] 1 WLR 346, [2002]
    1 All ER 351 382

R

R v Dudley and Stephens (1884) 14 QBD 273, 15 Cox CC 624 380
R v Henn & Darby [1981] AC 850, HL; [1978] 1 WLR 1031, [1978] 3 All ER 1190,
    [1978] 2 CMLR 688, CA 326
R v Kirk (Case 63/83) [1984] ECR 2689, [1984] 3 CMLR 522, [1985] 1 All ER 453,
    ECJ 181, 324
R v Montila [2004] UKHL 50, [2004] 1 WLR 3141, [2005] 1 All ER 113, [2005] Crim
    LR 479, [2005] 1 Cr App R 425, HL 305, 312
R v Ponting [1985] Crim LR 318 176
R v Secretary of State for the Home Department, ex parte Brind [1991] 1 AC 696,
    [1991] 2 WLR 588, [1991] 1 All ER 720, HL 330
R v Secretary of State for the Home Department, ex parte Fire Brigades Union [1995]
    2 AC 513, [1995] 2 WLR 464, [1995] 2 All ER 244, HL 166
R v Secretary of State for the Home Department, ex parte Manjit Kaur
    [2001] ECR I-237, [2001] CMLR 24, [2001] All ER (EC) 250, [2001] INLR
    507, ECJ 187

PAGE

R v Secretary of State for the Home Department, ex parte Zamir [1980] AC 930, [1980] 3 WLR 249, (1980) 124 SJ 527, HL 380

R v Secretary of State for Transport, ex parte Factortame [1990] 2 AC 85, [1989] 2 WLR 997, [1989] 2 All ER 692, [1989] 3 CMLR 1, HL 196, 199, 327

R v Secretary of State for Transport, ex parte Factortame (No 2) (Case C-213/89) [1991] 1 AC 603, [1990] 3 WLR 818, [1991] 1 All ER 70, [1990] 3 CMLR 375, ECJ 196, 199, 327

R v Secretary of State for Transport, ex parte Factortame (No 4) (Case 48/93) [1996] QB 404, [1996] 2 WLR 505, [1996] All ER (EC) 301, (1996) 1 CMLR 889 (ECJ) 166, ECJ 196, 199

R v Secretary of State for Transport, ex parte Factortame (No 5) [2000] 1 AC 524, [1999] 3 WLR 1062, [1999] 4 All ER 906, HL 196, 199

R v Secretary of State for Transport, Local Government and the Regions ex parte Factortame (No 8) [2002] EWCA Civ 932, [2003] QB 381, [2003] 2 Lloyd's Rep 225, [2002] 4 All ER 97 379

R v Sheer Metalcraft Ltd [1954] 1 QB 586, [1954] 2 WLR 777, [1954] 1 All ER 542, Surrey Assizes 281

R (Jackson) v Attorney-General [2005] UKHL 56, [2006] 1 AC 262, [2005] 3 WLR 733, [2005] 4 All ER 1253, HL 23, 316

R v (Quintavelle) v Secretary of State for Health [2003] UKHL 13, [2003] 2 AC 687, [2003] 2 WLR 692, [2003] 2 All ER 113, HL 303

R (Westminster City Council) v National Asylum Support Service [2002] UKHL 38, [2002] 1 WLR 2956, [2002] 4 All ER 654 312

RHM Bakeries (Scotland) Ltd v Strathclyde Regional Council 1985 SC (HL) 17, 1985 SLT 214, HL 447

Reed International v IRC [1976] AC 336, [1975] 3 WLR 413, [1975] 3 All ER 218, HL 308

Reynolds v Dyer 2002 SLT 295, 2002 SCCR 322 257

Ritchie v Petrie 1972 JC 7, 1972 SLT 2, HCJ 302

River Wear Commissioners v Adamson (1877) 2 App Cas 743, 47 LJQB 193, 37 LT 543 318

Rondel v Worsley [1969] 1 AC 191, [1967] 3 WLR 1666, [1967] 3 All ER 993, HL .. 421

Royal Bank of Scotland v Gillies 1987 SLT 54 338

Royal Four Towns Fishing Association v Dumfriesshire Assessor 1956 SC 379, 1956 SLT 217 170

Royal Scholten-Honig (Holdings) v Intervention Board for Agricultural Produce [1977] 2 CMLR 449, ECJ 378

Rylands v Fletcher (1868) LR 3 HL 330, HL............................. 447

S

S v HM Advocate 1989 SLT 469; sub nom Stallard v HM Advocate 1989 SCCR 248 .. 441

SA Roquette Freres v Council EC (Case 138/79) [1980] ECR 3333, ECJ 188

Saif Ali v Sydney Mitchell & Co (A Firm) [1980] AC 198, [1978] 3 WLR 849, [1978] 3 All ER 1033, HL 422

Schorsch Meier GmbH v Hennin [1975] QB 416, [1974] 3 WLR 823, [1975] 1 All ER 152, CA 196

Scottish Cinema and Variety Theatres v Ritchie 1929 SC 350, 1929 SLT 323 302

Scottish Water v Clydecare Ltd, 2003 SC 330, IH 303

Secretary of State for the Home Department v JJ & Others [2006] EWCA Civ 1141, [2007] QB 446, [2006] 3 WLR 866, CA 229

Secretary of State for the Home Department v MB [2006] EWCA Civ 1140, [2007] QB 415, [2006] 3 WLR 839, [2006] NLJR 1288, CA 229

Shields v E Coomes (Holdings) Ltd [1978] 1 WLR 1408, [1979] 1 All ER 456, [1978] ICR 1159, CA 196

Short's Trustee v Keeper of the Registers of Scotland 1994 SLT 65, 1994 SCLR 135, IH 311

Simmenthal (No 2) (Case 106/77) [1978] ECR 629, [1978] 3 CMLR 263, ECJ 191

PAGE

Singh v West Midlands Passenger Transport Executive [1988] 1 WLR 730, [1988] ICR
   614, [1988] IRLR 186, CA 307
Sloan, Petr 1991 SLT 527 338
Smith v M 1982 SLT 421; sub nom Smith v McC 1982 JC 67, 1982 SCCR 115 448
Smith v Scott 2007 SLT 137, IH (Registration of Voters Appeal Court) 120
Stallard v HM Advocate. *See* S v HM Advocate
Starrs v Ruxton 2000 JC 208, 2000 SLT 42, 1999 SCCR 1052 .... 65, 74, 95, 99, 320
Stauder v City of Ulm (Case 29/69) [1969] ECR 419, [1970] CMLR 112, ECJ 322
Stewart v Secretary of State for Scotland 1995 SLT 895, 1996 SLT 1203, 1998 SLT
   385 100
Stirling v Earl of Lauderdale (1733) Mor 2930 358
Stirling District Council v Allan 1995 SLT 1255 329
Stirling Park & Co v Digby Brown & Co 1995 SCLR 375, 1996 SLT (Sh Ct) 17 171
Strathern v Padden 1926 JC 9 319
Sugden v HM Advocate 1934 JC 103, 1934 SLT 465 .... 168, 369, 370
Sutherland v Nicol. *See* Nicol's Trustees v Sutherland
Swaire v Demetriades 1942 SC 1 387
Sweet v Parsley [1970] AC 132, [1969] 2 WLR 470, [1969] 1 All ER 347, HL ... 314, 316

T

T, Petitioner; sub nom AMT, Petitioner 1997 SLT 724, 1996 SCLR 897, [1997] Fam
   Law 225, 1 Div 325, 330
Taylor's Executrices v Thom 1914 SC 79, 1913 2 SLT 337 378
Tehrani v Argyll and Clyde Health Board (No 1) 1989 SLT 851, OH 177
Thomas v National Union of Mineworkers (South Wales Area) [1986] Ch 20, [1985] 2
   WLR 1081, [1985] 2 All ER 1 175
Tudhope v McCarthy 1985 JC 48, 1985 SCCR 76, 1985 SLT 392 370
Tyrer v United Kingdom (1978) A/26, (1978) 2 EHRR 1, ECHR 374

U

Ulhaq v HM Advocate 1990 SCCR 593, 1991 SLT 614 338
United Kingdom v EC Council (Case 131/86) [1988] ECR 905, [1988] 2 CMLR 364,
   ECJ 185
United Kingdom v EU Council (Case C-84/94) [1996] ECR I-5755, [1996] 3 CMLR
   671, [1996] All ER (EC) 877, ECJ 180

V

Vacher & Sons v London Society of Compositors [1913] AC 107, 82 LJKB 232, 107
   LT 722 305
Van Duyn v Home Office (Case 41/74) [1974] ECR 1337, [1975] Ch 358, [1975] 1
   CMLR 1, ECJ 193, 325
Van Gend en Loos. *See* NV Algemene Transport en Expeditie Onderneming van Gend
   en Loos v Nederlandse Administratie der Belastingen (Case 26/62)
Viola v Viola 1988 SLT 7, 1987 SCLR 529, OH 308
Virtue v Commissioners of Police of Alloa (1874) 1 R 285 .... 362, 363
Von Colson and Kamann v Land Nordrhein-Westfalen (Case 14/83) [1984] ECR
   1891, [1986] 2 CMLR 430, ECJ 195, 328

W

Walker v Strathclyde Regional Council 1986 SC 1, 1986 SLT 523, OH 382
Walkingshaw v Marshall 1991 SCCR 397, 1992 SLT 1167 197
Wan Ping Nam v German Federal Republic Minister of Justice 1972 JC 43, 1972 SLT
   220 338
Watt v Annan 1978 JC 84, 1978 SLT 198, HCJ 370

PAGE

Webster v Dominick 2005 JC 65, 2003 SCCR 525, 2003 SLT 975 .... 356, 370
Weir v Jessop 1991 SCCR 242, HCJ 378
Weir v Jessop (No 2) 1991 SCCR 636, 1992 SLT 533, 1991 JC 146 379
West v Secretary of State for Scotland 1992 SC 385, 1992 SLT 636, 1992 SCLR 504,
    1 Div 448
Westwater v Thomson 1992 SCCR 624, 1993 SLT 703 197
Wilkie v Scottish Aviation Ltd 1956 SC 198, 1956 SLT (Notes) 25, 1 Div 11
Wills' Trustees v Cairngorm Canoeing and Sailing School Ltd 1976 SC(HL) 30, 1976
    SLT 162, HL 359
Wilsons and Clyde Coal Co v Scottish Insurance Corporation 1949 SC(HL) 90, 1949
    SLT 230, [1949] AC 462, [1949] LJR 1190, 65 TLR 354, 93 SJ 423, [1949] 1 All
    ER 1068, HL 377
Windsor, Petr 1994 SLT 604, 1994 SCCR 59 338
Wood v Gray & Sons. *See* Darling v Gray & Sons
Wright v Paton Farrell [2006] CSIH 7, 2006 SLT 269 409
Wylie v HM Advocate 1966 SLT 149 338

X

X Insurance Co Ltd v A and B 1936 SC 225, 1936 SLT 188 407

1. Introduction

WHY HAVE LAW?

Law is everywhere. It is, like the air we breathe, part of our environment. But unlike the air it is man-made. Why is it made? There is no one universally agreed answer, but a plausible one that would fit most societies is this. People live together in communities. They have competing wants and limited resources to satisfy them. Therefore they make arrangements to share things out and minimise or repress conflict. These arrangements can take various forms, such as morality, etiquette, conventions and law. Law consists of rules. These are not necessarily fair or accepted by all. They may be written by a small elite who wield some form of power and impose them on a reluctant majority. But some such arrangements are indispensable. The bigger and more complex the community, the more the scope for conflict; and so the more likely there are to be rules of law. As one writer puts it, society is not a suicide club.

SOME KINDS OF LAW WE ALL KNOW

If law is everywhere about us, we must be enveloped in it from our earliest days. In a family the parents have power over young children by virtue of their greater size and strength and knowledge. Ideally the relationship is imbued with love. But it still involves the children doing what they are told on such matters as bed-time, dress, going to school, and play-mates. If the parents are consistent in what they require the children to do, then unwritten rules emerge. They can still be rules, even though exceptions may be made for special occasions or they are relaxed as the children grow older. In school too the pupils find themselves in a regime of rules, concerning time-tables, holidays, absentee notes and so on. In many schools there will be no list of school rules as such. But the children are taught by the teachers what a rule is when the consequences of unacceptable behaviour are explained to them and they are told what conduct to

1

avoid for the future. If they still do not conform, then some punishment, such as loss of privileges, will be imposed and as a last resort exclusion from the school.

As children grow older and become more self-reliant they become aware of a system of control that affects nearly everything that people do outside their homes. Probably it first impinges on them when as pedestrians they become aware of the rules that make drivers of vehicles behave more or less consistently in certain situations; stopping at a red light or giving way to someone on a pedestrian crossing or obeying the lollipop man's signal. Sooner or later they will also watch the result of not complying, when police stop and question the errant driver.

SO WHAT EXACTLY IS LAW?

Already from these simple situations we can see some of the elements of law. It seems to be the words of someone in authority who has the power to intervene in other people's affairs. It imposes patterns of conduct on other people; and if they do not comply something unpleasant is liable to befall them. A single example of these effective words is called a rule or a law. Some people would want to add that the law must be fair to be a true law. Others would say that if the law comes from a person or institution whose authority is generally recognised, then that is good enough. Some laws actually compel conduct, whether you like it or not. For example, a speeding motorist may be stopped by traffic police and warned to obey the speed limit. A persistent offender will be fined by a judge and may be disqualified from driving. But a lot of law simply provides opportunities to do things effectively. If you want to buy a house, there are rules you must observe to obtain the desired result. You don't need to go near a court. You can ignore such laws if you choose, but you are likely to find that somebody takes your house from you or you cannot get anyone to buy it from you. So some laws are primarily compelling ones and some are primarily enabling ones. But if you ignore either kind, some harm or loss or detriment is likely to befall you. Some laws are very precise; they tell you exactly what you can and cannot do. Others shade off into discretion. Thus, on divorce the matrimonial property is to 'be shared fairly' between the parties (Family Law (Scotland) Act 1985, s 9(1)(a)). The couple will be the best people to decide what will be a fair sharing of their belongings. But if they cannot, then judges are available to do it for them.

We have only just touched on some of the most profound questions in the subject called jurisprudence or legal philosophy, which university students of law will have to study later. There are many aspects of this topic which will then be examined, such as: must the law-maker obey his own laws?; is there any duty to obey the laws of a tyrant?; what law is to be obeyed during and after a revolution? But for our purposes in this book that picture of the standard form that law takes will suffice.

However, there is a variant of law that we must mention at this stage. It is law without a law-giver. It simply rests on the general observance of some pattern of behaviour. The person who steps out of line will be criticised and may suffer some harm, such as being ostracised. In a narrow street where all the cars are parked on one side to let the traffic flow, a driver who parks on the other side will soon be made to feel unpopular. This is custom or convention. It is unwritten law and is associated with an early stage of legal development, when means of making law and imposing punishments had not yet been developed. So we can call it embryonic or inchoate law. Yet, paradoxically, some of the most basic parts of the United Kingdom's constitution exist only in the form of conventions, such as the duty of a Prime Minister whose government is defeated on a matter of confidence in the House of Commons to offer his resignation to the Sovereign.

THE LAW OF A STATE

So far we have been describing a very simple model of law. But of course in a modern state it is much more complex. Indeed, to issue and uphold its own laws is one of the marks of a state. The laws of a state are arranged in a hierarchy of authority and importance. In the United Kingdom the highest tier of law has for centuries been the statutes or Acts issued by Parliament. But since the United Kingdom accepted the Treaty of Rome and entered the European Community, and the consequences of this decision were spelled out by Parliament in the European Communities Act 1972, there is a higher tier of law, that of European Community law (also called European Union Law), which takes precedence over United Kingdom law. In theory, Parliament could repeal the European Communities Act and free itself of that level of law. But the problems of disengaging itself from the European Union make that possibility highly unlikely. Likewise, the United Kingdom Parliament has tied its hands by incorporating substantial parts of the European Convention on

Human Rights in the Human Rights Act of 1998. That Parliament could repeal that Act but is most unlikely to do so. Parliament has devolved some of its power to make law to the Parliament of Scotland since 1999.

Much modern statute law is of an outline kind. The details are provided in regulations drawn up by government departments under the authority of a parent Act. They can thus be varied easily, for example to take account of inflation. Most social security law is of this kind. As we shall see, there are many other subordinate forms of enacted law, such as laws made by courts for their own procedure, by local authorities and by transport undertakings.

Alongside the law created on purpose, there is a kind of law which is extracted as a by-product from something else. To justify their decisions in disputed cases judges issue judgments applying the existing law to the new situation which has come before them. In so doing they make law in a limited sense in that they clarify or extend the existing law, including the law emerging from the decisions of previous judges. Lawyers reading such published judgments try to formulate a brief rule of law which epitomises the reason underlying the decision. Judges in their judgments have to respect what Parliament appears to have enacted, if anything, on the subject; and their statements of the law and even (though rarely) their decisions could be overridden by Parliament. They also have to adhere to expositions of the law in courts higher than their own. So this judge-made law is also arranged in tiers of authority.

As well as this structure of enacted and judge-made law – what we might call official law – which is of general application, there are sets of law applying to people in particular circumstances; for example, members of the armed forces, of the universities, of the established Churches of Scotland and of England and of certain professions such as medicine, law and teaching. The laws of these bodies require some degree of state approval and the decisions of their courts and tribunals are usually subject to final appeal to the courts of the land.

There are also many other bodies which have a legal structure which in a limited way imitates that of the state; for example, trade unions and professional associations, the non-established churches, and sports associations. But only if they act in an oppressive way or fail to observe the basic rules of natural justice, as laid down by the law courts, do they become subject to the law of the land.

The laws of such private organisations do not have to be obeyed. If, as a member, you do disobey them the worst that can happen is that you will be made to leave the organisation. But all the other kinds of law mentioned above have a pedigree which could be traced back to the ultimate source of legal authority which in the United

Kingdom we refer to by the symbol of the Crown and personify in the person of the monarch. If you come within the scope of such an official law, you have to comply or take the prescribed consequences.

IS LAW A GOOD OR A BAD THING?

A modern law system extends to every corner of a nation, and in limited ways beyond its boundaries. It touches the lives of every inhabitant and to some degree even those of temporary residents such as tourists. Most laws probably strike the law-abiding citizen as restrictive. They stop them from doing what they want to do. Yet provided laws as a whole are generally respected they create a climate of security in which people can go about their everyday affairs, confident that they are not going to be harmed in their persons or property. If they are, something will be done about it. For example, we can be reasonably sure in this country, though not perhaps in Madrid or Rome, that if we drive through a road crossing on the green light we are not going to collide with someone driving across on a red light.

The other kind of laws, those which enable us to do things and get results, are more obviously beneficial. They could be compared to the telephone network which enables us to make contact with people all over the country and even beyond. This sort of law enables us to perform transactions with people everywhere, whom we may never have seen and know little about, with some assurance that they will be honoured; and if not, we shall be able to get some redress. From Scotland we might send to a nursery firm in Cornwall for some plants, in the confidence that they would send the plants ordered to us, properly packed. If they did turn up dead on arrival, we would have a good chance of getting our money back. If we were paying by credit card or cheque we would be counting on the bank to make payment on our behalf. Again, we might get married in Scotland and, armed with a marriage certificate, we could be assured of being treated as married here and elsewhere in the world. It is this comprehensive system of law that enables people to enter transactions like these with assurance.

LAW IS ALWAYS SUBJECT TO CHANGE

One of the problems about law is discovering what exactly it is at any given point of time. If one is trying to do exactly what the law requires or to discover the law that should settle a dispute, then it is vitally important to ascertain all the rules applicable at the relevant date. Why so? Surely it might be thought the law is as clear and certain as the law-maker can make it? The trouble is that law is always subject to change so that it can be kept up to date. This is true of individual rules of law. That means that although a new statute may get plenty of publicity in the media, what may not be so clear is how it amends previous statutes, or when it comes into force (for different parts of it may be operative from different dates), or whether it has any retrospective effect. So lawyers have to rely on publications such as the monthly periodical *Current Law* to keep them abreast of legal changes. The Internet is proving a valuable aid in this regard.

But although law is always evolving, it is mainly at the margins. There are broad core areas of the law, such as the law of contract and of property, and the main crimes such as murder and theft, where change is minimal. These heartlands of the law enable it to have a conserving and a stabilising role in societies. The very existence of the modern nation-state depends on reliable rules of law and the means to find them and enforce them. Thus, the law of companies enables property to be set apart for certain economic purposes and for the ownership of that property to be fragmented among many people and other companies, without putting at risk the rest of their assets. Without that device the capitalist or free enterprise system could not flourish.

In this book we are more concerned with structures and with broad movements and trends in the law, although some rules will be mentioned; and we shall have to strive to state them as accurately as possible at a named date. There are different kinds of legal change. There is the step-by-step kind of change, which we may call incremental. Most judge-made law is of that kind. There is innovative change, when a new area of legal regulation is opened up, for instance, by the Sex Discrimination Act of 1976; or an existing one is drastically changed, such as making divorce rest on the breakdown of the marriage, instead of the commission of a matrimonial fault. And there is evolutionary change, which takes the form of broad trends such as the increasing role of civil servants in detailed law-making. Of course, if all the laws were in a constant state of flux it would defeat the purposes of law to create certainty and security. But a certain amount of change can be lived with in the interests of keeping the law in line with people's expectations.

Another way in which a small element of uncertainty creeps into the law arises out of laws which remain on paper but are not actually enforced. Thus, in 1972 the Lord Advocate let it be known that he would not initiate prosecutions of male adults for engaging in private homosexual activities by agreement in Scotland, in circumstances such that they would not be criminal in England. The police, like prosecutors, in the nature of their duties have much discretion, but in 1982 they publicly declined to operate the powers conferred on them in the Transport Act 1982, s 27, to issue fixed penalty notices for a variety of minor traffic offences, including speeding. In 1993 (now under the Road Traffic Offenders Act 1988, s 54) they announced that they would now do so. Bodies affected by a new law may protest that they need time to prepare for it. Thus the Freedom of Information (Scotland) Act 2002 affecting all governmental and many quasi-governmental bodies did not come into force until 1st January 2005. This shows that legal institutions have the power to vary the operation of legal rules.

LAW AND POWER

Law is indissolubly linked with power; that is, the ability of a person or group to determine the behaviour of others. From what we have already said about laws, they are obviously ideal instruments by means of which to control others. Power may take many and varied forms. Sometimes it is visible and very forceful, as when massed policemen, their arms linked, try to confine demonstrators to one street and stop them marching, then handcuff those they arrest. Sometimes it is more subtle. Those who are in charge of the mass media have the power to influence what people think, and thus do, by their ability to select which facts to publicise and which opinions to advance. Power may be exercised by an individual or by a group or class. The trade union movement used to attribute its power against employers to the ability of its members to take strike action. But now strikes must be preceded by a strike ballot, otherwise the union funds are put at risk, and employees are free to join or not join a trade union. An individual employer still has the power to dismiss an employee but if he does so unfairly he may have to pay the employee compensation. These forms of power are legitimate in that they are either authorised by law or at least not forbidden by it. But the power a bank robber exercises when he holds up the staff of a bank would be regarded as illegitimate.

LAWS AS WAYS OF GETTING THINGS DONE

In a modern democratic society there is a constant ferment of debate on things that are wrong and how to correct them. For example, road accidents have long been blamed on driving with excessive alcohol in the system. Now there is concern about the effect of drugs, whether medicinal or forbidden, on driving. People who sleep on the streets regardless of the weather are seen as an embarrassment and a scandal. Pressure groups, television documentaries and articles in the newspapers draw attention to such social evils. Political parties may put them into their election manifestos. The method of correction usually uses law. It may be simply some new use of existing legal powers which have been conferred on officials such as the police or head teachers or environmental protection officers. Or it may require new parliamentary legislation. Relying on law assumes that, for the most part, people respect law and approve of the objectives that are embodied in particular laws. If they ignore a law then some sanction can come into operation to compel or persuade them to comply. It need not be as overt as imprisonment. It might be the payment of compensation to someone hurt by the failure to obey the law. In the case of professionals it might be loss of promotion or humiliating publicity. So the legitimate power of law is drawn upon to achieve reforms in all walks of life. But the job is never done. There are always calls for new laws and the amendment of existing ones. Whole new areas may be made subject to law, such as racial relations and sexual and age discrimination. The law is always on the move.

2. Scotland – nation and state

In this chapter we shall be looking in a broad-brush manner at the history of Scotland and seeing the ways in which law has been entwined with it. In so doing we may hope to find the answer to the question: how did the peculiar, indeed unique, association enjoyed by the legal system of Scotland within the United Kingdom arise?

NATION AND STATE

A nation is a cultural concept, rooted among people and their belief that they have a shared identity that distinguishes them from other peoples. It is manifested in what they produce as a people – their art, music and literature, their language, their pastimes and games, in their beliefs about themselves and their place in the world. A nation may or may not have the organs of government which signify a state; a central administration holding sway over a defined area; armed forces to defend its boundaries; police and courts to maintain order within them. That apparatus is the sign of a state and if it is functioning effectively gives it a claim to recognition by other states. It marks a society which claims independence from all others, although in the modern world of instant communications, mutual economic dependence and treaties and alliances that independence is more apparent than real.

When we examine the law in Scotland certain unique problems confront us. Most Scots would claim that Scotland is a nation. Certainly in most sports (though not yet at the Olympic Games) it counts as a nation. But it is not in itself a state. In the Scottish Executive it has only some of the apparatus of a state; part of that of the United Kingdom of Great Britain and Northern Ireland. Its representatives as MPs participate in the Parliament of the United Kingdom. Since May 1999 it has also had its own Parliament sitting in Edinburgh and dealing with matters devolved to it by the United Kingdom Parliament. It does have its own courts, but it shares with the rest of the United Kingdom common highest courts in civil and devolution cases. Most of its tribunals are part of a United Kingdom organisation. It has its own legal profession. Some of its laws are peculiar to Scotland, some are common to the whole of Britain (ie England, Scotland and Wales), some are shared with the rest of the United Kingdom (ie with Northern Ireland as well). Some are separate in form, but almost identical in substance. It will be one of our main tasks to tease out these similarities and differences.

THE EMERGENCE OF SCOTLAND

The emergence of a Scottish nation and later a Scottish state was a slow and painful process lasting several centuries. It began in the 11th century when four rival peoples had by warfare coalesced into one kingdom under King Malcolm II (1005–34). They were the Picts of the east of Scotland, the Angles of the south-east, the Scots of Dalriada in the west and the Britons of the south-west.

Custom

The law before David I (1124–53) was probably entirely custom and in the Celtic, Gaelic-speaking areas of the west was spoken to by hereditary oracles called Brehons. In the nature of things customary law, being unwritten, is hard to identify later. But numerous references to *leges et consuetudines* (laws and customs) in the statutes of the 12th and 13th centuries testify to the existence and recognition of some law other than the enacted written law[1]. Custom is also often referred to in charters. Some of it, especially in charters, is local[2]. Some of it is general; what in England was called the common law, a term which in Scotland is used both for the law common to the whole of Scotland and less frequently the Roman or civil law common to Europe[3]. Stair, the 17th century authoritative institu-

---

1 Thus, the *Laws of the Four Burghs* (of Edinburgh, Roxburgh, Berwick and Stirling) are more properly the *Leges et Consuetudines Quatuor Burgorum* and were adopted by many other Scots burghs. See APS I, 333. The *Laws of the Marches* were the outcome of a process of recognition in 1249 by magnates from England and Scotland of the laws and customs of the marches (or frontiers). See APS I, 413–416, conveniently and fully translated in DM Walker *A Legal History of Scotland* (1988) vol I pp 63–66.
2 For example, Malcolm IV in a charter to the Abbey of Scone of 1164 allowed it to have three tradesmen with the same liberties and customs as those of his Burgh of Perth (Barrow, *Regesta of Malcolm IV*), No 243).
3 For numerous medieval examples, see DM Walker *A Legal History of Scotland* vol II (1990) pp 252–254. Later Stair was also to use 'common law' as the law 'common to many nations' (*Institutions of the Law of Scotland* (ed 1981) I, 1, 11).

tional writer on Scots law, uses the term 'common law' to mean primarily, as in England, 'our ancient and immemorial customs'[4]. As examples he includes the law governing most rights of succession as being 'anterior to any statute'[5]. To these might be added the early ways of trying criminal accusations - the ordeal, trial by combat and even the early jury. Custom flourished for centuries in the law observed by mariners and traders among nations, where there was no sovereign authority to enact it, and to a minor extent this is still so. But most maritime law is now embodied in judicial precedent (the authoritative statement of the law by a court), statute and international convention. Customs of trade may sometimes be used to interpret a contract[6]. In employment law the custom and practice of a workplace may be paid regard to by employment tribunals and courts. Thus, custom had a formative role in the law of Scotland and despite the spread of written law still has a minor part to play.

EARLY MEDIEVAL SCOTLAND

Custom with its local roots could be a divisive force. But through a documentary form of law uniformly introduced and enforced from the centre the country was to become much more united. This came about through the arrival of the Normans who pacified England within a few years of their victory over King Harold at Hastings in 1066 and then began a peaceful penetration of Scotland. The marriage of Margaret, an English Saxon princess[7], to Malcolm III of Scotland and the marriages of their sons, Alexander I and David I, to English noblewomen led to the coming to Scotland of many families hailing from Normandy, such as the Bruces, the Stewarts (formerly Fitzallans) and the Grahams. Margaret's piety drew many religious orders to Scotland during her reign and thereafter. The Scottish kings then followed Norman practice in conferring lands upon these incomers, in return for their homage and the promise of armed knights in time of war. These tenants-in-chief could create their own sub-tenants. At the lowest level were the peasants, the husbandmen and cottars who tilled the land and whose return was in produce and days of labour on their overlord's land. These land rights carried with them the right to hold a court. In this way disputes as to tenure and

4 Stair *Institutions* I, 1, 16. See p 136 infra.
5 Stair *Institutions* I, 1, 16.
6 See, eg, *Wilkie v Scottish Aviation* 1956 SC 198 (custom as to remuneration of chartered surveyor followed if reasonable, certain and notorious).
7 Though born in Hungary.

succession could be settled. The kings also conferred on religious houses extensive lands. For them the return was usually in prayers and masses.

Feudal tenure

This system was known as feudal tenure. Worked out initially in relation to land, it was soon to be extended to towns. Burghs were royal creations, part of a deliberate policy to maintain peace and raise standards of life. This plan had three elements: royal castles manifesting the king's authority and power; sheriffs there resident to represent the king in administration, tax-gathering and law enforcement; and townships whose inhabitants were encouraged to engage in trade and manufacture. They too were given plots of land, for which they paid a return in rent and in other obligations such as attendance at the burgh court.

In this way a legal device, rooted in the staple resource of land, carried the monarch's authority throughout the country. It was a centralised form of government in that all rights derived from the Crown and the forms of land tenure were uniform everywhere. The Royal Chancery issued the charters conferring the lands or confirming them; and when any kind of dispute arose it ordered in the form of legal writs called brieves an inquiry in the local court. After hearing evidence from local people it reported back as to the true state of affairs. But it was also decentralised in so far as the monarch gave his tenants-in-chief powers similar to his own within their territories. By the 14th and 15th centuries these so-called regalities were to be a source of division and conflict in the country.

Thus, feudalism reinforced class stratification, at least in the rural areas. Burghs were more loosely bound into the system. The burghers had a strong sense of community, focused on their town church and burgh court, and often maintained a doughty independence from adjacent large land-owners, even those who had the powers of sheriffs.

Feudalism in time tended to disperse power, for the successors of those who were entrusted with lands by the sovereign did not always remain faithful to him or his successors. But it did give Scotland many of the signs of statehood, even although they and that concept were not fully developed until the 16th century. It emphasised the loyalty owed by everyone in the country to the person of the king, who was both leader and the symbolic embodiment of the nation. It facilitated the raising of an army when needed. It sustained courts in every community. Yet paradoxically, at the centre, the *curia regis* or royal court was just an informal gathering of a varying number of those clerics and titled laymen who gave counsel to the king. Out of it grew eventually the Scots Parliament, central law courts and the Privy Council[8].

The pervasiveness of the linked institutions we call feudalism has been equalled by its durability. Its concept of concurrent interests in land is still the basis of Scottish land law, for example, between landlord and tenant or owner-occupier and security holder. In 1991 the Scottish Law Commission (which is charged with the reform of Scots law) published a discussion paper entitled *Property Law: Abolition of the Feudal System*. This led to the Abolition of Feudal Tenure etc (Scotland) Act 2000 which was brought into force in stages. From this era too we derive the cleavage in Scots property and succession law between, on the one hand, the law of land, all buildings attached to land, trees and growing crops, mines and quarries and, on the other, all other items of value; that is between heritable and moveable property, respectively.

Documents of title

The distinctive form of law derived from this period is the charter, the all-important document of title which evidenced the rights over land of the wealthy, both individuals and institutions such as religious houses. The stout charter-chest can still be seen in many castles. In the 19th century, groups of (usually) titled people formed clubs, such as the Maitland and the Bannatyne, to publish the surviving charters and other documents of title, often of their own families, and these form invaluable historical records, as well as supplying a chain of ownership. Today many owner-occupiers still have their title deeds, though often deposited as security with a building society which holds a standard security (a form of mortgage) over the home. From a legal proposition of the most general kind, that the Crown is the ultimate owner of all the land of Scotland, fragments of that ownership descend to the level of the home-owner and give him legal rights. Tenants of lands, homes, factories etc likewise have the enjoyment of that property, though limited in duration and other ways.

Feudalism and independence

Feudalism also led to a growing sense of Scots independence from England, though it was from England that the feudal institutions had

8 See pp 17, 20, 26.

been imported. At one level it was a disagreement over feudal law that precipitated the Wars of Independence. On the death in Orkney en route to Scotland of the Maid of Norway, who was to succeed to the Scottish throne following the accidental death of Alexander III in 1286, Robert Bruce, the Lord of Annandale, and John Balliol, the Lord of Galloway, were in dispute as to who had the right to succeed to the throne of Scotland. Edward I of England claimed to be over-lord of Scotland and in support of his claim could argue that the contenders and other Scots nobles, like the Comyns, owned lands in England for which they paid him homage. Eventually Bruce and Balliol and certain lesser claimants conceded that Edward was lord superior of Scotland and promised to abide by his decision. After many sessions of legal argument Edward gave judgment in favour of John Balliol who then paid him homage at Newcastle.

The humiliation implied in the outcome of this so-called Great Cause was emphasised by Edward who went on to hear appeals on questions of Scottish feudal rights, insisting that King John Balliol be present. When war broke out between England and France Scots envoys signed an alliance with the French. Edward invaded Scotland in 1296, stripped John of the symbols of his kingship and removed the Scots records and Stone of Destiny to Westminster. There then followed the Wars of Independence, with Scotland's defeat under William Wallace at Falkirk in 1298 and victory under Robert Bruce against Edward II at Bannockburn in 1314. This formative period in Scotland's development ended in 1328 with a peace treaty signed at Edinburgh and Northampton, prior to which Edward III accepted that Scotland was to be 'separate in all things from the kingdom of England, assured forever of its territorial integrity, to remain forever free and quit of any subjection, servitude, claim or demand'.

Beliefs sustaining legal independence

The victory at Bannockburn gave a great boost to Scotland's sense of nationhood. This is manifested in the sonorous prose of the Declaration of Arbroath of 1320. In it the nobility, the barons, free-holders and whole community of the kingdom of Scotland beseeched Pope John XXII to persuade Edward III of England to allow the Scots to live in peace and liberty. They are portrayed as a nation (*nacio*) of ancient lineage, governed by a succession of 113 kings of native stock, and under the patronage of St Andrew, brother of St Peter. Mythology much of it may be, but it gave the Scots a certain pride of ancestry and confidence as a people for the future. Its rhetoric is echoed in a populist form as Scots supporters sing

'Flower of Scotland' at international rugby and football matches. Confidence that Scotland is still a nation underlies the Scotland Act 1998 which affirms that Scotland should retain a separate judicial system from that of England[9].

The Declaration was composed by Bernard de Linton, Abbot of Arbroath and Chancellor of Scotland[10]. Leading churchmen had given their support and recognition to King Robert Bruce, speaking on behalf of the people and commons of the Kingdom of Scotland, in a declaration of 1310. A century earlier the Church had successfully fought off the claims of the Archbishop of York to jurisdiction over the dioceses of Scotland by securing from Pope Honorius III in 1218 a bull declaring the bishops of the Scottish Church to be directly subject to Rome. So the Church had an interest parallel to that of the state in proclaiming the independence of the Scottish nation.

Bernard de Linton wrote a poem in celebration of the victory of Bannockburn and later in the century another churchman, John Barbour, Archdeacon of Aberdeen, further boosted the national sentiment in his epic poem *The Bruce*. In it he gives an account of the Wars of Independence, portraying Bruce as the hero and the English kings as holding the Scottish people, rich and poor, in a state of 'thryllage' or serfdom, until led to freedom by Bruce[11].

Rather than stressing the stratification of society, imposed by feudalism, Barbour portrays one 'kynrik' or country and one folk, certain of whose members are chosen to act for the common weal (or good). This theme is to be found too in the Declaration of Arbroath. According to it, it was 'the consent and assent of all the people', as well as divine providence and (very questionably) right of succession, that made Robert Bruce King of the Scots. The class divisions of feudalism were no doubt real enough, but an attempt was being made to subsume them into a united national consciousness.

THE LATER MIDDLE AGES

The years following the Treaty of Edinburgh and Northampton were turbulent ones politically, though not without cultural achievements, in poetry, architecture and learning. Edward III went back on his

9 S 37. Article XIX Union with England Act 1707.
10 The Declaration of Arbroath, in Latin with an English translation, is printed in Lord Cooper *Selected Papers 1922–1954* (1957) p 334.
11 See Archibald AH Duncan *The Bruce, An Epic Poem*.

word and the 1330s were a decade in which English troops captured
Scottish castles and were ousted from them one by one. The Scots
made an alliance with the French and thus became embroiled in the
Hundred Years War. There were many dynastic feuds. Several kings
such as David II and James I came to the throne in childhood. Both
of these kings spent periods in captivity in England. Yet throughout
these vicissitudes there was no doubt that Scotland remained a
nation and had much of the apparatus of a state, though it func-
tioned imperfectly. The chroniclers of the 14th and 15th centuries,
John of Fordoun, Walter Bower, and Andrew Wyntoun, all
churchmen, recount Scotland's history in strongly nationalist terms.

Emerging statehood

One way in which statehood was evidenced was in boundaries. The
River Tweed and the Solway Firth became accepted natural divisions
between Scotland and England, though Berwick on the north bank
of the Tweed remained English. In between there were disputed
marches, east, middle and west. These were policed by wardens, the
Scottish ones being appointed by Parliament or the Council from
the families of the Humes, the Kerrs and the Maxwells. They kept
rough and ready order, at times engaging in warfare, at times
upholding truces. Although raids were frequent and there was strife
as to the exact boundaries, there was no doubt that here was an
international frontier.

Treaties too evidence Scotland's international standing. Thus,
before James IV married Margaret Tudor, daughter of Henry VII, in
1503, a Treaty of Peace was signed between the two monarchs,
promising 'a true, sincere, whole and unbroken peace, friendship,
league and alliance'. But no union was contemplated. If the King of
England waged war against another country, the King of Scotland
promised to refrain from invading England, but might still give
succour to England's enemy.

Courts, central and local

By the 16th century Scotland had developed many of the judicial
institutions of a legal system. Some were akin to those of England;
others adapted from continental models. The development is one
from local and diverse institutions to centralised and uniform ones.
Many of them emanated from the feudal system. Participation in the
doing of justice was one of the returns made for the right to hold
lands, large and small. At the top it meant attendance by the king's

tenants-in-chief, lay and ecclesiastical, at the king's court, the *curia regis*. It advised the monarch on all matters of government. Out of it, by the 15th century, there emerged various combinations of Lords – of Council and of Session[12]. In 1532 they were placed on a permanent footing, financed out of church revenues, as the Court of Session, which remains the premier civil court in Scotland.

From the reign of the first effective feudal king, David I (1124–53), an attempt was made to maintain order throughout Scotland by travelling civil and criminal courts presided over by judges called Justiciars. These courts operated very irregularly, perhaps because the Justiciars were also magnates with more pressing interests and ambitions of their own. Repeated attempts were made over the centuries to make them travel on circuit or ayre, 'on the grass and on the corn' (in spring and autumn). The civil side of the Justiciars' work had decayed by the 15th century. The revival of their criminal jurisdiction was one of the achievements of James VI. Eventually central criminal justice was put on a permanent footing with the founding of the High Court of Justiciary in 1672, composed for the most part of Court of Session judges in the role of Lords Commissioners of Justiciary.

The inadequacies of the central courts were remedied to some extent locally. Trusted nobles and churchmen were granted from the 14th century powers of regality enabling them in their own territory to exercise justice on the gravest crimes, the pleas of the crown which normally had to await the coming of the Justiciar's court. Regality courts could repledge or recall their own subjects from other courts[13]. Some, such as those of St Andrews and the Abbeys of Dunfermline and Arbroath, even had their own chancery. The surviving regalities were finally abolished in the Heritable Jurisdictions (Scotland) Act 1746. Although they could be divisive in the hands of unruly noblemen, the records of the best regalities run by religious foundations suggest that they provided a high quality of justice[14].

At the level of the shire or county, sheriffs existed as local judges, civil and criminal, from the reign of David I and remain as the

---

12 On the antecedents and creation of the Court of Session, see RK Hannay *The College of Justice*, republished by the Stair Society in 1990. For a vivid account of the part played by a leading churchman in judicial decisions, see LJ Macfarlane *William Elphinstone and The Kingdom of Scotland, 1431–1514*.

13 ID Willock *The Origins and Development of the Jury in Scotland* (Stair Society, vol 23, 1966) p 84.

14 See JM Webster and AAM *Duncan Regality of Dunfermline Court Book, 1531–1538; Court Book of the Regality of Broughton 1569–1573*.

mainstay of Scottish justice to this day. But like the lords of regality, the office of sheriff became a hereditary one, which could be turned against the king and his policies[15].

Sheriffs were in competition with the burghs which were created by the early medieval kings as centres of royal influence and economic development through trade and manufacturing. They enjoyed their own courts over which provosts and baillies presided. At the principal or head courts of both burgh and sheriff courts, usually held four times a year, all the adult males with a title to land had to attend. This was known as suit of court. From them jurors would be selected[16].

Until the 15th century the burgh courts were supervised by the Chamberlain, a high officer of the king's household, who also heard appeals from the burgh courts. In the later Middle Ages wealthy magnates set up their own burghs, free of the king's influence and strengthening their own power. Burgh courts are the predecessors of today's district courts. Lesser landowners, called barons or lairds, also had the right and the duty to do justice in barony courts, and usually appointed a baron-baillie to act as judge in their name. In both civil and minor criminal matters he would be assisted in establishing the facts by the suitors of court, those tenants who were bound to attend[17].

As well as these courts of the land, there operated in Scotland a parallel set of courts set up by the Church. Every bishop had his own court, with a judge called the official and in larger dioceses local archdeacons also. As well as dealing with internal church disputes, it had jurisdiction over marriage, legitimacy, wills and moveable property, and contracts made under oath. Appeal lay to the supreme courts of the Catholic Church in Rome. Because of the unreliability of the courts of the land, people often voluntarily submitted their disputes to the arbitrament of the ecclesiastical courts[18] and registered agreements in their records.

15 For a comprehensive account of the functions of the sheriff and the records of a well-run sheriff court, see WC Dickinson *The Sheriff Court Book of Fife, 1515–1522* (Scottish History Society).

16 For a similar account of burgh courts, prefacing the earliest surviving records of a burgh court, see WC Dickinson *Early Records of the Burgh of Aberdeen, 1317, 1398–1407* (Scottish History Society). On burgh juries, see ID Willock *The Origins and Development of the Jury in Scotland* p 52.

17 See, eg, WC Dickinson *The Barony Court Book of Carnwath, 1523–1542* (Scottish History Society).

18 See further Simon Ollivant *The Court of the Official in Pre-Reformation Scotland* (Stair Society).

The substantive law

Unless courts are just going to decide cases on a whim or according to what seems just and reasonable, they need law to apply, general formulae which will enable cases to be determined with consistency. Feudal law, except in the individualised form of deeds, is rather scanty; but it has a voluminous procedural law, stating the manner in which decisions are to be reached. Thus, it had an order of succession to land on the death of the holder. The procedure of determining who was the entitled successor to particular lands was commenced by a claimant obtaining a brieve, a short document issued by the chancery of the king or of a regality. It ordered the sheriff or other judge to make inquiry of faithful men, the inquest or jury, whether the deceased died 'vest and seized' of certain lands, and by what tenure, and what was the relationship of the claimant to the deceased. Most of the law was of this procedural character. When much later in 1605 the first book giving a narrative account of Scots law was written it was the *Jus Feudale* or *Feudal Law* of Sir Thomas Craig. Criminal law was simpler. Killing, stealing, robbing and raping were crimes. The rules of law were concerned more with detailed procedures than deciding whether certain acts constituted a crime.

Law from the courts

If law was to emerge from the decisions of courts, there had to be judges sitting regularly and giving reasoned decisions on what the law meant which were in some way recorded and stored. There had also to be people knowledgeable about the law and able to argue from it; in other words, a legal profession. Its history is described in Chapter 14. It was not until the early 19th century that such a fully fledged system of judicial precedent emerged. But in the 16th and early 17th centuries, judges began to keep notebooks, initially for their own convenience, of decisions which demonstrated the practice of the courts, like a form of custom. These were called *Practicks*. The fullest are those of Sir James Balfour and Sir Thomas Hope, who wrote *Major* and *Minor Practicks*, and Robert Spotiswoode. All of these were eventually printed. But printing was slow to be applied to the law and for a long time they circulated in handwritten copies. Some *Practicks* are mere collections of decisions of the highest courts. Others, called by historians *Digest-Practicks*, contain extracts from statutes, Roman law and Canon law as well[19].

19 The largest and most authoritative *Practicks* are those of Balfour of probably 1579, but not printed until 1754. See PGB McNeill *The Practicks of Sir James Balfour* (Stair Society, vols 21, 22).

Law from Parliament

Long before these personal collections of rules of law appeared, a book of Scots law of venerable antiquity existed. This was *Regiam Majestatem*, a rather disorderly collection of laws from various sources. Some of it is native Scots law taken from Scots statutes of the 12th and 13th centuries. But the major source is the *Tractatus* or *Treatise on the Laws and Customs of England*, attributed to Glanvill, the Justiciar of Henry II, some of the borrowings being unchanged and others amended to fit Scottish circumstances. Other sources include writers on medieval Roman and Canon law. It is uncertain how this collection began; it may well have been merely collections made by a clerk of court for his own use. But by the 15th century it was regarded as one of 'the bukis of law of this realme' and a commission was appointed to 'mend the lawis that nedis mendment'[20]. The return of James I from captivity in England produced a spurt of legislation from Parliament in 1424 and subsequent years, much of it designed to improve the quality of justice and some of it apparently inspired by English examples[21]. The substantive law was still very incomplete and a statute of 1473 deplored the 'divers obscure matters that are now in our law'[22]. The first printing press was introduced into Scotland in 1507, but it was not until 1541 with the printing of the Black Acts that it was applied to legislation. Thus, the problem of identifying the authentic text of an Act was eventually solved.

The study of law

Despite the political and dynastic upheavals, the vitality of the cultural life of Scotland in the 15th century was attested to by the founding of three universities, all under papal bulls; in St Andrews in 1413, Glasgow in 1451, and Aberdeen in 1494. All were founded on the initiative of local bishops; James Kennedy, the second founder of St Andrews, William Turnbull of Glasgow and William Elphinstone of Aberdeen were all graduates in Canon law, that is, the law of the Church. All the universities taught some law from the beginning, mainly to clerical students, who thus no longer had to travel to continental universities such as Paris and Orleans. But their existence justified a statute of 1496 requiring barons and freeholders to spend

20 APS II, 10; one of several such Acts.
21 On the content of that statute law, see JJ Robertson 'The Development of the Law' in Jenny Brown *Scottish Society in the Fifteenth Century*.
22 APS II, 105.

three years in the 'sculis of art and jure' (ie law) 'that thai may have knawlege and understanding of the lawis'[23]. With some interruptions the teaching of law in Scottish universities has continued to the present day.

Scots law is often said to have been influenced by Roman law – sometimes referred to as civil law. In so far as this is true, the influences have come through academic study in the universities. The first channel was through the Canon law of the Catholic Church which provided a complete and self-sufficient legal apparatus from the 12th to the mid-16th centuries and made up for many of the deficiencies of the native law. It employed the terminology and procedures of the later Roman law which reached its peak of development under the Emperor Justinian in 6th-century Byzantium. A second channel was through the *Regiam Majestatem*, the compiler of which supplemented his mainly English materials with extracts from continental writers on Roman law (see above). The third channel was through legal study by Scots in continental universities, where as a matter of course the law worthy of study was taken to be updated Roman law and not the local customary law. In the early Middle Ages, Bologna and Pisa were favoured, in the 14th and 15th centuries, Paris and Orleans, and after the Reformation, Utrecht and Leiden in the Protestant Netherlands. Many Scots, such as William Elphinstone, also taught in these overseas universities. Their influence is to be found in the often cumbersome Romanistic pleadings used in the Scots courts and in the style and phraseology of writers such as Sir Thomas Craig and Viscount Stair (though the latter denied that Roman law formed part of the law of Scotland)[24]. But influence of Roman law on Scots law has been very limited and spasmodic in comparison with that of English law[25].

THE REFORMATION

The Reformation brought about several changes in political and thus legal doctrine. The latent concept of the state emerged in England, France and Spain and a long struggle began to align

---

23 APS II, 238. On the place of law in the first Scottish universities, see DM Walker *A Legal History of Scotland* vol II, pp 277–285.
24 Stair Inst I, 1, 12: 'though it be not acknowledged as a law binding for its authority, yet being, as a rule, followed for its equity'.
25 For a slightly more favourable account, see P Stein 'The influence of Roman law on the law of Scotland' 1963 JR 205. He concludes 'many parts (of Scots law) still bear an unmistakeably Roman stamp'.

nations and states. In those countries which accepted the doctrines of Martin Luther, religion became in effect a department of state and all subjects were required to follow the religion of their prince. In this respect, England followed Lutheranism. The Sovereign became the head of the Church of England, to which all subjects had to belong. Allegiance to the Pope was made a matter of treason. Scotland, on the other hand, followed the doctrines of John Calvin, as applied in Geneva. He distinguished two kingdoms, a civil one and a spiritual one, the latter with Christ as its only head. These two jurisdictions were complementary.

The magistrates of the civil power should submit to the ministers of the ecclesiastical power in matters of conscience and religion, just as the ministers submitted to the magistrates in matters of civil and criminal law. As expounded in the Second Book of Discipline, drawn up by Andrew Melville in 1578, this doctrine threw a challenge to the king, which was taken up by James VI who was something of a theologian. It lay behind many of the divisive religious conflicts of the 17th century and tended to dilute the concepts of nation and patriotism. In place of bishops, Presbyterianism chose government by committees − in ascending order the Kirk Session, the Presbytery, the Synod and the General Assembly. They provided many Scots men with experience of argument from theological principles and a belief in the principles of equality and community. Arguably the Scots resistance to laws in the making of which they have had only a minor part or which seem to embody excessive individualism derives in part from this group experience. It certainly made natural and acceptable the theological slant to the work of Viscount Stair, the late 17th century consolidator of Scots law[26].

In the ten years before and after the Reformation Act of 1560 there was popular hostility to the French counsellors and soldiers who accompanied Mary of Lorraine, the Queen Regent, and later her daughter Queen Mary. This was more than equalled by hatred of the English, following the invasions of Scotland by the Earl of Hertford in 1544 and 1545 and by the Earl of Somerset in 1547, during which many churches and towns were destroyed. When the Reformation came it took a distinctively Scottish course which owed nothing to the example of England and arguably strengthened the Scots sense of nationhood, albeit as a branch of a reformed universal church.

26 See p 29.

UNION OF THE CROWNS

The first of the three major steps which brought about the present constitutional position of Scotland was the Union of the Crowns in 1603. Queen Mary of Scotland had one child, James. When she fled to England and was imprisoned there by her cousin, Queen Elizabeth, her son was educated by tutors, including George Buchanan, an intellectual of European renown. At the age of 12 James took up the powers of kingship and was an able and vigorous monarch in trying to pacify the more disorderly parts of his realm and play off the various political and religious factions. On the execution of Mary in 1587, James became heir to the English throne, a prospect he had long relished. When Elizabeth died in 1603, James immediately made a ceremonial procession to London, feted in every town. He returned to Scotland only once, in 1617. During his reign James VI and I took as close an interest in the government of Scotland as that of England. The introduction of Justices of the Peace into Scotland in 1609 and the creation in 1617 of the still extant Register of Sasines, providing a register of all deeds concerning title to land (outside the burghs till 1681), were two of his lasting innovations. Above all, looking at his reign over Scotland as a whole, he gave stable central government, which it had not known during many centuries of factional strife.

Throughout his reign over the two kingdoms James cherished a scheme for their union. He derived it from his belief in the Divine Right of Kings. Since God had appointed him to rule the two realms, they should be treated as one. In his first address to the English Parliament in 1603 he fancifully compared himself to a husband wedded to the whole island of Britain as his wife. In 1604, the two Parliaments at his request appointed Commissioners from Scotland and England to discuss the project of unification. One of the Scots, Sir Thomas Craig, author of the *Jus Feudale*, wrote a treatise in 1605 arguing for union on mainly practical grounds[27]. In it he asserted 'that at the present day there are no nations whose laws and institutions more closely correspond than England and Scotland' (at p 304). Although the Commissioners reported in favour of a fuller union, the proposals were opposed by both Parliaments and nothing came of them.

One of the issues driving the king to raise the question of unification in some form was the legal status of Scots in England. Nationality was by now such a strong force that Scots and English

27 *De Unione Regnorum Britanniae Tractatus*, with translation by CS Terry (Scottish History Society). See also BP Levack 'The Proposed Union of English and Scots in the 17th Century' 1975 JR 97.

were treated as foreigners in each other's country, a handicap felt much more by Scots than English. Despairing of finding a solution through the English Parliament, James arranged a collusive case before the highest English judges called *Calvin's Case*[28]. Land in London was bought for an infant born in Edinburgh in 1606. Its seizure by others was challenged. The judges held that *post-nati*, ie persons born in Scotland since the accession of James to the throne of England, were entitled to hold land in England, since they owed allegiance to him as King of England and he owed them protection. This limited form of naturalisation removed one of the grievances of Scots in England.

THE 17TH CENTURY; RELIGIOUS FEUDS

Throughout most of the 17th century disputes about religion took precedence over nationhood. James following out his doctrine of the Divine Right of Kings (to rule) contemplated a single church in England and Scotland led by bishops appointed by him. This provoked resistance in Scotland in his reign and even more so in that of his successor, Charles I. Charles was about to introduce Episcopacy in Scotland. The Scots of all classes reacted in 1638 by signing a National Covenant, which echoed some of the arguments of the Declaration of Arbroath in portraying the Scots as a chosen people, like the Jews, covenanted to God. This elevated form of nationalism was not long persisted in as a matter of policy, but it led to the raising of a Scottish army, which gave a boost to the concept of Scottish identity. The Scots troops invaded the North of England and occupied Newcastle. In the face of this threat Charles gave way and in 1641 ratified laws of the Scots Parliament against Episcopacy. Emboldened by this success, the Scots Covenanters then sought to impose their Presbyterian form of church government on England. Commissioners of the English Parliament, by now in conflict with the king, sought the support of the Scots. In a Solemn League and Covenant signed in 1643 the Scots and English agreed that the Church of England should be reformed on the model of the reformed faith practised in Scotland, so that there would be one form of church government throughout Britain. The Scots took this as acceptance of Presbyterianism.

This incursion into English affairs was to lead to years of skirmishes and minor battles among the armed sectarians, as an offshoot of the English Civil War. Most Scots, though rejecting the

28 (1608) 7 Co Rep 1a.

ecclesiastical claims of Charles and his son, were shocked at the English Parliament's execution of the king in 1649 and refused to accept the ensuing Republic under Oliver Cromwell. They also were concerned that Cromwell declined to endorse Presbyterianism and instead showed a tenderness to the consciences of most believers (except of course Catholics). The period of the Commonwealth from 1649 to 1659 was thus for Scotland one of military occupation and a forced union with England.

Some Scots welcomed that unity. But when the monarchy was restored in 1660 in the person of Charles II, it was a restoration of the status quo and the two Parliaments resumed their separate existence. The religious feuds continued, but no longer reinforced nationalism, for Scots were much divided as to whether Scotland was still covenanted to impose Presbyterianism on England. Constitutional issues then came to the surface. Charles ruled in Scotland through the Scottish Privy Council, which had more power than it had enjoyed since the Middle Ages. It exercised both legislative and judicial functions, thus challenging the Parliament and the Court of Session respectively, and purported to do so under the royal prerogative, the residual powers of the king as the fountain of justice.

Resentment against this autocratic style of government eventually led to the dethroning of Charles' successor, his brother James VII (in Scotland) and II (in England). His successor (and son-in-law), William of Orange, was invited to Britain by some English nobles, prompting James's precipitate flight. The question was thus posed: who was now the King of Scotland? The Estates of Scotland (or Parliament) answered by offering the Crown to William and his spouse Mary. In a long preamble they denounced the abuses by James, who was in any case disqualified as a 'papist'. He had thus 'invaded the fundamental constitution of the Kingdom, and altered it from a legal limited Monarchy, to an arbitrary despotic Power' leading to 'the violation of the laws and liberties of the Kingdom, inverting all the ends of Government'. The Estates then declared William and Mary to be King and Queen of Scotland, confident they would preserve the rights they had asserted. Thus, the Estates were appealing to a fundamental law, by which sovereignty resided in the people (represented by the Estates of Parliament), who conferred the Crown on one who would respect that fundamental law. Indeed, the whole document is styled the Claim of Right and is the Scottish equivalent of the English Bill of Rights[29].

29 See APS IX, 38.

For much of the 17th century men's energies were thus taken up with argument and warfare on essentially religious issues. Amid the clash of arms the laws were often silent. What did emerge from this epoch of legal significance was a constitutional settlement in which the autocratic powers claimed by the Stewart monarchs were rejected and parliamentary government put in place. From it by gradual extensions of the franchise the form of parliamentary democracy now in existence in the United Kingdom emerged.

THE 18TH CENTURY

Union of the Parliaments

The inconveniences of governing two kingdoms under one king became more obvious in the reign of William, who was often absent on the continent. Scots resented their exclusion from England's foreign trade and engaged in a disastrous attempt to establish a colony at Darien in Central America. When William was succeeded by Anne, who outlived all her many children, matters came to a head, for the English Parliament, without consulting the Scots, passed the Act of Succession in 1701, declaring that the Electress Sophia of Hanover and her offspring should succeed to the English throne. So Scots who wished the Union of the Crowns to continue would have to accept the English choice. Those who did not would have to find an alternative. James VII and II and his descendants could provide one.

Faced with this deterioration in relations, Queen Anne took the initiative and instructed that commissioners should be chosen from each country to negotiate a complete union. The Scots commissioners chosen were wholeheartedly in favour, their price being that Scots should have complete equality in trade with England. The English were luke-warm. Negotiations collapsed when the Scots demanded an 'equivalent' or compensation for taking on a share of the English national debt. The Scots Parliament reacted by passing in 1703 an Act of Security declaring that on Anne's death it would nominate a successor from the royal house of Scotland provided he or she was a Protestant. The English retaliated by passing the Aliens Act 1705, making Scots aliens in England and restricting trade between the two countries.

It seemed as if the two countries were on a track leading to complete separation. But in 1706 Anne restarted negotiations, this time nominating the commissioners herself, with on each side a majority in favour of an incorporating union under one Parliament.

Working on the drafts of the earlier meetings, a draft treaty was produced within a few months[30].

The resultant articles of union then had to be approved one by one by the Estates of Scotland in Parliament. They were unpopular with several groups, as well as with the ordinary people of the towns. The Presbyterians of various persuasions resented the lack of protection for that form of church government. They were placated by the passing of an Act for Securing the Protestant Religion and Presbyterian Church Government, which was declared to be 'a fundamental and essential condition of any Treaty or Union ... in all time coming'[31]. In the same Act the then four universities of Scotland were to 'continue within this Kingdom for ever'. The legal profession had already had its doubts met by articles preserving the private law of Scotland and forbidding Scottish cases to be heard in any court 'in Westminster Hall'. Noblemen who saw their offices of state about to disappear were won over with sinecures, pensions, arrears of salaries (paid out of the agreed equivalent) and the retention of their hereditary rights of dispensing justice on their own lands. But the greatest lure of the union was the promise of freedom of trade with England and its colonies, which could be presented as the means to raise living standards in Scotland to equal those enjoyed in England.

The articles of union were debated by the one-chamber Scots Parliament over several months and each was voted on separately by the nobles, barons and burgesses[32]. They were all approved, with minor amendments, on 16 January 1707, together with the Act on Presbyterian Church Government. The English Parliament, urged by Queen Anne, then with less deliberation ratified the Treaty and passed an Act of Union in terms corresponding to and incorporating the Scots Act[33]. The Scots Privy Council by a proclamation dissolved the Scots Parliament on 28 April 1707 and on 1 May the United Kingdom of Great Britain, as defined in Article II, came into being. There was no corresponding dissolution of the English Parliament, but the existing members of the English Parliament, unlike members of the Scots, automatically became members of the Parliament of Great Britain and it followed the procedure of the English Parliament.

The main features of the Treaty of Union are these. The two kingdoms were united under the name of Great Britain, the succession to

---

30 The Articles of Union are printed in G Donaldson *Scottish Historical Documents* (1970) p 268.
31 Scots Statutes Revised, 201.
32 Minutes of the debates are printed in APS XI, 322.
33 APS XI, 446.

the monarchy being conferred on the Electress Sophia of Hanover and her descendants, as the English Parliament had decreed. There was to be one Parliament of Great Britain, in the Commons of which there should be 45 elected Scots representatives, and in the Lords 16 peers elected by their fellows. All subjects of Great Britain were to have full freedom of trade and navigation in Britain and the Dominions. The same customs and duties were to apply throughout the kingdom and the same coinage and weights and measures. The Court of Session and Court of Justiciary were to remain in all time coming in Scotland. 'No causes in Scotland [were to] be cognisable by the Courts of Chancery, Queen's Bench, Common Pleas or any other Court in Westminster Hall', a sentence the meaning of which was to be later the subject of debate[34]. The Scots Privy Council was to continue until altered by Parliament (which promptly abolished it). Heritable jurisdictions and offices were reserved to their owners. Laws concerning 'Public Right, Policy and Civil Government may be made the same throughout the whole United Kingdom', but 'no alteration be made in Laws which concern private Right, except for the evident utility of the Subjects within Scotland' (Article XVIII). The rights and privileges of the royal burghs of Scotland were preserved. Laws and statutes of either kingdom so far as inconsistent with the Articles were void[35].

Rational exposition of the law

Apart from Craig's defence in Latin of feudal law, writing about the law as distinct from collections of laws in the 17th century had scarcely gone beyond the stage of *Digest-Practicks* (see p 19). Sir George Mackenzie, Lord Advocate under Charles II and founder of the Advocates' Library (the precursor of the present National Library of Scotland), was a man of learning who wrote much on morality, religion and heraldry. But in writing his *Laws and Customs in Matters Criminal* he gathered together pieces of law from many varied sources under subject-headings with only minor analysis. James Dalrymple, Viscount Stair, then with one massive and masterly work transformed the civil (ie non-criminal) law of Scotland from uncoordinated fragments of law from various sources of uncertain weight and priority into a coherent and rational system of law, expounded in magisterial style. This work was *The Institutions*

---

34 APS XI, 411.
35 For text with subsequent amendments, see *Scots Statutes Revised* 203.

of the Law of Scotland of 1681 (extensively revised and republished in 1693)[36].

Stair's achievement is summed up in the sub-title 'Deduced from its originals, and collated with the Civil [ie Roman] Canon and Feudal Laws, and with the Customs of Neighbouring Nations'. Stair had been a Regent (or Professor) of Philosophy at Glasgow University from 1641 before embarking on a legal career which carried him to the top post of Lord President of the Court of Session in 1671. In 1681 he refused to take an oath under the Test Act 1681, had to resign and retired in 1682 to Leiden in the Netherlands, where he remained until the deposition of James VII and II in 1688. He then returned to Britain in the company of the future King William of Orange who re-appointed him Lord President[37].

Stair's concept of a work expounding as a system the whole of a nation's civil law had no counter-part in England until William Blackstone's *Commentaries* of 1765, but he may have been inspired by the similar treatment of the civil law of the Netherlands by Hugo Grotius, who is celebrated as the founder of international law. Stair's achievement thus put Scots law in line with the major systems of law which took Roman law as their inspiration. In Scotland his example was followed by the *Institute of the Law of Scotland in Civil Rights* of Andrew McDouall, Lord Bankton, of 1751, the *Institute of the Law of Scotland* of John Erskine, Professor of Scots Law at Edinburgh, of 1773, and the *Commentaries on the Law of Scotland and the Principles of Mercantile Jurisprudence* of 1804 and the *Principles of the Law of Scotland* of 1829 of George Joseph Bell. The weakness of legal literature on the criminal side was remedied by David Hume (nephew of the philosopher of the same name) in his *Commentaries on the Law of Scotland Respecting Crimes* of 1797, which performed the same organising role for criminal law as Stair had done for civil law a century earlier. Erskine, Bell and Hume were all holders of the Chair of Scots Law at Edinburgh University and evidence the contribution that the Universities of Edinburgh and, to a lesser extent, Glasgow (in William Forbes and others) were making to the development of Scots law, following the establishment of Chairs of Law there in the early 18th century.

As such they were part of the movement in scholarship called the Enlightenment in which Scotland played a leading role through the writings of men such as David Hume, the philosopher, Adam Smith,

---

36 The 1693 text was used in a new edition, edited by DM Walker in 1981.
37 For a fuller account of his life, see *Stair Tercentenary Studies*, edited by DM Walker (Stair Society, 1981).

the economist and jurist, John Millar and Adam Ferguson, the fore-
runners of modern sociology. Stair, though founding his work on
theological assumptions that were undermined by the philosopher
Hume, had in common with the Enlightenment movement of the
next century his claim that the constitution rested on rational foundations and his imposing order on the hitherto disorderly and
incomplete civil law of Scotland. Within the 18th century the most
prominent   contributor   from   the   legal   profession   to   the
Enlightenment   movement   was   Henry   Home,   Lord   Kames
(1696–1782). Kames was an enthusiastic polymath, whose interests
extended to agricultural improvement, transport, town planning,
history, philosophy and literature, as well as law and its science,
jurisprudence. His main work on the law is his *Principles of Equity* of
1760, in which in typical Enlightenment fashion he precedes his
account of equitable procedures in Scots law and English law with a
discussion of the principle of utility under which courts have a role
to play in advancing the well-being of people[38].

THE 19TH CENTURY

The transformation of the social life of Scotland through the
Industrial and Agricultural Revolutions could not fail to have an
impact on its legal system and in several ways it adapted itself to
meet the challenge. The upsurge of trade and manufacturing made
new demands on the legal concepts of contract and property.
Innumerable daily deals for the supply and transformation and
transport of commodities required an environment in which they
could be entered into with confidence that they would be carried
out. Insurance and bankruptcy laws had to be available to cope when
they were not. But land law, still rooted in the feudal law handed
down from the Middle Ages, was ill-adapted to industrial needs and
in the hands of rapacious landlords could become an instrument of
oppression in rural areas, most notoriously in the Highland
Clearances. Police forces were rudimentary, until the Police
(Scotland) Act 1857 required all counties and the larger burghs to
maintain a local force. Thus, conditions of law and order in which
industrial and commercial activity could flourish were secured.

At the start of the century the law could enable people to come

---

38 For biographies of Kames, see Ian S Ross *Lord Kames and the Scotland of his Day*
(1972) and William C Lehmann *Henry Home, Lord Kames, and the Scottish
Enlightenment* (1971). On the Enlightenment as a whole see *The Scottish
Enlightenment* Arthur Herman 2002.

together in business only by means of partnership and unincorpo-rated joint stock companies. Their resources could be pooled in the enterprise, but each individual's own entire assets remained fully liable if it failed. From the creditor's point of view there was the handicap that each contributor to the enterprise had to be sued separately. By means of several statutes this brake on commercial enterprise was removed by 1862 through the creation of incorpo-rated companies, which have an existence in law distinct from that of the individuals who as shareholders are their members. Their personal liability for the company's debts is limited to the value of their shares, including any unpaid ones. Banks, however, were excluded from incorporation until after the disastrous collapse of the City of Glasgow Bank in 1878 which brought ruin to many in the West of Scotland.

Restructuring of the courts

Early in the century the Court of Session was restructured and thus became better able to deal with the later upsurge of commercial liti-gation. It had sat since its inception in 1532 as a single court of fifteen judges, one of whom in turn sat in the 'Outer House' to take evidence, while the rest sat in the 'Inner House'. In 1808 the Inner House was made an appellate court, sitting in two divisions, each of four judges[39]. The remainder dealt alone with cases at first instance, that is, on first hearing. Procedure was also facilitated by cutting down the length of written pleadings. Later in the century, shorthand writers were admitted to record evidence. Appeals from the Court of Session to the House of Lords, which had begun immediately after the Union of 1707 and flourished in the 18th century, were curtailed by the Court of Session Act of 1808. Many of the sheriff courts had been poorly served since the abolition of heritable jurisdictions in 1747, for the sheriffs were Edinburgh advocates, who seldom attended, but acted through unqualified resident sheriff-substitutes. From 1825 this abuse was remedied in that sheriff-substitutes had to be advocates or solicitors of at least three years' standing.

Growth of case law

The smaller appellate courts led to the judges feeling an onus upon each of them to justify his decision; and as the century wore on these

---

39 On the reform of the Court of Session, see Nicholas Phillipson *The Scottish Whigs and the Reform of the Court of Session* (Stair Society, vol 37) ch V.

tended to become fuller and supported by the authority of past cases and, in their absence, of the class of authorities who became recognised as institutional writers. From 1821 the judgments, mainly of the Inner House, were collected and published in annual volumes which form part of the series now known as Session Cases. In this manner the essential requirement for the emergence of a practice of judicial precedent, namely accurate reports of litigation and reasoned judgments upon it, gathered by advocates in a standardised form, was met. Previously it had been left to the initiative of individuals, of whom two of the best qualified were Stair and Kames, to publish such decisions as they selected. Now the material was available and the structure was in place to operate a system of judicial precedent. In the 19th century the typical form of law was thus the published judgment. As more and more issues arose for decision from the industrial and commercial community, Scots advocates cited and Scots judges used more and more English decisions to justify their judgments and thereby gave the business users of the law a legal environment which was nearly uniform throughout Great Britain. Statutes such as the Mercantile Law Amendment Act of 1856 and the Sale of Goods Act of 1893, applying throughout Great Britain, accentuated this trend.

THE 20TH AND 21ST CENTURIES

While the decisions of judges still play a creative role, now in most of the law there is less scope for innovation and development than before. In part this is because more law is already settled. But chiefly it is because of the dominance of enacted law, both in changing existing areas of law such as family law, and in opening up new areas of legal regulation; for example, road traffic law, planning law, social security law, race and sex discrimination, employment protection, misuse of drugs and new forms of taxation. In these areas the role of the courts is a secondary one, clearing up ambiguities in the law that comes from Parliament. The courts too play a less dominant role than before, because much of the work of decision-making is entrusted to specialised tribunals, such as immigration tribunals, employment tribunals, and Commissioners of Income Tax. Road traffic law remains with the courts, but the volume of cases has been lessened by procedures allowing many minor criminal, including road traffic, offences to be dealt with by the acceptance of a penalty offer, recourse to the courts being at the option of the alleged offender.

Nearly all these new areas of statutory law are common to Great

Britain or the United Kingdom and represent the notional will of the whole electorate as mediated through the United Kingdom Parliament. Thus, they diminish the proportion of the law prevailing in Scotland which is distinctively Scots. Most of the tribunal systems operate on a British basis and so offer little or no scope for a distinctive Scottish contribution. Occasionally in road traffic and drug law the Scots courts will differ from their English counterparts, but such disagreements do not usually last long.

Parliaments are ill-equipped to deal with these demands for new and complex legal regulation. Much of such law calls for a response to changing circumstances; for instance, new drugs, new vehicles, new forms of disability. For this reason and the sheer volume of regulations required, most enacted law takes the form of regulations classed as statutory instruments and produced by government departments, under powers delegated by Parliaments, but with little or no parliamentary scrutiny. Often, as in the Social Security Act 1986, the Act itself is a mere framework, authorising the creation of benefits through easily amended statutory instruments such as in that example income support and housing benefit.

During the years of Conservative rule from 1979 to 1997 a ground-swell of discontent arose at the imposition of policies on Scotland which were opposed by the majority of MPs elected in Scottish constituencies. This first took the form of a pressure-group called the Campaign for a Scottish Assembly. This demand was taken up in a formal way by the formation of a Scottish Constitutional Convention composed of representatives of certain political parties, local authorities, trade unions and churches. It published a Claim of Right deliberately echoing that of the late 17th century and asserting the right of the Scottish people to determine the form of government that best suited their needs. The Labour government that returned to power on 1 May 1997 was, with the Liberal Democrats, pledged to create a Scottish Parliament. This commitment was fleshed out in a White Paper, *Scotland's Parliament*. Its terms were put to a referendum of voters registered in Scotland and supported by a large majority. The first Scottish Parliament was elected in May 1999 and exercises authority over all matters which are not specifically reserved to the United Kingdom Parliament. During its first fixed term of four years the Parliament passed over 62 Acts. The Parliaments elected in 1999 and 2003 produced governments that were coalitions of the Labour and Liberal Democrat parties, which together held a majority of the seats. But in 2007 the Scottish National Party, whose aim is the independence of Scotland, obtained the largest number of votes, but in seats won only one more than the Labour

Party. It formed a ministry, acknowledging it would have to secure the approval of at least some of the other parties to any legislation it proposed.

The continuing parts of the law of Scotland have the means of being kept up to date through the research and reports of the Scottish Law Commission, regardless of whether they engender appeals to the courts[40]. It has been supported by a resurgence of the academic study of law in the university law schools, substantial evidence of which is to be seen in the volumes of the Scottish Universities Law Institute (SULI) and *The Laws of Scotland: Stair Memorial Encyclopaedia,* both initiated by Sir Thomas Smith. But, as we shall see, there have been some difficulties in securing the enactment of the Commission's draft Bills, which should be remedied by the Scottish Parliament. Other changes to Scots law have sometimes been made as part of mainly English measures, such as the Unfair Contract Terms Act 1977 and the Criminal Justice Act 1988. Even today, Acts which apply throughout Britain and have special applications to Scotland, such as the Proceeds of Crime Act 2003, may be passed in the Westminster Parliament.

The United Kingdom's membership of the European Community created a layer of legal regulation above that emanating from Parliament and thus diminished to some degree the identity of the Scots law[41]. The characteristics of the law produced by the European Commission have much in common with the statutory instruments produced by United Kingdom ministries. They are difficult to discover and to understand because of their technical expression and lack of a context. They are prone to frequent unannounced change. Any disadvantage emerging to the detriment of the issuing authority can quickly be corrected by amendment, sometimes with retrospective effect. The legal profession tends to be reluctant to become involved with regulations. Thus, this law is weighted in favour of its creators, who are also its enforcers, and any rights it appears to confer on individuals are purely theoretical. We may call this law bureaucratic law, and with its adjunct in tribunals it is the typical legal product of the 20th century.

However, just as the volume of law of all kinds seems to be in danger of collapsing under its own weight, computer technology has come to the rescue in the form of data retrieval bases. These have been in operation for over ten years in the form of LexisNexis, WESTLAW and others which give access to decisions (some unreported) and statutory materials in the United Kingdom,

40 See ch 8 below
41 See p47 below.

Commonwealth countries, USA, France and to a minor extent the European Community. *Statutes in Force* and the Land Register of Scotland can also be accessed by computer. A database of sentences passed on offenders in various circumstances has been provided for High Court judges to promote consistency in sentencing. Judgments of the Court of Session and High Court are now available on the Internet on the day of publication.

CONCLUSION

It is a far cry from the trading customs of Scottish burghs in the 12th century to a print-out of the latest statutory instrument in the early 21st. All they have in common is the capacity to change people's behaviour, at the behest of those who control them, from what it would otherwise be. But that is the tenuous essence of law. Scotland in its chequered but well-documented history has generated the full range of forms that law can take.

3. Institutions – the constitutional background

CONSTITUTIONS AND CONSTITUTIONAL REFORM

Any legal system has to be understood against its constitutional background, a fact particularly true for any of the three legal systems of the United Kingdom. This is because the United Kingdom is most unusual in being a unitary rather than federal state, yet having within it three separate legal systems[1]. This situation clearly pre-dates devolution, being built into the constitution of the United Kingdom.

In the first edition of this book, it was remarked that the United Kingdom constitution had been disparagingly described as a 'medieval theme park'. There have been very considerable changes since then, though it is still a matter of discussion how apt that description remains. Some long-announced changes appear stalled, such as reform of the House of Lords. Others, only appearing on the horizon at the time of the last edition of this book, and with more effect on the legal system, have already been legislated for, but have not yet come into effect, that is, the replacement of the Appellate Committee of the House of Lords, and (in part) the Judicial Committee of the Privy Council, by a 'Supreme Court of the United Kingdom'.

Yet others still with very considerable effect on the legal system have come into effect, however, such as the embedding of human rights, in the form of the European Convention on Human Rights.

---

1 Federal states are those containing a number of sub-units of varying, but considerable, degrees of autonomy. Thus in Germany, there are 16 'states' (*Länder*), such as Baden-Württemburg, Bavaria, and so on, each of which has its own Government, Parliament, court system and legal powers, and together they make up the Federal Republic of Germany (*Bundesrepublik Deutschland*), which has a federal Government, Parliament, court system and legal powers (thus arguably constituting 17 legal systems in all). Similarly, in the United States, there are 50 'states', such as Alabama, Alaska, Arizona, and so on, making up the (federal) United States of America (thus arguably constituting 51 legal systems in all). Such arrangements are to be distinguished from devolution.

In addition, the evolution of the European Community into a more ambitious and wider-ranging European Union has had a continuing effect. These latter examples mean that, while the Scottish legal system is the focus, 'Europe' is a constitutional dimension which must be examined.

The change with most obvious effect on the United Kingdom legal systems has, however, been devolution, introduced in varying degrees, and for somewhat disparate reasons, to Scotland, Wales and (with more difficulty) Northern Ireland, though not so far to England[2]. When introduced into Scotland, devolution was seen by its architects as an antidote to separation from the rest of the United Kingdom. For so long as this antidote remains effective, while the Scottish legal system is the focus, the United Kingdom remains another constitutional dimension which must be examined.

This chapter therefore considers the relevant aspects of the constitutional background to the Scottish legal system, firstly in relation to the United Kingdom, including Scotland, and then in relation to 'Europe'[3], including the United Kingdom.

THE UNITED KINGDOM

The state is properly called 'the United Kingdom of Great Britain and Northern Ireland'. This title was assumed after what is now the Republic of Ireland seceded in 1922. It does not include the Channel Islands and the Isle of Man, which are technically dependencies of it. The preceding title, 'the United Kingdom of Great Britain and Ireland', was created when Great Britain and Ireland were formally amalgamated by the Union of 1801.

'Great Britain' comprises Scotland, England and Wales. This title was adopted when the two previous states (Scotland, and England and Wales, respectively) were combined in 1707, after sharing monarchs since 1603 (when the failure of the Tudor dynasty to produce an heir brought the Stuart dynasty to England as well as Scotland). Wales had been conquered by England in the 13th century, and was legally and administratively combined with it in the 16th century[4].

---

2   This last fact more than any other distinguishes devolution from federalisation. For a useful brief history of the devolution legislation, see CMG Himsworth & CR Munro *The Scotland Act 1998* (W Green/Sweet & Maxwell, 2nd ed 2000).

3   Deliberately in question marks, to indicate an ambiguity discussed below.

4   See Jones, Turnbull & Williams 'The Law of Wales or the Law of England and Wales?' (2005) 26 Stat LR 135-145.

The laws and legal institutions of Scotland and of England and Wales were not merged by the Union of 1707. Thus, they remain separate 'law areas', with separate court systems (as does Northern Ireland), and it is necessary to distinguish Scots law and English law (and Northern Irish law). However, a single legislature was created by the 1707 Union (and continued by the 1801 Union[5]). This legislature is common to all the law areas and much legislation is passed which applies to the whole of the United Kingdom, or of Great Britain. It makes sense, therefore, to speak of 'United Kingdom law' and 'Great Britain law' in fields such as tax and social security law which are common to the whole United Kingdom, or to Great Britain, as well as speaking of 'Scots law' and 'English law' (and 'Northern Ireland law')[6].

In 1973 the United Kingdom acceded to the European Community, which was itself incorporated into the European Union[7] in 1992. This has had considerable legal and governmental effects in the three and a half decades of United Kingdom membership. The principal effect, so far as the legal system is concerned, is that there are institutions generating and judging the law created by the European Union ('European Union law' or 'Community law'), and this law can apply in the United Kingdom and, indeed, displace Scots or English law (or Northern Ireland law).

United Kingdom government and Parliament

The Crown and government

'The Crown' is a term used to mean, in effect, the state. It is a symbol of the power of the state, which was formerly vested in the monarch. Thus, for example, prosecution of crime is said to be on behalf of 'the Crown'. For very few purposes does 'the Crown' refer to the monarch personally. When reference is made to the Queen's formal powers and duties, the terms 'Sovereign' or 'Her Majesty' are often used.

5   Or rather, perhaps, created in 1801, out of the merger of the Parliaments of Great Britain and of Ireland.
6   'British' is a very ambiguous word in constitutional terms, and has no specific legal meaning, save in specific contexts, such as 'British citizenship', as created by the British Nationality Act 1981. On the Treaty and Acts of Union, see ch 2.
7   The European Union was considered as comprising the 'three pillars' of: the European Community; the 'Common Foreign and Security Policy' of EC Member States; and 'Police and Judicial Co-operation in Criminal Matters' (previously 'Justice and Home Affairs') among EC Member States. However, the trend is to integrate the "three pillars": this is discussed in more detail below.

Government is carried on in the name of 'the Crown', so the Crown often comes to mean the government of the United Kingdom. This comprises the Prime Minister and some 25 senior ministers (those in charge of departments usually being called 'Secretary of State'[8]) who form the Cabinet, and up to 100 or so junior ministers (usually called 'Minister of State' or 'Parliamentary Under-Secretary of State') and unpaid 'Parliamentary Private Secretaries'. By a 'convention of the constitution' (that is, an unwritten rule of the constitution[9]), members of the government must be members of one or other House of Parliament. The Prime Minister is appointed by the Sovereign. However, her discretion is extremely constrained, for there is another strong convention of the constitution that she appoint the person who can command a majority in a vote in the House of Commons. In practice this means the leader of the party which won the last general election[10]. The other ministers are also appointed by the Sovereign, but in practice on the nomination of the Prime Minister. It is the United Kingdom government which proposes most legislation in the United Kingdom Parliament (including some which relates to Scotland, either because it relates to the whole United Kingdom or to Great Britain, or because it has been asked to by the Scottish Executive, typically 'piggy-backing' upon similar legislation for England and Wales[11]). The United Kingdom government is sometimes referred to as 'Whitehall'[12], after the name of the street in which most central government offices are situated.

Secretary of State for Scotland. Before devolution, the Scottish Office, headed by a Secretary of State for Scotland, was the

8   Thus, eg, Secretary of State for Foreign and Commonwealth Affairs ('Foreign Secretary ') etc. There is no fixed number or identity of these offices. In 2007, for instance, the ancient 'Home Department' was split into two with responsibility for courts, prisons, etc transferring to the Department for Constitutional Affairs (itself a recent creation) simultaneously renamed 'Ministry of Justice', while 'security' functions such as immigration and counter-terrorism, remained with the Home Office. (By mid-2007, the Transfer of Functions Order which might have been expected, had not been published). Like those noted below in relation to the Lord Chancellor and Department for Constitutional Affairs, these changes were introduced with remarkably little discussion, but considerable controversy.

9   And is not to be confused with the European Convention on Human Rights, discussed below.

10   Thus, when Mr Blair, Prime Minister by virtue of leading the Labour Party which had won the previous three elections, resigned in 2007, and Mr Brown was the only candidate for leadership of the Labour Party, it was clear that only Mr Brown could be appointed Prime Minister

11   See the discussion of legislative process in Ch 7.

12   The phrase 'Westminster Government' is also commonly used.

United Kingdom government ('Whitehall') department responsible for Scotland. Responsibility for most Scottish matters, including the legal system, is now, however, devolved to the Scottish Executive (and Scottish Parliament). However, a Scotland Office[13] remains in Whitehall, under a Secretary of State for Scotland, despite the reduction in his functions, and he is able to participate in decisions on matters reserved to the United Kingdom government as they affect Scotland[14]. Under the devolution legislation, he can forbid any action proposed by a member of the Scottish Executive which he believes would be incompatible with any international obligations, including Community law and rights under the European Convention of Human Rights, and likewise to order action to be taken to give effect to such obligations[15]. Similarly, he can also revoke Scottish delegated legislation which he believes to be incompatible with international obligations or with the interests of defence and national security or which purports to modify reserved matters[16]. Thus, he can be said to have a supervisory function to ensure that the Scottish authorities do not exceed their powers. However, while the Secretary of State may be said to have a number of roles (including representing Scotland in Westminster and Whitehall, and vice versa; resolving issues between the two; determining whether proposed Scottish legislation is within devolved powers and challenging legislation which is not; and being the channel of funds from the United Kingdom government to the Scottish Executive and negotiating in relation to them), it has been doubted whether, with devolution, there is a real role for the office[17].

13 Note the change of name.
14 See www.scotlandoffice.gov.uk/. The Secretary of State for Scotland in mid-2007 was Des Browne MP (freshly appointed in the re-shuffle after Gordon Brown replaced Tony Blair as Prime Minister), and the Scotland Office (also containing a Parliamentary Under-Secretary, and the Advocate-General for Scotland) was situated in Dover House, Whitehall, London, and Melville Crescent, Edinburgh. Since 2003, Secretary of State has been a part time job, held by another Minister with other responsibilities already (in the case of Des Browne, that of Secretary of State for Defence, and in the case of both his predecessors, Douglas Alexander, and Alistair Darling, that of Secretary of State for Transport: all three had the advantage of already being Cabinet Ministers with Scottish seats). This change was announced at the same time as the changes noted below in relation to the Lord Chancellor.
15 Scotland Act 1998, s 58.
16 *Ibid.*
17 However, in mid-2007, as a result of frictions between the new Scottish Executive formed by the Scottish National Party, and Labour Party Westminster Government, it was suggested that Gordon Brown, the new Prime Minister, might regard a full-time Secretary of State as necessary to manage Westminster and Whitehall relations with Holyrood.

Law Officers of the Crown – Advocate-General for Scotland, Attorney General and the Solicitor General (for England and Wales). The Law Officers of the Crown are the chief Government legal advisers. The devolution settlement also made provision for a new Law Officer, the Advocate-General for Scotland, to advise the Westminster government on matters of Scots law[18]. This was necessary because the Lord Advocate, who provided such advice before devolution, was translated to the Scottish Executive under the devolution settlement. There is no requirement that he be a Member of Parliament, nor even qualified in Scots law. Under the devolution legislation, he is one of those who can initiate court proceedings to determine any dispute or doubt that has arisen over the operation of that legislation[19], and can (as can the Attorney-General for England and Wales) raise proceedings before the Judicial Committee of the Privy Council which, despite its name, is a court, and is the ultimate authority on the meaning of the Scotland Act, including the question of whether a Bill of the Scottish Parliament is one which it has power to pass[20].

The Attorney General and the Solicitor General are Law Officers for England and Wales[21] (and, to maintain the former of the two 'conventions of the constitution' referred to above, are invariably members of one or other House of Parliament, though not necessarily in Cabinet[22]).

---

18 Scotland Act 1998, s 87: see www.oag.gov.uk/ The first Advocate-General for Scotland was Lynda Clarke, QC, MP, who remained in that office as Lady Clarke of Calton after the 2005 General Election, when her constituency was abolished. She became a judge in 2006 and was replaced by Neil Davidson, QC, who was not an MP, but was a former Solicitor-General for Scotland. Thus, the former of the two 'conventions of the constitution' referred to above does not appear to apply to this office. The Advocate-General for Scotland should not be confused with the European Court of Justice's Advocates General (discussed below).

19 Scotland Act 1998, Sch 6, Pt II.

20 Scotland Act 1998, s 33: but note below, and in Ch 4, in relation to the new "Supreme Court".

21 There is also an Attorney General (but no Solicitor General) for Northern Ireland. Under 'direct rule' since 1972 this has been the Attorney-General for England & Wales, but when devolution to Northern Ireland is complete, a separate office will be re-established.

22 In mid-2007, the Attorney General was Lady Scotland of Asthall, QC, previously Minister of State in the Home Office in the House of Lords, and freshly appointed in the reshuffle after Gordon Brown replaced Tony Blair as Prime Minister. She achieved a double whammy by being the first woman, and the first black person, to be Attorney-General (cf the Lord Advocate). Her predecessor was Lord Goldsmith, QC (also elevated to the peerage in order abide by the 'convention of the constitution'). The Solicitor General was Vera Baird QC, MP, previously Parliamentary Under Secretary in the Department of Constitutional Affairs. Her predecessor was Mike O'Brien, QC, MP who became Minister of State at the Department of Work and Pensions.

They may appear for the Crown in major litigation on behalf of the Crown, and provide legal advice on English law, but are likely to be asked to give legal advice on United Kingdom law, and indeed, international law, as well[23].

The other Law Officers, that is, the Lord Advocate and the Solicitor General for Scotland, are considered below.

Lord Chancellor and Secretary of State for Justice, and the Secretary of State for Home Affairs. In day-to-day terms, the Lord Chancellor and Secretary of State for Justice (two offices held by the same person) bears no responsibility for the Scottish legal system. He is the Cabinet minister responsible in England and Wales, firstly (as Lord Chancellor[24]), for appointments to the judiciary, and secondly (as Secretary of State for Justice), for courts, prisons, etc[25]. In addition to the Lord Chancellor and Secretary for

23 The advice of the then Attorney General (Lord Goldsmith) on the legality of the invasion of Iraq in 2003 became controversial, though remaining officially confidential.

24 Still, technically 'Lord High Chancellor of Great Britain', successor to the Lord Chancellors of Scotland and England & Wales. The former office of Lord Chancellor of Ireland was abolished upon Partition in 1922.

25 This situation dates only from 2007, and is the latest phase in a controversial story, too complicated to recount fully here. In brief, it chiefly involved: firstly the reduction of the role of Lord Chancellor (once a 'great office of state' involving headship of the judiciary in England & Wales and speakership of the House of Lords as well as membership of the Cabinet), in part because of increased interest in human rights against which this three-fold role offended (and more specifically, its breach of the 'doctrine of the separation of powers' whereby the three 'powers' of government - 'executive', 'legislative' and 'judicial') should be held by different bodies); secondly, the transformation of the old Lord Chancellor's Department into a 'Department for Constitutional Affairs'; thirdly, the creation of a 'Supreme Court of the United Kingdom' (discussed below and in Ch 4); fourthly, the splitting of the old Home Office into a Ministry of Justice (including the recently created Department of Constitutional Affairs) and a residual Home Office (noted above); and fifthly (as noted below) the first appointment of a non-barrister or advocate. For some further detail, see the Appendix to the Preface of the Third Edition of this book, Gretton 'Scotland and the Supreme Court' 2003 SLT 265-266, MacQueen 'Scotland and a Supreme Court for the UK?' 2003 SLT 279-282, Chalmers 'Scottish Appeals and the Proposed Supreme Court' (2004) 8 Edin LR 4-30, Bingham of Cornhill 'The Old Order Changeth' (2006) 122 LQR 211-223, recent editions of constitutional law textbooks, and the annotations to the Constitutional Reform Act 2005 in Current Law Statutes Annotated. See also references to the Appellate Committee of the House of Lords and the Supreme Court of the United Kingdom below and in Ch 4.

Justice[26], the Ministry of Justice also contains six other ministers[27]. However, because the responsibility for appointments to the judiciary includes appointments to United Kingdom tribunals, and because the Lord Chancellor has a wide range of disparate statutory responsibilities, his functions may touch upon the machinery of justice in Scotland.

Reflecting the history of the Lord Chancellorship, and constitutional significance of responsibility for judicial appointments (not to mention the controversial nature of the way in which the present arrangements were effected[28]), the recent legislation requires certain qualifications of an appointee, imposes a responsibility upon him to uphold judicial independence, and obliges him to take an oath[29].

The Secretary of State for Home Affairs (the 'Home Secretary') and his Department (the residual Home Office), bear no day-to-day responsibility for the Scottish legal system either. They continue to have some responsibility relating to the English legal system in relation to criminal law and sentencing, which is less likely to impinge on the Scottish legal system than the responsibilities of the Lord Chancellor and Secretary of State for Justice. Their other functions in relation to immigration and anti-terrorism do impinge, however.

The United Kingdom Parliament[30]

The Parliament of the United Kingdom comprises the Sovereign, the House of Lords, and the House of Commons. In this, it reflects the traditions of the English Parliament rather than the Scots. It is

---

26 In mid-2007, the Lord Chancellor and Secretary of State for Justice was Jack Straw MP, previously Leader of the House of Commons, and freshly appointed in the reshuffle after Gordon Brown replaced Tony Blair as Prime Minister. His appointment continued the change in status of the Lord Chancellorship, as he was the first person to be Lord Chancellor in modern times who was not a peer, nor either a barrister or an advocate (though he is a solicitor). His predecessor was Lord Falconer of Thoroton, who had presided over the manifold and rapid changes described above.

27 See http://www.justice.gov.uk/ . The other Ministers, following the reshuffle after Gordon Brown replaced Tony Blair as Prime Minister, were two Ministers of State (David Hanson, MP, and Michael Wills MP), and three Parliamentary Under-Secretaries, one in the House of Lords (Lord Hunt of King's Heath) and two in the House of Commons (Bridget Prentice MP and Maria Eagle MP).

28 See two previous notes.

29 Constitutional Reform Act 2005, ss 2, 3 & 17: see also the curious assertion of fact in s 1. The qualifications are, however, less than exiguous.

30 See www.parliament.uk/, also www.parliamentlive.tv.

sometimes referred to as 'Westminster', as the building it meets in is technically the Palace of Westminster.

The Sovereign is a ceremonial element of Parliament only. The House of Lords used to comprise all hereditary peers[31] (who latterly numbered some 750, though few sat regularly) and all life peers[32] (who numbered some 600). This had been regarded by many for a century or more as an indefensible anomaly, but several efforts to reform it over that period failed. As first stage of the most recent attempt, legislation[33] allowed all the life peers to continue to sit, but only 92 hereditary peers chosen by election from among themselves (giving an overall total of some 730), radically altering the composition of the House into a largely appointed one[34]. It also continued to contain certain Church of England bishops and the Lords of Appeal in Ordinary (for whom, see below). However, the matter has remained stalled since then, as dispute between those who seek a House wholly or largely appointed by the government, and those who seek one wholly or largely elected by the electorate, remains unresolved[35].

The House of Lords, as such, is to be distinguished from the Appellate Committee of the House of Lords. This is a court staffed by judges who are made life peers (mostly as 'Lords of Appeal in

---

31 From the Union until the Peerage Act 1963, while all holders of post-1707 peerages, and all holders of (pre-1707) English peerages, might sit in the House of Lords, only 16 elected 'representative' holders of (pre-1707) Scottish peerages could sit. The 1963 Act permitted all Scottish peers to sit.

32 Permitted by the Life Peerages Act 1958 (though there were some examples before that). Life peers are, in effect, nominated by the Prime Minister, typically as party political appointments from the major political parties, though not all are. In 2000, the government set up an extra-statutory House of Lords Appointments Commission to recommend non-political appointments ('people's peers'). It had nominated some 35 peers by mid-2007, including Sir Stewart Sutherland, Principal of Edinburgh University; Dame Ruth Deech, Independent Adjudicator for Higher Education; and Dame Elizabeth Butler-Sloss, first woman President of the Family Division of the English High Court. For details, see www.houseoflordsappointmentscommission.gov.uk. In 2006 an investigation was instituted into 'cash for honours', that is, the accusation that the Government rewarded donors to the Labour Party with honours, including peerages, but this was incomplete in mid-2007.

33 House of Lords Act 1999.

34 *Lord Gray's Motion* 2000 SC(HL) 46 unsuccessfully challenged the change as a breach of the Treaty of Union. Peers may now, however, seek election to the House of Commons (and the Scottish Parliament).

35 A White Paper *House of Lords Reform* (Cm 7027) was published in 2007, outlining different options. On votes which were merely indicative, the House of Commons preferred a wholly or largely elected House, but the House of Lords itself preferred a wholly or largely appointed one.

Ordinary') in order to sit in it, though it is to be replaced by a new 'Supreme Court of the United Kingdom'.

The House of Commons comprises 646 MPs, elected in single-member constituencies of roughly equal population. There are 59 Scottish constituencies, a number reduced in 2005 from an admitted overprovision of 72, to reflect the existence of the Scottish Parliament[36].

The United Kingdom Parliament is (subject to Community legislation) the legislature, in which most law for the United Kingdom is made. It is also the forum in which government policy is discussed, and provides the means by which governments are created. The party which can command the largest number of votes in the House of Commons is, by a convention of the constitution, entitled to form the government[37]. The system of simple majority voting in general elections has had the effect that the party which receives most votes in total usually has a disproportionate number of members returned. Coalition governments are therefore almost unknown, except in war-time.

The United Kingdom constitution has usually been said to display 'parliamentary supremacy' (alias 'parliamentary sovereignty'), that is, that there are no legal boundaries to Parliament's legislative power: it may pass any law to any effect[38]. As governments almost invariably have a majority in the House of Commons (indeed, that is why they are the government), and a convention of the constitution requires that the House of Lords not veto legislation which the Commons insist upon, there has long been in practice 'executive dominance of the legislature', or more bluntly 'governmental supremacy'[39].

---

36 Devolution has created the anomaly whereby the Scottish MPs can vote legislation relating to English Law while English and Welsh MPs cannot vote on legislation relating to Scots law, responsibility for which has been devolved to the Scottish Parliament. This is commonly known as the 'West Lothian Question' after Tam Dalziel, for many years MP for West Lothian, who is credited with drawing attention to it. It is a constitutional problem (though no greater than the anomaly preceding devolution whereby English MPs could outvote Scottish ones on a matter of Scots law: a sort of 'West Sussex Question').

37 Thus the 'convention of the constitution' that the Sovereign appoint as Prime Minister the person who can command a majority in a vote in the House of Commons

38 It has been argued that this is an English principle, which the Scots constitution never recognised (see eg *MacCormick v Lord Advocate* 1953 SC 396); also that it is a 19th-century invention. Be that as it may, it has been the UK constitutional orthodoxy for well over a century. Thus, the Scottish Parliament's power to make law derives from the Scotland Act which can be amended or repealed by the UK Parliament.

39 Lord Hailsham, a former Conservative Lord Chancellor, described it even more bluntly as 'elective dictatorship'.

Parliamentary supremacy as a constitutional principle is extremely unusual, for nearly all other states have a written constitution which, among other things, limits the powers of the legislature. In any case, accession to the European Community has required that Acts of Parliament be subordinate to Community legislation, apparently fatally compromising this 'supremacy'.

There is a House of Commons Scottish Grand Committee, comprising all Scottish MPs, which can debate government policy but, since devolution, has little to do[40]. There is also a Select Committee on Scottish Affairs, which consists of back-benchers, reflects party strengths, and scrutinises the policy and decisions of the Scotland Office, including its relationship with the Scottish Parliament[41]. This will no doubt continue for as long as the office of Secretary of State for Scotland remains.

The Scottish Parliament and Executive

Scotland now has a large measure of devolution[42]. There is a Scottish Parliament (sometimes referred to as 'Holyrood', as it is located is next to the Palace of Holyrood) and a Scottish Administration (in effect a Scottish government, a phrase it sometimes applies to itself, though it is not used in the legislation), led by a Scottish Executive (in effect, a Scottish Cabinet, again a phrase it sometimes applies to itself, though it is not used in the legislation either). The Act grants to these new devolved institutions the powers and responsibilities which used to be exercised by the United Kingdom Parliament and United Kingdom government.

Many issues arise concerning the nature and progress of devolution which cannot be addressed here. However, it can be noted that there are many legislative successes, such as the reform of landownership; that legislative procedures interestingly different from those of Westminster have been introduced; and that policies at variance with those of Whitehall pursued (as devolution was intended to permit). However, the early years were overshadowed by a rapid turnover of First Ministers, and the lateness and expense of the new Scottish Parliament building[43]. More recently, there have been suggestions of greater or lesser plausibility, that some reserved matters be devolved (for instance, drugs legislation, immigration

40 In mid-2007, it had not met for some years.
41 It produces several reports a year. In mid-2007, the most recent was on poverty.
42 See Scotland Act 1998.
43 It was completed some three years late and some ten times over budget.

policy and taxation and financial responsibilities). These issues have
been overtaken by the question of whether devolution is a successful
antidote to independence (as its authors intended), or a stepping
stone to it[44].

Devolved matters and reserved matters

The basic principle of Scottish devolution is that everything is
devolved unless specifically reserved. The powers and responsibilities devolved are essentially domestic ones, but the division is not
simple and unavoidably leaves a large number of debatable lands.
The legislation contains the detailed list of 'reserved matters'[45]. They
are divided into 'General Reservations' and 'Specific Reservations'.

The **General Reservations** are the Constitution, Political
Parties, Foreign Affairs, the Civil Service, Defence, and Treason.
These are clearly United Kingdom responsibilities. Some of these
have exceptions, however. An important one is that, while relations
with the European Community are reserved, 'observing and implementing international obligations, obligations under the Human
Rights Convention, and obligations under Community law' are not,
and are therefore devolved so far as Scotland is concerned.

The **Specific Reservations** are set out under 11 subject-headings, often with reference to particular statutes and again with exceptions. These are cases where there is tension between the wide sweep
of devolution on the one hand and the desire to reserve certain
specific matters on the other. They are therefore much more complicated, and are as follows:

A – Financial and Economic Matters
Council tax and non-domestic rates are not reserved, but money-
laundering is.

---

44 In the third Scottish Parliamentary election in 2007, the Scottish National
Party, committed to independence, won more seats in the Scottish Parliament
than any other. However, it only obtained one more seat than did the Scottish
Labour Party (47 to 46), and many fewer than the 65 which would give an
overall majority. It did not achieve a coalition with any other party, so formed a
minority Scottish Executive, but with a "Co-operation Agreement" with the
Green Party (2 MSPs), and an understanding with the Scottish Liberal
Democrat Party (16 MSPs), which enabled it to govern.
45 Scotland Act 1998, Sch 5: s 30(2) allows the list to be modified by 'Her Majesty
in Council' (in effect, the Westminster Government), and it has been, albeit in
only minor ways.

B – Home Affairs
A miscellaneous assortment is included, reflecting the interests of the former Home Office (including the current Home Office and Ministry of Justice). The Misuse of Drugs Act 1971 and legislation on drug-trafficking and international control of substances used for manufacture of controlled drugs are reserved, but confiscation orders are not, and nor are the prosecution of drug offences and police, social work and health involvement with controlled drugs.

Also reserved are the Data Protection Act 1998, elections, firearms, classification of films and video-recordings, immigration and nationality, the Animals (Scientific Procedures) Act 1986, most of the Official Secrets Acts, betting gaming and lotteries, emergency powers and extradition.

C – Trade and Industry
This is a lengthy list with many detailed exceptions. Among the reservations are business associations (covering limited liability companies), but not charities; insolvency (including preferred or preferential debts under the Bankruptcy (Scotland) Act 1985, but not other aspects of Scots bankruptcy law); anti-competitive practices law (but not so far as it affects the legal profession); intellectual property; import and export control; sea fishing; consumer protection; product standards, safety and liability (but not as concerns food safety or items used in agricultural and fisheries); weights and measures; telecommunications and wireless telegraphy (including the Internet); postal services; research councils; and industrial development.

D – Energy
Electricity, oil and gas, coal, nuclear energy and energy conservation are reserved.

E – Transport
Road transport (including the Road Traffic Act 1988 and Road Traffic Offenders Acts 1988, but not road safety), rail transport, marine transport (except ports and harbours), and air transport are reserved matters.

F – Social Security
Social security schemes, child support, occupational and personal pensions and war pensions are reserved matters.

G – Regulation of Professions
Regulation of architects, health professionals, as defined, and auditors are reserved matters, but not that of the legal profession.

H – Employment
Employment and industrial relations (except the Agricultural Wages
(Scotland) Act 1949), health and safety at work, and job search and
support are reserved matters.

J – Health and Medicine
Abortion, xenotransplantation (ie from a non-human species to a
human), embryology surrogacy and genetics, medicines, poisons
and welfare foods are reserved matters.

K – Media and Culture
Broadcasting, and public lending rights are reserved matters, but the
Scottish Arts Council, National Galleries, Libraries and Museums
are not.

L – Miscellaneous
Remuneration of judges, equal opportunities (including the Equal
Pay Act 1970, Sex Discrimination Act 1976, Race Relations Act
1976 and Disability Discrimination Act 1975), control of weapons
of mass destruction, the Ordnance Survey, and finally (and perhaps
unsurprisingly) Outer Space are reserved matters.

Thus, most obviously important for present purposes, responsibility for the legal system is devolved, save for the remuneration of
judges (and also, in fact, responsibility for the appointment of the
most senior judges: see below), as is regulation of the legal profession. Other noteworthy matters which are devolved are education
and training at all levels, the National Health Service (though regulation of the health professions is not), housing, the environment,
agriculture, forestry and fisheries, and the arts. Transport is reserved,
but with numerous exceptions.

The practical significance of the list of 'reserved matters' is as
follows: firstly, the list is the basis of the Scottish Parliament's
'legislative competence', that is, its ability to make law[46]. Secondly,
this legislative competence is, in turn, the basis of the Scottish
Executive's 'devolved competence', that is, its ability to exercise any
function (including making delegated legislation[47]). However, the
list of reserved matters does not actually define the legislative and

46 *Ibid* 1998, ss 29, 30.
47 For which, see Ch 10.

executive devolved competencies, which are considered separately below.

It should also be remembered that 'power devolved is power retained' and the United Kingdom Parliament retains its powers to make laws for Scotland, as the devolution legislation expressly declares[48].

The constitution and role of the Scottish Parliament and Executive (including their 'competences'), and the concept of 'devolution issues', are considered below in this Chapter, and Acts of the Scottish Parliament and 'Scottish Statutory Instruments' in later Chapters.

The Scottish Parliament[49]

Election of the Scottish Parliament. The Scottish Parliament, unlike the Westminster Parliament, has only one chamber. There are 129 Members of the Scottish Parliament ('MSPs')[50]. Also unlike MPs in the United Kingdom Parliament, MSPs are elected by two simultaneous ballots. The first ballot is by the 'first-past-the-post system' for 73 individual 'constituency members', on the Westminster model. But because 'first-past-the-post' tends to produce a result unrepresentative of the actual votes for each party, a further 56 'additional members' are elected by the somewhat complicated second ballot to remove this unrepresentativeness. For this ballot, there are eight 'regional' constituencies. Each political party draws up a list for each of these constituencies, and independent candidates may stand. The voters in each regional constituency vote for one of those lists, or for any independent candidate. Reflecting the voters' preferences between those lists (or independent candidates), the top-scoring names (selected on a mathematical formula designed to give each party about the same proportion of MSPs as their proportion of the total vote once the constituency member results are declared), provide seven 'additional' ('list' or

---

48 Scotland Act 1998, s 28(7). The (UK) Housing Act 2004 inadvertently amended Scots law in a devolved area. However unfortunate, this amendment was effective.
49 See www.scottish.parliament.uk/ and www.holyrood.tv/index.asp
50 It was intended that the number be reduced when the number of Scottish MPs was reduced in 2005, but this did not happen.

'regional') members for that constituency[51]. The relationship between 'constituency' and 'additional' MSPs has been a source of debate.

A person may be a member of both the House of Commons and the Scottish Parliament[52] and a member of the House of Lords may be elected to the Scottish Parliament[53].

The Parliament is elected for a fixed period of four years, the election being held on the first Thursday in May. Exceptionally it may be dissolved if two-thirds of the membership vote for a resolution to that effect, or if it fails to nominate a First Minister.

The law-making powers of the Scottish Parliament – 'legislative competence'. The devolution legislation declares that 'the Parliament may make laws, to be known as Acts of the Scottish Parliament'[54]. However, it limits this power by the concept of 'legislative competence', and any provision which is outside that competence is declared to be 'not law'[55]. The boundaries of legislative competence appear in what seems a simple list, but it requires some explanation. A provision is declared to be outside the legislative competence if it:

(i)   purports to apply outwith Scotland - This is an obvious limitation, but raises interesting questions where legislation concerns personal status which may have effect abroad, such as in relation to marriage or to recognition of professional qualifications.

(ii) relates to 'reserved matters' - These are described above. The question of whether a provision of an Act of the Scottish

---

51   The formula can be found in the Scotland Act 1998, ss 6–8. It is expressed more simply in Annex C of the White Paper, *Scotland's Parliament*. See also the hypothetical worked example in Page, Reid and Ross *A Guide to the Scotland Act* 1998 (1999) App 1. This method is one very likely to produce coalition governments, since the largest party is unlikely to have an overall majority. This happened in all three of the elections by 2007. In 2007, council elections were run at the same time as Scottish Parliamentary elections, producing two ballot papers with three votes, each based on a different system of voting. This in turn produced, in an election producing a very close outcome, a considerable number of spoiled papers, casting doubt on some individual results, though none was contested, in the event: see below.

52   In 2007, Alec Salmond, who had been MP for Banff & Buchan since 1987, was elected as MSP for Gordon, for which he had also been MSP from 1999-2001 (and as leader of the Scottish National Party, which achieved the largest number of seats, became First Minister: see previous note and below).

53   In 2007, George Foulkes (who had been a Labour MP in Scottish constituencies for 25 years and member of the 'Westminster' Labour Government for several years), elevated to the peerage as Baron Foulkes of Cumnock in 2005, was elected as a 'list' MSP for the Lothian 'regional' constituency.

54   Scotland Act 1998, s 28.

55   *Ibid.* s 29.

Parliament relates to a reserved matter or not is to be determined from the purpose of that provision (having regard
among other things, to its effects)[56]. This makes the boundaries
of legislative competence a little elastic. Legislative competence
is also potentially extended into reserved matters by providing
that if the Scottish Parliament makes an incidental foray into a
reserved matter in the course of making an Act modifying Scots
private law[57] or Scots criminal law[58], the offending provision is
not to be treated as dealing with a reserved matter if it makes
'the law in question apply consistently to reserved matters and
otherwise'[59]. This somewhat obscure piece of drafting seems to
mean that if the Scottish Parliament is legislating on, say, the
law of contract (which is devolved), and its legislation carries
implications for consumer law (which is not), then the legislation is nevertheless to be treated as not affecting reserved
matters[60].

(iii) is in breach of certain further specific restrictions – In addition
to the limit on reserved matters, there are further consequential
restrictions[61]. These, in effect, protect the actual devolution
settlement from amendment by the Scottish Parliament. The
most important is that (subject to exceptions) an Act of the
Scottish Parliament cannot modify (a) the Scotland Act itself,
(b) certain other basic provisions of existing law (including the
parts of the (English) Act of Union with Scotland 1706 and
(Scottish) Act of Union with England 1707 which relate to

---

56 *Ibid.* s29(3).
57 Defined as: the general principles of private law (including private international
law); the law of persons (including natural persons and unincorporated bodies);
the law of obligations (including those arising from contract, unilateral promise,
delict, unjustified enrichment and *negotiorum gestio*); the law of property
(including heritable and moveable property, trusts and succession); the law of
actions (including jurisdiction, remedies, evidence, procedure, diligence, recognition and enforcement of court orders, limitation of actions and arbitration);
and judicial review: *ibid.* s 126(4).
58 Defined as: criminal offences, jurisdiction, evidence, procedure and penalties
and treatment of offenders: *ibid.* s 126(5).
59 *Ibid.* s 29(4).
60 Thus, suppose that, in its wisdom, the Scottish Parliament sought to introduce
the English law 'doctrine of consideration' into Scots contract. It could do so in
relation to contract, as such, under its ordinary devolved powers without reference to this provision, but not to consumer contracts, or any other contracts
within reserved matters. This provision would allow it to do so even though it
would affect consumer contracts and any other contracts within reserved
matters.
61 Listed in Scotland Act 1998, Sch 4.

freedom of trade; the essential parts of the European Communities Act 1972; or any part of the Human Rights Act 1998; and (c) 'the law on reserved matters'. This last, in drafting of quite outstanding complexity and some uncertainty, is a belt-and-braces provision preventing the Scottish Parliament from amending Acts of the United Kingdom on reserved matters, or altering the common law on reserved matters (subject to exceptions).

(iv) is incompatible with Convention rights or Community Law. Another obvious limit to the legislative competence of the Scottish Parliament is the inability to pass Acts incompatible with Convention rights (that is, rights derived from the European Convention on Human Rights: see below) or Community law (that is, the law of the European Community: see below).

(v) would remove the Lord Advocate from his position as head of the systems of criminal prosecution and investigation of deaths – Finally, this curiously specific limit is designed to protect the Lord Advocate from improper pressure by the Scottish Executive in exercising his prosecutorial and related functions.

However, note that, within that legislative competence, the Scottish Parliament may amend or repeal Acts of the United Kingdom Parliament, typically those concerned with devolved matters[62].

The policing of the boundaries of legislative competence is considered below in relation to 'devolution disputes' and 'devolution issues', and in a Chapter 8 in relation to Acts of the Scottish Parliament.

Activities of the Scottish Parliament. The Scottish Parliament passed over 60 Acts in each of its first two sessions, on a variety of topics. While many of these were uncontroversial 'house-keeping' measures, some were very controversial. In the first session, they ranged from the abolition of feudal land-holding and fox-hunting, to reform of the means of appointing judges and the Scottish Qualifications Agency: in the second, from the prohibition of anti-social behaviour and prostitution in public places, to support for the Gaelic language and breastfeeders. However, a surprising amount of legislation for Scotland is still passed in Westminster (as discussed below and in Chapter s 7 and 8).

---

62 Acts of the United Kingdom may, of course, amend or repeal Acts of the Scottish Parliament, as its legislative omnicompetence (subject to Community law) is unaffected: Scotland Act 1998, s 27(8).

But the Scottish Parliament is not only a legislature, it is also a forum for discussion of important matters, and it has oral and written questions to Scottish Ministers on a wide range of devolved topics, and debates on a yet wider range (including reserved matters, such as defence, for topics for discussion are not limited to the Parliament's legislative competence).

The Parliament operates to a considerable extent through a committee structure, built in from the beginning as an improvement upon Westminster[63]. Some are mandatory (including Committees on European and External Relations, Finance and Subordinate Legislation), others concern the devolved areas (such as the Education, Culture and Sport, and Health Committee, the Community Care Committee, and Justice Committee[64]). It has made considerable efforts to involve the public in its activities, including special procedures to permit petitions on almost any matter of public interest, and actively employing IT.

Following the 2007 Scottish Parliamentary elections, with the question of independence in the air, and the Scottish National Party being the largest party in Parliament, it may be that aspects of the activities of the Scottish Parliament will change their nature[65].

The Scottish Administration and Executive[66]

Appointment of the Scottish Executive. There is a Scottish Administration headed by a Scottish Executive (comprising 'the Scottish Ministers'), which is in effect the Scottish Cabinet[67].

63 In the 1999-2003 and 2003-2007 Parliaments, the Executive coalition parties had a majority in these Committees. This will no longer be true in the 2007-2011 Parliament, as there is a minority Executive, so a minority on these Committees.

64 During the 2003-2007 Parliament, there were two Justice Committees but, at least initially, only one was established in the 2007-2011 Parliament.

65 While no doubt there will continue to be Scottish legislation in Westminster, its quantity may be reduced, and certainly the power to discuss matters outside the legislative competence may be exercised more.

66 See www.scotland.gov.uk.

67 Scotland Act 1998, s 44(1) although the term 'Scottish Executive' is sometimes used more loosely and widely to mean the whole Administration (as is the term 'Scottish Government', which has no statutory authority). The first two Scottish Executives (1999-2003 and 2003-2007, respectively) were Labour/Liberal Democrats coalitions, but the third is a Scottish National Party minority Executive (with limited support from Greens and even more limited from the Liberal Democrats). As noted above, the voting system makes coalitions very likely.

The devolution legislation states that the First Minister, that is, the head of the Scottish Executive, is 'appointed by Her Majesty from among' MSPs, following a nomination by the Scottish Parliament[68]. He appoints other Ministers to the Executive from among the remaining MSPs 'with the approval of Her Majesty' and the agreement of the Scottish Parliament[69]. However, the Lord Advocate and the Solicitor-General for Scotland (see below), who are also members of the Scottish Executive, and are also recommended by the First Minister to Her Majesty for appointment, need not be MSPs, though they may speak in the Parliament[70]. The ministers can be given titles showing their functions[71].

'Junior ministers' can also be appointed by the First Minister from among MSPs, but they are not part of the Scottish Executive[72].

The Scottish Ministers are supported by the staff of the Scottish Administration, who are civil servants of all levels. There is also a small number of non-career civil servant 'special advisers' who work to individual ministers or the Executive as a whole, and are appointed by them and leave with them. The Civil Service is a reserved subject, and civil servants remain members of the United

68 Scotland Act 1998, ss 45(1), 46. During the life of the first Scottish Executive, the First Minister changed twice. The initial appointment, Donald Dewar, architect of devolution, died in office: the second, Henry McLeish, resigned: the third, Jack McConnell also remained in office during the whole of rest of the life of the second. All three were leaders of the Labour Party in Scotland, the senior party in the Labour/Liberal Democrats coalitions. In the third Scottish Executive, the First Minister was Alec Salmond, in a minority administration: see previous note.

69 *Ibid.* s 47(1),(2). In the first two Scottish Executives, there were about a dozen Scottish Ministers at one time, including a Deputy First Minister, who was leader of the junior coalition party (initially Jim Wallace, followed by Nicol Stephen). In the third, there were (at least initially) only six, no doubt reflecting in part the smaller number of eligible MSPs supporting a minority Executive.

70 *Ibid.* ss 27(1), 48(1).

71 In mid-2007, titles included "Deputy First Minister and Cabinet Secretary for Health and Wellbeing" (Nicola Sturgeon, MSP) and "Cabinet Secretary for Finance and Sustainable Growth" (John Swinney, MSP). The title 'Cabinet Secretary' was presumably adopted to advertise the Scottish Executive as a 'Scottish Cabinet' and to imitate the use (elsewhere as well as in Westminster) of 'Secretary of State' to denote a senior member of Government. For the Minister of Justice and the position of the Lord Advocate, see below.

72 In the first two Scottish Executives, there were up to another dozen Junior Ministers at one time. In the third, there were (at least initially) a similar number, two attached to most 'Cabinet Secretaries', but one to the rest. Although officially 'Junior Ministers', and not 'Scottish Ministers', they have been referred to (presumably in distinction to the 'Cabinet Secretaries') simply as 'ministers'.

Kingdom Home Civil Service and subject to the same terms of service[73].

Functions of the Scottish Executive – 'devolved competence'. The purpose of the Scottish Executive is to run Scotland over broadly the same range of functions as the United Kingdom government's pre-devolution Scottish Office did. This apparently straightforward proposition needs clarification, however.

Firstly, where governmental functions were conferred before devolution upon the Secretary of State for Scotland or other members of the United Kingdom government, they are now conferred upon the Scottish Ministers, so far as they are to be exercised within the 'devolved competence'[74]. Thus, where a pre-devolution Act of the United Kingdom Parliament refers to 'the Secretary of State', in relation to devolved matters it is implicitly amended to read 'the Scottish Ministers' instead. This 'devolved competence' thus covers the same range of topics as permitted by the Scottish Parliament's 'legislative competence'.

Secondly, these functions now conferred upon the Scottish Executive are exercised by them exclusively. However, there are two important exceptions to this. In the first place, there is a variety of disparate matters, from road safety information and training to the funding of scientific research *via* arrangements for employment and training, which are 'shared powers', and are therefore carried out on a shared basis by the Scottish Executive and the United Kingdom government[75]. In the second place, although it is important to realise that the carrying out of Community law obligations is devolved, and they are therefore normally carried out in Scotland through the Scottish Ministers' functions, the United Kingdom government can also still act to carry them out in Scotland[76]. These two provisions further obscure the already complicated difference between reserved and devolved matters.

73 Scotland Act 1998, s 51.
74 *Ibid.* ss 52–54. For certain purposes the First Minister and the Lord Advocate (in the latter case, in order to preserve his independence as head of the criminal prosecution service) are in a special position. Also, in a belt-and-braces provision, by s 57(2), the Scottish Executive is explicitly denied the power to do any act (including making delegated legislation) incompatible with Convention rights or Community law, although they are in any case outwith their delegated competence because they are outwith the Scottish Parliament's legislative competence.
75 *Ibid.* s 56.
76 *Ibid.* s 57

However, thirdly, although certain matters are clearly reserved to the United Kingdom government, there are powers enabling it to transfer reserved matters to the Scottish Executive[77]. This process, which clearly enables the United Kingdom government without further legislation to extend the functions of the Scottish Ministers beyond the devolved competence (further blurring the reserved/devolved boundary), is sometimes referred to as 'executive devolution'.

Fourthly, the United Kingdom government can, in any case, make an 'agency arrangement' for the Scottish Ministers (and vice versa)[78]. This means that the Scottish Ministers carry out specified functions on behalf of the United Kingdom government; or concurrently with the United Kingdom government; or are carried out by the United Kingdom government but only in agreement with, or after consultation with, the Scottish Ministers (and vice versa). This renders the reserved and devolved distinction yet more opaque.

Fifthly, in any case further Acts of United Kingdom and Scottish Parliaments may add further functions.

Finally, as an interesting long-stop measure, the Secretary of State (in effect, the United Kingdom government) may direct that a proposed action not be taken, if he has reasonable grounds to believe it would be incompatible with international obligations (which would include the European Convention on Human Rights, and obligations under the various treaties constituting the European Union), or to order that a particular action be taken in order to give effect to such obligations[79].

Thus, there is a good deal of latitude in working out at ministerial and Civil Service level the exact interface between Whitehall and the Scottish Administration, and the pattern of devolved executive powers is extremely complex[80]. Electricity provides a good

77 *Ibid.* s 63. By mid-2007, there had been more than a dozen 'Scotland Act 1998 (Transfer of Functions to the Scottish Ministers, etc) Orders' under s 63, transferring a variety of functions under legislation from the Small Landholders (Scotland) Act 1911 (SI 1999/1750) to the Fire Service Act 1947 (SI 2006/304). There are also powers to transfer functions from the Scottish Ministers to the United Kingdom government in s 108 which had not been exercised by mid-2007.

78 *Ibid.* s 93. By mid-2007, there had been some twenty 'Scotland Act 1998 (Agency Arrangements) (Specification) Orders' under s 93, creating arrangements relating to functions ranging from the funding and conduct parliamentary elections (SI 1999/1512), to certificates for NHS charges for personal injuries (SI 2006/3338).

79 *Ibid.* s 58.

80 In addition to the functions of the Scottish Executive, as such, the Scotland Act 1998, ss 88–90 creates a regime for 'cross border public authorities', that is, bodies which operate on a UK or GB basis and are concerned with reserved and devolved matters, such as the Council on Tribunals.

example[81]. The generation and supply of electricity is a reserved matter, so is outwith the devolved competence of the Scottish Ministers. However, the power to grant consents for generating stations and overhead lines in Scotland has been transferred to the Scottish Ministers, though not as part of the general conferring of powers, but rather by an order transferring responsibility[82]. But the same order provides that powers to require certain statistical information are to be exercised concurrently by Scottish Ministers and the Secretary of State, though it also provides that the power to license suppliers of electricity remains a power of the Secretary of State, but only after consultation with the Scottish Ministers.

Interestingly, 'inter-governmental relations' within the United Kingdom have been concluded to have no statutory basis, resting in practice (at least during the first two Scottish Executives) on a Memorandum of Understanding, various 'concordats' and a Joint Ministerial Committee, and while these relations were intensive, they were in general highly informal, which may cause problems when different parties form the United Kingdom government and the Scottish Executive[83].

Law Officers of the Crown – Lord Advocate and Solicitor-General for Scotland. There are two specifically Scottish Law Officers[84], the Lord Advocate and the Solicitor-General for Scotland[85],

---

81 The authors are grateful to their colleague Colin Reid who supplied this example, fully explained in his 'Devolution and the Environment' in Ross (ed) *Environment and Regulation (Hume Papers on Public Policy vol 8, no 2)* (David Hume Institute, 2000) at 104.

82 Ie not under ss 52-54, but under s 63, of the Scotland Act 1998.

83 House of Lords Committee of the Constitution Second Report 2002–03, HL Paper (2002–03) no 28, (*House of Lords Constitution Report*). The Memorandum of Understanding was published as Cm 5240 (2001), and it and the concordats can be found on the Scottish Executive website at www.scotland.gov.uk/concordats.

84 In contradistinction to the Advocate-General for Scotland, who is part of the United Kingdom Government.

85 See www.crownoffice.gov.uk/ (also http://www.scotland.gov.uk/About/Ministers). In mid-2007 the Lord Advocate was Elish Angiolini, QC who performed a multiple whammy by in being the first solicitor, the first procurator fiscal, and the first woman to hold the office, as well as having been, immediately before, the first woman, and first solicitor, to be Solicitor-General for Scotland, first solicitor QC and the first to remain in office after a change of government (see next note). Unlike her predecessor, however, she was not in the 'Cabinet'. The Solicitor-General for Scotland, in mid-2007, to whom none of the above applies, was Frank Mulholland, QC.

both being ancient offices[86]. (The other Law Officers were considered above). They have two roles. Firstly, they responsible for providing the government with legal advice on Scots law and able to sue and be sued on behalf of it. Secondly, they are head and depute head of the prosecution service and responsible for fatal accident enquiries. Until devolution, they were members of the United Kingdom government and the Lord Advocate, at least, was either an MP or peer.

They are now, as noted above, *ex officio* members of the Scottish Executive, and may speak in the Scottish Parliament, but need not be MSPs. In their first role, they must be politically acceptable to the Executive (before devolution, to the United Kingdom government). However, in their second, they hold quasi-judicial office and must be independent of the Executive. Their position is therefore constitutionally odd[87].

Minister for Justice. As legal powers generally have been devolved, one Scottish Minister has always been a Minister of Justice[88]. He is responsible for the Scottish legal system, both civil and criminal justice, including the courts (though prosecution is a

---

86 For the history of these offices, see *Laws of Scotland: Stair Memorial Encyclopaedia*, 'Constitutional Law' and 'Criminal Procedure'. For recent Scottish Law Officers, see White 'The Career Path of Recent Scottish Law Officers' 2006 SLT 144-147 and 'The Career Path of Recent Scottish Law Officers Revisited' 2007 SLT (forthcoming): also next note.

87 The anomaly is less than it was, as the Lord Advocate's powers are more restricted than was once the case. In the 18th century, they were essentially Governors of Scotland on behalf of the Westminster government, and were for a long time party political appointments. In more recent times, they still had considerable powers in appointing judges (and not infrequently appointed themselves: on the appointment of judges now, see below). In 2007, as noted, the Lord Advocate (but not the Solicitor General) was retained by the incoming Scottish National Party minority administration, although appointed by the previous Labour/Liberal Democrat coalition. As also noted, this was the first occasion ever on which an incoming administration (whether during or before devolution) had not appointed a new Lord Advocate, thus marked an important stage in the de-politicisation of the offices. As further noted, the Lord Advocate was no longer in the 'Scottish Cabinet', noteworthy in that a non-nationalist Lord Advocate advising a nationalist Executive on the boundaries of the Scottish Parliament's legislative competence and the Executive's own devolved competence might have an interesting time.

88 In the first Scottish Executive, it was Jim Wallace (also Deputy First Minister), who was leader of the Liberal Democrats (the junior partner in the coalition), and an advocate. In the second, it was Cathy Jamieson, (of the Labour Party, the senior partner in the coalition), who was not a lawyer. In the third, Scottish National Party minority Executive, it was Kenny Macaskill, a solicitor, as 'Cabinet Secretary for Justice', and assisted by one (Junior) minister, Fergus Ewing, also a solicitor (but unlike some other Departments in that Executive, no other (Junior) minister).

matter for the Lord Advocate, as discussed above, and judicial appointments, discussed below, are a matter for the First Minister).[89]

Financial arrangements. Checks as to income and expenditure by the Scottish Administration follow the well-tried United Kingdom model. There is a Scottish Consolidated Fund[90], into which all Scottish Administration income is paid, and out of which all Scottish Administration expenditure is paid. Such payments must be authorised by some enactment and under Treasury rules, and there is an Auditor General for Scotland to check that all expenditure is properly authorised. The main source of income is the Block grant from the Treasury, to be spent as determined by the Executive and authorised by the Parliament. It can be supplemented or reduced if the Parliament votes in favour of a tax-varying resolution moved by a member of the Scottish Executive varying the basic rate of income tax payable by Scottish tax-payers by no more than 3 pence in the pound, up or down, for one assessment year[91].

Devolution disputes and 'devolution issues'

Plainly, there is scope for a lot of questions to arise concerning the relative powers of the Scottish Executive and Scottish Parliament and the United Kingdom Government and Parliament. To avoid such problems so far as possible, as noted above, an extra-statutory 'Memorandum of Understanding' and 'concordats' were devised, that is, working arrangements on such matters as relations with the European Union and application of Community law[92]. Also, prob-

---

89 The remit was expressed on the Scottish Executive website in mid-2007 as "criminal law and procedure, youth justice, criminal justice social work, police, prisons and sentencing policy, legal aid, legal profession, courts and law reform, anti-social behaviour, sectarianism, human rights, fire and rescue services, community safety, civil contingencies, drugs policy and related matters, liquor licensing, vulnerable witnesses, victim support and civil law, charity law, religious and faith organisations": see www.scotland.gov.uk/About/Scottish-Cabinet.

90 Scotland Act 1998, s 64(1).

91 *Ibid.* ss 73-75. In mid-2007, this power had never been exercised. With the advent of a (minority) Scottish National Party Executive in 2007, this may be the occasion of debate.

92 See Cm 5240 (2001) and www.scotland.gov.uk/concordats. As noted above, when both the United Kingdom government and the Scottish Executive were of the same political hue, or largely so, as was the case for the first two Scottish Executives, all such problems can be worked out relatively simply and amicably. However, when they are not, the risk of friction will be intensified, particularly if the Executive (although a minority one) is committed to independence.

lems in relation to making delegated legislation can be aired through the normal processes of approval of such legislation[93].

In any case, since any Act of the Scottish Parliament beyond its legislative competence is *ultra vires* (that is, 'beyond the powers'), it is void. Indeed, as noted, the devolution legislation expressly says that any such purported Act 'is not law'[94]. Any action of the Scottish Executive beyond its devolved competence is in a similar position[95]. Thus such matters may arise in the course of ordinary civil litigation (for example, answers in a claim for damages) or criminal prosecution (for example, a defence to a prosecution). They may also arise through a person directly challenging such Act or action through judicial review (for which, see below)[96]. Such cases may include challenges in terms of human rights (for which, see below)[97] or otherwise.

However, there are specific devices for dealing with devolution disputes. Firstly, there are various scrutiny devices in the process of enactment of Acts of the Scottish Parliament to try and ensure they are within its legislative competence. These are dealt with below, when such Acts are discussed[98].

Secondly, there are special procedures to deal with what are called 'devolution issues'. These are defined rather elaborately[99] and can take any one of six forms, that is, questions as to:

- whether or not an Act of the Scottish Parliament (or part of one) is in fact within its legislative competence (thus recognising the scrutiny in the enactment process might not have worked);
- whether or not a governmental function is one which is conferred on Scottish Ministers, the First Minister or the Lord Advocate (in other words, whether it is one which has been devolved);
- whether or not the actual exercise of a governmental function by a member of the Scottish Executive is within its 'devolved competence' (for which, see above);

---

93 See Chs 7 & 8.
94 Scotland Act 1998, s 29.
95 Though there is no equivalent of s 29. As noted, the advent of a Scottish National Party Scottish Executive in 2007 might make such an action more likely.
96 Attempts to subject Acts of the Scottish Parliament to judicial review have been unsuccessful: see *Adams v Scottish Ministers* 2003 SC 171 (OH), 2004 SC 665 (IH), *Friend v Lord Advocate* 2004 SC 78 (OH), 2006 SC 121(IH): see also Winetrobe 'The Judge in the Scottish Parliament' 2005 PL 3-12.
97 The power to do this under the Scotland Act 1998 is expressly preserved by s 100: see *Adams v Scottish Ministers* and *Friend v Lord Advocate* (and previous note).
98 See Ch 9.
99 Scotland Act 1998, Sch 6.

- whether or not such an actual exercise would be incompatible with Convention rights or Community law;
- whether or not a failure to act is incompatible with Convention rights or Community law; and
- any other question about whether a function is within the devolved competence or relates to Scotland or which concerns reserved matters (for which, see above).

Where a 'devolution issue' thus defined arises in any court or tribunal of whatever level[100], then (provided it is not dismissed there as 'frivolous or vexatious'), it can be separated from the rest of the proceedings, and intimation made to the Lord Advocate and Advocate-General for Scotland in case they wish to participate. These separated proceedings are as elaborate as the definition of 'devolved issues'.

A court or tribunal faced with a devolution issue may decide the matter itself, or may refer it to the Inner House (in civil proceedings) or High Court acting as an appeal court (in criminal proceedings)[101]. At least in the early years of devolution, any such case was likely to be referred unless very straightforward[102]. The court to which reference is made must decide the matter itself, but its decision can be appealed in all cases to the Judicial Committee of the Privy Council[103]. If the Inner House or High Court acting as a court of appeal are faced with a devolution issue directly, they may also either decide it themselves or refer it to the Judicial Committee of the Privy Council. If they decide it themselves, the matter can be appealed to the Judicial Committee of the Privy Council (unless appeal would normally be to the Appellate Committee of the House of Lords). In the early years of devolution, there were in fact hundreds of devolution issues raised, mostly criminal cases concerning human rights, as discussed below.

---

100 Devolution issues have arisen in District Courts, for example: see *eg Kelly v Clark* 2003 SC(PC) 77.
101 For these courts, see below.
102 Incidentally, a problem occurs where the devolution issue arises in the middle of a trial, for halting proceedings for some months for such a reference is impractical.
103 In the future, the new 'Supreme Court of the United Kingdom': see below and Ch 4. As this, and the following references, show, the Judicial Committee of the Privy Council had imposed upon it a role akin to a Constitutional Court. This was one strand of reasoning, and complication, in the setting up of the new 'Supreme Court'.

In any case, the Lord Advocate[104] or the Advocate-General for Scotland may institute proceedings on a devolution issue on their own initiative (and the Lord Advocate may defend proceedings instituted by the Advocate-General[105]); they (and the law officers of England and Wales, and of Northern Ireland) may require any court or tribunal to refer such a case direct to the Judicial Committee of the Privy Council; and they (and those other law officers) may forestall a dispute by referring to the Judicial Committee of the Privy Council action proposed by a member of the Scottish Executive before it happens.

Interlinking of 'human rights' with the concept of 'devolution issues'

'Human rights' are dealt with below. However, it is useful to recall here that, as noted above, the powers of the Scottish Parliament and Scottish Executive are limited by the devolution legislation to, among other things, actions compatible with Convention rights, ie, rights derived from the European Convention on Human Rights[106]. Inevitably, some legislation passed by the Scottish Parliament will turn out to be incompatible, despite the scrutiny during the enactment process designed to weed it out[107]. Equally, some actions of the Scottish Executive will too (including making delegated legislation and performing administrative acts whether by Ministers themselves or by their civil servants). These are thus *ultra vires*, ie 'beyond the powers' the Parliament and Executive have, and may be dealt with as described above as 'devolution issues'.

And it is thus worth noting, that, while Convention rights came into full force throughout the whole United Kingdom in 2000, they were brought partly into force in Scotland in 1998, as part of the devolution arrangements. One result of this is that all the early

---

104 Given the Lord Advocate's membership of the Scottish Executive, and the opportunities to challenge a non-Executive Bills before the royal assent (for which, see Ch 8), such occasions are likely to be rare.
105 Indicating, in effect, a disagreement between the UK government and the Scottish Executive which has not been resolved by other means.
106 Scotland Act 1998, ss 29(2)(c),(d), 30, Schs 4, 5 (which define the 'legislative competence' of the Scottish Parliament) and ss 54 and 57(2) (which, read with s 53, define the 'devolved competence' and rule-making power of the Scottish Executive) respectively. (As noted, s 29(1) roundly declares the legislation outside the legislative competence 'is not law'.) There is no saving provision for those adversely affected by such a finding. Remedial action does not arise. Fresh legislation would have to be made.
107 As described in Ch 8.

human rights cases in United Kingdom law are Scottish ones, arising as 'devolution issues' under the devolution legislation. As noted above, some hundreds were initiated, though few made their way as far as the Judicial Committee of the Privy Council[108]. The vast majority were challenges to actions of the Scottish Executive, not the Scottish Parliament. In particular, they were challenges to decisions by the Lord Advocate to prosecute, and related decisions, so arose in criminal cases, relied on the right to a fair trial under Article 6 of the European Convention on Human Rights (see below), and were referred from, or via the High Court[109]. This is discussed further in relation to the human rights legislation, in Chapter 7.

'EUROPE' – THE COUNCIL OF EUROPE AND THE EUROPEAN CONVENTION ON HUMAN RIGHTS

'Europe', in quotation marks, is a useful, but ambiguous term. It is useful to refer to two separate institutions which have strongly modified, and continue to modify, the Scottish legal system. These two institutions are the Council of Europe (and its principal product, the European Convention on Human Rights), and the European Union (including the European Community, once referred to as 'the Common Market', and its principal product 'Community law').

It is ambiguous because these two separate institutions are frequently confused in public discussion. In particular: the Council of Europe's European Court of Human Rights is thought to be the same as the European Union's European Court of Justice; and the European Convention on Human Rights is thought to be a product of the European Union, and part of Community law. Neither of these things is true. The ambiguity is therefore embraced here deliberately to draw attention to the necessity of distinguishing. Appendix 3 assists in this.

This section therefore deals with the Council of Europe and the European Convention on Human Rights, and the next deals with the European Union, including the European Community.

---

108 By mid-2007, less than 20 were reported.
109 Early examples included *Starrs v Ruxton* 2000 JC 208 (Temporary Sheriffs), *HM Advocate v McNab* 2000 JC 80 and *HM Advocate v McLean* 2000 JC 140 (both delays in prosecution), *HM Advocate v Montgomery and Coulter* 2000 JC 111 (pre-trial publicity), and *Brown v Stott* 2000 SLT 379 (self-incrimination).

The Council of Europe and the European Convention on Human Rights

The Council of Europe[110] and 'human rights'[111]

The Council of Europe has had a considerable effect upon the Scottish legal system, most noticeably since the passing of the Human Rights Act 1998. Like the European Union (including the European Community), but in a different way, it has introduced what amounts to a new source of law, requiring to be treated in a different fashion, and overriding existing Scots law.

The first thing to note is that the Council of Europe is not the same thing as the European Union (including the European Community) which is dealt with below. Set up in 1948 in the aftermath of the Second World War by ten Western European states, it is a treaty organisation, intended to promote unity through democracy and human rights. The United Kingdom was a founder member[112]. Membership has now expanded to nearly 50 Western, Central and Eastern European states[113], and it has links with other states. Its decision-making body is a Committee of Ministers comprising the Foreign Ministers of the signatory states. It also has a representative deliberative Parliamentary Assembly[114]. In addition, there are a Secretary-General and a Commissioner for Human Rights, both

110 See http://www.coe.int/.
111 'Human rights' has become a popular phrase to describe certain obligations considered by their exponents to be more fundamental than ordinary law, indeed perhaps more fundamental than law itself. There are important questions to be asked as to what makes a claim a 'human right', and who decides, which cannot be considered here. However, it should be noted that numerous international treaties assert a range of human rights, fundamental freedoms and the like, including the United Nations Universal Declaration of Human Rights (1948), and related documents like the International Covenant on Civil and Political Rights and International Covenant on Economic, Social and Cultural Rights (both 1966), not to mention a host of others on specific rights such as those concerned with the treatment of prisoners, the death penalty, torture, genocide, prisoners of war, children and so on. Further, the European Union is expanding into the field, by introducing legislation on race and gender discrimination; requiring Member States to adhere to respect for human rights, democracy and the rule of law; 'proclaiming' its own Charter of Fundamental Rights (though without any means of enforceability at present); and possibly one day acceding, in its own right, to the European Convention on Human Rights and Fundamental Freedoms.
112 See Appendix 3.
113 It extends eastwards far enough to include Azerbaijan, Georgia, the Russian Federation and Ukraine among its members.
114 See http://assembly.coe.int/. The Parliamentary Assembly of the Council of Europe some times refers to itself as 'PACE', which is slightly confusing as this acronym is used in England and Wales to refer to the Police and Criminal Evidence Act 1984.

elected by the Parliamentary Assembly. The Secretary-General has, among other things, the function of monitoring states' compliance with the European Convention on Human Rights (see below), and the Commissioner has the function of promoting observance of that Convention. Most importantly, it set up the European Court of Human Rights[115] to judge 'human rights' cases.

The Council of Europe has promoted the creation of treaties among its members. There are nearly 200 to date, and they cover a wide variety of subjects, ranging from terrorism to nationality, and from social security to cybercrime. However, the first and most important of these treaties is the European Convention for the Protection of Human Rights and Fundamental Freedoms (commonly called the 'European Convention on Human Rights', abbreviated to 'ECHR'). The United Kingdom was joint first signatory in 1950, the Convention came into force in 1953, and it has been signed by all Council of Europe members. The ECHR is an attempt to implement the United Nations Universal Declaration of Human Rights of 1948, and requires its signatories to 'secure' (that is, not to allow breach of) certain specified human rights, such as a right to life, freedom from torture or inhuman or degrading treatment, a right to liberty and security of person, and a right to family life. There are amending Protocols which add further rights, but the United Kingdom has not signed up for all of these.

The European Convention on Human Rights ('ECHR')

The ECHR is designed to limit the actions of government bodies and officials by declaring certain obligations which the signatories accept as binding. The United Kingdom has accepted (subject to certain derogations, that is, 'disapplications') the following obligations in the Convention itself[116]:

---

115 See http://www.echr.coe.int/echr/.
116 Those listed below in quotation marks are quoted verbatim. The full text, and details of derogations, etc, can be found through the Council of Europe website (see above). In particular, note that the United Kingdom has not ratified the Fourth Protocol (Art 1: 'No one shall be deprived of his liberty merely on the ground of inability to fulfil a contractual obligation'; Art 2: Freedom of movement within the state, and freedom to leave it; Art 3: No expulsion of nationals or deprivation of their right to enter the country) nor even signed the Seventh Protocol (Art 1: Expulsion of aliens only after a reasoned decision with appeal and representation; Art 2: Right to have criminal convictions reviewed by a higher tribunal governed by law; Art 3: Compensation for those wrongly convicted of a crime; Art 4: No one subjected to double jeopardy in criminal proceedings; Art 5: Equality of rights and responsibilities of spouses). This is because United Kingdom law is inconsistent with them.

Article 1 All signatory states agree to secure to everyone within their jurisdiction the rights and freedoms listed.

Article 2 Everyone's life shall be protected by law, except where the death penalty is provided by law or where death results from defence from unlawful violence, to effect arrest, to prevent escape from detention, or in quelling a riot or insurrection.

Article 3 'No one shall be subjected to torture or to inhuman or degrading treatment or punishment'.

Article 4 'No one shall be held in slavery or servitude. No one shall be required to perform forced or compulsory labour'.

Article 5 'Everyone has the right to liberty and security of person' except under lawful arrest or detention. In such cases he must be given reasons and must be brought promptly before a judge.

Article 6 Everyone is entitled to a fair and public hearing in civil and criminal law. Everyone charged with a criminal offence is presumed innocent until proved guilty.

Article 7 No one shall be guilty of an offence which was not one under national or international law when it was committed, except for an act which was criminal according to general principles of law recognised by civilised nations.

Article 8 'Everyone has the right to respect for his private and family life, his home and correspondence' (subject to certain exceptions).

Article 9 'Everyone has the right to freedom of thought, conscience and religion' (subject to certain exceptions).

Article 10 'Everyone has the right to freedom of expression' and opinions (subject to certain exceptions).

Article 11 'Everyone has the right to freedom of peaceful assembly and to freedom of association with others' (subject to certain exceptions).

Article 12 'Men and women of marriageable age have the right to marry and to found a family'.

Article 13 Everyone whose rights or freedoms have been violated to have an effective remedy before a national authority.

Article 14 'The enjoyment of the rights and freedoms set forth in this Convention shall be secured without discrimination on any ground such as sex, race, colour, language, religion, political or other opinion, national or social origin'.

Article 15 In time of war or other public emergency threatening the life of the nation, measures limiting the application of the rights may be taken, except from Article 2 (other than in respect of deaths from lawful acts of war), Article 3, Article 4 (in respect of slavery or servitude), and Article 7.

Article 16 Restrictions may be imposed on the political activity of aliens.

Article 17 Nothing must be done that is aimed at the destruction or limitation of the rights.

Article 18 Permitted restrictions to the rights and freedoms must not be used except for the purposes for which they are prescribed.

In addition, the United Kingdom has agreed to secure the following additional rights and freedoms in the First Protocol to the Convention:

Article 1 The peaceful enjoyment of possessions is protected. No one can be deprived of possessions, except in the public interest.

Article 2 'No person shall be denied the right to education'. The right of parents shall be respected.

Article 3 Free elections shall be held at reasonable intervals by secret ballot.

It has also agreed to secure the following additional right or freedom in the Sixth and Thirteenth Protocols to the Convention (which overlap):

Article 1 'The death penalty shall be abolished. No one shall be condemned to such penalty or executed'.

Certain of the Articles and Protocols are subject to qualifications. Thus, the right to peaceful enjoyment of possessions is subject to the right of the state to control the use of property and to secure the payment of taxes. They are also subject to possible derogations and reservations (that is, *ad hoc* exceptions and exclusions[117]).

However, the underlying message is clear, and the United Kingdom, its government and Parliament, the Scottish Executive

---

117 In the early days of the ECHR, the United Kingdom derogated from obligations in relation to colonies. However, the two most important derogations, resulting from terrorist activities, were from Art 5. During the 'Troubles' in Northern Ireland, the United Kingdom entered a derogation from Art 5(3) concerning judicial control over arrest and detention powers there under the Prevention of Terrorism (Temporary Provisions) Act 1984, after an adverse ECtHR decision (*Brogan v UK* (A 145-B) [1989] 11 EHRR 117), in order to continue using those powers (finally repealed by the Terrorism Act 2000). It also entered a derogation from Art 5(1)(f) concerning detention in any part of the United Kingdom through the Human Rights (Designated Derogation) Order 2001, SI 2001/3644 to allow ss 21–23 of the Anti-Terrorism, Crime and Security Act 2001 (passed in the wake of '9/11') which permitted those subject to deportation as 'suspected international terrorists' to be detained indefinitely if they could not be deported because it would subject them to the risk of torture (thus breaching Art 3) or it was impossible because no state will take them, or like reason. However, in *A & Others v Secretary of State* [2004] UKHL 56 the Appellate Committee of the House of Lords declared that those powers were disproportionate and discriminatory, so could not justify derogation, rendering the legislation incompatible with the ECHR, and the derogation was withdrawn.

and Scottish Parliament, and all other 'official' institutions, are bound by its terms.

Thus, the United Kingdom has, for over fifty years, committed itself to promoting a number of rights and freedoms, commonly enumerated as: 'the right to life (including abolition of the death penalty)', 'freedom from torture', 'protection from slavery', 'liberty and the security of persons', 'a fair trial', 'the principle of legality', 'respect for private and family life', 'freedom of expression', 'a right to peaceful assembly', 'the right to marry and to found a family', 'peaceful enjoyment of possessions', 'the right to education', the 'right to free elections' and the right to an effective remedy for any breach, and non-discrimination in the application, of the law. Some of these can be derogated from 'in time of war or other public emergency threatening the life of the nation, and reservations can be entered to some.

Some of the rights and freedoms are defined with a degree of explicitness (for instance the 'right to a fair trial'), while others are not (for instance the 'right to private and family life'). This means courts are required to interpret them, and certainly, some such interpretations have been surprising. However, a considerable case law has grown up in the different signatory states and, most importantly, from the European Court of Human Rights itself, and it is important to realise that these are a set of rights and freedoms held against the organs of the state, rather than against other people.

Enforceability of the ECHR

But what does the agreement to 'secure' these rights mean?

Enforceability of the ECHR by states and by individual petition. All signatory states, including the United Kingdom, agree to secure to everyone within its jurisdiction the rights and freedoms declared in the ECHR[118]. That agreement, being a matter of international law, did not make the Convention part of the law of the United Kingdom. It merely allowed states to refer to cases the Court of Human Rights ('ECtHR') in Strasbourg (and which is discussed below in Chapter 7).

Inter-state cases have been rare however[119], and much more important is the 'right of individual petition', which allows individ-

---

118 Art 1, ECHR.
119 One of significance, nevertheless, was *Ireland v UK* (1979-80) 2 EHRR 25, which concerned treatment of detainees in Northern Ireland.

uals claiming that they have been treated in a manner which contravened one or more Articles of the Convention, and who have exhausted possible remedies in their local courts, to petition the ECtHR[120].

There have been a considerable number of petitions from Scotland, concerning trials, prisoners' rights, and other matters, and there are a number of examples of enforcement by individual petition following a judgement of the ECtHR. *Campbell and Cosans*[121] concerned corporal punishment in schools. The parents of Campbell, who went to school in Bishopbriggs, objected to the use of corporal punishment and sought assurance from Strathclyde Regional Council (then the relevant local authority) that it would not be inflicted upon their son. This was refused. Cosans, who went to school in Cowdenbeath, refused to submit to corporal punishment, a form of punishment which Fife Regional Council (then the relevant local authority) permitted. He was suspended. The petitioners claimed corporal punishment breached Article 3 of the ECHR (inhuman or degrading punishment) and Article 2 of the First Protocol (requirement for respect for parents' right to ensure education is in conformity with their religious and philosophical beliefs). The matter eventually went to the ECtHR, which held that Article 3 had not been breached, but (though by a majority only) that Article 2 of the Protocol had been.

The case was adjourned on the question of compensation, with a view to the parties agreeing a sum. More importantly, after this case, the law on corporal punishment in state schools was abolished[122], indicating that the United Kingdom was 'securing' the right generally, and not simply compensating the applicants. However, the process from petition to judgment took seven years, and from petition to the change of law, a decade.

It is important to remember that the implementation of the content of the ECHR by the United Kingdom Human Rights Act 1998 (discussed below) does not remove a victim's right of individual petition. It merely requires the victim, when exhausting possible remedies for their grievances in the courts of the United Kingdom before petitioning, to invoke any remedies under that Act. However, the existence of the legislation is likely to reduce considerably the number of individual petitions.

---

120 Art 34, ECHR: the United Kingdom accepted this right from 1966.
121 (1982) 4 EHRR 293.
122 Education (No 2) Act 1986, s 48.

Enforceability of the ECHR through Community law.
Although the ECHR and its institutions are separate from the
European Union and its institutions, and although the European
Union is experimenting with its own 'fundamental rights', the
ECHR may be enforceable through European Community law. This
is discussed in Chapter 6 in relation to Community law.

**Enforceability of the ECHR through United Kingdom law –
'embedding'.** Before the Human Rights Act 1998, the Scottish
courts had, over time, changed from the view that the ECHR was
not legislation, so could be ignored, to the view that it should be
used, at least by way of requiring statutes to be interpreted in conformity with it. However, the position has been further changed radically by the Human Rights Act 1998. It is sometimes said that this
'incorporates' the ECHR into United Kingdom law. This is
misleading terminology, for it implies that its terms have 'direct
effect', as Community law has (for which see Chapter 6). However,
instead it may be said to 'embed' it[123], by cutting and pasting most of
the contents of the ECHR, and its First and Sixth Protocols, into the
United Kingdom Act, calling them 'Convention rights', with a
unique status, and putting them into a somewhat unusual United
Kingdom Act[124].

These Convention rights have nevertheless become part of United
Kingdom law and, broadly speaking, United Kingdom law is
intended to be 'compatible' with them (though, as we shall see, the
United Kingdom still retains a 'let out' clause, by which its law may
remain incompatible).

This compatibility is sought in various ways. The legislation
imposes requirements firstly in relation to parliamentary scrutiny
during the process of legislation of all subsequent Acts of the United

---

123   The distinction is not obvious, but crucial. If the terms were 'incorporated' and
had 'direct effect', then the United Kingdom could not alter them, but they
could be altered by agreement of the other members states of the Council of
Europe. But they are 'embedded', and have no 'direct effect', so the United
Kingdom can alter them unilaterally, and does not have to accept alterations
agreed by the other member states.

124   Human Rights Act 1998, s 1 and Sch 1. The Act omits Arts 1, 13 and 15 of the
Convention, and all other Protocols. Arts 1 and 15 are omitted because it was
thought that they do not add anything to the obligations listed in the Schedule.
Omission of Art 13 is more controversial. It can be seen, like Arts 1 & 15, as
adding nothing. However, another view is that it was omitted because judges
might use it to extend the range of remedies available. The Act also omits the
other Protocols because either they are purely procedural, or because, in the
case of Protocols 4 & 7, because the United Kingdom has not ratified them.

Kingdom, secondly in relation to statutory interpretation, and thirdly in relation to legislation by devolved bodies. These are dealt with in the relevant sections in Chapter 7.

The legislation also creates rights for victims of breaches of Convention rights, which are dealt with here. It makes it 'unlawful for a public authority to act in a way which is incompatible with a Convention right' (subject to exceptions)[125] and allows a 'victim' to 'bring proceedings against the authority ... in the appropriate court or tribunal' or to 'rely on the convention right ... concerned in any proceedings' (within certain time limits)[126]. Thus, he can both sue and defend himself on the basis of Convention rights. 'Public authority' is defined so as to include any court or tribunal (including the Appellate Committee of the House of Lords), and 'any person certain of whose functions are of a public nature' (other than the Westminster Parliament or a person exercising functions on its behalf)[127]. This is clearly very wide and 'public authority' includes the Scottish Parliament, all government departments (including the Scottish Executive), local authorities, quangos, universities etc (and including the Law Society of Scotland and the Faculty of Advocates). 'Victim' is also defined widely as 'any person, non-governmental organisation or group of individuals'[128]. Such challenges have been attempted even against Acts of the Scottish Parliament[129].

Where a court or tribunal finds an act of a public authority unlawful, it can 'grant such relief or remedy, or make such order' as it considers 'just and appropriate', subject to certain limitations[130].

Human Rights Act cases in Scotland. The immediate effect of the Human Rights Act 1998 was considerable. A large amount of litigation arose, mostly by way of devolution issues (because the cases were initiated in the period between the coming into force of the Scotland Act 1998 and the complete coming into force of the Human Rights Act, as noted above) and mostly concerning the criminal law. As much publicity has been given to the notion that

125 Human Rights Act 1998, s 6.
126 *Ibid.* s 7.
127 *Ibid.* s 6(3),(4).
128 *Ibid*, s7(7) (echoing Art 34 ECHR).
129 But by mid-2007, only unsuccessfully: see *eg A v Scottish Ministers* 2002 PC 63 (judicial review of Mental Health (Public Safety and Appeals) (Scotland) Act 1999 sought for incompatibility with Convention right Art 5), *Adams v Scottish Ministers* 2002 SCLR 881 (judicial review of Protection of Wild Mammals (Scotland) Act 2002 sought for incompatibility with Convention right Arts 8 and 14 and Protocol 1, Art 1).
130 Human Rights Act 1998, s 8.

embedding of the ECHR has thrown the legal system into turmoil, and produced ridiculous results, it is worth noting that many of these decisions affirmed the law as fulfilling the requirements of the Convention rights, such as *Brown v Stott*[131] and *Clark v Kelly*[132]. In the former, despite doubts in courts below, the Judicial Committee of the Privy Council concluded that requiring a driver to take a breath test did not breach the privilege against self-incrimination and therefore prejudice the right to a fair trial[133]. In the latter, it decided that the position of the clerk of court and legal adviser (a local authority employee with limited security of tenure) in the District Court did not compromise the right to an independent and impartial tribunal[134].

However, some did have far-reaching effects. The best-known example was *Starrs v Ruxton*[135], and it does illustrate the considerable power of the Act. The case concerned Temporary Sheriffs, that is, advocates or solicitors appointed to serve part-time, and who undertook some 25% of the criminal work of the court. As they were appointed by the Lord Advocate, a member of the Scottish Executive and (of more immediate relevance) the head of the prosecution service, their appointments were clearly acts of a public authority. On an appeal from a decision by a Temporary Sheriff, the High Court of Justiciary decided that, because their appointments were short term, and they could be sidelined by being given no work, or dismissed at will, Temporary Sheriffs lacked security of tenure. This breached the Convention right to an independent and impartial tribunal[136]. As a result, Temporary Sheriffs ceased to be appointed or used, and the office was abolished, and replaced by that of 'Part-time Sheriff' with greater security of tenure[137].

Scottish Commission on Human Rights. Following lengthy consultation[138], the Scottish Parliament passed the Scottish Commission on Human Rights Act 2006, creating such a

131 2001 SC(PC) 43.
132 2003 SC(PC) 77.
133 Human Rights Act 1998, Sch 11 (embodying Article 6, ECHR).
134 See previous note.
135 2000 JC 208.
136 Human Rights Act 1998, Sch 1 (embodying Art 6, ECHR). The decision had an incidental effect on the District Court, where it was concluded, without litigation, that the reasoning excluded councillors from sitting as JPs because District Courts were run by local authorities. It did not have effect on the Court of Session, however: see *Clancy v Caird* 2000 SC 441.
137 Bail, Judicial Appointments, Etc (Scotland) Act 2000.
138 See *Protecting Our Rights; a Human Rights Commission for Scotland* (Scottish Executive 2001) and *Scottish Human Rights* (Scottish Executive 2003).

Commission comprising a Chairman and four other members[139]. Its job is not, however, to enforce, or assist in enforcing the Human Rights Act 1998, or other legislation, but to 'promote human rights and … to encourage best practice in relation to human rights', by publication and dissemination of information, conducting research, providing training, monitoring practice, conducting enquiries, etc[140]. This role is designed to mesh with that of the (Great Britain) Commission for Equality and Human Rights (a merger of the former Commission for Racial Equality, Equal Opportunities Commission and Disability Rights Commission), set up by the Equality Act 2006, with its functions in relation to Scotland somewhat restricted to take account of devolution.

'EUROPE' – THE EUROPEAN UNION, INCLUDING THE EUROPEAN COMMUNITY

As noted above in relation to the Council of Europe and the European Convention on Human Rights, 'Europe', in quotation marks, is a useful, but ambiguous term, because it refers to two separate institutions which have strongly modified, and continue to modify, the Scottish legal system, that is, the Council of Europe (and its principal product, the European Convention on Human Rights), and the European Union (including the European Community, once referred to as 'the Common Market'), which are frequently confused in public discussion.

As noted, in particular, the Council of Europe's European Court of Human Rights, and the European Union's European Court of Justice are often confused. Also the European Convention on Human Rights is thought to be a product of the European Union, and part of Community law, which is not true.

Therefore, this ambiguity is embraced here deliberately to draw attention to the necessity of distinguishing, and Appendix 3 assists in this, and while the last section was concerned with the Council of Europe and the European Convention on Human Rights, this section is concerned with the European Union, including the European Community, and its principal product 'Community law'.

---

139 Scottish Commission on Human Rights Act 2006, s 1 & Sch 1 (not in force in mid-2007).
140 *Ibid.*, ss 2-4 (not in force in mid-2007).

The European Union, including the European Community[141]

The European Union has had a considerable effect upon the Scottish legal system since United Kingdom accession to it (or rather, to the European Communities). Like the Council of Europe, though in a different way, it has introduced what amounts to a new source of law, requiring to be treated in a different fashion, and overriding existing Scots law.

The European Union (including the European Community, once referred to as 'the Common Market') is not the same thing as the Council of Europe. It is only readily understood by considering its evolution from the original treaties to the present day, firstly in terms of institutional origins and changes, and secondly in terms of original membership and changes to it (although these two sets of changes have affected each other). After that, the institutions of the European Union require to be considered.

Evolution from the original treaties to the present day

Institutional origins and changes: In the 1950s, six European states[142], set up three 'communities', that is, the European Coal and Steel Community ('ECSC'), the European Atomic Energy Community ('Euratom'), the European Economic Community ('EEC'). They were set up under three separate treaties[143], the main one of which was the EEC Treaty, sometimes referred to as the 'Treaty of Rome'. Each community had its own separate institutions to carry out its purposes of promoting economic and political integration (to a degree still disputed among the Member States).

After a Preamble reciting that the Member States are 'Determined to lay the foundations of an ever closer union among the peoples of Europe' and similar sentiments, and Article 1, actually establishing the Community, the EEC Treaty, continues:

> Article 2 'The Community shall have as its task, by establishing a common market and an economic and monetary union and by implementing common policies or activities referred to in Articles 3 and 4, to promote throughout the Community a harmonious, balanced and sustainable development of economic activities, a high level of employment and of social protection, equality

---

141 See Appendix 3. The European Union website is at http://europa.eu.int/.
142 *Ie* Belgium, France, Germany, Italy, Luxembourg and the Netherlands.
143 These can be found at http://eur-lex.europa.eu/en/treaties/index.htm and click on 'Founding Treaties'.

between men and women, sustainable and non-inflationary growth, a high degree of competitiveness and convergence of economic performance, a high level of protection and improvement of the quality of the environment, the raising of the standard of living and quality of life, and economic and social cohesion and solidarity among Member States'.

Article 3 refers to prohibition of customs duties, a common commercial policy, an internal market with free movement of goods, persons, services and capital, etc, and Article 4 to adoption of a common economic policy and a single currency.

Thus, in the words of the EEC Treaty[144], the EEC sought 'ever closer union' through 'a common market and an economic and monetary union', requiring 'prohibition of customs duties, a common commercial policy, an internal market with free movement of goods, persons, services and capital, etc,' and not least 'a common economic policy and a single currency'.

In 1965, the 'Merger Treaty' merged the institutions of the three communities, while leaving them technically separate, but under the new collective title of 'the European Communities'.

In 1986, the 'Single European Act' altered significantly some internal procedures (for instance, introducing qualified majority voting of Member States in some matters, instead of unanimity) and sought to extend co-operation over a new area of 'justice and home affairs' under the title 'European political co-operation'.

In 1993, the Treaty on European Union[145] (the 'Maastricht Treaty') created the European Union ('EU'). It is important to note how this was done, and what it means (and not least the difference between 'EEC', 'EC' and 'EU'). After a Preamble reciting that the Member States 'Resolved to mark a new stage in the process of European integration undertaken with the establishment of the European Communities', and similar sentiments, Article 1 establishes the European Union and continues:

'This Treaty marks a new stage on the process of creating an ever closer union among the peoples of Europe, in which decisions are taken as openly as possible and as closely as possible to the citizen.

---

144 For the current version, see also http://eur-lex.europa.eu/en/treaties/index.htm under "European Union – Consolidated Versions of the *Treaty on European Union and of the Treaty Establishing the European Community* (consolidated text) *Official Journal C 321E of 29 December 2006*".
145 For the current version, see previous note.

The Union shall be founded on the European Communities, supplemented by the policies and forms of co-operation established by this Treaty. Its task shall be to organize, in a manner demonstrating consistency and solidarity, relations between the Member States and their peoples'.

Article 2 sets the objectives of economic and social progress, high employment and balanced and sustainable development through the creation of an area without internal frontiers; to assert an identity on the international scene through a common foreign and security policy; to maintain and develop an area of freedom, security and justice etc.

Thus, firstly, this Treaty sought to re-emphasise the aim of 'closer union' of Member States by renaming the three communities ('the European Communities') as simply 'the European Community' ('EC') and by institutional changes within the Community. Secondly, it sought to embed co-operation between member states outwith the Community in the justice and home affairs area (now renamed 'police and judicial co-operation in criminal matters') and extend co-operation over another such area, that is, foreign and security policy. Joint action in these areas is by 'intergovernmental co-operation', that is by agreement among governments as such, involving the Community institutions to only a limited degree, and thus without the degree of integration achieved in the Community. These two areas were described as second and third 'pillars', respectively, being added to the first pillar of the EC itself. The EU is the resulting edifice, comprising all three pillars. In addition to these changes the Treaty sought to include the principle of subsidiarity, whereby, in areas in which either Member States or the Community might act, it is the Member States which should do so.

In 1997, the Treaty of Amsterdam amended the aims of the EC and EU in a number of ways, extending the EU competence, creating some new 'social' rights, such as a right against discrimination, and transferring questions of 'external borders' (that is, immigration, visas and asylum) from 'third pillar' to 'first', allowing there to be Community law on the subject[146]. It also renumbered the Articles of the EC Treaty (as amended), which makes reference to them hazardous. However, a principal result is to blur the distinction between the pillars. It also encouraged different member states to integrate at different speeds (known as 'variable geometry') and assists non-member states which are associated with the EC/EU and likely to become members.

---

146 The United Kingdom, however, opted out of much of this transfer.

In 2000, the Treaty of Nice, largely concerned with recent and impending expansion of the EU, extended majority voting in the EC, further encouraged 'variable geometry', and made alterations to the European Court of Justice. However, from the point of view of the legal system, it was principally concerned with two matters. Firstly, as an alternative to acceding to the ECHR (discussed above), the EU adopted a 'Charter of Fundamental Rights'. This contains provisions similar to those in the ECHR, but goes beyond it to include 'social rights' in relation to education, employment, asylum, data protection and the freedom to conduct business. Nevertheless, this Charter does not have legal force, although it may influence decision-making, and is intended by some Member States to have some such force in the future. Secondly, the Treaty of Nice prepared the way for enlargement of the EU, by the accession of ten states with effect from 2004.

In 2003, a 'Draft Treaty establishing a Constitution for Europe' was published, to introduce further institutional change, in general involving closer integration, but seeking to involve Member States' Parliaments into the EC law-making process and adopting the 'Charter of Fundamental Rights'. However, following rejection of this by referendums in the Netherlands and France, it was put into abeyance.

In mid-2007, however, in an attempt to steer a course between avoiding resuscitation of the 'Draft Constitution' on the one hand and institutional stasis on the other, at a European Council meeting, it was agreed to convene an Inter-Governmental Conference ('IGC') to draft a new 'Reform Treaty'[147].

147 See Council of the European Union 'Brussels European Council 21/22 June 2007 Presidency Conclusions' (23 June 2007) 11177/07. The principal matters the IGC was enjoined to include were: 'double majority' voting (ie requiring a majority of Member States representing a majority of the population of the whole EU) for matters to be decided by majority; extension of majority voting to a number of new areas; a 'President' of the EU elected by the Council for a two and a half year term, to replace the six month alphabetical rotation; appointment of a 'High Representative of the Union for Foreign Affairs and Security Policy', who would be a Vice-President of the EU to represent a common EU policy on such matters and run the foreign aid budget; reduction in the size of the Commission so that only two-thirds of Member states are represented at any one time (but only from 2014); a legal personality for the EU; reference to, but not incorporation of, the Charter on Fundamental Freedoms, from which there might in any case be opt-outs (which the UK is likely to use); a longer period for national legislatures to examine draft legislation; reference to 'solidarity' in relation to energy supply problems; criteria for the accession of new Member States; and reference to increasing and decreasing EU competences and the possibility of withdrawal.

Original membership and changes to it: As noted, the EEC started with six original Member States in the 1950s. At the same time as all the institutional changes indicated above, there were considerable changes of membership. By means of a number of 'Accession Treaties' coming into force in 1973 (when the United Kingdom acceded), 1981, 1986, 1995 and 2007, the original Member States were successively joined by groups of others[148], and more accessions are likely[149].

Further, in the midst of this, with effect from 1994, the EC also created the 'European Economic Area' ('EEA') with the remaining members of a rival organisation, the European Free Trade Area ('EFTA')[150]. This arrangement allowed the EFTA members to participate in benefits of EC membership, such as the free movement of workers, goods and services within the EC, but without participating in the EC institutions.

In 2002, Switzerland, though not a member of EFTA, also joined the EEA, by a bilateral agreement.

The current European Union: These institutional and membership changes affected each other in various ways, most particularly in that institutional change was required by changes in membership, for institutions designed for six very similar Member States had difficulty in coping with twenty-seven much less similar ones. As a result, however, for some years, the EU has appeared to be in a state of continuous revolution, and the whole enterprise is becoming more complex and difficult to understand.

The most important effect of all this as far as the Scottish legal system is concerned is that some Community law has 'direct effect'. The meaning of this term is discussed below in Chapter 6. For the moment, it can simply be described as the process whereby Community law becomes part of the law of Scotland without the intervention of either Westminster, or Holyrood, Parliaments (and is thus incapable of being changed unilaterally by the United Kingdom, but is possibly capable of being changed by agreement of the other Member States).

---

148 *Ie* Denmark, Ireland and the United Kingdom (1972), Greece (1981), Spain & Portugal (1986) and Austria, Finland & Sweden (1995), Cyprus, Czech Republic, Estonia, Hungary, Latvia, Lithuania, Malta & Poland (2004) and Bulgaria & Romania (2007). Thus, by 2007, membership had more than quadrupled, and totalled 27.

149 Croatia & Turkey are 'candidate countries', and Albania, Bosnia-Herzogovina, Montenegro & Serbia (including Kosovo) are 'potential candidate countries'.

150 Iceland, Liechtenstein & Norway.

The Institutions of the European Union

The European Commission[151]: The Commission, which sits in Brussels, exists to further the interests of the Community. Sometimes described as the 'Executive' of the EU, it is better regarded as the top grade of its civil service. It initiates and implements Community policy (including legislation), but can legislate under its own powers as well as under powers delegated by the Council of Ministers[152]. Its deliberations, however, are confidential.

There are 27 Commissioners, one from each Member State, nominated by the Member States, subject to the approval of Council of the Union and the European Parliament[153]. Nevertheless, Commissioners are required to owe their political allegiance to the Community, not the nominating government[154].

One Commissioner is President, others may be Vice-Presidents, and each has responsibility for an area of Community policy[155]. The Commission is accountable to the European Parliament, insofar as Commissioners can be removed by a no confidence vote of that body[156]. Each has a small personal 'Cabinet', and they are supported by a Civil Service with some 25 directorates-general and other agencies such as the Legal Service and the Translating Service.

The European Commission should not be confused with the European Commission on Human Rights (discussed above).

The Council of the Union (sometimes referred to as 'the Council of the European Union' and formerly called the 'Council of Ministers')[157]: The Council of the Union, which also sits in Brussels, exists to represent the Member States, and co-ordinate

---

151 See http://europa.eu.int/comm./ . See also Appendix ?.
152 It can legislate by itself under Art. 202 EC, for example, through a system of technical and specialist bodies, known as 'comitology' (though 'comitocracy' might be a better name), from which the European Parliament is excluded. As noted below, it is difficult to say what 'the legislature' of the EU is.
153 Change to the size, and means of appointment to, the Commission is one of the matters which increased membership necessitates.
154 Some are more successful at this than others.
155 In mid-2007, the UK Commissioner was Peter Mandelson (a former Labour Cabinet Minister), who is responsible for trade policy.
156 In 1999, the entire Commission resigned to avoid being dismissed by the Parliament, after allegations of fraud and mismanagement, though most were re-appointed. In 2004, the Parliament objected to a nominee as Commissioner for Freedom, Security and Justice as his views were thought incompatible with the fundamental human rights, so blocked appointment of all Commissioners until he was replaced.
157 See http://europa.eu.int/.

their views. It must give final approval to most Community legislation (so has a central role in the legislative process of the EU under the 'first pillar'), and to inter-governmental decisions (under the 'second' and 'third pillars': see above)[158]. Voting may require unanimity, but may be by 'qualified majority voting' ('QMV'), a complicated weighted system for legislative measures (which will be amended in the light of the enlargement of the EU) to allow larger states a greater say without squeezing out the smaller[159]. Its deliberations are also secret.

It comprises one minister from each Member State's government. Membership is not constant. For discussions on agriculture, it will be Agriculture Ministers, for those on trade, Trade Ministers, and so on. The Presidency rotates every six months. The Council of the Union has a general secretariat, with several directorates-general and a legal service. Although individual members are accountable to their national governments and parliaments, it is not clear that the Council of the Union as a whole is accountable to anyone.

The Council of the Union, as well as suffering from a variety of names itself, is easily confused with the European Council, which is a semi-formal quarterly meeting of Member State heads of government, designed to further political co-operation, and not strictly speaking an institution of the EU. It is also easily confused with the Council of Europe which is, of course, nothing to do with the EU (as discussed above).

COREPER (the 'Comité de réprésantants permanents' or 'Committee of Permanent Represetnatives)[160]: COREPER is the French acronym usually used for the Committee of Permanent Representatives and is not, strictly speaking, one of the EU institutions, but a name given to the regular meetings of top civil servants of Member States. Because meetings of the Council of the Union are infrequent, involve different ministers on different occasions, and because ministers have other responsibilities, Council of the Union work is carried on between meetings by Permanent Representatives (sometimes referred to as 'Ambassadors') from each member state, who are national civil servants, and their staff[161].

---

158 Indeed, it could be regarded as the legislature of the EU.
159 Details are given on the Council's website.
160 There is no COREPER website.
161 In mid-2007, the UK Permanent Representative was Sir John Grant, described as 'Ambassador Extraordinary and Plenipotentiary Permanent Representative of the United Kingdom'.

The significance of COREPER is great. It deals with all business going to the Council of the Union and, if it is unanimous, the Council will rubber-stamp its decision.

The European Parliament[162]: The European Parliament, despite its name, is not the legislature of the Community, but a supervisory, consultative and deliberative body. It participates in the legislative process for Community law, but is only consultative for 'second' and 'third pillar' matters (see above). It exists to represent the population at large of the Member States, and is directly elected every five years[163], so provides the EU with some democratic legitimacy[164]. It must be consulted on some proposals. The Treaty on European Union gave it a veto in certain legislation, and 'co-decision' with the Council of Ministers in other legislation, and the Amsterdam and Nice treaties strengthened it further. MEPs sit in political groupings[165], but there are no 'government party' and 'opposition parties'.

As noted, appointment of the European Commission must be approved by the European Parliament. The Commission must also report to the European Parliament and answer its questions, and it could be dismissed by the European Parliament in a vote of censure[166]. The Council of the Union must also make certain other reports to the European Parliament, which also has powers in relation to the Community budget. The European Parliament may also review the activities of other EU institutions, and appoints a European Parliamentary Ombudsman.

The European Parliament sits for only a short part of the year, and most of its work is done by committees. It has a secretariat, with five

---

162 See http://www.europarl.eu.int
163 There are 785 MEPs, 78 from the United Kingdom, which is divided into 12 constituencies of which Scotland is one, originally returning 8 MEPs, a figure reduced in 2005 to 7 upon the accession of new Member States which required representation. In mid-2007, it was suggested that a further reduction to 6 might occur when further Member States acceded.
164 The need to improve such legitimacy, by engaging with the citizens of Member States, has become an EU priority.
165 Such as the 'Group of the European People's Party' (Christian Democrats) and 'European Democrats' (to which the United Kingdom Conservative Party MEPs belong), 'Socialist Group in the European Parliament' (to which the United Kingdom Labour Party MEPs belong), 'Group of the Alliance of Liberals and Democrats for Europe' (to which the United Kingdom Liberal Democrats belong) and 'Group of the Greens/European Free Alliance' (to which the United Kingdom Green Party and Plaid Cymru and Scottish National Party MEPs belong).
166 As noted above in relation to the Commission, this power to dismiss has been exercised, in effect if not technically, in both 1999 and 2004.

directorates-general. As a result of a compromise, the European Parliament itself sits in Strasbourg, the committees in Brussels, and the secretariat in Luxembourg.

The European Court of Justice (the 'Court of Justice of the European Communities') and Court of First Instance[167]: The European Court of Justice ('ECJ') exists to ensure that Community law is correctly interpreted, and is observed. Since 1989 there has been attached to it a Court of First Instance ('CFI'), which was created because of the large workload, and consequent enormous delays, in the ECJ itself. For certain cases, there is a right of appeal from it to the ECJ on a point of law.

The ECJ, which sits in Luxembourg, is not to be confused with the European Court of Human Rights (ECtHR), which sits in Strasbourg. Both are discussed below in Chapter 4.

Other Community bodies: There is also a Court of Auditors, which is a formal Community institution, and two advisory important bodies, the Economic and Social Committee ('ECOSOC') and the Committee of the Regions. ECOSOC represents functional interests, that is, 'the various economic and social components of civil society, and in particular producers, farmers, carriers, workers, dealers, craftsmen, professional occupations, consumers and the general interest'[168]. It gives its opinion on draft legislation and under the Treaty of Amsterdam can be consulted by the European Parliament. The Committee of the Regions, created under the Treaty on European Union, is a consultative body representing regional and national bodies[169]. It operates through 'Commissions' on a variety of topics such as 'territorial adhesion' and 'economic and social policy'.

---

167   See http://curia.eu.
168   See http://www.eesc.europa.eu/.
169   See http://www.cor.europa.eu/.

4. Institutions – courts, tribunals, judges and procedure

UNITED KINGDOM COURTS, TRIBUNALS AND RELATED INSTITUTIONS

This Chapter (supplemented by Appendix 2) examines in detail the courts and tribunals which apply, or may make, Scots law; their judges (including questions of judicial appointments and judicial training and competence); and the procedures they follow (at least in outline). It is also useful in this Chapter to at least glance over the border and consider in outline courts in the other parts of the United Kingdom.

Courts in general

The courts are a major set of institutions in any legal system. So are the judges who sit in them and the procedures they follow, for the courts' operation is only comprehensible in the light of these aspects. This is particularly true in a common law, or hybrid, system in which the courts not only apply the law, but also make it[1].

It is to be noticed that courts in any jurisdiction, and their relationship, are commonly represented in diagrams (as in Appendix 2). These diagrams are two dimensional, and these dimensions represent something important. The vertical dimension is the more obvious. It indicates that courts are in a hierarchy. Thus some courts are 'higher', that is, more powerful than other, 'lower' ones. This is most obvious in the simple sense that ('higher') appeal courts may overturn the decisions of ('lower') 'courts of first instance', as courts which are not appeal courts are sometimes called, though the picture is more complicated in that, for instance, there may be more than one level of appeal. It is also to be noted that courts of first instance

---

1 A matter discussed in Ch 5.

usually have only one judge, while appeal courts usually have more, though there are important exceptions to this.

The horizontal dimension is less obvious, but indicates that at any level within the hierarchy, there may be several courts. At it simplest, by definition, there can only be one final court of appeal in any hierarchy, but there may be a large number of 'courts of first instance', typically because they are local courts, spread out across the land. (Thus, in Scotland, for instance, there is room for confusion with reference to 'the Sheriff Court', as there are 49 separate locations in which there is a Sheriff Court).

The vertical dimension has a further significance in a common law, or hybrid, legal system, in that it is the appeal courts, broadly speaking, which may make the law[2].

Scottish, United Kingdom and European courts and tribunals

There are two hierarchies of courts in Scotland: the civil and the criminal[3]. England and Wales and Northern Ireland have their own civil and criminal hierarchies, somewhat similar to the Scottish ones, but separate.

Nevertheless, five of the resulting six hierarchies are connected at the top in the final court of appeal. The normal Scottish civil hierarchy of courts ends with final appeal to a court called the 'Appellate Committee of the House of Lords' ('ACHL': commonly but misleadingly referred to simply as 'the House of Lords'), as do both civil and criminal courts of England and Wales, and Northern Ireland. This, incidentally, sits in London. However, the sixth hierarchy, normal Scottish criminal hierarchy, does not, as it ends within Scotland in the High Court of Justiciary. However, to complicate the position further, certain specialised questions concerning devolution arising in either civil or criminal proceedings, instead of going to the ACHL, or the High Court of Justiciary, may go to another court called the 'Judicial Committee of the Privy Council' ('JCPC'), which also sits in London. (In a further complexity, the ACHL, and (in part) the JCPC, will become the 'Supreme Court of the United Kingdom', as discussed in Chapter 3 and below).

Also, from all courts in the United Kingdom there is the possibility of a 'preliminary reference' to the European Court of Justice in rela-

---

2 See Ch 5.
3 It is sometimes suggested that there are three, that is, civil, criminal and 'administrative', the last-mentioned dealing with legal disputes involving government. However, the administrative is regarded here as a sub-set of the civil.

tion to European Community law (as also discussed in Chapter 3 and below). Also, again, a person who considers that his rights under the European Convention on Human Rights have not been protected, and who has taken the matter through the relevant United Kingdom courts unsuccessfully, may petition the European Court of Human Rights for a remedy (as again discussed in Chapter 3 and below). Neither of these types of proceeding is an appeal.

All these courts, whether in other parts of the United Kingdom, or of Europe, apply, or make, Scots law, so must be regarded as Scottish courts, even if they are not within Scotland.

In addition to the courts, as such, there are a number of 'tribunals', generally organised on a United Kingdom basis. These deal with certain types of legal dispute, but are not regarded as courts. Well-known examples are the Employment Tribunals and tribunals dealing with social security. Tribunals vary considerably in structure and personnel, but in general are less formal than courts, and litigants are often unrepresented by lawyers. There may be appeal from them to the courts.

Dissatisfaction with the efficiency of the administration of criminal justice in Scotland led to several reports on the subject[4] which have produced significant changes in the structure running of the criminal courts still, at the time of publication, coming into effect. Dissatisfaction with the administration of civil justice is in a similar position[5]. So is dissatisfaction with the method of appointing JPs, Sheriffs and Judges[6].

Judicial Appointments and Judicial Independence

The appointment of judges raises important issues. In brief, who is to appoint them, and by what means? In some countries, at least some judges are elected. This raises interesting questions which cannot be pursued here. In most countries, they are all appointed by

---

4 Chiefly *Improving Justice: 2002 Review of the Practices and Procedures of the High Court of Justiciary* (2002) (the 'Bonomy Report' produced by Lord Bonomy, a judge) and *The Summary Justice Review Committee - Report to Ministers* (2004) (the 'McInnes Report', produced by Sheriff Principal McInnes), though by no means all their recommendations were adopted, and an *Independent Review of Disclosure* by Lord Coulsfield (another judge) was set up in 2006, to report in 2007 on the disclosure of evidence in criminal cases.

5 See chiefly, the *Civil Courts Review* under Lord Gill, the Lord Justice-Clerk, in early 2007: see www.scotcourts.gov.uk/lordgill/index.asp.

6 This is discussed below in relation to Judicial Appointments and Judicial Independence.

the Government. But if they are appointed by the Government, what is to make it appoint judges who are impartial, and in particular, what is to stop it appointing judges who are favourable towards it (a question of very considerable importance in a final court of appeal where, by definition, bias cannot be corrected on further appeal)? In short, how is 'judicial independence' to be preserved? These questions have become more obvious with the embedding of human rights into United Kingdom law through the Human Rights Act 1998 (discussed in Chapter 3). Courts with an international dimension raise further difficulties in that, for instance, all states accepting their jurisdiction are likely to want to be represented on the bench.

There are also three particularities about the appointment of judges in common law or hybrid countries (for the meaning of which, see Chapter 5). Firstly, in such jurisdictions, there is usually heavy reliance upon 'lay' (that is, non-professional) judges, at least in the criminal courts. This fact is less evident in Scotland than in some other jurisdictions. Nevertheless, lay justices in the District Court (and in future the JP Court) take about a third of all criminal proceedings[7]. Secondly, there is a major difference in relation to professional judges. In civil law countries, the judiciary is a distinct branch of the legal profession (so law graduates may opt for that choice upon graduation). In common law or hybrid countries, however, judges are usually only appointed after having pursued a successful career, typically as a court lawyer (so are invariably of a much maturer age and with the perspective of a participant). Thirdly, there is a further, consequential, major difference in relation to professional judges. In civil law countries, there is likely to be a career path within the judicial hierarchy, from minor courts to major ones. In common law or hybrid countries, however, there are usually few prospects of promotion within the judicial hierarchy. Thus, for example, a Sheriff cannot expect to reach the Court of Session bench (though it has happened), and within the Court of Session, while all Outer House judges may have some expectation of becoming Inner House judges, not all will, and in any case, it remains a 'collegiate court'.

All three of these particularities have a bearing upon the underlying tension between Judiciary and Government, in that all three may be seen in practice as limiting the power of the Government over the Judiciary. In short, they can be seen as helping to preserve judicial independence, and such considerations explain a considerable emphasis upon the adequacy of arrangements to protect this independence in recent years.

7 In England & Wales, a more extreme example, magistrates take some 90%.

In particular, there have been concerns in recent years over the implications of the change in status of the Lord Chancellor, and the creation of a department in the United Kingdom Government with responsibility for both the appointment of judges and the running of prisons[8]. This has been seen by some as increasing executive control over the judiciary, for instance possibly tempting that Government to seek to improperly influence judges to assist penal policy but, in any case, putting the courts in direct competition with prisons, and other Departmental responsibilities, for resources. Such fears have certainly generated United Kingdom legislation[9] which requires 'the Lord Chancellor, other Ministers of the Crown, and all with responsibility for matters relating to the judiciary or otherwise to the administration of justice' to 'uphold the continued independence of the judiciary', and which allows the 'chief justice of any part of the United Kingdom' (which in Scotland is the Lord President of the Court of Session) to 'lay before Parliament written representations on matters that appear to him to be matters of importance relating to the judiciary, or otherwise the administration of justice'[10]. Similar fears have also been expressed in Scotland in relation to appointments here, and further, related legislation may occur in Scotland, as noted below.

So far as Scotland is concerned, several methods of appointment are used though, to a large extent, these are variations upon the themes adumbrated above (including trenchant assertions of executive attempts to improperly control the judiciary[11]). There are different methods employed for the Appellate Committee of the House of Lords (to be replaced by yet further different ones with the setting up of the new Supreme Court of the United Kingdom), for the senior Judges (and for appointment to the Inner House of the Court of Session) and for other Judges, for Sheriffs, and for Justices of the Peace. These are discussed below, in relation to each court. However, one important recent innovation deserves mention here, because it introduced radical change, rendered the process more uniform and more reliable, and demonstrates well some of the tensions in the appointment process. This is the Judicial Appointments Board for Scotland ('JABS').

8 For which, see Ch 3.
9 Constitutional Reform Act 2005, s 3.
10 *Ibid*, s 5. This does apply to Scotland, but 'matters within the competence of the Scottish Parliament' are excepted.
11 These criticisms were prompted by aspects of two Consultative Papers, *Judicial Appointments: an inclusive approach* (Scottish Executive, 2000) and *Strengthening Judicial Independence in a Modern Scotland: a consultation on the unification, appointment, removal and management of Scotland's judiciary* (Scottish Executive, 2006)

After a consultation exercise in 2000, and brief use of an *ad hoc* formal Selection Board, JABS was set up in 2001[12]. Its creation marked a very big change in the method of appointment, for formerly, the procedure was very opaque and did not always create confidence[13]. It receives guidance from ministers, but decides its own procedure[14]. Its function is to provide the First Minister with a list of candidates recommended for appointment as Judge of the Court of Session, Sheriff Principal, Sheriff or Part-Time Sheriff (but not as Justice of the Peace) and to do so on merit, while considering ways of making representative recommendations. The Board comprises a mixture of lay members (including the Chairman), Judges, Sheriff Principals and Sheriffs, advocates and solicitors[15]. Although it has not been in operation for long, a surprising number of judges and Sheriffs have been appointed through its recommendations already[16].

However, a separate, more elaborate process is planned for the Supreme Court, and another, still more elaborate, for Justices of the

---

12 See www.judicialappointmentsscotland.gov.uk. There are also a separate Judicial Appointments Commission for England & Wales (see www.judicialappointments.gov.uk/), and Northern Ireland Judicial Appointments Commission (see www.nijac.org/Live/NIJAC_Site.htm). (For a precursor, see McNeill 'Trials of Judges' 2003 SLT 108-109). Note also that the illness of the Lord President in 2006 generated legislation ensuring his responsibilities can be carried out by the Lord Justice-Clerk during a vacancy of the office, or its holder's incapacitation, ie Senior Judiciary (Vacancies and Incapacity) (Scotland) Act 2006.

13 See, for example, see Stott *Lord Advocate's Diary* (1991), pp 173, 195.

14 Note its 'Principles' at http://www.judicialappointmentsscotland.gov.uk/judicial/JUD_Main.jsp?pContentID=443&p_applic=CCC&pMenu0=43&p_service=Content.show&: also the very useful Judicial Appointments Board 'The Judicial Appointments Board for Scotland: a view from the inside' 2006 SLT 79-81.

15 In mid-2007, the Chair was Sir Neil McIntosh (a retired senior local government official); the lay members were a personnel specialist (Barbara Duffner), a businessman (Sir Robert Smith), a legal academic (Prof Alan Paterson, of Strathclyde University), and an academic administrator (Prof Joan Stringer, Principal of Napier University); the judge was Lord Wheatley; the Sheriff Principal, Sheriff Principal Bruce Kerr; the Sheriff, Sheriff Douglas Allan; the advocate was Valerie Stacey, QC (Vice-Dean of the Faculty of Advocates); and the solicitor was Michael Scanlan (a former President of the Law Society of Scotland and Temporary Sheriff).

16 By mid-2007, these included 12 Judges (more than a third of the total), and three Sheriff Principals (half of the total): see http://www.judicialappointmentsscotland.gov.uk/judicial/JUD_Main.jsp?pContentID=494&p_applic=CCC&pMenu0=45&p_service=Content.show&. The judges appointed included Lord Malcolm who, as Colin Campbell QC, had been a member of the JABS, so an additional 'independent assessor' was appointed for consideration of his case: see JABS Annual Report 2006-2007, paras 32 & 33.

Peace. Also, as noted above, further changes may be expected in Scotland[17].

Judicial Training and Judicial Competence

As noted in relation to judicial appointments, in common law and hybrid jurisdictions, being a judge cannot be embarked upon as a career path, and most of those appointed must have achieved some success in another, albeit related, job. Unsurprisingly, therefore, traditionally, there was no training and professional development for Judges or Sheriffs (though there has been for JPs for some time).

Since 1997, however, for Judges and Sheriffs, there has been a Judicial Studies Committee[18] to provide this. The Committee

17 See Draft Bill attached to by *Proposals for a Judiciary (Scotland) Bill* (Scottish Executive, 2007), available at www.scotland.gov.uk/Publications/2007/02/13115213/0. (This followed the Consultation Papers on judicial appointments and independence referred to above, which included proposals that there be a 'unified judiciary' of which the Lord President would be formal 'head', and thereby take on a more managerial role). Clause 1 of the Draft Bill repeats, in relation to the First Minister, Lord Advocate, Scottish Ministers 'and all with responsibility for matters relating to the judiciary or otherwise to the administration of justice' the obligation found in the Constitutional Reform Act 2005, s 3, to 'uphold the continued independence of the judiciary', though not the power in s 5 of the 'chief justice' to 'lay before Parliament written representations on matters that appear to him to be matters of importance relating to the judiciary, or otherwise the administration of justice'; cll 2-10 & Sch 1 set JABS on a statutory footing as a means of appointing all judges except the Lord President and the Lord Justice-Clerk (and JPs), and declare the Board 'is not to be subject to the direction or control of any member of the Scottish Executive' (though there may be ministerial 'guidance' on procedures) and re-iterate that selection is to be on merit and good character, but should also to encourage diversity; cll 11-12 & Sch 2 set up means of appointing the Lord President and the Lord Justice-Clerk which are radically different from current practice in that they would no longer be appointed by Her Majesty on the recommendation of the Prime Minister, but by the First Minister on the recommendation of a panel comprising the Chair of JABS, one other lay member, and (in the case of the Lord President) two further judges nominated by the First Minister or (in the case of the Lord Justice-Clerk) the Lord President and one judge nominated by the First Minister; cll 13-14 concern re-employment of retired judges and Sheriffs (giving Sheriff Principals the power to re-appoint the latter); cll 15-20 concern removal of judges and Sheriffs, modifying the existing arrangements; cll 21-24 concern vacancy, incapacity or suspension of the Lord President, again modifying the existing (recent) arrangements. This Bill was drafted for the outgoing Executive before the 2007 election . In mid-2007, it was not clear if the incoming Executive would seek to continue it (nor, of course, how far the Scottish Parliament might amend it if they did).

18 See www.judicialstudies-scotland.org.uk/ (and for England and Wales, www.jsboard.co.uk, and see also www.etjn.net).

comprises a mixture of Judges (one being Chairman), Sheriff Principals and Sheriffs (one of whom is 'Director of Judicial Studies'), lay members and a civil servant from the Justice Department of the Scottish Executive[19]. It organises induction courses for Sheriffs and Judges, refresher courses and seminars on specific topics, and publishes annual reports.

For JPs, training is described below in relation to the District Court (and JP Court)

The Scottish courts

The District Court/the Justice of the Peace Court[20]

District Courts are local courts dealing with minor crime (and no civil matters), staffed by justices of the peace ('JPs') who are not qualified lawyers[21]. (In Glasgow, there are also salaried stipendiary magistrates, who are). The District Courts deal with about a third of all criminal proceedings in Scotland, although these proceedings all concern minor crime[22]. District Courts are to be abolished and replaced by Justice of the Peace Courts ('JP Courts')[23], though to a large extent this is simply an exercise in renaming and re-organising.

The court. District courts were created by the District Courts (Scotland) Act 1975, as an amalgamation of the previous 'burgh

19 In mid-2007, they were Lords Brodie (Chairman) and Menzies, Sheriff Principal Dunlop, Sheriffs Mitchell, Newall, Crowe (Director of Judicial Studies), Fletcher & Stoddart, Dr McClure (lay member) and Mr Robert Gordon (Scottish Executive Justice Department).
20 Most of the relevant law on District Courts is in the District Courts (Scotland) Act 1975, as amended by the Bail, Judicial Appointments Etc (Scotland) Act 2000. The law on Justice of the Peace Courts is chiefly in the Criminal Proceedings (etc) (Scotland) Act 2007, Part 4.
21 As noted, such 'lay' involvement, also manifested in juries, has been seen as a particular feature, and strength, of the administration of justice in common law and hybrid jurisdictions, but is a good deal more prominent in England & Wales.
22 In 2004-5, some 151,000 people were proceeded against in a criminal court, of whom 47,000 (35%) were dealt with by the District Courts (including the Stipendiary Magistrates in Glasgow): *Scottish Executive Statistical Bulletin: Criminal Justice Series* CrJ/2006/3 (April 2006), Table 3. This position had not changed much over the preceding years, but was significantly less than a decade earlier, largely because of an increase in the use of alternatives to prosecution like 'fiscal fines'. In England & Wales, some 90% of all criminal proceedings are before lay JPs.
23 In mid-2007, these changes had not taken place. However, the changes were intended to be rolled out over the following two years, commencing in Lothian and Borders, and Grampian, Highlands and Islands.

courts' and 'police courts' (in the burghs) and 'justice of the peace courts'[24] (in some landward areas).

They are run, somewhat anomalously, by local authorities rather than centrally. The structure of local authority areas has altered since District Courts were set up, so their territorial jurisdiction no longer closely coincides with local authority boundaries, and some local authorities have several District Courts[25]. In cities and towns the justices sit usually alone (as in the old burgh and police courts), and in the landward areas usually in twos or more (as in the former justice of the peace courts). A legally-qualified assessor (usually the clerk of court) is always present to offer legal advice, but not to take part otherwise[26]. Frequency of sitting is decided locally. In rural areas only a few court days a month may be required, while in the cities the court sits every weekday, and sometimes two or more courts may sit simultaneously.

Every District Court must have a Justices' Committee. This decides the duty rota of JPs, makes training arrangements, and takes other steps to secure the effective administration of justice. The clerk of the court, and if necessary, deputes, are appointed by the council. The clerk of the court must be a solicitor or advocate, and (as noted above) usually acts as legal assessor. The council must also appoint a clerk of the peace (who may be the clerk of court), to advise the JPs generally on the performance of their duties, and to carry out administrative duties for the Justices' Committee. The council is also responsible for providing suitable premises for the court, and for servicing it.

The First Minister has oversight of the work of JPs generally, advised by the Central Committee on Justices of the Peace, chaired by the Lord Justice-Clerk. The First Minister has specific obligations in respect of training JPs, although most arrangements are made locally.

Prosecutions in the District Court are undertaken by the Procurator Fiscal Service, which can thus decide, in respect to minor crime, whether the District Court or the Sheriff Court is the appropriate forum.

---

24 There is possible confusion in that the name 'JP Court' is now being resuscitated for the rather different successor body.
25 For example, Fife has District Courts in Cupar, Dunfermline and Kirkcaldy. For the locations of District Courts, see the annual *Scottish Law Directory* ('the White Book') (LexisNexis UK).
26 District Court clerks of court and their (principal) deputes are listed in the entry for the relevant court in the White Book (see above). For discussion of the role of clerk to the district court, and indeed, general discussion on its origins, see *Kelly v Clark* 2003 SC(PC) 77.

The new JP Courts, which will replace District Courts, will be organised on a very different basis, cutting the local authority link. It will then be for the Scottish Ministers to provide for JP Courts, and these Courts will be managed by the Scottish Courts Service (an Executive Agency of the Scottish Executive Justice Department[27]), as the Sheriff Courts are[28]. They are to be organised according to Sheriffdoms, normally with one JP Court in each Sheriff Court District[29], and Sheriff Principals are to administer them[30]. Each Sheriffdom will have a Sheriffdom Legal Adviser, and deputes, for the JP Courts, and each JP Court will, like the District Court, only sit with a clerk of court who (save where there is a stipendiary magistrate) will act as Legal Adviser[31].

Prosecutions will continue to be undertaken by the Procurator Fiscal Service.

Justices. Under the District Court regime, the First Minister appoints most justices, in the name of the Sovereign and upon the recommendation of local Justice of the Peace Advisory Committees ('JPACs'). There are few formal requirements for appointment, save an obligation to live in or near the district (though there has been a tendency in some areas to seek 'political balance'). The JPAC's role is to ensure that appointees are honest, sensible, local people. In

27 See www.scotcourts.gov.uk/courtsadmin/scs.asp.
28 Criminal Proceedings (etc) (Scotland) Act 2007, ss 59-61.
29 *Ibid.* s 59. For Sheriffdoms and Sheriff Court Districts, see below. In mid-2007, the legislation specifying the location of JP Courts had not been made. In many cases, the Justice of the Peace Courts will simply occupy the premises of the preceding District Courts, and so fall into the relevant Sheriff Court District and Sheriffdom. Thus, for example, the District Courts in Cupar, Dunfermline and Kirkcaldy will no doubt become the JP Courts in the Sheriff Court Districts of Cupar, Dunfermline and Kirkcaldy, respectively, all within the Sheriffdom of Tayside, Central and Fife. However, there are difficulties in some areas, for example, where local authority areas fall into two Sheriffdoms, and there is in any case a policy to co-locate JP Courts and Sheriff Courts where possible. Thus it is likely that, for example, the former Midlothian District Court (sitting latterly in Loanhead) and Edinburgh District Court (sitting in its own premises in Edinburgh) will be integrated as a 'City of Edinburgh and Midlothian JP Court' and move to share premises with Edinburgh Sheriff Court. The location of all JP Courts will no doubt appear on the Scottish Courts website at www.scotcourts.gov.uk, and in the White Book (see above) in due course.
30 *Ibid.* s 61: For Sheriff Principals, see below.
31 *Ibid.* s 63: the clerks may also have such other functions as the Scottish Ministers confer. No doubt the names of the Sheriffdom JP Court Legal Advisers (and their principal deputes) will appear at www.scotcourts.gov.uk, and in the White Book (see above) in due course.

addition to this, councils may also nominate up to a quarter of their members to serve as justices, but these constitute only a small proportion of all justices. Stipendiary magistrates are all appointed by the council, and must be solicitors or advocates of at least five years' standing, but there are very few of these as only Glasgow has appointed them. The Judicial Appointments Board for Scotland has never been involved.

There are about 4,000 justices in all, and they are formally divided into 'full' justices, who actually sit on the bench, and 'signing' justices (including all those appointed by councils), who may only sign warrants and other documents. The Justices' Committee selects justices for the bench-sitting duty rota from among those 'full' justices who are suitably trained. 'Full' justices may be removed only on specified grounds, and after investigation by a tribunal appointed by the Lord President of the Court of Session and chaired by a Sheriff Principal[32]. 'Signing' justices are on a 'supplemental list', and at the age of 70, all justices are in any case put on that list. A justice may also be placed on that list by reason of infirmity or negligent attention to duties. In practice only a small proportion of justices, perhaps 10%, sit on the bench.

Under the JP Court regime, lay JPs continue, but are to be appointed to a Sheriffdom 'in the name of Her Majesty' by the Scottish Ministers for a renewable period of five years, until reaching the age of 70[33]. The Judicial Appointments Board for Scotland remains uninvolved. The Scottish Ministers may make provision concerning the appointment process and residence[34], and have set up a JPAC for each Sheriffdom, appointed and convened by the Sheriff Principal, but with a specified membership, and no JP may be appointed unless recommended by a JPAC. However, transitionally, while all existing JPs will cease to hold office, most 'full' JPs are likely

---

32 This division and security of tenure were introduced after the High Court of Justiciary decided in *Starrs v Ruxton* 2000 JC 208, that Temporary Sheriffs did not constitute 'an independent and impartial tribunal', contrary to Art 6 ECHR. A particular problem was presented by those justices who were appointed by virtue of being councillors.

33 Criminal Proceedings (etc) (Scotland) Act 2007, s 67. This constitutes the biggest change from the recommendations of the McInnes Report (see above). It preferred their replacement with a system of 'sub-Sheriffs', rather like the existing stipendiary magistrates. However, strong lobbying from certain interests influenced the Scottish Executive's final plans: see *Smarter Justice, Safer Communities, Summary Justice, Next Steps* (Scottish Executive 2005).

34 *Ibid.* s 67. This power was exercised in the Justice of the Peace (Scotland) Order 2007 (SSI 2007/210).

to be re-appointed[35]. 'Signing' JPs and those on the 'supplemental list' will not.

There is also to be a Justices Training Committee ('JTC') for each Sheriffdom, the members of which are to include the members of a Justices Appraisal Committee ('JAC'), but also a Sheriff, and a clerk of court as legal adviser, convened by the convenor of the JAC, and which is to provide an annual training plan for JPs[36]. There is also, therefore, to be a JAC for each Sheriffdom, appointed by the Sheriff Principal, with a specified membership, the convenor of which need not be (and is unlikely to be) the Sheriff Principal, and which is to establish an appraisal scheme for JPs[37]. The Judicial Studies Committee is not directly involved[38].

The work of the District Court. The District Court hears cases concerning offences which a statute has declared competent to it, and which occur within its area. This includes a number of common law offences (such as, subject to limitations, minor assault, breach of the peace, and theft), and statutory ones (such as minor road traffic offences).

All cases are prosecuted by summary procedure[39]. As all such cases are competent in the Sheriff Court as well, it is the procurator fiscal who decides which cases go to which court in the light, among other things, of the limits to the district court's sentencing powers[40]. A justice may impose up to 60 days' imprisonment and/or a fine at level four of the standard scale[41]. A stipendiary magistrate, however, has the same powers as a Sheriff in summary criminal proceedings.

Appeal is possible, against conviction and/or sentence, to the High Court of Justiciary, sitting as an appeal court. It is available both to the person convicted, and (on a point of law only) to the prosecutor.

---

35 Under the Criminal Proceedings (etc) (Scotland) Act 2007, s 67(7), all existing JPs lose office on a day to be specified by the Scottish Ministers and all 'full' justices whose names were on the duty rota are to be re-appointed unless declining to serve. (No date had been specified by mid-2007, but it was expected to be 31 December 2007).
36 Justice of the Peace (Scotland) Order 2007 (SSI 2007/210). All re-appointed JPs (see previous note) will have to undergo a training course.
37 *Ibid.*
38 It may provide some training, however, and in mid 2007, was producing a Draft *Justices' Bench Book* and Draft *Competences for Justices of the Peace*.
39 For which, see below.
40 Thus, speeding under 100mph in a 70mph limit might go to the District Court; above that figure to the Sheriff Court.
41 In mid-2007, level four of the standard scale under the Criminal Procedure (Scotland) Act 1995, s 225, as amended, was £2,500.

The JP Court will likewise hear cases concerning offences which a statute has declared competent to it, and which occur within its area. However, the range of competent offences is likely to increase, and the relevant area will be the Sheriffdom[42] (though in practice no doubt likely to be restricted to the Sheriff Court District).

The Sheriff Court[43]

Sheriff Courts are local courts with very wide jurisdiction, both civil and criminal, and legally qualified judges. There is a Sheriff Court in every city and most towns[44]. Thus, for many purposes it is the most important court in the land. In its civil jurisdiction (largely overlapping that of the Court of Session) it deals mostly with debt and divorce. However, many of these cases are simple, and much of a Sheriff's time may be taken up with the small proportion of difficult and important cases which may be debt or divorce or some other matter. In its criminal jurisdiction (largely overlapping that of the High Court of Justiciary on the one hand, and that of the District Court, and in future, JP Court, on the other), it deals with about two-thirds of all criminal proceedings[45].

The court. Sheriff Courts are organised into six Sheriffdoms, based on the former local government regions[46]. Each Sheriffdom (except Glasgow and Strathkelvin) is divided into several Sheriff Court Districts, giving 49 Sheriff Courts in all[47]. The First Minister decides how many Sheriffs there shall be in each Sheriffdom, and

---

42 Criminal Proceedings (etc) (Scotland) Act 2007, s 62.
43 Much of the relevant law is to be found in the Sheriff Courts (Scotland) Acts 1907 and 1971, as amended. Information on Sheriff Courts is available at www.scotcourts.gov.uk.
44 Their location is given at www.scotcourts.gov.uk and in the 'White Book' (see above).
45 In 2005-6, some 151,000 people were proceeded against in a criminal court, of whom 82,000 (61%) were dealt with by Sheriff summary proceedings, and 3,800 (3%) by Sheriff and jury: *Scottish Executive Statistical Bulletin: Criminal Justice Series* CrJ/2006/3 (April 2006), Table 3.
46 The Sheriffdoms of Glasgow and Strathkelvin; Grampian, Highland and Islands; Lothian and Borders; North Strathclyde; South Strathclyde; Dumfries and Galloway; and Tayside, Central and Fife.
47 For instance, the Sheriffdom of Tayside, Central and Fife is divided into the Sheriff Court Districts of Alloa, Arbroath, Cupar, Dundee, Dunfermline, Falkirk, Forfar, Kirkcaldy, Perth and Stirling. For locations, see www.scotcourts.gov.uk which gives addresses and maps, and for a complete list, the 'White Book' (see above).

Sheriff Courts often have more than one[48]. Sheriffs are appointed to a Sheriffdom[49], and usually sit in only one Sheriff Court District, but may sit in more in areas with little business. There are also, however, 'floating Sheriffs', part-time Sheriffs and honorary Sheriffs.

The First Minister has overall responsibility for the efficient organisation and administration of the courts[50], which he discharges through the Scottish Courts Service, an Executive Agency of the Scottish Executive Justice Department[51]. It is responsible for provision of staff, court-houses etc. However, each of the six Sheriffdoms has a Sheriff Principal who is responsible for the speedy and efficient disposal of business[52], and each Sheriffdom has a regional sheriff clerk, and a sheriff clerk (and deputes if necessary) for each court, who run it day-to-day[53].

Sheriffs. The office of Sheriff is ancient, and Sheriffs were long a principal part of local law and administration. The office became largely hereditary in the Middle Ages, but Sheriffs appointed 'Deputes' to do the work, and they in turn appointed 'Substitutes', a sort of three rank system. Heritability was finally abolished after the 1745 rebellion[54]. No-one was thereafter appointed to the office of Sheriff (the top rank), but the office of Sheriff Depute (the second rank) was continued, and its holders were called by that title until the 19th century, when they became known simply as Sheriffs (or as 'Sheriffs Principal'). The appointment was part-time, and held by advocates[55]. In 1971 they became formally entitled Sheriffs Principal, and the post became full-time[56].

The Sheriff Deputes continued to appoint Substitutes (the third rank) after the heritable jurisdictions were abolished. These Substitutes became the full-time Sheriffs, with the title 'Sheriff Substitute', salaried and legally qualified from the early 19th

---

48 Sheriff Courts (Scotland) Act 1971, s 14 (as amended), read with Scotland Act 1998, s 53. Glasgow and Strathkelvin Sheriffdom (and Sheriff Court District) has 22 Sheriffs.
49 *Ibid*, ss 7, 9 (as amended).
50 *Ibid*, ss 1, 24, 25 read with Scotland Act 1998, s 53.
51 See www.scotcourts.gov.uk/courtsadmin/scs.asp.
52 Sheriff Courts (Scotland) Act 1971, ss 15-17 (as amended). For the identities of Sheriff Principals, see www.scotcourts.gov.uk.
53 The identities and addresses of sheriff clerks are given at www.scotcourts.gov.uk, and in the 'White Book' (see above).
54 Heritable Jurisdictions (Scotland) Act 1746
55 Undoubtedly the most famous Sheriff was Sir Walter Scott, appointed Sheriff-Depute of Selkirk in 1799.
56 Sheriff Courts (Scotland) Act 1971, ss 4, 6 (as amended).

century, but appointed by the Crown only later. In 1971 the Sheriff Substitutes finally fell heir to the title Sheriff[57]. The actual means of appointment, clear in formal terms, was somewhat obscure in practical ones, involving consultations with the Dean of the Faculty of Advocates and Sheriffs Principal, until the Judicial Appointments Board for Scotland was set up in 2002.

Today, the 'right of appointing' Sheriffs, including Sheriffs Principal (but excluding part-time and honorary Sheriffs), 'is vested in [Her] Majesty and shall be exercised by [the Scottish Ministers]'[58], after consultation with the Lord President and recommendation by the Judicial Appointments Board[59]. Those who have been advocates or solicitors for at least ten years are eligible to be appointed Sheriff[60], but few are appointed with less than a couple of decades of experience, or more in the case of Sheriff Principals (who are usually appointed from among QCs and those who are Sheriffs already). Vacancies are now publicly advertised. Sheriffs may hold office until the age of 70[61]. They are salaried[62].

In addition to ordinary Sheriffs, full-time salaried 'floating Sheriffs'[63], appointed to a particular Sheriffdom or as 'all-Scotland floating Sheriffs', may be directed to sit anywhere to relieve pressure of business. There are also up to 60 part-time Sheriffs, appointed by the Scottish Ministers from those qualified to be Sheriffs, for five-year terms[64] (and are normally to be re-appointed), who may sit in

---

57 *Ibid*, s 4.
58 Sheriff Courts (Scotland) Act 1907, s 11 (as amended). In mid-2007, there were some 140 full-time Sheriffs (including some 30 'floating Sheriffs'), some 20 of them women. A list of their identities, Sheriffdoms and Sheriff Court Districts is found at www.scotcourts.gov.uk and in the 'White Book' (see above).
59 Sheriff Ian Macphail, appointed Sheriff Principal of Lothian and Borders in 2002 (but now Lord Macphail in the Court of Session), was the first to be so appointed.
60 Sheriff Courts (Scotland) Act 1971, s 5 (as amended).
61 *Ibid*, s 65A (as inserted by Judicial Pensions and Retirement Act 1993, Sch 6, para 10).
62 In mid-2007, Sheriff Principals received £129,900 and Sheriffs, £120,300.
63 In mid-2007, there were some 30 floating Sheriffs: see www.scotcourts.gov.uk.
64 Sheriff Courts (Scotland) Act 1971, ss 11A-11D (as inserted by the Bail, Judicial Appointments etc. (Scotland) Act, s7). Part-time Sheriffs replaced the former 'Temporary Sheriffs' after it was decided in *Starrs v Ruxton* 2000 JC 208 that the latter did not provide the 'independent and impartial tribunal' required by Art 6 of the ECHR, because of their lack of tenure. The method of appointing, terms of office and means of removal of part-time Sheriffs are laid down in the Bail, Judicial Appointments, Etc (Scotland) Act 2000. In mid-2007, there was still no published list of the actual number, or their identities, but all appointments since 2002 can be found at www.judicialappointmentsscotland.gov.uk.

any Sheriff Court District, and are expected to sit for between 20 and 100 days a year. If solicitors, they would not normally be used in the Sheriff Court District in which they practise. Like the floating Sheriffs, they add flexibility to the system, and a part-time appointment provides judicial experience for possible appointees to a full-time post.

Honorary Sheriffs are appointed by the Sheriff Principal[65]. They require no legal qualification (although many are senior solicitors). The office is honorary but may involve some judicial duties. In that role Honorary Sheriffs have the same powers as other Sheriffs.

Sheriffs can be removed from office[66]. The Lord President and the Lord Justice-Clerk on their own initiative, or on that of the First Minister, may investigate the fitness for office of any Sheriff or Sheriff Principal. They report that he is fit for office, or that he is not 'by reason of inability, neglect of duty, or misbehaviour', in which case the First Minister may make a statutory instrument[67] (subject to annulment by the Scottish Parliament) removing him. This has only been done twice. In 1977, a Sheriff was removed for having organised local political plebiscites, and in 1992 another was removed for inability[68]. A part-time Sheriff may be removed if, at the request of the Scottish Ministers, the Lord President of the Court of Session appoints a tribunal (consisting of a Court of Session judge, a person of at least ten years' legal experience, and another person) which finds him unfit on the same grounds as for removal of a Sheriff. Honorary Sheriffs are appointed by the Sheriff Principal, so may be removed by him.

The Judicial Studies Committee[69] now provides training and professional development for Sheriffs.

The work of the Sheriff Court. In civil proceedings, the basic principle is that a pursuer must bring his case in the Sheriffdom of the defender's domicile. This is much broadened, however, to include other connections with the Sheriffdom, such as that the relevant contract was performed there, or the relevant delict occurred there[70].

65 The identities of Honorary Sheriffs are given in the entry for the relevant Sheriffdom in the White Book (see above).

66 Sheriff Courts (Scotland) Act 1971, s 12 (as amended).

67 For the nature of statutory instruments, see Chs 9 & 10.

68 See the Sheriff (Removal from Office) Order 1992, SI 1992/1677 and *Stewart v Secretary of State* 1995 SLT 895, 1996 SLT 1203, 1998 SLT 385.

69 See www.judicialstudies-scotland.org.uk/, and see above.

70 Sheriff Courts (Scotland) Act 1971, s 7, Civil Jurisdiction and Judgments Act 1982, Pt II & Sch 8 (as substituted by Civil Jurisdiction and Judgments Order 2001 (SI 2001.2929) Sch 2 para 6).

Within these limits, a Sheriff Court may take almost any kind of civil case, including contract, delict, property and divorce[71] (though that has its own grounds of jurisdiction). It also hears appeals from, or review of, a large number of local authority and other administrative decisions, such as licensing appeals. There are some types of case it cannot hear[72]. On the other hand, it has 'privative' (ie exclusive) jurisdiction in relation to actions for sums of £1,500 or less[73], and to many statutory applications and appeals. As a civil court, it employs 'small claims', 'summary cause' and 'ordinary cause' procedures[74] for cases of different levels of complexity and value, and also summary application procedure for the great variety of emergency and administrative applications under common law and legislation.

Appeal in civil cases depends upon the procedure used. In small claims, appeal is to the Sheriff Principal on a point of law only, and no further. In summary causes, it is to the Sheriff Principal on a point of law only and thence (by leave only) to the Inner House of the Court of Session and thereafter to the Appellate Committee of the House of Lords ('ACHL'). In ordinary causes, it is to the Sheriff Principal and then (generally as of right) to the Inner House, or direct to the Inner House, and thereafter in either case, on a point of law only, to the ACHL. The number of appeals is small compared with the number of cases dealt with[75].

In criminal proceedings, in broad terms, the Sheriff Court has jurisdiction only over offences occurring within the Sheriffdom. Also, there are certain offences, the main ones being murder and rape, which cannot be tried in a Sheriff Court. There are limits too

---

71 In 2002 (the last year for which figures were available in mid-2007), there were some 10,500 divorce actions ended by final judgment in the Sheriff Courts (compared with only 136 in the Court of Session): see *Civil Judicial Statistics Scotland 2002* (Scottish Executive Justice Department 2004).

72 For instance, by virtue of the Insolvency Act 1986, s 120(3), the Sheriff Court cannot hear petitions to wind up a company with fully paid up share capital of greater than £120,000.

73 Sheriff Courts (Scotland) Act 1907, s 7 (as amended).

74 See *ibid*, ss 35-38, 41-42. In 2002 (the last year for which figures were available in mid-2007), there were some 32,000 small claims initiated, 36,500 summary causes and 28,000 ordinary causes: see *Civil Judicial Statistics Scotland 2002* (Scottish Executive Justice Department 2004). The meaning of 'small claims', etc, is considered below in relation to court procedure.

75 In 2002 (the last year for which figures were available in mid-2007), there were 12 small claims appeals, 29 summary cause appeals and 281 ordinary cause appeals disposed of by Sheriff Principals, and 59 appeals from Sheriff Courts disposed of by the Inner House: see *Civil Judicial Statistics Scotland 2002* (Scottish Executive Justice Department 2004), Chapter 3. Eighty per cent of appeals were unsuccessful.

on a Sheriff's sentencing powers. In summary proceedings, a Sheriff can impose up to three months' imprisonment and/or a fine at level five of the standard scale[76], and in solemn proceedings (used in serious cases with a jury), five years' imprisonment (or in some cases more[77]) and/or an unlimited fine[78] (and may remit to the High Court for heavier sentence[79]). Within these limits, however, a Sheriff can try any criminal case, and by summary or solemn procedure, as appropriate[80]. Prosecution is by the Procurator Fiscal Service, and the fiscal chooses between summary or solemn procedure where a choice is available.

Appeals in criminal cases may be against conviction and/or sentence, and are to the High Court of Justiciary. In summary proceedings, the person convicted can appeal against conviction and sentence or other disposal. The prosecutor may appeal, but only on a point of law, against conviction or sentence. In solemn procedure, only the person convicted may appeal. Appeals are a small proportion of cases heard.

The High Court of Justiciary[81]

The High Court of Justiciary is the trial court for major crime, and the final appeal court for all crime, in Scotland. As a trial court, it goes on circuit to a number of towns and cities, with a single judge. It deals with a very small proportion of all crime, although all that it does deal with is serious[82]. As an appeal court (called the Court of Criminal Appeal in appeals under 'solemn procedure'[83]), it sits only in Parliament House in Edinburgh[84], usually with a bench of three judges, although a larger bench can be convened to review prece-

---

76 But, for instance, six months for a second or subsequent offence of dishonest appropriation or personal violence: Criminal Procedure (Scotland) Act 1995, s 5.
77 Particular statutes may impose different sentencing powers *ad hoc*.
78 Criminal Procedure (Scotland) Act 1995, s 3(3) (as amended).
79 *Ibid*, s 219(8).
80 For 'summary' and 'solemn' proceedings, see below.
81 Much of the relevant law is found in the Criminal Procedure (Scotland) Act 1995.
82 In 2005-6, some 151,000 people were proceeded against in a criminal court, of whom 800 (0.5%) were dealt with by the High Court: *Scottish Executive Statistical Bulletin: Criminal Justice Series* CrJ/2006/3 (April 2006), Table 3.
83 For 'solemn' proceedings, see below. See also Shiels 'The Origins of the Court of Criminal Appeal' 2006 SLT 215-218.
84 That is, the building erected in 1639 for the Scottish Parliament, in the Edinburgh High Street, behind St Giles, and vacated upon the Union of Parliaments in 1707, now with an annexe across the road in the Lawnmarket.

dents[85] which are doubted. The judges are the same as those who staff the Court of Session. It is the supreme criminal court for Scotland, and will remain unaffected by the creation of the 'Supreme Court of the United Kingdom'[86].

The court. In 1672, the High Court of Justiciary was set up to replace the previous system of lay 'Justices-General' (earlier called 'Justiciars') appointed to tour the country dealing with crime (and other matters) of particular concern to the Sovereign. The sovereign might directly interfere in the business, and the system was ineffective even by the standards of the day. The High Court originally comprised the Lord Justice-General (a layman who often did not sit[87]), the Lord Justice-Clerk (originally the clerk of court to the lay Justiciars), and five Lords Commissioners of Justiciary from among the Court of Session judges.

In 1837, the office of Lord Justice-General was passed to the Lord President of the Court of Session, and in 1887 all Court of Session judges became Lords Commissioners of Justiciary and the court took its present form.

The court may sit anywhere in Scotland. It used to go on four fixed circuits, but now sits where the Lord Justice-General determines after consultation with the Lord Advocate. Half a dozen Lords Commissioners will be on circuit much of the time (but with a permanent presence in Glasgow), sitting singly with a jury, and three more sitting in Edinburgh hearing appeals.

The Lord Justice-General is responsible for the administration of the court, acting through the Principal Clerk of Session and Justiciary and his staff, who may act as clerks of court on circuit.

High Court of Justiciary judges ('Lords Commissioners of Justiciary'). The Lord President of the Court of Session is the Lord Justice-General, and all Court of Session judges ('Senators of the College of Justice') are also High Court judges ('Lords Commissioners of Justiciary') *ex officio*[88]. Temporary Judges of the Court of Session are also Temporary Judges of the High Court[89].

---

85 For the meaning and significance of 'precedent', see Ch 12.
86 Thus preserving the anomaly that civil appeals from Scotland can go on a further appeal, but criminal cases cannot, creating the further anomaly that the Supreme Court of the United Kingdom is thus a misnomer.
87 The office became hereditary in the Dukes of Argyll.
88 For their identities, see www.scotcourts.gov.uk, the 'White Book' (see above), or the bound volumes of Session Cases and Scots Law Times.
89 See previous note.

As with Court of Session judges (and Sheriffs) the Judicial Studies Committee[90] now provides training and professional development.

The work of the High Court. As a trial court, the High Court of Justiciary has jurisdiction over all offences in Scotland (unless excluded by statute). Thus, its jurisdiction overlaps that of other criminal courts, and it is the prosecutor's decision in most cases whether a case goes to the High Court or elsewhere. However, no other court may try certain offences, principally murder and rape, and the High Court also wields the *nobile offi-cium* (see Chapter 12) and, possibly, a 'declaratory power' to create new offences (see also Chapter 12), although this is very constrained if indeed it still exists. On the other hand, it does not deal with offences triable by summary proceedings, so trials are always by solemn procedure, before a single judge and a jury of 15. Prosecution is by one of some 20 Advocates-Depute in the name of the Lord Advocate[91], but occasionally by the Lord Advocate or the Solicitor-General[92].

Appeal from the High Court sitting as a trial court is to the High Court sitting as a court of appeal, which usually comprises three judges, but may comprise only two, and is often called 'the Court of Criminal Appeal'. It also sits as the appeal court from all summary proceedings in the District Court (and in future, the JP Court) and the summary and solemn proceedings in the Sheriff Court. In practice, one or other of the Divisions of the Inner House of the Court of Session, under their presiding judges, almost always provides the criminal appeal court. There is no further appeal save in a devolution case (as discussed below).

The Court of Session[93]

The Court of Session has jurisdiction over most civil matters in Scotland, but sits only in Parliament House[94] in Edinburgh. It comprises the 'Outer House' and the 'Inner House'. Judges of the former (known as 'Lords Ordinary') sit singly, and deal with cases

---

90 See www.judicialstudies-scotland.org.uk/, and above.
91 For the identities of Advocates-Depute, see the 'White Book' (see above).
92 For example, the Lord Advocate, Colin Boyd QC, led the prosecution of the Lockerbie bombers.
93 Much of the relevant law is found in the Court of Session Act 1988.
94 See above in relation to the High Court of Justiciary.

at first instance. Judges of the latter sit on one or other of two 'Divisions' (though there may be an 'Extra Division'), normally with three judges, and chiefly hear appeals (although they also hear petitions in which one party seeks some special permission, usually without opposition). Also, as with the High Court of Justiciary, a larger bench can be convened to review precedents[95]. The Court of Session is the supreme civil court in Scotland, although appeal from it to the Appellate Committee of the House of Lords is possible (and in future, the Supreme Court of the United Kingdom).

The court. The date traditionally taken to be the year of the court's foundation is 1532. Since the late 15th century the King's Council had been sitting intermittently to dispense civil justice. Its lack of funding, and the limited availability of the nobility around the time of the Kings James IV and V, impeded its efficiency. An Act of 1532 (later called the College of Justice Act) made arrangements for a central royal court under the name of the 'College of Justice' to be set up[96]. It comprised fifteen men (eight, including the Lord President, being clerics) appointed as 'Lords of Council and Session' to be professional judges, supported financially by church endowments and exhorted to sit daily. But it was not until an Act of Parliament of 1541, confirming that of 1532 and a Bull of Pope Paul III of 1535, that the court began to function regularly with some semblance of sufficient funding.

At first it dealt only with cases at first instance, with possible appeal to the Privy Council, and it had no jurisdiction over marriage and some other matters, which were then dealt with by ecclesiastical courts. It rapidly expanded its jurisdiction, however, and became an appeal court as well. The leading writer on Scots law, Viscount Stair, referred to the court in his *Institutions* of 1681[97] as 'the Session' or 'the College of Justice'. By the time of the Union of 1707, it was called the 'Court of Session'.

Until the Union rendered Parliament House vacant[98], 'the Haill

---

95 For the meaning and significance of 'precedent', see Ch 12.
96 On this complex subject, see RK Hannay, *The College of Justice* (Stair Society, 1990).
97 *Institutions*, IV, 1, 22.
98 See above in relation to the High Court of Justiciary.

Fifteen' usually sat in an inner room in the Edinburgh Tolbooth[99], save for one or two judges dealing with witnesses and preliminary matters outside, reporting back to them. This practice persisted when the court moved into the adjacent Parliament Hall within Parliament House. They would send one of their number in turn to hear evidence on the other side of a partition and report back to them. Thus the titles 'Inner' and 'Outer House' arose. In 1808 and 1825 a number of reforms resulted in the court taking its present form. It is still 'collegiate' in that decisions are given in the name of the whole court, judges from one House may sit in the other, and all are said to be of equal status (although Inner House judges are paid slightly more, and the Lord President most of all).

There is provision for 34 Court of Session judges[100], but additional temporary judges. One judge is always seconded to the Scottish Law Commission as whole- or part-time chairman[101]. The more junior Court of Session judges (that is, those who are not members of the Inner House) sit as Lords Ordinary in the Outer House. But they will not do so every working day. Some may be sitting as Lords Commissioners of Justiciary in the High Court of Justiciary, usually away from Edinburgh on circuit. Others may be sitting in other judicial capacities, such as Chairman of the Employment Appeal Tribunal, and yet others may be undertaking other functions, such as judicial inquiries[102].

---

99 Or rather, it sat in the Tolbooth itself till 1560, but from 1564 to 1640 in an upstairs room in an annexe to St Giles church, referred to as the 'Over' or 'Upper Tolbooth' (the High Court of Justiciary sitting in a lower room). McQueen 'Two Visitors in the Session, 1629 and 1639' in McQueen (ed) *Miscellany IV* (Stair Society, 2002) reproduces two 17th-century accounts by English visitors, including a sketch map of the lay-out of the 'Upper Tolbooth'. One of the visitors (Sir C Lowther) recorded (p163) that in the Outer House 'is allway grete noyse and confusion, but the Inner House very orderly ... it onely medleth with things not determined or where his [*scil* the Outer House judge's] judgment is disliked'. The other visitor (Sir W Brereton) also recorded (at p166) that 'I observed the gretest rudeness, disorder and confusion that ever I saw in any court of justice, no, not the like disorder in any of our sessions, for here two or three plead and speak together, and that with such a forced, strained voice as the strongest only caries it ...'.

100 Court of Session Act 1988, s1(1) (as amended by the Maximum Number of Judges (Scotland) Order 2004 (SSI 2004/499), Art. 2).

101 In mid-2007, Lord Drummond Young.

102 Lord Cullen of Whitekirk, Lord President 2001-5, while a judge, had conducted the Public Inquiry into the Piper Alpha disaster between 1988 and 1990, the Public Inquiry into the Dunblane Primary School shootings in 1996, and the Ladbroke Grove Rail Inquiry in 1999, for instance.

The Inner House comprises the 'First' and 'Second' Divisions, which are, despite their titles, of equal status. The First is composed of the Lord President of the Court of Session and four senior judges, and the Second, the Lord Justice-Clerk and four other senior judges[103]. Both have a quorum, and normal complement, of three (for the others may be performing other tasks). An Extra Division may also be convened. Also, occasionally, a Court of Seven (or more) Judges is convened for a point of special difficulty, or where overruling a precedent[104] of a Division is in contemplation.

The Lord President is responsible for administration of the court, acting through the Principal Clerk of Session and Justiciary and his staff.

Court of Session judges (Senators of the College of Justice). The judges of the Court of Session, the senior permanent Scottish judges, are technically 'Senators of the College of Justice'[105]. The power of appointment lies with Her Majesty, and under arrangements introduced upon devolution, on the recommendation of the First Minister and after consulting the Lord President[106] and receiving recommendations from the Judicial Appointments Board for Scotland[107]. Those eligible are Sheriffs and Sheriffs Principal of five years' standing, and advocates and solicitors with five years' right of audience in the Court of Session[108]. Vacancies are now advertised. On appointment judges take the courtesy title 'Lord' or

---

103 Both, until recently, only three others.
104 For the meaning and significance of 'precedent', see Ch 12.
105 For their identities, see www.scotcourts.gov.uk, the 'White Book' (see above), or the bound volumes of Session Cases and Scots Law Times. In mid-2007, the Lord President was Lord Hamilton, and the Lord Justice-Clerk, Lord Gill.
106 Scotland Act 1998, s 95(4). See, however, the Draft Bill attached to by *Proposals for a Judiciary (Scotland) Bill* (Scottish Executive, 2007), available at www.scotland.gov.uk/Publications/2007/02/13115213/0.
107 The first two judges appointed under the new system were Phillip Brodie QC, who took the courtesy title of Lord Brodie, and Alistair Campbell QC, who took the courtesy title of Lord Bracadale. However, see below on the appointment of Lady Smith.
108 Until the Law Reform (Miscellaneous Provisions) (Scotland) Act 1990, s 35, it was not clear who was eligible. There was no legislation on this matter, but Art. 19 of the Treaty of Union permitted (on various conditions) advocates, Writers to the Signet and Principal Clerks of Session to be appointed. Only senior advocates who were not Sheriffs had been appointed for many years, so the 1990 Act broadened eligibility considerably. However, advocates as such are not mentioned in the 1990 Act, so while they are undoubtedly still considered eligible, it is presumably on the basis of the Treaty of Union, Art. 19

'Lady'[109]. They are not thereby members of the House of Lords[110]. Some follow a tradition of taking a territorial or family title instead of their surname, which may some times be justified as avoiding the surname of another judge[111]. In addition, Temporary Judges may now be appointed by the First Minister from among retired judges for a year at a time up to the age of 75 and also from those eligible to be appointed as full-time judges (usually senior Sheriffs or practising advocates)[112]. The latter do not have the title of 'Lord' or 'Lady'.

109 In mid-2007, there had been five women judges (four of whom were still sitting): Lady Cosgrove (appointed 1996, having been a Sheriff and Temporary Judge, and the first woman judge, also becoming the first woman to serve in the Inner House, in 2003: retired 2006); Lady Paton (appointed 2000, direct from the Bar, having been an advocate-depute and standing counsel to various Government departments); Lady Smith (appointed 2001, direct from the Bar, having been a Temporary Sheriff and an advocate-depute: she was appointed by a temporary formal selection process which briefly preceded the Judicial Appointments Board); Lady Dorrian (appointed 2005, direct from the bar having also been an advocate-depute and standing counsel to Government departments); and Lady Clark of Calton (appointed 2006, having been standing counsel to Government departments and Advocate-General for Scotland).

110 Nor are they knighted, as are their equivalents in England & Wales. However, several judges were already life peers for other reasons, typically as law officers required to sit in the House of Lords (not being MPs), such as Lord McCluskey, Lord Cameron of Lochbroom, Lord Rodger of Earlsferry and Lady Clark of Calton. Also, recent Lord Presidents not previously ennobled have received peerages, ie Lord Hope of Craighead and Lord Cullen of Whitechurch.

111 The practice may be increasing in popularity, for among judges sitting in mid-2007, nearly a quarter of the Court of Session bench had taken advantage of it: Lord Kingarth was Derek Emslie, Lord Abernethy was John Cameron, Lord Eassie was Ronald Mackay, Lord Carloway was Colin Sutherland, Lord Bracadale was Alistair Campbell, Lord Kinclaven was Alexander Wylie, Lord Uist was Roderick Macdonald, and Lord Malcolm was Colin Campbell. This practice incidentally raises the subject of Scottish judicial dynasties. Lord Clyde (appointed 1985, Lord of Appeal in Ordinary 1996–2001) was son of the late Lord Clyde (Lord President 1954–72) and grandson of another late Lord Clyde (Lord President 1928–35). Lord Kingarth (appointed 1997) and Lord Emslie (appointed 2001) are both sons of the late Lord Emslie (appointed 1970, Lord President 1972–89). Lord Wheatley (appointed 2000) is the son of the late Lord Wheatley (appointed 1954, Lord Justice Clerk 1972–85).

112 Judicial Pensions and Retirement Act 1993, s 26(4)–(7); Law Reform (Miscellaneous Provisions) (Scotland) Act 1990, s 35(3). In mid-2007, there were some ten retired judges available. In 2004, one retired judge who was available to sit as a Temporary Judge, Lord Morrison, resigned from that role because of the high usage of Temporary Judges which indicated, in his opinion, that more permanent judges should be appointed. Since then the number of permanent judges has risen from 32 to 34.

Appointment to the Inner House is by the Lord President and Lord Justice-Clerk, with the consent of the Scottish Ministers and 'after such consultation with judges as appears to them to be appropriate in the particular circumstances'[113]. However, the Lord President of the Court of Session and the Lord Justice-Clerk 'continue to be' appointed by Her Majesty on the recommendation of the Prime Minister, after consulting the Lord President and the Lord Justice-Clerk, unless the office is vacant[114]. Occasionally they are appointed straight from the Bar, but otherwise from among existing judges[115].

Senators are paid[116]. They are required to retire at 70 and when they do so they retain their title. Provision is now made for the removal of a judge of the Court of Session. Formerly it was thought that only an Act of Parliament could prematurely remove a judge[117]. However, now, it is provided[118] that if the removal of a judge is contemplated, the First Minister must convene a tribunal of at least three persons, chaired by a member of the Judicial Committee of the Privy Council, which is to report whether the judge is unfit for office 'by reason of inability, neglect of duty or misbehaviour'. If such a report is made, the First Minister may recommend to the Scottish Parliament that the judge be removed and if it so resolves he shall make a recommendation to Her Majesty to that effect. The procedure is similar to that for the removal of a Sheriff.

The Judicial Studies Committee[119] now provides some training and career development of judges.

---

113 Court of Session Act 1988, s 2(6) (as amended).
114 Scotland Act 1998, s 95.
115 In mid-2007, the Lord President (Lord Hamilton) was appointed from the First Division; his immediate predecessor (Lord Cullen) was previously Lord Justice-Clerk; his predecessor in turn (Lord Rodger, now a House of Lords judge) was appointed from the Outer House, but his further predecessor (Lord Hope, now also a House of Lords judge), was appointed from the Bar where he was Dean of the Faculty of Advocates. The current Lord Justice-Clerk (Lord Gill) was an Outer House judge, and Chairman of the Scottish Law Commission; his immediate predecessor was Lord Cullen (see above), whose predecessor (Lord Ross) was appointed from the Inner House.
116 In mid-2007, the Lord President received £200,800; the Lord Justice-Clerk, £194,000; and other Senators, £184,000.
117 The position in England was covered by the Supreme Court Act 1981, which does not apply in Scotland.
118 Scotland Act, s 95(6)-(11). See, however, the Draft Bill attached to by *Proposals for a Judiciary (Scotland) Bill* (Scottish Executive, 2007), available at www.scotland.gov.uk/Publications/2007/02/13115213/0, discussed above in relation to judicial independence.
119 See www.judicialstudies-scotland.org.uk/, and see above.

The work of the Court of Session. The Outer House of the Court of Session is a court of first instance, and can hear most types of civil case. Therefore many cases can be brought either there or in the Sheriff Court, and pursuers choose on the basis of cost, importance, convenience etc. Some cases, however, such as judicial review over certain administrative bodies, and exercise of the *nobile officium* (for which, see Chapter 12), are reserved to the Court. Some others though, such as actions for £1,500 or less and a number of appeals from administrative decisions, are reserved for Sheriffs. There is a limited degree of specialisation among the Court of Session judges, for instance, in judicial review cases and in intellectual property, commercial and patent cases there are special provisions to enable them to be dealt with quickly[120]. Most cases, however, are personal injury cases[121].

The Inner House of the Court of Session is primarily a court of appeal from the Outer House, Sheriffs Principal and Sheriffs, certain specialised courts (such as the Scottish Land Court), and a variety of tribunals (such as the Employment Appeal Tribunal and the Social Security Commissioners). As a court of first instance, it hears 'special cases', that is, certain ones in which the facts are agreed, and only the law is disputed (for example, on the interpretation of a will), and certain petitions, generally purely formal (such as to appoint solicitors as notaries public), but also including those seeking variation of trusts.

Appeal from the Outer House to the Inner House is as of right and is called a 'reclaiming motion', as one part of the collegiate court is reviewing the decision of another part. Thereafter it is to the House of Lords, provided it is from a final judgment, or the judges were not unanimous, or the Inner House gives leave. Where the appeal originated in the Sheriff Court, there are restrictions on appeal to the Inner House. It may go thereafter go to the Appellate Committee of the House of Lords on a point of law. The number of appeals (as from other courts) is not large[122].

---

120 In mid-2007, the 'Commercial Judges' were Lords Clarke, Mackay of Drumadoon, and Drummond Young.

121 In 2002 (the last year for which figures were available in mid-2007), there were 4,855 causes initiated in the Outer House and 204 in the Inner House. By far the biggest category was personal injury (2,419 actions initiated), but there were also 1,292 petitions initiated in the Outer House, and 59 in the Inner House: *Civil Judicial Statistics Scotland 2002* (Scottish Executive Justice Department 2004).

122 In 2002 (see previous note), there were 145 appeals to the Inner House from the different courts and tribunals: *Civil Judicial Statistics Scotland 2002* (Scottish Executive Justice Department 2004).

The Court of Session has the power of judicial review over the decisions of lower courts and tribunals and of government, on grounds of procedural impropriety, such as *ultra vires* (acting beyond one's powers), or lack of 'natural justice' (for instance, not hearing both sides of the case)[123]. This process is considered further below in relation to civil procedure.

It can also exercise the *nobile officium* (see Chapter 12).

Appellate Committee of the House of Lords/Supreme Court of the United Kingdom[124]

Subject always to the decisions of the European Court of Justice on Community law matters, the final court of appeal from civil courts (but not from criminal courts, except in England and Wales and Northern Ireland) is that commonly referred to as 'the House of Lords'. However, it is in fact the 'Appellate Committee of the House of Lords' ('ACHL'), comprising a number of judges, which is the actual court. It sits in the Palace of Westminster, that is, the United Kingdom Parliament building in London. However, in 2003, it was announced, as one of a number of related matters, some controversial, and all with limited discussion, that the Government intended to replace the Appellate Committee by a 'Supreme Court', and a Consultation Paper was issued[125],

---

123   In 2002 (see previous note), there were 160 judicial review proceedings initiated: *Civil Judicial Statistics Scotland 2002* (Scottish Executive Justice Department 2004).

124   The relevant law on the Appellate Committee is largely found in the Appellate Jurisdiction Act 1876 (as amended): that on the Supreme Court (which in effect rebrands the Appellate Committee as a 'Supreme Court') is the Constitutional Reform Act 2006, Part 3 which, in mid-2007, had been passed by the United Kingdom Parliament, but was not likely to come into force till late 2009.

125   For the circumstances of the announcement, and critiques of the Consultation Paper, (CP/113) see the Appendix to the Preface of the Third Edition of this book, recent editions of constitutional law textbooks, House of Commons Constitutional Affairs Committee *First Report of Session 2003-04 'Judicial Appointments and a Supreme Court (court of final appeal)'* HC Paper (2003-04) No 48, Gretton 'Scotland and the Supreme Court' 2003 SLT 265-266, McQueen 'Scotland and a Supreme Court for the UK?' 2003 SLT 279-282, Chalmers 'Scottish Appeals and the Proposed Supreme Court' (2004) 8 Edin LR 4-30, Bingham of Cornhill 'The Old Order Changeth' (2006) 122 LQR 211-223, and the annotations to the Constitutional Reform Act 2005 in Current Law Statutes Annotated. See also references to the Appellate Committee of the House of Lords and the Supreme Court of the United Kingdom below and in Ch 3.

followed by legislation[126]. This legislation sets up a 'Supreme Court of the United Kingdom'[127], which will take over the existing jurisdiction of the ACHL, and part of that of the Judicial Committee of the Privy Council, and have judges of similar status. It will sit in the old Middlesex Guildhall, opposite the United Kingdom Parliament, in Parliament Square[128].

Fears have been expressed that a Supreme Court would anglify Scots law and have other defects[129]. However, there are provisions in the method of appointment (considered below) designed to ensure an adequate Scottish presence on the court, and it is also provided that its operations are not 'to affect the distinctions between the separate legal systems of the parts of the United Kingdom' and that a 'decision of the Supreme Court on appeal from a court of any part of the United Kingdom … is to be regarded as the decision of a court of that part of the United Kingdom'[130].

The court. There was no Scottish House of Lords, as Scottish peers did not meet as a separate body. The present House of Lords is descended from the House of Lords of Great Britain, set up in 1707, but following the traditions of the English House, which heard

126 Constitutional Reform Act 2005, Part 3. (Part 1 of the Act oddly asserts that, *int. al.* it "does not adversely affect … the constitutional principle of the rule of law"; Part 2 deals with the position of the Lord Chancellor (and was referred to in Ch 3 in that regard); Part 4 with appointment to, and discipline of, the judiciary, chiefly in England & Wales; Part 5 with judicial appointments and removals in Northern Ireland; Part 6 with other matters, including the Judicial Committee of the Privy Council; and Part 7 with general matters.

127 *Ibid*, s 23(1). There is a good deal of room for confusion in the title. Firstly, it was initially assumed by some commentators that the United States Supreme Court was the model, which implied party political appointments and the power to over-ride the legislature: much effort went into seeking to rebut this. Secondly, the term 'Supreme Courts' has been used in Scotland semi-officially to refer to the Court of Session and the High Court of Justiciary in the title of a long-standing solicitors' body called 'the Society of Solicitors to the Supreme Courts of Scotland' ('SSC'), and also (rather curiously further including Accountant of Court's Office) in *Scottish Court Service; an introduction* (Scottish Court Service, n.d.)). Thirdly, the term has been used officially (if rarely) in England & Wales to refer to the High Court of Justice, Crown Court (formerly 'the Assizes') and Court of Appeal, set up in broadly their present form by the Supreme Court of Judicature Acts 1873 & 1875 (which accounts for the change of title of the Supreme Courts Act 1981 to the 'Senior Courts Act 1981' by the Constitutional Reform Act 2005, Sch 11).

128 The other two sides, interestingly, are formed by Westminster Abbey (God) and the Treasury (Mammon).

129 See references above in relation to the Consultation Paper.

130 Constitutional Reform Act 2005, s 41: any 'devolution matter' is excepted from this, so that a decision on the boundaries of devolution binds all parts.

appeals from the courts. There was dispute as to whether the new House could hear appeals from Scottish courts, but it quickly assumed jurisdiction[131], and there were many Scottish appeals until the twentieth century. The House of Lords only grew into a professional court in the 19th century, when a convention grew up that lay peers should not sit on appeals, judges were ennobled in order to hear such appeals, and finally the ACHL was set up in 1876[132].

The ACHL usually sits as a bench of five, in a committee room in the House of Lords, but judgment is given in the Chamber itself.

The Supreme Court of the United Kingdom, noted above, will be successor body to this arrangement, but with the existing link with Parliament intentionally severed (as open to the criticism as incompatible with human rights and, more specifically, breaches the 'doctrine of the separation of powers')[133].

Judges of the Appellate Committee of the House of Lords/Supreme Court of the United Kingdom. The ACHL comprises the Lord Chancellor[134], Lords of Appeal in Ordinary, and any other peers who have held high judicial office. Collectively, but informally, they are referred to as 'the Law Lords'.

Lord Chancellors are members of the government[135]. They are therefore, in some sense, political appointments, and they have been either active members of the ruling party who are legally qualified (such as Lord Hailsham), or persons of distinction in the law who are at least sympathetic to that party's objectives (such as the Conservative Lord Mackay of Clashfern and the Labour Lord Irvine of Lairg). Their tenure therefore depends upon the continued trust

---

131 The first reported case, *Greenshields v Magistrates of Edinburgh* (1710–11) Rob 12, was in 1710. An Episcopalian minister was imprisoned by the magistrates, at the behest of the Presbytery, for using the Anglican form of service. The Court of Session upheld their decision, but the House of Lords set its stamp on the matter by overturning it.

132 Appellate Jurisdiction Act 1876.

133 The argument was more forceful in relation to the Lord Chancellor: see the arguments on this in Ch 3, and the references above to the circumstances of the announcement of the proposal.

134 In mid-2007, the Lord Chancellor (and Secretary of State for Justice) was Jack Straw MP, previously Leader of the House of Commons, and freshly appointed in the reshuffle after Gordon Brown replaced Tony Blair as Prime Minister. As the first person to be Lord Chancellor in modern times who was not a peer, nor either a barrister or an advocate (though he is a solicitor) his appointment was the latest stage in the change in status of the Lord Chancellorship. His predecessor was Lord Falconer of Thoroton, who had presided over the earlier manifold and rapid changes described in Ch 3).

135 See references to the Lord Chancellor in Ch 3.

of the Prime Minister and the outcome of general elections. Recognition of objections in terms of human rights and, more specifically, the 'doctrine of the separation of powers', and thus the independence of the judiciary, to such persons sitting as the most senior judge in the highest court in the land mean that no Lord Chancellor is ever likely to sit again[136]. The ACHL is now chaired by a 'Senior Lord of Appeal in Ordinary' or 'Second Senior Lord of Appeal in Ordinary', who also have administrative responsibilities.

Up to 12 Lords of Appeal in Ordinary[137] (including the Senior, and Second Senior, Lords of Appeal in Ordinary) are appointed as peers for life from among those who have 'held high judicial office' for at least two years, or have been practising advocates (or barristers in England and Wales or Northern Ireland) for 15 years[138]. By convention, at least two are Scottish[139]. Thus, as the Appellate Committee of the House of Lords normally sits as a bench of five, Scottish appeals have usually been heard by a majority of non-Scottish judges. Lords of Appeal in Ordinary are appointed by the Crown on the recommendation of the Prime Minister, but there is, however, no formal selection procedure or scrutiny of appointments[140]. They hold office until the age of 70, but remain eligible on

136 This is a recent position, however. Lord Falconer (see previous two notes) issued a self-denying ordinance to this effect. However, he, and previous Lord Chancellors (in mid-2007, only Lord Irvine of Lairg) remained technically eligible.

137 The curious suffix 'in Ordinary' simply indicates that they are paid.

138 A list of their identities is also to be found at http://www.parliament.uk/judicial_work/judicial_work.cfm, and in the 'White Book' (see above). Those appointed as Lords of Appeal in Ordinary are almost invariably already judges, but Lord Reid of Drem (appointed 1948, retired 1975), who had been both Solicitor-General for Scotland and Lord Advocate (while an MP, thus acquiring no peerage) and Dean of the Faculty of Advocates, was appointed direct from the Bar.

139 In mid-2007, they were Lord Hope of Craighead and Lord Rodger of Earlsferry. The Scottish presence may, in principle, be increased by use of retired Scottish Lords of Appeal in Ordinary still eligible to sit and Scottish judges who happen to hold peerages (and three retired Scottish peers who had held high judicial office were then still eligible to sit, that is, Lord Mackay of Clashfern, Lord McCluskey and Lord Cameron of Lochbroom).

140 The Lord Chancellor's Department paper *Judicial Appointments* (2002) declared that they are 'appointed by the Queen on the recommendation of the Prime Minister, who receives advice from the Lord Chancellor. Before giving advice the Lord Chancellor customarily [sic] consults serving Lords of Appeal in Ordinary and other senior members of the judiciary'. The Judicial Appointments Board for Scotland has no formal role, nor has the Judicial Appointments Commission in England and Wales.

a temporary basis up to the age of 75[141]. They remain peers for life, and are salaried[142].

Peers who have 'high judicial office' include past Lord Chancellors, retired Lords of Appeal in Ordinary, if not disqualified by age, and judges of the Court of Session (and their equivalents in England and Wales and Northern Ireland) who happen to hold peerages[143]. Typically, these are judges who have received peerages through holding some other office attracting a peerage before appointment to the bench[144]. The availability of such judicial peers is unpredictable.

The Supreme Court of the United Kingdom will initially comprise the existing Lords of Appeal in Ordinary, with the Senior Lord as President and Second Senior as Deputy President[145], all other members being called 'Justices of the Supreme Court'[146]. Thereafter, a complicated procedure applies which demonstrates the relationship, always difficult and rendered more uneasy by the circumstances in which the new provisions emerged, between Government and Judiciary.

That is that those who have held 'high judicial office' for at least two years or been a 'qualifying practitioner' for at least fifteen years, are eligible for appointment[147]. There will be a formal selection procedure, whereby the Lord Chancellor convenes a 'Selection

---

141 In mid-2007, there were none, but a few years earlier, Lord Clyde was still available.
142 In mid-2007, the Senior Lord of Appeal in Ordinary received £200,800 (the same as the Lord President of the Court of Session) and the other Lords of Appeal in Ordinary received £194,000 (the same as the Lord Justice-Clerk).
143 A list of their identities is to be found at at http://www.parliament.uk/judicial_work/judicial_work.cfm, and in the 'White Book' (see above). In mid-2007, there were five retired Lords of Appeal in Ordinary who were still eligible to hear appeals and six other peers who hold, or had held high judicial office and who were still eligible to hear appeals, five of whom were Scottish (including one former Lord Chancellor (Lord Irvine of Lairg), one former Lord President (Lord Cullen of Whitekirk), and three current Court of Session judges (Lord Hardie, Lord Mackay of Drumadoon, and Lady Clark of Calton: see next note).
144 For example as Lord Mackay of Drumadoon, a former Solicitor-General for Scotland and Lord Advocate, and Lady Clark of Calton, a former Advocate-General for Scotland
145 Constitutional Reform Act 2005, s 24.
146 *Ibid*, s 23.
147 *Ibid*, s 25(1). 'High judicial office' is defined (with presently irrelevant exceptions) as being a judge of the Court of Session, or its equivalents in England and Wales, and Northern Ireland: s 60; 'qualifying practitioner' means an advocate or solicitor-advocate, or their equivalents in England and Wales, and Northern Ireland: s 25(2).

Commission' comprising the President (as chair) and Deputy President of the Supreme Court, and one representative each from the Judicial Appointments Board for Scotland, the Judicial Appointments Commission (for England and Wales) and the Northern Ireland Judicial Appointments Commission, nominated by that Board or Commission itself (one of whom must be non-legally qualified)[148]. The Selection Commission determines its own procedure, but must consult such other 'senior judges'[149] as are inel-igible for appointment (failing which, the most senior of the relevant court), the Lord Chancellor, the First Minister of Scotland and the Secretary of State for Northern Ireland, and must select on the basis of merit, though also ensuring knowledge among the Supreme Court of the legal system of each of the constituent parts of the United Kingdom, and having regard to any guidance given by the Lord Chancellor[150]. The Commission reports to the Lord Chancellor in a form which he approves[151]. The Lord Chancellor may accept or (on grounds of 'suitability') either reject the selection or require the Commission to reconsider it and, following any rejec-tion or reconsideration, the Commission has effectively the same choices (though cannot re-nominate a rejected recommendation), but after any third nomination by the Commission, the Lord Chancellor must accept it[152]. His acceptance is indicated by noti-fying the Prime Minister[153], who must 'recommend' such person[154]. Recommendation is presumably to Her Majesty (though the legisla-tion does not actually say so), as it is she who appoints the judges[155].

The work of the Appellate Committee of the House of Lords/Supreme Court of the United Kingdom. The Appellate Committee is the final court of appeal from the Scottish civil courts (and their equivalents, and from the criminal courts, in England and

---

148 *Ibid*, s 26(5)-(8) and Sch 8.
149 That is, the Lord President of the Court of Session, the Lord Justice-Clerk, and their equivalents in England & Wales and Northern Ireland: s 60(1).
150 Constitutional Reform Act 2006, s 27.
151 *Ibid*, s 28.
152 *Ibid*, ss 29-31: 'suitability' means lack of evidence of suitability, evidence that the candidate is not the best person, or lack of evidence that the Court will have knowledge of all three United Kingdom jurisdictions (in all cases, in the opinion of the Lord Chancellor): s 30.
153 *Ibid*, s 29.
154 *Ibid*, s 26.
155 *Ibid*, s 23.

Wales and Northern Ireland). Appeals to it are few[156]. This does not make them unimportant, as they usually lay down broad principles which other courts must follow[157]. The House of Lords also has a rarely exercised jurisdiction at first instance in cases of impeachment and claims to peerages.

The Supreme Court of the United Kingdom will hear any appeal from Scotland which the ACHL could hear[158].

The Judicial Committee of the Privy Council/Supreme Court of the United Kingdom[159]

The Privy Council is the surviving remnant of the former English Privy Council, the Privy Council of Scotland having been abolished[160]. It was an advisory body to the sovereign at a time when sovereigns wielded real political power. The Privy Council, as such, still has a shadowy existence as a dignified, rather than useful, part of the United Kingdom constitution. Membership is a form of honour for certain ministers of the Crown, senior opposition politicians, senior judges and others. 'Prerogative Orders in Council' (for which, see Chapter 5) which are used for some constitutional legislation are technically Orders of the Sovereign in Privy Council. It does, however, have various committees which do have important functions. One, for instance, exercises certain regulatory powers over Scottish Universities. Another is the Judicial Committee.

The court. The Judicial Committee of the Privy Council ('JCPC'), set up in 1833 is, in effect, a court. As such, it has a very miscellaneous jurisdiction.

In part this is 'imperial'. At one time, the colonies of the British Empire, and later the Commonwealth countries (other than the United Kingdom itself), had a final right of appeal to the Judicial Committee, which was thus a sort of central imperial court. A couple of dozen small Commonwealth countries retain a possibility of appeal on a variety of different conditions, as it is useful for such

---

156 In 2002 (the last year for which figures were available in mid-2007), there were 7 appeals from Scotland initiated, and 13 disposed of: *Judicial Statistics Scotland 2002* (Scottish Executive Justice Department 2004).
157 See Ch 12.
158 Constitutional Reform Act 2005, s 40(3).
159 The most important legislation in relation to the Privy Council is the Judicial Committee Act 1833, the Appellate Jurisdiction Act 1887, the Judicial Committee (Amendment) Act 1895 and the Appellate Jurisdiction Acts 1908.
160 See www.privy-council.org.uk.

jurisdictions, with few judges and few cases, to have an 'external' appeal court. These include Antigua, the Bahamas, the Falkland Islands and Gibraltar, as well as the Channel Islands and the Isle of Man (which technically are not part of the United Kingdom).

In part, the jurisdiction is in relation to professional discipline, as it acts as a final court of appeal from certain professional disciplinary bodies, such as the Disciplinary Committee of the Royal College of Veterinary Surgeons.

In part the jurisdiction is ecclesiastical, as it deals with appeals against certain actions of the (Church of England) Church Commissioners (and in principle, of the Church of England itself, though this jurisdiction has not been exercised for many years).

In part the jurisdiction is now in relation to devolution. This recently acquired jurisdiction has increased the significance of the Judicial Committee has considerably. In brief, firstly, there is a specific power for the Advocate-General for Scotland or the Lord Advocate, during the passage of a Bill through Parliament, to refer to the JCPC the question of whether that Bill is in fact within the Parliament's competence[161]. Secondly, in any case, in relation to 'devolution issues' generally (that is, questions as to whether the Scottish Parliament or Scottish Executive have exceeded their powers) there are a variety of procedures[162]. The devolution issue may be raised by the Advocate-General or the Lord Advocate, as such, or by any person adversely affected in any existing proceedings. In any case, the court may decide the issue itself, or refer it to the Inner House (if a civil matter) or the High Court (if criminal), from which it may be appealed to the JCPC. Thus the Judicial Committee has taken on a role as a sort of Constitutional Court in relation to devolution. This jurisdiction, however, is in the future to be transferred to the new Supreme Court of the United Kingdom.

As, strictly speaking, it is a committee of an advisory body rather than a court, the judgments of the JCPC used to conclude with words tendering advice to the Sovereign in Council. By the same token, traditionally, there was a single 'judgment', but occasionally the right to give a dissenting judgment is exercised. In devolution cases, however, the format has followed that of the Appellate Committee House of Lords, and this practice will no doubt be followed in the Supreme Court of the United Kingdom.

Members of the Judicial Committee of the Privy Council/ Supreme Court of the United Kingdom. Membership of the

161 See Chs 3 & 6.
162 *Ibid.*

Judicial Committee comprises all the Lords of Appeal in Ordinary (the Appellate Committee of the House of Lords judges), the Lord Chancellor, Lord Justices of Appeal and any members of the Privy Council who hold or have held high judicial office in the United Kingdom or (save in devolution cases) have been judges in the highest courts of those Commonwealth territories from which appeals still go to the JCPC[163]. Appeals are in practice nearly always heard by three or five of the Law Lords and so it is effectively the same court as the Appellate Committee of the House of Lords and can therefore include those trained in Scots law, and presumably always would in relation to a Scottish devolution matter[164].

The membership of the Supreme Court of the United Kingdom is dealt with above in the relation to the Appellate Committee of the House of Lords.

The work of the Judicial Committee of the Privy Council/ Supreme Court of the United Kingdom. There was a small but steady flow of appeals from Hong Kong until 1997 when it was returned to China, but the number and size of countries using it as their final court of appeal has diminished and this work therefore declined[165]. As the law of these countries is based on English law, such appeals have in fact clarified some points of English law, chiefly criminal law (as several such countries retain the death penalty against which appeal to the JCPC is very likely[166]).

For present purposes, the devolution jurisdiction is much more important. Although there have been hundreds of devolution cases (mostly criminal cases involving the human rights legislation), very few have gone as far as the JCPC[167]. It follows that it is unlikely that the Supreme Court will be called upon to exercise this jurisdiction often[168]. Nevertheless, the significance of this small number of cases is considerable.

163 Judicial Committee Act 1833 (as amended).
164 There is no formal requirement for the Judicial Committee to reflect any balance between the constituent parts of the United Kingdom in a devolution case (but note the method of appointing Justices of the Supreme Court).
165 There still appear to be a significant number of cases per year, however, mostly from the Bahamas and Jamaica: see http://www.privy-council.org.uk/output/ Page34.asp.
166 For example, the law of provocation was reviewed in *A-G for Jersey v Holley* [2005] JCPC 23, an appeal from Jersey. This has caused difficulties, however, considered in Ch 12 in relation to the system of precedent in practice in the criminal courts.
167 By mid-2007, there had been 17.
168 On the other hand, the coming into power of an SNP Scottish Executive might lead to some pushing at the boundaries, with consequential litigation.

Other courts in Scotland

There are several specialised courts of special jurisdiction, most of which are rarely convened.

There are the closely associated **Scottish Land Court**[169] and **Lands Tribunal for Scotland**[170] (which, despite its name, is really a court). The former deals with disputes over agricultural tenancies and crofting lands, has a legally qualified chairman who is not, but has the same status as, a Court of Session judge[171], and three lay members with agricultural experience, including at least one Gaelic speaker, and there is appeal on a point of law to the Inner House[172]. The latter is concerned with disputes over tenants' 'right to buy', compensation for compulsory purchase, and other such matters, and also has a legally qualified President[173], and three lay members[174]. In addition, there are a **Lands Valuation Appeal Court**[175], concerned with disputes arising out of local rates, comprising three Court of Session judges, and there is no appeal[176], and **Court of Teinds**[177], concerned with disputes over teinds (or 'tithes'), comprising five Court of Session judges[178].

Further, there are the **Registration of Voters Appeal Court**[179], comprising three Court of Session judges, and the **Election**

169 See www.scottish-land-court.org.uk/.
170 See www.lands-tribunal-scotland.org.uk/.
171 In mid-2007, it was Lord McGhie.
172 In 2002 (the latest figures available in mid-2007), it disposed of 131 cases: *Civil Judicial Statistics Scotland 2002* (Scottish Executive, 2004).
173 In mid-2007, it was also Lord McGhie.
174 In 2002 (the last year for which figures were available in mid-2007), it disposed of 93 cases: *Civil Judicial Statistics Scotland 2002* (Scottish Executive, 2004).
175 The Lands Valuation Appeal Court has no website.
176 In 2002 (the last year for which figures were available in mid-2007), it disposed of 2 cases: *Civil Judicial Statistics Scotland 2002* (Scottish Executive, 2004).
177 The Court of Teinds has no website.
178 In 2002 (the last year for which figures were available in mid-2007), it appears that there had been no actions before it for some years: *Civil Judicial Statistics Scotland 2002* (Scottish Executive, 2004).
179 The Registration of Voters Appeal Court has no website, and in 2002 (the last year for which figures were available in mid-2007), it appeared that there had been no causes before it for some years: *Civil Judicial Statistics Scotland 2002* (Scottish Executive, 2004). However, see now *Smith v Scott* 2007 SLT 137, a decision of the Inner House, sitting as the Registration of Voters Appeal Court, in which it made a declaration of incompatibility (for the meaning of which, see Chs & 7), to the effect that the Representation of the People Act 1983, s 3(1) was incompatible with Art 3 ECHR insofar as it prevented any prisoner from voting.

Petition Court[180], comprising two Court of Session judges, not to mention the **Court of the Lord Lyon**[181], concerned with heraldry.

European Court of Human Rights[182]

The relevant meaning of 'human rights', and the role of the Council of Europe, are dealt with in Chapter 3. It was observed there that the most important treaty the Council of Europe has generated is the European Convention on Human Rights and Fundamental Freedoms ('ECHR'). The content of the ECHR was also discussed., and the fact that thereby, the United Kingdom has committed itself to promoting a number of rights and freedoms, commonly enumerated as: 'the right to life (including abolition of the death penalty)', 'freedom from torture', 'protection from slavery', 'liberty and the security of persons', 'a fair trial', 'the principle of legality', 'respect for private and family life', 'freedom of expression', 'a right to peaceful assembly', 'the right to marry and to found a family', 'peaceful enjoyment of possessions', 'the right to education', the 'right to free elections'. It has also committed itself to ensuring a right to an effective remedy for any breach, and non-discrimination in the application, of the law.

The primary means of so doing is now through the ordinary courts of the land, by relying on the Human Rights Act 1998 (as discussed further in Chapter 7). However, before that came into effect (apart from the rare inter-state actions), the only method an individual could employ was a petition to the European Court of Human Rights ('ECtHR'), which is thus the principal institution set up under the ECHR. This right of individual petition, however, continues to exist (provided the applicant has exhausted all national remedies), and in any case, the judgments of the ECtHR on the interpretation of the ECHR remain the most authoritative, and the powerful guide to national courts.

The court. A chief means of enforceability of the ECHR, whether by inter-state actions or individual petitions, is thus through the

---

180 The Election Petition Court has no website, and in 2002 (the last year for which figures were available in mid-2007), it appears that there had been no causes before it for some years: *Civil Judicial Statistics Scotland 2002* (Scottish Executive, 2004).

181 See   http://www.lyon-court.com/lordlyon/ll_homeTemplate.jsp;jsessionid= DCB8BF147D0DE9ED9F877048355FCC56?p_applic=CCC&p_service=C ontent.show&pContentID=220&.

182 See www.echr.coe.int/echr/.

ECtHR, which sits in Strasbourg (so is occasionally referred to as 'the Strasbourg Court'). It is not to be confused with the European Court of Justice, which is considered below.

Judges of the European Court of Human Rights. The European Court of Human Rights has one judge from each of the signatory states[183]. However, they are not representatives of their states, though they will be familiar with its legal system. They are appointed by the Parliamentary Assembly of the Council of Europe (for which, see Chapter 3) for a period of six years, and sit full-time[184]. The full Court elects its President and two Vice-Presidents for a period of three years[185]. The Court is divided into five 'Sections', each led by a Vice-President or a 'Section President'. Within each Section, Committees of three judges are set up for 12-month periods. However, in cases of major importance, or where a respondent state requests, it is possible for the case to be referred to a Grand Chamber of 17 judges[186]. The official languages of the Court are French and English only.

The work of the European Court of Human Rights[187]. After a preliminary sifting, a three-judge Committee considers the 'admissibility' of an application, that is, whether the applicant had exhausted remedies in his own state and whether a violation of one or more Articles had been validly raised, etc[188]. A high proportion of applications fail at this stage.

---

183 In mid-2007, there were 46 judges.
184 In mid-2007, the United Kingdom judge was Sir Nicholas Bratza, an English High Court judge and a Vice-President of the Court.
185 In mid-2007, the President was French (Jean-Paul Costa) and the Vice-Presidents Greek (Christos Rozakis) and British (Sir Nicholas Bratza: see previous note).
186 Art 43, ECHR.
187 Until Protocol 11 to the ECHR in 1998, a petition was considered first by another body, the European Commission on Human Rights ('EComHR') which, having decided whether or not the petition was admissible, would seek a friendly settlement. If it failed to achieve a settlement, it considered whether or not to pass the matter to the ECtHR, or to the Committee of Ministers. If it did so, the ECtHR might proceed to a judgment, or the Committee to a decision, respectively. In all of this complicated procedure, enforceability depended upon the state in question agreeing to comply with the conclusion of Commission, Court or Committee. This is important to know, because reports of pre-1998 ECtHR cases carry opinions by the Commission as well as the Court.
188 Art 35, ECHR.

If the application against a state is admitted (or the Committee is divided), it goes before a seven-judge 'Chamber' (formed of the members of a Section), which includes a judge from the respondent state (unless it is referred to a Grand Chamber). This considers written submissions, may hear evidence, and formally decides on admissibility, and on the merits of the case. Decisions in a Chamber are by majority, and dissenting judgments can be issued (as in the United Kingdom, but contrary to the practice in most countries of Continental Europe).

States agree to abide by the judgment of the ECtHR, though enforcement remains a matter of the state honouring its obligation to abide by the judgment, a process supervised by the Committee of Ministers (for which, see Chapter 3) which thus ensures that the judgments of the Court are complied with and corrective measures introduced where necessary, as there is no other enforcement machinery[189].

European Court of Justice (the 'Court of Justice of the European Communities') and Court of First Instance[190]

The European Union (including the European Community) was discussed in Chapter 3. As noted there, it has had a considerable effect upon the Scottish legal system since United Kingdom accession, and has introduced what amounts to a new source of law, requiring to be treated in a different fashion than, and overriding, existing Scots law.

The court. The European Court of Justice ('ECJ') sits in Luxembourg, and is not to be confused with the European Court of Human Rights (ECtHR), considered above, which sits in Strasbourg. As noted in Chapter 3, it exists to ensure that Community law is correctly interpreted, and is observed. Since 1989 there has been attached to it a Court of First Instance ('CFI'), which was created because of the large workload, and consequent enormous delays, in the ECJ itself. For certain cases, there is a right of appeal from it to the ECJ on a point of law.

The judges of the European Court of Justice (the 'Court of Justice of the European Communities') and Court of First Instance. Currently, the ECJ has 27 judges, one nominated

189 Art 46, ECHR
190 See http://curia.europa.eu/

by each Member State[191] for a renewable six year term, and one is elected President[192]. This may change, however, in consequence of the enlargement of the European Union.

The ECJ normally sits in 'Chambers' of three or five judges under an elected President, but may form a 'Grand Chamber' of 13, for a case of great significance, or where a Member State requests it, or may even sit as a 'Full Court'. Nevertheless, it is, like the Court of Session, a 'collegiate court'.

There are also eight Advocates General, an office for which there is no United Kingdom equivalent[193]. They present to the judges a fully reasoned preliminary judgment after hearing the parties' arguments. The ECJ's judgment, given thereafter, is by no means bound to follow the Advocate General's view, but is likely to[194]. The difference between the two styles of judgment has importance for judicial reasoning and the operation of precedent. This is discussed in Chapter 3 but, for the moment, it may be noticed that Advocate General's judgments, being the work of one person, are frequently more clearly reasoned and comprehensible, while those of the ECJ, although flowing from a draft prepared by one judge as *'rapporteur'*, are ultimately a compromise between the several judges, and may be a good deal less so.

The CFI has 27 further judges, each also nominated for six years by a Member State[195], with another elected President[196], but no separate Advocates General (though a judge may act as Advocate General).

The work of the European Court of Justice (the 'Court of Justice of the European Communities') and Court of First Instance. Between them the ECJ and CFI decide several classes of case.

---

191 In mid-2007, the United Kingdom ECJ judge was Konrad Schiemann, formerly a Court of Appeal judge in England.
192 In mid-2007, the President was the Greek nomination, Vassilios Skouris. For some years in the 1980s, the President was a Scottish judge, Lord Mackenzie-Stuart.
193 Advocates-General of the ECJ should not be confused with the Advocate-General for Scotland (see Ch 3). In mid-2007, one of the Advocates-General was Eleanor Sharpston QC, an English barrister and legal academic.
194 The difference between the two styles of judgment has importance for judicial reasoning and the operation of precedent. This is discussed in Ch 12.
195 In mid-2007, the United Kingdom CFI judge was Nicholas Forwood QC, an English barrister.
196 In mid-2007, it was the Danish nomination, Bo Westerdorf.

Firstly, there are various types of 'direct action', in which the ECJ or CFI hears the whole proceedings. These include actions against Community institutions (for instance, where an institution is accused of acting *ultra vires* or otherwise improperly; appeals against penalties imposed by Community institutions; actions for damages against Community institutions for wrongful acts; 'staff cases' by those employed by Community institutions, against their employer[197]; and 'enforcement actions' brought by Community institutions against member states alleged to have failed to carry out their Treaty obligations[198]. The CFI has usually heard staff cases[199], competition law cases, and anti-dumping cases, other cases going to the ECJ. (Thus, generally, the ECJ hears cases brought by states and institutions, the CFI hears cases brought by individuals.)

Secondly, and of much more importance in the context of the Scottish legal system, the ECJ (and possibly in the future the CFI) hear preliminary references under Article 234[200]. Here the proceedings neither start nor finish in the Court, but in ordinary national courts and tribunals. To explain this, it must be recalled that Community law may have 'direct effect'. This is discussed in more detail in Chapter 3, but means, among other things, that it is to be applied by the usual national courts. As these courts stretch from Shetland to the Peloponnese, the possibility of conflicting decisions is great. Article 234[201] therefore permits any national court hearing a case involving the validity or interpretation of Community law to send that question (but not the rest of the dispute) to the ECJ for an authoritative ruling, which binds that national court. The national court nevertheless decides all questions of fact, and any questions of national law, and gives the final judgment. Final courts of appeal in Member States are required to make preliminary references, subject however, to the *acte clair* doctrine, which dispenses with it where the

---

197 However, these may now be heard by the 'European Civil Service Tribunal', the first of the 'Judicial Panels' attached to the CFI, and with appeal to it, set up by the Treaty of Nice.

198 For example, Art. 141 (numbered 119 before the Treaty of Amsterdam) requires sexual equality in employment, and the EC Equal Pay Directive (75/117) furthering that policy, was made in 1976. The European Commission considered that the relevant United Kingdom legislation, the Equal Pay Act 1970, did not fulfil the requirements of Community law and successfully brought enforcement proceedings against the United Kingdom (Case 51/81 *Commission v UK* [1982] ICR 578).

199 But see above.

200 Numbered 177 before the Treaty of Amsterdam.

201 See previous note.

law is clear (whether because it is inherently clear or because there is already a clear ruling).

Procedure in both ECJ and CFI follows civil law rather than common law patterns (for example, relying heavily upon written submissions, with very limited oral argument), and the language of the case is usually that of the applicant, although both use French as their working language.

COURT PROCEDURE

In broad terms, both civil and criminal procedure in Scotland are 'adversarial' (or 'accusatorial'). In other words, the judge does not actively seek to discover what happened and what the law is on the subject, but leaves it to the parties to put their best case before him. This is to be contrasted with 'inquisitorial' proceedings, in which the judge does undertake such enquiries. While Scots law generally follows the 'adversarial' path, some proceedings are certainly 'inquisitorial', and there has been a general trend towards more 'inquisitorial' proceedings for some years (as also in England and Wales), largely through a desire for 'case management' by the judge, with a view to speeding up proceedings.

Usually, parties are represented by a lawyer. In the Court of Session, and the High Court of Justiciary, these must be advocates, or solicitor-advocates. In other courts, they may be advocates, but are much more likely to be solicitors[202]. To support litigants with limited funds, there is both civil and criminal 'legal aid'[203].

With few exceptions, all court proceedings are public, and may even be televised[204], though this has rarely happened.

---

202 For the difference between advocates and solicitors (and solicitor-advocates), see Ch 14.
203 For which, see Ch 14. In criminal cases, it is interesting to note that the prosecution is funded by the state, and the accused is usually assisted by legal aid also provided by the state.
204 The Lord President and Sheriff Principals have given permission for television cameras to be used in court if, broadly speaking, the programme is educational or documentary, the proceedings do not show witnesses or juries, proceedings are not disrupted, the presiding judge approves (and he may set further conditions), and the parties approve: see 1992 SLT (News) 249 and 332. However, it has hardly ever been done (though see White 'Small Earthquake in Peru - not many killed' 1994 Scolag 59-60.

Civil procedure[205]

Most civil disputes, that is, disputes concerning contract, delict, succession, and the like, are settled out of court, because litigation is slow, expensive and uncertain (though a private settlement may be adopted by the court at the request of the parties). Decisions of courts affect such settlements, as they show how the dispute might be determined if it were litigated, and litigation may be started as a threat to induce settlement.

Civil procedure is (as noted) usually adversarial. Thus, the person who initiates the case (the pursuer), bears the burden of proof (which is on the balance of probabilities) and puts before the court the evidence and arguments he considers appropriate to support his case, and to entitle him to a remedy. The person called upon to answer the claim (the defender), may put his evidence and arguments to show why a remedy should not be granted. In principle, the judge is referee, intervenes little, and decides if the pursuer has proved his case.

The precise procedure depends upon the remedy sought and the court used. In most forms, the pursuer initiates matters by issue of a 'summons' or an 'initial writ', specifying the parties and the remedy sought. The defender must reply to this or risk judgment against him by default. In practice, most proceedings are undefended, so the pursuer may not have to prove his case.

Where proceedings are defended, there may be 'written pleadings', that is, answers by the defender to the pursuer's claims, and possibly further interchanges, to specify more closely the facts and law in dispute. When these are complete, the proceedings continue in court in order to determine the result. These proceedings may be a 'proof' in the case of disputed facts (or possibly, in the Court of Session, a jury trial with a jury of 12), or a 'debate' in the case of disputed law.

Proof depends upon witnesses and other evidence. Witnesses are 'examined in chief' by the side which calls them, and 'cross-examined' by the other side. Examination in chief is designed to bring out the witness's story in his own words. Cross-examination is designed to cast doubt upon it, and may do so by asking leading questions, that is, questions suggesting an answer. In legal debate, the parties'

---

205 Most of the relevant law is in the Sheriff Courts (Scotland) Act 1907, Act of Sederunt (Small Claim Rules) 2002, SI 2002/133, Act of Sederunt (Summary Cause Rules) 2002, SI 2002/132, Ordinary Cause Rules 1993, SI 1993/1956, Court of Session Act 1988 and Rules of the Court of Session 1994, SI 1994/1443 (all as amended).

lawyers argue as to what the applicable law is, which requires them to refer to relevant sources of law such as Acts of Parliament and precedents.

There may be 'proof before answer', whereby facts are determined before legal debate, and 'pleas to the relevancy', in which the defender argues that even if the facts are true, they do not entitle the pursuer to the remedy sought[206]. Commonly, a judge will not give an *ex tempore* judgment, but 'take it to *avizandum*', that is take time for consideration.

Decisions by the judge on matters which arise as the case proceeds are called 'interlocutors'. At the end of the proceedings the judge states his findings of fact and law, and expresses, in greater or lesser detail, the arguments which he considers justify his decision. (This process, discussed more fully in Chapter 12, characterises legal reasoning, and thus the nature and importance of law reports, in a common law or hybrid system). This in turn leads to the final interlocutor in which, if he upholds the pursuer's claim, the judge grants decree against the defender and authorises enforcement.

The principal forms of civil procedure for disputes are small claims, summary cause, and ordinary procedure in the Sheriff Court, and Court of Session procedure[207].

Small claims procedure, an attempt at a truly simple and cheap procedure, is for sums less than £750 (excluding aliment claims, that is, claims for financial support by family members usually arising out of matrimonial proceedings)[208]. A *pro forma* summons initiates procedure, but thereafter it is largely at the Sheriff's discretion, and intended to be informal. It may not be in practice, as complicated questions of law may arise and be dealt with by Sheriffs in strict legal fashion.

Summary cause procedure, an earlier attempt at simplicity, is for sums between £750 and £1,500[209]. It is more formal (and the actual

---

206   Thus, in the celebrated *Donoghue v Stevenson* 1932 SC(HL) 31, the presence of the snail in the bottle was never admitted or proved. Stevenson's argument was that, even if there were a snail, it did not entitle Mrs Donoghue to any remedy from him.

207   These are found in updated form in the '*Parliament House Book*' (Parliament House book: statutes and regulations for Scottish lawyers: 5 volumes, loose-leaf) and at www.scotcourts.gov.uk/library/rules/index.asp .

208   For the number of small claims, see above in relation to the Sheriff Court. The great majority are raised by large businesses, such as mail order companies and public utilities, against individuals. In mid-2007, the upper limit had not been increased since the procedure was introduced, so represented about half of its original value.

209   For the number of summary causes, see above in relation to the Sheriff Court.

rules are lengthy and complicated). Nevertheless, many summary causes are straightforward, and the Sheriff has a large discretion over procedure.

Ordinary cause procedure and Court of Session procedure are similar. They are much more formal, and there are full written pleadings. The summons must state the remedy sought (called 'craves' in Sheriff Court procedure and 'conclusions' in Court of Session procedure), the facts averred (called the 'condescendence'), and the rules and principles which, applied to those facts, in the pursuer's view entitle him to a remedy (called the 'pleas-in-law'). The defender enters formal defences, and these claims and counterclaims form the 'open record', which is 'adjusted' (that is, amended) by the parties to identify the points of agreement and, as closely as possible, the issue between them, resulting in the 'closed record', upon which any proofs or debate proceed. This process may take months.

There have long been criticism of delays and lack of expertise in specific area associated with such a generalist court. In response, since 1994, three specialist judges[210] using a simplified commercial procedure with an 'inquisitorial', and informal, approach, have sat as 'commercial court' judges. In addition there are judges designated for intellectual property (that is, copyright, patents, etc) cases[211]. However, in 2007, a new major review of the civil courts was set up under the Lord Justice-Clerk, to look specifically and costs of litigation, use of mediation and other methods of dispute resolution, better 'case-management' and further specialisation[212].

In addition to these proceedings of an adversarial nature, which are usually contentious[213], there are also the usually non-contentious petition procedures[214]. There is a large number of types of petition. Very many are of a formal nature, such as those to the Court of Session seeking appointment of a trustee where a trust lacks one, or to the Sheriff Court for confirmation as executor of a will[215]. Others

---

210 In mid-2007, Lords Clarke, Mackay and Drumadoon, and Drummond Young (part-time).
211 In mid-2007, Lords Nimmo Smith and Kingarth.
212 See www.scotcourts.gov.uk/lordgill/index.asp. This followed a Scottish Executive paper *Modern Laws for a Modern Scotland: a report on civil justice in Scotland* (Scottish Executive, 2004) (see http://www.scotland.gov.uk/Resource/Doc/165338/0045028.pdf).
213 Not all actions between parties are contentious. Many divorces are, for example, in effect by agreement.
214 But petition procedure may be contentious, as with judicial review, for instance, on which, see below.
215 Admission to the Law Society of Scotland requires petition to the Court of Session, which is organised as a 'block petition' with a large number of names, from time to time.

concern the dissolution of companies and sequestration of bankrupts. Others yet, involving contentious issues, include seeking interdict, an order forbidding a person or persons from acting in an unlawful way.

One form of petition (noted above in relation to the Court of Session) that deserves particular mention is 'judicial review'. In a nutshell, judicial review is a procedure whereby the Court of Session exercises its 'supervisory jurisdiction' over government departments and local authorities and other 'official' decision-takers. These have become common in many areas, such as environmental and planning law, and immigration law. It is not an appeal, but a procedure whereby the court is asked to quash an official's decision because it was taken in a wrong fashion. Typical ways in which the decision was wrongly taken those taken are *ultra vires* (acting beyond one's powers), or with a lack of 'natural justice' (for instance, not hearing both sides of the case). It has become a powerful remedy against improper government action, no less since the embedding of human rights into Scots law.

Remedies

The most common remedies are an order to pay a sum owed (such as the price under a contract); specific implement (an order requiring a person to carry out a legal obligation other than payment of money, for example, delivering goods contracted for); damages (an order to pay compensation, for example for injury done); declarator (a declaration that an individual or corporate body has a specific right or duty, for example that a local authority is obliged to house a homeless person); interdict (an order forbidding the commission of a wrong, for example publishing a defamatory statement); reduction (an order nullifying a document, for example an invalid will); aliment (an order to give financial support to dependants); divorce; and adoption.

There is also a large number of specific remedies under statute for specific circumstances. The Court of Session may provide a remedy in exceptional and unforeseen circumstances (the *nobile officium*).

Appeal

It is possible to appeal against almost every decision taken at first instance, and often thereafter further appeal is possible. Appeals are nevertheless a small proportion of cases heard[216].

---

216 See relevant references in relation to individual courts.

Appeals may be on both law and fact, but are often limited to points of law, in part because of the difficulty of reopening the facts, for appeal is never by way of a complete rehearing (although appeal from a jury trial might result in a new trial).

An appeal court can usually affirm the decision below, substitute its own judgment, or remit the case to the lower court for further procedure (such as proof) or final decision in the light of the appeal court's judgment.

Diligence and expenses

A court's order is usually obeyed. If it is not, the pursuer can 'do diligence', that is, enforce it. There are several forms of diligence. Most common are charges (formally requiring payment) and arrestment (impounding a debtor's funds held by a third party, such as a bank). The former method of 'warrant sale', technically 'poinding' (pronounced 'pinding') and sale, whereby sheriff-officers, or (if decree is from the Court of Session) messengers-at-arms, removed and might sell the debtor's moveable property, has been repealed and replaced by 'debt arrangement and attachment'[217]. Diligence is also possible against heritable property by 'inhibition' (forbidding sale of it), followed by 'adjudication', that is, its transfer to the creditor. Exceptionally there can even be diligence against the person, that is, imprisonment for debt, although this is available only for aliment, and is very rare.

Courts generally have discretion to award expenses, and usually the losing party is required to pay the 'judicial expenses' of the winning party (that is, those in connection with the action), although that sum is usually less than the actual expenditure.

Criminal procedure[218]

Criminal proceedings are held in public, but the judge is entitled to exclude all those not immediately involved in cases of rape and the like[219].

217 Debt Arrangement and Attachment (Scotland) Act 2002
218 The relevant law is largely found in the Criminal Procedure (Scotland) Act 1995 and the Act of Adjournal (Criminal Procedure Rules) 1998, SI 1998/513.
219 Criminal Procedure (Scotland) Act 1995, s 92(3).

The public prosecution system[220]

Criminal proceedings are almost always brought by the Crown through the public prosecution system. Private prosecutions are possible with the consent of the Lord Advocate, failing which, if brought by someone with a direct interest, with the consent of the court, but are extremely rare.

The Lord Advocate, assisted by the Solicitor-General for Scotland[221], is in charge of public prosecutions, through the Crown Office[222], which is effectively the headquarters of the Procurator Fiscal Service (the whole being called the Crown Office and Procurator Fiscal Service (COPFS). There is also a recently created Inspectorate of Prosecutions in Scotland ('IPIS')[223].

In District and Sheriff Courts, prosecutions are brought by COPFS. Previously organised on the basis of the six Sheriffdoms, the Procurator Fiscal Service is now organised on the basis of the eight police forces, save that Strathclyde is divided into four, giving a total of eleven areas[224]. Each of these has an area procurator fiscal who administers the service within that area and is the procurator fiscal for the Sheriff Court District in which he is. Prosecution is carried normally out by depute procurators fiscal[225].

In the High Court of Justiciary, prosecutions are brought by Advocates-Depute (*alias* 'Crown counsel') or, on occasion, the Lord Advocate or the Solicitor-General for Scotland in person. Advocates-Depute are advocates employed (temporarily and part-time) to prosecute on the Crown's behalf[226].

---

220 See www.crownoffice.gov.uk/.
221 These offices are discussed in Ch 3.
222 The Crown Office is situated in Chambers Street, Edinburgh. It produces annual 'reviews', and a Prosecution Code explaining how it exercises its discretion. These are available from www.crownoffice.gov.uk/, though not always easy to find. At the beginning of the 21st century, the COPFS was undergoing considerable change as a result of various criticisms.
223 See www.scotland.gov.uk/Topics/Justice/ipis. The members are all former employees of COPFS. IPIS also produces annual reports, 'office inspection reports' on individual procurator fiscal offices, and 'thematic reports' on general issues, all available from the website.
224 Ie, Argyll & Clyde, Ayrshire, Central, Dumfries & Galloway, Fife, Glasgow, Grampian, Highlands & Islands, Lanarkshire, Lothian & Borders and Tayside.
225 The identity of procurator fiscals can be found in the 'White Book', and on www.crownoffice.gov.uk/ (though it is not easy to find).
226 In mid-2007, there were some 20 Advocates-Depute. There identities are given in the 'White Book'. They are now divided into the categories of Senior Advocate-Depute, Advocate-Depute and Ad Hoc Advocate-Depute. This provides something of a career path for prosecutors.

Public Defence Solicitors' Office[227]

In 1998, in response to the rising cost of criminal legal aid, the Scottish Legal Aid Board was given powers to employ solicitors, on a limited basis, and as a five year pilot scheme, to provide criminal legal assistance instead of paying solicitors in private practice for criminal cases in the District and Sheriff Courts[228]. This scheme was set up as a 'Public Defence Solicitor's Office' ('PDSO') in Edinburgh, and considered a sufficient success to expand to cover a large proportion of the country[229]. Initially, a proportion of cases (randomly selected) was directed to PDSO. However, it now relies on word of mouth, so offers essentially the same services to those accused of criminal offences, on the same terms, as do private solicitors (including the duty solicitor rota to provide initial assistance to those taken into custody)[230] but, effectively, in competition with them. This is somewhat controversial[231].

The PDSO is fully discussed in Chapter 14.

Procedure

Criminal proceedings are (like civil) generally adversarial. Thus, it is not the judge who seeks to discover if there has been a crime or not[232]. It is for the prosecution to decide what crime it considers may have been committed, and it bears the burden of proof (which is beyond reasonable doubt). It therefore seeks and presents to the court the evidence it considers sufficient to prove it. The defence generally need prove nothing, but is entitled to have the case against it proved, to cast doubt on prosecution evidence, and to bring

---

227   See www.pdso.org.uk/: also www.slab.org.uk/pdso/.
228   Legal Aid (Scotland) Act 1986, s 28A (inserted by Crime and Punishment (Scotland) Act 1997, and as subsequently amended).
229   In mid-2007, there were nine offices, in Aberdeen, Ayr, Dumfries, Dundee, Edinburgh, Falkirk, Glasgow, Inverness & Kirkwall: the addresses of each office are to found on www.pdso.org.uk/.
230   As employees of the Scottish Legal Aid Board, PDSO's salaried solicitors are answerable to it, but they are operationally independent, and normal professional ethics apply to them, though in addition, there is a 'Code of Conduct for Public Defence Solicitors in Scotland', available on www.pdso.org.uk/.
231   Legal Aid (Scotland) Act 1986, s 28A(9A) requires a report on the progress of the scheme to be laid before the Scottish Parliament before 31 December 2008.
232   Civil law systems tend to use inquisitorial procedure, whereby a judge (other than the judge at any resulting trial) actively pursues the investigation.

evidence if it chooses[233]. Indeed, it may move that 'there is no case to answer' at the end of the prosecution evidence, seeking to have the case dismissed for want of proper evidence. Traditionally, the judge is referee and intervenes little. He charges the jury if there is one, that is, reminds them of the main evidence presented and instructs them on the applicable law. It is, however, entirely for the jury to decide what conclusions they draw from the facts, and thus whether the prosecution has proved its case.

The two forms of criminal procedure are summary and solemn. Most common law offences are triable by either procedure. Statutory offences are declared by statute to be triable by one or both. The District Court uses only summary procedure, the Sheriff Court both, and the High Court only solemn. It is for the prosecution to decide which procedure and which venue is appropriate[234].

In both forms the prosecution must serve on the accused a precise accusation, to which he pleads guilty or not guilty. If he pleads not guilty, a later date is fixed for trial. The trial may require facts to be proved, and law to be determined. These are done in essentially the same way as in civil proceedings, although the burden of proof, which is on the prosecutor, is higher ('beyond reasonable doubt'), and the accused must generally be present. Facts are proved by evidence, from witnesses and otherwise, and the law is determined by argument. After evidence has been given, the prosecution and defence address the court. At the end of the trial, the accused may be found guilty, not guilty, or the charge be found not proven. A verdict of not proven is equivalent to an acquittal, and an acquitted person may not be retried. If found guilty, before sentence is passed, a list of previous convictions (if any) is produced by the prosecutor, and any plea in mitigation (that is, information tending to suggest a lenient sentence should be passed) is made by the defence.

In summary proceedings, the procurator fiscal details the charge in a complaint. The accused may appear in court to plead to this, but in many cases will plead by letter or be represented by a solicitor instead of appearing. If he pleads not guilty, a later date is fixed for

---

233   There has been an increasing trends towards more inquisitorial procedures, for example by requiring both sides to disclose evidence to each other before trial. The law and practice in relation to disclosure was, in mid-2007, being examined by a Committee chaired by Lord Coulsfield: see www.scotland.gov.uk/Topics/Justice/criminal/disclosure-review.

234   England & Wales and Northern Ireland are markedly different, in that, albeit to an increasingly limited extent, in the case of an 'either way' offence (that is, one which may be tried by either procedure) the accused may be able to choose a jury trial: this is the so-called 'right to trial by jury', which has never existed in Scotland.

trial, which is conducted before a Sheriff, JP or Stipendiary Magistrate, without a jury. If found guilty, the court sentences him.

In solemn procedure, the procurator fiscal drafts a petition alleging a named person committed a specified crime, and requesting authority to arrest him. The accused appears before the Sheriff in private for a brief first examination. Usually no plea or declaration is made and the accused is released on bail or committed in custody for trial (in which case, the trial must begin within 140 days[235]). There may be further judicial examination before the Sheriff in which the prosecutor may put a limited range of questions to the accused, to discover if he is going to use certain defences, or concerning any alleged confession. The accused is not on oath, and can decline to reply. The prosecutor then drafts the indictment detailing the charges upon which the accused will be tried (which is served upon the accused) and decides if the case is to go to a Sheriff or the High Court. In either case there will be a jury. There must then be a 'preliminary hearing', to deal with issues of 'competency' or of 'relevancy' of the indictment (for example, arguing that the facts alleged in the indictment disclose no crime known to the law[236]), and for 'case management' (that is, for the judge to assure himself that proper progress towards the trial has taken place).

The trial diet follows on similar principles to that in summary proceedings, but after the evidence and the addresses by the prosecution and defence, the judge charges the jury (as described above) before they retire to consider their verdict.

Because of a considerably increased workload, and consequential delays and difficulties, there have been several reports in recent years, seeking more efficient disposal of business, which have produced some legislation[237].

---

235 Until the Criminal Procedure (Amendment) (Scotland) Act 2004, s 6(5)(b), the limit was 110 days. This remains remarkably speedy compared with many systems.

236 As happened in *Khaliq v HM Advocate* 1984 JC 23, where the accused were charged with supplying glue-sniffing kits to children.

237 *Improving Justice: 2002 review of the practices and procedures of the High Court of Justiciary* (2002) (the 'Bonomy Report' produced by Lord Bonomy, a judge) resulted in the Criminal Procedure (Amendment) (Scotland) Act 2004 (though by no means adopting all the recommendations, but see www.scotland.gov.uk/Resource/Doc/166328/0045282.pdf.). *The Summary Justice Review Committee - Report to Ministers* (2004) (the 'McInnes Report', produced by Sheriff Principal McInnes: see www.scotland.gov.uk/Resource/Doc/47171/0031637.pdf.), resulted in the Criminal Proceedings (etc) (Scotland) Act 2007 (though again by no means adopting all the recommendations). The *Independent Review of Disclosure* by Lord Coulsfield (another judge) is to report in 2007 on the disclosure of evidence in criminal cases (see http://www.scotland.gov.uk/Topics/Justice/criminal/disclosure-review).

Guilty pleas

However, the great majority of those charged, whether under summary or solemn procedure, are not tried, because they plead guilty, usually at an early stage. (Indeed, if this were not so, the courts could not cope.) This plea may result from 'plea negotiation', an informal procedure whereby the accused, through his agent, agrees with the Crown to plead guilty (so there is a conviction), but only to some charges, amended charges, or lesser charges (so he may expect a lesser sentence). The court takes no part in this negotiation[238]. In any case, early guilty pleas are now encouraged by an obligation upon sentencers to consider a reduction of sentence for a guilty plea, with a greater reduction the earlier the plea[239].

Diversion schemes

The pressure upon the criminal courts has led to diversion from prosecution schemes[240]. The police may make a conditional offer of a fixed penalty to the accused in certain minor road traffic offences[241], and a procurator fiscal may do so in certain other offences triable in the district court[242]. Accepting it avoids going to court and risking a higher penalty on conviction. However, it may be declined, and the accused may be summoned to court and there seek acquittal. These are popularly referred to as 'fiscal fines'. They are separate from other diversion schemes, such as the fixed penalty

---

238 The position is somewhat different in England & Wales, where he may do so in certain circumstances.

239 Criminal Procedure (Scotland) Act 1995, s 196 (as amended).

240 Thus, the vehicle defect rectification scheme deals with 30,000 road traffic offences a year; police fixed penalty conditional offers with another 280,000; and there is an unknown number of police warnings, references to other agencies and cases dealt with by detecting agencies (such as the Television Licensing Authority) all without their being reported to the procurator fiscal: further, of the 328,000 crimes and offences recorded by the police in 2004-5, there were procurator fiscal warnings in 32,000 cases, 'fiscal fines' in 23,000 cases; procurator fiscal fixed penalty conditional offers for motor vehicles offences in 10,000 cases; other forms of diversion in 1,000 cases; and simple 'no pros' (that is, a decision not to prosecute or do anything else) in 61,000 cases: *Scottish Executive Statistical Bulletin: Criminal Justice Series* CRJ/2006/3.

241 These vary, depending upon the offence, from £30 to £200: Fixed Penalty Order 2000, SI 2000/2792 (as amended).

242 Criminal Procedure (Scotland) Act 1995, ss 302, 303 (as amended by the Criminal Proceedings, Etc. (Reform) (Scotland) Act 2007, s 50: not in force in mid-2007).

notice for parking and similar offences, whereby a traffic warden affixes a notice to an illegally parked car, rendering the owner liable to a fine. In addition, somewhat controversially, a variety of new variations are to be introduced (as well as 'fines enforcement officers')[243].

In any case, it has long been accepted that fiscals are able to issue directly, or through the police, a formal warning, which is not recorded as a conviction. Fiscals may also divert cases to social work or psychiatric services. Further, a fiscal is always entitled to decide not to prosecute although there appears to be sufficient evidence, if the offence is trivial, or it is otherwise not in the public interest to prosecute.

Penalties

The principal penalties are: a fine (unlimited, or to a maximum permitted by statute); admonition (a warning); imprisonment or detention in a young offenders' institution; a community service order; probation; and a compensation order in favour of the victim, which may be combined with another penalty[244]. Imprisonment or a supervised attendance order (requiring attendance at a certain place for some form of training) can be imposed to replace an unpaid fine.

Sentence is often deferred. This may be a brief deferral of, normally, some three weeks for social background, psychiatric, or other reports, or a lengthy one (such as six months) for good behaviour or restitution to a victim. In the latter case, it is in effect a sentence in itself, as the penalty is likely to be reduced if there has been good behaviour or restitution of property stolen or damaged.

Appeals and the Scottish Criminal Cases Review Commission[245]

A person convicted after summary procedure may appeal as of right to the High Court of Justiciary sitting as an appeal court by 'stated

---

243 See Criminal Proceedings, Etc. (Reform) (Scotland) Act 2007, ss 50-54 (not in force in mid-2007)
244 In 2004-5, of 135,000 main penalties imposed, there were 85,000 fines imposed (63% of all disposals); 16,000 imprisonments, including 3,000 in young offenders' institutions (12%); 14,000 admonitions (11%); 9,500 probation orders (7%); 5,500 community service orders (4%); 1,500 compensation orders (1%); 1,300 restriction of liberty orders (1%); 1,000 absolute discharges (1%) and 1,000 drug treatment and testing orders (1%): *Scottish Executive Statistical Bulletin: Criminal Justice Series* CRJ/2006/3..
245 See www.sccrc.org.uk/home.aspx.

case'[246] on the ground of 'miscarriage of justice'. If convicted after trial, he may appeal against conviction and/or sentence; if after a guilty plea, against sentence only. He may seek to introduce new evidence unavailable at trial, but this is rare. He may also appeal by way of a 'bill of suspension' on the ground of procedural irregularity.

The prosecutor may also appeal, on a point of law only, against conviction or sentence by stated case or, on the ground of procedural irregularity, by 'bill of advocation'.

A person convicted after solemn procedure (again whether by guilty plea or trial) may appeal in like terms, save that the appeal is usually by 'note of appeal'. The prosecutor may not appeal at all against conviction, but after conviction, the Lord Advocate may appeal against sentence on the grounds of undue leniency.

The High Court is entitled to dismiss an appeal and affirm the verdict and sentence, quash a conviction, substitute conviction of a lesser offence, or impose a lesser or (unless appeal was against conviction only) a heavier sentence. It may authorise a retrial but is unlikely to do so if there was any fault on the part of the prosecution or the evidence was weak. It is for the Crown within two months to decide whether to prosecute again.

Two other procedures exist which are related to appeals. Both have been used, but rarely. Firstly, the Lord Advocate may refer any question of law which has arisen in a trial by solemn procedure resulting in an acquittal to the High Court for an opinion. This 'Lord Advocate's Reference' is not an appeal, so cannot overturn the acquittal, but the person acquitted may appear, and the High Court can give an authoritative view on the point of law.

Secondly, the Scottish Criminal Cases Review Commission[247] has

---

246 In a stated case, the charges are listed and procedure outlined, and the judge lists the facts he found, or were admitted, indicates the reasons for his decision, and asks a question such as 'On the facts admitted or proved, was I entitled to convict the accused?'.

247 Set up under the Criminal Procedure (Scotland) Act 1995, s 194A & Sch 9A (inserted by the Crime and Punishment (Scotland) Act s 25), and sitting in Glasgow with eight members (in mid-2007, the Very Rev Dr Graham Forbes, Provost of St Mary's Edinburgh; Professor Peter Duff, Aberdeen University; Sir Gerald Gordon, formerly Sheriff, Professor and procurator fiscal, and author of *Criminal Law of Scotland*; Sheriff Ruth Anderson; David Belfall, former Home Office civil servant; James McKay, former Chief Constable of Tayside; Graham Bell QC, practising advocate and former Advocate-Depute; Robert Anthony QC, another practising advocate and former Advocate-Depute) and support staff.

powers to refer a case to the High Court for re-consideration after the appeal process has been exhausted (or, exceptionally, where it was not invoked). A person concerned may refer a conviction or sentence to the Commission, and it decides whether or not to accept such application. If it does accept it, the Commission receives any representations, and may make its own inquiries through its staff (and this may involve interviewing witnesses and taking evidence on oath, and using the services of expert advisers) as well as examining the trial and appeal papers. It only refers the matter to the High Court if it believes a miscarriage of justice has occurred and that it is in the interests of justice to make the reference. This might be because of new evidence which has emerged since the appeal. If the Commission does not refer the case, it gives its reasons to the applicant. If it does refer the case, it gives its reasons to the High Court, copied to the applicant and Crown Office. However, the Commission does not represent the applicant in the High Court re-consideration, which is conducted much as an ordinary appeal. Thus the applicant requires to obtain representation (for which legal aid will be available) or conduct it himself. The Commission publishes an annual report[248].

Expenses

Generally speaking, criminal courts cannot award expenses. The expenses of prosecution are paid by the prosecution. Those of the defence are usually paid from criminal legal aid (including *via* PDSO).

---

248 No longer, seemingly, available from www.sccrc.org.uk/home.aspx (nor are 'case studies' still available). However, by mid-2007, it had received several hundred cases, and had issued final decisions in most of them, 50 or so of which they referred the case to the High Court. Some of these have resulted in the High Court concluding that there had been a miscarriage of justice: eg *Boncza-Tomaszewski (aka Fraser) v HM Advocate* 2000 SCCR 657. Its most high profile case however, is that of the 'Lockerbie Bomber', commenced in 2007: see www.sccrc.org.uk/ViewFile.aspx?id=175. In mid-2007, the Commission had referred the case to the High Court, but the High Court had had no opportunity to consider the referral: see www.sccrc.org.uk/viewfile.aspx?id=293, which contains a summary of the main reasons for the referral. It was noted that the report leading to the referral was over 800 pages long, and there were 13 appendices to it.

TRIBUNALS, OTHER RELATED INSTITUTIONS, ENGLISH AND WELSH AND NORTHERN IRELAND COURTS

Tribunals[249]

In modern times the state has entered into, or extended, numerous legal relationships with its citizens. Personal taxation and social security are two obvious examples. These give rise to legal rights and duties, on which disputes may arise. These disputes might have been entrusted to the courts, like any other justiciable issues. But courts would have been swamped by the number of such disputes and arguably forced to change in character to cope. They might have been left to the government departments concerned to decide internally at a higher level. But that would have contravened the principle of 'natural justice', that no-one should be judge in his own cause. So in fact a new type of decision-making body has been devised. They are independent and impartial like the courts, but less formal and more accessible. These are the tribunals.

Tribunals are now enormously varied in subject-matter, extent and degree of formality. Among those that cover major areas. The General Commissioners and the Special Commissioners of Income Tax deal with disputes on matters of personal taxation. National Health Service Tribunals and Service Committees handle complaints by patients against medical and related practitioners. These could affect any citizen. Others affect only people in special occupations and capacities, such as the Police Appeals Tribunal for Scotland which handles appeals by constables against dismissal and other penalties, and the Immigration Tribunal system which hears appeals from individuals refused entry into the United Kingdom and related decisions. One is simply and misleadingly called the Appeals Service. Its remit is indicated by its being created by the Social Security Act 1998 s 4 and schedule 1. It has very wide jurisdiction including all benefits under the Act. Recently Tax Credit and some Child Support Agency appeals have been added. It has some unusual features. Its composition depends on the subject-matter. Thus in a Disability Living Allowance or Attendance Allowance case there must be a lawyer (who presides), a medical practitioner, and an expert in disability (who might be blind). Sometimes there will be an accountant. But often there will just be a lawyer, where there are no special features except whether the words of the Act cover the appellant. All members are drawn from a panel nominally appointed by the Lord Chancellor. Oral hearings are held in most Scottish cities and large towns. But sometimes a case is decided on the case-papers in private by appropriate tribunal members.

Although most tribunals stem from central government functions, a few relate to local authority activities. Housing Benefit Review Boards deal with questions about entitlement to or the amount of housing benefit, and Education Appeal Committees were set up to hear complaints arising out of parents' requests that their children be placed in a certain school.

The tribunal format has been extended to situations where private citizens are in dispute with each other or with a company or other corporate body. Industrial Tribunals were set up under the Industrial Training Act 1964 to handle questions arising from the imposition of levies on employers to help finance schemes of training in particular industries such as haulage contracting. In this and other roles they were so successful that in 1971 they were extended to claims for compensation for unfair dismissal brought by ex-employees against employers. This remains their largest type of business but, under various Acts of Parliament, and now called Employment Tribunals, they have about 15 kinds of jurisdiction, including complaints of discrimination on grounds of gender or marital status, of failure to give equal pay, to supply written particulars of a contract of employment, to make a redundancy payment and to give time off work to safety representatives. Another private relationship in which tribunals are involved, though now less so than in the past, is that between landlord and tenant. Rent Assessment Committees establish fair rents when the parties cannot agree on them.

Characteristics

Since tribunals have such diverse functions it is not easy to generalise about their characteristics. Moreover, the strengths of some of them have been somewhat weakened with the passage of time. However, there would be general agreement that the following features are among the advantages of most kinds of tribunal and are in fact exhibited in most of them.

Informality. In comparison with courts all tribunals are informal. At some, such as Children's Hearings and those dealing with benefits, all the participants sit round a table and a relaxed discussion is encouraged, though not always achieved. Employment Tribunals, have become increasingly formal. The chairman and members sit on a raised dais, and evidence by the parties and witnesses they have summoned is usually given on oath and always subject to cross-examination. The Lands Tribunal for Scotland is also formal in its layout and presided over by a judge of Court of Session rank.

Representation. Informality tends to be eroded by the participation of lawyers accustomed to the procedure of courts. Employers in Employment Tribunal cases usually find it worthwhile to employ a lawyer; and appeals to the Employment Appeal Tribunal, which is chaired by a Court of Session judge, and from there to the Court of Session, are not infrequent. This means that judgments by Employment Tribunal chairmen have to be fully supported in law and in facts established in evidence. It also means that case law from the courts and Employment Appeal Tribunal feeds back into the tribunals and will be invoked by lawyers there.

On the other hand, lawyers scarcely ever appear before Children's Hearings, which have remained relatively informal. But people appearing before them are allowed and encouraged to bring a friend or relative to help them bring out the points they wish to make. More formal representation is given by appropriate non-lawyers before some tribunals, such as a trade union official at an Employment Tribunal. A guidance teacher might accompany a child at a Children's Hearing. Some Citizens Advice Bureaux also offer help at the less formal tribunals.

Cheapness. Unlike civil courts, where a fee usually has to be paid to initiate proceedings, tribunals are almost entirely free. Unlike courts again, the loser does not have to pay the winner's expenses. A minor exception is in Employment Tribunal procedure. If a party has acted frivolously, vexatiously or otherwise unreasonably (on which there may have been a finding at a pre-hearing assessment of the case) then he may be ordered to pay the other side's expenses, which might include the fees of the employer's lawyer.

Speed. Tribunals are intended to provide a rapid settlement of disputes. Unfortunately, for a variety of reasons, they do not always fulfill that expectation. As in courts, one side may use delaying tactics in the hope that the opponent will give up or evidence may be lost. In tribunals dealing with social security benefits, upsurges in claims and cuts in staffing can produce long delays. Thus, claims for the disability living allowance introduced in 1992 far exceeded expectations and led to the operation of disability appeal tribunals being held up and thus decisions being subject to long delay.

Specialisation. All tribunals are specialised to some extent, some highly so. Thus, there is at one extreme the National Appeal Panel for Entry to the Pharmaceutical Lists. Others cover a range of related questions, such as the Employment Tribunals which handle nearly all disputes arising in the workplace and involving individuals (and received 8,461 cases in Scotland in 2005). People with relevant background knowledge can be appointed to sit on tribunals and, given a sufficient flow of cases, can apply and extend that knowledge in contentious situations. So the part-time lay members of Employment Tribunals are appointed from panels nominated by organisations representative of employers and of employees. In Scotland, these are the Confederation of British Industry and the Scottish Trade Union Council. Appeal Tribunals on disability benefits have a medically qualified member and one with knowledge or experience of the needs of disabled people.

Legal authority

Despite the appearance of informality of many of them, tribunals are vested with legal powers, just as much as are courts. The rules of law which they apply can be very complex, especially in the social security area. Their decisions are just as enforceable as court decrees and sentences. Appeal to the courts on a point of law is usually possible, as is judicial review by the Court of Session, that is, an inquiry on the adequacy of the procedure, but both are uncommon. In their conduct of cases, tribunals are bound to observe the same broad standards of fairness to all parties as courts. They must clearly state their decisions in writing, usually amplified by their findings on the facts and the reasons for the decision (in the case of Children's Hearings, only if requested to do so).

For all these reasons nearly all tribunals are now presided over by a legally qualified chairman. (A conspicuous exception is Children's Hearings.) For example, Employment Tribunal chairmen must be solicitors or advocates of at least seven years' standing. There is a danger that lawyer-chairmen may come to dominate the proceedings, unless the lay members have the confidence to make their own distinctive contribution.

Supervision

In their early days each tribunal was set up on an *ad hoc* basis, usually on the initiative of a government department. It could thus come under the influence of the department and conform to its expectations. The department's ascendancy could be exacerbated when it appointed the chairman and members, as was the case with the now extinct National Insurance Appeal Tribunals and Supplementary Benefit Appeal Tribunals. In 1957, the Franks Committee[250] urged that common standards of openness, fairness and impartiality should be observed by all tribunals. It scrutinised the mode of appointment and procedure of all the then tribunals and made recommendations for improvement. To provide a permanent form of supervision the Committee proposed a Council on Tribunals.

Such a Council, with a Scottish Committee, was set up and now operates under the Tribunals and Inquiries Act 1992[251]. It is consulted by departments and other bodies setting up or changing tribunals and sees the draft statutory instruments authorising them[252]. It also pays visits to tribunals and inquiries. However, since it has some 70 tribunals and comparable bodies such as the Civil Aviation Authority (which grants licences) under its supervision (of which some are under the direct supervision of its Scottish Committee), plus office-holders such as the Data Protection Registrar and the Director General of Fair Trading[253], visits to any single tribunal are few and far between. It does not have power to correct individual complaints, but these may indicate a failure to follow procedures which can be taken up with the organisation concerned.

Many tribunals are organised on a Great Britain basis. But a few, such as Children's Hearings, the Crofters Commission and the Lands Tribunal for Scotland, are peculiarly Scottish. Others such as Employment Tribunals, Pensions Appeal Tribunals and Criminal Injuries Compensation Adjudicators, have a Scottish organisation, similar to that operating in England and Wales. The Scottish Committee of the Council on Tribunals supervises these bodies in the same manner as the parent Council. The Council has seventeen members, all prominent people with a variety of backgrounds and

---

250 *Report of the Committee on Administrative Tribunals and Enquiries* (1957) (Cmnd 218).
251 Its Statement of Purposes includes ensuring that tribunals and inquiries are: open, fair and impartial; accessible to users; have the needs of users as their primary focus; offer cost effective procedures; are properly resourced and organised; and are responsive to the needs of all sectors of society: see *Council on Tribunals Annual Report 2001–02*. (The Scottish Committee seems more generous: see *Council on Tribunals Scottish Committee Annual Report 2001–02*.)
252 It has issued Model Rules of Procedure for Tribunals (Cm 1434) which in early 2003 it was updating.
253 Tribunals and Inquiries Act 1992, Sch 1, Pts I and II and *Annual Reports*.

other public appointments (six of whom, together with four other persons, constitute its Scottish Committee) with a staff of a dozen[254]. During 2005–06 they considered some 25 statutory instruments, and paid numerous visits to tribunals and inquiries (including some in Scotland, several to Children's Panel Hearings). Notice is given of the proposed attendance of a member, who writes a report to the Committee. The Scottish Committee also responded to an Executive consultation on Children's Hearings. It found some major items for concern, such as courses of action decided but not implemented.

Tribunal performance

Tribunals as a whole are big business. It is impossible to give precise total figures since figures are supplied to the Council by each tribunal organisation or their sponsoring department, where they still exist. Some use the calendar year and some the civil service financial year to the end of March. But cases received from within Britain annually certainly exceed half a million; for example 201,000 in the Asylum and Immigration Appeal Tribunal and 181,000 on social security claims. Not all proceed to a decision because some are withdrawn as incompetent or a change in the applicant's circumstances.

Not all Great Britain tribunals have even one sitting in Scotland in a year, for example the Betting Levy Appeal Tribunal. But Employment Tribunals for Scotland in 2005-06 received 8,461 applications of which 7,232 were withdrawn, presumably because they led to a settlement. In Scotland in 2005, 50,529 reports were received on children in need by Reporters, but only 5,793 proceeded to a Children's Hearing.

However, relatively little research has been carried out on their performance. One large-scale piece of work[255] gave the results of a study commissioned by the Lord Chancellor's Department focusing on the then Social Security Appeal Tribunals, Immigration Adjudicators, Industrial (now Employment) Tribunals and Mental Health Review Tribunals (not found in Scotland). The researchers found that appellants did not regard the tribunals as informal, which they equated with being able to talk freely about the fairness of the

---

254 For a list of members, see the current annual report of the Council and its Scottish Committee.
255 Genn and Genn *The Effectiveness of Representation at Tribunals* (1989).

decision in question. Instead they found themselves up against incomprehensible law in Social Security Appeal Tribunals and Immigration Adjudications and a formal procedure, with a confident opposing lawyer familiar with it in Employment Tribunals. In all four tribunals the presence of a representative significantly increased the probability that appellants and applicants would succeed in their cases; but in Employment Tribunals this was dependent on the respondent being unrepresented. In Employment Tribunals, barristers and solicitors had the greatest impact on success, and in Social Security Appeal Tribunals lay agencies specialising in welfare law.

Another report[256], commissioned by the Independent Tribunal Service, reported the same feeling of disappointment at the formality of the proceedings among appellants, who had the additional disadvantage of being disabled and for various reasons found it a stressful experience. They had medical as well as legal jargon to contend with. The average clearance time for all cases in 1990 was 27 weeks, leading to hardship and anxiety for appellants. Representatives found little scope for advocacy skills, but had a useful role in marshalling evidence for the appellant.

It would seem that some formality is inseparable from any system which expresses entitlements in legal form and thus makes them open to disputed interpretation.

The future

In 2001, a major review of tribunals operating in England and Wales was undertaken by the government[257]. It made numerous recommendations, summed up as offering a more independent system, a more coherent system, and a more user-friendly system. In particular, appointments to tribunals should be undertaken by the Lord Chancellor, to ensure greater separation between them and the government authority whose policies and decisions are being tested. Further, there should be a single over-arching structure for tribunals in a Tribunals Service. Also, tribunal procedure should be altered to assist users to present their own cases. There were also numerous recommendations in relation to specific tribunals. The Tribunal Service has had an inauspicious beginning, since time could not be found for the necessary legislation. Nevertheless such was the support for it that in April 2006, using administrative powers, it was

---

256 Sainsbury *Survey and Report into the Working of Medical Appeal Tribunals* (1992).
257 *Tribunals for Users: One System, One Service: Report of the Review of Tribunals by Sir Andrew Leggat* (2001) (the '*Leggat Report*').

set up as an executive agency under the aegis of the then new Department of Constitutional Affairs. The links between tribunals and the departments with which they are associated are gradually being dissolved to emphasise their independence. It was intended that the Council on Tribunals should have a wider remit as The Administrative Justice and Tribunals Council but that awaits legislation.

The Tribunal Service's relationship to Scotland is somewhat confused. It covers tribunals in England and Wales and British ones, but not Scottish ones operating under separate Scottish legislation, such as the Education (Scotland) Act 1980 and the National Health Service (Scotland) Act 1978. Some of the benefits emerging under the Tribunal Service are being obtained through the Scottish Tribunals Forum which was set up by the Lord President under the Chairmanship of the now retired judge, Lord Abernethy. Its membership embraces persons from tribunals operative in Scotland in both reserved and devolved areas and Scotland only and Great Britain ones. Thus it enables matters of common concern to be discussed in a Scottish legal context.

Other related institutions

Arbitration and alternative dispute resolution

A popular alternative to litigation in some areas of industry and the professions is arbitration. Indeed, a number of trade and professional bodies have arbitration schemes for their members, including the building and engineering industries, the Scottish Motor Traders' Association, and the Association of British Travel Agents. The Law Society of Scotland also offers an arbitration scheme. Arbitration may also be international, between companies in different countries.

Essentially, arbitration is the submission of a dispute to a private judge (called an arbiter), whose decision is final. The courts are thus largely excluded. Arbitration may have advantages for those in dispute. The matter is disposed of privately and probably more rapidly than in the courts. The award may be a compromise acceptable to all parties, rather than (as commonly occurs in litigation) finding a winner, and thus a loser. No precedent is set for later disputes. The dispute may be on technical matters, so the arbiter can be someone technically qualified. Arbitration may also be cheaper than litigation, although this depends upon the procedure used, which may be quite formal, with the parties legally represented, and a lawyer as arbiter.

Commonly, arbitration is contractual; that is, the parties to a contract have agreed that any dispute arising out of the contract shall be dealt with thus. Probably the contract will be a standard form contract used in such cases, incorporating an arbitration scheme. The arbiter is likely to be identified by office (for example, the president for the time being of a professional association), but may be nominated by the parties. The parties may be able to nominate an arbiter each, in which case there may also be appointed an 'oversman' to determine the matter if the arbiters cannot agree. What disputes can be arbitrated, what procedure followed, and what awards made, are matters for the parties.

Although the aim is to exclude the courts, there is a good deal of law on the subject, and the courts do have a role. For example, an arbiter may be required to 'state a case', that is, to obtain a legal opinion from the Court of Session. Also, although there is no appeal to the courts from the arbitration, the award may be open to challenge on the grounds of procedural irregularity, such as want of honesty or impartiality on the part of the arbiter. Further, an arbiter's award may be enforceable by the courts. International arbitrations are decided under the Model Rules laid down by international agreement by the UN Committee on International Trade Law. There are also statutory arbitration schemes, for example under the Agricultural Holdings (Scotland) Act 1991.

While arbitration is as old as litigation, recently 'alternative dispute resolution' has come to prominence. 'ADR' is said to be widely used in many countries for many types of issue, from commercial to family disputes. Because of this wide usage, however, it is difficult to give exact meaning to the term. It refers to a variety of means of settlement alternative to litigation. These means include a repertoire of processes such as arbitration, conciliation, mediation and negotiation, all of which have semi-technical definitions. The means may also include variations upon, and combinations of, that repertoire (and indeed of litigation as well). Thus, for example, one ADR method is described as 'med-arb' or 'concilio-arb', in which mediation is used, failing which, arbitration[258]. In Scotland the Law Society keeps a Register of Accredited Mediators called ACCORD. There is also a Group called CALM (Comprehensive Accredited Lawyer Mediators). Family Mediation Scotland supports branches in some parts of Scotland where trained lay volunteers try to bring

---

258 For a review of ADR, see the memoranda prepared for the English Law Society called 'Alternative Dispute Resolution' (1991) and 'Alternative Dispute Resolution: Second Report' (1992).

about agreement mainly on the relationships of divorcing or separated parents with their children.

Because ADR is argued for in such a variety of disputes, it is a matter for discussion which means or combinations of means are appropriate for each dispute. This in turn depends upon the perceived disadvantages of litigation, but these are not the same in all disputes. For example, in a commercial dispute between trading partners of roughly equal power, confidentiality may be all-important to both, and be a reason to avoid litigation, while cost is irrelevant. In one between a consumer and a supplier, however, firstly, the perspectives of the two disputants may be very different from each other, and secondly, from the consumer's point of view, it is cost that may be all-important and a reason to avoid litigation, and confidentiality may be irrelevant. Considerations are different again in, say, family disputes where privacy may be predominant. In all cases the possibility of greater speed, however, is usually an advantage.

The significance of ADR probably does not lie in the novelty of the means of dispute resolution that it offers. Arbitration, conciliation and mediation have long been widely used in the United Kingdom in industrial disputes, for example, and were a strongly preferred alternative to litigation until legislation in the 1980s. The Advisory, Conciliation and Arbitration Service (ACAS) is well known and active in the field, and is the descendant of government services set up for this purpose as long ago as the late 19th century.

The significance lies rather in the existence of a conscious search for alternatives to litigation, premised upon a dissatisfaction with litigation, perhaps parallel to that which caused the enormous growth in tribunals a generation ago. This is important to the study of a legal system for it may indicate a declining relevance and use of courts, and the growth of alternative quasi-legal institutions. This particularly affects a legal system reliant upon precedent. It may also have importance in relation to civil liberties, in questions as to how far individuals may seek to use private means of dispute settlement, and whether stronger disputants may be enabled to force weaker ones into unsatisfactory arrangements.

Ombudsmen[259]

A method of redressing grievances imported from Scandinavia (via New Zealand) in the last few decades is the ombudsman, that is, an

---

259 A directory of Ombudsmen can be found on the British and Irish Ombudsman Association website at www.bioa.org.uk.

official who is not a judge, but who can examine critically the conduct of officials in a more effective way than could a court or tribunal (though usually only after the complainant has exhausted all other remedies). The first ombudsman, technically called the Parliamentary Commissioner for Administration (PCA), was appointed in 1967 under the Parliamentary Commissioner Act of that year[260].

The PCA is appointed by the Crown, and may be removed only by an address of both Houses of the UK Parliament, so has protection of tenure similar to that of a judge, though most appointees have been civil servants. The PCA is entitled to investigate complaints of injustice resulting from 'maladministration' (a term given a technical meaning) by government departments in the exercise of their administrative functions. Various areas are specifically excluded from oversight, including foreign relations, the investigation of crime, and appointment and discipline within the Civil Service. Nor may the PCA investigate where the complainant has a legal remedy which could reasonably be pursued (such as an appeal against refusal of a benefit). On the other hand, the PCA has powers equivalent to those of the Court of Session to require production of papers and the attendance of witnesses (save in relation to Cabinet proceedings).

A complainant cannot approach the PCA directly, however, but only via an MP, who is not required to pass the complaint on. The PCA's conclusions after investigation are passed back to the MP, though he may also make a special report to Parliament. This indirect approach was the result of MPs' jealousy of Parliament's role as the place where grievances against government are dealt with. Thus, also, the PCA cannot order any remedy where maladministration is found, and it is up to the department concerned what it does. There is a Public Administration Select Committee which reports to the House of Commons, and which in practice assists in obtaining a remedy. The PCA issues an annual report and reports on specific issues.

In 2001–02, the PCA received the highest ever number of complaints, at 2,319 (an increase of nearly a quarter over the previous year), and settled 1,988 complaints. A proportion of complaints received each year is clearly outside the PCA's jurisdiction (109 in 2001–02), and in a further substantial number of cases,

---

260 The PCA website is at www.ombudsman.org.uk. The PCA in 2006 was Ann Abraham (previously Legal Services Ombudsman for England and Wales, and before that Chief Executive of the National Association of Citizen's Advice Bureaux). She is simultaneously Health Service Ombudsman for England and Wales.

after consideration of the papers the matter is taken no further, for example because there is no evidence of a continuing injustice to the complainant (812 in 2001–02). Where, after consideration, there does seem to be maladministration producing such injustice, the PCA makes inquiries. Many complaints are settled by this means, whether in favour of the complainant (344 in 2001–02) or otherwise (437 in 2001–02). Others require a statutory investigation, which may result in settlement or in a conclusion that no worthwhile remedy can be given (91 in 2001–02) or in a report which is sent to the MP who initiated the matter and the offending body (195 in 2001–02). Many complaints are received concerning the Department of Work and Pensions (53% in 2001–02), frequently concerning disability- or incapacity-related benefits and non-payment of Child Support Agency payments. Other complaints are spread over a wide range of government departments.

There is also a Scottish Public Services Ombudsman[261], an office set up by the Scottish Public Services Ombudsman Act 2002 to replace the Scottish Parliamentary Ombudsman, the Health Service Ombudsman for Scotland, the Local Government Ombudsman for Scotland, and the Housing Association Ombudsman for Scotland. Consequently, the office covers a very wide range of organisations, including the Scottish Administration, health service bodies, local authorities, further and higher education, and a variety of other governmental bodies from the Audit Commission for Scotland to the Water Industry Commissioner for Scotland (via the Crofters' Commission, the Parole Board for Scotland and the Scottish Arts Council). It also includes a large number of 'cross-border public authorities', that is, Great Britain or United Kingdom ones, some of whose activities relate to devolved matters, such as the Criminal Injuries Compensation Authority, the National Consumer Council and the Unrelated Live Transplant Regulatory Authority. There is also a Scottish Legal Services Ombudsman (discussed in Chapter 7).

In addition, there is a UK-wide Financial Ombudsman Service (replacing the former Banking, Building Society, Insurance and Investment Ombudsmen) and Pensions Ombudsman, and several other ombudsmen whose jurisdiction relates to England and Wales only. Some of these schemes are closer to arbitration than to the usual role of an ombudsman.

---

261 The website of the Scottish Public Services Ombudsman is at www.scottish ombudsman.org.uk. The SPSO is Alice Brown, a political scientist at Edinburgh University, and there are three deputes.

Principal English and Welsh courts

Civil courts

Magistrates' courts are organised on a county basis, with lay justices of the peace ('JPs') assisted by a legally qualified clerk, but also in many urban areas with full-time District Judges. There are some 700 JPs in all and some 100 District Judges. They deal with certain family law matters including adoption proceedings (when they are termed 'Family Proceedings Courts'), recovery of charges from public utilities, and act as a licensing court for alcohol licensing. They are not equivalent to any Scottish Court.

County Courts, of which there are some 300, are found in all major towns. They are roughly equivalent to Sheriff Courts, and take a wide variety of civil cases within their areas, subject to certain limitations. District Judges may hear cases up to a limited figure, Circuit Judges hear above that limit, and there are small claims procedures. Many County Courts (though not all) deal with divorce.

The High Court of Justice is roughly equivalent to the Outer House of the Court of Session (and not to be confused with the Scottish High Court of Justiciary). However, it sits not only in London, but also in a number of provincial centres. It comprises three Divisions, but these are not like the Divisions of the Inner House, as they are distinguished in terms of jurisdiction. They are called, respectively, Queen's Bench (which includes the Commercial Court, the Admiralty Court and the Administrative Court), with some 70 judges, headed by the President of the Queen's Bench Division'[262]; Chancery, with some 20 judges headed by the 'Chancellor of the High Court'[263]; and Family (once known as the Probate, Divorce and Admiralty Division), also with about 20 judges, headed by the President of the Family Division[264].

The judges without titles are styled 'Mr Justice' ('J', after the surname; 'JJ' in the plural: thus, for instance, 'Lightman J', and 'Lightman and Pumphrey, JJ'[265]). The High Court takes important

---

262 In mid-2007, Sir Igor Judge: until the Constitutional Reform Act 2005, the head was the Lord Chief Justice (for whom, see below).

263 In mid-2007, Sir Andrew Morrit: until the Constitutional Reform Act 2005, the head was technically the Lord Chancellor and in practice the Vice-Chancellor.

264 In mid-2007, Sir Mark Potter: this title has not been changed recently, but the President is now also 'Head of Family Justice' as noted below.

265 Though English High Court judges are made knights or dames, as appropriate, on appointment. Thus Lightman J is Sir Gavin Lightman.

civil litigation at first instance, and each Division has a small appeal jurisdiction. This is exercised by two or more judges and, confusingly, is known as the 'Divisional Court' (thus 'the Divisional Court of Queen's Bench' rather than 'Queen's Bench Division').

The Court of Appeal (Civil Division) chiefly takes appeals from the County Courts, a number of tribunals, and the three Divisions of the High Court, and is roughly equivalent to the Inner House of the Court of Session. It has some 40 judges, called Lords Justices of Appeal (abbreviated to 'LJ' after the surname; 'LJJ' in the plural, and not to be confused with the Lords of Appeal in Ordinary of the Appellate Committee of the House of Lords[266]: thus, for instance, 'Auld LJ'[267]), and is headed by the 'Master of the Rolls' ('MR': thus 'Sir Anthony Clarke, MR'). They sit in threes, usually.

The Appellate Committee of the House of Lords hears further appeals from the Court of Appeal, but also occasionally, with the consent of the parties, on questions of statutory interpretation of general public importance, direct from the High Court (for which there is no Scottish equivalent procedure).

As in Scotland, there have been criticisms of the way civil procedure operates, and there were major changes in it recently[268].

Criminal courts

Magistrates' courts, essentially the same courts as for civil purposes, try minor offences, which constitute the overwhelming majority of all criminal cases, with restricted sentencing powers. Their nearest equivalent in Scotland is the District Court (soon to be JP Court), but they take a much greater proportion of cases, so overlap with Sheriff Summary Courts. As the 'Youth Court', they try those aged between 14 and 17 years (as there is no equivalent to the Children's Hearings).

They also act as a 'Court of Committal', for which there is no Scottish equivalent. Any serious crime is tried 'on indictment' (roughly similar to solemn procedure) before the Crown Court, but traditionally, the person had first to appear before examining magistrates whose function was to decide if there were a prima facie case

---

266 Discussed in Ch 4, and shortly to be replaced by the 'Supreme Court of the United Kingdom'.

267 Who is, in fact, Sir Robin Auld.

268 See *Access to Justice: interim report* (1995) and *Access to Justice: final report* (the 'Woolf Report': 1996), largely effected in new Civil Procedure Rules. There were also been a review of the Court of Appeal and another of civil justice and legal aid in 1997.

against the accused. If they decided there was, the case was committed to the Crown Court for trial. If not, the accused was discharged. However, the unwieldiness of the proceedings means that they are now considerably watered down, and the process has lost much of its purpose.

Crown Courts (descended from the old 'Assizes' and 'Quarter Sessions'), which sit in some 90 locations, hear more serious criminal cases, including all trials on indictment, and are organised on a circuit basis so are the rough equivalent of the Sheriff Solemn Court, and High Court of Justiciary in Scotland. However, there are several levels of judge (High Court judges, Circuit Judges and Recorders), as the courts are organised into three tiers, reflected in the seriousness of the cases they may try. The 'Old Bailey' is the popular name for London Crown Court, technically known as the Central Criminal Court (which is situated in a street called 'Old Bailey'). Crown Courts also hear appeals from Magistrates' Courts.

The Court of Appeal (Criminal Division), headed by the Lord Chief Justice ('LCJ': thus 'Lord Phillips of Worth Matravers, LCJ'), hears appeals against conviction and sentence, and other matters, from the Crown Court (so is the rough equivalent of the High Court of Justiciary acting as the Court of Criminal Appeal), and the Appellate Committee of the House of Lords is the final court of criminal appeal[269] (though not in Scotland).

Again, as in Scotland, there has been criticism of the administration of criminal justice, which has had significant effects[270].

Judicial offices

Recent changes, in part flowing from the change in status of the Lord Chancellor[271] have created new judicial offices.

The Lord Chief Justice is now also the 'President of the Courts of England & Wales' and as such, responsible for conveying the views of the England and Wales judiciary to the Government, for training of this judiciary ('within the resources made available by the Lord Chancellor') and for 'maintenance of appropriate arrangements for the deployment of the judiciary in England and Wales. The Lord Chief Justice is also now 'Head of Criminal Justice' in England and

---

269   And, as noted, is discussed in Ch 4, and shortly to be replaced by the 'Supreme Court of the United Kingdom'.

270   See *Review of the Criminal Courts in England & Wales* (the 'Auld Report': 2001), some of the recommendations of which were effected in the Criminal Justice Act 2003.

271   For which, see Chs 3 & 4, and above.

Wales (or appoints a Court of Appeal judge to hold that office, after consultation with the Lord Chancellor)[272].

The President of the Family Division is now also 'Head of Family Justice', and has a Deputy appointed by the Lord Chief Justice[273].

Principal Northern Ireland Courts[274]

Civil Courts

Magistrates Courts, County Courts and the High Court and the Court of Appeal operate in a similar fashion to their equivalents in England and Wales.

Magistrates Courts were originally staffed by lay Justices of the Peace. However, for two hundred years or more, there have been professional 'Resident Magistrates' who largely, but not completely, replaced them over time. Magistrates Courts deal with maintenance proceedings between husband and wife and related matters, small debts, land disputes and licensing within their area. Appeal is either to the County Court or the Court of Appeal (on a point of law only).

County Courts deal with the general range of civil matters including contract, delict and divorce (as well as appeals from Magistrates Courts) within their area. Appeal from County Courts is by way of a re-hearing to the High Court or by case stated to the Court of Appeal (on a point of law only).

The High Court, with three Divisions (as in England and Wales) hears the broad range of important civil matters from anywhere in Northern Ireland. Appeal is to the Court of Appeal or in some cases, direct to the Appellate Committee of the House of Lords.

The Court of Appeal hears appeals, as described above, with appeal to the Appellate Committee of the House of Lords.

Criminal Courts

Magistrates Courts, the Crown Court and the Court of Appeal also operate in a similar fashion to their equivalents in England and Wales

Magistrates Courts (usually staffed by 'Resident Magistrates', as noted above in relation to civil matters) undertake committal proceedings in respect of major crime, acting as a sieve for the

272 Constitutional Reform Act 2005, s7.
273 *Ibid*, s 8.
274 For further detail, see eg Dickson *The Legal System of Northern Ireland* (SLS Publications, 5th ed 2005)

Crown Court, but try summarily (that is, without a jury), the vast majority of criminal cases themselves, within their area. Appeal is either to the County Court (by way of a re-hearing) or to the Court of Appeal (on a point of law only).

County Courts hear the appeals just noted, but have no original jurisdiction in criminal matters.

The Crown Court hears major criminal cases on indictment (that is, with a jury) after the committal proceedings in the Magistrates Court. Appeal is the Court of Appeal and, thereafter to the Appellate Committee of the House of Lords

5. Sources of law

THE MEANINGS OF 'SOURCES OF LAW'

'Sources of law' is a widely used phrase. It has several meanings, all of which have their importance, and each of which must be distinguished.

Historical sources

Legal rules and principles do not spring into existence, fully formed. They have their origins in political, moral and social ideas. Specific pieces of legislation (for example, the Race Relations Act 1976), and fundamental organising legal principles (such as contract), encapsulate such ideas. Thus, any legal provision has historical sources. Chapters 1, 2 and 15 look further at the process by which such ideas become law.

Formal sources

The most common use of the phrase 'sources of law', however, relates to the form in which the law appears. The formal sources of any legal system will be specific to it. Thus, the formal sources of Scots law are not identical to those of English law, and a good deal more different from those of, say, French law. The formal sources of Scots law are conventionally divided into major and minor, reflecting their relative importance.

The major formal sources can be said to be:

(a) legislation, including:
- Acts of the United Kingdom Parliament, two of which, the Human Rights Act 1998 and the European Communities Act 1972, have special status;
- laws made by Ministers of the Crown and others under powers delegated to them by the United Kingdom Parliament;

- Acts of the Scottish Parliament also made under powers delegated by the United Kingdom Parliament;
- laws made by the Scottish Ministers and other, again under powers delegated by the United Kingdom Parliament;
- laws made by the Scottish Ministers and others, but under powers delegated by the Scottish Parliament; and
- European Community legislation of various types;

(b) precedent, that is, rules of law produced by courts without reference to the UK Parliament or any other legislature.

The minor formal sources can be said to be:

(a) prerogative legislation (that is, remnants of the former power of the Crown before the rise of Parliament in the 17th Century, now exercised by the government, most of them being executive in form, but some being undeniably legislative);
(b) 'Institutional Works' (that is, certain writings on the law by individual authors who have won respect in the courts and elsewhere, their writings therefore being treated as authoritative); and
(c) custom (that is, practices observed by certain groups of people, or by people generally).

This typology of formal sources is the basis upon which, broadly speaking, most of the rest of this Chapter, and Chapters 6 to 13 proceed. Its importance is, incidentally, reflected in the most significant feature of a law library, which is visible at a glance. Half the books are textbooks, monographs, commentaries and other books about the law. The other half are the law itself, that is, they are collections of legislation, and reports of cases etc. It is the most characteristic part of a law student's work that he must 'look up the law', that is, find not just summaries of the law and comments on it but the actual legal provisions themselves.

Other uses of the term 'sources of law'

Before considering the various sorts of 'formal source' in detail, it should be noted that the term 'sources of law' can be used in yet other senses. For example, it is sometimes used to indicate that a rule is to be found in a specific piece of legislation or a particular precedent (that is, a particular decided case), as when the legal rules on how a valid marriage is contracted are said to have as their source the Marriage (Scotland) Act 1977, and the legal rules on what constitutes a contract to have as their source a large number of identifiable cases in which they were laid down. This usage does not have a conventional name, might be termed the 'locational source'.

Quasi-sources

Also before considering the various sorts of 'formal source' in detail, it should further be noted that some rules, although not actually rules of law, are similar to rules of law in some important ways. These require examination, if only to distinguish them, and can be described as 'quasi-sources'.

RANKING OF SOURCES

If there is more than one source of law, they might contradict each other. This would be, quite literally, intolerable, for it would be impossible to discover what the law was on any topic. So to prevent contradiction, the sources must be ranked in an order of precedence, the higher 'trumping' the lower.

Unfortunately, the details of how this ranking works are now very complicated. Nevertheless, ten principles broadly express this ranking:

1 Legislation – 'Convention rights'

'Convention rights' is the name given to the rights and freedoms contained within the European Convention on Human Rights (for which, see Chapter 3), which have been cut and pasted into the Human Rights Act 1998 (an Act of the United Kingdom Parliament) and made enforceable in United Kingdom courts. Their special significance is expressed in the first principle, that is, that courts, government and other public authorities must interpret all other laws, both existing and future, so far as possible consistently with them. There is an important exception to this, however, in that, if other Acts of the United Kingdom Parliament (but not other laws) cannot be interpreted consistently with them, they override them.

2 Legislation – 'Community law'

This is the law created by the European Community (for which, see Chapters 3 and 6 and Appendix 3). The second principle is that all other existing and future law is valid only in so far as it is consistent with Community law. This is required by the European Communities Act 1972. (However, Community law is still to be interpreted consistently with the European Convention on Human Rights in conformity with the first principle).

3 Legislation – United Kingdom Parliamentary legislation

This is the law passed by the United Kingdom Parliament, in Acts of Parliament. The third principle is that, subject to the first two, the United Kingdom Parliament may pass any Act, to any effect, that it wishes, and this legislation is therefore more powerful than the law created by any of the following means.

4 Legislation – Scottish parliamentary legislation

This is law passed by the Scottish Parliament in Acts of the Scottish Parliament. The fourth principle is that, as the Scottish Parliament has law-making power only by virtue of the United Kingdom Parliament delegating such powers in the Scotland Act 1998, Acts of the Scottish Parliament are valid only in so far as permitted by the delegation in that Act.

5 Legislation – other delegated legislation

This is law made by members of the United Kingdom government, or the Scottish Executive, or other governmental bodies such as local authorities, in the form of Statutory Instruments (and Scottish Statutory Instruments), by-laws etc. It also is possible only by virtue of the United Kingdom Parliament (or, in the case of the Scottish Executive and Scottish local authorities, the Scottish Parliament) delegating appropriate powers. The fifth principle is that, as with the fourth, such legislation is thus valid only in so far as it is permitted by the delegation in the relevant legislation.

6 Legislation – Earlier and later legislation

The sixth principle is that, within any of the above classes of legislation, later legislation may repeal or amend earlier inconsistent legislation implicitly, even if it does not do so explicitly.

7 Judicial precedent – precedent and legislation

This is the law made by judges in deciding cases in courts, in the absence of legislation. The seventh principle is that such law is valid only in so far as it is compatible with legislation, in any of its forms.

8 Judicial precedent – higher and lower courts

Precedents can be laid down, in general, by any court. However, in general, it is those created by courts relatively high in the hierarchy, that is, appeal courts, which will have attention to paid to them. Thus, the eighth principle is that higher courts can, despite the seventh principle, overturn the law created by judicial precedent in lower courts. (Note, incidentally, that a form of judicial precedent operates in cases interpreting legislation, that is, working out a meaning where the legislation is unclear, for such interpretations become embedded as precedents, and this principle applies in such cases.)

8 Judicial precedent – earlier and later judicial precedent

Those operating the system of judicial precedent, from whatever time, assume that no precedent contradicts any other, so are reconcilable until proved otherwise. The ninth principle is, therefore, to strive to maintain the whole body of judicial precedent as a coherent and consistent whole.

9 Minor sources

This is law made by a variety of disparate bodies (as described above). The tenth principle is therefore that law made by the minor sources may be drawn on in default of any of the above. Recourse to minor sources is so rare that there is no need for a principle to rank between them.

THE MAJOR FORMAL SOURCES OF LAW

Legislation and precedent: civil law, common law and mixed systems

It may be useful to start consideration of the major formal sources of law with the distinction between the 'civil' and 'common law' families of legal systems, for this throws light upon the relationship between legislation and precedent.

Civil law systems claim to be the intellectual heirs of Roman law, and many of their legal rules are descended from it. 'Civil law' is a translation of the Latin *ius civile*, the name given by Roman lawyers to the bulk of their law. In general, civil law systems are codified systems, in the sense that much law is set out in logical, reasoned and encyclopaedic form in legislative 'codes'. In such a system, in principle, not only do all legal rules derive from legislation (principally the codes), but also the underlying principles of the system are set forth there. In such systems, precedent is not recognised as a source of law at all, or at least only as a minor, supplementary one. The legal systems of most of Continental Europe, such as Belgium, France, Germany, Italy and Spain, and to a large extent those parts of the rest of the world which were colonised by these European powers, such as the countries of South America, are civil law.

Common law systems are usually seen as the heirs of English law. English law itself never adopted Roman law as other European countries did. The native law it developed depended heavily upon precedent. Indeed, only in the 19th century did legislation become a significant source of law. The name given to the kind of law created by precedent, 'the common law', is the very name identifying this type of legal system. Thus the rules, and the principles underlying them, are found in precedent. For example, the organising concepts of law such as contract, and the basic rules on the creation of contracts, the effect upon them of error by a party, and on performance or non-performance of contracts, and so on, are found in precedent. Legislation merely alters the application of those principles, to a greater or lesser extent, in respect of specific contracts (such as sale of goods, consumer credit or insurance contracts). Even great new areas of law such as company law, which were created by legislation, depend upon underlying common law rules and principles. English law was exported to colonies, and thus became the type of law found in much of the rest of the world, including most of the countries of North America, and the British Commonwealth.

Scots law forms one of a small group of 'mixed' or 'hybrid' systems, which partake of both civil and common law. Other mixed or hybrid systems are, because of the vagaries of their colonial history, the state of Louisiana, South Africa, the province of Quebec, and Sri Lanka. Scots law is said to be a civil law system, in so far as Roman law, and the law of civil law countries, influenced it in the past, through the writings of the Institutional Writers and the fact that, when law teaching in Scottish universities was less than lively, law students commonly repaired to France (before the Reformation) and the Netherlands (after it) for their instruction. However, it is not codified and since the 19th century, but especially since the mid-20th century, it has accepted precedent as a source of law on the common law model.

Legislation

'Legislation' is surprisingly hard to define. It is both a process and a product. As a product, it is easiest to say that, so far as Scotland is concerned, legislation is the law created by certain European Community institutions, by the United Kingdom and Scottish Parliaments and by those to whom the United Kingdom and Scottish Parliaments have delegated legislative power. This, however, begs the question of what these bodies have in common.

It is better therefore to say that legislation is deliberately and formally created law. Acts of the United Kingdom Parliament have commonly been regarded as the standard example, in as much as throughout the United Kingdom, they prevailed over all other forms of law until the coming of European Community law (and still prevail over the European Convention on Human Rights). Legislation as a product is produced by legislation as a process. It is thus commonly, but not necessarily, produced by a deliberative body (sometimes referred to as a legislature, and sometimes elected). It nearly always deals in general rules rather than specific cases. While in civil law countries the whole law can be presumed to be the result of legislation (often in the form of encyclopaedic codes), in common law countries, which admit precedent as a formal source of law, this is not so, for the purpose of legislation is to change (or sometimes restate) the law. Legislation in common law countries is thus essentially *ad hoc*.

The various types of legislation applying in the United Kingdom are discussed in Chapters 6-10.

Precedent

Precedent is law created incidentally, by an adjudicative body (usually a court), in the course of judging disputes in an area where there is no legislation. It is to be found, therefore, in specific cases dealing with specific facts, and the actual rules of law applied must necessarily be inferred from those facts, typically by other judges in other cases appealing to precedent, as further described in Chapters 12 & 13 and Appendix 1. Acceptance of precedent as a means of creating law effectively defines common law legal systems. These inferred rules purport to express timeless principles inherent in the system, rather than specific contemporary policy. While it is possible for the law to be changed through precedent, the process is usually slow, limited and uncertain, so legislation is usually sought for this purpose. Thus, the underlying principles of the legal system are to be found in the common law, that is the law created by precedent, rather than in legislation, which merely modifies or adds to it. Indeed, common law can be put into abeyance by legislation, but not wholly destroyed, for it takes force again if the legislation replacing it is repealed.

THE MINOR FORMAL SOURCES OF LAW

The minor sources are prerogative legislation, the Institutional Works, and custom.

Prerogative legislation

Generally speaking, the Crown (that is, in practice, the government of the day) has no power to create law, for under the 'doctrine of the separation of the powers', creating law is the job of another body, that is, Parliament. However, it does have some limited residual powers, dating from a time before the separation of the powers was thought sound theory, and when monarchs could thus legislate without reference to Parliament. These powers are part of the 'royal prerogative', which is the name given to the ill-defined bundle of legal powers which the Crown has[1].

These powers are chiefly executive rather than legislative, and include the Sovereign's power to appoint ministers to form a government, and the powers of the government (in the name of the Crown) to conduct foreign affairs including, for example, the power to sign treaties and declare war[2].

Among these prerogative powers, certain residual legislative ones exist, however. Although they are undoubtedly legislative, they are minor, so are dealt with here, rather than in Chapters 6-10. They are residual in that, as noted above, they are the remains of the broad legislative powers claimed by the Crown before the 'Glorious Revolution', that is, the constitutional settlement of 1688-89 in both England and Scotland (which had shared a king from 1603). In this settlement, Parliament took most of these powers away from the Crown, and what remains could also be removed by Parliament. The

---

1 In *Laker Airways v Department of Trade* [1977] 1 QB 643, Lord Denning described the royal prerogative as 'a discretionary power to be exercised for the public good' and so was examinable by the courts.

2 In mid-2007, as one of his first acts as Prime Minister, Gordon Brown announced a review of such powers with a view to transferring some of them to Parliament.

prerogative powers therefore continue to exist on sufferance[3], and there remains no general right on the part of the Crown to legislate[4], only a limited right to do so in relation to certain topics. These topics include the colonies, internal governmental matters, and possibly certain emergencies and otherwise.

Examples of its use are therefore few and disparate. One, concerned with colonial legislation, was the constitution of Hong Kong from its acquisition by the United Kingdom until it was handed back to China in 1997. This constitution was latterly contained in certain acts of prerogative legislation (called 'Letters Patent')[5]. All legislation made in Hong Kong by the Governor in the Legislative Council (Hong Kong's Parliament) was therefore valid by virtue of the fact that the Letters Patent created the post of Governor, set up the Legislative Council and provided for its composition, and gave legislative powers to the Governor in Legislative Council.

A second example, concerned with internal governmental matters, is the principal regulations for the internal operation of the Civil Service[6], and a third, concerned with emergencies, is certain legislation made on the outbreak of war in 1914, when no standing emergency legislation existed[7], and somewhat more recently at the time of the Falklands emergency[8].

A fourth example was the former Criminal Injuries Compensation Scheme. When the government decided in 1964 that persons suffering injuries as a result of criminal acts should receive some compensation from the state (being unlikely to obtain it from the criminal) it used the prerogative to set up a scheme of awards, based on the level of damages that the courts in Scotland or in England would grant. The justifications for circumventing Parliament were that the scheme was experimental and the costs to the state uncer-

3   See, for example, the English case of *Attorney-General v de Keyser's Royal Hotel* [1920] AC 508.
4   Claim of Right 1689; *Grieve v Edinburgh and District Water Trustees* 1918 SC 700, 1918 2 SLT 72; also the English *Case of Proclamations* (1611) Co Rep 74.
5   Letters Patent of 14 February 1917 (as amended); also Royal Instructions of 14 February 1917 (as amended) etc; see Wesley-Smith *Constitutional and Administrative Law in Hong Kong* (1987) vol 1, ch 4.
6   For example, the Civil Service Orders 1982, 1991 and 1995. It has been suggested that these ought to be replaced by a 'Civil Service Act', ie an Act of Parliament. Note also the Diplomatic Service Orders in Council of 1991, 1994 (two), 1995 & 204.
7   For example, the Trading with the Enemy Proclamation 1914.
8   Requisitioning of Ships Order of 4 April 1982.

tain. In fact, dissatisfaction with this arrangement led eventually to the Criminal Injuries Compensation Act 1995[9].

While acts of prerogative legislation answer to a variety of names[10], such as 'Letters Patent', 'Royal Instructions', 'Proclamations' and 'Royal Warrants', they are usually issued in the form of (prerogative) 'Orders in Council', that is, Orders purportedly made by the Sovereign on the advice of the Privy Council[11]. The title 'Order in Council' is misleading. Firstly, the involvement of the Sovereign and the advice of the Privy Council are fictional as the content is dictated by the government of the day. Secondly, the same name is used for another much more common type of legislation, that is (delegated) Orders in Council, a form of delegated legislation (see Chapter 9).

The Institutional Works

In the 17th century, Scots law was an untidy amalgam derived from various sources. It included old unwritten custom, written custom and other rules recorded in medieval writings, such as that called *Regiam Majestatem*[12], which were considered authoritative, *ad hoc* Acts of Parliament of various vintages, and decisions of the Court of Session, at least in so far as available in occasionally published collections known as the '*Practicks*'.

Scots law was not the only system with such characteristics, and the advantages of a systematic treatment were clear to lawyers and

---

9 The story is in fact more complicated, and instructive on the relationship of prerogative and legislation. A statutory scheme to replace the non-statutory one was introduced by the Criminal Justice Act 1988, ss 108-117. However, it was not brought into effect, and some time later, the Secretary of State announced that he was not going to bring it into force, but would introduce a new non-statutory scheme. In *R v Secretary of State for the Home Department ex parte Fire Brigades Union* [1995] 2 All ER 244, the Appellate Committee of the House of Lords held that, while he was not obliged to bring the statutory scheme into force, it was an abuse of the prerogative power to introduce an inconsistent non-statutory scheme under the royal prerogative. The Criminal Injuries Compensation Act 1995 therefore repealed the relevant portions of the Criminal Justice Act 1988, and introduced the scheme as a statutory one.

10 Acts of prerogative legislation are cited by name and date, as the examples above show. Some are bound in the annual volumes of *Statutory Instruments*, so can be cited by that reference. They do not appear on Westlaw or LexisNexis.

11 The Privy Council, originally a sort of forerunner of the Cabinet, is almost fictional in that it never meets as a whole, and the title 'Privy Councillor' is a sort of honour bestowed upon leading politicians, judges and bishops.

12 See Ch 2. It appears that *Regiam Majestatem* was heavily based upon an earlier English work, called *Glanvil* after the name of its presumed author. '*Regiam majestatem ...*', meaning 'Royal Majesty ...', are its opening words.

others across Europe. A widely known model for systematising native law was the *Corpus Iuris Civilis* (which can be roughly translated as 'the Body of the Civil Law'). This was a codification of late Roman law, produced in the 6th century AD in Constantinople (which was by then the capital of the Eastern part of the Roman Empire) under the auspices of the Emperor Justinian. It comprised four parts, two of which were of greater importance than the rest. The *'Pandects'* (or *'Digest'*) was a reconciliation of the commentaries of the major Roman legal writers of previous centuries. The *'Institutiones'* was a general introductory book on Roman law, dedicated to law students.

In Scotland such attempts to produce a systematic treatment took place from the mid-17th to the early 19th centuries. The writers of these works have become known as 'Institutional Writers', as several of their works adopted the title *'Institutes'* or *'Institutions'* in imitation of the title of Justinian's *'Institutiones'*, even though they might imitate the *'Digest'* in content. Their work remade Scots law.

It can be debated whether a particular writer or work is institutional. However, undoubtedly Stair's *Institutions of the Law of Scotland* is regarded as the greatest, and certain works are in all lists.

They are[13]: Sir Thomas Craig's *Jus Feudale* (1655); Sir George Mackenzie's *Laws and Customs of Scotland in Matters Criminal* (1678); James Dalrymple, Viscount Stair's *The Institutions of the Law of Scotland* (1681); Andrew McDouall, Lord Bankton's *An Institute of the Laws of Scotland* (1751–53); Professor John Erskine's *An Institute of the Law of Scotland* (1772); Baron David Hume's *Commentaries on the Law of Scotland Respecting the Description and Punishment of Crimes* (1797); Professor George Joseph Bell's *Commentaries on the Law of Scotland and Principles of Mercantile Jurisprudence* (1804) and *Principles of the Law of Scotland* (1829); and Archibald Alison's *Principles of the Criminal Law of Scotland* (1833) and *Practice of the Criminal Law of Scotland* (1833)[14]. Sometimes

---

13 All dates given are of the first edition. Later editions may be more authoritative. The first edition of Stair's *Institutions* was defective, for example, and the second, published in 1693, is more reliable. In any case, later editions of all the works are usually preferred.

14 References to Stair are usually cited by name, book, title and section, for example, 'Stair I, 1, 22' (or, more traditionally 'I, i, 22'), but sometimes in the form 'Stair *Institutions* I, 1, 22'. Bankton (commonly abbreviated to Bankt) and Erskine's *'Institute'* are cited in essentially the same way, for example, 'Bankt I, 5, 28' and 'Erskine III, 1, 2' (and Erskine's *'Principles'* similarly, but with *'Prin'* inserted). Bell's *'Commentaries'* are cited as, for example, 'Bell *Comm* I, 343', but his *'Principles'* (which has continuous paragraphing throughout), as 'Bell *Prin* 267'. Hume is cited as, for example, 'Hume 1, 52'.

included are Mackenzie's *The Institutions of the Law of Scotland* (1684); Erskine's *Principles of the Law of Scotland* (1759); and Henry Home, Lord Kames' *Principles of Equity* (1760).

The current significance of these works is that, at least since the middle of the 19th century, they have been accorded a special status. That is, they are regarded not as commentaries upon, illustrations of, opinions about, or textbooks concerning, the law, but as in themselves actually constituting the law[15]. Thus, in effect, the Institutional Writers have been regarded as akin to legislators.

While it is undeniable that the Institutional Writers are sources of law, explicit recognition of the position is actually limited to a small number of 19th-century cases, decided at a time when attitudes to the nature of law were different from today's, buttressed by a few authoritative, but less than comprehensive, 20th-century cases[16]. No works have been added to the canon since the middle of the 19th century and none deleted, although, so far as institutional authority depends upon judicial recognition, in principle either event could occur.

When an Institutional Work is cited, the question of its weight in comparison with other sources arises. There is little guidance on the answer. Lord Normand, a distinguished Scottish judge, observed in an often quoted[17] published lecture of 1941 that they were as respected in court as decisions of the Appellate Committee of the House of Lords. However, because there are few cases explicitly dealing with the authority of the Institutional Writers, judges have rarely discussed the matter explicitly. Clearly, the Institutional Works carry less weight than any legislation and, given their status, it is unlikely that any judicial decision will flatly contradict them, but in many areas, such as family law and employment law, social and moral changes have been so substantial as to reduce their persuasiveness considerably, or justify use of the maxim *cessante ratione*

15 It is unusual for legal systems to regard such writers as sources of law. South African law appears to be the only other system which does so. There, rules may be regarded as legal rules simply by virtue of having been written by one of the 'old authorities', chiefly internationally renowned Dutch writers on law, such as Grotius (Hugo de Groot 1583–1645): see *The Laws of Scotland: Stair Memorial Encyclopedia* vol 22, para 435, and Cairns 'Institutional Writings' in Kiralfy and MacQueen *New Perspectives in Scottish Legal History*.

16 For example, *Sugden v HM Advocate* 1934 JC 103, 1934 SLT 465; *Fortington v Lord Kinnaird* 1942 SC 239, 1943 SLT 24.

17 For example, in *The Laws of Scotland: Stair Memorial Encyclopedia* vol 22, 'Sources of Law (Formal)', para 437.

legis, cessat ipsa lex[18], and the deference suggested by Lord Normand now seems exaggerated[19]. Thus, they may be regarded as potentially decisive, but only where no legislation or clear precedent exists, and in areas of law in which the principles have not altered significantly since the institutional writers were at work.

In any case, although Institutional Works were of enormous importance in the past, it would be very unusual for any court today to justify its decision solely by reference to one. Indeed, although the High Court refers to Hume's works from time to time in relation to major common law offences[20], it is unusual for Institutional Writers even to be cited in court, in part because the tide of precedent and statute has washed over so much law in the last hundred years (although those precedents may themselves be built on the Institutional Writers' views, which are thus embedded in the law through a different route). Their role is thus, perhaps, to supply a moral and intellectual sheet anchor for the law, providing stability while not excluding change.

Other, non-institutional, works may be referred to in argument or decision in court, and increasingly are. Indeed, some highly respected but non-institutional works, such as Gloag's *Law of Contract* (2nd edn, 1929) and McBryde *The Law of Contract in Scotland* (2nd edn, 2001), are cited more frequently than Institutional Works. But in such cases, if the judge adopts the rule described, he is not accepting it as the actual law, but making it law by his decision. Thus, in *Black v Carmichael* 1992 SLT 897, the judges accepted a statement in Gordon's *Criminal Law* (2nd ed 1978[21]) at para 14–63 that in theft it is the owner's loss, not the thief's gain, that is important. In *Morgan Guaranty Trust Co v Lothian Regional Council* 1995 SLT 299, Lord President Hope acknowledged 'the work of academic lawyers whose detailed research and vigorous criticism has already had a marked influence on debate among the judiciary'.

---

18 *Ie*, approximately, 'if the reason for the law ceases, so does the law'.
19 See *HM Advocate v Stallard* 1989 SCCR 248, 1989 SLT 469. The learned commentator on the SCCR report of that case observed that 'it is not necessary to convene a Full Bench [*ie* an enlarged bench of judges, capable of giving more authoritative decisions] to depart from a proposition of Hume, which was repeated by later authorities and has been unchallenged by any authority for almost two centuries'.
20 As in *Khaliq v HM Advocate* 1984 JC 23, where Hume was relied upon, and *HM Advocate v Stallard* (see note above), where he was mentioned only to reject him.
21 See now 3rd ed, 2000 & 2001 (2 vols).

Custom

The common law (in the sense of law not created by Parliament) emerged from unwritten custom. Institutional Writers digested it in their works, and judges adopted it in their judgments, which clearly made it law which was common to the whole country. However, local custom might also be recognised. For example, Stair and other Institutional Writers recognised 'udal tenure', a form of land-holding found only in Orkney and Shetland, as custom enforceable through the courts[22].

It remains possible for custom to be a source of law. Nevertheless, because most rules once referred to as customs, such as 'legitim' (rights held by a deceased person's children to his moveable property), have now been enshrined in precedent, and thus incorporated into the common law, even that possibility exists only in limited circumstances. It is thus very rare today to assert the existence of a custom, and the leading case, *Bruce v Smith* (1890) 17 R 1000 (which concerns the rejection of a claim by the owner of land abutting the shore in Shetland, by virtue of owning the land, to one third of the value of pilot whales driven onto that shore and slaughtered), is well over a century old.

In so far as a custom might still be declared enforceable in the courts, it must pass certain tests. The custom must not contradict the general law[23], it must be certain[24], it must be generally accepted or acquiesced in as being obligatory[25], it must be reasonable (although what this means is not clear and might be difficult to decide), and it must have continued for a long time, although no particular period is required and interruption is not fatal. But a custom may be regarded as falling into desuetude, or by losing authority by contrary usage[26]. Any enforceable custom is likely to be restricted to a locality or trade, because any more general custom will either have been absorbed into the common law by judicial precedent, or be regarded as contrary to the general law.

Although the test of an enforceable custom has been laid down by precedent, it is of the essence of the idea of custom that it can be binding without judicial recognition. Explicit recognition of a

---

22 Stair IV, 22, 2.
23 *Anderson v McCall* (1866) 4 M 765.
24 Erskine I, 1, 44.
25 *Bruce v Smith* (1890) 17 R 1000.
26 *Bruce v Smith* (1890) 17 R 1000; *McAra v Edinburgh Magistrates* 1913 SC 1059, 1913 2 SLT 110; *Royal Four Towns Fishing Association v Dumfriesshire Assessor* 1956 SC 379, 1956 SLT 217.

custom is very rare, but one modern example is *Stirling Park & Co v Digby Brown and Co* 1996 SLT (Sh Ct) 17. A firm of solicitors, as agents for a client, instructed sheriff officers to serve a charge and carry out a 'poinding' (that is, impounding a debtor's goods) in order to recover a debt. The solicitors did not pay the sheriff officers' fees and expenses, and were sued. On appeal a Sheriff Principal held there was a custom to that effect 'so certain, uniform, notorious and reasonable' as to be binding on the solicitors, as if it were part of a contract.

Legislation may implicitly or explicitly delegate to custom, as when a statute uses words such as 'reasonable', which give judges a wide interpretive discretion. For example, by virtue of s 8(4)(a) of the Employment Rights Act 1996, part of the test of whether an employee was unfairly dismissed is that the employer 'in the circumstances ... acted reasonably ...'. In applying this test, judges have regard to what is commonly called 'custom and practice', that is, what is commonly regarded as acceptable in that employment.

In addition, custom-like rights may be recognised in other ways. Rights of way, for example, may arise from prescription, that is, continuous use over a period, now fixed by statute at 20 years[27]. Also, trade practices may be incorporated into a contract.

Most important of all, however, as a 'historical source', custom may affect the law in a major fashion without being explicitly recognised. Judges' views of what people, generally or within a particular milieu, consider acceptable will influence the way they take their decisions, both in applying and developing precedent, and in statutory interpretation. An example may be Lord Atkin's implicit, but clear, adoption of Christian morality in his 'neighbour test'[28] in *Donoghue v Stevenson* 1932 SC(HL) 31.

QUASI-SOURCES

As well as the major and minor sources of law, there are also what are called here 'quasi-sources'. This term refers to a great and amorphous variety of rules and principles which are not unequivocally law, which therefore do not fit into the generally accepted categories of formal sources of law, but which are nevertheless connected to law, look like law, or are treated much as if they were law.

27 Prescription and Limitation (Scotland) Act 1973, s 3.
28 See Matthew xix, 19 and the Catechism in the (English) Book of Common Prayer.

Constitutional conventions

One of the most important types of quasi-source is constitutional conventions. The United Kingdom has no single document called 'the constitution'. Constitutional laws, therefore, are found in the same sources as other laws, chiefly legislation (such as the Scotland Act 1998) and precedent. There are no fundamental laws such as exist in, for example, Germany and the United States[29]. Unwritten rules affect the way in which the constitution operates in practice in all states, no doubt. Because of the unwritten nature of the United Kingdom constitution, these unwritten rules, usually termed 'conventions of the constitution', have assumed special significance.

For example, there is no law requiring there to be a Prime Minister, let alone stipulating how he or she is to be appointed. In law there is simply a power on the part of the Sovereign to appoint ministers. Nevertheless, there is an unwritten rule, a constitutional convention, that the Sovereign will appoint the person who can command a majority of the votes on an issue of confidence in the House of Commons[30]. Indeed, it is only by convention that members of the government must normally have a seat in one or other House of Parliament[31] and that the Speaker of the House of Commons is an impartial chairman once elected to that office by the House, although he will invariably be an MP who is a member of a political party. Another important convention is that the Sovereign should not refuse assent to a Bill which has passed both Houses of Parliament. Indeed, the role of the Sovereign as one who 'reigns but does not rule', that is, one who acts in accordance with the basic constitutional conventions, has grown up by convention only.

Conventions are created by behaviour which becomes strictly observed because thought to be right, but by the same token can be tacitly altered by simple non-observation. For example, until the

29 It has been argued that various documents, such as the Acts of Union of the two Parliaments which created Great Britain in 1707, in fact form at least part of a constitution, and are fundamental law. Also, accession to the European Community has considerably altered the constitutional map, and the EC and EU Treaties bear to be the constitution of the United Kingdom as well as any other document. Further, the embedded position of the Human Rights Act (see Ch 7) was intended to make it, in some sense, fundamental.

30 To command a majority in the House of Commons requires in practice that one be an MP, and leader of the party which won the last general election. As party leaders are elected by party members according to various rules, it is an interesting question as to whether such party rules are part of the constitution of the United Kingdom, and thus quasi-sources.

31 This convention has occasionally not been observed for brief periods, and the ease of creating life peers provides a means of avoiding embarrassment.

beginning of the 20th century, the convention was that a Prime Minister might be a member of either House, as long as his party had a majority in the House of Commons. Thus, the Marquess of Salisbury was Prime Minister from 1895 to 1902 because the Conservative Party had a majority in the Commons. However, at some time in the 20th century, it became accepted that the Prime Minister must be a member of the elected House, and the convention altered, so no peer has been thought eligible since at least the middle of that century. Indeed, the Earl of Home renounced his peerage in 1963 and successfully sought election for Kinross and West Perthshire solely in order to be eligible to become Prime Minister (an aim he achieved shortly thereafter).

The Scottish Parliament and Administration may be expected to develop practices which will be observed with a sense of duty and so become constitutional conventions. The relationship between them and the United Kingdom Parliament and government will, if it is to be harmonious, require to be regulated by fresh conventions[32].

Constitutional conventions are certainly not enforceable by courts, but can be argued to be law in so far as they are respected and acted upon and thus, like laws, have a certain obligatory character. Like a jigsaw, they interlock with one another and so give a certain coherence to the public life of a society. They are part of the political morality of the state. Indeed, 'unconstitutional' in the United Kingdom more readily fits a breach of convention than one of ordinary law.

Administrative quasi-legislation

Governments produce among other things, guidance, guidelines, advice, plans, information upon their intentions, and so on. Various regulatory agencies set up by government do likewise. Within this mass of communications there are rules and principles, not contained in legislation, but intended to be acted upon, and often directed to officials. Indeed, the process is sometimes referred to as administrative rule-making or (somewhat misleadingly, insofar as the point is that it is not law) 'soft law'[33]. To some extent, its growth parallels that of delegated legislation, for it has increased through an

---

32 Indeed, the 'Sewel Convention', discussed in Ch 7, is an example of a recent creation.

33 The learned editor of the entry on Legislation in *The Laws of Scotland: Stair Memorial Encyclopaedia of the Laws of Scotland* vol 22, paras 233ff used the phrase 'ersatz legislation' ('**Ersatz**, *m.* substitute ...' Chambers New German Dictionary).

increase in the activities of government and regulatory agencies, but it may also have grown through a desire to influence activities through self-regulation rather than directly.

On the other hand, some of this guidance etc reflects a need for comprehensibility, which the United Kingdom style of legislative drafting does not promote, and is aimed at the general public, or those engaging in particular occupations or activities.

There are concerns over the growth of administrative quasi-legislation. While legislation comes under Parliamentary and other scrutiny (albeit sometimes of a limited kind), quasi-legislation may come under less or none. Indeed, it may actually be secret, and in any case may be seen as reflecting too cosy a relationship between government and some interest-groups. Although any government must be entitled to produce internal rules for its civil servants, some quasi-legislation may appear to be legislation by government, outside the royal prerogative and without recourse to Parliament.

This quasi-legislation includes many types of communication, including codes of practice, professional codes of conduct, government circulars, and perhaps the Citizen's Charter.

Codes of practice

The Highway Code is a well-known example, though not necessarily typical, of a code of practice, one form of administrative quasi-legislation which is increasingly common. Such codes are in general relatively brief, but systematic and reasonably comprehensive sets of precepts, produced by government or a regulatory agency, and addressed to the public. They are produced in order to allow a particular activity to be carried out more safely, or better in some other way, so are written in standard English for the layman rather than in watertight drafting for the lawyer and judge.

Usually they are required or permitted by an Act of Parliament, and may require parliamentary approval. They are not, however, legislation, but paraphrases or interpretations of it, or embellishments upon it. They have varying legal force. Some offer only guidance, and are wholly unenforceable, as, for example, the Secretary of State's 'guidance' to be issued under the Transport Act 1985, s 125 in relation to the transport needs of disabled persons. Others are indirectly enforceable, for example, the Highway Code. The Road Traffic Act 1988, s 38 stipulates that a breach of the Highway Code renders no-one liable to criminal proceedings, but may be relied upon in civil or criminal proceedings to assist in establishing liability. In short, failure to signal a right turn, for example, is not an offence, but if an accident occurs in the course of such a manoeuvre, it can be used to help prove the offence of careless driving or negligence creating liability to compensate somebody injured. Other examples of codes, breach of which may result in some form of liability, are the code of practice on employment under the Race Relations Act 1976, and the Code of Practice on Picketing, now under the Trade Union and Labour Relations (Consolidation) Act 1992, s 199 (as amended), which by s 207 courts and tribunals are bound to 'take into account'[34].

Professional codes of conduct

Suppliers of services organised as a profession often have a registration procedure as a precondition of practice, and a code of conduct, breach of which may be punished, and may even result in deregistration. It is part of the orthodox notion of a profession that the code of conduct is produced and enforced by the profession itself. This is modified in some cases by legislation requiring and otherwise controlling such a code.

For example, under ss 34, 35 and 53 of the Solicitors (Scotland) Act 1980 (as amended), the Law Society of Scotland is required to make such rules, usually called practice rules and accounts rules. Breach, judged by the independent Scottish Solicitors' Discipline Tribunal, may constitute professional misconduct, attracting one of a range of penalties, including 'striking off the roll', that is deregistration. (This procedure is more fully dealt with in Chapter 14.)

Government circulars

Government circulars form a miscellaneous category of quasi-legislation, comprising a variety of advice and guidance, diversely titled, issued as a formal letter to officials in central or local government, or in the National Health Service, or to police, or otherwise[35]. Some are very important, for example, Crown Office Circulars to procurators fiscal are presumed (for they are secret) to detail procedures to be followed and how discretion is to be exercised in prosecuting offences. At the other extreme, Scottish Home and Health

---

34 Applied as to number of picketers in *Thomas v National Union of Mineworkers* [1986] Ch 20 at 70.
35 In 2006, for instance, the Home Office published over 40 circulars (most relating to police in England and Wales): see www.knowledgenetwork.gov.uk/ HO/circular.nsf/ViewTemplate%20For%20HOCircularsWeb?OpenForm.

Department Circular 6/1992 (ref: CPF/2/7) dated 30 April 1992 to chief executives of islands and district councils informed them of rates of travelling and subsistence allowances to be paid to justices of the peace.

Circulars are not legislation, so cannot vary the enacted law. Thus, in *Inglis v British Airports Authority* 1978 SLT (Lands Tr) 30, a woman claimed compensation for depreciation in the value of her house by reason of the construction of a new runway at Edinburgh Airport. The Airports Authority resisted her claim, relying on advice as to its obligations contained in the Scottish Development Department Memorandum No 85/1973. The Lands Tribunal described the memorandum as 'an administrative circular', and decided it was mere guidance to public authorities as to the scope of the relevant legislation on compensation, and could not be used as an aid to construe the wording of a statute. So compensation was awarded.

There are few other cases directly in point, but some decisions from the Appellate Committee of the House of Lords in English cases broadly support the conclusion. In *Gillick v West Norfolk and Wisbech Area Health Authority* [1986] AC 112, the health authority, following advice from the Department of Health and Social Security in Circular HSC(IS)32 (memorandum of guidance on family planning), gave contraceptive advice to young people, including those under 16. Mrs Gillick (who had five children under 16) sought a declaration that this was unlawful. Although this point was not the main issue in the case, the Appellate Committee of the House of Lords concluded that it could issue a declaration correcting erroneous advice on the law issued by government departments in a public, non-statutory document such as a circular. This clearly involved concluding that such legal advice could be wrong, and that a circular could not alter the law.

However, it is certainly the case that some circulars can be enforced indirectly. For example, if local planning authorities ignore planning circulars, their decisions can be overturned on appeal.

Also, circulars addressed by central government to civil servants are from the Crown to Crown servants, and from employers to employees, and may be enforced through disciplinary proceedings[36]. Thus, in *Palmer v Inverness Hospitals Board* 1963 SC 311 a circular of the Department of Health concerning hospital disciplinary proceedings was held to create a right to a hearing, which could be read as part of the contract of employment of a dismissed house surgeon. In

36 See *R v Ponting* [1985] Crim LR 318.

Tehrani v Argyll and Clyde Health Board (No 1) 1989 SLT 851 the suspension of a hospital consultant on full pay in accordance with a Scottish Home and Health Department circular was not disputed, but in the absence of reasons and the brief duration of the suspension beyond that envisaged in the circular were held to be not unreasonable.

Chartermarks and benchmarks

One interesting example of quasi-legislation emerged through the 'Citizens' Charters', an idea produced by the Conservative Government of the early 1990s, and adopted by the Labour Government of the late 1990s, designed as a means of setting and raising standards in the provision of public sector services by mechanisms such as performance targets, publication of information, and encouragement of means of complaint and redress. There are now some hundreds of 'national charters', from HM Revenue and Customs 'Travellers [*sic*] Charter' to the Forestry Commission's 'Woodland Grants Scheme Applicants Charter for England'.

Such charters, while indicating good practice, and how to complain about service, do not create legal rights or new means of redress in themselves, however. Nor do they have any parliamentary approval.

6. Legislation – European Community law

THE INSTITUTIONAL BACKGROUND

The institutional background of European Union (including European Community) institutions are discussed in Chapter 3 (among other things, distinguishing them from the Council of Europe and the European Convention on Human Rights). This Chapter deals with the meaning and types of Community law, the Community legislative processes, the relationship between Community law and national systems in general and with United Kingdom law in particular, and with the publication and citation of Community law.

THE MEANING, TYPES AND STYLE OF COMMUNITY LAW

The meaning of 'Community law'

European Community law is usually called simply 'Community law'. As discussed in Chapter 3, the Community was set up by various Treaties in order to promote certain aims. The most important aims are explicitly stated in the opening Articles of the original European Economic Community Treaty of 1957, which, as amended and now called the European Community Treaty (or Treaty on the European Community: 'TEC'), remains in force. The Preamble speaks of the intention 'to lay the foundations of an ever closer union among the peoples of Europe', and the Treaty Articles specify numerous policies to that end, including free movement between Member States of goods, persons, capital and services, and non-discrimination against their nationals on the ground of nationality or sex.

In order to fulfil these aims, the Treaties do something of enormous significance, that is, they give the Community the power to make its own law. Community law is thus a 'separate legal order' from those of the Member States. However, Community law exists only for the purpose of achieving the aims specified, so any piece of Community legislation might be *ultra vires*, that is, beyond the powers granted to the Community's institutions by the various Treaties, and thereby invalid[1]. It is important to realise that anything done within the Community must be justified by reference to a Treaty provision. Nevertheless, the Community's aims are so broad, and so broadly interpreted by the European Court of Justice, that this is not a major limitation in practice.

The subsequent creation of the European Union out of the European Community and other elements, and later developments (as discussed in Chapter 3) have complicated the matter considerably. For present purposes, what requires noting principally is that the second and third 'pillars' of the European Union operated 'intergovernmentally' (between Member States) rather than 'supranationally' (above Member States) as the European Community (the first 'pillar') does. Thus, they did not create Community law, so were not subject to the jurisdiction of the European Court of Justice.

Thereafter, however, the Treaty of Amsterdam allowed the United Kingdom to opt out of parts of an amended first 'pillar' (so as not to be bound by them)[2], and also allowed Member States to conclude agreements between only some of their number and not others (creating further areas in which some Member States are bound, but

---

1   Articles 230 and 231 (numbered 173 and 174 before the Treaty of Amsterdam) allow the European Court of Justice to review the legality of acts of the Commission and the Council of Ministers on specified grounds including *ultra vires*, and to declare them void. For example, the UK sought to have the 'Working Time Directive' (EC) 93/104 (which imposes regulation of working hours, rest breaks, night work and annual leave) set aside as *ultra vires* because it was based on Art 118a of the Treaty (now Art 138: which concerned health and safety at work and required only a qualified majority vote, from which the United Kingdom in fact abstained), when it should have been based on Art 100 or Art 235 (now Arts 94 and 308 post-Amsterdam) which allow legislation to fulfil the purposes of the Treaty in areas not specifically covered, and requires unanimity, and thus could be vetoed by the United Kingdom). In Case C–84/95 *UK v EU Council (working time)* [1996] 3 CMLR 671, the European Court of Justice rejected the argument on the facts, however, as health and safety were the essential objectives of the Directive.

2   Indeed, complexity was even greater, for the Treaty of Amsterdam transferred a large part of the third 'pillar' to the first 'pillar', which was the part the UK (and Ireland and Denmark) were allowed to opt out of (though they might also opt in to bits of it later if they wished, and the UK, at least, has taken advantage of this possibility several times).

not others)[3]. It also integrated the third 'pillar' more closely to the first, giving the European Court of Justice a restricted role in relation to it. Thus, the term 'European Union law' is used by some commentators, and indeed, the European Union itself. However, for most purposes, it is only the law of the Community with which we are concerned, so the title 'Community law' is retained here.

'Community legislation' (as opposed to 'Community law') is not a term much used, no doubt because all the founding Member States were civil law states, in which precedent is, broadly speaking, not a source of law, so for whom 'legislation' and 'law' can be equated[4].

Community law and the European Convention on Human Rights

The European Convention on Human Rights ('ECHR') is fully considered in Chapters 3 and 4. However, here it should be noted that, although the ECHR and its institutions are separate from the European Union and its institutions (and the European Union is experimenting with its own 'fundamental rights'), the former may be enforceable through the latter.

In Case 11/70 *Internationale Handelsgesellschaft* [1970] ECR 1125, the European Court of Justice (not the European Court of Human Rights) held, in a creative decision, that respect for the fundamental freedoms enshrined in the ECHR was an integral part of the general principles of law which it had to uphold. In Case 4/73 *Nold* [1974] ECR 419, the Court went further and declared that international Treaties for the protection of human rights to which Member States were signatory could supply guidelines to be followed within the framework of Community law. A United Kingdom case, Case 63/83 *R v Kirk* [1984] ECR 2689, concerned penalties for illegal fishing. Regulation 170/83 appeared to permit a retrospective penalty, but the court interpreted the Regulation to exclude this, expressly by reference to Article 7 (non-retroactivity of criminal law) of the ECHR.

Therefore, Community law will be applied by the European Court of Justice subject to the ECHR. As such decisions are binding on the

---

3 While the Treaties refer to this as 'flexibility', 'enhanced co-operation' and 'closer co-operation', it is popularly termed 'variable geometry'. In any event, UK has the reputation for being one of the less co-operative Member States.

4 The creative role of the European Court of Justice means that, while it would be very unorthodox to refer to 'Community precedent', there is effectively Community law which is not legislation. This is discussed in Ch 12.

courts of Member States, Scots courts must loyally apply the same principle when deciding Community law cases.

Types of Community legislation and their forms

Four types of Community legislation can be said to exist: Treaties; Regulations; Directives; and Decisions. (In addition, other Community documents of no clear legal force are also issued.) The Decisions referred to are those of Commission or the Council (for which, see Chapter 3), not of the European Court of Justice ('ECJ'). The powers of the ECJ, which also develops Community law, are dealt with in Chapter 4. (Under the second 'pillar' created by the Treaty on European Union, the European Union may adopt 'common strategies', 'joint actions', 'common positions' and 'systematic co-operation', and under the third 'pillar', may adopt 'common decisions'; 'framework decisions' and 'decisions' and 'conventions', which may variously resemble Regulations, Directives and Decisions, but are not part of Community law, so are not considered here.)

Treaties

The Treaties, sometimes referred to as the Community's 'primary legislation', form its constitution (although some parts concern very detailed provisions of other sorts, for instance on customs duties). They have lengthy names, but are often referred to by abbreviations, such as 'the TEC'. The principal ones[5] are:

- the European Economic Community Treaty of 1957 (the EEC Treaty, once often referred to as the Treaty of Rome, but now, after many amendments, referred to as the EC Treaty or 'TEC');
- the Merger Treaty of 1965;
- the First Accession Treaty of 1972, and subsequent Accession Treaties;
- the Single European Act ('SEA') of 1986;
- the Treaty on European Union ('TEU', often referred to as 'the Maastricht Treaty') of 1992;

5   For the purpose and significance of these Treaties, see Ch 3. Other Treaties entered into by the Community (such as the Lomé Convention, with West African states), and possibly some entered into between Member States (such as the Convention on Jurisdiction and Enforcement of Judgments) are also relevant. Other agreements, such as the 'Luxembourg Accord', by which Member States promised informally not to exercise majority voting where one of them claims its vital national interests are involved, are not Treaties.

- the Treaty of Amsterdam ('ToA') of 1997; and
- the Treaty of Nice ('ToN') of 2000.

The original EEC Treaty was drawn up in the four languages of the original six Member States. More recent Treaties are drawn up in the official language of each Member State. Each version has to be equally authentic, which has caused problems where there are discrepancies.

The form of all the principal Treaties is broadly similar[6]. They start with a series of statements of purposes[7]. They may be divided into Parts, subdivided into 'Titles' and 'Chapters'[8], but the basic unit is the Article. Articles are usually numbered sequentially throughout, ignoring the parts, titles etc[9]. The Treaty of Amsterdam also renumbered the Articles of the principal Treaties, which means that commonly Articles are referred to by both pre- and post-Amsterdam numbers, as, for example, 'Article 18 (ex 8a)' or 'Article 234 (ex Article 177) (or 'Article 8a (now 18)' or 'Article 177 (now Article 234)')'[10]. To avoid confusion between Treaties, Articles may be referred to as, for example, 'Article 205 EC' or 'Article 205 (TEC)' to identify the Treaty in question.

The Articles may be brief or lengthy[11], and may be divided into paragraphs and sub-paragraphs. These in turn may be identified by

6 The structure of the TEU is more confusing than most, but this has been overtaken by the amendments in the ToA.

7 The TEC Preamble commences 'Determined to lay the foundations of an ever closer union among the peoples of Europe ... ', and the opening Articles specify the establishment of a common market, and a variety of specific policies to that and other ends, such as the elimination of customs duties, and the approximation of the laws of Member States

8 The TEC is divided into six numbered and named 'Parts', 'I – Principles', 'II – Citizenship of the Union' etc. Parts III and V are divided into 'Titles' (Part V into XXI Titles), several of which are divided into 'Chapters' (Part V, Title VII is divided into five Chapters), and some of those even further into 'Sections' (Part V, Title I, Chapter 1 is divided into five Sections).

9 The numbering of the TEU, however, had its Articles identified by letters ('Article A', 'Article B' etc, including 'K.1','K.2', etc, and even 'K.3(2)(c)'). This system is obsolete, having been replaced by numbers by the ToA (see below), but contemporary literature necessarily contains reference to the letter form.

10 Or in relation to TEU articles, for example, 'Article 33 (ex K.5)'. Indeed, some Articles have changed number more than once. The SEA introduced an Article 8a, renumbered by the TEU as Article 7a, renumbered again by the ToA as Article 14. The possibilities of confusion are thus great. Good Community law textbooks contain 'Tables of Equivalences' to permit correct identification.

11 The TEC has over 300 articles. One of the shortest, Article 281 (ex Article 210) reads 'The Community shall have legal personality'. One of the longest is Article 272 (ex Article 203) which extends over two pages.

number and letter in the United Kingdom fashion (for example, Article 39(3)(b) (ex Article 48(3)(b)) or otherwise (for example, Article 43 (ex Article 52) which has two paragraphs identified by neither number nor letter, while Article 40 (ex Article 49) has no numbered paragraphs, but four lettered ones expanding upon the first). This can make citation of specific passages difficult[12]. Commonly the Treaties also have numbered 'Annexes' and unnumbered 'Protocols'. These are essentially Schedules, containing material too detailed or too specific for the body of a Treaty, though they may reflect the fact that unanimity was not achieved on a matter, but the majority are going ahead anyway as between themselves[13].

As is common with Treaties generally, some Articles are simple exhortation. Others are specific enough to be applied by courts, and may therefore have 'direct effect' (for which, see below).

Article 249 (ex Article 189) specifically permits the Commission and the Council of Ministers, under various powers elsewhere in the Treaty, to make Regulations, Directives and Decisions, which are collectively referred to as 'acts', but sometimes colloquially as 'secondary legislation'. The difference between each type is significant for the legal effect they have in Member States, which is dealt with below.

Regulations

Regulations[14] are the principal means by which the Community legislates, and there are thousands made every year[15].

Regulations start with a title in a form exemplified in the following: 'COMMISSION REGULATION (EEC) No 417/85 of 19 December 1985 on the application of Article 85(3) of the Treaty to categories of specialization agreements'. There follows a preamble opening with the name of the initiating institution and closing with the formula indicating enactment, for example, 'THE COMMISSION OF THE EUROPEAN COMMUNITIES ... HAS

---

12   Thus, there may be circumlocutions such as 'point (1)(b) of the first sub-paragraph of Article 63'.
13   The TEC and TEU jointly have 36 Protocols, including specific material such as the Statute of the European Court of Justice (Sixth Protocol), but also others recording the special position of the United Kingdom, Ireland and Denmark who declined to accept certain aspects of freedom of movement of persons (Second to Fifth Protocols).
14   The name 'Regulation' is also given to one type of UK delegated legislation (for which, see Ch 9). The two should not be confused.
15   In 2006 there were over 2000 Regulations.

ADOPTED THIS REGULATION'. These two items are separated by a recital of the Treaty provisions giving authority for the Regulation to be made, the consultative procedure followed, and the reasoning which has produced the proposal, in a series of statements, possibly covering more than a page, and beginning 'Having regard to ... ' or 'Whereas ... '.

This lengthy preliminary exists because Article 253 (ex Article 190) requires legislative acts of the Community to state the reasons on which they are based and to refer to any proposals or opinions required by the relevant Treaty to be obtained. This in turn allows the European Court of Justice to review the validity of them[16].

The actual provisions of the regulation follow in numbered Articles, often grouped into 'sections' or 'titles', in much the same fashion as in the Treaties. The last Article usually declares the date on which the regulation comes into force, but if there is no declaration, then by virtue of Article 254 (ex Article 191) it comes into force on the twentieth day following publication in the *Official Journal*. Unless a Regulation stipulates that it is to cease having effect on a certain date, it continues in force until amended or repealed.

After the body of the text, a Regulation has the formula: 'This Regulation shall be binding in its entirety and directly applicable in all Member States', which reproduces part of Article 249 (ex Article 189), and indicates its 'direct effect'. Regulations terminate with a statement of the place and date of its making, and the name of the Commissioner responsible.

Directives

Directives are much less frequent than regulations[17], but no less important. They were originally intended to be policy statements delivered by Community institutions to a particular Member State government or to Member State governments generally. However, they may be drafted to leave little discretion to the Member State

---

16 Regulation (EC) 3595/85 concerned tariff preferences for developed countries. In Case 45/86 *Council v Commission* [1987] ECR 1493 (the 'Generalised Tariffs case'), the European Court of Justice annulled the Regulation because the recital was insufficiently concise, clear and relevant on the relevant issues of law and fact. Directive (EC) 86/113 concerned minimum sizes for battery hens' cages. Community officials altered the reasons recited after the Council of Ministers had approved it. The United Kingdom successfully challenged the validity of this Directive on this ground in Case 131/86 *United Kingdom v EC Council* [1988] 2 CMLR 364.

17 In 2006 there were 140.

and, as a result of creative adjudication by the European Court of Justice, the distinction between Regulations and Directives is now blurred.

The form of a Directive is much the same as that of a Regulation[18]. By virtue of Article 249 (ex Article 189), Directives take effect from the date of notification to Member States, but because they may require action on the part of Member States, a period for implementation, often two years, is allowed. Directives also finish with a different formula from Regulations, reflecting their different original purpose, as follows: 'This Directive is addressed to the Member States'.

Decisions

Decisions (that is, decisions of the Commission or the Council of Ministers, not of the European Court of Justice), of which there are hundreds made each year[19], were originally intended to be individualised executive decisions, addressed by Community institutions to Member States, companies or individuals. Most are of limited scope and importance, but some have laid down rules rather like Regulations so, as with Directives, the distinction between them and Regulations may be blurred.

The form of Decisions is essentially the same as Regulations. As with Directives, a Decision applies only to its addressees, and takes effect upon notification to them. They usually end with the words 'This Decision is addressed to ... ', followed by the words 'Member States', or a particular addressee or addressees, such as 'the Federal Republic of Germany and the United Kingdom'.

Other Community documents

The Commission and Council of Ministers may also, by virtue of Article 211 (ex Article 155), make 'Recommendations' and deliver 'Opinions', but Article 249 (ex Article 189) makes it clear these are not legislative.

---

18 For example, 'EIGHTH COUNCIL DIRECTIVE of 10 April 1984 based on article 54(3)(g) of the Treaty on the approval of persons responsible for carrying out the statutory audits of accounting documents (85/253/EEC)'. They are sometimes given more memorable colloquial names, such as 'the Equal Treatment Directive' (76/207).

19 In 2006 there were just over 1,000.

Some other types of document have exceptionally been held to be legislative when the European Court of Justice has sought to further Community aims at the expense of legal exactitude[20].

The content of such documents is sometimes referred to as 'soft law' which is a misleading term since they are not law at all.

THE COMMUNITY LEGISLATIVE PROCESSES

Legislative powers of the Community and the Community legislative process

Authority to make Community legislation, and the method of legislation, must be found in the Treaties. Some Articles of the Treaties give specific powers to the Commission and the Council of Ministers to legislate. For example, Article 94 (ex Article 100) allows the Council of Ministers, acting on a proposal from the European Commission (and in some cases consulting the European Parliament) to issue Directives to achieve approximation of laws of Member States.

Other Articles impose obligations without expressly giving the power to legislate. For example, Article 137 (ex Article 118) requires the Commission to promote co-operation in employment and other fields. However, the European Court of Justice has held that the obligation implies the power to legislate to fulfil that obligation[21].

In any case, where there is no clear power, Article 308 (ex Article 235) says that the Council of Ministers, acting according to a certain procedure, can legislate if it is necessary to attain one of the objectives of the Community. Given the breadth of the Treaty objectives and the breadth of the interpretation which they have been given, this power is very wide.

---

20 For example, a Resolution of the Council of Ministers in Case 22/70 *Commission v Council (the ERTA case)* [1971] ECR 263, [1971] CMLR 335. An interesting example is the United Kingdom 'Declaration' as to who are 'United Kingdom nationals' for the purpose of free movement of workers within the Community. This was appended to the United Kingdom Treaty of Accession. The definition, like the title, was different from any existing form of United Kingdom nationality. The declaration was amended in 1982 to take account of the British Nationality Act 1981 (see OJ C23, 28.1.1983: also Cmnd 9062). It is a unilateral declaration, and not a Treaty, nor a United Kingdom statute, nor had Parliamentary approval, nor was a decision of a court. However, the European Court of Justice accepted it in *R v Secretary of State for the Home Department, ex parte Manjit Kaur* [2001] ECR I–237.

21 Cases 218, 283–285/85 and 287/85 *Germany v Commission* [1988] CMLR 11.

The actual legislative process depends upon the Treaty provision giving the power to legislate, and varies with the type of legislation, but is always complicated.

Basic legislative procedure

In basic form, the idea for legislation comes from within the Commission. Its staff draft a proposal in consultation with interested parties, including Member States. As those drafting are not necessarily lawyers, and drafts are translated into all Community languages, the possibility of misunderstanding is high.

The proposal is sent to the Council of the Union, which passes it on to the European Parliament. The European Parliament remits the proposal to one of its committees for a report, which may contain suggested amendments, upon which the Parliament votes. Members of the Commission may appear in order to explain the proposal. The European Parliament's views are sent back to the Council, which passes them on to one of its working groups, co-ordinated by COREPER, comprising national civil servants who examine it in the light of individual national interests.

COREPER's aim is to produce a version acceptable to all. If this is achieved, the Council rubber stamps the proposal. If it is not, the Council seeks a compromise which is voted on (by a complicated weighted voting system), or refers the matter back to COREPER. Thus, the final version is that agreed by the Council, rather than that desired by the Commission, or that which the European Parliament would accept. Indeed, despite its name, the powers of the European Parliament are not great, and it is certainly not the Community legislature[22].

'Co-operation procedure'

The Single European Act introduced for certain purposes a yet more complicated 'co-operation procedure' (alias 'Article 252 (ex Article 189c) procedure')[23], which increases the power of the European Parliament to amend proposals. After the existing consultation procedure with the European Parliament (the 'first reading'), the Council produces a 'common position'. The Parliament may (in the 'second reading') accept this (by an absolute majority); it may reject

---

22 Where its opinion is required, failure to obtain it invalidates the legislation, however: Case 138/79 *SA Roquette Freres v Council* [1980] ECR 3333.

23 This unfortunately uses the terms 'first' and 'second reading', which have a very different technical meaning in UK legislative procedure.

it, in which case it can be adopted only by a unanimous vote of the Council; or it may (by an absolute majority), seek amendment which the Council (by a qualified majority) may accept or reject.

'Co-decision procedure'

The Treaty on European Union further increased the European Parliament's power through a more successful 'co-decision procedure' (alias 'Article 251 (ex Article 189b) procedure' and modified by the Treaty of Amsterdam) in some situations. In simplified form, it operates as follows: the Commission's proposal, after initial consultation, is submitted to the Council and the European Parliament simultaneously. If the Parliament (by an absolute majority) rejects it, the Council may convene a Conciliation Committee of equal numbers of representatives of Council and Parliament, assisted by the Commission, with a view to agreeing within six weeks a text acceptable to the Council (by a qualified majority) and to Parliament (by an absolute majority). If it fails, the proposal falls unless the Council adopts its original position, or as amended by the Parliament, within a further six weeks. However, the Parliament by an absolute majority may veto this within six months.

'Assent procedure'

The Single European Act also introduced a simple procedure which maximises the European Parliament's power, essentially by giving it a veto, which applies since the Treaty on European Union only to a narrow range of issues, such as those under Article 49 (ex Article O) on membership of the European Union.

Popular accountability

What is clear is that, despite the increased role of the European Parliament, the Community legislative process has little direct accountability to the electors of the Member States. It is an example of the Community's 'democratic deficit'.

The role of the European Court of Justice[24]

The European Court of Justice may hear an enforcement action brought by the Commission against a Member State appearing not

24 For the composition and powers of the European Court of Justice, see Chs 3 & 6.

to be fulfilling its Community obligations (for example, by failing to implement a Directive[25]). It may also hear a preliminary reference under Article 234 (ex Article 177) from a national court or tribunal with a view to ensuring consistent decisions on validity and interpretation throughout the Community and some other types of action.

The full importance of Article 234 (ex Article 177) depends upon the principle of 'direct' effect of Community law.

THE RELATIONSHIP BETWEEN COMMUNITY LAW TO NATIONAL SYSTEMS IN GENERAL, AND UNITED KINGDOM LAW IN PARTICULAR

The relationship between Community law and national systems in general[26]

The Treaties give remarkably little explicit guidance on the effect Community legislation is to have on Member States' own law.

Direct applicability, primacy and direct effect

Regulations are said in Article 249 (ex Article 189) to be 'binding' and 'directly applicable'. This was intended to mean that they should be incorporated into national law without national legislation, unlike Directives (which though 'binding upon Member States' were intended to be incorporated by way of national legislation), and also unlike Decisions (which are 'binding upon those to whom [they] are addressed').

However, certain ideas were implicit in the structure of Community law, and the European Court of Justice has ingeniously

---

25 For instance, Article 141 (ex Article 119) requires sexual equality in employment, and the Equal Pay Directive (Council Directive 75/117), furthering that policy, was made in 1976. The Commission considered that the Equal Pay Act 1970 did not fulfil the requirements of Community law, and successfully brought enforcement proceedings (Case 61/81 *Commission v United Kingdom* [1982] ECR 2601). As a result, the 1970 Act was amended by the Equal Pay (Amendment) Regulations 1983, SI 1983/1794. (These were UK delegated legislation regulations, not Community regulations.) However, the Commission considered that the UK legislation did not fulfil the requirements of the Equal Treatment Directive (76/207) either and brought further successful enforcement proceedings (Case 165/82 *Commission v United Kingdom* [1984] 1 CMLR 44). These resulted in the Sex Discrimination Act 1986.

26 It should be recalled that 'Community law' is possible only under the EC Treaty, within 'the Community' and not under the second and third 'pillars' of the European Union, despite the partial incorporation of the third 'pillar' into the 'first'.

built upon them in various decisions[27]. 'Primacy' is thus regarded as a basic principle, that is, that Community law is intended to supersede national law where the two conflict.

Further, Community legislation is intended, provided that certain conditions are fulfilled, to have 'direct effect'. This term does not appear in any of the Treaties, but is hallowed by usage. It means that individuals may bring and defend cases in court on the basis of legislation if it has that characteristic.

These ideas taken together involve that, at least in Community law terms:

(a) Community legislation can be law in every Member State;
(b) it may be so without the need for national legislation;
(c) it may therefore be so against the wishes of the national legislature;
(d) such Community legislation supersedes any existing contrary national law;
(e) the existence of such Community legislation prevents a national legislature from passing valid contrary legislation in future;
(f) Community legislation is applied by the ordinary courts and tribunals of the Member State;
(g) the ordinary courts of the Member State must apply such Community legislation even if there is contrary national law;
(h) such Community legislation may, under appropriate circumstances, be invoked before ordinary national courts by individuals and companies against other individuals and companies, and against Member States.

These conclusions can be exemplified by Case 26/62 *Van Gend en Loos* [1963] ECR 1. Community law, in the form of Article 25 (ex Article 12) obliged Member States not to raise existing customs duties. However, the Dutch government altered the law to raise them in respect of certain chemicals. Van Gend en Loos was a company which had to pay the higher rate. It therefore sued the Dutch government. On an Article 234 (ex Article 177) preliminary reference, the question of the relationship of national law (here Dutch) and Community law went to the European Court of Justice. It decided that Article 25 (ex Article 12), being clear and unconditional, had 'direct effect' and that the Treaty provision took precedence over Dutch law. Thus, the Dutch tax tribunal hearing the case had to ignore Dutch law, and apply Community law instead.

---

27 Chiefly Case 26/62 *Van Gend en Loos* [1963] ECR ; Case 6/64 *Costa v ENEL* [1964] ECR 585; Case 11/70 *Internationale Handelsgesellschaft* [1970] ECR 1125; and Case 106/77 *Simmenthal (No 2)* [1978] ECR 629.

In practice, national courts may apply Community law without the rigour the European Court of Justice would like. On the other hand, the Court has not yet exhausted its ingenuity, as *Francovich* and other decisions (discussed below) show.

Vertical and horizontal direct effect

Direct effect is complicated by a division into 'vertical' and 'horizontal', worked out by the European Court of Justice in relation to Directives.

Community law may place an obligation with direct effect upon a Member State. If it does, but the obligation is not fulfilled, a person or company which suffers as a result can sue the Member State. This (on the assumption that the Member State is 'above' the person or company) is described as 'vertical direct effect', and *Van Gend en Loos* is an example.

Community law may place an obligation with direct effect upon a person or company. If it does, but the obligation is not fulfilled, another person or company which suffers as a result can sue the first one. This is referred to as 'horizontal direct effect' (on the assumption that the individuals or companies are on the same level). An example is Case 43/75 *Defrenne v Sabena* [1976] ECR 455. Article 141 (ex Article 119) requires equal pay between the sexes. Defrenne was an air stewardess employed by Sabena, a Belgian airline. She discovered she was being paid less than the male stewards, so sued Sabena. On an Article 234 (ex Article 177) preliminary reference, the European Court of Justice held that Article 141 (ex Article 119) (as well as being vertically directly effective) was directly effective as between persons and companies (that is, horizontally directly effective).

Direct effect and different types of Community legislation

The conditions under which Community legislation has direct effect are not explicitly laid down in the Treaties (nor whether it be vertical, horizontal, or both), but must be inferred from the decisions of the European Court of Justice.

Broadly, there are two conditions necessary to create direct effect. Firstly, the legislation must be clearly and specifically enough drafted for a court to be able to apply it[28]. Secondly, it must create an

---

28 Thus, for example, in Case 126/86 *Gimenez Zaera* [1987] ECR 3697, Article 2 (which remains Article 2) was found to impose insufficiently precise obligations to create direct effect.

unqualified right or duty and not require action by some other body before a court can apply it.

Direct effect and the Treaties. The Treaties are binding upon the signatory Member States. However, certain articles of the Treaties also have direct effect. The *Van Gend en Loos* case decided that Article 25 (ex Article 12) had direct effect, although the EEC Treaty itself made no mention of its effect, and Article 25 (ex Article 12) itself certainly did not say that an aggrieved person could sue a Member State for breach of it. Where a Treaty Article has direct effect, it is likely to be both vertical and horizontal.

Direct effect and Regulations. Regulations were undoubtedly intended to have direct effect (at least if the conditions were fulfilled). Article 249 (ex Article 189) describes a Regulation as having 'general application' and 'being binding in its entirety and directly applicable in all Member States'. Occasionally, however, a Regulation is drafted in unspecific language, or requires action by another body before a court could apply it, so is not directly effective[29].

Direct effect and Directives. Directives are in a more complicated and uncertain position. Article 249 (ex Article 189) says they are 'binding as to the result to be achieved, upon each Member State to which [they] are addressed, but shall leave to the national authorities the choice of form and methods', and time for implementation (perhaps two years) is given. As this implies, originally they were not intended to be directly effective, for they apparently require action by some other body (the national authorities) before a court could apply them.

However, Member States have a poor record of compliance with them, and the European Court of Justice, in a number of major cases in the 1970s such as Case 41/74 *Van Duyn* [1974] ECR 1337[30], inven-

---

29 Case C–403/98 *Azienda Agricola Monte Arosu Srl v Regione Autonoma della Sardegna* [2001] ECR I–103.

30 Free movement of workers between member states is a fundamental principle of the Community, enshrined in Articles 39–41 (ex Articles 48–50), and given flesh by Regulations and Directives. Directive 64/221 allowed a member state to limit this free movement on grounds of public policy if the personal conduct of the individual warranted it. Van Duyn was a Dutch Scientologist. Scientology is a quasi-religious cult employing pseudo-scientific learning, invented by L Ron Hubbard, an American science-fiction writer. The Home Office wished to discourage Scientology without banning it, and refused van Duyn leave to enter. She sued the United Kingdom government to vindicate her right to free movement. The European Court of Justice (on an Article 234 (ex Article 177) preliminary reference) upheld her argument, declaring the Directive directly effective, and therefore nullifying any contrary UK law.

tively reinterpreted the law to give them direct effect in certain circumstances. Directives are now regarded as directly effective provided they are sufficiently clear and specific, require no specific action by another body, and their time limit for implementation has expired.

But because Directives are addressed to Member States, they have been held only vertically directly effective, and not horizontally. This was settled in Case 152/84 *Marshall v Southampton and South West Area Health Authority* [1986] ECR 723. Marshall was a dietician employed by the health authority. She was required to retire at the age of 62, although men were not required to do so until the age of 65. National legislation, the Sex Discrimination Act 1975 s 6(2), expressly permitted this discrimination. A Directive, the 'Equal Treatment Directive' (76/207), did not. The European Court of Justice, on an Article 234 (ex Article 177) preliminary reference, held the differential breached the Directive, and that where the employee was employed by a public body, she was employed by the Member State (to which the Directive was addressed). It was therefore in breach of Community law and could be sued. However, a private employer cannot breach a Directive, because it is addressed to, and therefore binding only upon, Member States[31]. Thus, in general terms, an individual or ordinary commercial company cannot be sued for breach of a Directive.

However, in Cases C–6/90 and C–9/90 *Francovich v Italy* [1991] ECR I–5357, the court was again inventive and decided that where a Member State has failed to implement a Directive, it may be liable to pay compensation to individuals harmed by non-implementation. Directive 80/987 required Member States to approximate laws guaranteeing the protection of employees' unpaid remuneration upon insolvency of the employer. The European Court of Justice held that the Directive was unspecific as to who was responsible for fulfilling the guarantees, therefore it was not directly effective. However, it also decided that the TEC, in particular Article 10 (ex Article 5)[32], made Member States liable for injury caused by their own infringements of Community law, provided that three conditions are fulfilled. They are: that the Directive gives rights to the individual;

---

31 A question remains as to what organisations are part of the Member State for this purpose. In Case C–188/89 *Foster v British Gas* [1991] QB 405, the European Court of Justice decided (and the House of Lords therefore held) that British Gas, when still nationalised, was so. The English Court of Appeal, applying the test laid down by the ECJ in *Doughty v Rolls-Royce plc* [1992] 1 CMLR 1045, CA, held that Rolls-Royce, when in form a commercial company, but wholly owned by the government, was not. What of universities?

32 'Member States shall take all appropriate measures, whether general or particular, to ensure fulfilment of the obligations arising out of this Treaty ...'.

that the content of those rights can be identified from the Directive; and that it was the non-implementation which caused the harm complained of. This reduces the importance of the vertical/horizontal distinction, and provides possible enforcement even where a Directive has no direct effect. Indeed, yet further cases have blurred the very distinction between 'vertical' and 'horizontal' direct effect.

In addition, in another line of cases including Case 14/83 *Von Colson & Kamann v Land Nordrhein-Westfalen* [1984] ECR 1891 ('Van Colson') and Case C–106/89 *Marleasing SA v La Comercial Internacionale de Alimentacion SA* [1990] ECR I–1435 ('*Marleasing*'), the European Court of Justice was developing another principle. This is that, because Directives were addressed to Member States, they were addressed to all organs of the Member State. Courts, as one such organ, should therefore decide cases 'in the light of directives', even if the Directives were unimplemented. This is sometimes called 'indirect effect' because it falls between having direct effect and not having direct effect.

Direct effect and decisions. Decisions were originally intended to be essentially executive decisions. Article 249 (ex Article 189) declares a Decision to be 'binding in its entirety upon those to whom it is addressed'. Nevertheless, in Case 9/70 *Grad v Finanzamt Traunstein* [1970] ECR 825, the European Court of Justice declared a Decision directly effective. The position of Decisions is probably the same as that of Directives.

The relationship between Community legislation and United Kingdom law in particular

The issues in the relationship of Community legislation and national systems described above operate in relation to all Member States. Their operation raises particular questions in the case of the United Kingdom, however. These are described below, save for the way in which statutory interpretation is affected, which is dealt with in Chapter 11.

Community legislation with direct effect and United Kingdom law

Community law did not become directly effective (let alone achieve primacy) in the United Kingdom as a result of the United Kingdom joining the Community by signing the Treaty of Accession in 1972. In United Kingdom law, Treaties have no effect in national law[33]. Legislation was required to change it.

33 *The Parlement Belge* (1879) 4 PD 129; *Attorney-General for Canada v Attorney-General for Ontario* [1937] AC 326; *British Airways v Laker Airways* [1984] 3 All ER 39. For the special position of the European Convention on Human Rights, see Chs 3 & 7.

That legislation was supplied by the European Communities Act 1972 (now as amended). The most important provision is s 2(1), which is unfortunately drafted in turgid and dense language. The gist of it is, however, clear. It provides that all directly effective Community legislation (whether already made or to be made, and whether in Treaty, Regulation, Directive or Decision form), creates 'enforceable Community rights', that is, it has direct effect in the United Kingdom, and will be enforced by courts and tribunals, and that United Kingdom law is to be applied subject to it. Devolution to Scotland and elsewhere has made no difference to this.

These central provisions are supported by s 3(1) and (2). These provide firstly that judges are to be presumed to know the content and significance of the Treaties, of the *Official Journal of the European Union*[34] (in which the other legislation is published), and of decisions of the European Court of Justice. Secondly, they provide that questions of the validity and interpretation of Community law, if not actually sent to the European Court of Justice for an Article 234 (ex Article 177) preliminary reference, must be decided in accordance with the decisions of the court and the principles laid down by it.

In a long series of cases over the following years United Kingdom courts, chiefly the English Court of Appeal, struggled to take on board the full implications of the legislation[35].

Full acceptance of the implications of s 2(1) of the European Communities Act 1972 seems to be shown in the *Factortame* cases[36]. These cases concerned 'quota-hopping' under the Community's fisheries policy. Spanish vessels were registered in the United Kingdom to enable them to fish the United Kingdom national quota. Parliament passed legislation introduced by the government (the Merchant Shipping Act 1988) which, together with delegated legislation under it (the Merchant Shipping (Registration of Fishing Vessels) Regulations 1988, SI 1988/1926), imposed a nationality condition upon registration. The Spanish companies adversely

---

34 Previously *Official Journal of the European Community*.
35 See, for example, *Bulmer (HP) Ltd v Bollinger (J) SA* [1974] Ch 401; *Schorsch Meier GmbH v Hennin* [1975] QB 416; *Felixstowe Docks v BT Docks Board* [1976] 2 CMLR 655; *Shields v E Coomes (Holdings) Ltd* [1979] 1 All ER 456; *Macarthys v Smith* [1979] ICR 785. The various postures of Lord Denning (who as Master of the Rolls, president of the Court of Appeal, had a pivotal role) are interesting.
36 *R v Secretary of State for Transport, ex parte Factortame* [1990] 2 AC 85 (HL); Case 213/89 *R v Secretary of State for Transport, ex parte Factortame (No 2)* [1991] 1 AC 603 (ECJ); Case C- 48/93 *R v Secretary of State, ex parte Factortame (No 4)* joined with *Brasserie du Pêcheur SA v Federal Republic of Germany* [1996] QB 404 (ECJ); and *R v Secretary of State for Transport, ex parte Factortame (No 5)* [2000] 1 AC 524 (HL).

affected sued the United Kingdom government for breach of Articles 12 (ex Article 6: non-discrimination on grounds of nationality) and 48 (ex Article 58: right to establish a business) of the EEC Treaty. Proceedings were lengthy and complicated, involving two preliminary references under Article 234 (ex Article 177), and appeals as far as the Appellate Committee of the House of Lords. There were also separate enforcement proceedings by the Commission[37].

The outcome, however, was that the House of Lords accepted that an Act of Parliament contradicting, and passed after, certain Community legislation, could not be enforced by United Kingdom courts. Moreover, because Community law had to be enforced, courts were entitled to issue orders carrying it out, even though national law gave no such right. This was revolutionary in that it appears to have abandoned the principle of parliamentary supremacy. Nevertheless, if Parliament decided to withdraw the United Kingdom from the EC, or explicitly and clearly passed legislation in defiance of Community law, the judges would probably still apply Parliament's expressed will in preference to Community law.

Article 234 (ex Article 177) references. United Kingdom courts have the same power and obligation as courts in any Member State to refer questions of the validity or interpretation of Community law to the European Court of Justice under Article 234 (ex Article 177), and reference is usually discretionary. Scottish devolution has made no difference to this. When the choice exists, there is no clear authority from any United Kingdom court on when it is appropriate to refer. In an English case on Great Britain legislation, *Garland v British Rail Engineering Ltd* [1983] 2 AC 751, the Appellate Committee of the House of Lords suggested there should be reference where a novel point of law arose, or where there is no constant series of decisions from the European Court of Justice.

There have been few references from Scotland. In *Walkingshaw v Marshall* 1992 SLT 1167, concerning illegal fishing, the High Court of Justiciary, on appeal from the sheriff court, made a reference. In *Westwater v Thomson* 1992 SCCR 624, also concerning illegal fishing, the High Court of Justiciary held that the point at issue was too plain to require a reference to the European Court of Justice. In *Brown v Rentokil Ltd* 1996 SLT 839 a previous decision of the court made a reference unnecessary.

---

37 Case C–246/89 *Commission v UK* [1991] ECR I–4585).

Community legislation without direct effect and United Kingdom law

Not all Community legislation has direct effect, but it is nevertheless intended to apply within all Member States. Directives, for example, are intended to be implemented by the Member State (although they may acquire direct effect if they are not).

Implementation may be by Act of the United Kingdom Parliament or of the Scottish Parliament. For instance, the Consumer Protection Act 1987 implements Directive 85/347, the Products Liability Directive. However, the European Communities Act 1972 (as amended), in addition to providing that direct effect should operate in the United Kingdom, also provides in s 2(2) a short-cut method of implementation of legislation which does not have direct effect. The provision is almost as difficult to understand as s 2(1). However, again, the gist is clear, for s 2(2) delegated from the United Kingdom Parliament to the United Kingdom government the power to implement any Community right or obligation by delegated legislation[38]. Thus, the United Kingdom government can implement a Directive without an Act of Parliament and the statutory instrument is the 'form and method' chosen to implement the Directive. This power has been widely used. An example is the Equal Pay (Amendment) Regulations 1983, SI 1983/1794, which were designed to amend the Equal Pay Act 1970 to conform to the Equal Pay Directive 75/117, after the enforcement proceedings in Case 61/81 *Commission v United Kingdom* [1982] ICR 578.

The restrictions upon the use of s 2(2), found in s 2(4) and Sch 2, are that the power may not be used to: impose or increase taxation; make retrospective legislation; allow further delegation (unless for the making of procedural rules for courts and tribunals); or create criminal offences carrying greater than a certain penalty. Thus, any Directive requiring any of these things to be done would necessitate an Act.

The Scotland Act 1998, by s 53, transfers to the Scottish Ministers functions in relation to observing and implementing obligations under Community law, with respect to devolved functions. However, there is a reserve power in s 57(1) enabling ministers of the United Kingdom government to exercise these functions too, presumably to avoid the possibility that a failure of the Scottish Ministers to act would put the United Kingdom in breach of its Community obligations.

---

38 Commonly by Statutory Instrument (for the meaning and significance of which see, see Ch 9), but also through the Legislative and Regulatory Reform Act 2006 (for which see Ch 9).

Direct effect, parliamentary supremacy and the role of the United Kingdom Parliament

The primacy and direct effect of Community legislation appear irreconcilable with the parliamentary supremacy traditionally professed by the United Kingdom Parliament. (No such problem arises with the Scottish Parliament which does not profess parliamentary supremacy.) In Community law terms the United Kingdom Parliament irrevocably gave up parliamentary supremacy in the 1972 Act (if not by signing the Treaty of Accession), and the United Kingdom judges' reaction in the *Factortame* cases appears to acknowledge that fact. In United Kingdom constitutional terms it is less clear for, despite *Factortame*, there can be little doubt that the United Kingdom judges would give effect to conscious and explicit repeal of the European Communities Act 1972, and thus to the removal of direct effect, whatever the Community law position.

In respect of legislation with direct effect, neither the United Kingdom Parliament nor the Scottish Parliament has in formal terms any role, for all national legislatures are bypassed in such cases, and Community institutions do not necessarily, or as a matter of course, even keep them informed.

In respect of legislation without direct effect, the United Kingdom Parliament and, in relation to devolved (ie non-reserved) functions, the Scottish Parliament, have roles in that either a statute or a piece of subordinate legislation may be required to implement the obligation under the European Communities Act 1972. However, 'executive dominance of the legislature' means that the government or executive can normally get through the legislation it wants.

There are two committees of the United Kingdom Parliament directly concerned with Community matters. Both produce reports prolifically. The House of Commons European Scrutiny Committee[39] looks at Community documents (including legislation and legislative proposals), seeks to monitor the activities of United Kingdom ministers in the Council of the Union, and keeps EU developments under review generally. It can form sub-committees, take evidence, and it has a number of expert advisers. It can recommend a proposal be debated on the grounds of its legal or political significance, in which case it normally will be, and the government will not normally assent to the proposal in the Council of the Union until it has been. However, while the Committee produces reports

---

39 Formerly called the House of Commons Select Committee on European Legislation.

on a wide variety of subjects (such as the mobile phone 'roaming' costs, fisheries 'by-catches' and discards, and the transfer of sentenced persons[40]) and generates discussion, it is not clear that it makes much difference, given the quantity of documents and the secrecy of Commission and Council proceedings, the fact that its views are not part of the input into Community legislation, and related reasons.

The House of Lords Select Committee on the European Union[41] has broader terms of reference, and is more powerful. It has half a dozen sub-committees examining different aspects of the EU[42]. Its reports (on, for example, missing trader fraud, European foreign policy and improving the mental health of the population[43]) are useful and robust, but again are not part of the formal input into Community legislation.

Other Committees may consider such questions as they arise during consideration of other matters.

In respect of Community legislation, the United Kingdom Parliament is thus primarily in the position of a well-informed pressure group upon the United Kingdom government and European Commission.

The Scottish Parliament has a European and External Relations Committee[44]. Its terms of reference are: to consider and report on proposals for European Community legislation, the implementation of such legislation, and any other European Union issue (as well as questions of other links the Scottish Administration has with other countries and territories). It has produced reports such as those on the scrutiny of Community legislation, the European Commission's Green Paper on a maritime policy, and the European Commission's strategy for growth and jobs[45]. It also produces 'Europe Matters', an electronic newsletter available on its website[46].

---

40 See www.parliament.uk/parliamentary_committees/european_scrutiny.cfm. By mid-2007, it had produced 23 Reports in that year alone.

41 Formerly called the House of Lords Select Committee on the European Communities.

42 These change from time to time, but in mid-2007 were on: Economic and Financial Affairs and International Trade; the Internal Market; Environment and Agriculture; Law and Institutions; Home Affairs; and Social Policy and Consumer Affairs.

43 See www.parliament.uk/parliamentary_committees/lords_eu_select_committee.cfm. By mid-2007, it had produced 21 Reports in that year alone.

44 Lack of a Scottish dimension in UK representation in the European Union institutions has been a source of complaint in the Scottish Executive and Parliament.

45 www.scottish.parliament.uk/s3/committees/europe/index.htm.

46 www.scottish.parliament.uk/business/committees/europe/news/news04-07.pdf.

PUBLICATION AND CITATION OF COMMUNITY LAW

Publication and citation of Community legislation in general

The Community publishes the *Official Journal of the European Union*[47]. Certain legislative material must be published in it, and it is the main means of publishing all official information. The *Official Journal* appears in three parallel series.

The first of these series is the 'L' (for 'Legislation') series, and itself now[48] contains up to four sections, that is: 'Acts adopted under the EC Treaty/Euratom Treaty whose [*sic*] publication is obligatory'[49] (for material required to be promulgated through the *Official Journal*); 'Acts adopted under the EC Treaty/Euratom Treaty whose [*sic*] publication is not obligatory'[50]; 'Acts adopted under the EU Treaty'; and, occasionally, 'Other Acts'.

The second of these series is the 'C' (for 'Communication') series, and contains, among other things, Council of the Union and Merger Decisions, Court of Auditors reports, and European Court of Justice and Court of First Instance judgments[51]. The C series has an electronic section called the 'C E' series which contains documents only published electronically, and which contains European Parliament minutes and resolutions, and Council of the Union 'Common Positions'.

The third of these series is the 'S' (for 'Supplement') series, which contains tenders and awards for public works and supply contracts. Debates of the European Parliament are published as an Annex to the *Official Journal* up to May 1999, after which they appear online and on CD-ROM (see below).

The *Official Journal* is officially distributed, on subscription, by EUR-OP, the Office for Official Publications of the European Communities in Luxembourg[52]. The *Official Journal* 'L' and 'C' series appear daily on paper in numbered issues, and are also available on a hybrid CD-ROM/Internet version monthly, with an annual cumulative version from 1999. There is a hard copy monthly and annual (cumulative) alphabetical and methodological index published in arrears. It is accompanied by a twice-yearly, two-

---

47 Formerly *Official Journal of the European Communities*.
48 There was a simpler subdivision in the past.
49 Formerly 'Acts whose publication is obligatory'.
50 Formerly 'Acts whose publication is not obligatory'
51 Until September 2006 it also contained European Parliament minutes and resolutions.
52 See http://publications.europa.eu.

volume, *Directory of European Community Legislation in Force*. The monthly and annual index, and the *Directory*, are included in the subscription to the *Official Journal*. The 'S' series is available in a twice-weekly CD-ROM format, or online on the TED (Tenders Electronic Daily) database[53] and no longer on paper.

Single copies of the *Official Journal* can be purchased from The Stationery Office ('TSO'), the United Kingdom government's publishing agency. Two multi-volume 'Special Edition' series of the *Official Journal* (one for 'Acts whose publication is obligatory', one for the rest) were produced upon United Kingdom accession, containing an authentic English language text of the legislation then in force. Much of this is still in force.

However, Community legislation and related documents are readily available online through EUR-lex[54]. EUR-lex gives access to draft legislative texts from the Prelex[55] and OEIL[56] databases, which help track the legislative progress of proposals. (The legislative sites of most Member States[57] are also accessible through another database, N-lex[58]).

An item in the *Official Journal* 'L' series is conventionally cited in the following form: 'OJ L180, 13.7.90, p 26', (or occasionally [1990] OJ L180, 13.7.90) that is, 'the item on page 26 of the 180th issue of the L series, which was published on 13 July 1990'. This is in fact the citation of a directive on the rights of workers exercising their rights of free movement within the Community. The 'C' series is commonly referred to by a different convention, for example 'OJ C80/1, 10.3.01', that is, series/issue/page/date (or even the more ambiguous '01/C 80/01', that is, year/series/issue/page number). This is the Treaty of Nice. Citations of items in the Special Edition include the abbreviation 'S Edn'.

The *Official Journal* and commercial derivatives, can be found in any of the 44 European Documentation Centres in universities throughout the United Kingdom, or in the European Information Points in the Public Information Relays (PIRs) within public libraries.

---

53 See http://ted.europa.eu.
54 See http://eur-lex.europa.eu/en/index.htm.
55 See http://ec.europa.eu/prelex/apcnet.cfm?CL=en.
56 See http://www.europarl.europa.eu/oeil .
57 Ie Austria, Belgium, Czech Republic, Denmark, Finland, Germany, Estonia, Greece, France, Ireland, Italy, Italy, Lithuania, Luxembourg, Malta, Netherlands, Poland, Portugal, Slovakia, Slovenia, Spain, Sweden & the UK.
58 See http://n-lex.europa.eu ('opened as an experimental site on 28 April 2006').

Publication and citation of Treaties

Treaties often bear a long official title, but an abbreviated form is usually used[59]. References to the EC Treaty ('TEC') are commonly given in the form 'Article 234 EC'. Because of the numbering of articles in the TEC and TEU effected by the Treaty of Amsterdam, the form is now commonly 'Article 234 (ex Article 177)'.

Community publication

The Treaties are published by the Community. New Treaties are published in the *Official Journal* 'C' series. Consolidated versions of the TEC and TEU, incorporating amendments to date, are also published in the 'C' series[60], and on the official Community website, EUR-lex[61]. Treaties are also likely to be published as a separate document by EUR-OP[62].

EUR-OP has also published several compilations. These include *Treaties Establishing the European Communities: Treaties Amending These Treaties: Documents Concerning Accession*, which is up to date to 1 July 1978 only, and *Treaties Establishing the European Communities, Single European Act, Other Basic Instruments: Abridged Edition*, up to date to 1 July 1987 'for reference purposes only and ... not binding upon the Community institutions'. Following the Treaty on European Union (the 'Maastricht Treaty') the European Community published a small volume of 'Selected Instruments taken from the Treaties [Book 1 Volume 1] in 1993. A new two-volume edition was published in 1995 to incorporate the provisions relating to the accession of Austria, Finland and Sweden. This was updated to January 1999 following the Treaty of Amsterdam. These compilations are also not legally binding, and are for reference only. EUR-OP also publishes the Collection of Agreements Concluded by the European Communities.

---

59 For example, the Treaty Establishing the European Economic Community (Rome, 25 March 1957) is usually referred to as the 'EEC Treaty', and by some as the 'Treaty of Rome'. It is now amended to become the Treaty Establishing the European Community, which is usually referred to as the 'EC Treaty' or 'TEC'.
60 OJ C325/E/1 (*et seq*), 29/02/06.
61 See http://eur-lex.europa.eu/en/index.htm.
62 For example, the Treaty on European Union (the 'Maastricht Treaty') was so published in 1992.

United Kingdom official publication

The United Kingdom government, through TSO, publishes the Treaties as Command Papers[63]. These include, for example, the *Treaty concerning the Accession of ... the United Kingdom ... to the European Economic Community* (Brussels, 22 January 1972; Cmnd 7460–7463, 1979) (UKTS Nos 15–18). It also produced *European Communities Treaties and Related Documents* in ten volumes up to date to 1972. Although reliable, these are not authoritative in Community law terms and are outdated.

United Kingdom commercial publication

Some commercial publishers produce compilations of the Treaties, which, although not authoritative, are in practice more useful, as they may be consolidated and annotated (that is, showing the current version, as amended, and comment). These include the multi-volume loose-leaf and CD-ROM *European Union Law Library* (Sweet & Maxwell), which contains the Treaties and many associated documents. Foster *Blackstone's EU Treaties and Legislation* (Oxford UP, 18th edn, 2007) also gives the texts up to date of publication. Texts of relevant parts of the Treaties may be found in encyclopaedias and textbooks on subjects with a significant Community law dimension[64] and extracts in 'cases and materials' books, such as Craig and de Búrca *EU Law: texts, cases and materials* (Oxford University Press, 3rd edn, 2003).

There are also several online subscription services such as Westlaw.

---

63 Command Papers are formal government policy documents and the like, produced 'by Command of Her Majesty'. They are numbered up to 9,999, so new series are commenced every few years. Different series are distinguished by preceding initials. Currently these are 'Cm'; for the previous series they were 'Cmnd'; before that 'Cmd'. Some sets of Command Papers are published or republished in subordinate series, such as the United Kingdom Treaty Series (UKTS).

64 For example, *Butterworths Immigration Law Service,* a looseleaf encyclopaedia on immigration law, contains Community legislation relevant to the subject, and is continuously updated. Macdonald and Webber (eds) *Macdonald's Immigration Law and Practice* (6th edn, 2005), a textbook, contains similar material, updated to the date of publication.

Publication and citation of Regulations, Directives and Decisions – 'secondary legislation'

Community publication

Regulations bear a title, but are usually cited in the following form: 'Council Regulation 1251/70/EEC', or simply 'Regulation 1251/70/EEC'[65], which refers to the 1,251st Regulation of 1970, initiated by the Council of Ministers of the EEC (now 'Council of the Union'). It is useful to cite them by the Official Journal reference as well (in this case 'OJ L124, 30.6.70, p 24 (S Edn 1970 (II), p 402)').

Directives and Decisions also bear little-used titles and are cited with the abbreviated year preceding the sequential number, for example 'Council Directive 90/364/EEC (OJ L180, 13.7.90, p26)'. Because the series are now published in separate sequences, with the same 'year/number' citation, the simple form '90/364' is ambiguous, making the correct *Official Journal* citation vital. Directives are sometimes given semi-official names, such as 'First Directive on Company Law Harmonisation' (Cl Dir 68/151/EEC); popular names, such as 'the Equal Pay Directive' (Cl Dir 75/117/EEC); or at least abbreviated names, for example 'the Directive on Animal Semen' (Cl Dir 87/328/EEC). Commonly, however, indication of the initiating body is dropped, as in 'Dir 64/221' (which contains the 'public policy proviso' exception to the free movement of workers), giving no hint that it was initiated by the Council.

Regulations must be published in the *Official Journal*, as 'Acts adopted under the EC Treaty/Euratom Treaty whose publication is obligatory'. Although Article 253 (ex Article 191) EC only requires Directives and Decisions to be notified to their addressees, in practice they appear in the section 'Acts adopted under the EC Treaty/Euratom Treaty whose publication is not obligatory', so are available generally. Up-to-date texts, containing amendments and excluding repeals, are not officially produced, unless there is consolidating legislation, but the EUR-OP *Directory of European Community Legislation in Force* also provides the means of updating.

Again, however, secondary legislation is readily found online through EUR-lex (see above).

United Kingdom official publication

HMSO (predecessor to TSO) produced *Secondary Legislation of the European Communities: Subject Edition*, a multi-volume version of the

---

65 The form '1251/70' is too ambiguous and unhelpful.

texts, digested into subject headings, but this has not been updated since 1979, so is of very limited value.

United Kingdom commercial publication

Commercial publications are therefore, as with the Treaties, in practice the most useful compilations. These include the multi-volume loose-leaf *Encyclopaedia of European Community Law* (Sweet & Maxwell) which contains most Community legislation, gives annotations and is continually updated, and works such as Foster *Blackstone's EU Treaties and Legislation* (Oxford UP, 18th edn, 2007) and Rudden and Wyatt *Basic Community Laws* (9th edn, 2004). Also, as in the case of the Treaties, encyclopaedias and textbooks on subjects with a significant Community law dimension may contain texts of relevant Regulations etc, as may 'cases and materials' books.

The online subscription services such as Westlaw also contain the secondary legislation.

Publication and citation of other related materials published by the Community

The Community also publishes an enormous quantity of information relating to its legislative and other activities. This includes the annual *General Report on the Activities of the Union* and monthly *Bulletin of the European Union*. The latter (published on-line only since 2006) contains an account of current proposals and other material. The 'COM' series of Commission documents includes proposals and discussion papers from the European Commission on EUR-lex, and there are very many regular and *ad hoc* publications. The European Parliament also published its Working Documents on paper form to 1990 and on microfiche to 1997, since when they can be found only online.

7. Legislation – United Kingdom Parliamentary Legislation (including the Human Rights Act 1998)

THE INSTITUTIONAL BACKGROUND

The institutional background of United Kingdom Government and Parliament (and of the Council of Europe and the European Convention on Human Rights) were dealt with in Chapter 3. This Chapter deals with the nature and style of United Kingdom legislation (including the Human Rights Act 1998), the United Kingdom Parliament legislative process, and the publication and citation of United Kingdom legislation.

THE NATURE AND STYLE OF UNITED KINGDOM PARLIAMENTARY LEGISLATION (INCLUDING HUMAN RIGHTS LEGISLATION)

Parliamentary legislation, human rights, Community law and devolution

Acts of Parliament, often referred to as 'statutes', are usually regarded as the normal form of legislation in the United Kingdom[1]. The United Kingdom is a state, and does not exist in order to fulfil certain specified policies but, rather, to run its territory and population in all their complexity. Thus, Acts of Parliament range over many subjects and touch on almost every aspect of life. On the other hand, such Acts rarely deal in fundamental principle, for the underlying principles of the legal system are found in the common law[2]. The lack of a written constitution underlines the point. Legislation is thus

---

1   In terms of sheer quantity, however, delegated legislation is much greater: see Chs 9 & 10 below.
2   For which, see Chs 4 & 12.

principally a means of changing the law, and of stating new law in detail, and such changes and detail may vary widely and rapidly with changing political priorities of different governments. As noted in Chapters 3 and 6, traditionally, there has been argued to be 'parliamentary supremacy', that is, that there are no legal boundaries to Parliament's legislative power, only boundaries created by the political prudence and the morality of its members[3]. In law, it may pass any Act to any effect. In practice, the position is more complicated.

Firstly, 'parliamentary supremacy' means that the United Kingdom Parliament may legislate on 'human rights' issues, and it has. However, 'human rights' has come to be seen as a means of limiting the ability of legislatures to enact laws, thus at least touching upon parliamentary supremacy (as well as limiting the ability of government to take decisions). The European Convention on Human Rights (ECHR) is thus such a limit, indeed is one of the two principal sources of such limits in the United Kingdom context. The nature of the ECHR and its institutions are discussed in Chapter 3, and the relationship between the ECHR, the Human Rights Act 1998 and Acts of Parliament sketched in Chapter 4, but is considered in detail below. It should be recalled that the Human Rights Act 1998 may limit, but certainly in fact preserves, parliamentary supremacy.

Secondly, 'parliamentary supremacy' means that the United Kingdom Parliament may legislate on matters within the remit of the European Union (including the European Community). However, the idea of the 'direct effect' of Community law is specifically designed to limit the powers of the legislatures of Member States on matters within the Community competences, and thus, in the United Kingdom case, to limit parliamentary supremacy in those areas. It should be noted that, unlike any state, the European Community exists for relatively specific (albeit evolving) purposes. The Treaties therefore include statements of underlying principles and relatively constant (if also evolving) policies. On the other hand, such relative constancy is in part because Community institutions are much less answerable to any electorate. Also, because it exists for relatively specific purposes, the range of Community legislation is narrower than that of parliamentary legislation. The nature of the European Community and its institutions was also discussed in Chapter 3, its relationship with Acts of Parliament sketched in Chapter 5, but is considered in detail in Chapter 6 (including how far parliamentary supremacy is compromised).

---

3   The Legislative and Regulatory Reform Act 2006, discussed in Chapter 9, shows the breadth of this power in a paradoxical fashion.

Thirdly, the introduction of devolution means that the devolved legislatures are taking over responsibilities within their competences, and thus removing from the United Kingdom the need to legislate on those matters, though not the right to do so[4]. Thus, in relation to Scotland, Acts of the Scottish Parliament are gradually taking over the role of normal legislation in those areas not reserved to Westminster (although in the first years of devolution a remarkably large proportion of legislation applying to Scotland has continued to be made at Westminster). The nature of devolution and its institutions was also discussed in Chapter 3, with the relationship with Acts of Parliament again sketched in Chapter 5, and they will be considered in detail in Chapter 8 (including that parliamentary supremacy is clearly preserved).

United Kingdom Acts of Parliament, their types and form

Most statutes are technically 'public, general' statutes, and discussion in this chapter relates exclusively to such statutes unless otherwise stated. 'Local', 'personal', 'private' and 'hybrid' legislation (which are not 'public, general') and particular types of public general Acts are discussed below as 'Special cases'.

There are on average some 50 Acts of Parliament passed in a year[5]. Many Acts repeal or amend existing legislation, so the annual increase is not as great as this rate of production suggests. Acts also vary enormously in length. Effectively, the shortest possible is two sections. Recent examples include the Census (Amendment) (Scotland) Act 2001, the Criminal Defence Service (Advice and Assistance) Act 2001 and the Civil Defence (Grants) Act 2002. There is no theoretical maximum, and many have hundreds of sections, for example the Enterprise Act 2001 with 281 sections, the Capital Allowances Act 2001 with 581 sections, though by far the longest so far is the Income and Corporation Taxes Act 1988, which approaches 1,500 sections (though, as a Consolidating statute – for the meaning of which, see below – it is not typical). The average length of statutes is increasing.

Statutes also vary enormously in age. The great majority of Acts in force are relatively modern, but there are still many older ones, and even a few dating from the Parliaments of Scotland and England,

---

4   The United Kingdom Parliament may, of course, continue to legislate in devolved areas if it chooses: Scotland Act 1998, s 28(7).
5   In 1997 there were 69 and in 2001 only 25. These represent the extremes in recent years.

which ceased to exist in 1707[6], and the Parliament of Great Britain which lasted from 1707 to 1801.

There is a conventional structure to a modern UK Act of Parliament, described in the following paragraphs[7].

Short Title, Chapter Number and Arrangement of Sections

United Kingdom Acts commence with a 'Short Title', for example the 'Scotland Act 1998'. The Short Title is a 19th-century invention, but all earlier statutes still in force have been given them retrospectively by the Short Titles Act 1896 and the Statute Law Revision (Scotland) Act 1964. It is the relatively brief name almost invariably used to identify the Act. Short Titles include the year of enactment, which may be important as Acts of similar Short Title may be passed in different years and may be in force at the same time[8]. (Nevertheless, when there can be no doubt which Act is being referred to, a form such as 'the 1971 Act' is common, and an example of this usage is noted below in relation to Marginal Notes). However, sometimes, when a series of related Acts exists, the last may give a collective title, for example the 'Official Secrets Acts 1911–89'[9] or simply 'the Immigration Acts'[10].

On the other hand, reflecting the *ad hoc* nature of legislation in a common law or mixed system, Acts on similar topics may have dissimilar names, for example, those concerned with statute

---

6 See below in relation to Acts of the original, pre-1707, Parliament of Scotland.

7 The Human Rights Act 1998, s 19, requires a minister introducing a Bill into Parliament to state whether or not it conforms to the requirements of that Act (for which, see below). However, there is no requirement that this statement, or an amended form of it, appear on the face of the Act.

8 For example, the British Nationality Acts of 1948, 1958, 1964, 1964 (No 2) and 1965 were all in force at the same time, and required reference to the British Nationality and Status of Aliens Act 1914 (itself amended by similarly entitled Acts in 1918, 1922, 1933 and 1943, which were all in force at the same time, too). All were repealed by the British Nationality Act 1981 (itself now amended, though by, *int al*, the British Nationality (Falkland Islands) Act 1983, the British Nationality (Hong Kong) Act 1997, and the Immigration, Asylum and Nationality Act 2006.

9 See Official Secrets Act 1989, s 16(2).

10 *Ie* the Immigration Act 1971, Immigration Act 1988, Asylum and Immigration Appeals Acts 1993, Asylum and Immigration Act 1996, Immigration and Asylum Act 1999, Nationality, Immigration and Asylum Act 2002 and Asylum and Immigration (Treatment of Claimants, etc) Act, 2004 and Immigration, Asylum and Nationality Act 2006 (but not the Special Immigration Appeals Commission Act 1997): see Immigration, Asylum and Nationality Act 2006, s 64(2).

law[11]. Short Titles often incorporate brackets, and almost all pre-devolution Acts applying only to Scotland are indicated in this way[12], though there are exceptions[13]. Other common uses of brackets are '(Amendment)', and '(Miscellaneous Provisions)'. An Act's Short Title is officially given to it by a Short Title provision (for which, see below) in a section towards the end of the Act (often in the 'Supplementary' or 'Miscellaneous and Supplemental' sections, for which, see below).

As well as a Short Title, Acts of the United Kingdom Parliament have a 'chapter number' which denotes the sequential number of that Act in the year. They are rendered variously as, for example, 'chapter 15', 'chap 15' 'ch 15' or 'cap 15'[14]. Taken with the year of enactment, it provides a unique reference number of that Act, known as the 'citation'. Thus, the citation '1998 c46' refers uniquely to the Scotland Act 1998[15].

An Act of greater length than a couple of sections is officially printed with an 'Arrangement of Sections', which is a contents list of Sections and Schedules and their Marginal Notes (for which, see below).

Long Title, Date of Royal Assent and Preamble

In addition to Short Titles, United Kingdom Acts also have 'Long Titles'. These were used well before Short Titles. In practice they may be brief or lengthy[16]. Their function is to indicate and delimit the subject matter of the Bill when first introduced into Parliament,

---

11 The principal ones include the Acts of Parliament (Commencement) Act 1793; Short Titles Act 1896; Parliament Act 1911; Consolidation of Enactments (Procedure) Act 1949; Acts of Parliament Numbering and Citation Act 1962; Royal Assent Act 1967; and Interpretation Act 1978.

12 *Eg* Criminal Procedure (Scotland) Act 1995. For transitional examples, see the Scottish Enterprise Act 1999 and the Mental Health (Scotland) Act 1999. A parallel convention applies to Northern Ireland legislation. Curiously, none applies to legislation applying only in England.

13 Modern examples include the Scotland Acts 1978 and 1998 (and there is the transitional example of the Scottish Enterprise Act 1999).

14 In medieval English constitutional theory, a parliament passed only one statute, so, if it covered different topics, each was distinguished as a 'chapter' (in Latin *'caput'*).

15 But see below 'Publication and citation of parliamentary legislation: Acts of the Parliaments of Great Britain and the United Kingdom'.

16 The long title of the Official Secrets Act 1989 runs to 20 words and reads 'An Act to replace section 2 of the Official Secrets Act 1911 by provisions protecting more limited classes of official information'. That of the Water Act 1989 runs to some 200 words.

and they may be an aid to interpretation of a statute. At the end of the Long Title is given, in square brackets, the 'Date of Royal Assent', that is, the date on which the Act is actually formally enacted[17]. However, while this is the date of enactment, confusingly, it is not necessarily (or indeed, generally) the date or dates on which the Act actually comes into force, for which, see below in relation to 'Commencement'.

Preambles to Acts were formerly used to show their purpose. Very occasionally, a modern Act may have a preamble, commencing with the word 'Whereas ... ', and outlining the reasons for it[18]. This precedes the Long Title.

The Enacting Formula

United Kingdom Acts of Parliament do not have lengthy recitals of their origins at the beginning, as Community legislation does. They do, however, have an 'Enacting Formula' immediately before the actual substantive provisions. It is a validating incantation, recording enactment. There are four forms of it: one is the basic, the others are used in taxation legislation, government expenditure legislation, and legislation under the Parliament Act 1911, respectively[19].

Sections, Marginal Notes and Marginal References

The basic unit of a United Kingdom Act is the 'Section', and Sections are numbered sequentially throughout the Act. Draftsmen

---

17 Thus, for example, after the Long Titles of the Official Secrets Act 1989 and Water Act 1989 appear '[11th May 1989]' and '[6th July 1989]' respectively.

18 The Welsh Language Act 1967 has the following: 'Whereas it is proper that the Welsh language should be freely used by those who so desire in the hearing of legal proceedings in Wales and Monmouthshire; that further provision should be made for the use of that language, with like effect as English, in the conduct of other official or public business there; and that Wales should be distinguished from England in the interpretation of future Acts of Parliament ... '. Private Bills (for which, see below) always have a Preamble, however: see, for example, the British Railways Act 1992.

19 Its basic form, reflecting the relationship of the three parts of Parliament until the 19th century, reads 'Be it enacted by the Queen's most Excellent Majesty, by and with the advice and consent of the Lords Spiritual and Temporal, and Commons, in this Parliament assembled, and by authority of the same as follows ... '. Amusingly, the Finance Acts, which permit taxation, refer to taxes 'freely and voluntarily given', and the Consolidated Fund and Appropriation Acts, which permit government expenditure, to funds 'cheerfully granted'. Legislation under the Parliament Acts omits reference to the Lords but inserts 'in accordance with the provisions of the Parliament Act 1911'.

aim at exactitude (in 'fixed verbal form': see Appendix 1), rather than comprehensibility. They break down the content into 'Sub-sections', 'Paragraphs' and 'Sub-paragraphs' as necessary[20], and use typographical devices to express grammatical, and thus logical, structure. This use of numbers, letters and indentation thus typifies statutory language. The principal convention on nomenclature and labelling is as follows (although the sub-section level is sometimes omitted in a short but sub-divided Section, so that the draftsman goes straight from Section to Paragraph):

section	1	(**emboldened**)
sub-section	(1)	(unemboldened)
paragraph	(a)	(unemboldened)
sub-paragraph	(i)	(unemboldened)

As well as assisting in exact expression of meaning, this convention allows precise identification of provisions, for example, 'Race Relations Act 1976, s 1(1)(b)(iii)', that is, 'section 1, sub-section 1, paragraph b, sub-paragraph ii of that Act' (or, where the draftsman has gone straight to paragraphs, 'Nationality, Immigration and Asylum Act 2002, s 5(b)', that is, 'section 5, paragraph b' of that Act).

Where an amending Act inserts a whole new Section, it is identi-fied by a capital letter after the preceding number. A new section after 's 1' is thus 's 1A', and its Sub-sections would be rendered 's 1A(1), 1(A)(2)' and so on[21]. Thus, ss 128-139 of the Immigration and Asylum Act 1999 inserted 11 new sections between ss 28 and 29 of the Immigration Act 1971, which therefore appear as 'ss 28A–29K' of that Act. A similar principle applies to inserted Sub-sections etc. Thus, s 140(3) of the Nationality, Immigration and Asylum Act 2002 inserted a new paragraph between s 87(3)(e) and (f) of the Immigration and Asylum Act 1999, which therefore appears as 's 87(3)(ea)' of that Act.

Every section has a Marginal Note. This is a signpost rather than a description, and is the form of words used in the relevant entry in the Arrangement of Sections.

---

20 In grammatical terms, the sentence contained in the Section is broken into its constituent clauses and phrases. The main clause is likely to start or finish the section. The subordinate clauses form the various Sub-sections etc, reflecting their relationship with the main clause. Much of the skill of drafting is finding a suitable means of expressing visually the internal and grammatical logic of the intended provision.

21 It follows that a 's 1(a)' and 's 1A' in any statute are entirely separate provisions. Indeed, there might be a 's1(a)' and a 's 1A(a)' which are equally separate. Obviously, this can be a source of confusion.

Where a section in one Act refers to another Act, for instance to amend it, an abbreviated citation to that other Act may given in the margin. For example, s 22 of the Immigration and Asylum Act 1999 affects the Asylum and Immigration Act 1996, so, in the margin of the former, next to s 22, appears '1996 c49', the citation of the earlier Act. However, the practice also exists of giving short title, year and chapter number in the text itself.

These conventions are used in official editions of United Kingdom Acts. Usage may vary somewhat in commercially produced ones or in textbooks. For example, Marginal Notes may not be in the margin, but follow the section number; Marginal References may not appear at all; 'section' is usually abbreviated to 's' ('ss' in the plural); and the brackets round the sub-section number removed.

Headings

A variety of Headings may be used in the text of an Act. Groups of sections may be collectively labelled as Parts, with capital roman numerals and centred capitalised names. For example, ss 1–31 and ss 32–43 of the Immigration and Asylum Act 1999 are labelled as, respectively:

'Part I: IMMIGRATION: GENERAL'
Part II: CARRIERS' LIABILITY'

Occasionally, Parts are divided into 'Titles' or even 'Chapters'[22].

Whether or not an Act has Parts, smaller groups of Sections are likely to be labelled by a 'Cross-heading', centred and italicised. For example, within Part 1 of the Immigration and Nationality Act 1999, ss 1–5, 6-8 and ss 9-15 are cross-headed as, respectively:

> *'Leave to enter, or remain in, the United Kingdom'*
> *'Exemption from immigration control'*
> *'Removal from the United Kingdom'*

A common usage is to label (whether as a separate Part or, more usually, under a Cross heading) 'Supplementary' or 'Miscellaneous and Supplemental' the last few Sections which contain a number of operating instructions for the Act, such as the Interpretation Section, Repeals and Amendment Provisions, and others described below.

---

22 An extreme example is the Capital Allowances Act 2001, which has 12 Parts, divided into 10, 20, 12, 6, 7, 5, 3, 5, 0, 8, 2 and 6 Chapters respectively.

Interpretation Sections

Interpretation Sections (usually identified by the Marginal Note), may appear anywhere in a United Kingdom Act, but are commonly found towards the end (often in the 'Supplementary' or 'Miscellaneous and Supplemental' sections)[23]. They specify meanings of words and phrases for the purposes of the Act. This may be necessary because the words are inherently vague, because they are used in an unusual sense, or because they have been invented for the purpose. For example, s 33 of the Immigration Act 1971 stipulates that '"aircraft" includes hovercraft', '"airport" includes hoverport', and '"port" includes airport', and also that '"Convention adoption" has the same meaning as in the Adoption Act 1976 and the Adoption (Scotland) Act 1978'. The meanings assigned may not actually be definitions, for sometimes the Section stipulates that one term 'means' something, sometimes that it 'includes' something, and occasionally that it 'does not include' something. The opening words of an Interpretation Section commonly, but unhelpfully, assign meanings 'unless the context otherwise requires'. Section 127 of the Scotland Act 1998 usefully gives a list of some 60 expressions used in the Act (such as 'cross-border authority', 'open power' and 'Scots private law') and in which sections their definition can be found[24].

Repeals and Amendments

United Kingdom Acts of Parliament continue in force unless repealed or amended, subject to an exception. Firstly, a provision in the Act may specify a terminal date, as did s 27 of the Prevention of Terrorism (Temporary Provisions) Act 1989 (and its predecessors). However, this is rare[25].

United Kingdom Acts, therefore, commonly repeal or amend earlier Acts, and no special process is required (and amendment

---

23 See Simamba, B 'The Placing and Other Handling of Definitions' (2006) 27 Stat LR 73-82.

24 A similar provision in Sch 1, Part 2 of the Capital Allowances Act 2001 lists 130 such expressions.

25 The Murder (Abolition of Death Penalty) Act 1965, most unusually, provided that 'This Act shall continue in force until the thirty first day of July nineteen hundred and seventy, and shall then expire unless Parliament by affirmative resolution of both Houses otherwise determines'. Such an affirmative resolution was forthcoming. Note also that an Act of the (pre-1707) Parliament of Scotland may fall into 'desuetude', that is, lapse through the growth of contrary practice: see *The Laws of Scotland: Stair Memorial Encyclopaedia* vol 22, para 129 and Ch 8.

does not only occur in Acts with '(Amendment)' in the short title). This follows from the doctrine of parliamentary supremacy, although the direct effect of Community law would appear to have limited this freedom.

Moreover, Delegated Legislation (for which, see Chapters 9 and 10) may repeal or amend an Act of Parliament, provided that Parliament has delegated the power to do so.

Two methods of amendment may be employed[26]. The 'textual' or 'direct' method simply substitutes a new provision for the old, a 'scissors and paste' process. It is generally preferred by the users of statutes as it shows the final form clearly. The 'referential' or 'indirect' method leaves the original text, but describes how it should be changed. It is preferred by Parliament as it shows what changes are proposed.

Repealing and Amending Provisions may appear anywhere in an Act, but commonly do so in a specific Section or Sections at the end of the Act (often in the 'Supplementary' or 'Miscellaneous and Supplemental' sections). Where there are numerous repeals and amendments, they are usually detailed in a Schedule, for example Sch 9 to the Social Security Act 1989 lists 18 Acts which it repeals to varying degrees. Indeed, where chiefly one Act is amended, and there are many amendments to other Acts, there may be two Schedules, as in Schs 4 ('Amendments of the Immigration Act 1981') and 7 ('Consequential Amendments') of the British Nationality Act 1981.

Occasionally, 'Statute Law Revision Acts' and 'Statute Law (Repeal) Acts' have been passed, which remove from the statute book obsolete and unnecessary legislation, which inevitably accumulates in a system in which legislation is generally *ad hoc*. These are discussed under 'Special cases' below.

Transitional Provisions

When a United Kingdom Act is repealed or amended, transitional difficulties may arise, for instance in relation to litigation which is in progress. Transitional Provisions, usually found at the end of an Act (often in the 'Supplementary' or 'Miscellaneous and Supplemental' sections), provide a solution, and the detail is often put in a Schedule. For example, s 169(2) of the Immigration and Asylum Act 1999 reads 'Schedule 15 contains transitional provisions and savings'.

---

26 Miers and Page *Legislation* (2nd edn, 1990) p 195, n 6 suggests that ss 60 & 61 the Wildlife and Countryside Act 1981 are paradigm cases.

Commencement Provisions

By virtue of the Acts of Parliament (Commencement) Act 1793, a United Kingdom Act comes into force on the Date of Royal Assent, unless it specifies otherwise[27]. They often so specify in a Commencement Section normally found at the end of the Act (often in the 'Supplementary' or 'Miscellaneous and Supplemental' sections). The simplest form of Commencement Section gives a specific date for commencement[28]. A rare variant is to declare that the Act comes into force at the same time as another Act[29], and a common one that it does so at a specific period after the Date of Royal Assent, typically three months[30]. A very common method nowadays is to delegate the power to the government to bring the Act into force, to be exercised through a Statutory Instrument (for which, see Chapter 9) known as a 'Commencement Order'. An Act may have different sections brought into force on different days, and use a mixture of commencement methods[31], and more than one commencement order, some of which may be years after the enactment which can make it difficult to discover if a particular provision is in force or not[32].

Short Title Provision

A provision at the end of a United Kingdom Act officially gives it its Short Title (for which, see above) by stating 'This Act may be cited as ... '[33]. No chapter number is given, for this cannot be known until enactment.

27 Thus the British Nationality Act 1958 (not specifying otherwise) came into force on the Date of Royal Assent (20 February 1958).

28 Section 34(2) of the British Nationality Act 1948 stipulated that it come into force 'on the first day of January nineteen hundred and forty-nine'.

29 Section 25 of the Company Directors Disqualification Act 1986 stipulates that it come into force on commencement of the Insolvency Act 1986.

30 Section 3(3) of the British Nationality Act 1964 stipulated that it come into force 'at the expiration of two months beginning with the date on which it is passed'.

31 Section 53(3) of the British Nationality Act 1981 stipulates that 'section 49 and this section shall come into force on the passing of this Act' (30 October 1981), and s 53(2) that the rest of the Act 'shall come into force on such day as the Secretary of State may by order made by statutory instrument appoint'. That power was exercised in the British Nationality 1981 (Commencement) Order 1982, SI 1982/933, which appointed 1 January 1983.

32 The Control of Pollution Act 1974 has had 20 commencement orders and is still not completely in force. The record is thought to be held by the Easter Act 1928 which is still not in force.

33 Thus s 149 of the Constitutional Reform Act 2005 stipulates 'The Act may be cited as the Constitutional Reform Act 2005'.

Extent Provisions

Because Acts of the United Kingdom Parliament do not necessarily apply to the whole of the United Kingdom (and, with the arrival of devolution, do so decreasingly) there are commonly 'Extent Provisions, stipulating to which law areas (for instance, England and Wales only, or Great Britain) they do apply. Such provisions can be complicated[34].

Acts may extend beyond the United Kingdom to dependencies. Commonly such Acts are extended to the Channel Islands and Isle of Man (which are not part of the United Kingdom), and to colonies as, for example, does the British Nationality Act 1981, by s 53(5).

An Act may even apply to activities by certain people outwith the territorial extent of the United Kingdom and its dependencies. For instance, the Official Secrets Act 1989 extends to the United Kingdom only, as such, but, by s 15, also applies to specified acts done by British Citizens and Crown servants abroad. Acts concerned with the security of the state and terrorism may extend and apply very broadly, usually by international agreement. The Taking of Hostages Act 1982, s 1 (which followed the International Convention Against Taking Hostages of 1979) declares 'A person, whatever his nationality, who, being in the United Kingdom or elsewhere' takes hostages contrary to the terms of the Act, commits an offence in the United Kingdom'. The Criminal Justice (Terrorism and Conspiracy) Act 1998 was co-ordinated with similar legislation in the Republic of Ireland and by s 5 enabled prosecutions in the United Kingdom of conspiracies to commit illegal acts in territories outside the UK.

The most extreme example appears to be the Outer Space Act 1986, which stipulates in s 1 that 'This Act applies to the following activities whether carried out in the United Kingdom or elsewhere ... (c) any activity in outer space'. 'Outer space' is defined in s 14, strangely, to include the moon.

---

34 Section 194(6) of the Water Act 1989 specified that Schs 2 and 5, ss 4, 13 and 23 'so far as relating to any scheme under either of those Schedules', s 95 and certain repeals extend to the United Kingdom. Section 194(7) specifies that certain other sections and schedules extend, or extend in part, to Great Britain. Section 194(8) specified that yet other provisions apply only to Scotland, and s 194(9) that yet further provisions extend only to England and Wales. Section 147 of the Constitutional Reform Act 2005 specified that ss 7, 8 & 9 'extend to England and Wales only', '[s]ection 6 and Part 5 extend to Northern Ireland only', but also that '[s]ubject to subsections (1) to (3), this Act extends to Northern Ireland'. It is thus a matter of inference whether ss 1-6, and 9-149 (minus Part 5) apply to Scotland.

Schedules

Many United Kingdom Acts have Schedules, which must be specifically incorporated into the Act by a Section. They are appendices, containing detailed matter too complicated for the body of the text, such as lists, tables and incidental rules. The British Nationality Act 1981, for example, has nine schedules[35].

Schedules may have Parts and cross-headings, as the body of an Act does, and are usually drafted in broadly the same manner as sections. The conventional labelling and nomenclature are as follows:

schedule	1	(unemboldened)
paragraph	(1)	(unemboldened)
sub-paragraph	(a)	(unemboldened)
sub-sub-paragraph	(i)	(unemboldened)

Repeal and amendment schedules are often in tabular form[36].

Explanatory Notes

Since 1999, 'Explanatory Notes' have been produced for almost every Act[37] by the sponsoring Government department. They are an attempt to explain in lay language what each provision of the Act does. They have, however, no official status, although (as discussed in relation to statutory interpretation in Chapter 11) they may be used in statutory interpretation.

THE UNITED KINGDOM PARLIAMENTARY LEGISLATIVE PROCEDURE

The proposal for legislation presented to the United Kingdom Parliament is called a 'Bill'. Any Bill is itself the result of a lengthy

---

35 Respectively: Requirements for Naturalisation; Provisions for Reducing Statelessness; Countries whose Citizens are Commonwealth Citizens; Amendments of the Immigration Act 1971; Form of Oath of Allegiance; British Dependent Territories; Consequential Amendments; Transitional Provisions; and Repeals. The Enterprise Act 2002 achieved 36 Schedules, and the Finance Act 2000 managed 40, but financial legislation is atypical.

36 Typically, a repeal schedule is in the form of a table of three columns, headed respectively 'chapter' (listing the citations of the Acts repealed); 'short title'; and 'extent of repeal' (which may be from a single word to 'The whole Act').

37 Technically, with every public general Act (for which see above) introduced by the government, and with at least some introduced as private members' Bills.

process. Indeed, commonly the changes imposed by the parliamentary process are small compared with what a proposal has already undergone.

Who seeks legislation and why?

The government's role in the initiation of legislation is central in the United Kingdom constitution. It is expected to legislate, and has something approaching a monopoly of the initiation of parliamentary legislation. Initiation by others is dealt with below under 'Special cases'.

Some government legislation is party political 'manifesto legislation', for example the community charge or poll tax, imposed by the Abolition of Domestic Rates (Scotland) Act 1987, or the introduction of 'human rights' and devolution in the Human Rights Act 1998 and Scotland Act 1998, respectively. Such legislation may be of enormous importance, but represents only a small proportion of all legislation[38]. Other legislation emerges as reaction to events. The Dangerous Dogs Act 1991 was a reaction to public pressure over a number of attacks by dogs; the Anti-Terrorism, Crime and Security Act 2001 was a reaction to the events of 11 September that year; the Terrorism Act 2006 was a response to the decision of the Appellate Committee of the House of Lords in *A v Secretary of State for the Home Department* [2004] UKHL 56, [2005] 2 WLR 87, which decided that detention under the Anti-Terrorism, Crime and Security Act 2001 was in breach of Article 5 of the European Convention on Human Rights (as effected through the Human Rights Act 1998). Much legislation in relation to asylum-seeking, in a number of Acts over several years (most recently the Immigration, Asylum and Nationality Act 2006) is a reaction to increased asylum-seeking. Such legislation may on occasion be symbolic as much as instrumental, but in any case represents only a small proportion of all legislation[39]. Yet other legislation, not clearly foreshadowed by the manifesto, or as obvious reaction to events may also appear, and be of considerable significance[40].

---

38 Rose *Do Parties Make a Difference?* (2nd edn, 1984) pp 72–73 concluded that only 8% of the Bills of the Conservative government 1970–72 were 'manifesto Bills', and only 13% of those of the Labour government of 1974–79. For an analysis on somewhat different lines, see Drewry (1989) 10 Stat LR 200. Such proportions are likely still to be broadly true.

39 See previous note.

40 The Constitutional Reform Act 2005 is of very great significance, but emerged for very unclear reasons: see the discussion of its introduction in Ch 3.

But the great majority of Bills originate in the normal processes of government. The constitution requires annual legislation to allow the government to raise and spend money. It also now requires the government to produce legislation to put into effect Community policy when Community institutions require it (although this is principally done by Delegated Legislation). Nevertheless, most legislation simply emerges from the departments of government. As they administer their responsibilities, they discover that the law is not having the desired effect, so legislation is promoted to change it. An important category of this is Statute Law Revision and Repeal and Consolidation which are discussed as 'Special cases' below.

It is useful to break up the legislative process into 'pre-Parliamentary' and 'post-Parliamentary'[41].

Pre-parliamentary stages of United Kingdom parliamentary legislation – 'the Whitehall stage'[42]

The pre-parliamentary stages of United Kingdom parliamentary legislation are of the utmost importance. It is then that the government decides what legislation it wishes, consults with interested parties, formulates specific proposals, and has them drafted by the Parliamentary draftsman into the Bill which will be presented to Parliament. Because the government has invested considerable resources into producing the Bill, it will be loath to accept amendments to it (though it may introduce amendments itself, reflecting second thoughts, or unfortunate results of the pressure the draftsman was under). Given executive dominance of the legislature, it will almost always get the Bill through Parliament in a form it wants, though often at a cost. Also, there is a limited amount of parliamentary time available for legislation, and governments would like to introduce much more legislation than there is parliamentary time for. In consequence, there is always a Committee of the Cabinet

---

41 There are some moves towards 'post-legislative scrutiny': see Law Commission 'Post-Legislative Scrutiny' (Law Commission Consultation Paper No 178 (2006) and Anon 'Post-Legislative Scrutiny' (2006) 27 Stat LR iii-vi

42 For fuller, readable accounts, see Miers and Page *Legislation* (2nd edn, 1990) chs 4 and 5 (now a little dated) and Zander *The Law-Making Process* (6th ed 2004), ch 1 (from which the phrase 'the Whitehall stage' is taken), also standard constitutional law textbooks, the lengthy Cabinet Office *Guide to Legislative Procedures* (Cabinet Office, 2004) www.cabinetoffice.gov.uk/secretariats/economic_and_domestic/legislative_programme/guide.asp, or much briefer www.parlianet.com/background/process_ns.asp.

to rank proposals for the coming parliamentary session. (There are also recently introduced Parliamentary procedures for 'Programming Motions', that is, for agreeing in advance how long each stage of each Bill might take, though the initiative has not been very successful).

Consultation is a major part of the pre-parliamentary stages (a topic dealt with in more detail in Chapter 15[43]). Advice is obtained from *ad hoc* or specialised bodies in highly institutionalised ways. Royal Commissions, composed of disinterested members of the great and good, were once a common method of investigating problems and suggesting solutions, but have largely fallen out of favour[44]. Committees of Inquiry, which are less high-powered, and departmental and inter-departmental committees and working parties of civil servants and others are much more common[45]. There has also been recourse to judges in recent years, at least in relation to possible legislation about courts and procedure[46]. The Law Commissions are of considerable importance in relation to certain types of legislation[47].

In addition, departments of government have continuing relations with a variety of interest and pressure groups, and it is in the dialogue with them that, within the government's priorities and predilections, proposals are formulated.

Consultation may be in part public. United Kingdom governments

---

43 And see previous note.
44 A major example was the Wheatley Commission, chaired by the then Lord Justice-Clerk, which reported in 1969 (Cmnd 4150), and resulted in the Local Government (Scotland) Act 1973 which set up a new local government structure in Scotland. Another was the Kilbrandon Commission, chaired by a Scottish House of Lords judge, which reported on devolution in 1973 (Cmnd 5460), but ultimately produced no change. Yet a third was the Wakeham Commission chaired by a former Conservative Cabinet Minister, which reported on the reform of the House of Lords in 2000 (Cm 4534), but also appears to have produced no change.
45 The Carnworth Report (*Enforcing Planning Control*) in 1989 led to the Planning and Compensation Act 1991. The North Report (*Road Traffic Law Review*) in 1988 led to the Road Traffic Act 1991.
46 The most obvious examples are *Access to Justice: interim report* (1995) and *Access to Justice: final report* (the 'Woolf Report': 1996) on civil procedure, many of the recommendations of which were effected in new Civil Procedure Rules (although this is Delegated, rather than Parliamentary Legislation) and *Review of the Criminal Courts in England & Wales* (the "Auld Report": 2001) on criminal procedure, some of the recommendations of which were effected in the Criminal Justice Act 2003.
47 Especially statute law revision and repeal, and consolidation. See also Ch 15.

sometimes issue Green Papers or other consultative documents[48], outlining options and soliciting comment (and sometimes also White Papers, that is, statements of firm policy[49], though some White Papers have 'green edges')[50]. Indeed, now some Bills are published in draft, which allows greater scrutiny.

Drafting is done by barristers and a few advocates employed as civil servants, and known collectively as 'Parliamentary Counsel' in the Parliamentary Counsel Office within the Cabinet Office[51]. At any time several will be on loan to the Law Commission, however. Draftsmen have been transferred to Edinburgh to draft the Bills of the Scottish Executive.

The draftsmens' role in legislation is pivotal. A United Kingdom government department, when its proposed Bill has a place in the queue, tells its own lawyers the policy the Bill is to promote, and these lawyers draft instructions for Parliamentary Counsel. Initial drafts of United Kingdom or Great Britain Bills are sent to the Advocate-General for Scotland's office for comment.

A team of two or three Parliamentary Counsel draft the Bill, and the 'Explanatory Notes' which nowadays accompany Bills, in liaison with the sponsoring department. This process may continue for months, or be hurried, depending upon the parliamentary legislative timetable. It has been suggested that there are five steps to drafting: understanding; analysis; design; composition; and revision[52]: also, that the Minister has the last word on matters of substance, the draftsman on matters of form.

---

48 The Children and Adoption Act 2006 (applying to England & Wales), was seemingly preceded by a consultation paper *Making Contact Work* (2001), an *Interim Response to the Report of the Children Act Sub-Committee* [ie the preceding paper] (2002), another consultation paper *Facilitation and Enforcement Group: final report* (2003), a Green Paper *Parental Separation: children's needs and parents' responsibilities* (Cm 6273) (2004), a White Paper *Parental Separation: children's needs and parents' responsibilities: next steps* (Cm 6273) (2005), a Parliamentary Committee Report *Report of a Joint Committee on the Draft Children (Contact) and Adoption Bill* (2005), a Government Reply to that (2005), another Parliamentary Committee Report *House of Commons Committee on Constitutional Affairs: Fourth Report for Session 2004-5 'Family Justice: the operation of family courts* (HC 2004-5 No 116 (2005), and a Government Response to that: see Current Law Annotated Statutes annotations.

49 *Smoking Kills* (Cm 1477) preceded the Tobacco Advertising and Promotion Act 2002.

50 However, it may be that Green Papers legislation have become less fashionable, and White Papers have certainly become more glossy, and therefore less useful.

51 See www.parliamentary-counsel.gov.uk/: also Bowman 'Why is there a Parliamentary Counsel Office?' (205) 26 Stat LR 69-81.

52 Thornton *Legislative Drafting* (4th edn, 1996) pp 112–13.

The draftsman works under considerable constraints. Firstly, the instructions must be put into legislative form so as to satisfy the government. This may require deliberate vagueness or ambiguity on occasion. Secondly, the Bill must be, so far as possible, legally effective and fit within the existing law without producing unintended contradictions. Thirdly, the Bill must be competent for the United Kingdom Parliament (and thus, despite parliamentary supremacy, should not unintentionally offend against 'Convention rights' under the Human Rights Act 1998, and must not against Community law. Fourthly, the Bill must fit into the parliamentary timetable, and shortage of time may lead to bad drafting and consequent need for extensive amendment in Parliament, requiring more of the draftsman's time. Fifthly, draftsmen see themselves as an elite, employing craft skills, which is said to lead to a certain conservatism in form and expression.

Parliamentary stages of United Kingdom parliamentary legislation – 'the Westminster stage'[53]

The Enacting Formula of an Act records that the three parts of the UK Parliament have agreed. To pass these three parts, several stages must be gone through.

A Bill may be introduced into either House of Parliament first, by any MP or peer (as appropriate). However, most Bills are government Bills (that is Bills introduced by a member of the government), and most (and certainly controversial Bills and those concerning taxation and expenditure) are introduced into the Commons first.

The stages in each House are called 'First' and 'Second Readings' ('1R' and '2R')[54], Committee Stage ('CS'), Report Stage ('RS') and Third Reading ('3R'). After a Bill has gone through all those stages in each House, there is a process of consideration by the House in

---

53 See again Miers and Page *Legislation* (2nd edn, 1990) ch 6 (now a little dated) and Zander *The Law-Making Process* (6th ed 2004), ch 2 (from which the phrase 'the Westminster stage' is taken): also standard constitutional law textbooks, the lengthy Cabinet Office *Guide to Legislative Procedures* ((Cabinet Office, 2004) www.cabinetoffice.gov.uk/secretariats/economic_and_domestic/legislative_prog ramme/ guide.asp, or much briefer www.parlianet.com/background/process_ ns.asp.

54 Unfortunately the 'co-operation procedure' for the European Community legislative procedure has adopted these titles for very different processes, as noted in Ch 6.

which the Bill was introduced of the other House's amendments, to produce an agreed version[55]. The Royal Assent follows automatically.

The whole process suffers from the fact that executive dominance of the legislature normally ensures that the Bill is largely unaltered (although hundreds of amendments may have been moved, unsuccessfully, by Opposition MPs) or only altered as the government wishes (by many amendments moved, successfully, by Government MPs). Parliament therefore largely rubber-stamps the government's proposals and, at least in the House of Commons, the legislative process often becomes a forum for the opposition to harry the government instead. To ensure that the current legislation gets through despite the Opposition's efforts to thwart it there is always also a Cabinet Committee, operating through the Whips (that is members of the government whose job is to maintain party discipline and convey to the government the concerns of backbenchers).

The First Reading is purely formal, but permits the Bill, traditionally hitherto confidential (though now Draft Bills are sometimes issued), to be published. Before the Second Reading, s 19 of the Human Rights Act 1998 requires the minister in charge of a Bill to make a written statement that, in his view, the provisions of the Bill are compatible with the 'Convention rights' under that Act (for which, see Chapter 3) or, if he cannot do so, state that the government wishes to proceed with the Bill nevertheless[56]. This is one of several devices designed to seek compatibility of legislation with those rights (see Chapters 3 and 5). The Second Reading, perhaps two weeks later, is designed as a debate on the principle of the Bill. Most Second Readings are unopposed, but a government will almost always win a vote, because it is government by virtue of having a majority in the House of Commons (and the House of Lords will not normally attempt to veto legislation which the majority in the Commons favours). The Committee Stage, which will often extend over several weeks, is usually taken by a 'Standing Committee' reflecting the party balance in the Commons[57], and a 'Committee of the Whole House' in the Lords. This stage is designed to examine the Bill in detail to see if it achieves its purpose, and is the

55 Indeed, in contentious cases, there can be 'Parliamentary ping-pong', whereby a Bill is passed back and forth several times. The record, seemingly, is six times: see Zander *The Law-Making Process* (6th ed, 2004) p56, n 14.

56 As was done in respect to the Anti-Terrorism, Crime & Security Act 2001, as discussed below in relation to the 'Special case' of human rights legislation.

57 It may be taken by a 'Committee of the Whole House', as the European Communities (Amendment) Bill 1992–93 (incorporating changes wrought by the Treaty on European Union) was; or by a 'Select Committee', which can take evidence. However, these committees are rarely used.

chief stage to put amendments. It may allow such examination on an uncontroversial Bill, but in other cases it may be political theatre, possibly with proceedings 'guillotined', that is terminated at a certain point, whether or not discussion has finished. In this case many clauses of the Bill will not be discussed at all. Also, increasingly, governments propose amendments to their own Bills ('legislating on the hoof'), which suggests that they have been ill-drafted, possibly through lack of time. The Report Stage is for the Committee to report its amendments to the Whole House (even if it has been a Committee of the Whole House, when it will be purely formal), although further amendments may be put. The Third Reading gives approval to the House's final formulation of the Bill. Because the first House to take any Bill has not approved any amendments made by the second House, there is a process of consideration of the other House's amendments. The House of Lords will usually concede to the reiterated opinion of the Commons. The Royal Assent has been purely formal for generations, but makes the Bill an Act (although it may come into force only later[58]).

A question raised by parliamentary legislative procedure is whether the unelected House of Lords should have a role[59]. One possible justification is that much legislation is not properly discussed in the Commons, so the Lords provides, in effect, a proper Committee Stage. This view has been prominent in discussions on House of Lords reform, and tends to characterise the Lords as a 'revising chamber' for legislation. Another is that it provides a sheet anchor to limit the wilder excesses of the Commons, which is dominated by the government of the day. This has not figured so largely in these discussions.

Enactment, the 'Sewel Convention' and 'Sewel Motions'

As noted above, and in Chapter 8, there is still a remarkable amount of legislation being enacted in relation to Scotland, and within the devolved legislative competence of the Scottish Parliament, but by the United Kingdom Parliament.

This is largely because of the existence of 'Sewel Motions'. In brief, during the passage of the Scotland Act 1998, the government, through Lord Sewel, its spokesman in the House of Lords, indicated

---

58 See 'Commencement provisions' above.
59 See *eg* Hope of Craighead 'What a Second Chamber Can Do for Legislative Scrutiny' (2004) Stat LR 3-18.

the expectation that a convention of the constitution would arise. This would be that, while the United Kingdom Parliament had power to legislate within the devolved competence of the Scottish Parliament, it would do so rarely and only with the consent of the Scottish Parliament.

However, the Scottish Parliament has in fact passed a large number of motions invoking the exception. As a result, in the first couple of years of its existence, the Scottish Parliament passed roughly as many 'Sewel Motions' as it passed Acts. Thus, arguably, as much Scots law was changed by Westminster as by Holyrood[60].

This may make sense if it includes Scotland in reforms introduced to the rest of the United Kingdom, applies international obligations, and so on. Nevertheless, it was completely unexpected. The phenomenon shows the strong centripetal United Kingdom tendencies in tension with notions of solutions tailored to Scottish wishes ('one size fits all' in tension with 'post-code solutions'), the more remarkable for being at least cheerfully acquiesced in by the Scottish Executive and Scottish Parliament. These centripetal tendencies may flow from a desire for uniformity, caused by electoral expectations, a reliance on UK administrative bodies, the need to avoid inconsistency, and a feeling that diversity should not be sought for its own sake. Moreover, there may be other reasons for not using the Scottish Parliament, such as doubt over the boundaries of devolution, impetus for reform coming from Westminster, a desire to avoid dislocation of the Scottish Parliament's legislative programme, avoidance of challenge, and simple economy of effort. Also, there remain Scottish MPs in Westminster to take care of Scottish interests.

Nevertheless, if all that the Scottish Parliament does is to pass a motion, with limited debate, accepting a Westminster Bill, it loses all control over what happens to the Bill thereafter. One of the problems devolution was set up to solve was Westminster passing legislation which applies to Scotland but is ill-suited to it. Perhaps this problem is being re-invented.

---

60 Clearly, one cannot simply compare number of Acts, as they vary in significance (and length), but the point is well made. For an analysis of 'Sewel motions' in the first few years of the Scottish Parliament, see Page and Batey 'Scotland's Other Parliament; Westminster legislation about devolved matters in Scotland' [2002] PL 501–23 (who noted that in the first three calendar years of the Scottish Parliament, 30 Sewel Motions were passed by the Scottish Parliament, which only passed 36 Acts of the Scottish Parliament in the same period!). The following text relies heavily on that analysis. See also Munro 'Thoughts on the "Sewel Convention"' 2003 SLT 194-196.

Special cases

There are a number of special cases of legislation which must be examined.

Human rights legislation

By far the most important special case is that of human rights legislation. For present purposes, 'human rights' can be taken to refer to the content of a particular treaty, the European Convention on Human Rights and Fundamental Freedoms (or 'ECHR'), made under the auspices of the Council of Europe, as considered in Chapter 3. As noted there, the United Kingdom, as a member of the Council of Europe, was one of the original signatories of the ECHR in 1950, and ratified it in 1951. (There are also amending Protocols which add further rights, but not all of these have been ratified by the United Kingdom.) Further, there is the possibility of 'individual petition' to the European Court of Human Rights asserting a state has breached its obligations under the ECHR. Thus the United Kingdom adheres to the ECHR and one form of remedy for breach. There are also possibilities of enforcement though Community law.

However, what is of present interest is human rights legislation which, in the United Kingdom, effectively means the Human Rights Act 1998. This is, in some senses, simply another Act of Parliament, and to be mentioned, if at all, in relation to Acts of Parliament in general. However, it has a special status, and has had radical effects, which makes it necessary to give it special mention[61].

As noted in Chapter 3, the Human Rights Act does not, as is sometimes said, actually incorporate the ECHR into United Kingdom law, for its terms do not have the 'direct effect' which Community law does (see Chapter 6). Nevertheless, it can be said to 'embed' human rights, for s 1 of that Act cuts and pastes most of the contents of the ECHR[62], and its First and Sixth Protocols[63], into its Sch 1, under the name of 'Convention rights'. These Convention rights are thus part of United Kingdom law by virtue of being in an Act of Parliament.

---

61 See also Feldman 'The Impact of Human Rights on the UK Legislative Process' (2004) 25 Stat LR 91-115.
62 It omits Arts. 1, 13 & 15. As noted in Ch 3, the omission of Art. 13, requiring 'an effective remedy before a national authority', is controversial. The government considered it added nothing, as the very Act itself provided the effective remedy. Another view is that it wished to avoid judges creating new remedies based on the Act.
63 That is, those protocols creating further rights which the UK has signed up to.

Further, in broad terms, United Kingdom law is intended to be 'compatible' with them (though not necessarily required to be). There are various means of seeking this compatibility. Firstly, the Act requires 'public authorities' (including United Kingdom Government and the courts) to act compatibly with Convention rights[64]. However, the United Kingdom Parliament is not a 'public authority' for this purpose (though the Scottish Parliament is, as noted below), so does not have to act compatibly[65] (though courts may issue a 'declaration of incompatibility' in litigation on legislation found to be incompatible). Secondly, imposes requirements in relation to parliamentary scrutiny during the process of legislation of all subsequent Acts, whereby every government Bill is required to have either a statement of compatibility or a declaration of non-compatibility[66]. This was noted above. Thirdly, the Act imposes requirements in relation to statutory interpretation[67], which is discussed in Chapter 11. Fourthly, specific requirements are imposed in relation to devolution[68], which are discussed in Chapters 3 and 8.

In addition to this requirement for 'compatibility', the Act also creates rights for victims of breaches of Convention rights, as was discussed in Chapter 3[69].

Financial legislation

The United Kingdom constitution requires that there be annual financial legislation. Thus, annual Finance Acts permit taxation and

64 Human Rights Act 1998, s 6.
65 As indeed it did not, as noted above, in relation to the Anti-Terrorism, Crime and Security Act 2001 which contained provisions incompatible with the Convention right to liberty and security of persons (Art. 5 ECHR), by permitting indefinite detention of certain persons. This therefore, required derogation from that part of the European Convention on Human Rights itself, seemingly effected by the Human Rights Act 1998 (Designated Derogation) Order 2001, SI 2001 No 3644. However, in litigation considering this derogation, the Appellate Committee of the House of Lords concluded, in *A and others v Secretary of State for the Home Department* [2004] UKHL 56, that it was incompatible with Convention rights and unlawful in UK law. The relevant provisions therefore ceased to be used, and were repealed by the Prevention of Terrorism Act 2005 which introduced 'control orders', a form of 'house arrest', which might be 'non-derogating' or (with the court's consent) 'derogating'. However, in mid-2007, it appeared that some non-derogating control orders might also breach the same Convention rights: see *Secretary of State for the Home Department v MB* [2006] EWCA Civ 1140, *Secretary of State for the Home Department v JJ & Others* [2006] EWCA Civ 1141.
66 Human Rights Act, s 19.
67 *Ibid*, ss 2 & 3.
68 Scotland Act 1998, 29 & 54.
69 Human Rights Act 1998, ss 7 & 8.

Consolidated Fund and Appropriation Acts permit government expenditure. The legislative procedure for these (which takes up much parliamentary legislative time) differs somewhat from the usual. It does not provide effective control over taxation and expenditure by government, however, and in any case control is increasingly shared with the European Community. (For the operation of this in relation to the Scottish Parliament, see Chapter 8).

Legislation under the Parliament Acts 1911 and 1949

The legislative powers of the House of Lords are constrained by the Parliament Acts 1911 and 1949. Firstly, Bills introduced into the United Kingdom Parliament certified by the Speaker as 'money Bills' (such as taxation and expenditure Bills), which by a convention of the constitution must always be introduced into the House of Commons, can be delayed by the Lords for one month only, after which they are deemed to have agreed to them. Secondly, other Bills (unless they fall into the third category) can be delayed for two sessions of Parliament only, after which they are deemed to be agreed. Thirdly, Bills to extend the life of the Parliament, and any private legislation, are unaffected by the legislation.

The Parliament Acts have rarely been formally invoked[70].

Statute Law Revision and Statute Law Repeal legislation

Legislation in a common law or mixed jurisdiction is *ad hoc*, and grows by accretion. Legislation on a topic may thus be widely scattered, and may become obsolete. While Acts of the pre-1707 Scots Parliament may fall into desuetude, others are considered immortal unless repealed. Later Acts of the United Kingdom Parliament may repeal all or part of earlier ones, but may do so implicitly.

After occasional initiatives over several centuries, in the early years of the 20th century (but somewhat earlier in England) serious attempts at weeding out were undertaken by the Statute Law Committee and others. They produced a number of Statute Law

---

70 However, the Lords did reject the War Crimes Bill in 1990, and again when it was reintroduced in 1991, so the Bill was deemed to have been passed and became law as the War Crimes Act 1991. The European Parliamentary Elections Act 1999 had a similar history, as did the Sexual Offences (Amendment) Act 2000, and the Hunting Act 2004. The Higher Education Act 1998 did not use the procedure, but was passed only after the government agreed to review the matter in dispute. For discussion, see *R (on the application of Jackson) v Attorney-General* [2005] UKHL 56 and Ekins 'Acts of Parliament and the Parliament Acts' (2007) 123 LQR 91-114.

Revision Acts, for example the Statute Law Revision (Scotland) Act 1906. A simplified parliamentary procedure, using a Joint Committee of both Houses for the Committee Stage, and permitting no subsequent amendments, later stages being 'on the nod', was created for them. These Acts collectively repealed thousands of Acts considered no longer in force or obsolete.

Responsibility for such activities was given to the Law Commissions when they were created in 1965. They have produced at the time of writing some ten Statute Law Repeal Acts, most recently in 2004, repealing hundreds more old Acts by the accelerated parliamentary procedure[71]. These Acts repeal those Acts considered 'no longer of practical utility', a somewhat more inclusive definition than used before.

Consolidation legislation

In conjunction with the weeding-out process, there have been attempts at 'consolidation', that is, at placing all provisions on a topic in a single coherent Act, and a large number of consolidating Acts were passed in the 19th century. However, the process of rendering provisions from a variety of Acts into a single coherent whole is difficult without at least marginally altering those provisions, in other words, without incidentally altering the law. Thus, although the same simplified legislative process, as for statute law revision, was made available, parliamentary jealousy meant it was little used. The Enactments (Procedure) Act 1949 permitted corrections and minor improvements (as defined in the Act) through the accelerated procedure.

The Law Commissions took principal responsibility for consolidation as well as statute law revision. Their initial hopes of large-scale consolidation were not fulfilled before devolution. It may yet be that the Scottish Parliament will be able to realise them through a simplified procedure. Nevertheless, even before devolution, the Scottish Law Commission had generated more than 20 Consolidation Acts applying solely to Scotland, for example the Prisons (Scotland) Act 1989 (indicating, incidentally, that consolidating Acts are not usually

---

71 Thus, its Schedule contained 10 Parts, each concerned with a different subject matter, eg Part I, Administration of Justice; Part II, Ecclesiastical Law; Part III, Education, and so on. Part VII concerned Scottish Local Acts (for 'local Acts' see below), and repealed some 75 Acts from the Edinburgh Poor Relief Act 1800 to the Zetland Masonic Sick and Widows and Orphans Fund Order Confirmation Act 1900, by way of the Mussel Fishery (Cockenzie) Order Confirmation Act 1894, the Dundee Gas Order Confirmation Act 1921 and the Merchants House (Crematorium) Order 1950.

explicitly so called in their Short Titles[72]). It has also joined with the (English and Welsh) Law Commission on many more applying to Great Britain or the United Kingdom, including the massive Income and Corporation Taxes Act 1988. Those consolidation measures recommended by the Law Commissions undergo a version of the accelerated legislative procedure even if their incidental amendments go beyond those permitted by the 1949 Act (although the enormous consolidating Companies Act 1985 used an *ad hoc* procedure laid down in the Companies Act 1981).

In addition, any government department may promote its own consolidating Bill, usually as a result of a report by a committee of inquiry, departmental committee or the like, for example the Highways Act 1959 which followed the *ad hoc* departmental *Report of the Committee on the Consolidation of Highway Law* (Cmnd 630). A more recent example is the Wireless Telegraphy Act 2006, consolidating the Wireless Telegraphy Acts of 1949, 1967 and 1998, the Marine Etc Broadcasting Offences Act 1967, part of the Telecommunications Act 1984 and part of the Communication Act 2003. One particular example of this is the 'Tax Rewrite', that is, the attempt to render tax law into a series of more comprehensible statutes, which the Inland Revenue (now HM Revenue and Customs) was obliged to undertake by the Finance Act 1995, s 160. This enormous task has produced legislation (for instance, the Capital Allowances Act 2001 and Income Tax (Earnings and Pensions) Act 2003), but has been a long drawn out process, doubtfully successful and, like all Consolidation legislation, gradually overtaken by amendments.

There are thus several means of introducing Consolidation Bills, and it has been calculated that about a third of all UK legislation since the Law Commissions were set up has been consolidating.

Consolidation is not a panacea. Firstly, an area of law may be large enough to require several consolidating statutes. The consolidation of customs and excise law in 1979 produced seven Acts. In any case, statutes never stand alone, and must cross-refer. Secondly, a Consolidating Act will soon be amended[73], and may require reconsolidation later. The Criminal Procedure (Scotland) Act 1995, was heavily amended in its first ten years such that it acquired, for example, ss 194A-194I, inserted between ss 194 and 195, 234A-234K between

---

72 The consolidating Criminal Procedure (Scotland) Act 1995 (replacing the similarly titled 1975 Act was, confusingly, preceded by a Criminal Law (Consolidation) Act 1995.

73 The consolidating Wireless Telegraphy Act 2006 was amended in its year of enactment by the Legislative and Regulatory Reform Act 2006.

ss 234 and 235, and 245A-245H between ss 245 and 246[74]. Thirdly, consolidation deals only with statute law, not common law.

It may be that pressure to consolidate has slackened in recent years[75].

Codification

Codification, in the sense of a single statute incorporating all the law on the subject from all the sources, legislative and common law, has been sought in some areas. There are a few late 19th-century United Kingdom examples, such as the Bills of Exchange Act 1882, all passed by ordinary legislative procedure. These Acts, however, suffer from similar problems to those of Consolidating Acts. The law continues to develop and is only comprehensible in the light of judicial interpretation of the Act, so the codification becomes outdated.

Such codifying statutes must not be confused with the 'codes properly so-called' found in civil law countries (for which, see Chapter 5). These, taking Justinian's codification of Roman law as their model, not only seek to reduce the entire law on a subject to a single mega-statute, but set it out in reasoned, encyclopaedic form, from first principles. They are the ultimate authority, changed only rarely and then with difficulty.

It is difficult to imagine such a code in a common law or mixed system. The whole grain of such systems runs against comprehensive, final, authoritative statements which reduce the judge's role to a mere mouthpiece.

There have, nevertheless, been attempts to 'codify' conducted by the Law Commission and others[76].

---

74 The consolidating Companies Act 1985 was probably amended more in the following four years than the preceding consolidating Companies Act 1949 was in the nearly 40 years of its life.

75 See Samuels, A 'Consolidation: a plea' (2005) 26 Stat LR 56-63

76 The Law Commissions Act 1965 enjoined the Law Commissions to 'codify', and the Government's White Paper Criminal Justice: the way ahead (2001), paras 3.27 and 3.57-59 enjoined 'codification', but it is not clear in either case what meaning is to be attached to that word. See, however, Law Commission Codification of the Criminal Law - a report to the Law Commission (Law Com No 143) (HC Paper 1984-5 No 270) (1985) and Law Commission Criminal Law: a criminal code (law Com No 177) (HC Paper 1989-90 No 299) (2 vols) (1989): also Toulson, R 'Forty Years On: what progress in delivering accessible and principled criminal law?' (2006) 27 Stat LR 61-72. For attempts in Scotland, see Ch 8.

The Legislative and Regulatory Reform Act 2006

This remarkable piece of legislation is discussed in Chapter 9. It should be noted here, however, that it allows the Government to amend existing legislation in order to remove vaguely expressed 'burdens', subject to vaguely expressed safeguards, with limited reference to Parliament.

Private Members' legislation

Although most Bills in the United Kingdom Parliament are introduced by the government, any MP or peer can, in principle, do so, and such legislation is called 'Private Members' legislation'. However, as governments and oppositions (as 'governments in waiting') have carved up parliamentary time, there is little left for private members.

Private Members may introduce Bills by two special methods. Firstly, the 'ten-minute rule' allows a private member on certain occasions to introduce a Bill and speak in favour of it for ten minutes, after which another can oppose it for ten minutes and a vote is taken. This procedure is usually used simply to air a grievance, rather than seriously to propose legislation.

Secondly, the Private Members' ballot is a device for prioritising between Private Members' Bills. Participants give in their names, and 20 are drawn from a hat. Standing Orders of the House of Commons allow up to a dozen Fridays for Private Members' Bills only and procedural rules make it easy to dispose of a Bill undebated, by filibustering. Only those with high places in the ballot are likely to receive enough time. In any case, the government's voting power ensures that no Bill it dislikes will get through Parliament, and Private Members have little access to Parliamentary Draftsmen.

Thus, Private Members' legislation is not a large proportion of all United Kingdom legislation. It has been as much as a third in the recent past, but this proportion is misleading, for what is ostensibly Private Members' Legislation may be covert government legislation, including Law Commission proposals, which has received drafting and other help. The Age of Legal Capacity (Scotland) Act 1991, introduced by Sir Nicholas Fairbairn MP (Perth and Kinross), is an example. So, more recently, is the Climate Change and Sustainable Energy Act 2006, introduced by Mark Lazarowicz MP (Edinburgh North and Leith). Private members coming high in the ballot are likely to be inundated with requests from interest groups to adopt their Bill. The Solicitors (Scotland) Act 1991, introduced by Alistair

Darling MP (Edinburgh Central), was a measure sought by the Law Society of Scotland, for example.

Overall, Private Members' Bills provide a continuing trickle of important legislation, perhaps half-covert government Bills, rarely party politically sensitive, but sometimes on campaigning issues which the government is at worst indifferent to or, as with the Abortion Act 1967, may favour without wishing to be seen to promote.

Local, Personal, Private and Hybrid legislation

The public/private distinction is extremely complicated but, broadly, it is used in two separate ways. Firstly, it is used to refer to the public nature of the contents of an Act. The Interpretation Act 1978, s 3 stipulates that every Act is a 'public Act' unless it otherwise states, and that if it is a public Act, when cited in court it does not have to be proved to be the law, but can be taken as read. Only Personal Acts, discussed below, are private in this sense, and given their rarity and limited effect, in practice this is an unimportant distinction.

Secondly, it is used to refer to the parliamentary procedure a Bill goes through. Public Bill procedure is used for legislation promoted by a member of either House, which will commonly be general in its application, but might apply to a locality only (though if it does, it might be hybrid), or even, rarely, to an individual. Private Bill procedure is used for UK legislation promoted by persons outwith Parliament, such as local authorities, who petition Parliament for legislation. This process involves a quasi-judicial procedure, in which promoters and objectors give evidence. Such a private Act in practice will always be 'Local', or 'Personal', not 'general'[77]. Such legislation was common until the 19th century, when promotion of legislation came to be seen as a function of government. It generally sought only to create exceptions to the law. Thus, for example, local authorities might seek exceptional powers through Local Private Acts, and individuals might seek naturalisation (and, in England, divorce) through Personal Private Acts. It is in this sense that the public/private distinction is usually made.

Personal Private legislation is extremely rare nowadays (though there were a few marriage enabling examples in the 1980s, such as the George Donald Evans and Deborah Jane Evans (Marriage

---

[77] Though the 'local' means, in practice, anything not 'personal', and personal means concerning an individual or small number of individuals.

Enabling) Act 1987), for individuals may now achieve naturalisation and divorce through quasi-judicial administrative procedures[78]. Local Private legislation still occurs every year, however (for example, the River Humber (Upper Pyewipe Outfall) Act 1992, the United Reformed Church Act 2000 and the HBOS Group Reorganisation Act 2006), though most of the need for it has gone as local authorities now have most of their powers given under public general legislation, such as the Local Government (Scotland) Act 1973, s 201 (which gives powers to write by-laws).

In any case, accelerated private legislation procedures have been invented to save parliamentary time. The chief one is 'Provisional Order procedure' under the Private Legislation Procedure (Scotland) Act 1936. This largely delegates the consideration of evidence to Commissioners, and the decision to the Secretary of State. If he makes the Provisional Order requested by the promoters, there must be a 'Confirmation Bill' (for example, the Pittenweem Harbour Order Confirmation Act 1992 and the Scottish Borders Council (Jim Clark Memorial Rally) Order Confirmation Act 1996) but it employs an accelerated procedure. There is also a special parliamentary procedure under the Statutory Orders (Special Procedure) Act 1945, which requires no confirmation Bill, but appears never to have been used.

The Scotland Act 1998 continues the Private Legislation Procedure (Scotland) Act 1936 but, by Sch 8, para 5 it cannot be used where the subject-matter is wholly within the competence of the Scottish Parliament. Thus, there was a Comhairle nan Eilean Siar (Eriskay Causeway) Order Confirmation Act 2000 and Railtrack (Waverley Station) Order Confirmation Act 2000.

Hybrid legislation is that which is partly public general, partly private (and local or personal). The Maplin Development Act 1973 was hybrid. It gave powers to the Secretary of State to acquire land on the Maplin Sands in the Thames Estuary for an airport, but did so in relation to a specific area, thus directly affecting individual interests. Hybrid Bills go through a modified public Bill procedure. Thus, the Maplin Development Act took its place in the Public General Act series as 1973 c64.

---

78 Non-marital examples include, for example, the Niall Mcpherson Indemnity Act 1954, c 29.

PUBLICATION AND CITATION OF GREAT BRITAIN AND UNITED KINGDON PARLIAMENTARY LEGISLATION

Publication of Acts of the Parliaments of Great Britain and the United Kingdom

Acts of the Parliaments of Great Britain and the United Kingdom (often bound with those of England) appear in a great variety of editions.

Chronological series

Public general Acts of the United Kingdom Parliament are printed and sold by The Stationery Office ('TSO') in single copies, and bound up in several volumes annually in a series called *Public General Acts and Measures*[79], which commenced in 1831. For almost all purposes, these can be taken as authoritative[80].

Most earlier legislation is of historical interest only. Diverse editions of earlier Acts were produced by various publishers, such as various editions of *Statutes at Large* covering various periods (for example, Ruffhead's, covering English legislation 1225–1707 and Great Britain legislation 1707–1800), and *Statutes of the Realm 1235–1713*, published by the Record Commissioners. These also contain English, but not Scots, Acts and some older editions are inaccurate.

Public General Statutes Affecting Scotland ('Blackwood's Acts') were published annually from 1848 to 1947, with a further three volumes published in 1948 covering the period 1707-1847. The third edition of *Statutes Revised*, published in 1950, contains Great Britain and United Kingdom (and English) Acts still in force in 1948.

All chronological series contain the original unamended text. This is useful for some purposes, but has the disadvantage that it is impossible to tell whether the provision has been repealed (and if so by what), or amended (and if so how).

Encyclopaedic series

The *Statutes in Force* volumes were published as a loose-leaf encyclopaedia, continually updated by the Statute Law Committee

---

79 The 'Measures' are legislation of the Church of England, which, for some reason, are bound in the same volume.
80 See, however, Rankine 'Errors in Acts' (1987) 8 Stat LR 53.

through the Statutory Publications Office. It attempted to provide the text of all public general Acts still in force and as amended (with minor exceptions). These were digested into 131 groups and sub-groups. A list of groups and Acts appears in the first volume.

New Acts were inserted, repealed ones removed, and amendments incorporated. An annual cumulative supplement noted amendments and repeals, and the text of heavily amended Acts was replaced from time to time. Unfortunately, the series was not easy to use, and was phased out in the 1990s in anticipation of the availability of an authoritative Statute Law Database (considered below). Despite the fact that the updating service ceased in 1991, and the last Acts were added were those for 1996, *Statutes in Force* can occasionally be useful for revealing changes made to older legislation.

Commercially produced reprints

The *Current Law Statutes Annotated* volumes (called *Scottish Current Law Statutes Annotated* until 1990) has been published since 1949 (and from 1948 in the case of England and Wales) by W Green and Sweet & Maxwell. The series reproduces all public general statutes chronologically with annotations. These include citation of parliamentary debates and sometimes lengthy and useful commentaries upon each section. Acts of the current year appear in a loose-leaf service file, and each year's Acts are bound into an annual volume or volumes.

Halsbury's Statutes (Butterworths) contains all United Kingdom Acts save those applying only to Scotland. This is unfortunate, as they are digested into subjects, well annotated, and updated through cumulative supplement, current statutes service, and noter-up volumes. Acts concerned with the constitutional structure and government of Northern Ireland, and Northern Ireland Acts which contain cross-border provisions, are reproduced and updated (though not necessarily annotated). In addition, the application of an Act to Northern Ireland is indicated in the preliminary notes. Acts of purely Scottish application, and those provisions of United Kingdom Acts which apply only to Scotland, are excluded.

There are also reprints of all, or most, statutes on a particular area, such as commercial law and family law. *The Parliament House Book* (W Green) is a six-volume loose-leaf encyclopaedia of information useful to practising Scots lawyers, including reprints of Acts of particular interest, in amended form. Acts included are also sold separately as *Parliament House Statutes Reprints*. There are also a number of specific area encyclopaedias, such as *Simon's Taxes*

(Butterworths). Unfortunately, not all of these contain the Scots law on the subject.

Textbooks and monographs may contain Acts of Parliament, or parts of them, relevant to their subject-matter. For example, Macdonald and Webber *Immigration Law and Practice in the United Kingdom* (6th edn, 2005) contains most of the relevant legislation, amended to the date of publication. Annotated Acts from the *Current Law* series are also sometimes published as books, as, for example, Himsworth and Munro *The Scotland Act 1998*.

Indexes etc

Each volume of *Public General Acts and Measures* contains alphabetical and chronological lists of the Acts included. The final volume for each year also contains a table of origins (formerly referred to as 'derivations') and destinations for consolidation Acts (that is, tables showing the relationship of original and consolidated provisions) although it has no official status; and a table of effects of legislation (that is, of repeals and amendments effected during the year).

The Stationery Office also publishes the *Chronological Table of Statutes* annually[81]. This lists chronologically all Scots, Great Britain and United Kingdom (and English) legislation to date, and indicates repeals and amendments.

(Scottish) Current Law Statutes Annotated volumes are individually indexed, as is the loose-leaf 'Service File'. In recent years, individual Acts have been indexed and for some time, the final volume for each year has had an index to all legislation in that year.

Halsbury's Statutes has a companion volume entitled *Is It In Force?*, also issued with the updating service to *The Laws of Scotland: Stair Memorial Encyclopaedia*. Each annual edition records, in respect of all sections of all statutes passed since 1980, whether they are yet in force, and to what extent.

Computerised retrieval of public general Acts

Acts of the UK Parliament since the first Act of 1988 are available in their original form (ie unamended or unrepealed where appropriate) at the Office of Public Sector Information website in full text, as are the Explanatory Notes on Acts which began life as government Bills. (Bills currently before the UK Parliament can be found in full text at

---

81 Until 1990, it produced an *Index to the Statutes* as well.

the Parliament website[82]). The Statute Law Database[83] is the official revised edition of the United Kingdom statute book that is, taking account of all repeals and amendments. Maintained by the Statutory Publication Office, part of the Ministry of Justice, it finally because available to the public in December 2006 after a long and controversial gestation.

The Westlaw database includes all public general Acts in force, in their amended form as appropriate. The BAILII database combines the coverage of unamended Acts from 1988, with older legislation derived from the Statute Law Database. The LexisNexis Butterworths database, mirroring *Halsbury's Statutes*, includes all Acts applying to the United Kingdom and to England and Wales only, but not those applying to Scotland only.

Justis [*sic*] United Kingdom Statutes database contains the full text of all Acts of Parliament, including repealed legislation.

Local, personal and private Acts

The Stationery Office publishes single copies of local and personal Acts and there is an Index to Local and Personal Acts 1797–1849 (2 volumes) and Index to Local and Personal Acts 1850–1995 (four volumes), a Chronological Table of Local Legislation 1797–1994 (4 volumes) and Chronological Table of Private and Personal Acts 1539–1997 (1 volume, containing all such legislation passed by Parliaments in Westminster). Public General Acts and Measures also contains an alphabetical list of local and personal Acts, but no text.

Local Acts have often been published in local compilations, for instance, Dundee Water Acts 1845–82, Dundee Municipal Statutes 1872–98, Dundee Gas and Corporation Acts 1868–1901, and Dundee Harbour Acts 1811–1912.

From 1992 local, personal and private Acts are published in *Current Law Statutes Annotated*.

Computerised retrieval of local, personal and private Acts

Local Acts since the first Act of 1991 can also be found in their original form (ie unamended or unrepealed where appropriate) in full text on the Office of Public Sector Information website ('OPSI')[84].

82 See www.parliament.uk.
83 See www.statutelaw.gov.uk.
84 See www.opsi.gov.uk

An electronic version of *Chronological Table of Private and Personal Acts 1539–1997*, updated to December 2005, is also available on the OPSI website.

Citation of Acts of the Parliaments of Great Britain and the United Kingdom

Before 1963 public general Acts were cited by the extraordinarily complicated regnal year method which the English Parliament used. In this, as well as (or instead of) the reference to the calendar year of enactment, there was reference to the Parliament that passed it, identified by the year or years of the reign of the contemporary Sovereign, calculated from the date of accession. Thus, the Prevention of Damage By Rabbits Act 1939 was correctly cited as '2 & 3 Geo 6 c44', that is, the 44th Act of the Parliament which started in the second year of George VI's reign, and ended in the third.

There were further complications. Until 1940 statutes were bound in volumes for each Parliament although this did not coincide with any calendar year. For example, the session 22 & 23 Geo 5 straddled 1932 and 1933. Thereafter, until 1963, the statutes were bound in annual volumes, although these did not coincide with any parliamentary year. For example, the volume for 1945 contained 8 & 9 Geo 6 c4 to c44 and 9 & 10 Geo 6 c1 to c21.

Since 1963, however, they have been cited in essentially the same fashion as used for Acts of the (original) Parliament of Scotland, by short title, year and chapter number, for example 'Criminal Procedure (Scotland) Act 1987 c46'.

Local and personal Acts are cited in the same form as public general, save that local Acts use lower case roman numerals (for example, the Price's Patent Candle Co Ltd Act 1992 cxvii), and personal Acts, italic numerals (for example, the Valerie Mary Hill and Alan Monk (Marriage Enabling) Act 1985 *c1*).

8. Legislation – Acts of the Scottish Parliament

THE INSTITUTIONAL BACKGROUND

The institutional background of devolution, and the Scottish Executive and Scottish Parliament, were dealt with in Chapter 3, and its relationship with Acts of the United Kingdom Parliament was noted in Chapter 7, with United Kingdom delegated legislation in Chapter 9 and with Scottish delegated legislation in Chapter 10. This Chapter deals with the nature and style of Scottish Parliamentary legislation, the Scottish Parliamentary process, and the publication and citation of Acts of the Scottish Parliament.

THE NATURE AND STYLE OF SCOTTISH PARLIAMENTARY LEGISLATION

Devolution and the nature of Acts of the Scottish Parliament

As noted in relation to Acts of the United Kingdom Parliament, a few Acts of the original pre-1707 Parliament of Scotland are still in force with, effectively, the same status as those of the United Kingdom Parliament[1]. However, this Chapter concerns Acts of the post-1998 Scottish Parliament.

Devolution is making Acts of the Scottish Parliament the normal method of legislating for Scotland (though existing Acts of the United Kingdom will remain the principal source for some time, and a surprising amount of law for Scotland continues to be enacted at

---

1   Though subject to the 'doctrine of desuetude', that is, that they can cease to have effect without explicit or implicit repeal by a later Act, if they have been ignored for a lengthy period, and there is evidence of contrary practice. The oldest Act of the Parliament of Scotland still in force is the Royal Mines Act 1424 (which provides that 'Item: gif ony myne of golde or siluer be fundyn in ony lordis landis of the realme and it may be prowt that thre halfpennys of siluer may be fynit pwt of the punde oe leide The lordis of parliament consentis that sik myne be the kingis as is vsuale in vthir realmys'.

Westminster, for reasons considered above in relation to Acts of the United Kingdom Parliament[2]). The 'legislative competence' of the Scottish Parliament was considered in Chapter 3, and its breadth noted, for, in respect of Scotland, all legislative powers that are not specifically reserved to the United Kingdom Parliament are devolved to the Scottish Parliament. So the Scottish Parliament has a plenitude of law-making power (and much greater than if it had been set up under the abortive Scotland Act 1978, which specified the powers to be devolved)[3]. The range of topics for legislation is thus wide. Indeed, as also noted in Chapter 3, in its first two sessions, the Scottish Parliament passed well over 100 Acts, on topics as diverse as the abolition of feudal land-holding and of fox-hunting, reform of the means of appointing judges and of the Scottish Qualifications Agency, prohibition of anti-social behaviour and of prostitution in public places, and support for the Gaelic language and for breastfeeders. The range may also include legislation on Convention rights and Community law[4].

The very concept of 'legislative competence' indicates, however, that Acts of the Scottish Parliament are 'subordinate' or 'delegated legislation' and this is expressly recognised in some legislation[5]. They are delegated legislation as they are made under powers delegated by the sovereign United Kingdom Parliament, in the Scotland Act 1998.

Pre- and post-enactment checks, described below, police those limits to legislative competence, and the Scottish Parliament is subject to the *ultra vires* doctrine (discussed elsewhere in relation to human rights, Community legislation, and other delegated legislation). In any case, power to override the Scottish Parliament still rests at Westminster for, as s 28(7) of the Scotland Act 1998 explicitly declares, 'This section does not affect the power of the Parliament of the United Kingdom to make laws for Scotland'.

However, their style of expression is that used by the United Kingdom Parliament, rather than that used in most delegated legisla-

2 As with the United Kingdom as a whole, the sheer quantity of (sub)delegated legislation (see Chapters 9 & 10) far outstrips the quantity of parliamentary legislation. See also references to the Sewel Convention and Sewel Motions below.

3 The position is further complicated in that the Acts of the Scottish Parliament may further delegate powers to the Scottish Executive and others, just as Acts of the Westminster Parliament may so delegate. Exercises of such powers by the Scottish Ministers, whether sub-delegated under Holyrood powers or delegated under Westminster powers, are called 'Scottish Statutory Instruments'. They are considered with other delegated legislation in Chapters 9 and 10.

4 Thus, for example, the Convention Rights (Compliance) (Scotland) Act 2001 was passed specifically to make aspects of Scots law conform to the European Convention on Human Rights

5 *Eg*, the Human Rights Act 1998, s 21(1).

tion. Also, they often make provision for areas such as criminal justice and land law which, until devolution, were dealt with in Acts of the United Kingdom Parliament, rather than in delegated legislation. Moreover, they are made by an elected, deliberative, body rather than by civil servants. Indeed, the powers of the Scottish Parliament are of such inherent significance, and the breadth of delegation so remarkable, as to justify separate treatment from other delegated legislation[6].

The 'Sewel Convention' and 'Sewel Motions'

It is worth recalling, nevertheless, that (as noted in Chapter 7) there has been much legislation enacted by the United Kingdom Parliament in relation to Scotland, even within the devolved legislative competence of the Scottish Parliament, through the medium of 'Sewel Motions', that is motions passed by the Scottish Parliament, in effect, requesting that Scotland be included in the Westminster legislation.

The arguments for this practice were rehearsed in Chapter 7, and will not be repeated here. However, it is important to note that, at least in the early years of the Scottish Parliament, Scots law was, arguably, changed as much by Westminster as by Holyrood, and that as the devolved institutions have no control over what happens to the Westminster Bill, they are arguably re-inventing one of the problems devolution was set up to solve.

Acts of the Scottish Parliament, their types and form

The types and forms of Acts of the Scottish Parliament are modelled upon those of United Kingdom Acts (to which reference should be made: see Chapter 7)[7]. Most are 'public'[8], and 'general'[9] in the sense

6   In *Adams v Scottish Ministers* 2003 SLT 366, at 385 J, K, Lord Nimmo Smith observed that '... despite the reference in the Human Rights Act to Acts of the Scottish Parliament being subordinate legislation, such Acts have, in my opinion, far more in common with public general statutes of the United Kingdom Parliament than with subordinate legislation as it is commonly understood. Indeed, the definition of "subordinate legislation" in the Scotland Act makes this distinction clear. The Parliament is a democratically elected body ... An Act of the Scottish Parliament, once passed, requires Royal Assent to become law ... [I]t might be better to regard it as *sui generis*'.
7   See also McCluskie, J 'New Approaches to UK Legislative Drafting: the view from Scotland' (2004) 25 Stat LR 136-143: also the speculative but interesting Jamieson, NJ 'The Scots Statute' (2006) 27 Stat LR 176-184.
8   *Ie* they go through the normal process of enactment unless they fall into the 'Private Bill' category: Standing Orders of the Scottish Parliament, r 9.17.1
9   *Ie* they are 'judicially noticed' so do not require proving in court: Scotland Act 1998, s 28(6).

that Acts of the United Kingdom Parliament are, and special types of Act are considered below. The normal legislative product in the first eight years of the existence of the Scottish Parliament was some 15 Acts a year, though they varied considerably in length. The very first Act of the Scottish Parliament had but three sections, and those in the first four years varied from two sections (University of St Andrews (Postgraduate Medical Degrees) Act 2002) to 100 sections (Land Reform (Scotland) Act 2003). Clearly, they do not yet vary much in age (though the continuation in force of Acts of the original Scottish Parliament should not be forgotten).

Short title, 'asp Number' and Contents List

Acts of the Scottish Parliament commence with a Short Title, normally containing brackets embracing the word '(Scotland)'[10], for example, the 'International Criminal Court (Scotland) Act 2001' (and may contain other bracketed words, as does the 'Mental Health (Public Safety and Appeals) (Scotland) Act 1999'). They also bear an 'asp' ('Act of the Scottish Parliament') Number, that is, a sequential number which, with the year of enactment, identifies the Act, for example, 'asp 10'. Thus '2002 asp 10' was the Fur Farming (Prohibition) (Scotland) Act 2002[11].

All but the shortest Acts have an official 'Contents' list of sections with their numbers and their marginal notes.

Statement of Enactment

Unlike Acts of the United Kingdom Parliament, there is no incantatory 'Enacting Formula', but each Act has a Statement indicating its parliamentary passage in the form: 'The Bill for this Act of the Scottish Parliament was passed by Parliament on 6th March 2002 and received Royal Assent on 11th April 2002'.

---

10 But not invariably, for example if the title is otherwise unequivocal, eg Scottish Public Services Ombudsman Act 2002. Note also that Acts of the Westminster Parliament exclusively concerning Scotland were usually identified by the parenthetic '(Scotland)' in the past (the last pre-devolution Act of the United Kingdom Parliament which applied exclusively to Scotland was the Mental Health (Amendment) (Scotland) Act 1999) and so no doubt will any in the future.

11 Short titles and asp numbers were required by the Scotland Act 1998 (Transitory and Transitional Provisions) (Publication and Interpretation etc of Acts of the Scottish Parliament) Order 1999, SI 1999/1379, arts 4, 5.

Long title and preamble

Acts of the Scottish Parliament also have a Long Title, delimiting the scope of the Bill introduced into the Parliament. Thus, the Fur Farming (Prohibition) (Scotland) Act 2002 has the Long Title 'An Act of the Scottish Parliament to prohibit the keeping of animals solely or primarily for slaughter for the value of their fur; to provide for the making of payments in respect of the related closure of certain businesses; and for connected purposes'.

Sections and Marginal Notes

The Section is the basic unit of Acts of the Scottish Parliament, and they are numbered sequentially through the Act. They may be broken into Sub-sections, Paragraphs and Sub-paragraphs for, as with Acts of the United Kingdom Parliament, the draftsmen aim at exactitude (rules in 'fixed verbal form') rather than comprehensibility, and use typographical devices to express the logic of the section. This also allows precise and unequivocal identification of provisions, for example 'Debt Arrangement and Attachment (Scotland) Act 2002, s 2(3)(a)(iii)'.

The United Kingdom convention of numbering a new Section or Sub-section inserted by an amending Act is employed. Thus the Criminal Procedure (Amendment) (Scotland) Act 2002, s 1(1) inserts new sub-sections 150(3A) and (3B) between the existing sub-sections 150(3) and (4) of the Criminal Procedure (Scotland) Act 1995[12].

Marginal References to legislation referred to in the text have not been used, the draftsman preferring to reproduce short title, year and chapter number or asp number in the text.

Headings

Groups of sections, as in the United Kingdom convention, may be grouped under 'Cross-headings', and into Parts and even Chapters. For example, the Land Reform (Scotland) Act 2003 has its 100 sections divided into 4 Parts, with 6, 2, 7 and 5 Chapters respectively.

No doubt 'Titles' will also be used if considered necessary.

---

12 This is an example of an Act of the Scottish Parliament amending an Act of the United Kingdom Parliament (both, however, identified by the parenthetic '(Scotland)').

Interpretation sections

Where words or phrases are inherently vague, or are used in an unusual sense, or have been invented for the purpose, an Interpretation Section may provide a meaning. Thus, the Abolition of Feudal Tenure (Scotland) Act 2000, s 72 defines, among other things 'land'[13].

Repeal and amendment

The standard United Kingdom conventions apply to Acts of the Scottish Parliament, that is, that Acts continue in force unless repealed or amended and no special process of repeal is necessary, so 'implicit repeal' is possible[14]. Also, while repeals and amendments may appear anywhere in the Act, commonly, a specific section at the end effects them, often in conjunction with a Schedule. For example, the Adults with Incapacity (Scotland) Act 2000, Sch 6 is headed 'Repeals' and contains a table indicating what provisions are repealed, and to what extent, and the Housing (Scotland) Act 2001, Sch 10, headed 'Modification of Enactments', contains a long list of repeals and amendments.

However, in the case of Acts of the Scottish Parliament, because of their delegated status, particular considerations concerning repeal and amendment should be noted. Firstly, because of the general possibility that they may be found to be outwith the Parliament's 'legislative competence', s 107 of the Scotland Act 1998 gives the United Kingdom government, in such cases, the power to make 'necessary or expedient' provision by ordinary delegated legislation (see Chapter 9). This clearly includes the power to repeal or amend. And, secondly, in any case, as s 28(7) reiterates, the United Kingdom Parliament retains the power to legislate for Scotland which even more clearly includes the power to repeal or amend Acts of the Scottish Parliament. (Indeed, the continued use of the United Kingdom Parliament to legislate for Scotland through 'Sewel Motions', considered above in relation to Acts of the United Kingdom Parliament, means that such legislation is in fact a

---

13 The Scotland Act 1998 (Transitory and Transitional Provisions) (Publication and Interpretation, etc of Acts of the Scottish Parliament) Order 1999, SI 1999/1379, Sch 2 contained a list of 'General Definitions' (including one of 'land') to be applied to Acts of the Scottish Parliament.

14 On the effects of repeal, see SI 1999/1379 (see previous note), Sch 1, paras 11–14. In principle, repeals are not retrospective and repeals of repeals do not revive the original provision.

frequent and regular occurrence.) Thus, repeal or amendment of Acts of the Scottish Parliament may well be by means other than further Acts of the Scottish Parliament.

Transitional, Commencement, Short Title and Extent provisions

In broad terms these operate, or will operate, in the same fashion as with United Kingdom statutes, save that the difficulty which Extent provisions deal with does not arise, as legislating outwith Scotland is beyond the Scottish Parliament's legislative competence. Thus, the University of St Andrews (Postgraduate Medical Degrees) Act 2002, s 2 states that it may be so cited, but contains no reference to commencement, so came into force on the date of Royal Assent[15], while the Scottish Qualifications Authority Act 2002, s 6, declares that it may be so cited, but that (other than s 6 itself) it comes into force 'on such day as the Scottish Ministers may by order appoint'[16].

Schedules

Schedules are attached to Acts of the Scottish Parliament in the same fashion, and for the same purposes, as to Acts of the United Kingdom Parliament. Thus, the Water Environment and Water Services (Scotland) Act 2002 has four Schedules, two split into two Parts each[17].

Explanatory Notes

Almost every Act has accompanying 'Explanatory Notes' (as United Kingdom Acts have since 1999), produced by the sponsoring government department and attempting to explain in lay language what each provision of the Act does. As with United Kingdom

---

15 30 July 2002 is indicated in the 'Statement of enactment' (see above).
16 Its royal assent was obtained on 6 June 2002. The Scottish Ministers, under s 6 of the Act, appointed 19 August 2002 for s 1(7)(a)(iii), (8), (9), by the Scottish Qualifications Authority Act 2002 (Commencement No 1) Order 2002, SSI/335, art 3(2). Thus, at that time, s 1(1)–(6), (7)(a)(i),(ii), (b) and ss 2–5 had not been brought into force.
17 'Matters to be included in river basin management plans' (split into 'Matters to be included in every plan' and 'Additional matters to be included in revised plans'); 'Controlled activities regulations' (split into 'List of purposes' and 'Supplementary provisions'); 'Sustainable urban drainage systems: further amendments'; and 'Modifications of Part III of the 1980 Act', respectively.

legislation, they nevertheless have no official status, although presumably they may presumably be used in statutory interpretation (as discussed in Chapter 11).

THE SCOTTISH PARLIAMENTARY LEGISLATIVE PROCESSES

Proposed Acts of the Scottish Parliament, by s 28(2) of the Scotland Act 1998, 'shall be known as Bills' and are the product of a lengthy process, as are Acts of the Untied Kingdom Parliament (for which, see Chapter 7), though with certain specialities.

Who seeks legislation and why?

The role of legislation in Scotland under devolution is intended to be, and likely to be, very much as is its role in the United Kingdom as a whole. Thus, most legislation comes from the Scottish Executive. This may be 'manifesto legislation' promised by the party forming (or forming part of) the Scottish Executive, for example the Abolition of Feudal Tenure, Etc (Scotland) Act 2000. One sort of legislation that was expected to figure largely in the early years (indeed, the expectation of which was part of the justification for devolution), was uncontentious reform for which the United Kingdom had failed to find time. There have been examples, such as the Adults with Incapacity (Scotland) Act 2000.

However, legislation may be a reaction to events, as was the very first Act of the Scottish Parliament, the Mental Health (Public Safety and Appeals) (Scotland) Act 1999. A person had been convicted of culpable homicide some years earlier, and was detained in the State Mental Hospital at Carstairs. Such detention was, under the relevant legislation, competent only where there was treatment capable of alleviating the subject's condition or preventing further decline. It was agreed that, on the facts, this person's treatment could not have this effect. As a result, a sheriff concluded that the detention was unlawful. The 1999 Act was designed to reverse this result.

The Bail, Judicial Appointments, Etc (Scotland) Act 2000 and the Convention Rights (Compliance) (Scotland) Act 2001 could also be seen in this light, but perhaps fall into the most common class of legislation, that is, legislation which simply emerges from the processes of government. In the early years of the Scottish Parliament, some of this is legislation simply setting up new institutions and procedures, such as the Public Finance and Accountability (Scotland) Act 2000, instituting governmental financial controls.

Pre-parliamentary stages of Scottish parliamentary legislation

As with United Kingdom legislation, the procedures before a Bill even appears are critical, for it is then that the Scottish Executive consults and decides what legislation it wishes to bring forward. This is discussed further in Chapter 15, though it may be remarked that the Scottish Parliament was set up with the intention of being more open to the population, and less bound by party political considerations, than is the United Kingdom Parliament[18].

The Scottish Executive was, until the 2007 Election, a coalition of two political parties, which puts additional strain upon the process of deciding what legislation to propose[19]. There is no Queen's Speech in the Scottish Parliament, and the practice in the first Parliament was for the Scottish Executive to outline its intended legislative programme in September. However, in the second, proposals were published from shortly after the election[20].

Parliamentary stages of Scottish parliamentary legislation and 'pre-enactment checks' on legislative competence

Any member of the Scottish Parliament may introduce a Bill and, when a Bill is introduced, s 31 of the Scotland Act 1998 requires the person introducing it to state that it is within the Scottish Parliament's 'legislative competence' (discussed in Chapter 3), and the Presiding Officer to decide separately whether or not this is the case (and he is required to give reasons where he decides a provision is not). These are the first two 'pre-enactment checks' on legislative competence[21]. Since legislation incompatible with the 'Convention rights' under the Human Rights Act 1998 (for which, see Chapter 3) is not permitted, this is also one of the devices used to seek compatibility between legislation and those rights (see again Chapter 3).

The Bill is also required by the Standing Orders of the Scottish Parliament to have 'accompanying documents', that is, a Financial

---

18 See *Shaping Scotland's Parliament; report of the Consultative Steering Group on the Scottish Parliament* (Scottish Office 1998), section 3.6 'Access and Information'. One specific example of this is the common use of Draft Bills, published for consultation.
19 As it was thereafter a minority Executive, different strains might be expected.
20 In mid-2007, it was too early to say what the practice would be for the third.
21 A position in marked contrast to that of the UK legislature which may not only validly pass legislation within the Scottish Parliament's legislative competence, but may do so inadvertently, as occurred in relation to the (UK) Housing Act 2004.

Memorandum giving best estimates of administrative, compliance and other costs, and (unless it is a 'Member's Bill': see below) 'Explanatory Notes' summarising the provisions and giving other necessary information, and a 'Policy Memorandum' giving the policy objectives of the Bill, describing why the Bill took the approach it did, the consultation which was undertaken, and an assessment of its effects on a somewhat mixed bag of factors, including equal opportunities, human rights, island communities, local government, sustainable development and any other relevant matter.

The Statement of Enactment records the date the Bill was introduced, and the date it received the Royal Assent, but is silent on what passes on and between those dates. However, s 36 of the Scotland Act 1998 lays down a procedure for enactment similar to that of the United Kingdom Parliament, though by no means identical[22]. One difference is clearly that there is no equivalent of the House of Lords. Another is that the various subject-based Committees of Parliament such as Education, and Justice (for which see Chapter 3) are more involved, and involved earlier.

Thus, s 36 requires (subject to exceptions) that standing orders include provision for:

-   a general debate (referred to as 'Stage 1', and equivalent to the United Kingdom Parliament's Second Reading);
-   a consideration of, and the opportunity for members to vote on, the details of a Bill (referred to as 'Stage 2' and equivalent to the United Kingdom Parliament's Committee Stage);
-   a final stage at which a Bill can be passed or rejected (referred to as 'Stage 3' and equivalent to the United Kingdom Parliament's Third Reading).

The Standing Orders of the Scottish Parliament fill in the detail.

Stage 1 effectively falls into two parts. In the first, the Bill is referred immediately to the relevant Parliamentary Committee (the 'lead committee') which considers and reports on the general principles to the Parliament as a whole, and any Policy Memorandum. (Where the Bill straddles the interests of more than one Committee, there is still a 'lead committee', but the other may also consider them, and in any case, the Subordinate Legislation Committee may also consider matters of delegated legislation: see below.) During this consideration, there can be public taking of evidence.

22 The procedures of other small countries and devolved legislatures were studied before the final procedure was fixed.

In the second part, the Parliament debates the general principles in the light of the Committee report, and may refer it back for a further report. If the Parliament disagrees with the general principles, the Bill fails. If it agrees, the Bill is remitted to the lead committee, or another committee, or a Committee of the Whole House, for Stage 2.

Stage 2, which must be at least two weeks later, considers each provision of the Bill, which must be agreed to, amended or rejected (though provisions concerning delegated legislation may be referred to the Subordinate Legislation Committee).

Stage 3, which must be at least two further weeks later if there have been amendments, may permit further amendments, and indeed may involve remitting the Bill back to Stage 2, but is essentially the decision as to whether to pass the Bill, as amended in Stage 2. If the decision is pushed to a vote, there is a quorum of one quarter of all MSPs.

Royal Assent is required by s 32, but s 33 gives to certain officials, in the four weeks following Stage 3, the right to refer a Bill to the Judicial Committee of the Privy Council (the final authority on disputes on the Scotland Act: see Chapter 3) for a decision as to whether Bill is within the Parliament's legislative competence. These officials are the Advocate-General for Scotland (the Scottish law officer of the Westminster government: see Chapter 3) or the Attorney-General (of England and Wales: see Chapter 3), either of whom might be concerned about an encroachment on Westminster's reserved powers, and even the Lord Advocate (the Scottish Executive's principal law officer: see Chapter 3), who, though a member of the Scottish Executive, might be unhappy with the form the Bill finally took. The Bill may not be presented for royal assent during this period. This is the third 'pre-enactment' check on legislative competence and, like the others, operates as another of the devices seeking to ensure compatibility between legislation and 'Convention rights' under the Human Rights Act 1998.

There is a fourth 'pre-enactment check' in that the Secretary of State (in other words, the United Kingdom government) may issue an order under s 35, forbidding the Presiding Officer from submitting a Bill for Royal Assent. This is different in kind from the other 'pre-enactment checks', for it is not in the hands of an official exercising a quasi-judicial function, but in those of a clearly party political person. However, the Secretary of State may take this grave step only if he believes on reasonable grounds that the Bill will transgress some international obligation (which would include a breach of the European Convention on Human Rights, or of Community law) or with the interests of defence or national security, or that, in modifying the law on reserved matters, it will have an adverse effect on them.

In addition to the 'pre-enactment checks', there are the 'post-enactment checks' considered in Chapter 3, whereby in any litigation concerning legislation which is in force, a 'devolution issue' may arise.

Special cases

Human rights legislation

There is no Scottish Parliament equivalent of the Human Rights Act 1998, for that Act applies to the whole United Kingdom in any case. One important result of this is, of course, that the legislative competence of the Scottish Parliament is limited by that Act (as noted above).

Financial legislation

The Scottish Parliament receives a block grant which is paid into the Scottish Consolidated Fund along with any other payments. Out of it the Scottish Administration pays all authorised expenditure.

As noted in relation to legislation of the United Kingdom Parliament, financial legislation has a particular constitutional status, and taxation is in any case a reserved matter. However, Part IV of the Scotland Act 1998 gives the Scottish Parliament the power to raise or lower the basic rate of income tax by 3p in the pound. Therefore, if this power is exercised, it must be by means of a 'Tax-Varying Resolution' of the Scottish Parliament, rather than an Act. Following United Kingdom constitutional convention, such Resolution would have to be annual.

Tax-spending powers (and any tax-raising powers other than varying the basic rate of income tax), can be exercised only through legislation, following United Kingdom convention of the constitution. Thus, any such legislation requires a 'Financial Resolution' before Stage 2 can be taken. Respecting the constitutional convention requiring annual Acts authorising expenditure, there has been an annual 'Budget (Scotland) Act'.

Consolidation, statute law repeal and statute law revision legislation

'Consolidation' etc are discussed above as special examples of United Kingdom legislation. Although there is insufficient legislation from the Scottish Parliament for these procedures to be needed in respect of it, the Scottish Parliament is, of course, entitled to seek to simplify the statute book by consolidating United Kingdom Parliament legislation within its legislative competence, and there are simplified procedures in the Standing Orders of the Scottish Parliament[23].

Members' legislation

Most legislation is introduced by government but, as noted in relation to the UK Parliament, any MSP may do so. The Scotland Act 1998 does not specifically refer to such Private Members' legislation, but the Standing Orders of the Scottish Parliament anticipate it, under the description 'Member's Bills'. Indeed, there have been some such Member's Bills[24], some of which have been enacted, though it is still early to conclude what role such Bills will usually fulfil.

Committee legislation

In addition, in an interesting innovation, committees themselves may introduce Bills on matters which they have enquired into, provided the Parliament agrees (and in which case the first part of Stage 1 is dispensed with). Again, it is still early to see how this innovation will develop[25].

23 These powers have been exercised. In 2003, following the Scottish Law Commission Report 'Report on the Consolidation of Certain Enactments concerning Salmon and Freshwater Fisheries' (Scot Law Com 188), the Salmon and Freshwater Fisheries (Consolidation) (Scotland) Act consolidated one Act of the Scottish Parliament (the Theft Act 1607), 23 Acts of the United Kingdom Parliament (the oldest dating from 1804) and four pieces of delegated legislation.
24 *Eg* the Council of the Law Society Act 2003 (introduced by David McLetchie MSP) and the Dog Fouling (Scotland) Act 2003 (introduced by Keith Harding MSP). There have also been unsuccessful attempts, eg the Gaelic Language Bill 2003 (introduced by Mike Russell MSP).
25 The Commissioner for Children and Young People (Scotland) Act 2003 was a Committee Bill, following the Education, Culture and Sport Committee's Report 'An Inquiry into the Need for a Children's Commissioner in Scotland' (2nd Report of 2002, SP Paper 508, 14 February 2002) and 'Report on the proposed Commissioner for Children and Young Persons Bill' (11th Report of 2002, SP Paper 617, 3 July 2002): the proposal was accepted by the Parliament on 25 September 2002 and introduced on 4 December 2002, and was successfully enacted 26 March 2003, receiving its royal assent on 1 May 2003.

Local, personal, private and hybrid legislation

Existing forms of Private Bill procedure are retained for those matters not within the competence of the Scottish Parliament. Thus, for reserved matters (which include oil and gas and most transport matters), the Private Legislation Procedure (Scotland) Act 1936 (discussed above in relation to United Kingdom Private, Personal etc legislation), continues unchanged, still requiring the decision of the Secretary of State and a UK Parliament Confirmation Act. The alternative procedure under the Statutory Orders (Special Procedure) Act 1945, which is partly devolved, also remains (though it appears never to have been used in Scotland, even before devolution).

However, for fully devolved matters, the public/private distinction applies to legislation of the Scottish Parliament as it does to the United Kingdom Parliament. There is provision in the Standing Orders of the Scottish Parliament for 'Private' legislation in this sense, that is, for Bills introduced by a promoter who is an individual person, a corporate body (such as a local authority or a trading company) or an unincorporated association (such as a club, society or trust which was not incorporated) for the purpose of obtaining particular powers or benefits in excess of, or in conflict with, the general law. This includes Bills relating to 'estate, property, status or style or otherwise relating to the personal affairs of the promoter'. In such case, the lead committee requires the promoter to deposit documents, give notice, deposit copies of the Bill for public inspection, give notice to interested parties and invite objections[26].

26 Thus there were the Robin Rigg Offshore Wind Farm (Navigation and Fishing) (Scotland) Act 2003, promoted by Offshore Energy Resources Ltd and Solway Offshore Ltd, and designed to allow them to interfere with public rights of navigation and fishing in order to construct and maintain the wind farm, and the Stirling-Alloa-Kincardine Railway and Linked Improvements Act 2004 promoted by Clackmannanshire Council and designed to construct a rail connection to Longannet Power Station and related works, including closing level crossings and roads, and purchasing land compulsorily.

Emergency legislation

There is special provision for 'emergency Bills' in the Standing Orders of the Scottish Parliament providing rapid enactment. No definition of 'emergency' is attempted[27].

PUBLICATION AND CITATION OF ACTS OF THE SCOTTISH PARLIAMENT

Publication of Acts of the (pre-1707) Parliament of Scotland

Chronological series

Acts of the original Parliament of Scotland, a few of which are still in force, are printed in a number of modern series. The *Acts of the Parliaments of Scotland 1124–1707* (alias the 'Record Edition') was published in the 19th century by the Commissioners of Public Records[28]. Acts and related documents, such as Charters, from 1135 are published in the several volumes of *Regesta Regum Scottorum* (Edinburgh University Press) which commenced in 1960. Each deals with the output during the reign of a monarch.

Those Acts still in force in 1964 appear in an HMSO reprint also called *Acts of the Parliaments of Scotland 1424–1707*.

Computerised retrieval of Acts of the (pre-1707) Scottish Parliament

The Statute Law Database[29] makes available the text of those Acts still in force, as amended.

---

27 However, the Criminal Procedure (Amendment) (Scotland) Act 2002, designed to overturn a particularly awkward decision on criminal procedure, *Reynolds v Dyer* 2002 SLT 295, 2002 SCCR 322, was passed by this means. The court decision was on 14 February, and the Bill was drafted by, and passed all its stages, on 27 February 2002. The learned annotator in the *Current Law* volume containing the Acts justly remarked that it is unlikely that the Westminster Parliament would have reacted that quickly.

28 Earlier editions include the *Laws and Acts of Parliament 1424-1681*, published by Sir Thomas Murray of Glendook ('*Glendook's Edition*'), itself based on those published a century earlier by Skene.

29 See www.statutelaw.gov.uk.

Citation of Acts of the (pre-1707) Scottish Parliament

Acts of the Parliament of Scotland are usually cited by Short Title and year, for example the 'Union with England Act 1706'. Different editions do not always agree on the chapter number[30] but, as so few are still in force, it is possible to omit it. In historical contexts they are sometimes cited by reference to the volume and page of the Record Edition, for example 'APS [ie 'Acts of the Parliaments of Scotland'] VIII, 80'.

Publication of Acts of the Scottish Parliament

Chronological series

Acts of the Scottish Parliament are printed and sold in individual copies by The Stationery Office ('TSO') and are bound into annual volumes so entitled, and these can be taken as authoritative.

Encyclopaedic series

It is understood that there are no plans to produce an encyclopaedic series.

Commercially produced reprints

The *Current Law Statutes Annotated* series reproduces all Acts of the Scottish Parliament, including private legislation.

The *Parliament House Book* and *Parliament House Statutes Reprints* include relevant Acts of the Scottish Parliament, and some textbooks and monographs will do likewise. In addition, the *Passage of Bills* series published by Astron most usefully contain all relevant accompanying documents, including Scottish parliamentary debates, and indeed the Bill as amended at different stages, with the Act itself in final form

Indexes etc

Annual volumes of *Acts of the Scottish Parliament* are indexed, but no indexes as such have yet been published.

---

30 The Royal Mines Act 1424, the oldest Scots Act still in force, is described in the Record Edition as c13, but in *Glendook's Edition* as c12.

Computerised retrieval of Acts of the Scottish Parliament

Acts of the Scottish Parliament are available in their original form (ie unamended and unrepealed) at the Office of Public Sector Information website in full text, as are the Explanatory Notes[31]. The revised text appears on the Statute Law Database[32]. Bills currently before the Scottish Parliament can be found in full text, and with links to 'accompanying documents' and 'policy memoranda' and references to the relevant Committees, at the Scottish Parliament website[33].

The Westlaw, LexisNexis Butterworths and Justis [*sic*] databases includes all Acts of the Scottish Parliament in force, in their amended form as appropriate, with sophisticated search facilities. The BAILII database also contains all such Acts.

Citation of Acts of the Scottish Parliament

Acts of the Scottish Parliament are cited by Short Title, year and 'asp' ('Act of the Scottish Parliament') number, for example 'Regulation of Care (Scotland) Act 2001 asp 8. Bills are cited as 'SP Bill', with the title, number, session and (in brackets) year, for example 'SP Bill 12 National Parks (Scotland) Bill [as introduced] Session 1 (2000)[34].

---

31 See www.opsi.gov.uk.
32 See www.statutelaw.gov.uk.
33 See www.scottish.parliament.uk/.
34 Style and Example taken from 'A Guide to recommended Citations for Scottish Parliament Publications' (May 2001).

9. Legislation – United Kingdom Delegated Legislation

THE INSTITUTIONAL BACKGROUND

The institutional background of delegated legislation was touched on in Chapters 3 (concerning the distinction between Parliament and Government) and 5 (concerning sources of law). The term 'United Kingdom delegated legislation' is used in this Chapter to mean delegated legislation other than Acts of the Scottish Parliament (which is, at least technically, delegated legislation, as discussed in Chapter 8 and below), and that made under powers delegated by the Scottish Parliament (which is thus, at least technically sub-delegated legislation, as discussed in Chapter 10). Therefore, broadly speaking, it deals with what might be regarded as the traditional sense of phrase, and considers the nature of such delegated legislation, its types and their form, *ultra vires* and judicial control of it, and its publication and citation.

THE NATURE OF DELEGATED LEGISLATION

The origins and purpose of delegated legislation

In the United Kingdom context, delegated legislation is legislation made by a body other than the United Kingdom Parliament (that is, 'the legislature'), under powers delegated to it by that Parliament. It is not a novel phenomenon. Its modern use dates from the early 19th-century Parliaments' reforming zeal, but it has proliferated in the last 50 years.

The reasons for having delegated legislation are various and interlocking, but the traditional ones can be summed up as speed and flexibility, and use of expertise. Parliamentary time is overburdened, so delegating the power to legislate bypasses the bottleneck. Moreover, much legislation requires frequent minor change, and it is a lot easier to amend most delegated legislation than any Parliamentary legislation. Much legislation is also complicated,

261

concerning subjects such as nuclear safety or teachers' superannuation, and Parliament has no collective expertise in most such areas. Therefore, delegation to experts, typically civil servants, but usually in consultation with outside interests affected by the proposals, may be sensible. One particular form of expertise is local knowledge, implying delegation to local authorities[1].

Other benefits said to accrue from delegation, for example its use for emergency powers, are usually variations upon those mentioned. One other advantage for a government (which already dominates Parliament and thus the legislative process) is said, cynically, to be further reduction in parliamentary control. Consultation with interested parties before and during drafting is as important with delegated legislation as with parliamentary, and because it is less often drafted against the clock, the standard of draftsmanship is often thought to be higher than for Acts.

Thus, traditionally, delegated legislation can be seen as a means by which the modern administrative machinery of government is reconciled (satisfactorily or otherwise) with democratic control. It also demonstrates the common characteristic of modern law, that is, that much of it is a form of procedural guide to officials and incomprehensible to the uninitiated, rather like a guide to computer software.

However, one important, non-traditional, purpose of delegation requires mention. A major feature of the structure of the United Kingdom has become devolution, introduced in varying degrees, and for somewhat disparate reasons, to Scotland, Wales and (with more difficulty) Northern Ireland (though not so far to England). The means adopted to devolve legislative power has been simply to delegate some of the legislative power of the United Kingdom Parliament to the new Scottish Parliament, thus making Acts of the Scottish Parliament technically, at least, delegated legislation[2] (and any delegation by it, sub-delegation). This, however, is dealt with in Chapters 8 and 10

Delegated legislation is sometimes referred to as 'subordinate legislation'[3] or even 'secondary legislation', which implies that it is less powerful than other forms. This is misleading for, provided the exercise of the delegated power is within the boundaries of the delegation and not *ultra vires*, legislation made under delegated powers is

1   For example, whether drinking alcoholic beverages in public in the centre of cities should be controlled or not is probably best left to local decision: see for example, the City of Dundee District Bylaws for Prohibiting the Consumption of Alcohol in Designated Places 1995 and equivalents elsewhere. See also, however, references to devolution below.
2   See next note.
3   The Scotland Act 1998 does so, for instance: see eg s 104.

as powerful as an Act of the United Kingdom Parliament. As illustrated below, it can be used to amend or even repeal Acts of Parliament

Not all grants of powers in Acts of Parliament are delegations of legislative powers, that is, of powers to write laws. They may be grants of executive or administrative powers, that is, powers to take decisions. For example, powers are granted by the Immigration and Asylum Act 1999, s 83(1),(2) to the Secretary of State to appoint (after consultation with the Lord Chancellor and the Scottish Ministers) an Immigration Services Commissioner with a duty to operate a register of persons qualified to provide immigration advice and services, and by s 85(3) and Sch 6 powers are granted to the Commissioner himself to determine whether a person is competent to provide such advice and services and, if so, to register that person as so qualified[4].

Nature and uses of delegated legislation

Delegated legislation, as noted above, is legislation made by a body other than the United Kingdom Parliament, under powers delegated to it by that Parliament. Such a delegate is not itself a source of law, so cannot legislate without such an act of delegation by that Parliament. There must therefore be a 'parent Act', as it is commonly called[5]. In practice, most Acts are 'parent Acts', though many have only few progeny.

In principle, delegation might be to any body, although commonly it is to 'the Secretary of State', that is, the government. In principle, delegated legislation may cover the same enormous range of subjects as do Acts of Parliament[6], although there are conventions which tend to restrict its use to, broadly speaking, more detailed matters, leaving the principles to the parent Act.

4   And the executive powers delegated to the Scottish Executive are likewise not, as such, legislative.
5   Thus the 'parent Act' of all devolved legislation in Scotland is the Scotland Act 1998.
6   Statutory Instruments (the principal form of delegated legislation) in 2007 concerned subjects as diverse as the air passenger duty and school admissions, by way of driving licences, insolvency practitioners, offshore installation safety zones, and road tolling. Among the first half-dozen statutory instruments of 2007 were the Animals and Animal Products (Import and Export) (England) (Amendment) Regulations 2007 SI 2007/3, the Cider and Perry and Wine and Made-wine (Amendment) Regulations 2007 SI 2007/4, and the Customs and Excise (Personal Reliefs for Special Visitors) (Amendment) Order 2007 SI 2007/5. The frequency of the word 'amendment' is not misleading.

Standard uses of delegated legislation

Much detailed domestic regulation is thus made by delegated legislation, for example the rules requiring headlamps of a certain size and power on cars, and the like[7], and speed limits[8]. Delegated legislation is often used to bring Acts of Parliament into force[9]. Much, however, is of minor significance, for example fixing fees for various services which may require frequent amendment[10].

Some delegated legislation is of major importance, however. Constitutions of newly independent ex-colonies were habitually laid down by this means[11]. 'Direct rule' in Northern Ireland operated from the 1970s through delegation of certain 'transferred powers' to the Secretary of State for Northern Ireland[12]. Equally, as noted above, devolution to Scotland operates through delegated powers (as more fully considered in Chapters 8 and 10). Much Community

7 For example, Road Vehicles (Construction and Use) Regulations 1986, SI 1986/1078 (as amended); Road Vehicles (Authorisation of Special Types) General Order 2003, SI 2003/1998) (as amended); Motor Vehicles (Tests) Regulations 1981, SI 1981/1694 (as amended) etc; and even the Pedal Cycles (Construction and Use) Regulations 1983, SI 1983/1176, made under various powers, now chiefly the Road Traffic Act 1988.

8 Chiefly the Motor Vehicle (Variation of Speed Limits) Regulations 1947, SR&O 1947/2192; Motorway Traffic (Speed Limit) Regulations 1974, SI 1974/502; 70mph, 60mph and 50mph (Temporary Speed Limit) Order 1977 and Temporary Speed Limit (Continuation) Order 1978, SI 1978/1548; and Motor Vehicle (Variation of Speed Limits) Regulations 1986, SI 1986/1175, made under various powers, chiefly now the Road Traffic Regulation Act 1984. Note that most of the Statutory Instruments imposing speed limits apply to very specific areas, eg the A34 Trunk Road (Chievely Interchange) (40 Miles Per Hour Speed Limit) Order 2007, SI 2007/233.

9 In other words, although the Act is law, having passed through Parliament, it has no effect until a further piece of legislation, the power to make which was delegated by the Act (typically to the government), is exercised: see 'Commencement provisions' in Chs. 7 & 8 and, for example, the Scotland Act 1998 (Commencement) Order 1998, SI 1998/3178.

10 For example, the Consular Fees (Amendment) Order 2006, SI 2006/1912, made under the Consular Fees Act 1980 s 1(1), fixes fees for passports.

11 For example, the original constitution of Zambia is in Sch 2 to the Zambia Independence Order 1964, SI 1964/1652, made under powers delegated to the government by the Foreign Jurisdiction Act 1890 and the Zambia Independence Act 1964.

12 Northern Ireland Act 1974, s 1(3), (4), and Sch 1(1)(b), read with the Northern Ireland Constitution Act 1973, ss 2, 3. The Northern Ireland Act 1998 replaced this with a new form of devolution, and (despite earlier interruptions, as manifested in the Northern Ireland Act 2000) in mid-2007, this appears to be working.

legislation (that which is without direct effect) takes effect in the United Kingdom by this means[13].

Controversial uses of delegated legislation

Some uses of delegated legislation are controversial. Firstly, governments often seek very wide powers of delegation, and may even propose 'skeleton Acts', that is, bare frameworks, the detail all to be provided by delegated legislation. Framework Acts, with clear principles, may not be objectionable. However, at some point, the provisions of the Act become too skeletal. An example of an Act which is controversial on this point was the Education (Student Loans) Act 1990[14]. This had but four sections and two fairly brief schedules, and could be summed up in s 1(1) which read 'The Secretary of State may make arrangements for enabling eligible students to receive loans towards their maintenance ... '. The term 'eligible students' was partly defined in s 1(2)(a), and various other terms were defined elsewhere, but s 1(2)(b) permitted the Secretary of State to impose on eligible students 'such other conditions as may be prescribed by regulations made by him' and Sch 2 permitted regulations to prescribe the maximum annual loan, the timing and manner of repayment, deferment or cancellation of liability etc, with few restrictions. Thus, the actual scheme was to be found, not in the Act, but almost entirely in delegated legislation[15].

Secondly, delegated legislation may be used to amend Acts of Parliament. This may be restricted to a power to amend earlier Acts in 'Transitional Provisions' (discussed in Chapter 7)[16], though it has been used to permit more major change, and indeed, even future amendment of the very Act giving the delegated powers[17]. Such uses have been termed 'Henry VIII clauses'.

Remarkable examples of the use of delegated legislation

There have been several examples of very wide delegation in recent years[18]. One remarkable example is the Scotland Act 1998[19], which

---

13 See 'Community legislation without direct effect and United Kingdom law' in Chapter 6.
14 Now replaced by the Teaching and Higher Education Act 1998.
15 In early 2003, there were 34 sets of such regulations in force.
16 *Eg* the Education Reform Act 1988, s 231.
17 *Eg* the Sex Discrimination Act 1975, s 80(1) permits amendment to listed provisions of the Act itself, and s 80(3) allows that list itself to be amended!
18 *Eg* the European Communities Act 1972, s 2(2) and the Human Rights Act 1988, s 10.
19 Delegation to Scottish authorities, including 'Scottish Statutory Instruments', are considered in Ch 10, as such.

includes (however inappropriately titled in historically accurate dynastic terms) 'HenryVIII clauses'. Thus, for example, s 30(2) allows Schs 4 and 5 to the Act itself to be amended; s 89 allows modification of the functions of cross-border public authorities set up by the Act if 'necessary or expedient'; s 104 allows any provision to be made which is 'necessary or expedient' in consequence of the Scotland Act or delegated legislation under it; s 105 allows modifications to legislation made before the Scotland Act which are 'necessary or expedient' in consequence of the Scotland Act; s 106 allows modification of the functions exercisable by the government which is 'appropriate' to enable it to be transferred to the Scottish Executive; s 107 allows 'necessary and expedient' amendments to be made in consequence of *ultra vires* legislation by the Scottish Parliament or action by the Scottish Executive; and so on, all by means of delegated legislation.

Moreover, s 113 extends the scope of all these, and other powers to make delegated legislation, in various ways. And s 114 allows amendment by delegated legislation of some of those very provisions which give the power to amend by delegated legislation. No doubt this can be justified in so far as the draftsmen could plead that it was impossible for them, or the Members of Parliament, to foresee all the necessary provisions. Certainly, some of these powers have been used extensively.

Another most extraordinary example is the Legislative and Regulatory Reform Act 2006 (largely replacing the Regulatory Reform Act 2001, itself amending the Deregulation and Contracting Out Act 1994)[20]. Part 1 of this Act gives power to the United Kingdom government, to make two sorts of 'Order'. The more controversial power[21], under s 1, allows it to make an order 'removing or reducing any burden' (including by 'repealing any enactment' or 'restating' it) if the burden 'result[s] directly or indirectly for any person from any legislation'. Moreover, by s 4, an Order can delegate (though not sub-delegate) powers, provided it is done by Statutory Instrument. The breadth of this is clearly enormous. It is underlined firstly by the definition of 'burden' in s 1(3), which is 'a financial cost', 'an administrative convenience' (which includes 'where legislation is hard to understand'), 'an obstacle to efficiency, productivity or profitability', or 'a sanction, criminal or

20 The original Bill was even more extraordinary. It emerged from a review of the Regulatory Reform Act 2001 called *Less is More: reducing burdens, improving outcomes* (Better Regulation Task Force 2005): see http://www.brc.gov.uk/upload/assets/www.brc.gov.uk/lessismore.pdf, and another report *Reducing Administrative Burdens: effective inspection and enforcement* (Treasury 2005).
21 The less controversial power, in s 2, to make an Order to secure that regulatory functions (as defined) are exercised to comply with certain principles (in Part 2 of the Act), is not considered here.

otherwise, which affects the carrying on of any lawful purpose'. It is equally underlined by the definition of legislation in s 1(6), which includes 'a public general Act or local Act (whether passed before or after the commencement of this section)' and 'any Order in Council, order, rules regulations, scheme, warrant, byelaw [*sic*] or other subordinate instrument made at any time under [a public general Act or local Act]' (subject to some exceptions[22]).

In s 3 there are, admittedly, 'preconditions' to an Order, that is, that the 'policy objective intended to be secured ... could not be satisfactorily secured by non-legislative means', 'the effect of the provision is proportionate to the policy objective', and the provision 'strikes a fair balance between the public interest and the interests of any person adversely affected by it', 'does not remove any necessary protection', 'does not prevent any person from continuing to exercise any right or freedom which that person might reasonably expect to continue to exercise' and 'is not of constitutional significance'. Also, by s 5, no order may impose, abolish or vary any tax (though it does allow the Treasury to 'vary the way in which a relevant tax has effect'), and by s 6, an order may not create a new offence punishable with imprisonment of over two years (by token of which it could do so for any period up to and including two years). Further, there are some Parliamentary controls (discussed below in relation to Statutory Instruments). Nevertheless, it remains that for vaguely state a purposes, and subject to vaguely stated safeguards, the Government can largely by-pass Parliament in amending existing legislation.

Control of uses of delegated powers

Concern about parliamentary control over delegation of powers to legislate produced what is now the House of Lords Select Committee on Delegated Powers and Regulatory Reform, and House of Commons Select Committee on Regulatory Reform. The former takes evidence and reports on whether a Bill 'inappropriately delegate[s] power or whether [proposes] an inappropriate level of parliamentary scrutiny', and reports to the House[23]. The latter

22 Part 1 of the Act itself and the Human Rights Act 1998 are excepted by virtue of s 8, and anything within the legislative competence of the Scottish Parliament by virtue of s 9.

23 In 2005-6, it issued 26 Reports, including one on the Legislative and Regulatory Reform Bill (see above). In the first half of 2007, it had issued 11 Reports, on subjects from Northern Ireland (St Andrews Agreement) Bill to the Building Societies (Funding) and Mutual Societies (Transfers) Bill. See also below in relation to 'Classification by degree of UK Parliamentary and governmental control and publicity'.

scrutinised Government proposals for regulatory reform orders under the Regulatory Reform Act 2001[24] and will doubtless do so in relation to the new orders under the Legislative and Regulatory Reform Act 2006.

TYPES OF UNITED KINGDOM DELEGATED LEGISLATION AND THEIR FORM

UK delegated legislation is very common. The total number of all forms of statutory instrument, the main type, rose from about 2,000 each year in the mid-1980s to approaching 4,000 in 2006[25]. Some apply only in Scotland, some only in Wales, some only in England, some only in Great Britain, and others in the whole United Kingdom[26].

Many have a limited life, and many others replace or amend earlier ones, often marginally, so (as with Acts of the UK Parliament) the actual quantity in force is not rising so steeply. They also vary enormously in length, from one page to (on occasion) hundreds. There may be an increasing propensity to delegate, and to delegate more important matters. For example, the Social Security Act 1986, s 20 created income support, but most of the detail of this benefit is found in a lengthy statutory instruments[27].

The form of delegated legislation varies with the type, although all mimic parliamentary legislation. There are two ways of classifying UK delegated legislation: by delegate and name; and by degree of parliamentary and governmental control and publicity.

Legislation delegated by the Scottish Parliament (technically sub-delegated, since delegated by Acts of the Scottish Parliament, themselves technically delegated legislation) can be fitted into this analysis, but deserves separate treatment, which follows in Chapter

---

24 In 2005-6 it issued some 10 Reports on 'regulatory reform orders' under the Regulatory Reform Act 2001, from the Regulatory Reform (Forestry) Order 2006 to the Draft Regulatory Reform (Agricultural Tenancies) (England and Wales) Order 2006, and in the first half of 2007 had issued as many more, from the Regulatory Reform (Game) Order 2007 to the Draft Regulatory Reform (Financial Services and Markets Act 2000) Order 2007.

25 The highest number ever, 4,642, was in 2001, but this is attributable to several hundred relating to the outbreak of Foot and Mouth Disease: see 'Statutory Instrument Statistics' on Her Majesty's Stationery Office website (see above).

26 Thus, there were over 600 Scottish Statutory Instruments (for which, see Ch 10) in 2006. Those applying only to England (or England and Wales) are not separately numbered, and those applying only in Northern Ireland raise other issues. Devolution has clearly increased the number of Statutory Instruments made.

27 Income Support (General) Regulations 1987, SI 1987/1967 (now amended).

10. It should also be noted that, rather confusingly, the term 'Scottish Statutory Instruments' is used to refer to such legislation applying exclusively to Scotland whether made under powers (sub)delegated by the Scottish Parliament, or under powers directly delegated by the United Kingdom Parliament.

Classification by delegate and name

In principle, the United Kingdom Parliament can delegate to any body (subject to any restrictions that Convention rights and Community law may impose). In practice, delegation is largely to four types of delegate: the government[28]; local government; the courts; and statutory bodies.

Delegation to government: orders, regulations, rules, etc

Most delegation is to the Secretary of State[29] or other minister, in other words, to government. It is of course the civil servants in the relevant department who actually draft the legislation. The resulting legislation may be termed 'Order' (for example, the European Communities (Designation) Order 2002, SI 2002/248); 'Order in Council' (for example, the Scotland Act 1998 (Transfer of Functions to the Scottish Ministers, etc) Order 1999, SI 1999/1750); 'Regulations' (for example, the Statutory Maternity Pay (Compensation of Employers) Amendment Regulations 2002, SI 2002/225); or 'Rules' (for example, the Immigration and Asylum Appeals (Procedure) Rules 2000, SI 2000/2333). Other titles are occasionally used, such as 'Scheme' (for example the Injuries in War (Shore Employment) Compensation (Amendment) Scheme 1990, SI 1990/1946), 'Directions' (for example the British Gas Corporation (Disposal of Wytch Farm Oilfield Interest) Directions 1981, SI 1981/1459) and 'Instrument' (for example the Foreign Compensation (People's Republic of China) Rules Approval Instrument, SI 1988/153).

There is no clear policy on which title to use, but Rules are usually procedural rules; Regulations of general application; and Orders brief. Confusion is possible with Orders in Council, where the

---

28 For the difference between Parliament and government, see Ch 3.

29 The title 'Secretary of State' is attached to most Cabinet ministers in charge of departments, as noted in Ch 3. There may therefore be nearly a dozen Secretaries of State. In principle, any Secretary of State could exercise powers so delegated. Commonly, one is clearly the relevant one. Before devolution, in a number of cases the function was carried out in Scotland by the Scottish Secretary, and in England by another. This can still occur, however.

nominal delegate is the Privy Council[30]. The title is usually used for delegated legislation of constitutional significance, but the same title is used for some prerogative (therefore not delegated) legislation[31]. The name 'Regulation' is also the name used for the principal form of Community legislation, unfortunately.

Delegation to local authorities: by-laws and management rules

Delegation to local authorities is common, giving powers to write laws for the good government and suppression of nuisance in their areas, for example, by requiring licensing of abattoirs, public houses, and taxi operations, and prohibiting ball games in parks. Such legislation is usually in the form of by-laws. The power to make by-laws is delegated by a variety of Acts relating to public health, transport etc, but most importantly by the Local Government (Scotland) Act 1973, ss 201–203 (as amended, chiefly by the Civic Government (Scotland) Act 1982). Breach of a by-law is commonly a criminal offence.

In addition to by-laws, local authorities may make less formal 'management rules' under the Civic Government (Scotland) Act 1982, s 112 for the control of their premises. Breach of them is not of itself criminal, but may lead to ejection and (after a hearing) an exclusion order, breach of which may be criminal. Since local government is a devolved responsibility, no doubt in time this legislation will be replaced by Acts of the Scottish Parliament which will delegate powers to local authorities.

Delegation to courts: Acts of Sederunt and Acts of Adjournal

Courts have delegated powers to make rules for their own organisation and procedure. The Lord President and other judges of the Court of Session are delegated such powers in respect of the Court of Session by the Court of Session Act 1988, s 5, and the legislation they produce is called Acts of Sederunt, for example the Act of Sederunt (Rules of the Court of Session Amendment) (Witnesses' Fees) 1999, SI 1999. They are granted similar powers under the

30 As noted in Chapter 3, in origin, the Privy Council was the forerunner of the Cabinet. It is, in this context, a dignified and mystifying title for the government, and is recipient on occasion of substantial delegated powers, for example to amend unilaterally (albeit after consultation) the constitutions of universities, under ss 202–208 of the Education Reform Act 1988. Cabinet Ministers, Bishops, senior judges and other worthies are appointed Privy Councillors as a form of honour.
31 For the meaning of which, see Ch 4.

Sheriff Courts (Scotland) Act 1971, s 32 in relation to the sheriff court, exercised, for example, in the Act of Sederunt (Ordinary Cause Rules, Sheriff Court) 1993, SI 1983/747.

The same judges in criminal guise are given parallel powers in respect of the High Court by the Criminal Procedure (Scotland) Act 1995, s 305, exercised in Acts of Adjournal, for example the Act of Adjournal (Criminal Procedure Rules) 1996, SI 1996/513[32].

However, this delegated legislation now appears in 'Scottish Statutory Instrument' form (discussed in Chapter 10).

Delegation to public corporations, statutory bodies and utilities by-laws

Some public corporations, statutory bodies and privatised utilities may be granted the power to make law. The Railways Act 1993, s 129 gave 'independent railway operating companies' power to make by-laws to regulate the use and working of railways. Smoking in a non-smoking carriage was a criminal offence by virtue of a rail operating company by-law which is invested with legal force by a delegation of law-making power by the United Kingdom Parliament under s 129(2)(c) of that Act[33].

Delegation to other bodies

There are many examples of delegated legislation which do not fit easily into the above four categories, for example the powers given by the Immigration and Asylum Act 1999, s 83(4) and Sch 5, Pt 1 to the Immigration Services Commissioner to make rules regulating the professional practice, conduct and discipline of those qualified to provide immigration advice and services, exercised in the 'Commissioner's Rules' published by the Commissioner[34]. These standards may appear to be internal professional rules rather than laws, and breach of them is not criminal. However, they are created under powers granted by Parliament, and breach can lead to professional disciplinary proceedings under a statutory procedure. Such proceedings could result in various penalties, including expulsion from the profession (and provision of such services by an expelled person would be criminal)[35].

32 In the 16th and 17th centuries courts were regarded as having inherent powers to produce such legislation, and did so upon subjects far removed from administration and procedure. See *Introduction to Scottish Legal History* (various authors) p 28.
33 '... an independent railway operator may ... make bye-laws [*sic*] ... with respect to the smoking of tobacco in railway carriages ...".
34 Available at www.oisc.org.uk.
35 As to Scottish solicitors, see Ch 14 below.

Classification by degree of parliamentary and governmental control and publicity

The United Kingdom Parliament has control over delegated legislation in so far as a parent Act is always required. Thus, the Bill which will become the parent Act is subject to such scrutiny as Parliament provides[36]. Firstly, therefore, Parliament accepts that the Bill should delegate at all. Most Bills delegate to a limited extent (for example, in relation to Commencement Orders: see Chapters 7 and 8). Secondly, the Parliament accepts the Bill's intended delegate. Thus, delegation under the Local Government (Scotland) Act 1973, s 201(1) (as amended) is to councils, and under the Solicitors (Scotland) Act 1980, s 34 to the Law Society of Scotland. Thirdly, Parliament accepts that the Bill makes the delegation as wide or as narrow as the draftsman has drafted it. Thus, delegation to the government under s 2(2) of the European Communities Act 1972 is solely for the purpose of putting into effect Community legislation, and then subject to certain exclusions. Fourthly, Parliament may require any procedure it likes by the delegate before exercise of the delegated powers. Thus, delegation to the government under the Social Security Act 1980 to produce certain social security regulations was, by ss 9 and 10 and Sch 3, to be exercised only after consultation with the Social Security Advisory Committee. Such consultation requirements are very common, although those required to be consulted may not be closely specified. Fifthly, the Parliament may require a degree of publicity for the resulting rules. And sixthly, Parliament may impose the possibility of a veto upon such legislation. These last two requirements are generally fulfilled either by requiring the delegated legislation to be in 'Statutory Instrument' form when the government is the delegate, or by separately delegating control to the government as 'confirming authority' when others are the delegates, as discussed below.

Thus, the most familiar classification of delegated legislation, that is, into Statutory Instruments and non-Statutory Instruments, is produced by the degree of parliamentary control[37]. This in turn

36 See above in relation to the House of Lords Select Committee on Delegated Powers and Regulatory Reform.
37 The picture is complicated by a common propensity to assume, inaccurately, that 'delegated legislation' and 'Statutory Instruments' are synonyms. The inaccuracy of this is exemplified by the 'Commissioner's Rules' under the powers given to the Immigration Services Commissioner by the Immigration and Asylum Act 1999, s 83(4) and Sch 5, Pt 1 to make rules regulating the professional practice, conduct and discipline of those qualified to provide immigration advice and services. These are not required to be in statutory instrument form, even though breach of them could result in removal of a person from the register of people qualified to give immigration advice and services, but they must be published by the Commissioner.

draws attention to the less familiar classification of by-laws into those subject to various types of confirmation.

The United Kingdom Parliament and Statutory Instruments

There is a complicated definition of 'Statutory Instrument' in the Statutory Instruments Act 1946 but, in essence, it is simple. A piece of delegated legislation is a Statutory Instrument if the parent Act says it must be. Thus, for example, the Immigration Act 1971, s 4(3) says that 'The Secretary of State may by regulations made by statutory instrument ... make provision for' certain things, including a requirement upon aliens to register with the police. The power was therefore exercised in a statutory instrument, the Immigration (Registration with Police) Regulations 1972, SI 1972/1758, and subsequent amending instruments. Legislative powers delegated to the government are usually required to be in Statutory Instrument form.

United Kingdom Statutory Instruments (with the exception of certain ones of only local or temporary effect[38]) are required by the Statutory Instruments Act 1946, ss 2, 3 and 4 to be dated, numbered, printed, published and sold. This may sound mundane, but if they were not numbered etc, how would one know they even existed?[39]

Statutory Instruments are also usually subject to certain parliamentary procedures principally laid down in ss 4–7 of the Statutory Instruments Act 1946 and designed to allow Parliament to be informed of their existence, and apply a veto if it wishes. (It cannot, however, amend other than in certain exceptional cases.)

Firstly, Statutory Instruments may be required to be laid before the Parliament (that is, made available to any MP) three weeks before coming into effect, showing the dates when it was made, when it was laid, and when it is intended to come into force. (In some cases they must be laid in draft, in some cases in final form.)

Secondly, Statutory Instruments may be examined by the Joint (ie Commons and Lords) Committee on Statutory Instruments[40],

---

38 For example, the Dundee–Aberdeen Trunk Road (A94) (Stracathro Junction) (Prohibition of Specified Turn) Order 1990, SI 1990/1829.

39 The Statutory Instruments Act 1946, s 3(2) created a special defence to prosecution for an offence laid down in a statutory instrument, that is, that it had not been published, nor reasonable steps taken to bring it to the notice of those likely to be affected.

40 Not to be confused with the House of Lords Select Committee on Delegated Powers and Regulatory Reform, for which, see above. There is a House of Commons Select Committee on Statutory Instruments, comprising the Commons members of the Joint Committee, for those SIs which require only House of Commons approval.

which concerns itself with 'technical scrutiny' of statutory instruments, that is, whether they are properly made and do not purport to do something constitutionally inappropriate. The Joint Committee cannot reject instruments, but may refer them to either House on any of nine extensive grounds (such as that the instrument is defectively drafted, or appears *ultra vires*). Such referral is, in fact, rare, but when it occurs, the Statutory Instrument may be debated (but still may not be amended). The Joint Committee also produces general reports on specific topics such as the consolidation of delegated legislation.

Thirdly, statutory instruments may be subject to a parliamentary vote. Briefly put, this may be either a 'negative' or 'affirmative' resolution procedure in one or both Houses of Parliament (or in a delegated legislation Standing Committee of one or other House). The 'negative resolution procedure', which is common, means the Statutory Instrument may be negatived by the parliamentary vote. The 'affirmative resolution procedure' means the statutory instrument does not come into force unless affirmed by a parliamentary vote. In neither case, however, may they be amended. This is the stage at which 'the merits' may be considered, that is, Parliament decides if it wants a statutory instrument which does what this one proposes to do (and does so possibly with the assistance of a report from the House of Lords Select Committee on Delegated Powers and Regulatory Reform, noted above).

Other Acts of Parliament may impose their own specific approval regimes. The European Communities Act 1972 requires statutory instruments made under s 2(2)[41] to undergo a negative resolution by either House unless there has been an affirmative approval of a draft instrument by each House.

Controls over powers of delegation under the Scotland Act are of considerable complication. Such legislation must be in Statutory Instrument form, but parliamentary approval is required in one of eleven different ways from 'Type A' (draft instrument has been laid before, and approved by resolution of, each House of the UK Parliament and laid before and approved by resolution of the Scottish Parliament) to 'Type K' (instrument subject to annulment by a resolution of the House of Commons)[42].

Somewhat less complicatedly, the Legislative and Regulatory Reform Act 2006 also requires Statutory Instrument form, and ss 13 and 13 require a Minister, before making an Order, to consult with,

41 That is, ones bringing into force Community law without direct effect.
42 Scotland Act 1998, s 115, Sch 7.

int. al. 'such organisations as appear to him to be representative of interests substantially affected by the proposals', the Law Commissions (for which, see Chapter 15) and 'such other persons as he considers appropriate'. Section 14 requires him to lay a Draft Order and Explanatory Document (the contents of which are prescribed, including the result of the consultation) before Parliament. And s 15 requires he recommend Parliamentary approval by 'negative resolution procedure', 'affirmative resolution procedure'; or 'super-affirmative resolution procedure', terms defined in ss 16–18 and implying increasing degrees of Parliamentary control

Parliamentary controls are, of course, subject to the fact of executive dominance of the legislature. Governments are therefore free to draft Bills delegating powers and making delegated powers subject to such procedures, safe in the knowledge that normally their majority removes the likelihood of the controls being effective. In an extremely rare event, the House of Lords rejected the Southern Rhodesia (United Nations Sanctions) Order 1968. However, after a threat to extend the Parliament Acts 1911 and 1949 to delegated legislation, it passed an identical order a month later. The Joint Committee on Statutory Instruments is, however, thought to have raised the standard of drafting.

Confirming authorities and by-laws etc

Local authority and public corporation by-laws are generally subject to approval by a 'confirming authority', the powers of which may be very wide, including powers to modify or reject on various grounds. The confirming authority is commonly stated in pre-devolution legislation to be the Secretary of State, that is, the United Kingdom government, but this is now commonly devolved to the Scottish Ministers in relation to Scotland by the 'general transfer of functions' under the Scotland Act 1998, s 53.

Thus the Secretary of State, as such, is confirming authority for independent railway operators' by-laws under the Transport Act 1962, s 67 (as amended), for provision and regulation of railway services is a reserved matter. However, the First Minister is now, under the Local Government (Scotland) Act 1973 (as amended), confirming authority for local authority by-laws (s 201(2)) after public consultation (s 202(4)–(7)), for local government is devolved. Again, under the Law Reform (Miscellaneous Provisions) (Scotland) Act 1990 the Secretary of State was (after consultation with the Director General of Fair Trading) the confirming authority for rules written by the Scottish Conveyancing and Executry Services Board setting standards of conduct for qualified conveyancers and executry practitioners because regulation of the professions is devolved (save for architects, health professions and auditors).

Local authorities are required by the Local Government (Scotland) Act 1973, s 202 (as amended by the Civic Government (Scotland) Act 1982, s 110) to publish, make available and sell copies of their by-laws, and by s 202A, required to review their by-laws every ten years. Independent railway operators are subject to similar requirements under the Transport Act 1962, s 67 (as amended).

Local authority management rules are, by virtue of the Civic Government (Scotland) Act 1982, ss 114 and 115, required to be displayed on the relevant premises and made available for inspection and sale.

Other rules made under a confirming authority procedure may not be subject to a requirement to be published.

The form of United Kingdom delegated legislation

In their form, statutory instruments and other forms of delegated legislation mimic parliamentary legislation, though the details vary according to the type in question.

Citation

Statutory Instruments commence with their citation in the form of a year and sequential number, for example '2002 No 3204' (commonly abbreviated to 'SI 2002/3204'). This may be followed by brackets enclosing a further reference number preceded by 'S', 'W' or 'Cy', 'NI', 'C', or 'L'. These indicate respectively that the instrument applies only in Scotland (as do some each year even after devolution[43]); applies only in Wales, *alias* Cymru (as do some also after devolution); applies only in Northern Ireland; is a Commencement Order (see Chapters 7 and 8[44]); or is a procedural instrument applying solely in England and Wales[45]. Thus, 'S13' would indicate the instrument is the 13th of that year applying solely to Scotland. However, while these conventions remain, since devolution, Scottish and Welsh statutory instruments are published in separate sequences (as considered below).

43 In 2006, there were 11, from the Parliamentary Constituencies (Scotland) Order 2005, SI 2005/250 (S1) to the Feeding Stuffs (Application of 200 Technical Additives, etc) (Scotland) Regulations 2005, SI 2005/3362 (S13).
44 In 2006, there were 147.
45 In 2006, there were 32.

Before the Statutory Instruments Act 1946, the equivalent class of delegated legislation was called 'statutory rules and orders', cited as 'SR&O'.

Name

In official editions of statutory instruments, after the citation, appear one or two headings, for example, 'FOOD' followed by 'MILK AND DAIRIES'. These are not part of the name but a guide to the subject-matter.

The name, equivalent to an Act's Short Title, is given thereafter, for example 'The Milk (Special Designations) (Scotland) Order 1988' or 'The Advice and Assistance (Scotland) (Prospective Cost) (No 3) Regulations 1988'[46]. Brackets are much favoured, enclosing 'Scotland', 'Amendment', 'Variation' and other things[47], including numerical sequences, as where an Act has several commencement orders[48].

Dates

After the name, statutory instruments list three dates, those of making, laying before Parliament, and of coming into force (unless the instrument is not required to be laid before Parliament).

Arrangement of Regulations, Articles or Rules

A statutory instrument of more than a few provisions is likely to have contents list, that is, an 'Arrangement of Regulations' (articles or rules) at the beginning. But the titles used there reappear as shoulder headings to the actual provisions.

46 There is a good deal of innocent amusement to be had in discovering the most unusual Statutory Instrument name. See for example, the Housing (Grants for Fire Escapes in Houses of Multiple Occupation) (Prescribed Percentage) (Scotland) Order 1990, SI 1990/2242, and the Water Bylaws (Milngavie Waterworks, Loch Katrine, Loch Arklet, Glen Finglas) Extension Order 1990, SI 1990/2250. See also Reid (correspondence) (2003) 24 Stat LR 93.
47 For example, the Town and Country Planning (Determination of Appeals by Appointed Persons) (Prescribed Classes) (Scotland) Amendment Regulations 1989, SI 1989/577. It is surprising that 'Amendment' is not bracketed.
48 For example, by mid-2007, the commencement orders for the Immigration and Asylum Act 1999 ran from the Immigration and Asylum Act 1999 (Commencement No 1) Order 1999, SI 1999/3190 to the Immigration and Asylum Act 1999 (Commencement No 16) Order 2004, SI 2004/297, without the whole Act yet being in force. Indeed, the twelfth Commencement Order (in 2003) actually followed the Nationality, Immigration and Asylum Act 2002 (Commencement (No 1) Order 2002, SI 2003/1, starting to bring into force the next major piece of immigration legislation.

Recital of delegated powers

By definition, the legislation is delegated, and if the legislation is in Statutory Instrument, it displays a recital of the powers under which it is delegated (and possibly of consultation carried out), for example, 'The Secretary of State, in exercise of the powers conferred on him by sections 37(1)(b), 38(1) and 143(1) of the Roads (Scotland) Act 1984 and of all other powers enabling him in that behalf, and after consultation with representative organisations in accordance with sections 37(6) and 38(2) of that Act, hereby makes the following Regulations ...'. This bears on the question of *ultra vires*, but its significance is reduced by the common use of 'and all other powers in that behalf'.

The substantive provisions – Regulations, Articles and Rules etc

The name of the basic unit of a statutory instrument varies with whether it is called Regulations ('Regulation'), an Order ('Article'), or Rules ('Rule'). Structure is in the same form as an Act, but sub-divisions of the basic unit are always called Paragraphs, Sub-para-graphs (and even Sub-sub-paragraphs).

In an instrument of any length, there are Shoulder Headings to each Regulation, rather like the Marginal Notes in an Act. Parts and Part headings are used in much the same way as in Acts.

Operating instructions such as interpretation, amending and repealing (known in Statutory Instruments as 'revoking') provisions may appear and, while most are placed at the end, as with Acts, interpretation paragraphs are usually placed at the beginning.

Schedules are common.

The Explanatory Note

Invariably, official editions of Statutory Instruments have an Explanatory Note appended. This is declared 'not part of' the instrument and they seldom provide any useful explanation.

ULTRA VIRES AND JUDICIAL CONTROL OF UNITED KINGDOM DELEGATED LEGISLATION

Law appearing in delegated legislation is as powerful as law appearing in Acts of Parliament, and therefore (subject to any requirements of Community law) cannot be struck down by the court. There is an important exception, however, in the *ultra vires* doctrine, a form of judicial control.

Judicial control of delegated legislation interlocks with parliamentary control. In practice, Parliament always limits delegation. Parent Acts delegate specific powers to specific persons, for specific purposes, to be exercised through specific procedures, possibly subject to specific publicity requirements and a veto.

If those limits are exceeded, the purported laws are *ultra vires*, that is, 'beyond the powers' which were delegated. In this case a court may strike them down. For example, *Malloch v Aberdeen Corporation* 1974 SLT 253 turned on the Education (Scotland) Act 1962 which delegated to the Secretary of State certain powers to make regulations for certain purposes[49]. Under these powers he made a regulation, the Teachers (Education, Training and Certification) (Scotland) Regulations 1967, SI 1967/1162, among other things purportedly requiring teachers retrospectively to register with the General Teaching Council for Scotland. Malloch, a teacher employed by Aberdeen Corporation, was dismissed for failure to register. He sued the Corporation, and the Inner House upheld his claim that the 1962 Act did not delegate the power to make such regulations, so that they were *ultra vires*[50].

In practice such striking down is rare. This is for several reasons. Firstly, the delegation may in practice be very wide, and give discretion to the delegate[51]. Secondly, the courts have regarded some

---

49 There was considerable related litigation, in part of which Mr Malloch most remarkably appeared as a litigant in person, in other words without benefit of legal representation, in the House of Lords: see 1973 SLT (Notes) 5.

50 See also *Marshall v Clark* 1957 JC 68 and *Magistrates of Ayr v Lord Advocate* 1950 SLT 102. An interesting English case is *Bugg v Director of Public Prosecutions* [1993] QB 473. RAF Alconbury By-laws 1985 and HMS Forest Moor and Menwith Hill Station By-laws 1986, made by the Secretary of State under Pt II of the Military Lands Act 1892, purported to exclude the public from certain military sites. Bugg was convicted of the offence of entering a place protected by the by-laws without permission, and convicted. On appeal, the Divisional Court of Queen's Bench held that there were two types of invalidity, substantive (where the by-law was invalid on its face because *ultra vires* or unreasonable) and procedural (where a procedural requirement, such as consultation, had not been followed). In the instant case, neither by-law set out with sufficient clarity the area it covered, and the Alconbury by-laws covered the area within a perimeter fence, but the fence had been moved in an attempt unilaterally to extend the area.

51 An extreme example was the Finance (No 2) Act 1940 which purported to give powers to the Commissioners of Customs and Excise to make such rules 'as appear to them necessary' in relation to deciding tax liability in the absence of a tax return. However, this was successfully challenged in an English case *Commissioners of Customs and Excise v Cure and Deeley Ltd* [1962] 1 QB 340. The powers under the Legislative and Regulatory Reform Act 2006 are not as wide, but still present little chance for an *ultra vires* challenge.

procedural requirements as merely directory rather than mandatory, that is they are required, but failure to follow them does not annul the regulations[52]. Thirdly, there may be attempts to oust the jurisdiction of the courts, that is, prevent the courts from pronouncing on the validity of the delegated legislation. For example, the Education (Scotland) Act 1980, s 114(2) (as amended by the Education (Scotland) Act 1981, Sch 6, para 13) provided that an instrument giving effect to a scheme under Part IV of the Act was to be conclusive proof that the scheme was not *ultra vires*.

CITATION AND PUBLICATION OF UNITED KINGDOM DELEGATED LEGISLATION

Citation

United Kingdom delegated legislation is cited in the manner described above under 'form of United Kingdom delegated legislation'.

Publication

Chronological series

Statutory instruments of general effect (and, since 1989, important local ones) are published by The Stationery Office ('TSO'), sold as individual copies and bound up in several annual volumes entitled *Statutory Instruments*. The volumes are grouped into 'Parts' and 'Sections' but, as the instruments are printed chronologically, and the sequence of instruments in each volume is printed on its spine, these names can be ignored. Statutory Instruments still in force in 1948 are available in *Statutory Instruments Revised*, published in 1950.

Encyclopaedic series

Halsbury's Statutory Instruments (Butterworths) is a multi-volume encyclopaedia. It covers instruments in force in the whole United Kingdom (or solely in England and Wales) under a large number of subject headings, but does not cover those instruments which apply solely in Scotland.

The full text of the more important instruments it covers is given. Others are outlined, and there are brief descriptions of the general effect of instruments on various topics.

Other commercially produced reprints

Acts of Sederunt and Acts of Adjournal (which appear as Statutory Instruments) are reprinted in The Parliament House Book (referred to in Chapter 8 in relation to commercially produced reprints of Acts) arranged by broad subject-matter, and until 1990 also in *(Scottish) Current Law Statutes Annotated*. (These now appear as 'Scottish Statutory Instruments': see Chapter 10.) Other subject-area encyclopaedias may contain relevant instruments. For example, *Butterworths Immigration Law Service* reprints all statutory instruments in force relevant to its subject-matter, updated as necessary, and the various editions of the principal textbook on the subject, Macdonald and Webber (eds) *United Kingdom Immigration Law and Practice* (6th edn, 2005, updated by supplement) have reprinted all those in force at the time of publication.

In April 2006, *Current Law Statutes Annotated* announced its intention of including annotated Statutory Instruments selected for their importance[53].

Indexes

Each volume of *Statutory Instruments* contains an index, numerical list and table of effects. There is also a monthly and annual *List of Statutory Publications* (formerly *List of Statutory Instruments*) with alphabetical and chronological tables.

Computerised retrieval

All Statutory Instruments since 1 January 1987 are available in full text at the Office of Public Sector Information website[54]. The Statute Law Database contains Statutory Instruments made from 1991 onwards but, unlike the Acts, these are not held in amended form.

The Westlaw, Justis [*sic*] United Kingdom Statutory Instruments and BAILII databases all contain full text of all Statutory Instruments (though coverage varies). The LexisNexis Butterworths database excludes all Statutory Instruments applying only in Scotland.

---

52 In English cases, requirements for publication were held directory in *Sheer Metalcraft Ltd* [1954] 1 QB 114, but requirements for consultation were mandatory in *Agricultural Training Board v Aylesbury Mushrooms Ltd* [1972] 1 WLR 190.
53 By mid-2007, none had appeared.
54 See www.opsi.gov.uk

Delegated legislation which is not in statutory instrument form

There are no general requirements for publication of delegated legislation which is not in statutory instrument form, but the requirements of publicity of by-laws and local management rules mean that they are likely to be reasonably available in the area to which they apply.

10. Legislation – Scottish Delegated Legislation

THE INSTITUTIONAL BACKGROUND

The idea of Scottish delegated legislation presents a few difficulties. In brief, firstly, United Kingdom delegated legislation (discussed in Chapter 9) may apply to Scotland simply because it applies to the whole of the United Kingdom, or to Great Britain. Secondly, in one sense, Acts of the Scottish Parliament are Scottish delegated legislation. Thirdly, an increasing amount of delegated legislation applying to Scotland is delegated by Acts of the Scottish Parliament, and is thus, technically, sub-delegated legislation. Fourthly, most delegation legislation applying in Scotland is in Statutory Instrument form, but those which apply only in Scotland are called 'Scottish Statutory Instruments'. Fifthly, however, this title is used whether the Statutory Instrument in question is delegated legislation made under a United Kingdom Act of Parliament, or sub-delegated legislation made under an Act of the Scottish Parliament. These issues are enlarged upon below.

The institutional background of delegated legislation was touched on in Chapter 3 (concerning devolution) and Chapter 5 (concerning sources of law). This Chapter deals with the nature of such legislation within the context of devolution, legislative control over it, its types and form, *ultra vires* and judicial control over it, and its citation and publication.

THE NATURE OF SCOTTISH DELEGATED LEGISLATION

Delegation, the Scotland Act 1998 and Acts of the Scottish Parliament

It is worth starting by recalling that devolution itself involves a massive delegation, for the Scotland Act 1998 delegated to the

Scottish Parliament and Scottish Executive all powers, legislative and executive, outwith the 'reserved matters'[1].

Acts of the Scottish Parliament are thus technically delegated legislation, because the United Kingdom Parliament set up the Scottish Parliament by statute, and delegated to that new Parliament some of its power to legislate for Scotland[2]. Devolution and Acts of the Scottish Parliament are discussed in the Chapter 8, however, so are not dealt with in this Chapter, though their status has to be borne in mind.

It must also be recalled that the Scotland Act 1998 did give the United Kingdom Government very wide powers to make delegated legislation to effect consequential changes to the law, including to the Scotland Act itself.

Delegated legislation in Scotland and devolution

The principles which apply to United Kingdom delegated legislation, discussed in Chapter 9. also apply to delegated legislation in relation to Scotland.

It might be thought that the position is therefore simple, and that, since devolution, all that happens is that the Scottish Parliament delegates to the Scottish Executive, which produces a new breed of delegated legislation replacing the earlier United Kingdom delegated legislation.

There is indeed a new breed of 'Scottish Statutory Instrument' ('SSI'), made by the Scottish Ministers and in some sense replacing United Kingdom Statutory Instruments ('(UK) SIs') made by the United Kingdom government, but the position has considerable complexities which need carefully disentangling, and produce some surprising conclusions[3].

Delegated legislation and 'reserved matters'[4]

Acts of the United Kingdom Parliament delegate powers to the United Kingdom government (typically in the form of 'the Secretary

1   For 'reserved matters' see Chapter 3.
2   This is made explicit in the Human Rights Act 1998, s 21(1), *sub voc.* 'subordinate legislation'.
3   The authors are grateful for the assistance derived from Himsworth 'Subordinate legislation in the Scottish Parliament' (2002) 6 EdinLR 356–379, Reid 'Who Makes Scotland's Law: delegated legislation under the devolution arrangements' (2002) 6 EdinLR 380–384 and Reid 'The Limits of Devolved Legislative Power; subordinate legislation in Scotland' (2003) 24 Stat LR 187-210.
4   See Ch 3.

of State') and other bodies in relation to 'reserved matters'. This was, of course, the position before devolution, and continues to be so since. The delegated legislation so produced was normally in the usual United Kingdom form of Statutory Instrument or by-law, etc (as appropriate) before devolution, and will normally continue to be so since. Such delegated legislation, both pre- and post-devolution, will continue to apply in Scotland[5], unaffected by devolution, subject to a particular complication.

The complication is that, as noted in Chapter 3, some functions within the 'reserved matters' can in fact be devolved by the United Kingdom government to the Scottish Ministers by the process known as 'executive devolution', under powers in the Scotland Act 1998, and others, while not transferred, can be used by Scottish Ministers under an 'agency agreement' with the United Kingdom government, also under powers in the Scotland Act 1998[6].

Delegated legislation and 'devolved matters'[7]

Existing delegated legislation on devolved matters

Acts of the United Kingdom Parliament, of course, also delegated powers before devolution concerning what have become 'devolved matters', to the Secretary of State, Scottish local authorities, Scottish courts and other persons and bodies within Scotland[8]. The delegated

5 Mostly, this will be legislation applying to the whole UK, or GB, but occasionally includes legislation applying solely to Scotland, typically because it concerns devolution: see *eg* Scottish Parliament (Disqualification) Order 2002, SI 2003/409 (S4) which specifies persons disqualified from being MSPs.

6 *Eg* the Scotland Act 1998 (Transfer of Functions to the Scottish Ministers) Order 1999, SI 1999/1750, which provided for the transfer of an enormous number of disparate functions of the UK government, so far as exercisable in relation to Scotland by the Scottish Ministers, or still by the UK government but with the agreement of the Scottish Ministers, and the Scotland Act 1998 (Agency Arrangements) Order 2002, SI 2002/261 (S1) which allows the Scottish Ministers to make arrangements on behalf of the UK government in preparing an emissions trading scheme for the implementing of the UK's obligations under the Kyoto Protocol on Climate Change.

7 For 'devolved matters', see Ch 3. Note that the Scotland Act 1998 does not define 'devolved matters', as they are simply all matters which are not 'reserved matters'.

8 Obvious examples delegation of powers to the Scottish courts to write their own procedures include Acts of Sederunt (*eg* Act of Sederunt (Rules of Court) (Consolidation and Amendment) 1965, SI 1965/321, made under the Administration of Justice (Scotland) Act 1933, s 16) and Acts of Adjournal (*eg* Act of Adjournal (Criminal Procedure Rules) 1996, SI 1996/513, made under the Criminal Procedure (Scotland) Act 1995, s 305).

legislation so produced was also normally in the usual United Kingdom form of Statutory Instrument or by-law, etc (as appropriate) before devolution. However, devolution did not remove this delegated legislation at a stroke. Thus, most of it is still in force. Indeed, it remains in force unless and until replaced.

However, that does not mean that such existing legislation is unchanged by devolution. As noted in Chapter 3, basic provisions of the Scotland Act 1998 perform a 'general transfer of functions' from United Kingdom government to the Scottish Ministers in relation to Scotland. Thus, they confer upon the Scottish Ministers the governmental functions previously granted to the Secretary of State and other members of the United Kingdom government in so far as they apply to Scotland[9]. Thus, where such delegated legislation gave powers and responsibilities to the Secretary of State, it must now be read as giving them to the Scottish Ministers[10]. So, where previously, the Secretary of State might be given the power to take a decision, or the responsibility for carrying out a duty, it is now normally the Scottish Ministers who may, or must, do so[11].

New delegated legislation on devolved matters

The devolution settlement envisages that, over time, the existing (UK)SIs will be replaced by SSIs in relation to devolved matters but, briefly put, the replacement occurs in three separate ways which require to be distinguished.

Firstly, it occurs by means of the Scottish Ministers exercising powers under existing United Kingdom legislation. The basic provisions of the Scotland Act 1998 just referred to, conferring upon the Scottish Ministers the functions previously granted to the Secretary of State, include not just powers to take decisions but also powers to make delegated legislation. Thus, where the United Kingdom government used to exercise these powers under United Kingdom Acts of Parliament, now the Scottish Ministers do, and they do so by

---

[9] Or rather, within the 'devolved competence' of the Scottish Ministers.

[10] To the extent that powers to make delegated legislation on subjects which are now devolved matters were delegated to any person or body other than the UK government, such delegation would be unaffected.

[11] Thus, for example, the Police (Scotland) Act 1967, s 4 requires that a police authority obtain the approval of the Secretary of State before appointing a new Chief Constable. This now means they must obtain the approval of the Scottish Ministers. Unfortunately, since this is not a traditional amendment, it is not picked up by the usual law-finding sources.

means of SSIs rather than (UK)SIs[12]. At least in the short term, this way of replacing (UK)SIs with SSIs is to be expected, simply because the Scottish Parliament has not had time to replace such United Kingdom legislation. However, it also includes examples which are by no means interim ones, for example conferring upon the Scottish Ministers the power to effect Community law which does not have direct effect[13].

Secondly, it occurs by means of the Scottish Ministers exercising powers to make delegated legislation (sub)delegated to them by Acts of the Scottish Parliament as such Acts gradually replace the existing United Kingdom legislation which delegates such powers[14]. Again, they do so by means of SSIs, and this means of replacement can be expected to increase in significance as the Scottish Parliament passes more Acts replacing United Kingdom legislation.

However, this process of replacement of United Kingdom legislation by Scottish legislation is slower than was expected, in part because the Scottish Parliament has in its early years used 'Sewel Motions' (discussed in Chapters 7 and 8) remarkably frequently, in effect handing back its delegated powers on certain topics to the United Kingdom Parliament. Thus, the third method of replacement is that where this happens, there is new United Kingdom legislation (whether as a result of 'Sewel Motions' or not) which delegates powers to make delegated legislation to the Scottish Ministers. Again, however, they do so by means of SSIs, rather than (UK)SIs[15].

---

12 Thus, for example, the pre-devolution Land Registration (Scotland) Act 1979 (Commencement No 12) Order 1998, made under powers in the Land Registration (Scotland) Act 1979, s 30(2), was issued by the Secretary of State for Scotland and was an SI (SI 1998/2980), while the post-devolution Land Registration (Scotland) Act 1979 (Commencement No 13) Order 1999 made under precisely the same powers was issued by the Scottish Ministers and is an SSI (SSI 1999/111).

13 Under the European Communities Act 1972, s 2(2): *eg* the very first SSI, *ie* the Environmental Impact Assessment (Scotland) Regulations 1999, SSI 1999/1 (implementing an EC Directive).

14 Such delegated legislation is technically sub-delegated, since Acts of the Scottish Parliament are technically delegated legislation.

15 Thus, for instance, the Tobacco Advertising (Commencement) (Scotland) Order 2002, SSI 2002/512 (C26), Tobacco Advertising (Commencement No 4) (Scotland) (Amendment and Transitional Provisions) Order 2003, SSI 2003/80 (C3) and Tobacco Advertising and Promotions Act 2002 (Commencement No 5) (Scotland) Order 2003, SSI 2003/11 (C5), all made by the Scottish Ministers under the Tobacco Advertising and Promotion Act 2002, s 22(1) (which gives 'the appropriate Minister' the power to do so) read with s 21 (which defines 'appropriate Minister in relation to Scotland as 'the Scottish Ministers'), brought that Act, a UK Act of Parliament passed in relation to Scotland by means of a 'Sewel motion', into force.

Note, however, that where the delegate is a local authority, or in some other cases, the delegated legislation was not in SI form before devolution, so is not to be replaced by SSIs[16].

Use of delegated legislative powers in Scotland

There are hundreds of SSIs every year so, as with the United Kingdom as a whole, it is a much more fecund source of law than Acts of Parliament[17]. They cover the expectedly wide range of topics, though concentrating on certain areas. In 2001, for example, three large groups dealing with the particular current issues of foot and mouth disease, shellfish poisoning and National Health Service reforms constituted almost third, and another fifth were local traffic orders. Other significant areas were fisheries and food, legal aid, the courts, the National Health Service (other than in relation to the specific reforms) and education, with a variety of quantitatively minor matters including adults with incapacity, housing, public finance, sports grounds, partnerships and wrecks[18].

The range of topics, it must be recalled, is not limited by the legislative competence of the Scottish Parliament, for SSIs may be made under powers granted to the Scottish Ministers by Acts of the United Kingdom Parliament, and may do so in connection with functions transferred to them which are within 'reserved matters' (see Chapter 3)[19]. Indeed, the commonest single parent Act was not an Act of the Scottish Parliament. This is perhaps not surprising, as the Scottish Parliament had been in operation for such a short time. What is surprising is that it was the European Communities Act 1972, which permits Community law without direct effect to be put into effect in the United Kingdom (see Chapter 3). Relations with the European Community are clearly a reserved matter, so the Scottish Ministers were exercising their power outside their normal devolved competence, under s 57 of the Scotland Act. A fifth of the SSIs, largely concerning agriculture and food, were made under that authority.

---

16 Thus, by-laws made by Scottish local authorities under the Local Government (Scotland) Act 1973, ss 201–203 (as amended) remain by-laws.

17 After a build up in the first three calendar years of the devolution, there were between about 550 and 650 per year. This compares with between 12 and 19 Acts of the Scottish Parliament over the same period.

18 See Reid 'Who Makes Scotland's Law?' (2002) 6 EdinLR 380–384 at 381.

19 Delegated legislation made under Acts of Parliament extending to Scotland by means of a 'Sewel Motion' (for which, see above) will relate to devolved matters, and the legislation will normally be in SSI form.

But, beyond SSIs, it must also be remembered that much delegated legislation made by the United Kingdom government continues to apply in Scotland, and indeed there may be more SIs than SSIs each year applying to Scotland[20]. This includes not only delegated legislation on reserved matters, for there is also delegated legislation on devolved matters. This is possible because the United Kingdom Parliament retains its power to legislate for Scotland on those matters which it might exercise by delegating in SI form, and in any case, certain powers (for example, to make delegated legislation to carry out obligations of Community law) are shared between the United Kingdom government and the Scottish Ministers.

CONTROLS OVER DELEGATED LEGISLATION AND SCOTLAND

(UK)SIs and SSIs

As explained above, Statutory Instruments ('SIs') will continue to apply in Scotland, unless and until replaced. This is the case whether the SI concerns a reserved matter or a devolved matter.

However, as also noted, where a power to make delegated legislation by SI is given to the Scottish Ministers (or any other Scottish public authority, such as the Scottish courts[21]), it is to be exercised by a Scottish Statutory Instrument ('SSI')[22]. This is the case whether the delegation is within the 'devolved competence' of the Scottish Ministers or within one of the examples of 'executive devolution' of 'reserved matters', and whether the power is in an existing United Kingdom Act of Parliament, an Act of the Scottish Parliament, or any new United Kingdom Act of Parliament[23].

---

20 Figures produced by Reid 'Who Makes Scotland's Law?' (2002) 6 EdinLR 8 380–384, suggest as many as a quarter of all SIs, say, 1,000 a year. It is not likely that this proportion has changed much.

21 Or, within the devolved competence, some other body. Thus the Act of Sederunt (Rules of the Court of Session Amendment No 7) (Miscellaneous) 1999, made by the Lord President of the Court of Session, is an SSI (SSI 1999/109). All previous Acts of Sederunt in modern times were SIs.

22 Scotland Act 1998 (Transitory and Transitional Provisions) (Statutory Instruments) Order 1999, SI 1999/1096, arts 2(1) *sub voc.* 'Scottish statutory instrument', read with art 4(2). Those made jointly with a member of the UK government are exceptions and there are some other exceptions. As this is an SSI made under a UK Act of Parliament (the Scotland Act 1998), it will no doubt in time be amended and even replaced by an SSI made under an Act of the Scottish Parliament: see below.

23 Unless such future Act decides otherwise.

Controls over (UK)SIs

(UK)SIs in existence were, of course, subject to the usual controls over SIs, discussed in Chapter 9.

Controls over SSIs

The significance of the concept of SSI is three-fold. Firstly, SSIs must be in a form broadly equivalent to (UK)SIs. Thus, they must be numbered, printed and sold[24].

Secondly, where the power is in an existing United Kingdom Act of Parliament, then the requirement for laying before Parliament, and for 'negative' 'affirmative' (or 'super-affirmative') resolution procedure', is a requirement in relation to the Scottish Parliament instead of the United Kingdom Parliament (or either House of it)[25].

Thirdly, where the power is in an Act of the Scottish Parliament, controls modeled on, but not identical with, those for (UK)SIs are imposed. Thus, there is a Subordinate Legislation Committee of the Scottish Parliament which combines the relevant roles of the House of Lords Select Committee on Delegated Legislation and Regulatory Reform to consider the powers granted in Acts, and of the Joint [Select] Committee on Statutory Instruments to provide technical scrutiny of the delegated legislation actually produced. In the former role, it may be involved in the enactment of Bills (as described above under the heading 'Acts of the Scottish Parliament'). In the latter role, it may be involved in the procedure for approval of the exercise of delegated legislation.

This procedure, laid down in the Standing Orders of the Scottish Parliament, has a provision for laying the delegated legislation before the Parliament, and possible discussion of it by the 'lead committee' (that is, the subject committee most concerned with the subject matter, which is likely to have been the lead committee for the enactment of the Act containing the powers) on the merits of the delegated legislation, and the Subordinate Legislation Committee on technical scrutiny on grounds similar to those used by the United Kingdom Joint Committee of Delegated Legislation (and the Parliament itself if either Committee refers a matter to it). It also has provision for equivalents to 'negative' and 'affirmative' resolution procedures.

---

24 Scotland Act 1998 (Transitory and Transitional Provisions) (Statutory Instruments) Order 1999, SI 1999/1096, arts 5–8.
25 Scotland Act, s 118.

The Subordinate Legislation Committee has raised a significant number of issues, though no delegated legislation has been rejected. One area in which issues have been raised was whether certain SSIs breached the Convention rights (see Chapter 3 and above), in particular, the Article 6 right to a fair trial. Interestingly, this was not in relation to criminal trials, which have been the overwhelmingly frequent source of Article 6 challenges to Scottish Executive action (see Chapter 3), but to a variety of matters including planning, pollution control, agricultural grants and appointments to official panels[26]. Another area in which issues have been raised was compatibility with Community law. The division between reserved matters and devolved ones did not produce much difficulty (though the question of whether the 'graduate endowment' for Scottish university students was a tax, and thus 'reserved', did arise in parliamentary debates).

Controls over by-laws

Controls over by-laws remain as they were before devolution, unless and until replaced, subject to the fact that where the Secretary of State was the confirming authority, it will now be the Scottish Ministers, by operation of the 'general transfer of functions'.

TYPES OF DELEGATED LEGISLATION IN SCOTLAND AND THEIR FORM

Delegated (and sub-delegated) legislation in Scotland does not provide the same variety of types as does its United Kingdom counterpart.

The form of delegated (and sub-delegated) legislation in Scotland

Delegated legislation made under Acts of the United Kingdom Parliament continue to be in the familiar form, even when applying to Scotland. Delegated legislation under Acts of the Scottish Parliament is in essentially the same form[27]. The only particularity worthy of remark is that SSIs are cited in a year-and-number

---

26 See Reid 'The Limits of Devolved Legislation Power; subordinate legislation in Scotland' (2003) 24 Stat LR 187-210.
27 Scotland Act 1998 (Transitory and Transitional) (Statutory Instruments) Order 1999 SI 1999/1096, art. 5.

manner, parallel to that of (UK)SIs, but commencing with the abbreviation 'SSI', for example 'SSI 2003/143', and use the 'C' abbreviation and sub-sequence of numbers for Commencement Orders. No distinction is made on the face of the instrument to distinguish those made under Acts of the United Kingdom and those made under Acts of the Scottish Parliament.

ULTRA VIRES AND JUDICIAL CONTROL OF DELEGATED LEGISLATION IN SCOTLAND

The same issues arise as with United Kingdom delegated legislation. However, two points require emphasis. Delegated legislation made in Scotland is as powerful as that made elsewhere, therefore it may amend Acts of the United Kingdom, even if it was made under an Act of the Scottish Parliament. On the other hand, the limits upon the Scottish Ministers are more exiguous, for the delegated legislation must be within the devolved competence, or an extension of it where the Scottish Ministers may exercise powers relating to reserved matters (see Chapter 3 and above: and *mutatis mutandis* in relation to other delegates), and not breach Convention rights or Community law.

CITATION AND PUBLICATION OF DELEGATED LEGISLATION IN SCOTLAND

Citation

Citation of delegated (and sub-delegated) legislation in Scotland is in the form described above under 'form of delegated (and sub-delegated) legislation in Scotland'[28].

Publication

Chronological series

Scottish Statutory Instruments ('SSIs') of general effect are printed and published by The Stationery Office ('TSO') as are (UK)SIs, and bound up in annual volumes as *Scottish Statutory Instruments*[29].

---

28   There is, again, innocent amusement to be had in discovering the most unusual statutory instrument name. See *eg* the Food Protection (Emergency Provisions) (Amnesic Shellfish Poisoning) (West Coast) (No 12) (Scotland) Order 2005, SSI 2006/6. (Note, incidentally, an example of an SSI title referring to one year, and the citation referring to the next).

29   Scotland Act 1998 (Transitory and Transitional) (Statutory Instruments) Order 1999 SI 1999/1096, arts 8 & 9.

Encyclopaedic series

No encyclopaedic series of SSIs yet exists.

Commercially produced reprints

No commercially produced reprints of SSIs yet exist.

Indexes

Each volume of *Scottish Statutory Instruments* contains an index, numerical list and table of effects. There is also a monthly and annual *List of Statutory Publications* with alphabetical and chronological tables.

Computerised retrieval

All SSIs are available in full text at the Office of Public Sector Information website[30].

30 See www.opsi.gov.uk.

11. Legislation – application, construction and interpretation: 'statutory interpretation'

THE APPLICATION, CONSTRUCTION AND INTERPRETATION OF LEGISLATION

Previous Chapters considered the various types of legislation which may apply in the United Kingdom generally, or Scotland in particular. This Chapter turns to difficulties in application and interpretation of such legislation. Most of the learning on this matter, and the cases, concern Acts of the United Kingdom Parliament, but such norms as emerge from that apply to other sorts of legislation, *mutatis mutandis*.

This is, in many ways, an unsatisfactory area of enquiry. There is some largely unacknowledged uncertainty as to what the enquiry is about (summed up in the distinction between 'construction' and 'interpretation'). Also, in any case and notoriously, the area includes a large number of purported 'rules', 'presumptions' and other principles, guidelines, and the like, which are applied inconsistently, often indicate incompatible solutions, and have no relative ranking to allow their reconciliation. Moreover, there have been considerable changes wrought by the effects of Community law, by the effects of the European Convention on Human Rights (as mediated by the Human Rights Act), and, in relation to Scottish legislation, by the exigencies of devolution as expressed in the Scotland Act 1998.

This Chapter is therefore unavoidably somewhat complicated, and considers the following:

(a) the need for application, including the ideas of 'construction' and 'interpretation';
(b) modes of construction and interpretation and their variation;
(c) the traditional mode of construction and interpretation in the United Kingdom, including the idea of 'the intention of Parliament'; the materials considered (such as *Hansard* and

'Explanatory Notes') to find it; and the techniques (such as 'Presumptions' and the three traditional 'Rules') applied to them;

(d) modification of construction and interpretation by United Kingdom courts under the influence of Community law, including construction and interpretation by the European Court of Justice, and the resulting construction and interpretation by United Kingdom courts in cases where there is a Community element (both where there is 'direct effect', and where there is not);

(e) modification of construction and interpretation by United Kingdom courts through the European Convention on Human Rights, as such, and more especially through the Human Rights Act 1998, including the concept of 'incompatibility'; and

(f) modification of construction and interpretation by United Kingdom courts through the Scotland Act 1998.

THE NEED FOR APPLICATION

Legislation is not self-applying: it must be applied by someone. This is regularly done by a variety of people, especially officials such as civil servants, local government officers and the police, as well as by lawyers. The way officials construe and interpret legislation is enormously important. The decisions of, say, local authority planning officers on the application of planning legislation affect the way that planning law operates in practice.

However, legal attention is usually directed exclusively at the way judges apply the law. There is good reason for this. Firstly, judges work from the authentic legislative texts and not from simplified guides, or explanatory material. Secondly, it is a central part of the judges' job and, by virtue of their experience, they have acquired expertise in it. Thirdly, judges give reasoned, public decisions published in the law reports. Fourthly, judges' decisions are impartial as between the parties. All these may apply to a greater or lesser extent to officials. However, fifthly, and most importantly, judges' decisions are uniquely authoritative, for they are signals to officials, including civil servants, local government officers, the police, tax inspectors, company secretaries, personnel managers, and the public at large, as to the correct view on the application of the legislation in question. They have the final word.

Much effort goes into the preparation and production of legislation, so it might be thought that it is easy to apply. Often this is the case, but by no means invariably, and there are remarkably few attempts to analyse what problems the application of legislation involves[1]. The reasons for the problems probably lie in the interplay of several factors. Some are inherent: rules concerning complicated matters will be complicated; no language is an instrument of complete precision; no draftsman can foresee all eventualities, and sometimes draftsmen make mistakes. Others are not: the United Kingdom tradition in drafting is to seek to cover all possibilities, at the expense of comprehensibility, while the civil law tradition (more obvious in Community law) involves looser drafting, giving more discretion to those applying it; the legislation may be an unhappy compromise, or it may be deliberately obscure[2]; much parliamentary legislation is ill-discussed because of the pressures upon parliamentary time; modern legislation is often a set of technical instructions to officials, and is not designed to be understood by lay people; frequent amendment may make comprehension difficult; United Kingdom or Great Britain legislation applying to Scotland has in the past often been a modified version of that drafted for England and Wales[3]. It may be that the Scottish Parliament will in future adopt a drafting style which avoids these pitfalls, though the drafting style adopted so far is deliberately the same[4].

These difficulties produce various problems. On the one hand, complexity may make legislation very resistant to comprehension. The legislative text may be unclear on its face, typically through numerous conditions and exceptions, exacerbated by frequent cross-reference, but also through ambiguity. On the other, it may be clear on its face, but produce a result which seems absurd, for example by apparently failing to cover certain situations (i.e. there is a *'lacuna'*[5] or *'casus omissus'*[6]). Further, sometimes it may reasonably be disputed

1   See, however, *eg* Kirby 'Towards a Grand Theory of Interpretation: the case of statutes and contracts' (2003) 24 Stat LR 95-111, Hunt 'Plain Language in Legislative Drafting: an achievable objective or a laudable ideal?' (2003) 24 Stat LR 112-124 and Barnes 'The Continuing Debate About "Plain Language" Legislation: a law reform conundrum' (2006) 27 Stat LR 83-132.

2   The Equal Pay (Amendment) Regulations 1983, SI 1983/1794, for example, were widely regarded as an unwilling response to the demands of Community law, drafted in obscure fashion, and involving a tortuous procedure in order to deter those seeking a remedy under them.

3   While devolution may have cured that defect, note the frequent use of 'Sewel Motions', discussed above in Chs 7 & 8 in relation to Acts of the United Kingdom and Scottish Parliaments, means that it may not.

4   See McCluskie 'New Approaches to UK Legislative Drafting: the view from Scotland' (2004) 25 Stat LR 136-143.

5   '1. A hiatus, blank, missing part ...' SOED (3rd ed, with corrections).

6   Roughly, an 'omitted case', *ie* a possible case omitted as not foreseen by the draftsman.

whether the text is in fact clear or not; or if it is clear, whether it in fact produces an absurd result or not. To compound the problem, no synthesised approach to a solution has been developed, but rather a series of disparate and potentially competing solutions, expressed in principles not 'in fixed verbal form' (see Appendix 1), and vague, in consequence of which broad, and not always acknowledged, notions of public policy and morality tend to influence outcomes. This is therefore an unsatisfying area of law. Various reforms have been proposed for many years, but have come to nothing, possibly because, while academic commentators and students are dissatisfied, the major players, that is, Parliament and the judges, are not.

The area, perhaps best referred to as 'application of legislation', is usually called 'statutory interpretation'. Arguably it involves two processes. Firstly, there is what is sometimes referred to as 'construing'[7] the rule, that is working out what the rule is by analysing closely what the draftsman actually wrote. This is rather like working out from a word-processing software manual the procedure for altering the margins of a document, or inserting footnotes, and has to be done whenever legislation is applied. Secondly, there is 'interpreting' the rule, that is, working out what the rule means in relation to the facts of a case when it is unclear. This is rather like trying to work out what the software manual means when it uses incomprehensible terms, or appears to leave out important stages from the instruction. The two processes are not easy to distinguish, and they overlap. Also, terminology is not constant, 'construction'[8] and 'interpretation' often being used interchangeably. Both processes are separate from the finding of facts, however. Indeed, interpretation assumes that the facts have been admitted or proved.

The idea of construction[9]

The construction of legislation has received less attention than the interpretation. Nevertheless, it may in practice cause difficulty more often for it is unavoidable, while interpretation is usually only necessary where the meaning of the legislation is unclear.

Legislation must be written, so there is always a text from which it may be extracted. The text must express the logic of the rule in its grammar and syntax. This is particularly obvious in the United

---

7   *Eg* Walker *Scottish Legal System* (8th ed, 2001), p 413 (esp. n 23).
8   'Construction' as in 'construing', not as in 'constructing': see previous note. There is even an ambiguity in the terminology used!
9   See previous note.

Kingdom drafting tradition because it seeks exactitude, and expresses the logic through typographical devices such as indentations as well as by division into Sections, Sub-sections etc.

A useful approach to construing legislation is therefore to remember that rules can be seen as 'if ... then' statements, that is, may be analysed into *protasis* and *apodosis*[10]; extract the facts of the *protasis* (which are likely to be separated into Sub-sections, or Paragraphs within a Sub-section) and determine their relationship, and distinguish the *apodosis* (which may be in head-words before any sub-divisions of the section, or in tail-words after them).

One commentator, an experienced former Parliamentary Draftsman, has taken this process further, and suggests that legislative provisions can be analysed into five aspects: case, condition, subject, declaration and exception[11]. In slightly modified form, his example, taken from the legislative provision on the production of driving licences, is as follows:

(a) Case – where a person is in charge of a motor vehicle (who is under consideration?).
(b) Condition – if so required by a constable (what must be true before the obligation or right applies?).
(c) Subject – that person (on whom does the obligation or right fall?).
(d) Declaration – shall produce his licence (what is the obligation or right created?).
(e) Exception – unless he is exempt from holding a licence (when does the obligation or right not apply?).

In straightforward cases, such analysis is done intuitively, but many cases are not straightforward. They are complicated by amendment; by cross-reference within the legislation (such as to Interpretation Sections); by cross-reference between pieces of legislation (particularly, in the United Kingdom context, between Acts of Parliament and delegated legislation); and by use of 'referential' rather than 'textual' amendment. Thus, for example, s 289E(2) of the (now repealed) Criminal Procedure (Scotland) Act 1975, itself inserted by the Criminal Justice Act 1982, read:

'Where the penalty or maximum penalty for an offence to which s 457A(1)(b) of this Act applies has not been altered by any enactment passed or made after 29th July 1977 (the date of the passing of the Criminal Law Act 1977), this section applies as if the

10 See Appendix 1.
11 *Bennion on Statute Law* (3rd ed, 1990): see also his *Statutory Interpretation: a code* (2nd ed 1992) and *Understanding Common Law Legislation* (2001).

amount referred to in subsection (5)(a) below were the greatest amount to which a person would have been liable on any conviction before that date'.

There is no law to assist on construing such complex rules. Patience and diligence are required, and analysis in the terms offered above is suggested[12].

The idea of interpretation

Construing legislation may leave open a number of interpretive questions in actual cases, for example, vagueness, or situations for which the draftsman appears not to have provided. What does a phrase like 'in charge of a motor vehicle' actually mean? Is a person alone in the front passenger seat without the car keys 'in charge'? Is a person in the back seat with the car keys? Unlike the problems of construction, this sort of problem has received much attention though not always providing useful answers.

For example, the Race Relations Act 1976 makes it unlawful in certain situations to discriminate against people on 'racial grounds', defined in s 3(1) as the ground of their 'colour, race, nationality or ethnic or national origins'. In *Mandla v Lee* [1983] AC 548 the question was whether discrimination against a Sikh was on this ground. The House of Lords finally decided that it was. Sikhs constitute an ethnic group, so discrimination against them is on the grounds of their '... ethnic ... origins'. In *Nyazi v Ryman Conran* [1988] Race Discrimination Law Reports 85, the same question arose in relation to Muslims, and it was decided that it was not unlawful discrimination. Muslims are a religious group, so discrimination against them is not on the grounds of their 'colour, race ... [etc]'. Thus, legislation requires to be interpreted in respect of any set of facts, which may show the precise meaning is unclear, so has to be resolved by the courts.

MODES OF CONSTRUCTING AND INTERPRETING LEGISLATION

So far as the United Kingdom is concerned, there is more than one mode of construction and interpretation. These are not Scottish and English modes, however, for there appears to be no significant

---

12 See also Twining and Miers *How To Do Things with Rules* (4th ed, 1999), especially App 2, which offers analysis in terms of algorithms.

difference between their approaches. It is possible that differences will develop with the growth of Acts of the Scottish Parliament, but this seems unlikely for several reasons. Firstly, much United Kingdom legislation (both in the forms of Acts of the United Kingdom Parliament and of delegated legislation), will remain in force in Scotland. Secondly, the propensity for this is willingly reinforced by the Parliament's use of 'Sewel Motions' (described in Chapters 7 and 8). Thirdly, in any case, the Scottish Parliament seems to be adopting United Kingdom drafting approaches[13]. And fourthly, the centripetal effects of the Appellate Committee of the House of Lords as final court of appeal are not diminished by devolution (and such effects are in fact increased by the use of the Judicial Committee of the Privy Council as final court of appeal in devolution cases). Nor is its impeding replacement by the new 'Supreme Court of the United Kingdom' (for which, see Chapter 3) likely to reverse this.

Thus, the modes are, rather, on the one hand the traditional mode which evolved over a lengthy period in the United Kingdom, without reference to other legal systems (save others of the common law family, which were largely seen as daughter systems of English law), and on the other a 'Community law mode' (which reflects the preoccupations of civil law systems), introduced through accession to the European Community, and the obligation to apply Community law (with or without direct effect).

It may be that a synthesis is emerging for, as noted above, the latter is having a marked influence upon the former. In any case, while the European Convention on Human Rights made surprisingly little difference for a surprisingly long time, further modifications have been imposed upon the mixture by the embedding of its content through explicit requirements of the Human Rights Act 1998 (which also reflects strong civil law influence in the case law of the European Court of Human Rights) and of the Scotland Act 1998 (which is clearly affected by some of the results of the mixing process). These will be addressed in turn.

THE TRADITIONAL MODE OF CONSTRUCTION AND INTERPRETATION OF LEGISLATION BY UNITED KINGDOM COURTS

As noted, there appear not to be separate Scottish and English traditions of construction and interpretation of legislation. Indeed, as the

13 See McCluskie 'New Approaches to UK Legislative Drafting: the view from Scotland' (2004) 25 Stat LR 136-143.

Appellate Committee of the House of Lords is final civil appeal court for both jurisdictions and much legislation covers both, it would be surprising if there were[14]. In the field of criminal law, however, where the Appellate Committee of the House of Lords has no jurisdiction in Scotland, occasionally Scottish and English courts give different interpretations to statutes which apply in both jurisdictions, as in *Ritchie v Petrie* 1972 JC 7 (concerning drunk driving) and *Kelly v MacKinnon* 1982 SCCR 205 (concerning possession of firearms). One effect of the lack of different traditions is that writers on the subject in Scotland cite English cases without remark.

Most discussions revolve around the interpretation of Acts of Parliament but, *mutatis mutandis*, the principles apply to delegated legislation as well. The important characteristics of United Kingdom legislation from the point of view of the application of legislation can be summed up in the phrase 'the intention of Parliament'.

'The intention of Parliament'

Courts commonly state that they seek to apply 'the intention of Parliament'[15]. This appears unhelpful in that the UK Parliament comprises 646 MPs and approximately as many unelected peers, many of whom may have voted against the legislation in question, and that legislation usually closely reflects the government's wishes. But, in so far as draftsmen seek exactitude couched in fixed verbal form (for which, see Appendix 1), Parliament's intention has traditionally meant the intention expressed in the text approved by Parliament[16].

This has constitutional significance. With statutory interpretation, the (unelected) judge is not making the law. He is applying that made by the (partly elected) Parliament. The point is expressed in a well-known exchange in the English case of *Magor and St Mellons RDC v Newport Corporation* [1952] AC 189 (HL), [1950] 2 All ER

---

14 See *Dalgleish v Glasgow Corporation* 1976 SC 32. As also noted, it is likely that its replacement by the new 'Supreme Court of the United Kingdom' will reverse this.

15 See Greenberg, D 'The Nature of Legislative Intention and the Implications for Legislative Drafting' (2006) 27 Stat LR 15-28.

16 The intention is traditionally that to be taken from the text at the time of enactment, not that of adjudication. This principle is referred to as *contemporanea expositio*: see, for example, *Montrose Peerage Case* (1853) 1 Macq 401. However, in some cases, the alternative 'speaking statute' view is now preferred: see *R (on the application of Quintavalle) v Secretary of State for Health* [2003] UKHL 13, [2003] 2 AC 687. Ancient statutes are expressed in style and vocabulary very different from today's however: see, for example, the words of the Royal Mines Act 1424, quoted in Chapter 8.

1226 (CA). Lord Denning (famous for his lack of respect for ortho-doxy) said in the Court of Appeal, at 1236, that he had 'no patience with an ultra legalistic interpretation which would deprive [the plaintiffs] of their rights altogether'. On appeal to the Appellate Committee of the House of Lords, Lord Simonds said, at 191, that '[t]he duty of the court is to interpret the words that the legislature has used; those words may be ambiguous but, even if they are, the power and duty of the court to travel outside them on a voyage of discovery are strictly limited', and referred to Lord Denning's 'naked usurpation of the legislative function under the thin disguise of inter-pretation'.

However, while courts still say that they seek to apply the intention of Parliament, the way they do it has changed significantly in recent years, in part under the influence of Community law, the Human Rights Act 1998 and the Scotland Act 1998, and they are now closer to Lord Denning's attitude than Lord Simonds'. This is demon-strated in, for instance, the English case of *Inco Europe Ltd and Others v First Choice Distribution and Others* [2000] 1 WLR 586, concerning the application of the (English) Arbitration Act 1971 to an arbitra-tion clause in a contract[17], and followed in Scotland by an Extra Division of the Inner House in *Scottish Water v Clydecare Ltd*, 2003 S.C. 330, concerning whether a nursing home was wholly a 'dwelling' for the purposes of recovering water and sewage charges under the Local Government (Scotland) Act 1994, ss 74 and 79. In *Inco*, the Appellate Committee of the House of Lords was prepared to read words into the statute on the ground that they considered it was clear that the draftsman had omitted them in error (*ie* there was a '*lacuna*' or '*casus omissus*'), Lord Nicholls declaring, at 592, that 'I am left in no doubt that for once, the draftsman has slipped up'. In *Clydecare*, Lord Osborne, giving the opinion of the court, explicitly agreed with Lord Nicholls, and asserted, at [30], that court would require to be persuaded that 'a fundamental error or draftsmanship has occurred in the legislation under consideration'.

Materials considered by United Kingdom courts in construing and interpreting legislation

The principal material the court considers is the legislative text itself and, although it may be crumbling, the orthodoxy has been that it considers no other text. It is applying the intention of Parliament as

17 For criticism of which, see Auchie 'The Undignified Death of the *Casus Omissus* Rule' (2004) 25 Stat LR 40-67. See also *R (on the application of Quintavalle) v Secretary of State for Health* [2003] UKHL13, [2003] 2 AC 687.

expressed in that text (in fixed verbal form). This renders other texts not so much useless as irrelevant. The difference of tradition with the European Court of Justice is obvious.

The legislative text

In so far as interpretation of legislation is a problem only where the meaning of the Act is unclear, a rule requiring first, and possibly last, resort to the unclear text seems paradoxical. However, reference to the legislation means reference to the whole legislative text in order to interpret the unclear word or phrase.

(a) **The Act as a whole.** Thus, an Act is a legislative unity which gives a context to any word or phrase. For example, the Race Relations Act 1968, s 3(1) made discrimination unlawful on the grounds of, among other things, 'national origins'. In *Ealing London Borough v Race Relations Board* [1972] AC 342, [1971] 2 WLR 71 the House of Lords considered whether this included discrimination against those not British subjects. The majority decided, on the basis of the general intent of the Act as a whole, that 'national origins' referred to the ineradicable characteristic of belonging to a 'nation', and not to holding a particular legal nationality, which was alterable.

(b) **Differences within the Act.** However, in some cases, courts have found the same phrase to mean different things in different parts of the same legislation. For example, the English Court of Appeal found that the word 'discrimination' bore different meanings in ss 1 and 4 of the Sex Discrimination Act 1975 (a Great Britain statute). On the other hand, Lord Justice-General Balfour in *Jacobs v Hart* (1900) 2 F(J) 33 at 37–38, concerning the Summary Procedure (Scotland) Act 1864, considered that Schedules, although annexed to Acts, could not alter the clear meaning of words in the body of the Act.

(c) **Interpretation sections and the like.** United Kingdom legislation also contains certain specific features which may assist in interpretation of legislation. Legislation is likely to have interpretation provisions. Thus, vague or unusual terms may be explained, for example 'racial discrimination', 'racial grounds' and 'racial groups' in the Race Relations Act 1976, s 3(3), and 'gender dysphoria' in the Gender Recognition Act 2004, s 25. There may be also lists and examples. Section 20 of the Race Relations Act 1976 makes discrimination unlawful in the provision of 'facilities and services'. Those terms are not defined, but s 20(2) says 'The following are examples of the facilities and services mentioned in subsection 1 ...'. Also, familiar, but inherently vague, terms may also be defined, such as 'sport' in the Gender Recognition Act 2004, s 19(3).

However, interpretation provisions can only assist where the draftsman has foreseen the difficulty, are usually preceded by the words 'unless the context otherwise requires', and may not be applicable to other Acts[18].

(d) Titles and preambles. Long and Short Titles are found in all United Kingdom Acts. Long Titles may be used to remove doubts, but not to raise them if a provision is otherwise clear, as held in *Kelly v Nuttal & Sons Ltd* 1965 SC 427 and more recently by the Appellate Committee of the House of Lords in *R (on the application of Quintavalle) v Secretary of State for Health* [2003] UKHL13, [2003] 2 AC 687 (per Lord Millet) at [41]. In practice, they are rarely useful. There seems to be no Scottish authority on Short Titles, but English authority declares that, as 'statutory nicknames', they cannot be used at all[19]. Preambles can be used[20], but are very rare (except in private legislation).

(e) Marginal notes, headings etc. Marginal notes (sometimes referred to as 'side notes'), cross-headings and the like are sometimes described as the 'unenacted' parts of an Act because they are not discussed in Parliament. In *Farqharson v White* (1886) 13 R(J) 29 (concerning the word 'month' in the Game Act 1773) and *Magistrates of Buckie v Dowager Countess of Seafield's Trustees* 1928 SC 525, (concerning the phrase 'any other place' in the Burgh Police (Scotland) Act 1892, s 90), the Inner House held such parts to be in the same position as the Long Title. Unenacted parts were also discussed by the Appellate Committee of the House of Lords in *DPP v Schildkamp* [1971] AC 1 and *R v Montila* [2004] UKHL 50. In the former, an English case on the Companies Act 1948, a Great Britain statute, the court resolved an ambiguity by reference to a cross-heading. No clear principle emerged, but the remarks of Lord Reid, a notable Scottish judge, are usually taken to indicate and confirm the position arrived at in the earlier Scottish cases, and it was subsequently applied in Scotland in *Hill v Orkney Islands Council* 1983

---

18 See references to legislation *'in pari materia'*, below.
19 *Vacher & Sons v London Society of Compositors* [1913] AC 107; *R v Boaler* [1915] 1 KB 21.
20 *Anderson v Jenkins Express Removals Ltd*, reported in *James Kemp (Leslie) Ltd v Robertson* 1967 SC 229 at 233–234 per Lord Mackintosh. The *locus classicus* is the English House of Lords case of *A-G v Prince Ernest Augustus of Hanover* [1957] AC 436, especially per Lord Normand (a Scottish judge), although the role of Scots law was overlooked in that case.

SLT (Lands Tr) 2, concerning the Tenants' Rights Etc Act 1980. In the latter, another English case, on the Criminal Justice Act 1988 (as amended), a largely England and Wales statute, the court (with Lord Hope, another Scottish judge, giving the opinion of the Court) decided that, while less weight might be attributed to cross heading and marginal notes, they should not be disregarded, as they were there for guidance (in particular in relation to the 'mischief' the legislation was intended to cure) so were part of the context of the Act which assisted in interpretation[21].

Other texts

The broad rule applied by United Kingdom courts is that only the legislative text approved by the UK Parliament is to be considered. A distinction has nevertheless been drawn between looking at other documents to discover the general background to the case (that is, for the 'mischief' referred to in the 'mischief rule'; see below) on the one hand, and looking at them to find Parliament's intention on the other. The former is permissible and, on occasion, freely done. The latter is not permissible. However, even to this exclusionary rule there are important exceptions, and the very rule is being eroded.

(a) Earlier judicial decisions on the legislation and legislation 'in pari materia'. It is the legislation which determines the meaning, not other judges' views[22]. However, earlier cases interpreting the same legislation may be used to extract its meaning and only a bold judge would depart from a series of similar decisions interpreting an Act, or even from a single decision of a higher court[23]. Previous interpretations are difficult to avoid as a means of seeking meaning, and are one of the most commonly used. They operate as precedents in essentially the same way as in the common law[24], as the Inner House decided, albeit with some difficulty, in

---

21 See Simamba, B 'Should Marginal Notes be Used in the Interpretation of Legislation?' (2005) Stat LR 125-130.
22 In the English case of *Farrell v Alexander* [1977] AC 59, at 97, Lord Edmund-Davies in the Appellate Committee of the House of Lords approved the remark of Lord Denning in the Court of Appeal [1976] QB 345, at 359, that 'where there is a conflict between a plain statute and a previous decision, the statute must prevail'.
23 In *Nicol's Trustees v Sutherland* 1951 SC(HL) 21 at 32 Lord Normand said that '[a] construction which recommended itself to Lord President Inglis [and a series of other notable judges] could only be rejected if on consideration by [the Appellate Committee of the House of Lords] it appeared an inescapable conclusion that the words of the statute were plain beyond doubt and that they had been repeatedly misunderstood by Judges who were not usually prone to such error'.
24 See Chs 5 & 12.

Dalgleish v Glasgow Corporation 1976 SC 32. However, as the Inner House also decided, in *AIB Finance Ltd v Bank of Scotland* 1995 SLT 2, subsequent legislation amending cannot be so used, as it cannot shed light on the intention of Parliament at the time of enactment of the legislation which is to be interpreted.

Other legislation concerning the same subject may also sometimes be used to interpret, as it can be assumed Parliament meant the same thing if it used the same words. In some cases, an Act specifically stipulates that it is 'to be construed with' another. That is also implied where Acts are given collective Short Titles. In general, however, this principle means that cases concerning the legislation *'in pari materia'*[25] can be used as precedents. Reinforcing this is a presumption, based on the Appellate Committee of the House of Lords' decision in *Barras v Aberdeen Steam Trawling and Fishing Co Ltd* 1933 SC(HL) 21, of 'statutory endorsement'. If a word or phrase has received a particular interpretation by the courts, and it is incorporated in subsequent statutes, then it may be assumed that Parliament was endorsing that interpretation. However, some doubt was cast upon this by the High Court in *Kelly v MacKinnon* 1982 SCCR 205. Consolidation Acts are a special case of legislation *in pari materia* with the Acts consolidated. They re-enact, though may do so with minor amendment.

There are exceptions and limits to the *pari materia* principle. In particular, there is the question of how *'pari'* the *'materia'* must be. For example, the Sex Discrimination Act 1975 and Race Relations Act 1976 concern different subjects but are drafted in large measure identically. Cross-reference to one is therefore sometimes made by the courts in order to interpret the other, as, for example, the English Court of Appeal did in *Singh v West Midlands Passenger Transport Executive* [1988] IRLR 186. On the other hand, Acts on the same subject may have differing interpretation provisions, as observed by the Inner House in *Lord Advocate v Sprot's Trustees* (1901) 3 F 440, (1901) 8 SLT 403 (IH).

There is also difficulty with delegated legislation, since it is not written for, nor normally expressly approved by, Parliament, so the words can be said to be 'the intention of Parliament' only with extreme difficulty. In *Hanlon v Law Society* [1981] AC 124, an English case before the House of Lords on the English legal aid legislation, at 193–194, Lord Lowry (a Northern Irish judge) suggested half a dozen principles to apply. These indicate that delegated legislation can be used to interpret its parent Act or related Acts, provided those Acts are ambiguous, or provided it can amend

25 Roughly, 'on a similar matter'.

them. In the former case, they cannot control the meaning of the Act but, if consistent, can confirm an interpretation, and are particularly reliable if they flesh out a skeleton Act. In the latter case (and if they are to have effect as if enacted in the Act), they are a clear guide.

(b) The Interpretation Act 1978, dictionaries and textbooks. The Interpretation Act 1978 gives certain standard definitions, such as that 'words importing the masculine gender include the feminine' and vice versa; that references to time are references to Greenwich Mean Time or British Summer Time, as appropriate; and the like. While useful, its application is limited[26], and the definitions are subject to the legislation expressing a contrary intention[27].

Dictionaries have always been admitted to find the ordinary meaning of words. However, they are not often helpful[28]. Textbooks on law are sometimes referred to, but they are evidence of what commentators thought, rather than guides to Parliament's intention. *The Laws of Scotland: Stair Memorial Encyclopaedia* (Butterworths) has created a great new source of information and argument.

(c) International treaties. International treaties may be incorporated into Scots law, and this is becoming more important with an increasing number of multilateral treaties directly affecting individuals[29]. Typically, they apply by express enactment in an Act of Parliament. For example, the Child Abduction and Custody Act 1985 incorporates the Convention on the Civil Aspects of International Child Abduction (and another treaty), and in *Viola v Viola* 1988 SLT 7 (OH) the judgment rests almost entirely upon the terms of the Convention. However, where there is express enact-

---

26 See Duperron 'Interpretation Acts - impediments to legal certainty and access to the law' (2005) 26 Stat LR 64-68.

27 For an example of which, see Lord Chancellor Loreburn and Lord Robertson in *Nairn v St Andrews and Edinburgh University Courts* 1909 SC(HL) 10, at 13 and 15-16 respectively.

28 In *Mandla v Lee* [1983] QB 1, at 9-10, Lord Denning in the English Court of Appeal relied upon three dictionaries to assign a meaning to 'ethnic' in the Race Relations Act 1976. His interpretation, relying heavily upon etymology, was roundly rejected as absurd by Lord Fraser of Tullybelton on appeal to the Appellate Committee of the House of Lords [1983] AC 548, at 560-565. In *Mandla v Lee*, Lord Denning also sought to rely on anthropological works. In *Reed International v IRC* [1976] AC 336, at 359, Lord Wilberforce, having found Dr Johnson's *Dictionary* (1755) unhelpful, referred to Palgrave's *Dictionary of Political Economy* (1896).

29 See *eg* Berman 'International Treaties and British Statutes' (2005) 26 Stat LR 1-12 and Eaton 'Enacting Treaties' (2005) 26 Stat LR 13-21

ment, and certainly where the treaty is incorporated into a schedule, as in this instance, the treaty is not an external aid at all.

English courts have in some cases considered that they might look at other, unincorporated versions of the treaty; commentaries on it (which might involve translation); and even the treaty's *travaux préparatoires*[30]. Indeed, there is Scottish authority in *Gatoil International v Arkwright-Boston Manufacturers Mutual Insurance* 1985 SC(HL) 1 (especially Lord Wilberforce, at 10 and 11, and Lord Keith of Kinkell, at 16). This concerned the Administration of Justice Act 1956 and the Brussels Convention Relating to the Arrest of Seagoing Ships. It suggested that even where the treaty is not expressly incorporated, so is external to the Act, it can be examined, and so possibly could some of its *travaux préparatoires*.

Such practice may be justified by the need for consistent interpretation in different countries (as is required of Community law). Treaties are, however, always aids to be used at the judges' discretion to interpret the legislative text and are not the text itself. Changes in attitude to treaties have been influenced by use of Community law in United Kingdom courts.

The European Convention on Human Rights has long been regarded as an exceptional case among treaties, and its position is considered separately below in relation to the effects of the Human Rights Act 1998

(d) Hansard. The publication known as '*Hansard*' is the verbatim account of proceedings in Parliament, so provides the obvious *travaux préparatoires* for Acts of Parliament. Traditionally, there has been a complete rejection of its use, following directly from the principle that the Act forms Parliament's final words which the judges must loyally apply. This was frequently and emphatically reiterated in the 1970s and 1980s by the Appellate Committee of the House of Lords in the face of attempts by Lord Denning in the Court of Appeal to alter the rule. The reasons for the exclusionary rule in relation to *Hansard* were summed up by the Law Commissions as relevance, reliability and availability[31]. It was commonly irrelevant in that it is unlikely that the precise question before the court was

---

30 Literally 'preparatory works', and used to refer to the published documentation of the negotiations leading to the treaty. The advantage of them is that they may show the reasoning which produced an agreed form of words. The disadvantage is that they are not what was actually agreed. For the views of the Appellate Committee of the House of Lords, see *James Buchanan & Co Ltd v Babco Forwarding and Shipping (UK) Ltd* [1978] AC 141; *Fothergill v Monarch Airlines Ltd* [1981] AC 251.

31 *The Interpretation of Statutes* (1969) Sco Law Com 1, Law Com 21, paras 53–62.

discussed; it was unreliable in that parliamentary debates are commonly attempts to persuade rather than to examine dispassionately, and contradictory statements may be made on any topic[32], and it was unavailable in that *Hansard* is available in few libraries. In broad terms, it might be thought that the first two criticisms remain, though the third must be modified as all parliamentary debates are now available on the Parliament website[33]. In any event, occasional exceptions to the rule nevertheless were discovered, most notably by the Appellate Committee of the House of Lords in *Litster v Forth Dry Dock and Engineering Co Ltd* 1989 S.C. (H.L.) 96, concerning reg 5(3) of a United Kingdom Statutory Instrument, the Transfer of Undertakings (Protection of Employment) Regulations 1981, SI 1981/1794. However, this Statutory Instrument sought to effect Community legislation, so raised special considerations. (*Litster* is discussed in relation to the construction and interpretation by United Kingdom courts of United Kingdom legislation which implements Community legislation without 'direct effect').

A major change in the exclusionary rule, prefigured by cases like *Litster* occurred, however, in *Pepper v Hart* [1993] A.C. 593, which concerned the Finance Act 1976, a United Kingdom statute. In a majority decision of the Appellate Committee of the House of Lords, Lord Browne-Wilkinson's leading judgment reiterated the reasons for excluding *Hansard* in terms of constitutional proprieties, practical difficulties and the need for a definite text. However, on the grounds that the courts' job is to apply the intention of Parliament, that Parliament cannot have intended an ambiguity, and the exclusionary rule thwarted the attempt to find the true meaning, a 'limited modification' to the existing rule was introduced. That modification is that where a statute is ambiguous, obscure or leads to an absurdity, statements by a minister or other promoter of the Bill may be referred to, if necessary with other parliamentary material, provided they are clear. The Lord Chancellor dissented, rehearsing the familiar arguments for the rule[34].

32 Lord Diplock in *Hadmor Productions v Hamilton* [1983] 1 AC 191 at 232, [1981] 2 All ER 724 observed that 'Lord Denning ... sought to justify the construction he placed on s 17(8) by referring to the report in Hansard of a speech made by a peer, who is a distinguished academic lawyer, Lord Wedderburn, when moving an opposition amendment (which was defeated) to delete the subsection from the Bill'.
33 *Ie* www.parliament.uk.
34 See Bates 'Judicial Application of *Pepper v Hart*' 1993 JLSS 251; Walker 'Discovering the Intention of Parliament' 1993 SLT (News) 121, Bates 'The Contemporary Use of Legislative History in the United Kingdom' [1995] Camb LJ 127, and Bennion 'Executive Estoppel: *Pepper v Hart* revisited' 2006 PL 1-12.

So far as Scotland, as such, is concerned, *Pepper v Hart* was applied in *Short's Trustee v Keeper of the Registers of Scotland* 1994 SLT 65. In this conveyancing case the 'Reid' and 'Henry Reports' which preceded legislation on the registration of titles, as well as aspects of the parliamentary process, were referred to in the both Outer and Inner House and found in the latter to be 'of limited assistance'. But in *AIB Finance v Bank of Scotland* 1995 SLT 2 and *Customs and Excise Comrs v Robert Gordon's College* 1995 SLT 1139 the *Pepper v Hart* exception was not utilised, since no ambiguity or obscurity could be found in the relevant statutes.

The modification refers explicitly to statements in Parliament, but if the views of the promoters of a Bill are to be considered, there seems no reason not to permit other governmental statements. In *Melluish v Fitzroy Finance* [1996] 1 AC 454 it was observed that the range of materials which might be looked at should not be widened. However, there have been further developments in relation to 'Explanatory Notes'.

(e) 'Explanatory Notes'. 'Explanatory Notes', written by the sponsoring Government Department, have long been attached to Statutory Instruments. They are designed to give a straightforward explanation of the meaning of the various provisions. They might be expected to be excluded on the traditional '*Hansard*' ground (discussed above) of relevance (for they often add little to what is in the text of the Statutory Instrument), though not the grounds of reliability (for Statutory Instruments, being delegated legislation, do not purport to be Parliament's intention), or availability (as they have always been printed with the Statutory Instrument). If this were the rule, again, some exceptions emerged. *Pickstone v Freemans plc* [1989] AC 66 concerned, *int. al.*, the Equal Pay (Amendment) Regulations 1983, SI 1983/1794, a United Kingdom Statutory Instrument. The Appellate Committee of the House of Lords took into account the words of the Minister introducing it because (as in *Litster*), it was seeking to effect Community law. Also, at least so far as Lord Oliver of Aylmerton was concerned, at 127, he concluded that the 'Explanatory Notes' could be used, and that, although not part of the Statutory Instrument, such a Note could be used, at least to identify the mischief[35] that the legislation sought to remedy.

Explanatory Notes have, since 1999, also been attached to Bills (and updated where Bills change during their passage through Parliament), and the resulting Acts. It might be thought that they

---

35 For the 'mischief rule', see below.

would fall at both the relevance (as adding little) and reliability (as clearly not expressing the intention of Parliament) hurdles, though still easily managing the availability hurdle (as they are available online with the relevant Bills and Acts).

In *R (on the application of Westminster City Council) v National Asylum Support Service* [2002] UKHL 38, [2002] 1 W.L.R. 2956, at [4]-[6], Lord Steyn described Explanatory Notes as 'not form[ing] part of the Bill, ... not endorsed by Parliament [and unable to be amended] by Parliament', though 'neutral in political tone ... aim[ing] to explain the text and not to justify it' and manifesting 'a procedure [which] has the *imprimatur* of the House of Commons Select Committee on Modernisation and the House of Lords Procedure Committee'. He went on to observe, explicitly invoking *Pepper v Hart*, that they are 'always admissible' in relation to the 'contextual scene of the statute and the mischief at which it is aimed'[36], for which purpose they might be more useful than government reports, Green and White Papers. Indeed, they might be quoted against the Government. What was 'impermissible', however, was 'to treat the wishes and desires of the Government about the scope of the statutory language as reflecting the will of Parliament'. This seems to reiterate the *Pepper v Hart* position that such texts may not usually be used, but, as an exception, may be where a statute is ambiguous, obscure or leads to an absurdity (though adding a further observation that they might be quoted against the Government as well as by it).

They have certainly been taken into account in a number of cases. In *Attorney-General for Jersey v Montila* [2004] UKHL 50, [2004] 1 W.L.R. 3141, for instance, Lord Hope, a Scottish judge, giving the opinion of the Appellate Committee of the House of Lords, at [35] went so far as to say that it has become 'common practice for their Lordships to ask to be shown the Explanatory Notes when issues are raised about the meaning of words used in an enactment'.

However, whether this is a satisfactory position is open to doubt, for it is possible to find statements in Explanatory Notes which do not seem to accord with the words of the enactment, yet may be used to interpret them[37].

(f) **Other government documents.** Arguments for excluding government documents such as White Papers, Royal Commission

---

36 See previous note.
37 See Munday 'Bad Character Rules and Riddles: "Explanatory Notes" and True Meanings of s 103(1) of the Criminal Justice Act 2003' [2005] Crim LR 337-354.

and other reports overlap those in relation to *Hansard*, but are stronger. They cannot be evidence of Parliament's intention. This position was taken in an English case on United Kingdom legislation before the Appellate Committee of the House of Lords, *Assam Railways and Trading Co Ltd v IRC* [1935] AC 445 (see Lord Wright at 457–458) and in a Scottish case, *Inglis v British Airports Authority* 1978 SLT (Lands Tr) 30. However, while in a complicated judgment in another English case the House of Lords preserved the rule in *Black-Clawson International Ltd v Papierwerke Waldhof Aschaffenburg AG* [1975] AC 591, some of its members were prepared to accept that in certain circumstances a draft Bill attached to a report, and possibly other documents, might be considered.

(g) The Reports of the Scottish Law Commission. These are a special instance where there is a case for invoking materials beyond the legislation in question for these reports now customarily rehearse the law before the legislation, identify its defects and offer a remedy in the form of a draft Bill with supporting arguments. If Parliament has in all material respects enacted the Bill drafted by the Commission, its Report would seem a useful means of discovering the meaning of the Act. In *McWilliams v Lord Advocate* 1992 SLT 1045, Lord Morton made full use of two Commission reports on the question whether a child had a right of action for injuries sustained before birth. However, the more common attitude of the judges, as exemplified in *Barratt Scotland Ltd v Keith* 1994 SLT 1343, has been to restrict reference to Law Commission publications to cases of ambiguity or other doubts. But, as has been pointed out[38], statutory language is neither clear nor unclear in the abstract. It depends on the context, and part of that context is the 'mischief' for which the Commission recommended a remedy. In *MacDonald v HM Advocate* 1999 SLT 533, it sufficed that it would be 'helpful' to refer to a Commission report.

Techniques employed by United Kingdom courts in construing and interpreting legislation

The techniques employed by the United Kingdom courts are usefully divided into 'Presumptions' and 'Rules', although there are problems with this classification, and an attempted synthesis is suggested.

---

38 Maher 'Statutory Interpretation and Scottish Law Commission Reports' 1992 SLT (News) 277.

Presumptions

There are a number of 'Presumptions'. These operate unless explicitly or implicitly excluded. In general they apply when there is doubt as to the meaning of the legislation, though some are so strong as to displace an apparently clear meaning. There is no exhaustive or official list of any of them, and they may contradict each other.

(a) **Legal presumptions.** Firstly, there are certain legal presumptions. They are so various as to defy easy classification, and different authorities give different examples[39]. These differences can be reconciled by regarding them as examples of just three broad overlapping presumptions, that is: against unclear alteration of settled law; against absurd results; and against injustice. Clearly, a judge is thus given considerable discretion as to whether there is in fact doubt as to the meaning of the legislation; as to whether (if there is doubt) any presumption applies to the particular situation before him; and as to whether (if it does apply to it) it is strong enough to displace any alternative interpretation. This discretion must also be seen against two background facts. Firstly, (as argued in Chapter 5), legislation is generally *ad hoc* and provides few broad principles, which must therefore be sought in the common law. Secondly, the operation of presumptions depends heavily upon the prevailing moral and political atmosphere.

A commonly cited example of a legal presumption fitting readily into one or more of the suggested three categories, is that against the creation of offences not requiring *mens rea* (that is, roughly, 'a guilty mind'). It is well illustrated by *Sweet v Parsley* [1970] AC 132, an English case on a United Kingdom statute, the Dangerous Drugs Act 1965. Section 5 of that Act created the offence of 'being the occupier'

---

39 Compare, for example, the list in *The Laws of Scotland: Stair Memorial Encyclopaedia* vol 12 'The Interpretation of Statute' paras 1126–1133 (against changing existing law, ousting or adding to courts' jurisdiction, taking away rights or imposing burdens, technical constructions of legislation, incorrect usage, and also against injustice, interpreting legislation to render it invalid, and absurdity) with that of 'principal' ones in DM Walker *The Scottish Legal System* (8th edn, 2001) pp 428–430 (against binding the Crown, altering fundamental principles of law, infringing international law, altering the jurisdiction of courts, rendering the legislation inoperable, retrospective operation, interfering with individual liberty, dispensing with *mens rea*, taking property without compensation, imposing a tax, altering rights of appeal, using precedents interpreting legislation now re-enacted, preventing a person from opting out of benefits etc). Compare further the 'judicial principles' referred to by Paterson, Bates and Poustie *The Legal System of Scotland: cases and materials* (4th ed, 2001) pp 384–386, and the 'presumptions of general application' and 'presumptions for use in doubtful cases' in Cross *Statutory Interpretation* (3rd ed, 1995) Ch 7.

or 'concerned in the management' of premises used for the offence of 'smoking of cannabis resin'. It was silent on whether such a person committed the offence if unaware of the smoking by others on the premises. Sweet, a non-resident landlord, wholly ignorant of the actual smoking by others on the premises, was convicted of the offence. The Appellate Committee of the House of Lords quashed the conviction on appeal, deciding that only the clearest words could exclude *mens rea* from such an offence, and that mere silence was insufficient. Lord Reid, a notable Scottish judge, observed, at 148, that 'there has for centuries been a presumption that Parliament did not intend to make criminals of persons who were in no way blameworthy ... '.

Nevertheless, there are many deliberately created (but usually merely regulatory) offences of strict liability, requiring no *mens rea*, for example speeding. Parliament may deliberately override any other presumption, such as that against retrospective legislation, which again clearly fits in one or more of the three suggested categories, as it did in both the War Damage Act 1965 and the War Crimes Act 1991.

An example of a legal presumption showing the effect of the prevailing *mores* is *Nairn v St Andrews and Edinburgh University Courts* 1909 SC(HL) 10. The Representation of the People (Scotland) Act 1868 gave graduates the right to vote for parliamentary seats representing their universities, in addition to their normal constituency votes. The Universities (Scotland) Act 1889 permitted universities to allow women to graduate. The two Acts taken together thus appeared to give women graduates the vote for university seats. However, at that time, women did not have the vote. The Appellate Committee of the House of Lords decided that male franchise was a fundamental constitutional provision, and it could be presumed that Parliament would only have altered it explicitly, not incidentally. This readily fitted into the suggested three broad categories of presumption in the early 20th century, but not in the early 21st.

(b) Linguistic presumptions. Secondly, there are certain linguistic presumptions[40]. Legislation in the United Kingdom is in

---

40 In this context, *The Laws of Scotland: Stair Memorial Encyclopaedia* vol 12, paras 1165–1174, especially 1169–1170, using somewhat different criteria, lists several relevant 'subsidiary principles of construction', and also refers under 'mandatory, directory and permissive enactments'; Cross *Statutory Interpretation* (3rd ed, 1995) pp 134–141 uses the term 'rules of language'; Paterson, Bates and Poustie *The Legal System of Scotland* (4th ed, 2001) pp 392–393 refer to 'the grammatical context' as part of the general context in which a statute must be construed; DM Walker *The Scottish Legal System* (8th ed, 2001) p 420 uses the term 'reference to context'.

English, and what are regarded as the standard grammatical and semantic rules of that language apply. There is a vast, unsatisfactory, case law on their application, however, including little Scottish authority, and these presumptions are rarely of help in practice.

Three such presumptions, tricked out in Latin, are orthodox to cite, and certain word usages deserve mention, that is, *'noscitur a sociis'*, *'eiusdem generis'*, and *'expressio unius, exclusio alterius'*. The first of these, *noscitur a sociis* means, roughly, 'a thing is known by its context' ('words of a feather flock together'), and the second, *eiusdem generis* ('of the same kind') is a special case of it. The third, *expressio unius, exclusio alterius* means 'if you don't say it, you don't mean it' (which might contradict a legal presumption such as that against injustice, as in *Sweet v Parsley*).

One example of the second (*eiusdem generis*) will suffice to illustrate their operation[41]. The presumption applies to a common statutory formulation, 'any A, B, C, or other X'. This strongly implies that X is the genus of which A, B, and C are species. Thus, s 11 of the Representation of the People (Scotland) Act 1832 referred to 'any house, warehouse, counting house, shop, or other building'. In *Duncan v Jackson* (1905) 8 F 323, the Inner House held that the genus expressed by 'or other building' was delimited by the species expressed by the words 'any house ...' etc. The genus was thus 'residential, commercial and agricultural premises'. It did not include a structure which, though a building in common parlance, and large, and made of stone and brick, was built to house a gas meter.

The words 'shall', 'may', 'and' and 'or' deserve attention. 'It shall be an offence ... ', a canonical formulation for creating criminal offences, really means 'It is an offence ... ' emphasising obligation rather than futurity. Also, used in relation to a procedure, 'shall' generally makes it mandatory (that is, obligatory), so failure to follow the procedure invalidates the outcome (rather than directory, that is, merely recommended), as held by the Appellate Committee of the House of Lords in *London and Clydeside Estates v Aberdeen District Council* 1980 SC(HL) 1, (which concerned a planning appeal procedure under the Town and Country Planning (General Development) (Scotland) Order 1959, SI 1959/1361). However, the presumption can be rebutted, as, for example, in *HM Advocate v Graham* 1985 SLT 498 (which concerned the lodging of copy indictments under the Criminal Procedure (Scotland) Act 1975). Where legislation says someone 'shall' do something, it also implies

---

41 For a recent example of express use of *expressio unius*, see *R (on the application of Jackson) v Attorney-General* [2005] UKHL 56, at [138] *per* Lord Rodger of Earlsferry.

he is given the power to do so. 'May' in legislative discourse generally denotes power or permission, without any obligation to use it, as held, for example, in *Patmor Ltd v City of Edinburgh District Licensing Board* 1988 SLT 850 (concerning gaming licences under the Gaming Act 1968). On occasion, however, permissive words have been interpreted as obligatory, as, for example, in *Gray v St Andrews and Cupar District Committees of Fife County Council* 1911 SC 266 (concerning the Highways (Scotland) Act 1771).

The words 'and' and 'or' appear unambiguous, but 'and' may in practice mean 'and/or'. The Food and Environmental Protection Act 1985, s 1(1), (2),(6) and Sch 1, para 1(d), taken together, permitted the Scottish Ministers to prohibit 'fishing for **and** taking fish' (emphasis added) under certain circumstances. They used that power to make, *int. al.*, the Food Protection (Emergency Prohibitions) (Amnesic Shellfish Poisoning) (East Coast) (No 4) (Scotland) Order 2003, SSI 2003/393, Art 4 of which purported to prohibit 'fishing for **or** taking scallops' (emphasis added)[42]. In *Colley v Poland* 2005 SLT 436, the High Court of Justiciary, on appeal, had to decide whether the words in the Statutory Instrument were competent, given the words in the Act.

'Rules'

Traditionally, three 'rules' of statutory interpretation have been said to exist: the 'Mischief Rule', the 'Literal Rule' and the 'Golden Rule'. All are based on English cases, but have been applied without comment in Scotland.

(a) **The '*Mischief Rule*'.** The Mischief Rule dates from the English *Heydon's Case* (1584) 3 Co Rep 7a. It is usually said to mean that, if a provision is unclear, the judge should look to the 'mischief' the Act was designed to overcome, and interpret it in order to 'suppress the mischief and advance the remedy'. Although it is often seen as a warrant for judges to rewrite legislation in a fashion they

---

42 The effect of the difference is, of course, that the Order would prohibit both fishing for scallops (even if none were caught), and the taking of fish (even inadvertently when not fishing for them, which was the essence of the original dispute), while arguably, the Act only permitted prohibition of catching fish when fishing for them. On the basis of normal English syntax (see para [15]), and that the legislation was for the protection of the public (a consideration that had led the Sheriff to decide the other way: see paras [16] & [17], and note references to the 'mischief rule' below), the Court decided that the Order was competent. It is curious that no major (or possibly minor) European language appears to have a word expressing the common and useful idea of 'and/or', and that the phrase became widespread only with the spread of computers.

find more palatable, it has been suggested that it is quite the contrary, having been developed as a means of compelling judges to focus on what Parliament intended rather than what they wish it had intended[43]. The rule has been explicitly applied in Scotland. For example, the Tweed Fishing Act 1859, s 10 allowed a court, where salmon had been poached, to order forfeit any 'boat, cart, basket or package' used to carry it[44]. In *Leadbetter v Hutcheson* 1934 JC 70 the High Court interpreted 'cart' to include a motor-cycle combination, in the words of Lord Morison (at 73) 'so as to cope with the mischief'[45].

(b) The *'Literal Rule'*. The Literal Rule emerged later, with the growth of the practice of drafting legislation 'in fixed verbal form'. The crystallisation of the idea is that Parliament is the law-maker *par excellence*, and judges simply apply that law. It asserts that the judge should apply the literal meaning of the legislation, but the title is best reserved for the implication that this meaning should be applied even if the result is absurd, or at least something common sense suggests Parliament did not intend, and probably therefore over-riding one of the presumptions. For example, the Finance Act 1933 taxed certain 'profits'. In *Ayrshire Employers Mutual Insurance v IRC* 1946 SC(HL) 1, the Appellate Committee of the House of Lords considered whether this included the 'surpluses' generated by mutual insurance companies. Even though reasonably sure that the government, the draftsman and Parliament all intended the legislation to tax them, it held that such surpluses were not regarded as profits elsewhere in the law, and it consequently applied a literal interpretation, thereby excluding them. In another example, the Misuse of Drugs Act 1971, s 5 made it an offence to possess cannabis resin. In *Keane v Gallagher* 1980 SLT 144, the High Court decided to apply 'the plain unqualified words' to uphold conviction of possessing a minute quantity, totalling 11 milligrams, which was too small to be usable.

(c) The *'Golden Rule'*. The Golden Rule implies that the literal meaning should be applied unless it produces, in Lord Blackburn's classical exposition of the rule in *RiverWear Commissioners v Adamson* (1877) 2 App Cas 743 (reiterating an earlier version), 'an inconsistency, or an absurdity, or inconvenience so great as to convince the court' that the intention of Parliament must have been different. Such an outcome will justify the court in applying another meaning

---

43   Miers and Page *Legislation* (2nd ed, 1990) p 171.
44   *Cf*, incidentally, Anon. 'Is a jet-ski a ship?' (2006) 27 Stat LT iii-vi.
45   See also *Colley v Poland* 2005 SLT 436, discussed above.

which the words will bear[46]. For example, in *Caledonian Railway Co v North British Railway Co* (1881) 8 R (HL) 23, at 25, the Lord Chancellor, Lord Selborne, observed:

> 'The more literal construction ought not to prevail if ... it is opposed to the intention of the legislature as apparent by the statute, and if the words are sufficiently flexible to admit of some other construction by which that intention will be better effectuated.'

In another example, the Prevention of Crimes Act 1871 distinguished between (more serious) 'crimes' and (less serious) 'offences'. Under s 7, it was a crime in itself for a person, within seven days of conviction of an earlier crime, to be found in such circumstances as to satisfy the court that he was going to commit an 'offence'. It did not expressly refer to those going to commit 'crimes'. In *Strathern v Padden* 1926 JC 9, the High Court (ignoring any relevant presumptions) rejected the interpretation that s 7 did not apply to those going to commit 'crimes', because that would be, in Lord Justice-General Clyde's words, at 13, 'absurd and irrational'. In *K v Craig* 1997 SLT 748, a case involving the discharge of a mental patient into community care, the court held that the reclaimer's contention that the literal wording of the Act required that a person who did not need to be detained must be released would 'lead to an absurd result'.

Problems with the 'Rules'

The problem for the 'Mischief Rule' is that, given the exclusion of most documents save the legislative text itself, it is not clear how Parliament intended to overcome the mischief. That for the 'Literal Rule' is that it denies there is any problem, and it is no help where the difficulty is ambiguous legislation. That with the 'Golden Rule' is that reasonable people can disagree on whether an outcome is absurd or merely inconvenient.

The problem with all three 'Rules' is that they are clearly alternatives, but there is no clue as to which should be preferred and when, thus giving the impression that they may be fig-leaves to cover the embarrassment of conclusions arrived at by other means. In any case, commonly judges do not refer explicitly to any 'Rule' and, when they do, sometimes it is to explain that fortunately all three

---

46 A weaker version of the golden rule might indicate simply a presumption that, where legislation is ambiguous, a 'sensible' interpretation is to be preferred to any other.

'Rules' point in the same direction. Academic commentators tend to explain them with examples promiscuously chosen from different judges, in different periods, in different courts, in different jurisdictions. The rules may thus appear mere talismans, arcane precepts extrapolated from certain cases of unknown representativeness, designed to render decisions beyond criticism.

It is, however, too cynical to dismiss the 'Rules' completely. Probably they are insufficiently subtle explanations of the complicated processes which judges employ to resolve the tension between the principle that the legislator is entitled to have his will carried out; the fact that this will cannot be exactly expressed and is frequently ill-expressed; the judges' impatience with ill-expressed legislation; their knowledge that legislation provides a poor reservoir of principle compared with the common law; and perhaps their residual reluctance to relinquish the overwhelming primacy in expounding the law that they once enjoyed.

Some commentators have suggested that the Rules should be seen as examples of two alternative approaches. One, a 'literal approach', regards the language of the text as primary, and tries to apply the actual words of the legislation, come what may. The other, 'a purposive approach', assumes that the legislator had a purpose which has to be applied, and that the words of the legislation are one piece of evidence of that purpose.

An attempted synthesis of the techniques employed by United Kingdom courts in construing and interpreting legislation

One respected academic commentator argued[47] that there is a single 'basic rule' with five parts. This view was developed exclusively from English cases but, as noted, separate Scottish and English traditions have not existed in modern times, and the learned author of the entry on the interpretation of statute in the *Stair Encyclopaedia* seems to take a consonant view[48].

This basic rule is:

(a) the judge must give effect to the grammatical and ordinary or, where appropriate, technical meaning of words, given their context;
(b) if the result is absurd, or contrary to the purpose of the statute, he may apply a secondary meaning;

47 Cross *Statutory Interpretation* (3rd ed, 1995) p 49.
48 See also Wilson 'Trials and Try-Ons: Modes of Interpretation' 1992 Stat LR 1.

(c) if necessary, the judge can read in missing words implied by words which are present and, to a limited extent, add to, ignore or alter words to prevent unintelligibility, absurdity, complete unreasonability, unworkability, or irreconcilability with the rest of the statute;

(d) in applying the above rules, the judge may have resort to the various materials and presumptions available;

(e) the judge must interpret a statute so as to give effect to directly applicable Community law.

This view does provide a more satisfying rule of thumb synthesised from judicial practice. However, it is not the orthodoxy. Nor does it appear to take account of the fact that, under the influence of Community law, and specific requirements of the Human Rights Act 1998 and the Scotland Act 1998, courts are nowadays taking a more purposive view of the construction and interpretation of legislation.

CONSTRUCTION AND INTERPRETATION OF LEGISLATION BY UNITED KINGDOM COURTS UNDER THE INFLUENCE OF COMMUNITY LAW

As noted above, since the accession of the United Kingdom to the European Community, and the obligation to apply Community law (with or without direct effect), another mode of construction and interpretation of legislation has been introduced. United Kingdom courts have therefore been faced with a problem in the interpretation of legislation with a Community law element. Their solution to the problem has had consequential effects upon interpretation of other legislation.

It is useful to commence with consideration of the European Court of Justice, however.

Construction and interpretation by the European Court of Justice

The European Court of Justice applies legislation in a manner closer to that employed in civil law countries than to that in common law countries, although the differences can be exaggerated.

---

49 Millett 'Rules of Interpretation of EEC Legislation' [1987] Stat LR 163. See also Tanner, E 'Clear, Simple and Precise Legislative Drafting: how does a European Community Directive fare?' (2006) 27 Stat LR 150-175.

Community legislation has been suggested to have four character-istics relevant to application of legislation[49]. Firstly, the Treaties exist for certain purposes, which they set out. Secondly, Community legislation is a single, separate, legal system, so must be uniformly applied in all member states. Thirdly, Community legislation is written in several different languages, all equally authentic, so literal interpretations may have to be discounted. Fourthly, the form of Community legislation is subject to certain requirements, in partic-ular, Article 253 (ex Article 190) which says that all secondary legis-lation must have a preamble outlining its origins. Collectively, these indicate that Community legislation may not be regarded as 'in fixed verbal form'.

Materials considered by the European Court of Justice in construing and interpreting Community legislation

The European Court of Justice looks, of course, at the legislative text itself. However, Community legislation is not always drafted with as great a degree of detail as United Kingdom legislation usually is, and there are not usually interpretation sections. For example, Article 39(1) (ex Article 48(1)) declares that 'Free movement of workers shall be secured ... ', but does not define 'worker'. A definition had to be worked out through a series of decisions.

This apparent vagueness may be unavoidable with many equally authentic texts in different languages, which are often the result of polit-ical bargaining[50]. Clear differences of meaning can occur, and may indeed be used to throw light upon meaning, as for instance in Case 29/69 *Stauder v City of Ulm* [1969] ECR 419, where there was a differ-ence between Dutch and German texts on the one hand, and French and Italian on the other. It may also be desirable, in that the concepts described are ones of Community law, not of any national system.

The Court also looks at other materials as well. The lengthy recitals at the beginning of secondary legislation required by Article 253 (ex Article 190) contain a list of the Treaty provisions under which they are made, the legislative history of proposals and opin-ions ('having regard to ...'), and a statement of the reasons for the

---

50 In Case 136/79 *National Panasonic (UK) Ltd v Commission* [1980] ECR 2033, at 2066, the Advocate General observed that 'what members of the Council [of the Union] do when they adopt regulation is to agree upon a text. They do not necessarily all have the same views as to its meaning'.

provision itself ('whereas ...')[51]. This expressly directs the court's attention to other specific documents (which are sometimes referred to as *travaux préparatoires*).

Indeed, the Court tends to look at any piece of legislation as part of a general scheme containing a reservoir of principles expressed in various legislative texts, rather than as a single free-standing text in fixed verbal form. For example, in Case 283/81 *CILFIT Srl v Ministry of Health* [1982] ECR 3415, at 3430, the court said 'every provision of Community law must be placed in its context and interpreted in the light of the provisions of Community law as a whole, regard being had to the objectives thereof and to its state of evolution at the date on which the provision in question is to be applied'. The last words imply that interpretation can change over time.

Not all *travaux préparatoires* are examined, however. Those of the Treaties themselves, and the proceedings of the Commission and Council, are not published. Debates of the European Parliament, though published, are rarely referred to. The opinions of individual members of the Commission, Council or Parliament or of their staff are not admissible, according to the Advocate General's opinion in Case 136/79 *National Panasonic (UK) Ltd v Commission* [1980] ECR 2033, at 2066, even if they negotiated or prepared the text in question.

As well as *travaux préparatoires*, decisions of the Court and opinions of the Advocates General are often cited in argument, though rarely in judgments. The Court usually follows its previous decisions, though it does so tacitly, and a series of consistent decisions produces a lasting interpretation. It is not bound by any previous decision, however, and occasionally contradicts itself, without formally overruling the previous decision, as it did in Case 25/62 *Plaumann & Co v Commission* [1963] ECR 95.

---

51 For example, Council Directive 64/221 (25/2/64) OJ 1964 p 850 (S Edn 1963–4) p 117, which contains the 'public policy proviso' permitting member states to limit free movement, commences ' ... Having regard to the Treaty ... especially Article 56(2), ... the Council Regulation 15 of August 16, 1964 on initial measures, ... the Council Directive of August 16, 1964 on administrative procedures ... governing entry ... of workers, ... the General Programmes for Abolition of restrictions on freedom of establishment ... the Council Directive of February 25, 1964 on abolition of restrictions upon movement, ... the proposal from the Commission ... the opinion of the European Parliament ... the opinion of the Economic and Social Committee ... ', and continues 'Whereas co-ordination of provision ... which provides for special treatment of foreign nationals on grounds of public policy ... should ... deal with the conditions of entry ... of nationals of Member States moving within the Community ... to pursue activities as employed or self-employed person ... [etc]'.

The court has also drawn on the constitutions of Member States, and national courts' interpretations of them, and on international treaties, in particular the European Convention on Human Rights, to produce 'general principles of law common to all Member States' such as certainty and proportionality, which it has applied in some cases, for example Case 63/83 *R v Kirk* [1984] ECR 2689, and Case 222/84 *Johnston v Chief Constable of the RUC* [1986] 3 CMLR 240. While it would be unusual to regard this as a form of Community common law, generated by precedent, it is difficult to regard it otherwise than as a source of Community law additional to Community legislation (see further in Chapter 12)

Techniques employed by the European Court of Justice in construing and interpreting Community legislation

The European Court of Justice seeks to apply not the literal meaning of the text before it, but what it considers the purpose of the legislation, as extracted from the legislation in question, related legislation, *travaux préparatoires*, its own previous decisions, and elsewhere.

It has been suggested that three techniques, termed 'teleological'[52], 'schematic' and 'literal', are employed, although in practice they intertwine, and are complementary, not alternative[53], and application is in the light of the 'general principles of law common to Member States' it has extracted from the European Convention on Human Rights and elsewhere.

The 'teleological' technique means that the court considers the general objective of the authors of the treaties, as revealed by the materials examined. The 'schematic' places the provision in question within a general legislative scheme, discovered from the materials examined, for implementation of those objectives. The 'literal' considers the text itself, but in a broad and naturalistic way[54]. Because no single technique is sufficient, a clear and unambiguous textual meaning can be rejected if the other techniques suggest something different. In Case 9/70 *Grad* [1970] ECR 825 at 839, for example, the court said 'It is true that a literal interpretation of ...

---

52 ' ... relating to ends or final causes; dealing with design or purposes...' SOED (3rd ed, with corrections).

53 See Millett 'Rules of Interpretation of EEC Legislation' [1987] Stat LR 163, also Miers and Page *Legislation* (2nd ed, 1990) pp 184–190.

54 It is unfortunate that this is described as 'literal' for, in United Kingdom practice on statutory interpretation, 'literal' is used to describe the approach which applies the literal meaning of a text, even if absurd, and without reference to any other consideration.

Article 4 ... might lead to the view that this provision refers to [a certain date]. However, such an interpretation would not correspond to the aim of the directives in question ... '.

This purposive approach, probably inevitable in its setting, has been reinforced by the fact that the court has been very '*communautaire*'[55]. It has seen its role as pushing the Community forward when Member States have dragged their feet. This is evident in the court's inventiveness in generating the 'general principles of law common to all Member States', and in a number of decisions which have been frankly legislative, such as Case 41/74 *Van Duyn v Home Office* [1974] ECR 1337, in which the court decided Directives might be directly effective, despite the apparently contrary wording of Article 189 and intention of the Treaty itself.

At least on occasion, therefore, the Court fairly explicitly decides cases on the basis of what it thinks the law should be rather than what it is.

Construction and interpretation by United Kingdom courts where there is a Community law element

Community law may bear on any legal issue in one of two ways. Firstly, Community law may have 'direct effect' (for the meaning of which, see Chapter 6), in which case it should be applied irrespective of existing Scots law. Secondly, Community law not of 'direct effect' is to be implemented by United Kingdom legislation. In either case, the court is required expressly or impliedly by the European Communities Act 1972, to interpret the law in the same fashion as the European Court of Justice would. This would seem to involve consulting various other texts, in particular *travaux préparatoires*, and adopting a purposive approach.

There are a few examples in the area of Community law and related treaties of United Kingdom legislation expressly referring to a specific other text. The Civil Jurisdiction and Judgments Act 1982, s 3(3) specifically requires that it be interpreted in the manner laid down in the European Communities Act 1972, and that regard be had to reports by named individuals on a relevant Convention and the United Kingdom Accession Treaty. A marginal reference (not reproduced in *Current Law Statutes Annotated*) gives the citation of these reports in the *Official Journal*. The Consumer Protection Act 1987, s 1 specifically requires that Part I of the Act be interpreted in accordance with a Directive.

---

55 *Ie*, roughly, 'Community-minded'.

As the following sections show, United Kingdom courts are likely to seek to act more like the European Court of Justice, and less in their traditional fashion, when applying both Community law with 'direct effect' and United Kingdom legislation implementing Community law. This, as noted, is having an effect upon the interpretation of United Kingdom legislation with no Community element.

However, how far lower-level United Kingdom courts will be able to cope with the possibility of *travaux préparatoires* in order to find the inferred purpose of the legislation may be questioned. Also, the United Kingdom tradition of lengthy judgments, with a wide possibility of dissent, and lack of Advocates General, all within a common law tradition, mean that there is unlikely to be complete conformity of practice. There is also the question of what, or whose, purpose a purposive interpretation seeks.

Construction and interpretation by United Kingdom courts of Community law with 'direct effect'.

Community legislation with 'direct effect' is to be applied by United Kingdom courts. The great majority of cases where United Kingdom courts have applied Community legislation with 'direct effect' appear to have raised no problems. Many cases have in fact been heard by tribunals, such as those heard by Social Security Commissioners (previously National Insurance Commissioners) on the application of Regulation 1408/71 on social security rights of those exercising their right of free movement between member states. Any problem has been reduced by the ready propensity in England (though less in Scotland) to resort to Article 234 (ex Article 177) preliminary references, which removes from the United Kingdom court the need to interpret.

Section 3(1) of the European Communities Act 1972 requires United Kingdom courts, where they do not send such a question to the European Court of Justice, to interpret Community law in the same way as that Court would. There are, however, examples in early cases of United Kingdom courts applying severely traditional interpretive methods to Community law with 'direct effect', as, for example, the English Court of Appeal did in *R v Henn & Darby* [1978] 3 All ER 1190. Article 28 (ex Article 30) prohibits quantitative restrictions upon imports between Member States and 'all measures having equivalent effect'. The then Lord Chief Justice, Lord Widgery, argued that a total prohibition was not a quantitative restriction as no quantity was mentioned[56].

56 On appeal to the House of Lords ([1981] AC 850, there was an Article 177 (now Article 234) preliminary reference, and the European Court of Justice interpreted the provision differently.

Cases where there is United Kingdom legislation and 'directly effective' Community legislation on the same topic have caused difficulty. The courts often argued that they were applying the United Kingdom legislation but, striving to avoid a conflict, interpreted it to conform to Community legislation. The English Court of Appeal did this, for example, in *Macarthys v Smith* [1979] ICR 785, (but did also make an Article 234 (ex Article 177) reference). This approach did not necessarily involve the United Kingdom courts in formally adopting the European Court of Justice's approach, but did do violence to the traditional United Kingdom methods of interpretation, and implicitly required a more purposive approach.

However, since the *Factortame* cases[57] the House of Lords appears to have fully accepted the implications of 'direct effect' (subject always to the question of explicit repeal of the European Communities Act 1972), and it seems likely that United Kingdom courts will consciously adopt interpretive styles closer to those of the European Court of Justice in the interpretation of Community law with 'direct effect'.

Construction and interpretation by United Kingdom courts of United Kingdom legislation which implements Community legislation without 'direct effect'

Community law without 'direct effect' is not applied, as such, by United Kingdom courts, but where such law has been implemented by United Kingdom legislation, that must be applied[58]. This is also now very common, for example, in the application of the VAT legislation by the VAT Tribunal, and otherwise.

No preliminary reference under Article 234 (ex Article 177) is possible in such a case, nor does the European Communities Act 1972 expressly require such legislation to be interpreted as the European Court of Justice would. However, while United Kingdom courts might regard such legislation as to be interpreted in the light of 'the intention of Parliament', clearly it is intended by Community

---

57 Case C–213 *R v Secretary of State for Transport, ex parte Factortame* [1990] 2 AC 85; Case C–213/89 *R v Secretary of State for Transport, ex parte Factortame* [1991] 1 AC 603. See also above.
58 In *Mayne & Others v Minister of Agriculture, Fisheries and Food* [2001] EHLR 5, the Divisional Court of Queen's Bench held that where a Statutory Instrument, effecting a Directive, imposed a criminal penalty, that penalty could not be used where the Directive was later amended, unless the Statutory Instrument clearly took account of that possibility. See, however, also *Department for the Environment, Food & Rural Affairs v ASDA Stores Ltd* [2003] UKHL 71.

law that such national legislation be interpreted in the fashion of the European Court of Justice, and the European Court of Justice itself so held in Case 14/83 *Von Colson and Kamann v Land Nordrhein-Westfalen* [1984] ECR 1891.

Lord Diplock in *Garland v British Rail Engineering Ltd* [1983] AC 751, an English case on Great Britain legislation, at 770-771, asserted a similar view. However, for many years United Kingdom courts generally took the traditional line. In *Duke v Reliance Ltd* [1988] AC 359, the Appellate Committee of the House of Lords was again applying Great Britain legislation, the Sex Discrimination Act 1975, in an English appeal. Although this Act had been passed shortly before Directive 76/207 (the Equal Treatment Directive), it was known that the Act was intended to implement it, and that the Draft Directive was available to Parliament. Nevertheless, Lord Templeman said that to interpret the 1975 Act in the light of the 1976 directive would 'distort' its meaning, and the House decided to ignore the Directive.

Shortly afterwards, however, in *Pickstone v Freemans plc* [1989] AC 66, a closely parallel English case, the Appellate Committee of the House of Lords took a different view. The case concerned s 1(2)(c) of the Equal Pay Act 1970, which had been added to that Act by a Statutory Instrument (the Equal Pay (Amendment) Regulations 1983, SI 1983/1794) made under s 2(2) of the European Communities Act 1972 expressly to implement Directive 75/177 (the Equal Pay Directive), which the United Kingdom had been found (in Case 61/82 *Commission v United Kingdom* [1982] ECR 2601) to be breaching. The Appellate Committee of the House of Lords consulted parliamentary materials to discover if the legislation had been introduced by the government in order to implement Community law and Lord Templeman said, at 121, 'the explanations of Government and the criticisms voiced by Members of Parliament in the debates which led to approval of the draft Regulations provide some indications of the intention of Parliament'.

The change of heart was yet plainer in a Scottish appeal to the House of Lords, *Litster v Forth Dry Dock and Engineering Co Ltd* 1989 S.C. (H.L.) 96 (discussed above in relation to the use of *Hansard* in statutory interpretation). Directive 77/187 required rights of employees to compensation for unfair dismissal to be preserved when their employing company was taken over. This policy was implemented in the Transfer of Undertakings (Protection of Employment) Regulations 1981, SI 1981/1794 in respect of those employed immediately before the takeover. Certain employees were dismissed one hour before the transfer of ownership of the employing company, apparently with a view to evading the

Regulations. The House of Lords held that United Kingdom courts should give a purposive interpretation to the Regulations because they were designed to implement Community obligations, and that this might involve departing from the strict and literal meaning of the words of the legislation.

Arguably there was no ambiguity in the regulations under consideration. However, Lord Oliver, giving the leading judgment, referred to the recital ('whereas ... ') at the beginning of the directive (at 106), and briefly to the French version of it (at 112). He said, at 105:

'If the legislation can reasonably be construed as to conform with [Community obligations] – obligations which are to be ascertained not only from the wording of the relevant Directive, but also from the interpretation placed on it by the European Court of Justice ... – such a purposive construction will be applied even though, perhaps, it may involve some departure from the strict and literal application of the words the legislature has elected to use.'

This still leaves open to doubt the position where the United Kingdom legislation cannot 'reasonably be construed to conform with' them, although in *Litster* the Appellate Committee of the House of Lords was prepared to read in words which were not in the text. Lord Templeman went even further, saying that United Kingdom courts are under 'an obligation to follow the practice of the European Court of Justice by giving a purposive construction to Directives and Regulations [*scil.* statutory instruments] issued for the purpose of complying with Directives'. Both Scottish judges (Lord Keith and Lord Jauncey) concurred[59].

MODIFICATION OF CONSTRUCTION AND INTERPRETATION BY UNITED KINGDOM COURTS THROUGH THE EUROPEAN CONVENTION ON HUMAN RIGHTS AND THE HUMAN RIGHTS ACT 1998

Statutory interpretation and the European Convention on Human Rights

The Scottish courts initially took the view that, as the Convention was not part of the law of Scotland, but merely an international

59 Nevertheless, in *Stirling District Council v Allan* 1995 SLT 1255, at 1259 D–E, the Inner House observed, *obiter* that, 'The [terms of the very same Directive] cannot affect the construction of the [the very same statutory instrument] except to the extent that there may be an ambiguity which may be resolved by reference to the Directive'.

treaty, they were not entitled to have regard to it, even as an aid in interpreting United Kingdom legislation[60]. However, in *T, Petitioner* 1997 SLT 724, at 733, Lord President Hope stated that where there was an ambiguity in United Kingdom legislation it would be appropriate to look at the European Convention so as to produce an interpretation in conformity with it[61]. He pointed out that under European Community law, to which the Scots courts were bound to give effect, 'general principles of law' included fundamental human rights. In *McLeod, Petitioner* 1998 SLT 233, on the recovery by the defence of police statements in the hands of the Crown, the High Court thought it prudent, in view of the impending enactment of the Human Rights Act 1998, to have regard to the case of *Edwards v UK* (1992) 15 EHRR 417 and found the judgment of the European Court of Human Rights in line with Scottish authority. English courts, incidentally, were much more ready to use the ECHR to assist in interpreting the law[62]. The position has now in any case been overtaken by enactment of the Human Rights Act 1998.

Statutory interpretation of legislation under the Human Rights Act 1998, and the concept of 'incompatibility'

By s 2 of the Human Rights Act 1998, any court or tribunal in deciding a question in connection with a Convention right must take into account 'any judgment, decision, declaration or advisory opinion' of European Court of Human Rights, that is to say, its case law (sometimes referred to, in French, as its *'jurisprudence'*)[63]. Thus, a common interpretation among signatories of the ECHR is encouraged, and it is a noticeable feature of most cases involving human rights issues, at least on appeal, that they quote decisions of the European Court of Human Rights, courts in other European countries discussing the ECHR, and indeed courts of yet other countries concerning other human rights conventions[64].

60 See *Kaur v Lord Advocate* 1980 SC 319, per Lord Ross, approved in *Moore v Secretary of State for Scotland* 1985 SLT 38.
61 Following Appellate Committee of the House of Lords decisions such as *R v Secretary of State for the Home Department, ex parte Brind* [1991] AC 696. See also *Anderson v HM Advocate* 1996 JC 29.
62 As, for example, in *Ex parte Brind* (see previous note). It was this dissonance which encouraged Lord Hope to take a new line in *T, Petitioner.*
63 Also the opinions of the European Commission on Human Rights and the Committee of Ministers of the Council of Europe under the earlier ECHR procedure (for which, see Ch 3).
64 *Eg* in *Starrs v Ruxton* 2000 JC 208, 2000 SLT 42, over 30 cases were cited, half of them from the European Court of Human Rights, or, in a few cases, elsewhere, such as Canada.

Further, by s 3(1), all legislation from whatever source 'must so far as is possible be read and given effect to in a way that is compatible with Convention rights'. There is a question as to what this means. Clearly, it means that where legislation is of uncertain meaning, it is to be interpreted to achieve compatibility. However, it may also mean that where the legislation is of apparently clear meaning, a court may add qualifications or exceptions to achieve compatibility. The full power of s 3 was realised in the English case of *Ghaidan v Godin-Mendoza* [2004] UKHL 30, [2004] 2 A.C. 557. The Rent Act 1977, Sch 1, para 4(2) gave certain rights to a 'surviving spouse'. In *Ghaidan*, the question was whether this included as same sex partner (before the creation of 'civil partnerships'). A majority of the Appellate Committee of the House of Lords decided to so interpret even though doing so meant effectively disregarding the meaning of the words[65].

So far, there is a certain parallel with the treatment of Community law. But what is the result of incompatibility? Delegated legislation (including Acts of the Scottish Parliament) found to be incompatible is thereby invalid, so has no effect. However, Acts of the United Kingdom ('primary legislation') are not so affected and continue in force unabated because s 3(2) declares that the duty to interpret compatibly 'does not affect the validity, continuing operation or enforcement of any incompatible primary legislation'. This is a fundamental difference from the treatment of Community law.

By s 4, if the Court of Session or the High Court (sitting as an appeal court) considers that a provision of such 'primary' legislation is incompatible with a Convention right, it can make a 'declaration of incompatibility'. (It can also make such a declaration with regard to a provision of delegated legislation if there is primary legislation which prevents removal of the incompatibility). By s 5, the Crown is entitled to be given notice of any intended declaration, so that it (including a member of the Scottish Executive) can intervene and make submissions.

So what is the result of a declaration of incompatibility? Such a declaration does not affect the validity of the provision at all. Nor does it bind the parties to the proceedings. It simply puts the government on notice that there is a conflict, in the opinion of the court, between a statutory provision and a Convention right. However, it may also thereby create an expectation that

---

65 For criticism of this, see van Zyl Smit 'The New Purposive Interpretation of Statutes: HRA Section 3 after *Ghaidan v Godin-Mendoza*' (2007) 70 MLR 294–317, who describes the process as 'abstract purposiveness'.

the Westminster Parliament will take steps to remove the incompatibility, as happened when the relevant parts of the Anti-Terrorism, Crime and Security Act 2001 were repealed by the Prevention of Terrorism Act 2005, after the Appellate Committee of the House of Lords declared them incompatible in *A v Secretary of State for the Home Department* [2004] UKHL 56, [2005] 2 A.C. 68.

This could be done by normal legislative activity (as occurred in the Anti-Terrorism, Crime and Security Act 2001 case) but, by s 10 and Sch 2, the appropriate Minister of the Crown may, 'where there are compelling reasons', use a special short-cut delegated legislation procedure (subject to the approval of both Houses of Parliament), to make a 'remedial order' amending the provision. Such a remedial order can operate retrospectively, though not so as to make a person guilty of an offence. The difference from the treatment of Community law is underlined.

These provisions are clearly framed so as to stress that the 'parliamentary supremacy' of Westminster (in so far as it has survived the 'direct effect' of Community law) is preserved, both as regards United Kingdom legislation encapsulating the content of the ECHR and Scottish parliamentary legislation[66].

MODIFICATION OF CONSTRUCTION AND INTERPRETATION OF LEGISLATION BY UNITED KINGDOM COURTS THROUGH THE SCOTLAND ACT 1998

Not only does the Human Rights Act 1998 impose a special requirement upon courts interpreting its terms, so does the Scotland Act 1998. Section 101 applies to any provision of an Act of the Scottish Parliament which could be read in such a way as to be outside the Parliament's legislative competence, and to any legislation made under powers delegated to the Scottish Ministers by the Act itself which could be read in such a way as to be outside the powers so delegated[67].

---

66 See further Arden 'The Interpretation of UK Domestic legislation in the light of the European Convention on Human Rights *Jurisprudence*' (2004) 25 Stat LR 165-179.

67 This provision is somewhat obscurely drafted, but seems to mean that s 101 applies not only to legislation made by Scottish Ministers under powers delegated to Scottish Ministers by the Scottish Parliament, but also all those made by them under powers devolved to them by the United Kingdom Parliament (and whether within their 'devolved competence' or not: for which, see Ch 3).

In such a case, s 101 stipulates that it 'be read as narrowly as is required for it to be within competence, if such reading is possible'. If such reading is not possible, clearly the legislation is *ultra vires*, so void[68], however, the aim is equally clearly to preserve the provision from this fate if at all possible.

The drafting is different from that of s 3 of the similar Human Rights Act 1998, considered above. Firstly, it specifically requires an ambiguity before the rule is invoked, which might suggest that this rule is not intended to operate on clear provisions, unlike the provision under the Human Rights Act. Secondly, it specifically enjoins a narrow interpretation which might have the effect of preserving provisions more readily than the provision under the Human Rights Act. Thirdly, s 29(3) of the Act requires that, on a question of whether a provision concerns a reserved matter, this is to be determined by reference to its purpose. There is also the question, since the Scotland Act s 57(2) requires the Scottish Ministers not to act incompatibly with Convention rights, as to whether in interpreting any provision, both the Human Rights Act, s 3(1) and the Scotland Act, s 101 appear to apply, but produce different answers.

However, all conclusions remain speculative, and we must wait for the courts to decide these matters[69].

68 Indeed, if it is a provision of an Act of the Scottish Parliament, it is specifically stated in s 29 to be 'not law'.
69 In mid-2007, no court was reported as having had to consider the meaning of s 101.

12. Precedent – *Ratio Decidendi*, *Obiter Dicta* and *Stare Decisis*

This Chapter considers the nature of precedent[1] as a source of law, and its mechanics, including most particularly, the key concepts of '*ratio decidendi*', '*obiter dicta*' and '*stare decisis*', and how they are applied in practice in the courts (including the European Court of Justice and the European Court of Human Rights, and differences as between Scotland and England and Wales), and the concept of 'the common law'.

'Law Reports', an essential feature of any system of precedent, are dealt with in the next Chapter.

PRECEDENT AS A SOURCE OF LAW

Precedent is a formal source of law[2]. It emerges from the justifications that judges provide for their judgments. As such it has an existence entirely independent of legislation. It can be distinguished from the role of judges in the construction and interpretation of statute (dealt with in Chapter 11). There the judges are not making law on their own, but seeking to find out and apply the intention of the legislature.

Rules of law created by precedent are not explicitly created as Acts of Parliament are, and written down in a single authentic text. They are created by judges in the course of deciding cases, primarily to justify their decisions, and have to be extracted from their written judgments. These judges may be reasonably explicit in explaining the rule they are applying, but they may not. In either case, they are not laying down a rule 'in fixed verbal form' (for which, see Appendix 1),

---

1 'Precedent' is spelt thus, and has the meaning described below. 'Precedence' and 'president' are perfectly respectable words, but mean something different. The surprisingly common tendency to confuse them is to be resisted.
2 See Ch 4.

and their words are not designed precisely to encapsulate the rule, but principally to describe its operation upon the facts of the case being decided. Usually they are only extending an existing rule, but it is not always clear what the historical source (see Chapter 4) of the rule is. It may come from custom, the judge's sense of morality, or elsewhere.

Thus, reasonable people may disagree on what rule has actually been laid down, and how it might apply to another case. The rule may have to be inferred from the decision. Indeed, it may only be possible to make this inference with confidence when a series of decisions on the same topic has been given; in other words, only from a series of precedents. This means, incidentally, that what look like hard and fast rules when written in a textbook may be the author's view, with the benefit of hindsight, of what the court found the more persuasive of two alternative propositions of law, both plausible enough to cause the parties to spend time, money and energy in litigating.

As a formal source of law, precedent carries its own authority. Lawyers and other users of the law will respect it as genuine law. Courts in the same judicial hierarchy will hear arguments based on similar cases already decided, and are obliged, or at least encouraged, to follow the rule that seems to emerge from an earlier case with similar facts. Why should this be so? The main reason is that there is a deep-seated sense, which no doubt everyone possesses to some extent, that like cases should be treated alike. It is perhaps the most basic meaning of 'justice'. When two people do the same act, and one is treated as having thereby committed a crime, and the other were not, one would expect a resultant outcry, testifying that the popular sense of justice has been outraged. Following past rules of law helps to prevent such criticism. Moreover, if a rule contained in a past case has been written about in law books and has been quoted by the legal profession or other regular users of law and come to be relied upon, then there would be at least a sense of annoyance if the rule were not applied by a court. These considerations are strengthened where the courts are arranged in a clear hierarchy. Respect will be felt for the more senior judges. If, as appellate judges, they have the power to overrule the decision of a lower court, the judge in the lower court will only reject the rule on some strong ground, such as that new social conditions have rendered an ancient rule unworkable or out of date.

Not all systems of law accept precedent as a formal source (and acceptance or non-acceptance of precedent is an essential difference between common law and civil law countries, as discussed in Chapter 5 and below). Scots law did not accept it until the 19th century (again, as discussed in Chapter 5 and below)[3], but precedent is an important formal source of law today. Many fundamental areas of law were largely created by precedent (albeit sometimes building upon the work of the institutional writers), and may still be developed by this means. Contract, delict and criminal law, for example, are of this nature. Their basic rules are not to be found written in Acts of Parliament, but have to be extracted from precedents. Thus, the basic rules on what contract is, how a contract is made, what the effect on it is of error by one party as to any of the terms, and so on, are found in, or inferred from, precedents. Acts of Parliament, such as those relating to the sale of goods and consumer credit, may be regarded as making modifications to this basic structure[4].

A problem about precedent is that the law can only develop if there are new precedents, and that depends upon litigants bringing cases to court in the areas needing development[5]. As Scotland has a population about one-tenth that of England and Wales, the potential for elaborating the law by means of judicial decisions is that much less. By the same token, the development of the law through cases requires that there be people with the resources and the determination to have their disputes settled by courts.

Nobile officium and declaratory power

Two exceptional exercises of legislative power by the courts require special mention, that is, the *nobile officium* and the declaratory power. The *nobile officium* is an exceptional 'equitable' power exercised by the Court of Session and High Court of Justiciary to provide a remedy where none exists, but the court feels it should. In the Court of Session, the power goes back to at least the time of Stair, at the end of the 17th century. He mentions in his *Institutions*, at IV, 3, 2, seven miscellaneous exercises of it. That varied character has continued to the present day. A modern, much cited, description of that is by Lord President Emslie: 'It may be exercised in highly special or unforeseen circumstances to prevent injustice or oppression. It cannot however be invoked in such a way as to defeat a

---

3 Indeed, the assertion that Scots law relies on principle rather than precedent implies a continuing doubt as to the role of precedent.

4 'The common law is a canvas on which a picture is being painted. The cloth may be obscured by layers of pigment, but it is ever apt to show through and without it the whole image crumbles', McBryde *The Law of Contract in Scotland* (2nd ed, 2001) para 1–15.

5 On the social limitations on Scottish case law, see Willock 'Making Law and Keeping to the Law' 1982 JR 237 at 250.

statutory intention, express or implied, or to extend the scope of an Act of Parliament'[6]. Petitions are heard by three judges of the Inner House[7].

On the criminal side the *nobile officium* (not always so described) is referred to by Alison in his *Practice* of 1833 as used 'in circumstances unforeseen for which the law makes no provision'. The Crown may seek its exercise as well as an accused[8]. Modern criminal instances of this power do tend to emphasise the avoidance of injustice or oppression as a justification for its use[9]. Examples of the absence of a remedy as such injustice or oppression include *Wylie v HM Advocate*, 1996 SLT 149, where the then lack of provisions on sentencing for contempt of court was held to justify invoking the *nobile officium*[10].

The declaratory power is an exceptional power held by the High Court of Justiciary to declare behaviour which it considers morally wrong to be a criminal offence, even though it was not, or not unequivocally, regarded as criminal before. This could be a wide and unpredictable power, and was so used in the formative years of Scots criminal law[11]. It is now very rarely invoked, if indeed it still exists. It is only invoked in cases closely analogous to existing crimes, and is difficult to distinguish from the application of existing vague offences to new circumstances, as for example in *Khaliq v HM*

---

6 *Humphries, Petr* 1982 SLT 481, applied in *L v Kennedy* 1993 SCLR 693, *Sloan, Petr* 1991 SLT 527 and *H, Petrs* 1997 SLT 3 (all Children's Hearings cases). Other modern examples include *Royal Bank of Scotland v Gillies* 1987 SLT 54 (reduction of decree obtained by petitioners).

7 *Institute of Chartered Accountants in Scotland, Petr* 2002 SLT 921.

8 Eg *Bryceland, Petr* 2003 SLT 54.

9 See eg *Perrie, Petr* 1992 SLT 655; *Windsor, Petr* 1994 SCCR 59; *Beglan, Petr* 2002 SLT 1175.

10 For another absence of statutory provision case, see *Wan Ping Nam v German Federal Republic Minister of Justice* 1972 JC 43, 1972 SLT 220. The Extradition Act 1870 allowed *habeas corpus* and no other remedy for review of a decision to extradite someone. A person arrested in Scotland and whose extradition to Germany was requested sought *habeas corpus* from the High Court. This was refused on the ground that it was a remedy unknown in Scotland. Nevertheless, looking at the intention of the Act, the court exercised the *nobile officium* and was prepared in principle to liberate the person if he could show good cause.

11 As such it was justified by Hume, the institutional writer on criminal law. In *Greenhuff* (1838) 2 Swin 236 its advantages and disadvantages were set out by the majority and the one dissenting judge Lord Cockburn. Its existence bears out the criticism of Bentham, the great political and legal philosopher of two centuries ago, that the common law operates as you train a dog. You wait till it does what you dislike, then you punish it. Any broad exercise of the declaratory power is liable to contravene Art 7 of the European Convention on Human Rights which forbids retrospectivity in crimes and punishments.

Advocate 1984 JC 23 which rendered criminal the selling of glue-sniffing kits as the wilful supply of potentially noxious substances[12].

Precedent and the common law

Precedent and common law are intertwined. Originally, at least in England[13], 'common law' meant custom which was common to the whole country, rather than purely local. Now, however, custom having crystallised into law through the decisions of judges, the basic meaning has come to be law which has been made by precedent, and this English law-based meaning has largely displaced any others. In a slightly extended form, the phrase refers to the minor sources as well, in other words, to all law that is not legislation. In both these meanings common law is contrasted with statute law.

Systems of law which accept precedent as a formal source are known as 'common law systems'. They are widespread because English law, the original common law system, was exported to most British colonies (not least those which later formed the United States of America). Thus, there is said to be a family of common law systems. It is contrasted with the family of civil law systems[14], that is,

---

12 See also *Ulhaq v HM Advocate* 1991 SLT 614. The offence does not seem to cover the supply of other noxious substances such as tobacco, but it is in the nature of the common law and the use of the declaratory power that it is not possible precisely to define what is prohibited. Note also the observation of Lord Clyde in *McLaughlin v Boyd* 1935 JC 19: 'It would be a mistake to imagine that the criminal law of Scotland countenances any precise and exact categorisation of the forms of conduct which amount to crime. It has been pointed out many times that such is not the nature or quality of the criminal law of Scotland'.

13 Originally in Scotland, the term 'common law' was used as a translation of the Latin '*ius commune*' and referred to canon law, that is, the law of the Christian church. In this sense there was a 'common law of Europe', as canon law was applied by courts throughout Christendom as a subsidiary source to 'municipal law', that is, national law. It was supported by Roman law, and the plural of '*ius commune*', that is, '*jura communia*', translated into Scots as 'the commoune lawis of the realme', was often used here and (translated into other languages) elsewhere, to describe canon law plus Roman law: see Dolezalek 'The Court of Session as a *Ius Commune* Court – witnessed by "Sinclair's Practicks", 1540–1549' in McQueen (ed) *Miscellany IV* (Stair Society, 2002). Modern Continental European lawyers sometimes use the phrase '*ius commune*' to refer to common principles of European civil law systems, seen as increasingly expressed through Community law.

14 It has been argued that this is a misleading term, used by English lawyers, and that the '*ius commune*' is better: see previous note.

those which claim Roman law as their intellectual progenitor and which, generally speaking, do not recognise precedent as a formal source of law. This family includes most European states, and countries formerly their colonies (such as the whole of South America).

Scots law is said to be one of a few 'mixed' or 'hybrid' systems, because it claims some Roman ancestry (like the civil law systems), but now uses precedent (like the common law systems). Other such systems are the state of Louisiana, the province of Quebec, South Africa and Sri Lanka.

European Community law, because it has been created largely in a milieu of civil law countries, operates essentially as a civil law system, with limited reliance upon precedent. 'Human rights law', as expressed in decisions of the European Court of Human Rights, also bears evidence of civil law reasoning.

There are other uses of the term 'common law'[15]. For example, in English law, it has a technical meaning more restricted than the basic meaning. For centuries in England there were two parallel sets of courts. The basic common law courts generated common law in this most restricted sense. The supplementary 'courts of Chancery' generated 'equity'. The two court systems were amalgamated in the 1870s, and English courts are now both common law and equity courts, but common law and equity are still said to be separate sets of rules or principles. Also, histories and theories of the common law (in any of its senses) are usually histories and theories of English law, and thus 'the common law' is sometimes taken to mean simply 'English law'.

Precedent and Scots law

Before the 19th century, Scottish courts were applying customary law (native and feudal), fortified by concepts of canon law and Roman law (the 'common law' in the original Scots sense[16]), rein-

---

15 Some phrases using the term 'common law' which have entered the popular language are misleading. 'Common law wife', referring to an unmarried partner, has no more meaning legal meaning than does 'bidie-in' or 'kippie-uppie'. Civil law also has several meanings, including 'non-criminal law' and Roman law. These meanings are also etymologically linked.

16 See previous notes. McQueen 'Two Visitors in the Session, 1629 and 1639' in McQueen (ed) *Miscellany IV* (Stair Society, 2002) recounts that an English visitor (Sir C Lowther) remarked that '[m]uch of their law is Acts of Parliament and Regiam Majestatem', presumably in contrast to the common law (English style) with which he was familiar in English courts. ('Regiam Majestatem' is a medieval collection of laws: see Ch 1).

forced and modified by statute, and consolidated by legal writers (Scottish, French, German and other), including, as time went on, those later regarded as 'institutional'[17].

Precedents were recorded in the *Practicks* which judges created for their own use from the earliest days of the Court of Session, and which were later published by them and others in collections. Such precedents were cited in court and Stair cited many in his *Institutions*. However, they were not the formal source of the law, but merely evidence of what it was. Indeed, the way the *Practicks* and early series of law reports were edited meant that nothing like the modern system of precedent could operate. For example, cases were commonly recorded without giving the judges' reasoning[18]. It can be very unclear, therefore, what rule or principle the judges considered they were applying.

In the 19th century reliance on institutional works did not wane, but reliance on precedent increased, and it became recognised as another, alternative, formal source of law. This reflected a number of factors, including change in the perception of the nature of law[19],

17 Lord Cockburn, in his *Memorials of His Times* (1856, reprinted 1971), critically examining the intellectual rigour of the preceding generation, recorded Lord Hermand, a judge appointed in 1799, as 'very apt to say "My Laards, I feel my law – here my Laards" striking his heart'. However, although well disposed towards Hermand on a personal level, Cockburn was a Whig, strongly opposed to the Tory dominance of Scotland of the time, manifested in the law by Hermand and others. For the 'Institutional Writers', see Ch 4.

18 Lord Cockburn (above at pp 164–165) also related of early law reporting that 'It had never [before the 19th century] been the practice to give any full and exact account of what passed on the Bench, but only results ... [T]heir Lordships were very jealous of this pretension [to full law reporting]. They considered it a contempt ... aggravated by the accuracy of the report. Mr Robert Bell ... was the first who advertised an independence in this matter ... This design was no sooner disclosed than he met with many threatening hints, and as much obstruction as could be given in open court. The hated but excellent volume at last appeared [*Bell's Cases*, in 1790], and ... he was actually called into the robing room, and admonished to beware. [Lord] Eskgrove's objection was "the fellow taks down ma' very words"'.

19 Legislation in its modern guise emerged at this time, and the creation of a distinct class of Institutional Writers, with Stair pre-eminent, emerged: see *The Laws of Scotland: Stair Memorial Encyclopaedia* vol 22, para 256 and Blackie 'Stair's Later Reputation as a Jurist' in *Stair Tercentenary Studies* (ed Walker) (Stair Society, vol 33, 1981). Law was seen less as immemorial custom, and more as the expression of Sovereign will. A parallel change in the status of precedent was also occurring in England: see *The Laws of Scotland: Stair Memorial Encyclopaedia* vol 22, para 252.

and the reorganisation of the Court of Session[20]. It has also been orthodox to blame the availability of appeal to the House of Lords (then very common) for various ills, including the descent from grace involved in abandoning Roman law and adopting precedent, although recent research has suggested otherwise[21]. The growth of law reporting in the modern form seems more likely to be a result than a cause of the growth of precedent, but the existence of full clear reports can only have encouraged recourse to precedent[22]. The Faculty of Advocates attempted, unsuccessfully, to introduce better reports than the *Practicks* from the early 18th century, but modern law reporting started with *Shaw's Reports* in 1821, which commenced the series now appearing as *Session Cases*. In the earlier reports, precedents and references to the Institutional Writers appear in the reported arguments of counsel rather than in the judgments themselves, but in the course of the 19th century fully reasoned judgments became reported. This allowed the operation of precedent in the contemporary sense, although only in the second half of the 20th century did explicit reliance upon precedent become a major feature, and Scots law clearly, in part at least, a common law system[23].

How do rules emerge from precedents? – precedent and adjudication

Precedents are cases which are assumed to be capable of laying down rules or principles, or extending existing ones. Although this assumption is central to the operation of a common law or mixed

20 The Court of Session sat as the unwieldy 'Haill Fifteen', with essentially written procedures from its foundation in 1532 to the Court of Session Acts of 1808, 1810, 1825 and 1830. (Lord Cockburn in his *Journal* vol I (1874) pp 221–222 referred to it as 'a mob of fifteen judges, meeting without previous consultation, and each impatient for independent eminence'. As indicated above, Cockburn's remarks cannot be taken as unbiased. However, there is other evidence. The Court of Session Acts gave it its present structure and the basis of its present procedure. These reforms made possible inconsistent judgments by different judges, Divisions or Houses created a hierarchy and thus posed questions of relative authority.

21 *The Laws of Scotland: Stair Memorial Encyclopaedia* vol 22, para 255.

22 Lord Cockburn in his *Memorials of His Times* (1856, reprinted 1971) attributed the rise in accurate reporting to the fact that 'the public, or at least the independent proportion of the legal profession, had begun to require something more [than the reporting of merely the results of cases]'.

23 Doubt as to the operation within Scotland has remained, at least until recently: see *eg* Maher 'Sir Thomas Smith, *stare decisis* and sheriffs' 2004 SLT 85-89.

legal system, there is not complete agreement about how the process occurs. Indeed, it is the central mystery of such a system, both in the sense of an obscure process and in the older sense of a jealously guarded trade skill.

The orthodoxy is as follows. There are many ways of resolving disputes. Violence is common in international affairs, spinning a coin in some other situations. What distinguishes court-based dispute resolution, and thus the operation of precedent, is adjudication. Precedents are created by judges in courts deciding disputes brought before them as cases, by means of adjudication.

Adjudication can be described as dispute resolution where a third party imposes a solution upon the disputants, whether they agree to his decision or not. This solution is not a compromise (so there are winners and losers), and is justified by reference to a rule of general application (rather than personal preference[24] or some random method). The decision must therefore fit into the matrix of previous similar cases. By the same token it is capable of use as a precedent in later cases of similar type. The decisions therefore form a more or less coherent system, and are not 'a wilderness of single instances'[25]. Adjudication also implies that the decision is taken by a judge, that is, someone professionally employed by the state to resolve disputes in this way[26].

Other methods of non-violent (and non-random) dispute resolution exist, such as conciliation, mediation and arbitration and other forms of 'alternative dispute resolution'. Some of them may be employed by courts from time to time. But they do not have all the features of adjudication, so do not generate precedents.

Because every case adjudicated is decided according to a rule or principle, the decision must reflect that rule or principle, which must therefore be discoverable from the judgment itself. This rule or principle is referred to as the *ratio decidendi*[27] (often abbreviated simply to

---

24 'Why does the judge not make his reason explicit by granting Mrs McTavish her divorce just because she has a ravishingly pert retroussé nose? Because such are not accepted as good reasons within the system for ... granting divorces', MacCormick *Legal Reasoning and Legal Theory* (1978) p 15. Lord Atkin is believed to have consulted his young children before deciding *Donoghue v Stevenson* 1932 SC(HL) 31, however.

25 'Mastering the lawless science of law/ That codeless myriad of precedent/ That wilderness of single instances/ Through which a few by wit or fortune led/ May beat a path to wealth and fame', Tennyson *Aylmer's Field* 1, 436.

26 An interesting and accessible account of the theory of precedent by a leading contemporary commentator is MacCormick *Legal Reasoning and Legal Theory* (1978). See also his later works.

27 The first word is pronounced 'ray-she-oh' or 'rah-tea-oh', the second 'dess-ee-dend-aye' or 'dess-ee-dend-ee'.

'*ratio*'). *Ratios*[28], being law, bind later judges under certain circumstances, that is, under these circumstances, later judges must apply them whether they wish to or not. In other circumstances, *ratios* are simply more or less persuasive, that is, may or may not be applied, at the discretion of the later judges, and depending upon whether they are persuaded by them. The principle that *ratios* may bind is called '*stare decisis*'[29].

This orthodoxy is made more comprehensible by viewing the central mystery in the light of the ideas of rules not 'in fixed verbal form', and of analysis of rules in terms of *protasis* and *apodosis*[30].

RATIO DECIDENDI AND *OBITER DICTA*

Commentators have often observed that defining the idea of the *ratio*, and identifying one in an actual case, are separate problems.

Defining '*ratio decidendi*'

The basic idea

A direct translation of '*ratio decidendi*' ('the reason for deciding') is unanimously agreed to be misleading, but there is no unanimity on a better one[31]. This is partly because commentators use the phrase to refer to slightly different things, partly because of lack of complete agreement on what the phenomenon actually is[32]. Also, usage is said to differ as between Scotland and England. This is important as most of the academic discussion has centred on English law[33], but it is noticeable that most commentators describe the concept and its operation using Scottish and English cases indifferently.

---

28 The plural in Latin would be *rationes decidendi* but this is rarely used.
29 Usually pronounced 'star-ray dee-sigh-sis'.
30 For which, see Appendix 1.
31 Walker *The Scottish Legal System* (8th ed, 2001) p 462 refers to seven possible translations.
32 Some argue that the phrase refers to the reasons advanced by the judge in the case; others that it is what later judges make of those reasons; yet others, that it is a combination of both: see, for example, *The Laws of Scotland: Stair Memorial Encyclopaedia* vol 22, para 335; MacCormick, *Legal Reasoning and Legal Theory* (1978) pp 86 and 215; Willock 'Judges at Work: Making Law and Keeping to the Law' 1982 JR 237, 246.
33 However, perhaps the leading commentator is MacCormick (see previous note), whose Scots credentials are impeccable.

For present purposes an adequate interpretation is 'the rule or principle of law for which a competent observer considers the case to be authority'[34]. There are, however, four riders to be added.

Four riders

Firstly, no *ratio* stands alone. It can only make sense within the matrix of other relevant precedents (that is, within the matrix of the common law). It is the reasoning adopted by a judge to decide the specific issue before him and justify his decision, and the judge must presume, and rely on, the surrounding law which it is not open to him to change. However, some cases which raise very wide issues go before appeal courts, giving them the opportunity to pronounce a rule or principle over a broad area.

Secondly, because of the way *ratios* are constructed, competent observers may genuinely differ as to what rule or principle is laid down. Common law rules are not 'in fixed verbal form', so that, although an authentic version of the judges' words is available, there is no single authentic version of the actual rule or principle. Moreover, judges may not even be very explicit as to what rule or principle they consider they are laying down. Thus, there may be 'wide' (more inclusive) and 'narrow' (less inclusive) versions of any *ratio*.

Thirdly, later judges and other commentators must interpret the apparent *ratio* of a case. This flows inevitably from the first and second riders, and from the fact that new cases appear all the time. It is an important truth that a precedent is what later judges say it is, and they decide upon the width of the *ratio*. All the judge actually laying down the precedent can do is to restrict the range of possibilities.

Fourthly, any *ratio* may nevertheless be regarded as wrong by other judges and commentators. A *ratio* can only be understood in the light of other *ratios*, and the law generally, and a judge is constrained to decide consistently with them. If he fails to do so, his decision does not properly fit into the matrix of the common law, by which token it is wrong. Whether the later judges can put the error right,

---

34 MacCormick *Legal Reasoning and Legal Theory* (1978), p 215, suggests that it is 'the ruling expressly or impliedly given by a judge which is sufficient to settle a point of law put in issue by the parties' arguments in a case, being a point on which a ruling was necessary to his justification (or one of his alternative justifications) of the decision in the case'.

however, depends upon whether it is binding upon them or not. Even if they cannot, they may still be able to avoid its effects by 'restrictive distinguishing' and other devices. These questions are dealt with below, in relation to *stare decisis*.

This interpretation and its riders are best understood by recalling the nature of the process of adjudication. A judge is required to decide the case before him according to some rule or principle (rather than by compromise, personal preference, or some random method). The judge may find the existing rules and principles, discoverable from the *ratios* of existing precedents, are clear enough to indicate the decision. In such a case, the judge's *ratio* in the new case adds nothing but another illustration to the existing law. However, the rules and principles may not be so clear, in which case the judge has the opportunity and duty to extend or restrict existing rules and principles, or lay down some new ones to decide the case, and the *ratio* of the new case will have some novelty. It thus develops the law. In laying down a new rule or principle, however, the judge is severely constrained by the need to fit into the matrix of existing common law, and is aware that the *ratio* may be cited in future as a precedent for other cases. Thus, the common law grows by the accretion of analogous cases.

Identifying a *ratio decidendi*

As noted, while it is the judge or judges in the precedent examined who uttered the words from which a *ratio* is to be extracted, it is later judges who, with the assistance of counsel representing the parties, have to identify it in later cases.

It would be helpful for such identification if judges explicitly identified the relevant rule or principle which they consider they are applying. Sometimes they do. Indeed, in recent years, there has been a general adoption of a common structure to opinions, with informal sections, identified by shoulder headings, and usually variations upon 'Introduction', 'Submissions of parties', 'Relevant legislation', 'Discussion' and 'Conclusion', 'Result' or 'Disposition'. This makes clear formulation of a *ratio* more likely.

Nevertheless, judges often do not explicitly identify the rule or principle, and even where they appear to do so, the statement must be treated with care, for reasons implicit in the definition of *ratio decidendi* and the riders to it.

Thus, while it is the words of judges which must be considered, it is a mistake to 'dig for buried treasure' by looking for a useful quotation from a judge which, wrenched from its context, provides a memorable and comprehensible, but possibly completely inaccurate, statement of the relevant principle[35].

These problems are best approached by considering four things: what the relevant facts are; what their appropriate level of generality is; how multiple *ratios* are to be dealt with; and wide and narrow *ratios* and the development of principles.

What are the relevant facts?

A useful way forward to confirm an apparently clear statement of rule or principle, or to infer a ratio where there is no clear statement, is to employ analysis in terms of *protasis* and *apodosis*[36] (although this approach is unorthodox). If a legal rule comprises a series of facts which (or some of which) must be fulfilled in order for the legal result to occur, then a *ratio* can be sought by identifying those facts the judges stated or implied to be 'relevant' or 'material' (that is, appeared sufficient for him to come to the conclusion he did), and excluding those which he stated or implied were not 'relevant' or 'material'. This approach has been elaborated largely in relation to English law and United States law[37], but is appropriate, if care be taken, in relation to Scots law[38].

35 The point is made in *Elabas v Secretary of State for the Home Department* 2004 SLT 1082 (Note), where, at [29], Lord Reed in the Outer House gave a lengthy disquisition on the citing of authority, including that proper citing of authority 'involves more than reading a *dictum* without explanation of its context (let alone reading a *dictum* without explaining that it comes from a minority or dissenting opinon, if that be the case'. See also Shields 'Elabas v Secretary of State for the Home Department' 2004 SLT 210. Indeed, searching for buried treasure is often the cause of embarrassing errors by students who fail to detect the difference in a law report between the arguments of counsel, often repeated by the judge, but not in reported speech (*eg* repeated as 'the guiding principle here is ...', instead of 'counsel for the pursuer argued that the guiding principle here is ...') and the judge's own opinion, and thus pull a misleading rabbit out of the misunderstood hat. The mistake is the more embarrassing if the judge goes on to later characterise the pursuer's argument as completely misguided and unsupported by authority.
36 See Appendix 1.
37 See, for example, Goodhart's 'The *Ratio Decidendi* of a Case' in *Essays in Jurisprudence and Common Law* (1931), and Llewellyn's very readable *The Bramble Bush* (1951), as well as Twining and Miers *How To Do Things With Rules* (4th ed, 1999).
38 *The Laws of Scotland: Stair Memorial Encyclopaedia* vol 22, para 344 expresses doubt but, subject to caveats, MacCormick in *Legal Reasoning and Legal Theory* (1978) appears to approve Goodhart's approach. Perhaps in modern conditions the assertion that Scots law relies on principle rather than precedent, while English law does the reverse, means that Scots lawyers are prepared to generalise further.

Thus, for example, assuming that a contract is constituted by an offer and its acceptance, to discover what can amount to an offer and what to an acceptance, sufficient to constitute a contract, it is useful to consider what actual communications were considered relevant or material by the judges in the relevant precedents, and what they considered not. (Have they considered an advertisement in a newspaper an offer, or the placing of priced goods in a shop window? Have they considered an acceptance can be constituted by actions without words, or leaving a voicemail message on a mobile phone?). In other words, what facts were adequate to allow the judges to decide that they constituted offer and acceptance?

What is the appropriate level of generality?

Identifying the right facts still leaves the problem of determining the right level of generality of the facts. If a ginger beer manufacturer is made liable for harm done to the ultimate consumer by noxious substances concealed, through negligence, in ginger beer, is this a liability upon ginger beer manufacturers only, upon manufacturers of any drink, manufacturers of any food or drink, or of anybody distributing anything which might contain hidden noxious substances?[39] The judge who laid down the precedent will have limited the range of possibilities, but it is the later judges who determine the actual level. The rule of thumb is to simply ask what, in the light of the judges' actual words, and all other precedents, is plausible.

How are multiple ratios to be dealt with?

Most discussion of the nature of the *ratio decidendi* assumes that there is one judge in the court. However, in appellate courts there will normally be more than one. If this is so, they may disagree on the decision (that is, essentially, on who wins), or agree on the decision, but disagree on the reasoning justifying that decision[40]. Increasingly, in Scottish appellate courts, both civil and criminal (assuming there are no dissenting judges) a single judgment is issued, usually written by the senior judge, likely to produce a single *ratio*. However, this is not always so, and it is not true of the Appellate Committee of the

---

39 This example relates, of course, to the famous *Donoghue v Stevenson* 1932 SC(HL) 31, discussed at greater length below
40 The dissenting opinion is an unavoidable, and important feature of common law systems: see Kirby 'Judicial Dissent - common law and civil law traditions' (2007) 123 LQR 379-440.

House of Lords[41], where there may be several judgments, almost inevitably differing more or less on what the *ratio* is. So, both in relation to some contemporary judgments, and most older ones, the problem of multiple *ratios* exists. The significance of this is great as appellate decisions are always more important than cases at first instance, because they come from higher in the hierarchy and therefore send out stronger signals as to what the law is. There are four possibilities to consider.

Disagreement on the decision – majority decisions. If the judges do not all agree on the decision, then the majority view prevails, although the problems of multiple *ratios* may arise within the majority. The views of the dissenting minority, while they can bind no-one, may throw light on those of the majority.

Agreement on the decision where there is an opinion of the court. Where all judges in a court agree on the decision, they can be assumed to agree on the reasoning producing that outcome. Then no problem arises. But sometimes, and quite commonly in the House of Lords, one full judgment will be given, but the other judges will add a few additional comments or ones which rephrase part of what the leading judge has said[42]. Then it is usually the leading judgment alone which is taken to contain the *ratio*.

41 A good example of the problem is *Macfarlane v Tayside Health Board* 2000 SC(HL) 1. A couple with four children, a number they considered sufficient, relied on a negligently inaccurate report on the success of a vasectomy, and produced a fifth. The mother sued for damages for pain and suffering from pregnancy and birth, consequential expenditure, and loss of earnings. The House of Lords held that the claim for pain and suffering was relevant (unanimously); the claim for expenditure consequential upon the pregnancy and birth was relevant (Lords Clyde and Millett dissenting) but that for expenditure consequential upon bringing up the child was not (unanimously); and the claim for loss of earnings consequential upon the pregnancy and birth were relevant (Lords Clyde and Millett again dissenting) but that loss of earnings consequential upon bringing up the child was not (unanimously). In respect of the consequential expenditure claim unanimously held irrelevant, in brief, Lords Slynn and Hope so concluded because they saw it as 'pure economic loss'; Lord Steyn relied on 'principles of distributive justice'; Lord Clyde on 'disproportionality'; and Lord Millett on the benefits of having a child invariably outweighing any detriments. Even on the merely majority issues, there was much variation as between the reasoning of the majority. Two other, more recent, complicated examples are the separate, but linked *A & Ors v Secretary of State* [2005] UKHL 71, [2006] 2 A.C. 221 and *A & Anr v Secretary of State* [2004] UKHL 56, [2005] 2 A.C. 68.

42 Lord Carmont (appointed to the Court of Session in 1934, entered the Inner House in 1937, and died in office in 1965), was said to concur so frequently that his motto was 'I came, I saw, I concurred'.

Agreement on the decision where there are separate judgments. In a significant proportion of House of Lords cases and older Inner House cases, the judges agree on the outcome, but deliver separate judgments. In such cases their reasoning may differ somewhat, or it may be difficult to tell whether they agree completely or not[43], in which case, there may be multiple *ratios*. The question is then posed as to what is the *ratio* of the case as a whole.

It is surprisingly unclear what is supposed to happen in such an eventuality, for there are few precedents explicitly on the question. The vagueness of rules not derived from statute, and the discretion of later judges to determine the *ratio* of precedents sometimes allows the issue to be avoided[44]. Three different situations must be distinguished:

(a) *Leading judgment.* If there is a leading judgment, that is, one more fully argued than the rest, and to which the other judgments merely add variations or emphases, the *ratio* extracted from it is likely to be treated as the *ratio* of the case, especially if that judge is more senior or more respected. The variations to it may be treated as persuasive rather than binding, or simply ignored.

(b) *No leading judgment but consistent reasoning.* If there is no leading judgment, and all judgments are broadly consistent, though not identical, then the *ratio* of the case is likely, according to some Scottish commentators[45], to be taken to be the highest common factor among the judges sitting and other parts of the judgments are ignored[46]. According to a commentator on English law[47], in such circumstances, the *ratio* of the case might be taken to be the sum of

---

43 In *Manuel v A-G* [1982] 3 All ER 786, an English case before the Chancery Division, Sir Robert Megarry VC (the President of the court), at 798, observed 'During the argument it was not surprisingly suggested to me on this point: (a) there was a majority for Lord Denning's view and that Kerr LJ was in a minority and (b) that there was a majority for the view of Kerr LJ and Lord Denning was in the minority. A third contention was that May LJ was agreeing with Lord Denning in his general view, but with Kerr LJ in his particular application. A variant is that May LJ ... '.

44 Paterson, Bates and Poustie *The Legal System of Scotland: Cases and Materials* (4th ed, 1999) at p 441 remark ' ... juggling with multiple ratios is one more technique which the wise judge acquires'.

45 *Ibid* p 440, and *The Laws of Scotland: Stair Memorial Encyclopaedia* vol 22, para 342. No authority is cited.

46 *Ie*, if Judge 1 finds facts A, B & C material, Judge 2 finds facts A, B & D material, and Judge 3 finds facts A, B & E material, the *ratio* is A+B.

47 Goodhart in 'Determining the *Ratio Decidendi* of a Case' in *Essays in Jurisprudence and the Common Law* (1931). Examples are given, but no authority cited.

all *ratios* of the judges sitting[48]. A third possible view is that the *ratio* is a version of the judgment which fits most neatly into the existing law[49]. In any case, clearly a wide discretion is left to judges in later cases.

(c) *No leading judgment and inconsistent reasoning.* If there is no leading judgment, nor any high degree of overlap in the reasoning of the judges, both the common factor and sum of the *ratios* approaches produce ridiculous results, and it is not possible to fit the decision neatly into the existing law. In this situation, the view cannot be avoided that the judges, though arriving at the same decision, do so by inconsistent reasoning, and there may be said to be no *ratio* for the case at all (or the case described as 'authority only for its own facts').

Commonly quoted are the words of Lord Dunedin in the English case of *Great Western Railways Co Ltd v Owners of the SS Mostyn* [1928] AC 57 at 73 '... if [the *ratio* of a case] is not clear, then I do not think it is part of the tribunal's duty to spell out with great difficulty a *ratio decidendi* in order to be bound by it'.

Multiple *ratios* and the single judge. Multiple *ratios* may also arise where a judge gives alternative lines of reasoning. Again, there is little authority as to how it is supposed to be treated, but probably the case then has two alternative, equally valid, *ratios*.

Wide and narrow ratios and the development of principles

A *ratio* may clearly be wide or narrow, or rather, widely or narrowly expressed. The fewer facts found to be material, and the higher the level of generality considered appropriate (and if the 'common factor' approach to multiple *ratios* be employed), the more inclusive, or 'wider', a *ratio* is[50]. Conversely, the more facts, the lower the level of generality (and if the 'sum of all facts' approach to multiple *ratios* be employed), the less inclusive, or 'narrower', it is[51]. As noted already in relation to the question of defining the *ratio*, the width can vary over time. In so far as *ratios* are not fixed and it is later judges who determine what they shall be taken to mean, a *ratio* may get

---

48 *Ie*, if Judge 1 finds facts A, B & C material, Judge 2 finds facts A, B & D material, and Judge 3 finds facts A, B & E material, the *ratio* is A+B+C+D+E.

49 *The Laws of Scotland: Stair Memorial Encyclopaedia* vol 22, para 342 describes this procedure as 'dubious'.

50 In the example above, only A & B have to be present. This is likely to include more cases.

51 In the example above, all of A, B, C, D & E have to be present. This is likely to include less cases.

wider or narrower as time passes. This can be shown in relation to *Donoghue v Stevenson* 1932 SC(HL) 31 (bearing in mind the definition of *ratio decidendi* and the riders to it).

Donoghue v Stevenson has for decades been cited as authority for certain propositions, and has been the basis of most of the modern law of negligence in Scotland and England. The decision does not, of course, stand alone. Like any other precedent, it has to be seen against the background of the earlier law. Before the decision, for example, it was not clear whether a manufacturer was liable to someone with whom he had no contract, and much of the judgment in *Donoghue* is spent reviewing the earlier precedents (different judges coming to different conclusions as to their significance). *Donoghue* settled the question, within limits, in the affirmative. The current view of *Donoghue*, and how far the principle attributed to it goes, equally can only be understood in the light of the numerous later precedents which have developed it.

As is the way with *ratios*, not all those of the judges in *Donoghue* are clear. Lord Atkin, for example, gives two different versions of his. One, most succinctly expressed at 44 (at the risk of falling into the trap of 'digging for buried treasure') is broad, and is his 'neighbour principle'. It includes few facts, and those at a high level of generality, and could be rendered as the following: 'If you act in such a way as to make it reasonably foreseeable that you will injure someone, if that person ought reasonably to be in your contemplation, and if such a person is in fact injured, then you are liable to compensate that other person for the injury suffered'. The other, most succinctly expressed (subject to the same risk) at 57, is narrower. It includes more facts, and at a lower level of generality, and could be rendered as the following: 'If you are a manufacturer of food and drink for consumption by the public, and if you produce such food or drink in sealed containers, then you are liable ...'.

However, later judges, after initially ignoring the decision, have generally asserted the broader version to be the principle. This is the more surprising because, firstly, the decision was by a bare majority of 3 to 2; secondly, it is not clear on the face of it that Lord Atkin's is the leading judgment; and thirdly, the other two judges of the majority, Lords Thankerton, especially at 59–60, and Macmillan, at 71, produced principles close to Lord Atkin's narrow version. The way *Donoghue* has been used subsequently by no means supports the 'sum of the facts' approach to the multiple *ratios* problem. It may be consistent with other approaches but, really, Lord Atkin's views have been retrospectively elevated to leading judgment status.

Later judges have used the broad version of *Donoghue* to give compensation for a variety of losses including those caused by negligent misstatements by banks, which were losses of profit rather than physical losses (*Hedley Byrne v Heller & Partners* [1964] AC 465) and losses caused by the escape through negligence of borstal[52] boys (*Dorset Yacht Co v Home Office* [1970] AC 1004). It is far from clear that even Lord Atkin would have accepted all such subsequent developments of his principle, and Lord Thankerton and Lord Macmillan's views are commonly simply discounted.

Not all such developments have proved lasting, however. *Donoghue* was used by the Appellate Committee of the House of Lords to justify the liability not only for wrongful acts, but also for the failure to act, in an English case concerning local authority building inspectors, *Anns v Merton Borough Council* [1978] AC 728, only for it to decide in *Murphy v Brentwood District Council* [1990] 1 AC 398 that it had decided *Anns* wrongly.

Thus, the views expressed in *Donoghue v Stevenson* have been a fecund source of principle in a wide area. The potential has been realised in some ways, but pinched off in others, but in all cases at the instance of later judges, and despite the fact that most of these developments could hardly have been foreseen by the original judges.

Defining and identifying '*obiter dicta*'

Obiter dicta[53], usually translated as 'things said by the way' (that is, 'in passing') is the phrase applied to any reasoning of a judge which is not part of his *ratio*. These include other observations upon the law, typically hypothetical examples. The problems of definition and identification of *obiter dicta* thus reflect those of *ratio decidendi*.

Obiter dicta have an importance. Although by definition they are never binding upon any court (not being a *ratio*), they may be persuasive, depending upon certain factors[54]. Also, given the difficulty of determining the *ratio* of a case, it may be that there is disagreement as to whether a particular piece of reasoning is *ratio* or *obiter*.

---

52 'Name of a town in Kent applied orig. to the system adopted there for reforming "juvenile adult" offenders': *Shorter Oxford English Dictionary*. Thus, in modern terms, a young offenders' institution.

53 '*Obiter dicta*', pronounced as spelt, is plural; the singular is '*obiter dictum*'. A noteworthy remark or remarks by a judge may be referred to as a '*dictum*' or '*dicta*' of his (as in 'Lord Reid's *dictum* in the case of ...'). Confusingly, this usage does not imply that such *dicta* are *obiter*.

54 Discussed below under '*Stare Decisis* – persuasiveness'.

STARE DECISIS

If precedent is a source of law, the *ratios* of precedents must, at least on occasion, bind later courts. In other words, on occasion, they lay down for the later court how a case is to be decided, and the later judge has no choice but to apply the rule or principle laid down. This doctrine is known as *stare decisis*, that is, 'to stand by what has been decided'[55]. There are stronger and weaker versions of *stare decisis*, and Scotland is said to employ a weaker.

Why have *stare decisis*?

There are several possible reasons for applying a doctrine of *stare decisis*. Some are unworthy, such as a desire on the part of judges to shuffle off responsibility for their decisions, or a form of ancestor worship. Others are less so, such as the efficiency of processing cases, enhanced by removing the need to decide every case anew when similar ones have been decided before. What most justifies *stare decisis*, however, is that it tends to ensure consistency. In other words, like cases should be decided alike, which as we have seen is a basic requirement of justice. Indeed, if like cases were not decided alike, in what sense would there be legal rules? On the other hand, consistency is bought at a price, for it may stultify development, and be seen to work injustice in individual cases.

What makes a precedent binding?

Not all precedents are binding. The binding nature depends upon two principal factors, that is, firstly, whether or not the *ratio* in question is 'in point', and secondly, upon the relative position in the court hierarchy of the court examining the precedent, to the court which laid down the precedent. Also, in Scotland it is said that a single precedent cannot bind, only a series of similar decisions, although as a *ratio* must always be seen as part of the matrix of the common law, it is rare for a precedent to be capable of being regarded as standing alone. In some cases it is not clear whether a precedent is binding or not, and there are exceptional cases where an apparently binding precedent is not so.

Precedents which are not binding may be 'persuasive', that is, they do not bind, but may persuade a judge to decide in conformity with

---

55   More fully rendered '*stare decisis et quieta non movere*', the additional words meaning 'and not disturb settled matters'.

them. Persuasiveness is a matter of degree, unlike bindingness, which is categorical.

'In point', 'follow', 'not follow', 'distinguish', 'explain', and related terms

A precedent is said to be 'in point'[56] when the issue (or an issue if there are several) in that case is the same as the issue (or an issue) in the case to be decided (the 'instant case'). This means that the material facts, at an appropriate level of generality, are the same[57].

Either a case is 'in point' or it is not (although this has to be decided in each instance, and inevitably the decision involves a discretion). If it is 'in point', then, depending upon the relationship of the two courts, it may be binding (in which case the judge may be said to be required to 'follow' it). If it is not, it cannot be binding, though it may be persuasive (in which case, the judge may choose either to follow it, or not to follow it).

A judge who decides a precedent is not in point is said to 'distinguish' it[58]. There is more than one way of distinguishing. There may be a factor in the rule or principle of the precedent which is absent in the instant case[59]. On the other hand, there may be a significant factor in the instant case which was absent in the precedent[60]. The latter form is sometimes called 'restrictive distinguishing', because its effect may be to restrict the width of the *ratio* of the precedent, whether by creating an exception, or more generally.

In addition to the limited repertoire of basic responses represented by 'follow', 'not follow' and 'distinguish', there are a number of variations such as 'apply', 'approve', 'disapprove', 'doubt', 'consider', and 'overrule'. These are also used by editors of law reports and others. They are broadly self-explanatory, although no official definitions exist[61]. For example, 'disapprove' and 'doubt' fall short of 'overruling' (and might be used where the court in the instant case could not overrule the precedent, possibly because it comes from

56 The term 'on all fours' is also sometimes used to mean the same thing.
57 Some commentators are keen to insist that it is the issues which are compared, and that material facts are but part of this, for example, *The Laws of Scotland: Stair Memorial Encyclopaedia* vol 22, para 344; DM Walker *The Scottish Legal System* (8th ed, 2001) especially p 465. With respect, this appears to ignore the question of the appropriate level of generality.
58 That is, he finds it distinctly different, not that he makes it admirable.
59 The precedent has material factors A, B & C: the instant case has only A & B.
60 The precedent has material factors A, B & C: the instant case has A, B, C & D.
61 See, however, the list of meanings given in each volume of *The Digest* (formerly *English and Empire Digest*) (3rd ed) in relation to English law.

another jurisdiction). 'Consider' may imply no particular attitude was taken, or that the person using the term does not wish to commit himself to a view.

'Explain' is of a slightly different nature. It is used where the judge in the instant case thinks the *ratio* of the precedent insufficiently clear, so he cannot decide the appropriate response to it until he has elucidated it. Thus, 'explain' is likely to be used in combination with any other term.

On occasion, judges have certainly resorted to restrictive distinguishing and interpreting a *ratio* in a precedent excessively narrowly to avoid applying a precedent. However, distinguishing is not itself improper. It is an essential part of the operation of precedent.

Relative position in the hierarchy of courts

Civil courts are in one hierarchy, and criminal courts in a similar, separate, one. There is a vertical dimension to these hierarchies in that some courts are 'above' others, and a horizontal one in that there will be one final court at the apex, but many courts at lower levels. The vertical dimension is created by the possibility of appeals and other factors (including special provision for cases of major importance). This dimension is important because not only may higher courts be able to overrule lower ones, but also, even when not overruling, higher courts send out stronger signals to lower courts and other users of the law as to what the law is on a given issue. The horizontal dimension is created by the need for multiple local points of entry to the system but not to have competing final courts of appeal. This dimension is important because there are relationships in the hierarchy other than 'above' and 'below'. There is also a possible relationship between the two hierarchies, and with courts outside the hierarchy, in other legal systems.

The hierarchy is not entirely simple. The Court of Session is above any Sheriff Court, although their jurisdiction is remarkably similar. Within the Court of Session, the Inner House is in some sense above the Outer House, for it hears appeals from it, but the court is a collegiate court and Courts of Five Judges (or other odd number) may be convened[62]. It is difficult to say in hierarchical terms what the

---

62 As membership of the Divisions of the Inner House was enlarged from four to five in 2002, it might be that the smallest augmented court would now be a Court of Seven Judges. However, a Court of Five Judges was convened in *Webster v Dominick* 2005 JC 65 and *Bott v MacLean* 2006 JC 85, more fully discussed below.

relationship between the Outer House and Sheriffs is succinctly. The relationship between the Appellate Committee of the House of Lords and the Judicial Committee of the Privy Council (newly revivified by devolution) is not entirely clear, though they have a common membership. (See Chapter 3).

Also, while civil and criminal courts are separate, there may be cross-reference of precedents. For example, whether a certain action is theft may depend upon who owned the item, which is a question of the law of property.

Further, it is difficult to fit the European Court of Human Rights into the hierarchy at all. By the Human Rights Act 1998, s 2, courts determining cases involving 'Convention rights' (see Chapter 3) must 'take into account' all decisions of that court (and of the former European Commission on Human Rights).

It is equally difficult to fit the European Court of Justice in. It must effectively be seen as above any Scottish court in matters of Community law, for preliminary references to it under Article 234 (ex Article 177) TEC are binding, and where one is not made, that court's interpretations must be followed.

Further, English cases, which are clearly outside the hierarchy, are frequently cited in Scottish cases.

Nevertheless, for the purposes of *stare decisis*, it can be said that certain courts are above, at the same level, or below, or in a different hierarchy from, certain others.

The interplay of precedents in point and the hierarchy of courts

The basic principles can be stated in the following propositions:

(*a*) a precedent which is 'distinguished' cannot bind, regardless of whether it comes from a court above, on the same level or below, and the question of following therefore does not arise;

(*b*) a precedent which is 'in point', if it comes from a court above (which includes the European Court of Justice and, effectively, the European Court of Human Rights), binds and it must therefore be followed;

(*c*) a precedent which is 'in point', if it comes from a court at the same level, is effectively binding if both courts are high in the hierarchy, and therefore is very likely to be followed, but does not bind if both courts are low in the hierarchy, and therefore may be followed or not followed, depending upon its persuasiveness;

(*d*) a precedent which is 'in point', if it comes from a court below (or from any court in another hierarchy), cannot bind, and therefore may be followed or not followed, depending upon its persuasiveness.

In all cases, however, the orthodoxy is that a single precedent cannot bind, only a series of consistent decisions.

Exceptional cases where a precedent is not binding

There are exceptional cases where a precedent, although apparently 'in point' and from a higher court (or one of the same level where such a precedent appears to bind) and therefore seemingly binding, will be taken not to be binding.

Firstly, where the precedent has been overtaken by legislation (Community, United Kingdom or Scots), it is no longer to be applied.

Secondly, where the precedent is *'per incuriam'*, it is not binding. This means that it was laid down by a court which had not considered all the relevant law, and had therefore come to an erroneous conclusion. Thus, in *Mitchell v Mackersy* (1905) 8 F 198, the Inner House overruled its own decision in *Gray's Trustees v Royal Bank of Scotland* (1895) 23 R 199, on the ground that it had been decided without reference to the House of Lords' decision in *Globe Insurance Co v Mackenzie* (1850) 7 Bell App 296. As the age of these cases suggests, the *per incuriam* rule is rarely applied, however.

Thirdly, age and defective reporting may render a precedent not binding. It is said that mere age of itself is insufficient, and ancient cases are relied upon from time to time. For example, *William Duncan v Town of Arbroath* (1668) Mor 10075 was explicitly followed in *Jacksons (Edinburgh) v Constructors John Brown* 1965 SLT 37[63]. Indeed, age might demonstrate consistent application and thus the fundamental nature of the principle the case embodies. However, because the doctrine of precedent only grew up in the 19th century, there is something odd about using 18th-century or even earlier cases as precedents (rather than as illustrations of a long consistent principle of law)[64]. In any case, they may disclose no clear *ratio*, and the form of the report of the case may be unclear or its contents suspect. Nevertheless, in *Morgan Guaranty Trust Co v Lothian Regional Council* 1995 SLT 299, cases of 1959 and 1975 were overruled, but a case of 1733 (*Stirling v Earl of Lauderdale* Mor 2930) was

---

63   And thus a case about a hirer's liability for damage to a machine was decided in part by reference to the Arbroath magistrate's liability for cannon buried in the sand to avoid capture by the English army.

64   See Styles 'Antique Judgments and Modern Judges' 1989 SLT (News) 393, examining *American Express v Royal Bank of Scotland (No 2)* 1989 SLT 650 in which the Lord Ordinary (Dervaird) felt bound to follow a mid-18th century Court of Session decision *Gordon v Murray* (1765) Mor 16818.

approved, along with the conclusions of Bankton[65], for the proposition that whether or not money was paid under a mistake of law or of fact, it must be repaid, unless it was a gift. A determined court may go a long way to examine alternative reports and other records of an ancient case, as the House of Lords did in *Wills' Trustees v Cairngorm Canoeing and Sailing School Ltd* 1976 SC(HL) 30, where *Grant v Duke of Gordon* (1781) Mor 12820 was considered.

Fourthly, a precedent may be robbed of authority where a court decides that the maxim *'cessante ratione legis, cessat ipsa lex'* applies. The phrase means, roughly, 'where the reason for a law ceases to exist, so does the law itself'. Clearly, this could be a device to run a coach and horses through the doctrine of precedent, and its application is in practice limited and rare. Indeed, it has been doubted whether courts ever do apply the maxim, apparent cases being in fact examples of courts' non-binding precedents which failed to persuade, or of common law overruled by legislation, or of *obiter dicta* etc. A clear example of its use, however, is *Commerzbank AG v Large* 1977 SC 375, in which the Inner House rejected the House of Lords' decision in *Hyslops v Gordon* (1824) Shaw's Appeals 451 that judgments for money must be expressed in sterling. In the opinion of the court, at 328, 'the case of *Hyslops*, decided as it was in the context of conditions which no longer apply, does not now bind this court. We are accordingly free to consider, in the context of the age of floating currencies and rapidly fluctuating exchange rates, the true objectives of our law ...'.

Persuasiveness

Decisions which do not bind may nevertheless be 'persuasive'. In other words, a judge may choose to apply the *ratio* of the precedent, even though he need not. *Obiter dicta* may also be persuasive.

Persuasiveness, unlike bindingness, is not categorical, but is a matter of degree. Various factors, which are difficult to disentangle, influence persuasiveness. The fundamental factor is perhaps how well decided the precedent seems to be: does the rule or principle applied seem a good one, emerging out of the existing law on the subject? This in turn depends on other factors. These include how convincingly the judges in the precedent have expressed themselves, but also upon how well respected those judges are, how high in the hierarchy the decision was taken, whether it was unanimous or not, and the subsequent judicial history of the precedent, that is whether intervening judges have approved it, doubted it, distinguished it, or otherwise.

---

65 That is, the Institutional Writer: see Ch 5.

THE SYSTEM IN PRACTICE – THE CIVIL COURTS

Subject to the exceptional cases just dealt with, in which an otherwise binding precedent does not bind, *stare decisis* operates in the civil courts as follows.

Sheriff Courts

Sheriff Courts are local civil courts with a local appeal to the Sheriff Principal. Appeals direct to the Inner House or on further appeal from an appeal to the Sheriff Principal are possible in many cases, but are rare, and each Sheriffdom forms its own small hierarchy. Thus, a Sheriff (including a Sheriff Principal) is bound to follow precedents from: the Sheriff Principal of his Sheriffdom (if he is not Sheriff Principal himself)[66]; the Outer House, possibly[67]; the Inner House, or any Court of Five or more Judges[68]; the House of Lords; and the Privy Council (on devolution issues). The Sheriff Court is also bound by preliminary references and the case law of the European Court of Justice in respect of Community law, and s 2 of the Human Rights Act 1998 requiring it to take into account the case law of the European Court of Human Rights in relevant cases.

The Court of Session

The Court of Session is a 'collegiate court'. Its judges (and their decisions) are therefore judges (and decisions) of the court as a whole. Appeals from Lords Ordinary to the Inner House are called 'reclaiming motions', whereby a larger bench reconsiders the decision of the single judge. Questions of difficulty or importance, or

---

66 See, incidentally Maher 'Sir Thomas Smith, *stare decisis* and sheriffs' 2004 SLT 85-89.

67 In *Jessop v Stevenson* 1987 SCCR 655 the High Court of Justiciary decided that a decision of a single High Court judge in a trial bound a sheriff. In *Cromarty Leasing v Turnbull* 1988 SLT (Sh Ct) 62 Sheriff Wilkinson held, by parity of reasoning, that in civil matters an Outer House judge bound a sheriff, and Sheriff Principal Ireland has said 'I have to accept [Jessop] as binding upon me': see 1990 SCLR 388. However, Sheriff Stoddart in *Farrell v Farrell* 1990 SCLR 717 took a different view. The matter remains unresolved.

68 See below in relation to the Court of Session.

69 Larger courts, sometimes referred to as 'Full' or 'Fuller Courts', of Seven Judges or more (typically one Division with three judges from the other) have been used in the past. For recent examples of Courts of Five Judges before the expansion, see *Cullen v Cullen* 2000 SC 395 (concerning legal aid) and *MT v DT* 2000 SLT 1442 (concerning child witnesses and since the expansion, *Webster v Dominick* 2005 JC 65 and *Bolt v Maclean* 2006 JC 85).

ones where (rarely) a Division is equally divided, have traditionally been heard by a Court of Five or more Judges[69] or even the Whole Court, although this is most unlikely[70]. There is therefore no straightforward hierarchy. There is also a lack of precedent on how *stare decisis* operates in a number of relationships. Nevertheless, broadly speaking, higher courts bind lower, and larger bind smaller, and the position appears as follows:

(a) a Lord Ordinary is bound to apply precedents from: the Inner House and any Court of Five or more Judges[71]; the House of Lords.
(b) a Division of the Inner House is bound to apply precedents from: either Division of the Inner House in all probability (for although the Inner House has never specifically pronounced on the matter, neither Division has departed from such a precedent for more than 50 years); a Court of Five or more Judges[72]; the House of Lords.
(c) a Court of Five or more Judges is bound by precedents from: another Court of the same or greater number of judges, in all probability[73]; the House of Lords.

The Court of Session is also bound by preliminary rulings and the case law of the European Court of Justice in respect of Community law, and the Human Rights Act 1998, s 2 requiring it to take into account the case law of the European Court of Human Rights in relevant cases.

The Appellate Committee of the House of Lords

The Appellate Committee of the House of Lords is the apex of the hierarchy of Scottish civil courts, and those of England and Wales, and of Northern Ireland except, in all cases, in relation to devolution cases. (Note that it is to be replaced by the 'Supreme Court of the United Kingdom' in the near future[74]. It is not clear that this will change the substance of what is described below, save in connection with the relationship between it and the Judicial Committee of the Privy Council, as considered below).

This fact raises three problems in relation to *stare decisis*, namely: whether a precedent laid down in a case appealed to the House of Lords from one hierarchy binds courts in another; whether the

---

70 The Whole Court has not been convened since *Bell v Bell* 1940 SC 229, and the larger size of the court and greater pressure of business make it extremely unlikely that it will ever be again.
71 See previous two notes.
72 See previous note.
73 See *The Laws of Scotland: Stair Memorial Encyclopaedia* vol 22, para 289.
74 See discussion of the new court in Ch 3.

House of Lords binds itself; and what is the relationship between the Appellate Committee of the House of Lords and the Judicial Committee of the Privy Council.

(a) *Appellate Committee of the House of Lords precedents from other United Kingdom hierarchies.* It is unclear how far precedents of the Appellate Committee of the House of Lords from one hierarchy in the United Kingdom bind courts in another hierarchy. This is partly because there are nowadays few appeals to the House of Lords from Scotland so the occasion for pronouncement does not arise, and partly because the vagueness of rules not 'in fixed verbal form' makes it difficult to know what the *ratio* of a case is, and easy to evade taking an unequivocal decision. The Appellate Committee of the House of Lords has in the past shown a propensity to modify Scots law to conform to English[75], and the Scottish courts willingly to acquiesce[76]. Also, it is remarkable how commonly English precedents are cited in Scottish decisions, even in some central areas of law such as delict and how, for example, the law of negligence has developed in common in Scotland and England out of *Donoghue v Stevenson* 1932 SC(HL) 31.

The matter was discussed by Lord Normand in the Appellate Committee of the House of Lords in *Glasgow Corporation v Central Land Board* 1956 SC(HL) 1, and by Lord Justice-Clerk Wheatley in the Inner House in *Dalgleish v Glasgow Corporation* 1976 SC 32. Four propositions as to the authority of House of Lords decisions in Scots courts can be distinguished:

(i) Judgments on questions of Scots common law are binding on Scottish courts;

(ii) Judgments upon questions of English (or Northern Ireland) common law are not binding upon Scottish courts. However, there are exceptions, dealt with as the third and fourth situations (and there may be further exceptions[77]);

---

75 Probably the most memorable example is the words of Lord Cranworth in *Bartonshill Coal v Reid* (1858) 3 Macq 266, at 285, where he said, apparently without irony, 'But if such be the law of England, on what ground can it be argued not to be the law of Scotland?'.

76 In *Virtue v Commissioners of Police of Alloa* (1874) 1 R 285 a Court of Seven Judges split 4:3 on whether they were bound by House of Lords' decisions in English cases. The majority, including both Lord President Inglis and Lord Justice-Clerk Moncrieff, thought they were. Some of the minority might have agreed, but were of the opinion that the English case could be distinguished, so the issue did not arise for them.

77 See references to the Exchequer jurisdiction in *The Laws of Scotland: Stair Memorial Encyclopaedia* vol 22, para 282.

(iii) Judgments upon questions where Scots and English (and Northern Ireland) common law are the same, are probably binding on Scottish courts. However, the problem in such cases is likely to be deciding whether the common law is in fact the same[78];

(vi) Judgments upon questions of the interpretation of Great Britain or United Kingdom legislation are probably binding upon Scottish courts (although the principle may not extend to criminal legislation).

(b) *How far the House of Lords binds itself.* Lower courts do not bind themselves. For example, Sheriffs are not bound by other Sheriffs (save their own Sheriff Principal). Higher courts may bind themselves. For example, the Inner House has never explicitly said it is bound to do so, but in practice Divisions follow their own judgments and those of the other Division. If the Inner House is contemplating departing from a judgment of one of its Divisions, then a larger court is convened. The Appellate Committee of the House of Lords is the highest court, and the arguments that it should bind itself are most powerful. As a final court of appeal sending the strongest signals to other courts, it would sow confusion by changing its mind. But also, by virtue of its finality, the conflict between the certainty of precedent and need for justice in the individual case will be most acute.

In the 19th century, the arguments for certainty prevailed. After many years in which it was the undeclared practice, in an English case, *London Street Tramways v London County Council* [1898] AC 375, the Appellate Committee of the House of Lords declared itself bound by its own precedents (subject to an exception in relation to cases decided *per incuriam*, for which, see above), and this has always been taken to apply both to the common law and to the construction and interpretation of statutes. The position was never declared in relation to Scots law. It cannot seriously be doubted to have been the same, however[79].

In the succeeding half century, particularly because of the enormous social changes, this position became irksome. In 1966, the Lord Chancellor issued a Practice Direction[80] concerning judicial

---

78 This was part of the problem in the split decision in *Virtue v Commissioners of Police of Alloa* (1874) 1 R 285. See also the history of the law of occupiers' liability, as recounted in Smith 'The Full Circle: the Law of Occupiers' Liability in Scotland' in TB Smith *Studies Critical and Comparative* (1962) p 154.

79 See, however, *First Programme of the Scottish Law Commission* (SLC 1, 1976) para 18: *The Laws of Scotland: Stair Memorial Encyclopaedia* vol 22, para 283 suggests it was this publication which precipitated the Practice Direction.

80 [1966] 1 WLR 1234. A Practice Direction is an administrative rule on the running of the courts. Not the least interesting aspect of this change is that it was effected by a mere Practice Direction.

precedent. This reiterated the desirability of certainty, but admitted that 'too rigid adherence to [it] may lead to injustice in a particular case' and might 'unduly restrict the proper development of the law'. It then declared that their Lordships 'propose to ... depart from a previous decision when it appears right to do so', but 'would bear in mind the danger of disturbing retrospectively ... contracts, settlements of property and fiscal arrangements ...'.

As this guarded wording prefigured, the Appellate Committee of the House of Lords has rarely used its new power. There have been less than a dozen cases, and only one in a Scottish appeal[81], that is, *Dick v Burgh of Falkirk* 1976 SC(HL) 1, where it overruled *Darling v Gray* (1892) 19 R(HL) 31. There is no clear policy behind these few cases, but attempts have been made to isolate relevant factors[82].

Thus, the House of Lords is bound by precedents from itself, subject to its power to depart from them under the 1966 Practice Direction.

(c) *What the relationship between the Appellate Committee of the House of Lords and the Judicial Committee of the Privy Council is.* The Appellate Committee and the Judicial Committee cannot both be at the apex of the hierarchy of courts. Since there is no point in making the Judicial Committee of the Privy Council the ultimate authority on devolution issues if the Appellate Committee of the House of Lords could ignore its decisions (the only likely area of law in which a clash could arise[83]), presumably, it will not. (This issue will no longer arise, of course, when the new 'Supreme Court of the United Kingdom' is instituted).

The Appellate Committee of the House of Lords is also bound by preliminary references and the case law of the European Court of Justice in respect of Community law, and s 2 of the Human Rights Act 1998 which requires it to take into account the case law of the European Court of Human Rights in relevant cases.

---

81 Paterson, Bates and Poustie *Legal System of Scotland: Cases and Materials* (4th ed, 1999) p 431 estimated that, between 1966 and their date of publication, it had been asked to reverse one of its precedents once or twice a year and, between 1996 and 1983, actually did so in nine cases (on average about once every three years). Since 1966, the House of Lords has heard well over 2,000 cases (though few of them Scottish appeals).

82 See, for example, *The Laws of Scotland: Stair Memorial Encyclopaedia* vol 22, para 285.

83 Problems could conceivably arise with the Judicial Committee's non-devolution jurisdiction, for which, see in relation to the system in practice in the criminal courts.

Judicial Committee of the Privy Council

The Judicial Committee of the Privy Council is the final authority on 'devolution issues'. (Note that this jurisdiction is to be replaced by the 'Supreme Court of the United Kingdom' in the near future[84]. It is not clear that this will change the substance of what is described below, save in connection with the relationship with the Appellate Committee of the House of Lords, as considered below). Its decisions on such issues must therefore be binding on all other courts.

Since devolution issues are a statutory matter, not common law, and the statute is United Kingdom legislation, there is unlikely to be a problem of using precedents arising in one jurisdiction in another. How far it binds itself is not clear, but since it has not claimed to, and draws upon the same personnel as the Appellate Committee of the House of Lords, it can be expected to take a similar line to that court if the question arises[85]. Since it has the role of final court of appeal in relation to devolution issues, it cannot be bound by the Appellate Committee of the House of Lords on such an issue[86]. (As noted above, this issue will no longer arise, of course, when the new 'Supreme Court of the United Kingdom' is instituted).

The Judicial Committee of the Privy Council is bound by preliminary references and the case law of the European Court of Justice in respect of Community law, and s 2 of the Human Rights Act 1998 which requires it to take into account the case law of the European Court of Human Rights in relevant cases.

Civil courts of special jurisdiction

Several courts of special jurisdiction exist, such as the Land Court and the Restrictive Practices Court. In general, these courts are not bound by their own precedents (and bind no other court), but are bound by precedents of the Inner House, to which appeals from them go; by those of the Appellate Committee of the House of

---

84 See discussion of the new court in Ch 3.
85 This may not be soon. By mid 2007, of nearly 20 devolution issue cases heard by the Privy Council, only one was not criminal. Note that the Constitutional Reform Act 2005, s 41, declares that: 'decision of the Supreme Court on appeal from a court of any part of the United Kingdom ... is to be regarded as the decision of a court of that part of the United Kingdom', but that any 'devolution matter' is excepted from this.
86 On other issues, the situation may be less clear: see below in relation to the system in practice in the criminal courts, but se previous note.

Lords; and also, in relation to Community law, by preliminary references and the case law of the European Court of Justice, and s 2 of the Human Rights Act 1998 which requires it to take into account the case law of the European Court of Human Rights in relevant cases.

Precedents from another jurisdiction

Precedents from English courts are frequently cited in Scottish courts, for instance in cases on delict, where the law is largely common law in both jurisdictions. Those from some other common law jurisdictions such as Australia, Canada, New Zealand and the United States are cited occasionally. Thus, in *Morgan Guaranty Trust Co v Lothian Regional Council* 1995 SLT 299 decisions from superior courts in Australia, Canada, and South Africa were mentioned by Lord President Hope as 'instructive'. Despite the apparent parallel of Scots law with other mixed systems, such as South Africa, precedents from such jurisdictions are not frequent.

All are in the same position in that, coming from a different jurisdiction, they cannot bind Scottish courts (save that decisions of the Appellate Committee of the House of Lords on the construction and interpretation of Great Britain or United Kingdom legislation are likely to be regarded as binding), though they may be persuasive. In any case, in judicial decisions and legal textbooks, not only are English cases often cited, but they are often cited without specific warning that they do not determine Scots law. The issue is clouded by the complexities of the position of the Appellate Committee of the House of Lords.

In relation to Community law, special considerations arise, as such law with 'direct effect' (for which, see Chapter 6) is intended to have the same meaning throughout the European Community. Thus, decisions of the European Court of Justice and the Court of First Instance bind United Kingdom courts, and decisions of courts in other Member States may be cited. However, precedent does not operate in Community law in the way it does in United Kingdom law, and the position of the European Court of Justice is dealt with below.

In relation to 'human rights' cases, other special considerations apply, for decisions of the European Court of Human Rights are required to be taken into account, and decisions from courts of other countries applying the European Convention on Human Rights and like documents are inevitably and frequently cited. The position of the European Court of Human Rights is looked at specifically below.

THE SYSTEM IN PRACTICE – TRIBUNALS

There are many tribunals, such as those for certain employment cases and for immigration cases. Commonly they form small *ad hoc* hierarchies in order to allow appeal within each tribunal system, for example, from Employment Tribunal to the Employment Appeal Tribunal. Tribunals do not bind themselves, but decisions of an appeal tribunal effectively bind the lower tribunal.

From most tribunal systems, there is appeal on a point of law to the Inner House, and thereafter to the Appellate Committee of the House of Lords (as, for example, from the Employment Appeal Tribunal). In any case, all tribunals are bound by the law laid down by the Inner House and Appellate Committee of the House of Lords.

Most tribunals operate on a Great Britain or United Kingdom basis (although the Employment Appeal Tribunal sits in Scotland and England separately, with a Scottish or English judge presiding, as appropriate). Most of the law applied by tribunals is common to the whole of Great Britain or the United Kingdom, and many more decisions are taken by them in England and Wales, so decisions of the English Court of Appeal and of the Appellate Committee of the House of Lords in English decisions arising out of tribunal cases are very persuasive[87].

In relation to Community law, tribunals are also bound by preliminary references and the case law of the European Court of Justice, and s 2 of the Human Rights Act 1998 which requires them to take into account the case law of the European Court of Human Rights in relevant cases.

THE SYSTEM IN PRACTICE – THE CRIMINAL COURTS

Precedent is considered to apply less rigidly in the criminal courts, in the interests of individualising criminal justice. On the other hand, criminal cases may turn upon civil court precedents. For example, whether or not an act is theft may depend upon ownership and thus the law of property. Subject to these points, and to the exceptional cases in which otherwise binding precedents do not bind, *stare decisis* operates in the criminal courts in the following fashion.

---

87 In *Brown v Rentokil Ltd* 1992 IRLR 302, Lord Mayfield, sitting in the Employment Appeal Tribunal, said 'this court, being part of a United Kingdom body in the field of employment law, would only depart from an opinion of the Court of Appeal on a matter which was purely related to an aspect of Scots law. Accordingly, we find [a certain decision of that court] binding upon us'.

The District Court

District Courts deal with minor local crime. Most cases turn upon the facts, so questions of law rarely arise. Appeal is to the High Court sitting as an appeal court, and there is no further appeal, save to the Judicial Committee of the Privy Council on a devolution issue. District Courts are bound by precedents from: a Sheriff possibly[88]; the High Court of Justiciary as a trial court probably[89]; the High Court of Justiciary as an appeal court; and the Judicial Committee of the Privy Council on a devolution issue.

In relation to Community law, the District Court is also bound by preliminary references and the case law of the European Court of Justice, and s 2 of the Human Rights Act 1998 which requires it to take into account the case law of the European Court of Human Rights in relevant cases.

District Courts are to be replaced by Justice of the Peace Courts[90], but this change will not affect what is described above.

The Sheriff Court

Sheriff Courts are local criminal courts dealing with the middle range of crime. Appeal is to the High Court sitting as an appeal court (called the 'Court of Criminal Appeal'), and there is no further appeal, save to the Judicial Committee of the Privy Council on a devolution issue. It used to be orthodox to say that a Sheriff was not bound by the High Court sitting as a trial court (with which it has a considerably overlapping jurisdiction). However, in *Jessop v Stevenson* 1987 SCCR 655, the High Court, sitting as an appeal court from a Sheriff's decision, held that Sheriffs were bound by it sitting as a trial court. This was controversial, but the High Court has taken no steps to retreat from it. Sheriffs are thus bound by precedents from the High Court of Justiciary as a trial court and as an appeal court; and the Privy Council on a devolution issue.

In relation to Community law, the Sheriff Court is also bound by preliminary references and the case law of the European Court of Justice, and s 2 of the Human Rights Act 1998 which requires it to

---

88 This is asserted by DM Walker *Scottish Legal System* (8th ed, 2001) p 447, but no authority is offered. *The Laws of Scotland: Stair Memorial Encyclopaedia* vol 22 is silent. There is a certain parity of reasoning with the position of the sheriff and the High Court as a trial court.

89 By a parity of reasoning with the position of the sheriff court.

90 See Ch 3.

take into account the case law of the European Court of Human Rights in relevant cases.

The High Court of Justiciary

The High Court of Justiciary, like the Court of Session, is a collegiate court, so hierarchy does not work within it in a straightforward way. It sits as a trial court with a single judge, trying major crime from anywhere in the country, with a jury. Appeal is to the High Court of Justiciary sitting as an appeal court (often called, without statutory warrant, the Court of Criminal Appeal) with two judges for sentencing appeals and three, or occasionally more, for appeals against conviction. There is no further appeal, save to the Privy Council on a devolution issue. Thus, the High Court of Justiciary, sitting as a trial court, is bound by precedents from the High Court of Justiciary sitting as an appeal court. The High Court of Justiciary sitting as an appeal court, is bound by precedents from itself sitting as an appeal court with a bench of similar size, or larger.

A larger court may be formed to overrule a precedent which has been found unacceptable or otherwise clarify the law. Formerly such occasions were rare. In *Sugden v HM Advocate* 1934 JC 103 and *Kirkwood v HM Advocate* 1939 JC 36, 'Whole Courts' of 12 (the full bench, less the Lord Justice-Clerk) in the former case, and 11 (the full bench, less the Lord Justice-General and Lord Pitman) in the latter were convened[91]. In *Sugden*, they were to overrule a decision of five judges in *HM Advocate v Macgregor* (1773) Mor 11146 that a prosecution could not be raised 20 years after the presumed date of the crime, and in *Kirkwood* they reviewed precedents from smaller benches on the significance for sentencing of a plea of diminished responsibility. Such 'Whole Courts' are unlikely ever to be convened again, as there are more judges and more pressures on judges' time.

However, smaller augmented courts have become more frequent in recent years[92]. A court of five judges revisited diminished respon-

---

91 The 'Haill Fifteen' of the original Court of Session was reduced to 13 in 1830 (though restored to 15 in 1948, and subsequently increased to more than double that figure: see Ch 3). Thus, in the 1930s, only 13 judges were available to act as Lords Commissioners of Justiciary.

92 A court of five judges was used in *HM Advocate v Al-Megrahi (No 4)* 2002 JC 99, the appeal from the Lockerbie Trial, but this was a unique occasion, for the trial had been before three judges and no jury. In mid-2007, that case was referred back to the High Court by the Scottish Criminal Cases Review Commission, so it remained to be seen what number of judges might deal with following stages.

sibility in *Galbraith v HM Advocate (No 2)* 2001 SLT 953 to consider whether a lengthy period of physical abuse could justify that plea. A court of nine judges was used in *McCutcheon v HM Advocate* 2002 SLT 27 to overrule a decision of seven judges concerning cross-examination in *Morrison v HM Advocate* 1990 JC 299. Another court of five judges was convened to declare that, in the light of Article 7 of the European Convention on Human Rights (as a 'Convention right' under the Human Rights Act 1998) 'shameless indecency' was too uncertain constitute a crime known to the law of Scotland in *Webster v Dominick* 2005 JC 65 and *Bott v MacLean* 2006 JC 85, thus overturning *Watt v Annan* 1978 JC 84 and *McLaughlin v Boyd* 1934 JC 19.

The request to convene a larger court is the more persuasive if made by counsel for both parties, as in *McFadyen v Annan* 1992 SCCR 186, where counsel for the appellant and the Advocate Depute in a case of oppression requested that the case of *Tudhope v McCarthy* 1985 JC 48 should be reconsidered. The interval between the reviewing and reviewed judgments is usually much less than the 160 years in *Sugden*. An extreme example, though on statutory interpretation, is *Elliott v HM Advocate* 1995 SLT 612 where, on 24 March 1995, five judges met and overruled the decision on 10 February 1995 of three judges in *Church v HM Advocate* 1995 SLT 604.

In relation to Community law, the High Court is bound by preliminary references and by the case law of the European Court of Justice, and s 2 of the Human Rights Act 1998 which requires it to take into account the case law of the European Court of Human Rights in relevant cases.

Judicial Committee of the Privy Council

The Judicial Committee of the Privy Council is the final authority on 'devolution issues' in criminal matters, as in civil. (As noted in relation to the civil courts, this jurisdiction is to be replaced by the 'Supreme Court of the United Kingdom' in the near future[93]. As there, it is not clear that this will change the substance of what is described below, save in connection with the relationship with the Appellate Committee of the House of Lords, as considered below). Its decisions on such issues must therefore be equally binding on all other courts (subject to the less rigid application of precedent in criminal cases).

---

93 See discussion of the new court in Ch 3.

As also noted in relation to the Judicial Committee of the Privy Council in civil matters, since devolution issues are statutory matter, not common law, and the statute is United Kingdom legislation, there is unlikely to be a problem of using precedents arising in one jurisdiction in another. The question of whether the Judicial Committee of the Privy Council binds itself is more of an innovation in criminal matters, for no appeal from the High Court was possible until that court acquired its devolution issue jurisdiction. Nevertheless, no doubt it remains that the Judicial Committee of the Privy Council can be expected to take a similar line as the Appellate Committee of the House of Lords does if the question arises[94]. (This issue will no longer arise, of course, when the new 'Supreme Court of the United Kingdom' is instituted[95]).

The Judicial Committee of the Privy Council is bound by preliminary references and the case law of the European Court of Justice in respect of Community law, and s 2 of the Human Rights Act 1998 which requires it to take into account the case law of the European Court of Human Rights in relevant cases.

Precedents from another jurisdiction

Precedents from courts in another jurisdiction are essentially in the same position as in relation to civil matters, save that Appellate Committee of the House of Lords' decisions in English cases on the construction and interpretation of legislation are likely to be regarded as persuasive only (though no doubt very highly persuasive), as there is no appeal to the House of Lords in criminal cases from Scotland.

---

94 There have been difficulties in English law concerning the Judicial Committee's non-devolution 'imperial' criminal jurisdiction (for which see Ch 4). In brief, what happens if the Judicial Committee decides a matter of criminal law from an overseas territory which is essentially the same as in English law, but does so inconsistently with the decisions of the Appellate Committee of the House of Lords (or *vice versa*)? This is discussed in Elvin 'The Doctrine of Precedent and the Provocation Defence: a comment on *James*' (2006) 69 MLR 819-842 and Conaglen and Nolan 'Precedent for the Privy Council' (2006) 122 LQR 349-353.

95 Note that the Constitutional Reform Act 2005, s 41, declares that: 'decision of the Supreme Court on appeal from a court of any part of the United Kingdom ... is to be regarded as the decision of a court of that part of the United Kingdom', but that any 'devolution matter' is excepted from this.

PRECEDENT AND THE EUROPEAN COURT OF JUSTICE

The European Court of Justice ('ECJ') and Court of First Instance ('CFI') do not readily fit into the hierarchy of courts. There is no appeal to them from any court, nor appeal from them (although there may be appeal from the CFI to the ECJ).

The ECJ is, however, the guardian of Community law, and by virtue of Article 234 (ex Article 177) TEC any court may, and final courts of appeal must (subject to the *acte clair*[96] doctrine), remit to it questions of the validity or interpretation of Community law for a preliminary reference. Also, by virtue of s 3 of the European Communities Act 1972, any such question, if not referred under Article 234 (ex Article 177), must be decided by any United Kingdom court 'in accordance with the principles laid down by and any relevant decision of' the ECJ. This means on the one hand that Scottish courts must in effect follow precedents of that court, and on the other, that a Scottish precedent, in point and otherwise binding, may have to be ignored.

In United Kingdom terms, decisions of the ECJ are, strictly speaking questions of the construction and interpretation of legislation rather than precedent on the common law model. Firstly, however, a form of precedent operates in relation to the construction and interpretation of legislation, for courts in practice use the decisions of earlier courts as a principal means of determining the meaning of legislation, often in preference to the actual words of the legislation (as discussed in Chapter 11). Secondly, the ECJ has developed certain 'general principles of law common to all Member States' which it requires to be applied to any decision on Community law. It has thus generated something approaching a Community law doctrine of precedent, as is evident from cases such as Cases 28–30/62 *Da Costa en Schaake NV and Others v Nederlandse Belastingadministratie* [1963] ECR 31 and Case 283/81 *Srl CILFIT and Another v Ministry of Health* [1982] ECR 4315 (as discussed in Chapter 6).

On the other hand (as also discussed in Chapter 6), the ECJ has decided, for example, in Case 4/69 *Alfons Lüttike GmbH v EC Commission* [1971] ECR 325, that it is not actually bound by its own decisions. This is because it sees itself as an instrument of the evolution of Community policy. In fact it is sometimes not clear whether

---

96 That is, where the Community provision is so clear it does not need interpretation.

the court is following or not following precedent. It does not cite other cases in its judgments, even when relying on them or when consciously rejecting them. The problem is aggravated by the fact that only a single judgment is given, which may reflect a compromise between several lines of reasoning, making it difficult to determine what principles are being applied. The Advocate General's opinion is printed with the judgment, and is able to avoid many of these difficulties. Thus, it is often cited as a form of precedent, though it lacks authority.

There is, in United Kingdom terms, no developed concept of *ratio decidendi* in the operation of Community law, and thus no clear operation of *stare decisis*. Thus, the ECJ and CFI are not bound by precedent in the English and Scottish sense.

PRECEDENT AND THE EUROPEAN COURT OF HUMAN RIGHTS

The European Court of Human Rights fits even less well into the hierarchy of courts than does the European Court of Justice, for not only is there no appeal to it from United Kingdom courts, nor any appeal from it, there is not even an equivalent of Article 234 (ex Article 177) TEC for preliminary rulings.

On the other hand, it is the authoritative interpreter of the European Convention on Human Rights ('ECHR'), the contents of the ECHR are enacted as 'Convention rights' by the Human Rights Act 1998, and s 2 of that Act requires its decisions to be taken into account by United Kingdom courts when deciding cases on Convention rights. Thus, its decisions are, in some sense, binding upon the United Kingdom courts. However, there is a notion of 'margin of appreciation'. This means that the Court accepts that the Articles of the ECHR cannot be applied mechanically to national situations, and a democratically elected government has some room for manoeuvre in balancing opposing interests and taking account of national conditions. There is not necessarily 'a uniform European conception of morals'[97].

However, while the European Court of Human Rights strives for consistency, it cannot be said to bind itself. Indeed, there are a number of complicating factors in determining whether it has actually been consistent. The Articles of the ECHR are generally brief[98],

---

97 *Handyside v United Kingdom* (1976) A/24, 1 EHRR 737, para 48.
98 Art 3 is simply 'No one shall be subjected to torture or inhuman or degrading treatment'.

and even the most specific is drafted in the form of a principle rather than a rule[99]. In any case, it is expressly asserted that the ECHR is 'a living instrument ... which must be interpreted in the light of present-day conditions'[100], that is, it is (according to taste) either 'dynamic' or simply 'mutable'.

Clearly, the European Court of Human Rights is not bound by precedent in the English and Scottish sense, either.

99 See *eg* Arts 5 and 6.
100 *Tyrer v United Kingdom* (1978) A/26, 2 EHRR, para 31.

13. Precedent – Law Reports

The previous Chapter considered the nature of precedent as a source of law, its mechanics, and the concept of 'the common law'. This Chapter considers 'law reports', that most essential feature of any system of precedent, including the issues of the nature and significance of law reporting, the citation of cases, the form and content of law reports, the principal series of law reports, and electronic reporting and computerised retrieval of law reports.

THE NATURE AND SIGNIFICANCE OF LAW REPORTS

Any system of precedent relies upon efficient law reporting. Unless the decisions in at least the most important cases, and the reasoning which produced them, are readily available, no doctrine of *stare decisis* can operate.

Law reporting also exists in civil law countries, where precedent is not, generally speaking, accepted as a formal source of law, and where at most a very weak doctrine of *stare decisis* operates. Its role in these countries is rather to illustrate how a code or other enacted law is being understood and applied. The form of law reports reflects this, being often more laconic, and reasoned in a formal stereotyped way in terms of the enacted law with usually no reference to precedents. The form of law reports of European Community law, or from the European Court of Human Rights are, however, far from laconic, though this may reflect the difficulty of obtaining a single opinion from a disparate body in the one case, and allowing broad discussion of principle from a disparate body in the other.

Within any common law system there is now so much legislation that law reports also perform the function of reporting decisions on the construction and interpretation of legislation. Indeed, in many branches of the law it is nowadays difficult to find a report concerned solely with common law.

Law reporting in Scotland

There has long been some form of reporting in Scotland, for the *Practicks* date to the mid-16th century, and reports intended for wide publication among the legal profession from the 18th. Modern law reporting, that is, full reporting of the judges' actual words, with a view to their use as precedents, is a 19th-century development, probably a reaction to the increased reliance upon precedent inherent in the growth of precedent as a formal source of law[1].

Curiously, given the fact that precedent relies upon it, law reporting has not been seen as an obligation of government, and (with a few exceptions[2]) was not done by any governmental body. However, in 1999 the Scottish Court Service introduced a new electronic form of reporting[3], and House of Lords judgments since 1996 are so available[4] and Privy Council judgments since 1999 (with some earlier ones)[5]. There are roughly equivalent systems operated by the English[6] and Northern Irish[7] Courts Services.

The most authoritative reports are produced by a non-profit-making semi-official body, the Scottish Council of Law Reporting (and in England by a parallel Incorporated Council of Law Reporting), but most reporting is done by commercial legal publishing companies.

There are some 70 series of law reports published in the United Kingdom. These are of various types. In addition to concentration on Scots law or English law, some aim at relatively rapid comprehensive coverage (such as the Scots Law Times), some at authoritative reporting of major cases from the principal courts (such as Session Cases), some at significant cases in a particular area of law, irrespective of the court or tribunal giving judgment (such as the Scottish Civil Law Reports and Scottish Criminal Case Reports or, focusing on a smaller area, such as the Industrial Case Reports).

1   See, for example, the prefaces to the first edition, and new and enlarged edition (1834) in vol 1 of Shaw's reports. Compare also an early report, such as *Huntar v Huntar* (1573) Mor 16233, which has 30 words only, as follows: 'The tutor dative is maid and gevin be the King, quha may dispose the samin at his awn plesour to ony persoun be his gift theirof under the quarter seill'.
2   For example, Reports of Patent, Design and Trade Mark Cases and Immigration Appeal Reports, published by The Stationery Office.
3   See www.scotcourts.gov.uk.
4   See www.parliament.uk.
5   See www.privy-council.org.uk.
6   See www.hmcourtservice.gov.uk.
7   See www.courtsni.gov.uk.

Nevertheless, it is only a tiny proportion of cases heard by courts and tribunals which is ever considered worthy of reporting.

Most series of reports are concerned with cases decided in England and Wales. However, because so much law is now in legislation, and so much legislation extends over Great Britain or the United Kingdom, such reports may be of value in Scotland.

CITATION OF CASES

Precedents, like legislation, have citations, that is, references which identify the case and help find a report of it[8].

Traditional citation

So far as Scotland is concerned, unlike the position with legislation, traditionally there has been no 'official' citation of cases, so citations relate not to the case itself, but to the report of it. Thus, while citations uniquely identify reports, any case may, if reported in more than one series of law reports, have several citations, presenting a forbiddingly prolific combination of names, numbers and letters, for example, *Wilsons and Clyde Coal Co v Scottish Insurance Corporation* 1949 SC(HL) 90, 1949 SLT 230, [1949] AC 462, [1949] LJR 1190, 65 TLR 354, 93 SJ 423, [1949] 1 All ER 1068.

A citation in traditional form refers to the names of the parties, and to the initial page of the report, in the appropriate volume, of the relevant series of law reports. Recently, there has been a tendency also to include initials to identify the court which heard the case, such as 'OH' for Outer House, but neutral citation (considered below) makes this unnecessary. Community law case citations also include a case number.

Names

Cases are usually known by the names of the parties, for example, *Junior Books Ltd v The Veitchi Company Ltd*[9]. These names are often abbreviated (for example, simply to *Junior Books v Veitchi*, or just *Junior Books*). In a case at first instance the pursuer's name comes first, but if the defender appeals, his name may come first. If the parties are acting in a particular capacity this may be recorded in the

8　For a discussion of some of the principles of citation, see White 'Bracketing the Target: the citation of multi-volume Session Cases' 2006 SLT 37-40.
9　1982 S.C. (H.L.) 244

citation, such as in *Aitken's Trustees v Aitken*[10], *Drummond's Judicial Factor v HM Advocate*[11] or *Taylor's Executor v Thom*[12]. Where the case concerns a petition, the name appears as, for example, *Petrie, Petitioner*[13].

Community law cases present special problems. Their names may be ambiguous, as in *Commission of the European Communities v United Kingdom of Great Britain and Northern Ireland*, for there are several cases of that name. Most Community law case names are not in English (and if translated, are not always consistently translated), so may have abbreviated names, as in *Van Gend en Loos*[14], or unofficial ones, such as '*the Isoglucose case*' (or just '*Isoglucose*')[15], even though that word may not be part of the name of either party. In any case they are referred to in Community practice by the case number.

A court lawyers' shibboleth[16] requires that the '*v*' between parties' names is not pronounced 'versus' or 'v', but 'against', or sometimes (particularly in England) 'and'. The first named party is not necessarily the pursuer, because if the defender loses at first instance and appeals, the names are reversed. Occasionally there is more than one piece of litigation between two parties, in which case it will be referred to with '*No 2*' after the names, for example, *Weir v Jessop*[17]

---

10 1927 SC 374. 'Trustee' and 'trustees' are usually abbreviated to 'Tr' and 'Trs'.

11 1944 SC 298. 'Judicial Factor' is usually abbreviated to 'JF'.

12 1914 SC 79. 'Executor', 'Executrix' (the feminine form) and 'Executors', are usually abbreviated to 'Ex' or 'Exr', 'Exx' or 'Exrx', and 'Exs' or 'Exrs', respectively.

13 1992 SLT 665. 'Petitioner' is usually abbreviated to Petr. There are further variations, such as 'Minuter'.

14 This case appears in the official European Court Reports at [1963] ECR 1 as Case 26/62 *NV Algemene Transport en Expeditie Onderneming van Gend en Loos v Nederlandse Administratie der Belastingen* (which means roughly, '*Ghent and Loos General Transport and Export Co Ltd v Dutch Tax Commission*'). In Common Market Law Reports ([1963] CMLR 105) the respondent appears reported in the table of cases as *Nederlandse Belastingadministratie*, and in the body of the volume as *Nederlandse Tariefcommisie*.

15 *Royal Scholter-Honig v Intervention Board* [1977] 2 CMLR 449.

16 '1. The Hebrew word used by Jephthah as a test-word by which to distinguish the fleeing Ephraimites (who could not pronounce the *sh*) from his own men, the Gileadites (Judges xii 4–6), 2. *transf*. a. A word used as a test for detecting foreigners, or persons from another district, by their pronunciation ... b. *loosely* A custom, habit, mode of dress or the like, which distinguishes a particular class or set of persons ... 3. (*fig*) A catchword or formula adopted by a party or sect, by which their adherents or followers may be discerned, or those not their followers may be excluded': *Shorter Oxford English Dictionary*.

17 1991 SCCR 242.

(concerning search of premises) and *Weir v Jessop (No 2)*[18] (concerning entrapment)[19].

There are variations. Where there are reporting restrictions, as with some cases involving children, or others whose identity is not to be publicised, initials may be used, as with *E v T*[20]. This can be confusing, as with the famous and very important *A v Secretary of State for the Home Department*[21], (concerning the legality of detention under the Anti-Terrorism, Crime and Security Act 2001, in the light of Article 5 of the European Convention on Human Rights) which is not to be mistaken for the equally famous and important *A v Secretary of State for the Home Department*[22] (concerning the inadmissibility of evidence obtained by torture, in the light of United Kingdom law generally, and Article 3 of the European Convention on Human Rights). This example is slightly unfair as it was the same anonymous 'A' in both cases, but the point remains[23].

Where procedure is by petition, as with the *nobile officium*, the case may be referred to in the form *McLachlan, Petitioner*[24]. Also, because it has been common in Scottish reports to record a married woman's maiden name as well, both may appear in the citation, at least in English-based sets of reports. Indeed, for this reason, in the English series called Appeal Cases, *Donoghue v Stevenson* 1932 SC(HL) 31 is cited as *M'Alister*[25] *(or Donoghue) v Stevenson* [1932] AC 562, and *Darling v Gray & Sons* (1892) 19 R(HL) 31, as *Wood v Gray & Sons* [1892] AC 576. The married name is politically incorrectly preceded by 'Mrs'.

In criminal cases, the names used are those of the nominal prosecutor and the accused. With cases heard by solemn procedure the prosecutor is always nominally 'Her Majesty's Advocate'[26], often

---

18 1991 SCCR 636.
19 The *Factortame* litigation probably takes the prize, as it runs to some ten cases, *ie* to *R. v Secretary of State for Transport*, Local Government and the Regions *ex parte Factortame Ltd* (No. 8) [2002] EWCA Civ 932, [2003] QB 381, plus *Factortame Ltd v Secretary of State for the Environment, Transport and the Regions (Costs) (No.2)* [2002] EWCA Civ 932, [2003] Q.B. 381.
20 1949 SLT 411.
21 [2004] UKHL 56, [2005] 2 A.C. 68.
22 [2005] UKHL 71, [2006] 2 A.C. 221.
23 Indeed, in mid-2007, Westlaw revealed 78 cases of 'A' and 'Secretary of State' names.
24 1987 SCCR 195.
25 'M', is an old-fashioned version of 'Mc'.
26 In civil cases, HM Advocate is referred to as 'Lord Advocate'. (In mid-2007, the Lord Advocate was Elish Angiolini, who was nevertheless referred to as 'Lord Advocate').

abbreviated to '*HM Advocate*' or simply '*HMA*', for example, *HM Advocate v McPhee*[27]. With cases heard by summary procedure, it is the senior procurator fiscal for the Sheriff Court District, for example, *English v Smith*[28] (Smith then being the regional procurator fiscal for Dundee). If the accused is convicted and appeals, the names are again usually reversed, for example, *Khaliq v HM Advocate*[29]. Older criminal cases are commonly cited only by the name of the accused, for example, *John Ballantyne*[30].

Similar conventions apply to English cases, but three variations are worth noting. Criminal cases are cited as '*R*' (*ie Regina* or *Rex*, that is 'Queen' or 'King' respectively), for example, *R v Dudley and Stephens*[31] (pronounced as 'Queen against Dudley and Stephens'). Judicial review cases (where the court reviews a decision of government or a tribunal) are in England technically brought by the Crown ('*R*') against the relevant person, on behalf of ('*ex parte*') the complainer, so are cited as, for example, *R v Secretary of State for the Home Department, ex parte Zamir*[32]. In proceedings where there is not a straightforward action by one person against another, the name of the principal party or other information is preceded by '*Re*' or '*In re*' (both meaning 'concerning' in Latin), for example, *In re an Arbitration between Polemis and Another and Furness Withy & Co Ltd*[33] (often abbreviated to simply *Re Polemis*).

Reference to location of the case

In principle, reference to location of the case is simple. Basically, the citation normally gives a year, possibly a volume number, an abbreviation for a series of reports, and a page number. Reference to any particular words of a judge is conventionally represented in the form '*per* Lord Dawson, at 17'. In some series of reports, pages have letters in the margin to allow more precise citation, as for example '*per* Lord Dawson, at 17C'.

If a case is cited in several series, there will be several citations. However, there are numerous complications. These are dealt with in relation to each series of reports discussed below.

27 1935 JC 46, 1935 SLT 179.
28 1981 SCCR 143.
29 1984 JC 23, 1984 SLT 137, 1983 SCCR 483.
30 (1859) 3 Irv 352.
31 (1884) 14 QBD 273, 15 Cox CC 624.
32 [1980] AC 930.
33 [1921] 3 KB 560.

'Neutral citation'

The availability of reports of cases online from electronic databases, including official ones as well as commercial publishers' ones, is having a variety of effects[34]. One of the most obvious is the creation of 'neutral citations', that is, citations which do not refer to any series of law reports at all so (presumably) are 'neutral' as between them.

These were created in England and Wales in 2001, and extended to Scotland in 2005, to accommodate the availability of judgments online (especially those from official databases), which may not (or may not yet) be reported in any series of law reports, and for which, so far as official databases are concerned, the page numbering given by any particular series of law reports is meaningless[35].

Names

Names are used in neutral citations in the same way as in traditional ones.

Reference to location of the case

In neutral citation location of the case is unique, official, identifying numbers for the purposes of citation. It is to be used for precedents cited by judges in their opinions, preceding any other form of citation (though the other forms may remain).

The broad form of neutral citations is similar to that of traditional citation, but indicates the year, the court and the case, rather than year, report and page. Thus '[2005] CSOH 1' indicates the first case of 2005 from the Court of Session, Outer House[36]. Similarly, '[2003]

---

34 In England & Wales, the Court of Appeal issued a Practice Direction in 2001 designed to limit the number of authorities cited, given their ready availability. See also the remarks of Lord Reed in *Elabas v Secretary of State for the Home Department* 2004 SLT 1082 (Note), at [29], in which he criticises the indiscriminate use of citation of cases made possible by electronic retrieval.

35 Both Scottish and English courts now permit use of a print-out of a case instead of a proper report: see next two notes.

36 The full list of abbreviations used in Scotland is 'UKPC D' for the Judicial Committee of the Privy Council (Devolution cases); 'UKHL' for the Appellate Committee of the House of Lords; 'CSIH' for the Inner House of the Court of Session; 'CSOH' for the Outer House of the Court of Session; and 'HCJAC' for the High Court of Justiciary, acting as an appeal court (see Court of Session Practice Note No 5 of 2004 and High Court of Justiciary Practice Note No 2 of 2004). Note, incidentally, the neutral citation has brought square brackets into Scottish citations for the first time.

EWCA Civ 1' indicates the first case of 2003 from the (England and Wales) Court of Appeal, Civil Division[37]. Further, every judgment has numbered paragraphs (the numbers running through the whole judgment, even if there are several judges). Thus, reference is made to a paragraph rather than a page, in the form '2005 CSOH 1 [7]' (or 'at [7]'), or '2001 EWCA Civ 10 [59]' (or 'at [59]'). The paragraph number is bracketed to avoid confusion with page numbers, which are not used.

FORM AND CONTENT OF LAW REPORTS

Law reports properly so-called

There is a great variety of modern law reports, Scots, English and United Kingdom, but they have a broadly similar form and content, as described below. This is broadly true of the summaries appearing on electronic databases, though the layout differs somewhat. Older published reports, and European Community and European Convention on Human Rights ones, are more dissimilar.

Names of the parties, their roles, and counsel

Reports commence with the names of the parties abbreviated (for the purpose of citation) and sometimes repeated in full. Their role in the proceedings, such as pursuer, defender, appellant or reclaimer (ie a person appealing from Outer House to Inner House), is explicitly noted in some reports and the surnames of their counsel, that is, their advocates[38]. (Initials are not given where only one advocate of that name is in practice.) The abbreviations 'QC' and 'AD' mean 'Queen's Counsel' and 'Advocate Depute', respectively.

Thus, for example, the first report in Session Cases for 1986 is headed *Walker v Strathclyde Regional Council* and continues:

37 Practice Direction on the Form of Judgments, Paragraph Marking and Neutral Citation of 11 January 2001 ([2001] 1 WLR 194, [2001] 1 All ER 193) and Practice direction – Neutral Citations of 14 January 2002 ([2002] 1 WLR 346, [2002] 1 All ER 351). The full list of abbreviations used is: 'UKPC' for the Judicial Committee of the Privy Council; 'UKHL' for the Appellate Committee of the House of Lords; 'EWCA (Civ)'; 'EWCA (Crim)'; EWHC (Ch)' for the Chancery Division; 'EWHC (Pat)' for the Patents Court; 'EWHC (QB)' for the Queen's Bench Division; 'EWHC (Admin)' for the Administrative Court; 'EWHC (Comm)' for the Commercial Court; 'EWHC (Admlty)' for the Admiralty Court; 'EWHC (TCC)' for the Technology and Construction Court; and 'EWHC (Fam)' for the Family Division.
38 For the role of advocates in litigation, see Ch 14.

William Stafford Walker and Mrs Rosalind Harriet Sneader or Walker, petitioners *Rodger, QC*

Strathclyde Regional Council, respondents *McFadyean, QC*

Case number and date

Beneath the parties' names or in the margin, the case number and date may be noted, for example, 'No 1' and 'Oct 1 1985'.

Names of judges and court

Usually beneath the names of the parties, or in the margin, will be noted the names of the judges and the court hearing the case, for example, 'Outer House' and 'Lord Davidson'.

Catch words

Under the names of the parties is a series of brief references to certain facts, terms or concepts and questions, and where any question of the construction or interpretation of legislation arises, to such legislation, for example:

> *Contract – Heritable property – Sale – Consensus in idem placitum – Whether consensus reached where purported withdrawal of offer verbally communicated between agents of parties – Whether subsequent formal acceptance of offer resulted in bargain being thereby concluded –Whether probative writ withdrawing offer required*

They are usually italicised or emboldened, and separated by dashes, and if the case concerns several disparate issues, there may be more than one series of references. There is no official name for them, but they are often referred to as the 'catch words'. Their function is to give at a glance an idea of what legal issues were raised in the case, and they are inserted by the editor of the reports.

Headnote

After the catch words appears in continuous prose the 'headnote' (sometimes referred to as the 'rubric'). It will contain in it the word 'Held' (usually italicised), and should be seen as divided into the part before and the part after that word. The part before is a précis of the facts and general argument in the case. The part after is a précis of the decision ('Held' meaning 'decided'). The latter therefore gives what appears to the editor of the reports to be the ratio *decidendi*. However, a headnote is only a précis of the case, and is written by the editor of the report. It is therefore unwise to rely entirely upon it.

A headnote may contain other italicised words, such as '*aff.*' or '*affirmed*', followed by the name of the court from which the appeal came, and '*opinion per*' a named judge, which indicates a view expressed by that judge alone. It will also record if any judge dissented, usually by giving his name after the italicised abbreviation '*diss.*', and possibly with some indication of his reasoning. A headnote may also indicate that a precedent cited has been followed, distinguished, approved or otherwise, and end with the decision, such as 'appeal dismissed'.

Where a case covers more than one distinct set of legal issues, there may be more than one distinct headnote.

Recital of facts and procedure and argument of counsel

More authoritative reports contain a recital of relevant facts, and of the procedure which brought the case to that court, and an abbreviated account of the arguments deployed by counsel[39]. This may be several pages long, and possibly longer than the actual judgment. It may explain why the dispute took the form it did. For example, one party may have conceded certain issues, which therefore do not have to be argued. Thus, it may throw light upon the breadth of the *ratio decidendi* or its persuasiveness.

Sometimes the report simply records that the facts are as described by the judge.

Cases and legislation cited

Some reports list the cases referred to by the judges in their judgments, and sometimes others cited by counsel in argument. Legislation referred to is often quoted in a footnote.

---

39 'Counsel' (not 'Council', which is different) means advocate (or advocates); see Ch 15. It is important to note that argument of counsel is not the opinion of the judge. As noted in Chapter 12, it is an embarrassing error to quote the former under the impression that it is the latter, the more so if the judge later characterises the pursuer's argument as completely misguided and unsupported by authority.

Opinions

The body of the report is formed by the opinion of the court, or separate opinions, where the judges have delivered them, preceded by their names (sometimes in the form 'Lord Davidson's opinion'). These are in the judges' own words, and are not written by the editor of the reports, as the rest of the report is. Thus, they are that part from which all legal reasoning, including extraction of *ratio decidendi* and assessment of persuasiveness, chiefly flow. As noted in Chapter 12, in recent years, judges have generally adopted a common structure to opinions, helpful in extracting *ratios*. Thus, they often comprise informal sections, identified by shoulder headings, and usually variations upon 'Introduction', 'Relevant legislation', 'Submissions of parties', 'Discussion' and 'Conclusion', 'Result' or 'Disposition'.

Not all of an opinion may be reported, however, if the report of the case is concerned with only part of the dispute. Also, a judge's recital of the facts may be omitted if an adequate summary exists, or they are recounted by another judge.

Disposal

Every piece of litigation must end in a decision. This appears in the opinion of the judge or judges, but may be separately recorded at the end by the editor, for example, 'appeal dismissed'.

Solicitors and counsel

The names of the firms of solicitors (or the public office, such as Crown Agent, of the person acting as solicitor[40]) acting for the parties is given at the end of the report. So may the names of counsel, if not recorded with the parties' names. This appears to be an ancient form of permitted advertising.

Commentary

Some specialised reports try to put the case in context and explain its implications. A modern development is the appearance of such commentaries in general reports, such as Scottish Criminal Case Reports and Scottish Civil Law Reports.

---

40 For the role of a solicitor in litigation, see Ch 14.

Reporter's name or initials

The report may terminate with the name or initials of the reporter, that is, the person responsible for the report of the case. Initials can be decoded from a list of reporters at the beginning of the volume.

Legal database summaries

Electronic legal databases usually give access to a report of a case already published in law reports properly so-called, which may be modified somewhat from the original, or a transcript, which is in the form usually used by the transcribing firm. In addition, they commonly give a summary of the case, which will contain much of the same information as is described above, but again, in the form usually used by the company operating the database.

PRINCIPAL SERIES OF LAW REPORTS

Scottish law reports[41]

Official reports

As noted above, with minor exceptions, there had never been any official reports of Scottish cases until the Scottish Court Service introduced electronic law reporting in 1999, by making decisions available on its website[42].

The opinions of judges in the Court of Session and High Court from September 1998 are contained on that site. New judgments are added about 2 pm on the date they are published. Important civil judgments from the Sheriff Courts from September 1998 (and Court of Session commercial cases from January 1988) and Fatal Accident Inquiries from March 1999 are also included.

Further, all judgments of the Appellate Committee of the House of Lords published since 14 November 1996 are available electronically on the day of publication from its website[43], and all Judicial Committee of the Privy Council judgments are similarly available[44].

---

41 Full lists of Scottish law reports which have existed, the dates they cover, and the abbreviated form of the name used for citation purposes, are to be found in Walker *The Scottish Legal System* (8th ed, 2001) p 493.

42 See www.scotcourts.gov.uk.

43 See www.parliament.gov.uk/.

44 See www.privy-council.org.uk.

These are published without catch words or headnotes (as it is editors of law reports who write these), which makes them harder to understand, but their rapidity of publication makes them extremely useful for updating and quick reference. (See also 'Electronic reporting and computerised retrieval of law reports' below).

Other reports

Session Cases and the 'nominate' reports. The principal law reports in Scotland are those produced by W Green, a commercial publisher, on behalf of the Scottish Council of Law Reporting. Although this publication is referred to generically as 'Session Cases', it comprises four parallel series, that is: Privy Council cases on appeal or reference on a devolution issue; Appellate Committee of the House of Lords cases on appeal from the Inner House; High Court of Justiciary cases ('Justiciary Cases'), usually on appeal; and cases, either at first instance or on appeal, heard by the Court of Session ('Session Cases').

Citations of reports in these series are given as 'SC(PC)', 'SC(HL)', 'JC'[45], and 'SC' respectively, with year and page number, for example '1942 SC(HL) 1'. These series have for many years been bound together in a single annual volume, misleadingly marked 'Session Cases' on the spine, the four series being separately paginated within it. Thus, there are separate reports cited '1942 SC(HL) 1' (*Crofter Hand Woven Tweed Co Ltd v Veitch*), '1942 JC 1' (*Duguid v Fraser*), and '1942 SC 1' (*Swaire v Demetriades*) respectively, all in the same volume[46].

The Session Cases series in its present form commenced in 1907 (covering 1906-7). It was, however, the continuation of privately produced reports in broadly the same form, in five sequential series sometimes collectively referred to as the 'nominate reports', but individually known by the name of the five editors. These are Shaw (1821–38), Dunlop (1838–62), Macpherson (1862–73), Rettie (1873–98), and Fraser (1898–1906). Reports are cited by the

---

45 From 1906 to 1916, Justiciary cases were cited 'SC(J)'.
46 Until the revivification of the Judicial Committee of the Privy Council by the creation of its devolution issue jurisdiction, there were only Appellate Committee of the House of Lords cases, Justiciary Cases and Session Cases series. In 2000, there were only Appellate Committee of the House of Lords, but no Judicial Committee of the Privy Council, cases reported, and in 2001, there were Judicial Committee of the Privy Council, but no Appellate Committee of the House of Lords, cases reported, so 2002 is the first year in which all four series appeared.

editor's name or, more commonly, initial ('Dunlop' or 'D' and 'Rettie' or 'R', for example), with the volume number within that series, and page number, the whole preceded by the year which, because inessential, is in brackets ('(1875) 2 R 595', for example).

From 1850 (that is, from volume 13 of Dunlop's reports), the series usually contains Appellate Committee of the House of Lords reports as well as Session Cases, bound in the same volume and separately paginated, and such reports are cited 'D(HL)' instead of 'D' etc, for example, '(1850) 13 D(HL) 1'. From 1874 (that is, from the first volume of Rettie's reports), they also contain Justiciary reports, similarly bound and separately paginated and cited 'R(J)' instead of 'R' (or 'R(HL)'), for example '(1874) 1 R(J) 8'.

The House of Lords and Justiciary cases, usually bound in with Session cases in the nominate reports, are sometimes bound separately. In any case, there used to be separate series of such reports, such as Macqueen's reports of House of Lords cases (1851–1865), and Adam's reports of Justiciary cases (1893–1916). Reports were cited in broadly the same way as in the nominate reports, with name or abbreviation, for example '(1852) 1 Macq 232'. They have not, however, been produced for many years.

Session Cases are also available on the Justis [sic] and Westlaw databases (considered below).

Scottish Criminal Case Reports and Scottish Civil Law Reports. The Scottish Criminal Case Reports and Scottish Civil Law Reports are two separate series published by the Law Society of Scotland, on a commercial basis, since 1981 and 1987 respectively. Citations of reports are given as 'SCCR' and 'SCLR' respectively, with year and page number, for example '2001 SCLR 26'. They cover cases considered worth reporting from any court in the country, and some have a commentary on them added by the editor or other commentator. The SCLR series contains brief 'Notes' of cases not deserving of a full report, and brief 'Quantum' notes on cases for which the chief interest is the 'quantum' (amount) of damages awarded, or means of its calculation.

These series commenced in part because of the then chronic delays in the production of Session Cases. They are produced in loose parts about six times a year, and bound into an annual volume at the end of each year.

Scottish Criminal Case Reports and Scottish Civil Law Reports are also available on the Justis [sic] and Westlaw databases (considered below).

Scots Law Times. The Scots Law Times is, like Session Cases, published by W Green, but as a purely commercial enterprise. It contains professional information and articles, but also law reports of devolution cases going to the Judicial Committee of the Privy Council, Scottish appeals (and occasionally English appeals) to the Appellate Committee of the House of Lords, and cases from the Court of Session, High Court of Justiciary, Sheriff Courts, Scottish Land Court and Lands Tribunal and the Lyon Court.

Citations of reports are given, with year and page number, as 'SLT' or 'SLT (Reps)' (Judicial Committee of the Privy Council, Appellate Committee of the House of Lords, Court of Session and High Court of Justiciary cases), and 'SLT (Sh Ct)', 'SLT (Land Ct)', and 'SLT (Lyon Ct)', for example, '2003 SLT 366'[47]. Articles and professional information are cited as 'SLT (News)'.

The Scots Law Times is produced weekly through the year, except when the Court of Session is on vacation. It thus provides rapid publication of reports. From the 1920s to 1990, it was produced in one annual volume, and some editions marked the News, House of Lords reports, Court of Session reports, etc sections by different coloured edges to the page. From 1991, it has been bound into two volumes *per annum*, one containing Judicial Committee of the Privy Council, Appellate Committee of the House of Lords, Court of Session and High Court of Justiciary reports, the other containing all other reports, and the News section[48]. The SLT law reports are also available on CD-ROM, and on the Westlaw database (considered below).

Greens Weekly Digest. Greens Weekly Digest has also been produced by W Green since 1986. It contains brief notes, though not a report, upon recently decided cases, under digested headings such as 'agency' and 'contract', and appears in weekly looseleaf parts thus providing rapid, but limited, information. Some libraries bind these into annual volumes. Citation of the notes is given as 'GWD', with

---

47 Citation of earlier volumes is confusing. The earliest volumes were cited by annual volume number, usually preceded by the year in brackets, for example '15 SLT' or '(1907) 15 SLT'. For some years until 1921, two annual volumes were produced, cited by year, but including the volume number, for example '(1915) 1 SLT'. See also next note.

48 In 2005, three volumes were published, one containing all Privy Council, House of Lords, Court of Session and High Court of Justiciary reports ,save one (with cases cited as '2005 1 S.C.(P.C.) 1', '2005 1 S.C.(H.L.) 1', '2005 1 J.C. 1' and '2005 1 J.C. 1', etc); a second containing but a single case (*McTear's Exrx v Imperial Tobacco* [2005] CSOH 69, to be cited as '2005 2 S.C. 1'); and the third, as usual, containing other containing all other reports, and the News section (cited as usual).

the year, issue, and paragraph number, for example, '2002 GWD 2–60'.

Earlier reports and compilations. Many reports other than the 'nominate' ones were produced in the 19th century and later, such as the Scottish Jurist (1829–1873) and Scottish Law Reporter (1865–1924). Reports in these series are cited in the same fashion as are the nominate reports, using the abbreviations 'SJ' or 'Sc Jur' and 'SLR' or 'Sc Law Rep'[49] respectively. They sometimes cover cases not found in other reports, or provide alternative reports.

Before the 19th century several major series existed to which reference is made, such as that of Lord Stair (cited, as are the nominate reports, with the unabbreviated name 'Stair'), that of Forbes (cited 'Forbes' in the same fashion) who was the first of a number of reporters appointed by the Faculty of Advocates, and the Faculty Collection (cited as 'FC' or 'Fac Col' with the date).

Reference may be made instead to the reports in Morison's Dictionary which, with 'synopses' and 'supplements', covers cases from the 16th to the early 19th centuries in some 40 subject-volumes. Citations of reports in Morison's Dictionary are given to the page numbers, which run continuously throughout all volumes, after the abbreviation 'Mor Dic', 'Mor', 'Mo' or (likely to cause confusion with Macpherson's reports) 'M', the whole often preceded by the year in brackets), for example '(1714) M 14757'. Most of these reports are very short and without reasoned judgments.

Cases in the 15th to 17th centuries are to be found in the *Practicks*, made by judges and others and published later, such as Balfour's *Practicks,* available in a modern edition published by the Stair Society.

Selected cases from Morison's Dictionary, the Faculty Collection, the earlier Session Cases and some other reports pre-1873 reports were reprinted as 'Scots Revised Reports'.

Community law reports

Official reports

Reports of cases before the European Court of Justice and the Court of First Instance, usually called the 'European Court Reports', are produced by the Office of Official Publications of the European Communities.

---

49 To avoid confusion with another, later, but overlapping series called the 'Scottish Law Review'.

The form and content of the reports differ somewhat from the common form in the United Kingdom. A summary appears which contains catch words and a précis of the principle applied, instead of a headnote. The opinion of the Advocate General (which has no analogy in United Kingdom practice) is normally included, and usually contains numbered sets of paragraphs, often grouped down into parts dealing with specific topics (such as 'jurisdiction', 'the first question' and 'costs'), and ending with a formal conclusion as to the law. The judgment of the court is given in more formal terms than in United Kingdom practice, specifying the nature of the proceedings and *dramatis personae*, and containing a decision, in numbered paragraphs, likely to be constructed in parts like the Advocate General's. It also ends with a formal conclusion preceded by words such as 'On these grounds ... '.

The reports are cited by case number (often in round brackets) as well as year in square brackets (indicating an essential part of the citation, following English practice) and page number, with the abbreviation 'ECR'. Since the Court of First Instance was instituted, the case numbers have been preceded by either 'C–'[50] if it is a case of the court, or 'T–'[51] if it is of the Court of First Instance. Community practice is to put the case number before the parties' names, for example, 'Case 24/62 *Germany v Commission* [1963] ECR 63' (*ie* the 24th case commenced in the court in 1962, reported on page 63 of the 1963 volumes of ECR)[52]. United Kingdom practice is to put it after, and in brackets, for example '*Germany v Commission* (Case 24/62) [1963] ECR 63'[53]. This distinction matters, for it is Community practice to index cases by the case number, United Kingdom practice to do so by the parties' names.

There are several numbered parts each year[54], but the bound volumes (several per year) supersede this numbering and, in any case, the pages run as a continuous sequence through all parts. The volumes are sometimes helpfully bound with the pages in each volume marked on the spine.

European Court Reports are the most authoritative reports, but have been slow to appear (although unbound copies of judgments

50 For 'Court', or rather, 'Cour', as in 'Cour de justice': see below.
51 For 'Tribunal', the CFI having been originally known in English as the 'Tribunal of First Instance', and still known in France as the 'Tribunal de première instance'.
52 Or 'Case C-59/91 *France v Commission*' or 'Case T-7089 *BBC v Commission*'
53 Or '*France v Commission* (Case C-59/91)' or '*BBC v Commission* (Case T-7089)'.
54 *EG* '2000-1' to '2000-12' (confusingly *via* not only '2000-5A' and '2000-5B', but also '2000-8/9A' and '2000-8/9B').

rendered in English may be much faster), and are produced without the editorial assistance of headnotes in the United Kingdom fashion. Thus, the Common Market Law Reports are often preferred.

Other reports

Common Market Law Reports. The Common Market Law Reports series is published by Sweet & Maxwell, on a commercial basis. It has similar but fuller coverage than the European Court Reports, including cases heard before national courts as well as those before the European Court of Justice and Court of First Instance. There published in numerous loose parts during the year, bound into a number of volumes at the end of the year, and reports have headnotes in the United Kingdom fashion.

The form and content are closer to United Kingdom practice than the European Court Reports, as in place of the summary there is usually a fuller précis of the issues, and the facts are more clearly spelled out. However, its basic form is determined by the form of the Advocate-General's opinion and the court's judgment. The actual translation of those items into English is not identical to that in European Court Reports.

The reports are cited in the same way as with the European Court Reports, but with the abbreviation 'CMLR' and the number of the volume for that year, for example, '*Clarke v Chief Adjudication Officer* (Case 384/85) [1987] 3 CMLR 277'[55] (a case before a United Kingdom tribunal which went to the European Court of Justice on an Article 234 (ex Article 177) preliminary reference), and '*Pickstone v Freemans plc* [1987] 2 CMLR 572' (a case heard only before United Kingdom courts). The final annual volumes have been a sub-sequence of 'anti-trust' cases for some years.

These reports may be bound in the usual United Kingdom fashion (English variant) with '[2001] 1', '[2001] 2' etc are printed on the spine. However, there is a separate single sequence number running from the first volume which may be used instead so that, for example, the volumes for 2001 are not marked '2001 1', '2001 2' and '2001 3', but '90', '91' and '92' (although also bearing the year).

Common Market Law Reports are also available on the Westlaw database (considered below).

All England Law Reports European Cases. This is an addition to the standard English set of All England Law Reports

---

55 Community practice would render this as 'Case 384/95 *Clarke v Adjudication Officer*'.

commercially produced by Butterworths, and contains decisions of the European Court of Justice and Court of First Instance.

The reports are cited by year (in square brackets, indicating an essential part of the citation), and page number, with the abbreviation 'All ER (EC)', *eg* '[2002] All ER (EC) 193'.

All England Law Reports are also available on the LexisNexis Butterworths database (considered below).

'Human rights' reports

Official reports

The official reports of the European Court of Human Rights appeared initially as 'Publications of the European Court of Human Rights: Series A: Judgments and Decisions and Series B; Pleadings, Oral Argument and Documents. Judgments of the Court' were cited as, for instance, '*Bryan v United Kingdom*, judgment of 22 November 1995, Series A no 335–A'. The volumes were numbered but this number was not used. However, the volumes also bore the number of the case or cases contained (in this case '335–338').

From 1996, the 'Series A' and 'B' titles were dropped, so citations were modified to, for instance '*Murray v United Kingdom*, judgment of 8 February 1996, Reports of Judgments and Decisions 1996–I'. Volume numbers now bear the year, and the citation indicated the case within that volume, as in *Hay v United Kingdom*, no 41894/99, ECHR 2000–XI'.

Other reports

European Human Rights Reports. The main commercial English language series of law reports on the application of the European Convention on Human Rights is the European Human Rights Reports (EHRR) published by Sweet & Maxwell. It contains full reports of judgments of the Court (and admissibility decisions of the former European Commission on Human Rights).

The annual volumes have a continuous sequence of numbers, so reports are cited in the standard fashion of year (in round brackets, indicating an inessential part of the citation), volume number and page[56], *eg* '(2000) 29 EHRR 245'. Sometimes the case number is included, *eg* '(A/121) (1988) 10 EHRR 29'.

---

56 Helpfully, while the sequence of page numbers appears on the top left and right of the pages, there is a running title giving the citation of the case, including its starting page number, at the top of every page.

Butterworths Human Rights Cases. This is another commercially produced series, related to the All England Law Reports series.

It is also available on the LexisNexis Butterworths database (considered below).

Other series of specialised reports

A considerable number of specialised law reports are produced, generally on a United Kingdom basis, concentrating upon specific areas of law. These include, for example, Building Law Reports, Estates Gazette Law Reports and Immigration Appeal Reports. Some may include comment, as does the Industrial Relations Law Reports. Many professional journals, and certain newspapers, carry brief law reports, sometimes with comment.

Specialised reports are usually cited by the year, the abbreviated name of the reports (such as 'Build LR', 'EGLR', 'Imm AR'), and the page number. In most, the year is essential so, following the English practice, it appears in square brackets, and may be followed by the volume number for that year, for example, '[1990] Imm AR' (*ie* Immigration Appeal Reports) and '[1992] 2 LL Rep' (*ie* Lloyd's Law Reports). In some cases the year is inessential, so is in round brackets, followed by the sequential number of the volume in the series, for example, '(1991) 94 Crim App R' (*ie* Criminal Appeal Reports)[57].

Newspaper reports are usually cited by the name of the newspaper and the date, for example, '*Independent*, 11 Feb 2003'.

English law reports

Official reports

As noted in respect to Scottish law reporting, there were, with minor exceptions, no official reports until the (English) Court Service made some decisions available on its website[58]. This is roughly equivalent to the Scottish system, for the decisions are without catch words or headnote, but unbeatable for rapid updating. However,

---

57 Note that, since the introduction of "neutral citations" (see below), Criminal Appeal Reports and other Sweet & Maxwell published reports cite by case number, not page number. Thus '(2002) 105 Crim App Rep 2' refers to the second case in that volume, not the second page.

58 See www.hmcourtservice.gov.uk: also www.courtsni.gov.uk for Northern Ireland courts.

only recent decisions are held and reference is made on to 'BAILII' (noted below) where they are available at no cost. As noted in relation to official Scots reports, all recent judgments of the Appellate Committee of the House of Lords are available electronically from its website[59], and all Judicial Committee of the Privy Council judgments from its website[60].

'The Law Reports'. The most authoritative English law reports are those produced by the Incorporated Council of Law Reporting. They are commonly, if presumptuously, referred to in England and Wales simply as 'the Law Reports'.

They comprise five series. The first of these is 'Appeal Cases' containing appeals heard by the Judicial Committee of the Privy Council and the Appellate Committee of the House of Lords (including Scottish ones). The second, third and fourth are, respectively, the 'Queen's Bench', 'Chancery' and 'Family'[61] series, containing cases heard by the three divisions of the (English) High Court, and appeals from them to the Court of Appeal. The fifth series is the 'Weekly Law Reports' ('WLR') which produces rapid reports of those cases to be more fully reported later in the other four series (annual volumes 2 and 3), and other cases (annual volume 1). Each of these appears initially in loose parts, bound into one or more volumes per annum.

Citation is given by year in square brackets (indicating an essential part of the citation), volume number for that year, the abbreviated name of the relevant series ('AC', 'QB', 'Ch', 'Fam'[62] and 'WLR'), and page number, for example, '*Anns v Merton London Borough Council* [1978] AC 728, [1977] 2 WLR 1024'.

For a period in the 19th century, a similar but more complicated system operated[63]. Before that, there were nominate private reports known by the name of the editor, rather as in Scotland. The more important were collected in various compilations, including the 'English Reports' (cited 'ER'), and 'All England Reports Reprint' (cited 'All ER Rep').

The Law Reports are also available on the Justis [*sic*], LexisNexis Butterworths and Westlaw databases (considered below).

---

59 See www.parliament.uk/.
60 See www.privy-council.org.uk.
61 What is now the 'Family Division' was before 1971, the 'Probate, Divorce and Admiralty Division'.
62 Until 1971, 'P' (but not 'PDA'): see previous note.
63 For details, see Sweet & Maxwell *Guide to Law Reports and statutes*.

All England Law Reports. The All England Law Reports is produced by Butterworths, a commercial legal publisher. It reports all cases considered worth reporting from any court in England and attempts more rapid production than the Law Reports. It is produced in weekly loose parts, bound into several volumes *per annum*. Citation of reports in the All England Law Reports is in the same fashion as for the Law Reports. *Anns v Merton London Borough Council* is also reported at [1977] 2 All ER 492, for example.

The All England Reports are also available on the LexisNexis Butterworths database (considered below).

ELECTRONIC REPORTING AND COMPUTERISED RETRIEVAL OF LAW REPORTS

Official sources

The United Kingdom

Electronic reporting as a new form of official reporting, is discussed above in relation to Scottish, English and Welsh, and Northern Irish 'official' law reporting, and 'neutral citations'.

Community law

Community law, so far as it emerges from United Kingdom cases, can be accessed from United Kingdom databases. All European Court of Justice cases and Court of First Instance staff cases from June 1997 are available from the European Court of Justice website[64].

'Human rights' law

'Human rights' cases emerging in the United Kingdom can be accessed from United Kingdom databases. All European Court of Human Rights cases are available from the European Court of Human Rights website[65].

---

64 See www.curia.europa/eu/.
65 See www.echr.coe.int.

Commercial sources

It should be noted that where judgments are obtained from official sources, as noted above, they do not contain catch words or headnotes.

The United Kingdom

The major law publishers make their own law reports available on their own online services. Thus All England Law Reports, published by Butterworths, are only available on LexisNexis Butterworths. Fleet Street Reports, however, published by Sweet & Maxwell, are only available on Westlaw. They also make third party content available under licence. Thus the Incorporated Council of Law Reporting licenses the Law Reports to appear on the Justis [sic], LexisNexis Butterworths and Westlaw databases.

The Justis database includes the Law Reports, Session Cases from 1930[66] and specialised series such as Family Law Reports. Many of their titles are are produced on CD-ROM.

The LexisNexis Butterworths database contains the full text of selected Scottish decisions of the Appellate Committee of the House of Lords, Judicial Committee of the Privy Council, Court of Session, High Court of Justiciary and Sheriff Courts from October 2000, and all cases reported in Scottish Civil Law Reports since February 1986.

It also contains cases from the (usually English-based) series of specialised United Kingdom law reports, such as the Industrial Relations Law Reports, and from the major English law reports ('the Law Reports') and All England Law Reports, as well as innumerable United States reports series.

Westlaw Scots Law, operated by Sweet & Maxwell and W Green, provides all Scots Law Times reports from 1893, and Session Cases from 1930. Westlaw, as such, also contains a wide variety of English and American material

Casetrack, operated by Smith Bernal who are official shorthand writers to the English courts, covers the Court of Appeal and the Administrative Court from April 1996, the High Court as a whole and the Employment Appeal Tribunal from July 1998, and the VAT Tribunal from January 2002.

---

66 In mid-2007, it was anticipated that this would shortly be extended back to 1907 (ie the beginning of Session Cases, as such), and sometime thereafter to 1873 (to include both Rettie's and Fraser's reports) and eventually beyond.

While all the above are subscription based services, BAILII is hosted by a charitable trust and is available at no cost. It covers Court of Session decisions, High Court of Justiciary decisions and significant civil and criminal Sheriff Court decisions, all from, effectively, 1998.

Community law

LexisNexis Butterworths and Westlaw can be used to access Community law cases including reported European Court of Justice and Court of First Instance cases.

'Human rights' law

LexisNexis Butterworths and Westlaw can also be used to access 'human rights' cases, including reported (and some unreported) European Court of Human Rights cases.

14. Legal services

THE NEED FOR LEGAL SERVICES

Although much modern law offers some kind of advantage to people, they may miss the benefits if they do not take them up in the right way. And the kind of law that holds out threats over people who do not obey them can easily be abused by the officials wielding the threats – in criminal law, the police, the prosecutors, the judges and the penal authorities who actually apply the sentences. In other words, laws may be abused or miss their intended objectives.

To avoid this it is important that the subjects of the law should know what the law is – or at least be able to discover it, to find out how it applies to their particular situation, and then to utilise it, if that seems to be in their interests, and comply with it if it has a penalty attached. They need knowledge, advice and sometimes representation.

In a simple society where the law is largely custom they could probably do all this for themselves. But as law becomes more comprehensive, it becomes less accessible. The sheer bulk of it is intimidating. How to find one's way about it is a problem. Even when one has found what seems to be the right bit of law, the words used may be technical and obscure. The draftsmen of statutes often seem to defeat their own ends; in trying to cover every possible situation, they end up with laws that are beyond the understanding of those who are expected to use them – even the lawyers and officials.

The laws in the statute books may not be enough, for they may have been interpreted in a certain way by senior judges if there has been a similar dispute in the past which has reached the stage of a court hearing. For instance, if a house purchaser claims he was misled by a favourable report by a surveyor instructed by a building society and is entitled to compensation, questions of what actually happened and the terms of contracts, of statute and of case law and the value of his loss will all have to be considered. Then if the claim seems a sound one, it may be pursued by negotiation, arbitration or litigation (in a court). Given that the defenders will be advised by legal experts, the house purchaser would not get very far without the help of a lawyer.

When an individual is on the receiving end of laws, then the need for knowledge, advice and representation is still greater, for there is an inequality between him and the professionals who are doing the job daily. This is especially so in criminal cases where prosecution is usually a rare or unprecedented occasion for the accused and moreover one which may lead to the loss of his liberty.

To meet these needs a class of experts in the law has arisen in all mature systems of law, ones which have reached such a stage of complexity that people cannot make their way through them unaided. They may be called by various titles. In Scotland lawyers come in two classes: advocates and solicitors. No-one can belong to both classes at the same time, though transfers from solicitor to advocate are quite common. In carrying out their functions they all act under law and have various privileges and duties. However, they do not necessarily meet the entire need for legal services and we shall examine later other more informal responses to that need.

HISTORY OF THE LEGAL PROFESSION

Advocates

How do we come to have two mutually exclusive categories of lawyer, both enabling people to make the best use of the law? In medieval Scotland, two specific needs for legal services emerged. These were speaking as a 'forspeaker' in a court on behalf of a person called before it, and authenticating the documents which described occurrences under feudal law, upon which the all-important titles to land depended.

It seems very likely that court pleaders, from whom the later profession of advocate emerged, appeared first in the ecclesiastical courts. By the 13th century they had elaborate procedural rules and a largely written procedure which obviously called for literacy. It was not peculiar to Scotland. It derived from the universal canon law of the Catholic Church. Canon law provided until the Reformation the Scots law on marriage and its annulment, legitimacy, succession to items other than land, and contracts supported by an oath. On other matters too its courts were often resorted to, as being impartial and usually free from the influence of local magnates.

Many of the occasional references to lawyers before the 15th century seem to have some connection with church courts. Thus, a Glasgow cleric, Adam Urri, was criticised in 1288 for practising civil law (ie Roman law) for personal profit, but repented before he died[1].

---

1 *Chronicle of Lanercost for 1288.*

The records of the Great Cause[2] around 1290 over the succession to the throne of Scotland and later those of a long litigation on titles to land in the Court of the Bishop of Aberdeen (as a secular lord) in 1382[3] show that men with a wealth of knowledge of civil in the sense of Roman law and of Canon law were available in Scotland. One such, Baldred Bissett, was a graduate of Bologna and an official or ecclesiastical judge in the Diocese of St Andrews in 1282. Later, in 1301, with two others he was in Rome presenting in legal arguments the Scottish case against Edward I to the Papal Curia[4].

In 1424, when James I returned from captivity in England and set about remodelling the Scottish legal system, there must have been sufficient lawyers around in the royal courts for judges to ensure that, as Parliament enacted, poor persons should have 'a leill and wyse advocate to folow sik pure creaturis causes'[5]. Advocates and forspeakers were also to swear that their cause was a 'gude and leill'(or true) one[6]. By 1455 advocates must have been recognised as professional participants in courts of some formality, for by an Act of that year forspeakers 'for meide' (or reward) were to wear 'habits of grene of the fashion of a tunicle and the sleeves to be open as a tabard'[7]. In 1479 there is the first mention of the King's Advocate, the ancestor of the Executive's chief law officer in Scotland today, the Lord Advocate[8].

When the Court of Session was established about 1532, eight men of 'best name, knawlege and experience' were selected to be 'general procurators', their number not to go above ten[9]. Others were admitted as individuals to practise before the court on satisfying the judges of their competence. The first sign of an organisation of these advocates is a mention in 1582 of Master John Sharp, 'dene of the

2   DM Walker *A Legal History of Scotland* vol II (1990) p 267; see p 14 above.
3   Stein '*The Influence of Roman Law on the Law of Scotland*' 1963 JR 205.
4   DER Watt *A Biographical Dictionary of Scottish Graduates Before 1410*. See generally HL MacQueen *Common Law and Feudal Law* ch 3.
5   APS II, 8.
6   APS II, 19.
7   APS II, 43.
8   APS II, 125 He is simply described as 'the Advocate', which is the manner in which the Lord Advocate is still referred to by the inhabitants of Parliament House. In 1579 he acquired his role as prosecutor of grave criminal offences on behalf of the Crown.
9   See RK Hannay *The College of Justice* p 137. In 1567 an Act narrated the great number of advocates in Edinburgh and restricted the number authorised to appear before the Session to ten, thus releasing others to appear in the other courts of Edinburgh (APS III, 41). See generally Gordon Donaldson 'The Legal Profession in Scottish Society in the 16th and 17th Centuries' 1976 JR 1.

advocattis of sessioun'[10]. Gradually they seem to have acquired a corporate identity and a monopoly of representation in the Court of Session. Their earliest extant minutes are of 1661[11], but the Faculty of Advocates had some form of existence as part of the College of Justice long before then – certainly by 1582, if not earlier.

Solicitors

The development of the advocates' profession is fairly simple to chart, as with the judges they have formed part of the College of Justice since its creation in 1532 and have thus been based (until recently) in Edinburgh. Solicitors on the other hand were and are to be found throughout Scotland and their corporate existence began as local societies of lawyers. Many of these still exist, but all practising solicitors must now be members of the Law Society of Scotland, which is the creation of statute.

The formation of societies of solicitors in the provincial towns is not well documented, except in Glasgow and Aberdeen. The term 'solicitor' is a relatively modern one. Lawyers in Glasgow specifically rejected it, preferring to be known as procurators, originally those who were licensed to appear before the Commissary Courts of the pre-Reformation Archdiocese of Glasgow. Reborn under a Charter of Queen Mary in 1563, the Commissary Court of Glasgow continued to dominate the legal life of the city. Lawyers in Glasgow, whether or not they regularly practised before the court, called themselves procurators and belonged to the Royal Faculty of Procurators in Glasgow, which still exists[12].

In Aberdeen the men of law called themselves advocates and belonged to the Society of Advocates in Aberdeen, which also still exists. It traces its origin to 1633 when the Sheriff of Aberdeen recognised 16 practitioners as being alone qualified to appear before him, but a list of advocates going back to 1549 survives[13]. A society was formed in 1685 and it received Royal Charters in 1774, 1799 and 1862[14]. The Dundee Faculty of Procurators and Solicitors was incorporated by Royal Charter in 1819. The members of none of these bodies, despite their titles, concentrated exclusively on court

10 RK Hannay *The College of Justice* p 144.
11 See JN Pinkerton The *Minute Book of the Faculty of Advocates* (Stair Society, vols 29 and 32).
12 See JS Muirhead *The Old Minute Book of the Faculty of Procurators in Glasgow*.
13 See article in (1969) 14 JLSS 325.
14 Collected in *Records of the Society of Advocates in Aberdeen* (New Spalding Club); Henderson Begg *Law Agents* p 12.

practice, but it was the right to appear in court that gave them their standing.

At the level of the Supreme Courts in Edinburgh non-advocates were also becoming involved in procedures. Advocates drafted the written pleadings or allegations and arguments on which they were to base their oral representations, but these documents had to be sealed with the Royal Signet. The Clerks of the Signet received fees for this transaction, which continued until 1933. They formed the Society of Writers to the Signet, which is now an organisation of solicitors, mainly in Edinburgh, where it has a fine hall and library. The Society of Solicitors in the Supreme Courts had a less auspicious beginning in the throng of 'agents' as they called themselves who throughout the 17th century crowded the courts offering to help litigants with their cases. The advocates resented their intrusion and obtained several Acts against the agents. Eventually they were tolerated and by the mid-18th century individual agents were formally admitted to assist litigants before the Supreme Courts[15]. As the Society of Solicitors in the Supreme Courts of Scotland they now operate under private Acts of Parliament. They have no special privileges but speak for the interests of many of those solicitors in Edinburgh who regularly instruct advocates to appear on behalf of their clients and those of firms outside Edinburgh.

Another common ancestor of the modern Scottish solicitor is the medieval notary. Notaries were licensed by the Pope or the Holy Roman Emperor (and usually by both) to record transactions of legal significance. Their record was enough to prove that the transaction had taken place as stated. The office of notary was recognised in courts throughout Europe. A supplication to the Pope in 1425 complained that there were few notaries in Scotland, to the detriment of the people, especially when documents had to be authenticated by a notary in order to be sent to the courts in Rome. Six new notaries were then created who might be priests[16]. In 1469 King James III decided to remedy this shortage by taking powers as, in effect, Emperor of Scotland to create notaries to operate within Scotland[17].

Notaries kept copies of all the deeds they drew up in what were called Protocol Books. These were preserved after the notary's death and formed a kind of public register and a safeguard against loss of or alterations to the originals. The many surviving ones give a vivid

15 Henderson Begg *Law Agents* p 8.
16 Henderson Begg *Law Agents* p 10.
17 DM Walker *A Legal History of Scotland* vol II (1990) p 272.

account of the variety of a notary's work[18]. The conveyancing and drafting side of the solicitor's work has its origin in the work of the notary. Their deeds still have international recognition. Until 1896 the office of notary was an additional qualification which many solicitors sought. Since then only enrolled solicitors have been eligible to become notaries. Most solicitors now do so[19].

There are thus two historic strands in the background of the present-day solicitor: admission by judges to provide services in their courts and the power to create authentic documents. Both of these privileges were sought by individuals. But there was no means of checking on the qualifications of those who applied and no means of training them. A first step towards remedying this deficiency was taken in 1825 when the Court of Session decreed that anyone seeking admission as a procurator before any court must first have served an apprenticeship for three years with a procurator, writer to the signet or solicitor.

There was still a lack of a prescribed curriculum and a means of testing proficiency in it. This was remedied in the Procurators (Scotland) Act 1865, which provided an easy means by which lawyers in every county could form an incorporated society. Having done so they were to hold examinations in general knowledge and law, with the approval of the local sheriff. But as the users of the law began to include companies and other organisations which operated nationally or in many localities, it was plainly unsatisfactory that the qualifications of new lawyers should be left to the initiative and variable competence of local societies. So, following a Royal Commission Report, their training and admission were closely regulated in the Law Agents (Scotland) Act 1873. Applicants for admission to a local society had to have served a five-year apprenticeship under a registered indenture or three years if they held a degree in arts or law. The Court of Session would nominate examiners to hold examinations in general knowledge and law. A registrar was appointed to keep a roll of enrolled law agents. The universities which had played little part in the education of lawyers were now given a role, in that applicants, whether or not graduates, must have attended the classes of Scots law and conveyancing in a Scottish university.

18 See, eg, *Selkirk Protocol Books* 1511–1547 (Stair Society, vol 40).
19 The admission and regulation of notaries public is now controlled by the Solicitors (Scotland) Act 1980, Pt V, as amended by the Law Reform (Miscellaneous Provisions) (Scotland) Act 1990, s 37. On the history of notaries in Scotland, see John C Murray *The Law of Scotland Relating to Notaries Public* ch 1.

The law agents as a whole had no voice. Having no collective say on who should be admitted to their number they were lacking in one of the essential indicators of a profession, which in the early 20th century they aspired to be. In 1933 by the Solicitors (Scotland) Act (giving official recognition to their now usual name) a General Council of Solicitors in Scotland was created, to be elected by all their local societies. It had power to hold examinations and to regulate the admission and enrolment of solicitors. It also made nominations to the Solicitors' Discipline (Scotland) Committee. In 1949, when a system of civil legal aid to help finance court actions was about to be introduced, it was decided that the legal profession should operate the scheme on behalf of the government. Yet the existing structure which did not represent all solicitors was felt to be inadequate. So a Law Society of Scotland was created by the Legal Aid and Solicitors (Scotland) Act 1949 to replace the General Council and exercise its powers and more. All solicitors wishing to practise as such must now hold a current practising certificate from it. The present law concerning solicitors is to be found in the Solicitors (Scotland) Act 1980, as amended by the Solicitors (Scotland) Act 1988, the Law Reform (Miscellaneous Provisions) (Scotland) Act 1990, the Council of the Law Society of Scotland (Scotland) Act 2003 and the Legal Profession and Legal Aid (Scotland) Act 2007 (not yet in force).

Thus, their separate histories explain the existence of two branches of the legal profession in Scotland. But they do not necessarily justify it. The advent of solicitor-advocates in the 1990s is one example of the drawing together of the two branches (see below p 412).

LEGAL PROFESSIONS?

From the standpoint of the state the main purveyors of legal services in Scotland are regarded as a single profession. The title of the Conservative Government's Consultation Paper of 1989 on the supply of legal services is *The Legal Profession in Scotland*, which it states 'comprises both solicitors and advocates'. In their responses to this document, which challenged many of their assumptions, the Faculty of Advocates and the Council of the Law Society of Scotland (speaking for solicitors) agreed that their members form two branches of the one profession.

But what is a profession? What justifies the use of this traditional title? Sociologists who range over the whole world in their scrutiny of societies find the term problematical, to the point of admitting defeat in trying to encapsulate the term in one meaning. But we can single out certain features of a profession as the term is habitually used in Scotland (and England too).

For our purposes a profession is taken to comprise those who possess a specialised body of knowledge and skills related to it. It sustains an organisation which enables it to define with greater precision that knowledge and those skills; to admit to its membership those who possess them to a sufficient degree; to impose on its members certain standards of behaviour; and to discipline those who fail to maintain them. The maintenance of these standards is regarded as a matter of such public benefit that the organisation is by law conceded certain privileges to be enjoyed by its members.

We shall examine each of these characteristics in turn, in relation to advocates and solicitors, and then look at the internal stresses and strains and the external pressures to which the legal profession is subject.

ORGANISATION OF THE LEGAL PROFESSION

Advocates

The Faculty of Advocates consists of those who have been admitted by the judges of the Court of Session to practise before it. They thereby have access to the other superior courts of Scotland, most importantly the High Court of Justiciary, in London to the House of Lords and Judicial Committee of the Privy Council (including devolution proceedings) and in Luxembourg to the Court of Justice of the European Union. They can also appear before all the lower courts of Scotland, but they share that right of access with solicitors. Certain solicitors may also appear in the superior courts[20].

The Faculty is in law a corporation, that is, it has a legal existence separate from that of its individual members. But it enjoys that status by custom. No statute created it. Nor does it have a written constitution. The conduct of its members was a matter of unwritten custom. But the Royal Commission on Legal Services in Scotland in its report in 1980 urged that the Faculty 'should promulgate an authoritative written guide to the professional conduct expected of advocates'. The Faculty responded in 1988 with the *Guide to the Professional Conduct of Advocates*, which, being available to the public, enables breaches of that conduct to be complained of.

In 2007 there were 759 members of the Faculty, of whom 458

20 See p 412 below.

practice as such. Each practises on his or her own. Partnerships are not permitted. Practising advocates are either seniors or juniors. They enter as juniors and after about 12 to 15 years of successful practice they may apply through the Lord President to be appointed by the Queen to the Roll of Queen's Counsel in Scotland, which, following English custom, was formed in 1897. As a QC or senior an advocate is entitled to require that he be accompanied by a junior to assist him in the conduct of a case, but he may choose not to be. Until 1977 a senior was invariably supported in court by one or more juniors, but this practice was adversely commented on by the Monopolies and Mergers Commission and then abandoned.

Advocates are to be found in and around the Advocates' Library in Parliament House, Edinburgh, where consulting rooms are available and at the High Court in Glasgow. They do not share accommodation, as do English barristers in 'chambers'. But most share the services of one of eleven clerks, through whom they are approached and who keep their diaries. Negotiations on fees are also conducted by the clerks. Fees are unregulated, except by statutory instrument in civil and criminal legal aid cases, where it is the state that pays. But they should be 'reasonable'. Practising advocates belong to a company called Faculty Services Ltd formed in 1971, which issues a note of the proposed fee to the instructing solicitor and if it is not disputed receives payment on their behalf.

It is unlawful for an advocate (or solicitor) to enter an agreement to be paid a proportion of, and out of, the proceeds of an action. This is widely used in the United States where it is known as a contingency fee. However, it is permissible for an advocate or solicitor to agree to give his services on the basis that he will be paid only if the action is successful; but there must be a reasonable prospect of success[21]. This is called a speculative action[22]. Because of the risk undertaken by the lawyer it is permissible for him to raise his agreed fee by up to 100 per cent[23].

Many advocates hold full-time appointments as judges, sheriffs, academic lawyers etc. They take little or no part in the running of the Faculty.

The Faculty is headed by its Dean, who is its elected leader and also makes rulings on professional conduct and has disciplinary powers and duties. He is assisted by an advisory Dean's Council. The other elected officers are the Vice-Dean, Clerk of Faculty,

---

21 *X Insurance Co Ltd v A and B* 1936 SC 225 at 239.
22 See Faculty of Advocates *Guide to the Professional Conduct of Advocates* (1988) 5.10, 9.6; McCulloch *'Fees for Speculative Actions'* 1994 SLT (News) 401. S.I. 1992/1897. The Parliament House Book, 42.17
23 Law Reform (Miscellaneous Provisions) (Scotland) Act 1990, s 36.

Keeper of the Library and Treasurer. They are elected at an annual
meeting of advocates held in January.

Solicitors

The Law Society of Scotland comprises all solicitors qualified in
Scotland. They are to be found throughout Scotland and a small
number in England and elsewhere. In 2007 the roll of members
numbered 12,126 of whom 9,847 held practising certificates. They
elect by district constituencies a Council numbering over 40
members, with co-opted and ex officio members, including 4 non-
lawyers, making a total of over 50. Elected members serve for three
years and may be re-elected[24]. From their number a President, who
is the main spokesman of the Society, is elected each year. A Vice-
President is also elected annually and usually becomes the next
President. The statutory objects of the Law Society include the
promotion of '(a) the interests of the solicitors' profession in
Scotland and (b) the interests of the public in relation to that profession', two goals which may in practice be difficult to reconcile[25]. The
Council conducts the business of the Society and, with the concur-
rence of the Lord President, the senior Scottish judge, can make
regulations affecting its members, which have the force of law.
    The Council puts much of its business through a plethora of
committees and working parties which report to it. They are
composed of Council members and others, the President and Vice-
President being members of them all.
    There are also other societies of solicitors, local and national.
Membership is voluntary and members do not now have any public
statutory privileges. They include the Scottish Law Agents Society,
the Society of Writers to the Signet, the Society of Solicitors in the
Supreme Courts and local societies such as the Glasgow Bar
Association and the Society of Advocates in Aberdeen.
    Certain solicitors also have the additional qualification of being
entitled to practise in the supreme courts and as such are colloquially called solicitor-advocates[26].

LEGAL EXPERTISE

The body of specialised knowledge which advocates and solicitors
profess to have is the law of Scotland, that is all the law from

24 Constitution of the Law Society of Scotland. Parliament House Book F360.
25 Solicitors (Scotland) Act 1980, s 1(2).
26 See p 412 below.

whatever source that prevails in Scotland. That includes both the substantive law and the procedural law. They should not advise on the law of any other country, even England, unless they are qualified in it.

Advocates

Advocates tend to be ready to accept instructions on any branch of the law of Scotland. But some are known to be specialists in criminal proceedings only, and are unlikely to be instructed in other cases. With some exceptions[27] they may receive instructions only from a solicitor, never directly from an individual client. They thus have no contractual relationship with the client, as the solicitor does. They have a professional loyalty to the client, but subject to the rules of professional practice, which include obligations to the court[28]. This has several consequences. They are not supposed to pick and choose among clients but should accept instructions when given, if free to do so and offered a reasonable fee, giving priority to the party who applies first. This is called 'the cab-rank rule' and it militates against specialisation at the Bar. Sometimes, of course, they are double-booked, for instance when a trial takes longer than expected. Then they will have to drop out of one commitment, often at very short notice, and the instructing solicitor will have to find a replacement. Advocates may not be sued for professional negligence when in court, although it is assumed on House of Lords authority in English cases that they may be in respect of forms of professional fault outside the court. And remarkably, according to a leading 19th-century judge, an advocate's 'legal right is to conduct the cause without any regard to the wishes of his client and what he does bona fide according to his own judgment will bind his client'[29] (that is, in court).

As well as their public appearances in courts of all levels, advocates are frequently consulted on questions of doubt which have arisen in the course of legal practice; for example, on the legality of a

---

27 From public authorities, their heads and members, from legal professionals outside Scotland, from certain charities, voluntary bodies, and trade unions. See summary in 2006 SLT (News) 233 and www.advocates.org.uk
28 *Anderson v HM Advocate* 1996 JC 29 at 35.
29 *Batchelor v Pattison and Mackersy* (1876) 3 R 914 at 918 by Lord President Inglis, cited with approval in *Brodt v King* 1991 SLT 272 and *Anderson v HM Advocate* 1996 SLT 150. See also *Wright v Paton Farrell* 2006 SLT 269 as to criminal trials. Inglis is described by his biographer, J.C. Watt, as the 'Great chief'.

proposed course of action or the meaning of a will or, most commonly, on the prospects of success in raising or defending an action. This is known as taking the opinion of counsel. The consultation is initiated by a written document, drafted by a solicitor, called a memorial, in which the facts are stated and copies of any documents are produced, possible legal authorities cited and then a number of questions posed. The advocate will answer these one by one, supporting his response by legal authority and argument. Advocates may also be consulted on the drafting and revision of documents intended to have legal effect, such as important contracts. Advocates frequently also take part in arbitrations, which are hearings of disputes by an arbiter in private, according to procedure agreed by the parties and at a time and place to suit them. They may also be instructed to represent interested parties at public inquiries including planning applications.

Solicitors[30]

Solicitors are sometimes described as the general practitioners of the law, but this is misleading. Certainly, anyone can consult any solicitor on any point of law, but they have techniques for sliding away from difficult and unremunerative problems. Indeed, they are warned in their Code of Conduct not to undertake work for which they lack the necessary knowledge and experience[31]. Their work is overwhelmingly concentrated in procedures which can be routinised in a standard set of steps, many capable of being carried out by unqualified staff (sometimes called para-legals). The law utilised can be treated as given and simply ensures the legal effectiveness of the transaction, provided the required steps have been correctly followed. When exceptionally a novel point of law does arise, it is likely to be referred to an advocate or in some subjects a specialised solicitor, such as a professor of conveyancing, to be researched. Thus, the work of solicitors can be concentrated in the more profitable areas of practice. By the use of advertising, which is now permitted within broad limits, the volume of desirable work such as the buying and selling of houses can be increased.

Advocates likewise are sometimes described as the consultants of the law and it is true that solicitors do consult them on difficult

---

30   On solicitors generally, see *The Laws of Scotland: Stair Memorial Encyclopaedia* vol 13, '*Legal Profession*'.
31   Code of Conduct, to be found in *The Parliament House Book* section F.

problems of law. But they are seldom consulted as specialists[32]. Their opinion is sought because they have the time to research a problem thoroughly and give a detached and reasoned answer to it, often with advice as to the course of action to take.

Nearly all solicitors engage in the buying and selling of property, both residential and commercial, and in drawing up the documents of offer and acceptance, called missives, the deed of transfer called the disposition, and the security, if any, over the property which enables the transaction to be financed. These and certain less frequent property transactions are called conveyancing. Nearly all also deal with the distribution of the estates of deceased people, which sometimes leads to the setting up and administration of a trust, under which assets are held for the benefit of someone or some public purpose. Many will form companies for clients, in which they may have a personal stake. This often leads to advising on all aspects of the law as it affects companies. Many are now licensed under the Financial Services Act 1986 to advise on financial investments, with their tax implications. Some firms avoid court work, some do it when their established clients require it, and a minority engage in it in a substantial way. Most civil cases relate to divorce and related family matters and actions for the recovery of debts. Criminal cases encompass all kinds from the most trivial to the gravest.

Since November 1996 all solicitors have been required by the Law Society to take steps to keep their professional expertise up to date, under the name of Continuing Professional Development. They must devote 20 hours each year to this end. At least 15 hours must be in group study. This usually takes the form of attendance at courses on new laws, which are organised by local faculties of solicitors, universities, training companies and some of the largest firms. Skills such as office management, accountancy, and client relations are also acceptable as being relevant to the solicitor's practice and 5 of the hours must be on management topics. Up to 5 of the 20 hours may be spent on private study, including the preparation of and reading of articles. Solicitors are obliged to keep record cards of their studies. The Law Society calls in a random selection of them for scrutiny[33].

Solicitors who have acquired expertise by specialising in a particular branch of law may apply to have this recognised by the Law Society by being known as Accredited Specialists. So far 18 areas of

32 A recent publication of the Faculty of Advocates, circulated to solicitors, provides a statement of the special knowledge claimed by each practising advocate. This may encourage the growth of specialisation.
33 See *The Parliament House Book* section F, 272. (Under review).

specialisation have been approved. They include agricultural law, child law, employment law, medical negligence law and pensions law. Holders of these qualifications are available to advise their fellow solicitors in their area of expertise.

Most solicitors also qualify as notaries public, for which no extra training or qualification is necessary. This enables them to perform such functions as receiving under oath written statements called affidavits which form the basis of the evidence in undefended divorces; receiving sworn statements from executors as to the items of property left by deceased persons; and drawing up and signing wills and other documents for blind people. Because of the international credibility of notaries they may also be asked by foreigners in Scotland to deal with documents under foreign legal systems[34].

The usual way in which persistent disputes with a legal basis are settled is by the judgment of a court or, less commonly, in private by an impartial arbiter[35]. However, since 1994 solicitors have been offering mediation services which help people in dispute to reach their own agreement. The Law Society sponsors a list of 20 trained and accredited solicitor-mediators in commercial cases called ACCORD. There is also a list of mediators called CALM who specialise in family disputes, such as the care of children on the breakdown of a marriage. There are 14 authorised insolvency practitioners

Solicitor-advocates

Until 1993 solicitors could not appear in the High Court of Justiciary, the Court of Session and other superior courts, though they were usually much involved in the preparation of cases in these courts and would sit in court, while their client was represented by an advocate. But now solicitors can seek what are called 'extended rights' enabling them to appear and speak in the superior courts. Solicitors who have not less than five years' continuous experience of court work may apply to practise in the superior civil or criminal courts or both. They must undergo an induction course, observe cases in the appropriate court(s), attend (subject to certain exemptions) a training course in the work of the courts, and pass examinations on subjects related to practice in the superior courts[36]. It is now permissible for a solicitor-advocate to be appointed an Advocate

34 See Brand '*The Modern Notary in Scotland*' 1997 JLSS 50.
35 See p 86.
36 See Admission as a Solicitor with Extended Rights (Scotland) Rules 1992. On the process of admission, see 1993 JLSS 234.

Depute. In 2006 there were 106 solicitor-advocates qualified to practise in the criminal courts, 60 in the civil courts and 2 in both. Like advocates, they are allowed to act according to their own discretion and judgment in the conduct of a client's case[37].

In the services that they profess to supply and do supply, advocates and solicitors define the law which matters to them. Predominantly it is the preservation and increase of substantial material assets, whether owned by individuals or corporations. That is what the clients set great store by and what they are willing to pay to defend and add to. In so far as most students of law in Scotland wish to enter the Scottish legal profession, the law courses which they elect to follow have to give prominence to those parts of the law which lawyers find remunerative.

ADMISSION TO THE LEGAL PROFESSION

Admission to the offices of advocate and solicitor is controlled by the Faculty of Advocates (nominally on a remit from the Court of Session) and under statute by the Law Society of Scotland, respectively. Both bodies require three stages of training, which are similar, but not identical. The first is the stage of knowledge of the law. For the Law Society this is in the law of Scotland, conveyancing, evidence, taxation and European Union law. The Faculty's requirements are more extensive, in that the subjects of the law of Scotland are fully specified, and in addition to the Law Society's requirements international private law, constitutional law, jurisprudence and the Roman law of property and obligations are demanded. The great majority of entrants to both branches provide evidence of their knowledge by the possession of a degree in law (LLB) from a Scottish university, with or without Honours, containing passes in the subjects specified. But both bodies also provide their own examinations in each required subject.

The second stage is study for and the acquisition of the Diploma in Legal Practice from a Scottish university. The course for the Diploma deals in a simulated way with the main forms of legal practice in Scotland. The course is uniform throughout the five participating universities, which share the same course materials. Much of the instruction is given on a part-time basis by practising solicitors. The Diploma courses are eight in number: conveyancing (in addition to that already studied in the LLB degree), accountancy, civil court practice, criminal court procedure, professional ethics,

37 *Anderson v HM Advocate* 1996 JC 29 at 35; 1996 SLT 155 at 158.

private client matters, and practice management, plus one of forma-tion and management of companies or public administration. In exceptional circumstances exemption may be granted from the Diploma, where there is sufficient relevant professional experience. The course has lasted one academic year, but has recently been reduced to the period from October to April.

The third stage is training in an approved legal office under a training contract. For an intending advocate it normally lasts 21 months; for an intending solicitor, two years. During that period the trainee attends a university for a further two weeks, takes a Professional Competence Course provided by the Glasgow Graduate School of Law and the Writers to the Signet Society or in two cases a large firm of solicitors. Professional Competence is attested by appraisal throughout the traineeship and a log-book record of all work performed by the trainee. The intending advocate then has to spend a further nine months approximately in pupillage (known colloquially as 'devilling'), learning from and assisting an established advocate. During this period he or she has to pass a further examination in evidence, pleading, practice and professional conduct. Any payment in respect of pupillage is forbidden. The Law Society, however, stipulates minimum salaries for each of the years of the solicitor's traineeship. These are often exceeded by local and other public authorities. Intending advocates can expect similar salaries from their firms.

The would-be advocate or solicitor has also to name persons who will provide a reference as to his or her fitness to enter the legal profession. Any criminal convictions or bankruptcy must be declared and will be investigated.

Thus, the two professional bodies determine whom they admit to their number and so to a form of public office with certain unique privileges. For the last two decades the numbers admitted have far exceeded the numbers leaving the solicitors' profession. The number of women admitted has for several years exceeded the number of men. The number of practising advocates has also grown steadily in recent years to about 460.

The Law Society held a consultation on the education and training of solicitors in 2006. From it substantial changes are likely to follow in due course.

STANDARDS OF PRACTICE AND BEHAVIOUR

It is difficult for the Law Society to supervise the activities of its members, once qualified and admitted. The work they may have the opportunity to do is very diverse, their numbers are large – over 12,000 in total, counting those with and without practising certificates – and they are scattered throughout Scotland and beyond. Advocates, on the other hand, being far fewer in number and concentrated in Edinburgh, and to a lesser extent Glasgow, around the courts, have a certain *esprit de corps* which enables standards of conduct to be absorbed informally by imitation or advice from colleagues, for example, as to clubs, sports and dress, though up to a certain point eccentricities and discreet deviant behaviour are tolerated.

The primary source of professional standards for the new advocate is the *Guide to the Professional Conduct of Advocates*, which was published in 1988, as a response to a recommendation by the Hughes Royal Commission in 1980. This slender publication of 26 pages also serves as an indication to the general public of behaviour to be expected of advocates. In 2003 it was said to be under revision.

The conduct required of solicitors could be ascertained in two ways: certain aspects of legal practice, for example, keeping accounts and advertising or 'touting' for business, were regulated in Law Society regulations and rules; and behaviour which amounted to professional misconduct could be ascertained from the decisions of the Scottish Solicitors' Discipline Tribunal[38]. Following criticism from the Royal Commission on Legal Services in Scotland in 1980 in its Report at 18.4 and the adoption of a Code of Conduct by the Bar Councils of the European Community in 1988 (known in Scotland as the Cross-Border Code of Conduct), the Law Society of Scotland in 1989 issued a Code of Conduct for Scottish solicitors, which was revised in 2002, taking account of the Cross-Border Code of Conduct[39].

The Code is 'a statement of the basic values and principles which form the foundation of the solicitor profession' and underlie the more specific rules, for example, on conflicts of interest between clients. It stipulates various obligations of the solicitor, which it acknowledges may conflict: to clients, to the courts, to the public and to the legal profession and its individual members. But the Code starts with an assertion of the independence of the solicitor in various senses. Thus, misleading arguments must not be put forward

38 See p 423 below. See also JH Webster *Professional Ethics and Practice for Scottish Solicitors* (3rd edn, 1996). Ian Smith and John Barton *Procedures and Decisions* (1995).
39 For the Cross-Border Code of Conduct Rules, see *The Parliament House Book* section F, 274 and for the *Code of Conduct for Scottish Solicitors*, see section F, 1002.

on behalf of a client because of the lawyer's duty to the court. He must give advice in the best interest of the client and not take action which he considers to be against that interest. He must not put forward advice which promotes his own interest. But many solicitors are literally dependent in being employed by the government, local authorities, banks, companies etc. Confidentiality towards clients is a fundamental duty, respected even by the courts. The concept of providing adequate professional services is extensively defined. Solicitors should not undertake work unless they can perform it adequately. That means they must have the requisite legal knowledge and skill, be able to complete the work within a reasonable period of time, and communicate effectively with the client and others. Having once undertaken work, they must not withdraw from it without good cause and, if the matter is before a court, normally with the agreement of the court.

There is also a Code of Conduct for Criminal Work, of 1996. It consists of short statements such as 'A solicitor should not accept instructions from more than one accused in the same matter', followed by longer explanatory guidance notes. The Scottish Legal Aid Board brought into operation in 1998 a Code of Practice affecting those solicitors who are registered to provide legal services remunerated by Criminal Legal Aid[40]. It stipulates in detail the manner in which these services are to be provided and the records which are to be kept[41].

Competition among solicitors has been encouraged by regulations of 1995 on advertising and promotion of their services. Formerly, any form of advertising was strictly curtailed. But since 1991 'a solicitor shall be entitled to promote his services in any way he thinks fit', with a few exceptions. He must not approach a person he knows or ought to know is the client of another solicitor. But that does not preclude the general circulation of promotional material, which may reach the clients of other solicitors. Advertising must be 'decent' and shall not claim superiority over another solicitor, compare fees with those of another solicitor, contain inaccurate or misleading statements, bring the profession into disrepute, identify any client without his consent, or be defamatory or illegal. The Council of the Society has power to order the withdrawal or cancellation of any offending material[42]. Breach of these rules can amount to professional misconduct[43].

40 See pp 427–428 below.
41 Crime and Punishment (Scotland) Act 1997, s 49.
42 For the rules on advertising and promotion, see *The Parliament House Book* section F, 248.
43 Ibid F, 249.

Misuse of clients' funds has led to the tightening up of the rules relating to clients' accounts. All account books must be properly written up and a reconciliation of the firm's books with bank statements be made every month. 'Books and documents' are defined to include computerised records. For each accounting period, usually every six months, a certificate must be produced to the Law Society, signed by the cash-room partner and another, as to the state of the firm's accounts[44]. Inspectors of the Law Society have the power to inspect accounts on giving written notice[45]. A guide to the Solicitors' (Scotland) Accounts Rules was issued with effect from 1 February 2002.

Detailed Practice Guidelines are issued by the Professional Practice Committee of the Society on many and varied subjects, such as conflicts of interest, confidentiality and the use of fax and e-mail for transmitting documents. These Guidelines are collected in *The Parliament House Book* section F.

NEW FORMS OF ORGANISATION

Most solicitors practise in partnerships, which means that each partner is fully liable for all the debts of the firm, a protection to some extent for clients. It is now possible for solicitors' partnerships to be formed under the Limited Partnerships Act 2000. Some practise as individuals. Under Rules of 2001 (replacing ones of 1997) it is possible for solicitors to form an incorporated practice, if recognised by the Council of the Society. Incorporation may take various forms but could limit the firm's liability to pay its debts, though it is still obliged to contribute to the Master Policy against professional negligence (see p 420 below) and its members to the Guarantee Fund (see p 419 below)[46]. It would also entail that the affairs of the practice be opened up to some degree of public scrutiny through the Registrar of Companies. So far thirty incorporated practices have been formed, most of them large firms. Their names can be found in the Scottish Law Directory.

It has been a matter of acute controversy whether solicitors should be allowed to practise along with members of other professions such as accountants and surveyors in multi-disciplinary practices (abbreviated to MDPs). In a discussion paper in 1987 the government floated the suggestion that it would be advantageous to consumers

44 *The Parliament House Book* section F, 1239.
45 *The Parliament House Book* section F, 1240.
46 *The Parliament House Book* section F, 1235.

to have one door to call at with their problems. The Law Society resisted the proposal strenuously in its response to the 1989 consultation paper *The Legal Profession in Scotland* on the grounds that it would erode the existing statutory protections to the public (see p 419 below), a position it still maintains. The Law Reform (Miscellaneous Provisions) (Scotland) Act 1990 by s 31(3) creates a curious compromise of the dispute in allowing the Law Society to regulate MDPs, but requiring that any regulation which would prohibit them should have the approval of the Secretary of State and the Director General of Fair Trading. The Law Society responded in 1991 by issuing rules forbidding solicitors to form a legal relationship with a person or body who is not a solicitor with a view to their offering jointly professional services, but allowing the Council to waive the rule in unspecified circumstances[47].

The possibility of MDPs has also been thrust on a reluctant Faculty of Advocates, whose members have always practised as individuals and continue to do so. But the 1990 Act, by s 31, states that any rule prohibiting partnerships among advocates or of advocates and other persons is subject to the approval of the Lord President and the Secretary of State for Scotland, who must consult the Director General of Fair Trading.

At the level of the Commission of the European Union there is also pressure on the legal professions to allow MDPs. But the Council of Bars and Law Societies of Europe (CCBE) has resisted such moves as threatening the independence of lawyers and confidential dealings with their clients.

A further novel form of practice which is provided for in the 1990 Act is the multi-national practice. Under a European Community Directive of 1977 (77/249) lawyers from one member state can appear in the courts of any other member state, though practical difficulties mean that this right is rarely used. Provision is made for testing the competence of and admitting qualified applicants[48]. Ironically, lawyers from England and Northern Ireland could not thereby appear in Scottish courts (nor vice versa). Provision is now made by s 30 of the 1990 Act for regulations to be made for the admission of legal practitioners qualified in England and Wales or Northern Ireland to appear and conduct litigation in Scottish courts. In *Hoekstra v HM Advocate (No 3)* 2000 SCCR 676, a case

47 *The Parliament House Book* section F, 5, 339–340. The Secretary of State for Scotland approved the multi-practice Rules, but stipulated that a review should take place after five years to ascertain whether competition had thereby been distorted. In England, following the Clement Report, solicitors are to be allowed to form partnerships with other professionals.
48 *The Parliament House Book* section F, 228.

concerning drug-smuggling at sea, three of the accused were represented by members of the Netherlands Bar. By s 32 of the same Act,
Scottish solicitors may enter multi-national practices with foreign
lawyers, defined so as to include those qualified in England or
Northern Ireland. The Council of the Law Society is to maintain a
register of such foreign lawyers.

PROTECTION OF THE PUBLIC

Professions are to a large extent self-regulating bodies. As such they
have traditionally set standards of conduct and policed their
members' compliance with them. In recent years Parliament, dominated by governments committed to extending market principles
and under pressure from the consumer movement, has taken more
interest in how professional standards are maintained. There has
been an increasing awareness that the knowledge and skills of professionals put them in a position of superiority over their clients and
that the competitive pressures on lawyers in particular mean that
there are temptations to take advantage of that relationship. Hence
some protections for the public against any abuses by members of
the Scottish legal profession have been adopted voluntarily and
some have been imposed on it.

Solicitors

The protections for the public against solicitors are: (a) the
Guarantee Fund; (b) claims for damages for professional negligence,
which may be met by compulsory insurance; (c) awards for inadequate professional services; and (d) refund of grossly excessive fees.

Guarantee Fund

Under the Solicitors (Scotland) Act 1980, s 43 the Law Society has
to maintain a fund from which grants of compensation may be made
to people who have suffered loss because of the dishonesty of solicitors (other than their partners or employees). The dishonesty may,
but need not, have led to a criminal conviction. The scheme is a last
resort, so any other remedies have to be pursued first. This
Guarantee Fund is maintained by annual contributions from solicitors, plus levies to meet exceptionally large claims[49] and borrowing.

---

49 *The Parliament House Book* section F, 280.

Professional negligence insurance

Solicitors, in common with other professional people, are bound to exercise the standard of skill and care which can reasonably be expected of a competent practitioner in their profession. If they do not, they may be sued for consequential loss, certainly by a client, and possibly by affected third parties as well[50]. Delay in performing legal transactions is the commonest form of such negligence. For example, failing to raise an action for damages for personal injuries within three years, failing to make an application for unfair dismissal compensation within three months, failing to register security documents. As well as such negligence, deliberate fault, such as fraud, will give rise to a claim for compensation.

It might be difficult to find a solicitor willing to raise a court action against a fellow practitioner. However, since 1975 the Law Society has had a panel of solicitors, to one of whom a complainer who cannot obtain advice or representation on such a claim is referred. The services of such a person (sometimes called a 'troubleshooter') have to be paid for, either in the normal way for professional services or through legal aid.

Although a claim against a solicitor may eventually have to be decided in court, the great majority are settled by negotiation, under the threat of court action. Since November 1978 the Law Society has required all its members to be covered by a Master Policy of professional indemnity insurance, thus ensuring that legitimate claims will be met[51]. Proof that the premium has been paid must be exhibited each October when applications for renewal of the practising certificate are made. The number and size of claims has soared and so inevitably there have been regular increases in the premiums. Premiums are calculated on a complex formula related to number of partners and staff. To encourage care, there is a low claims discount financed out of loadings on the premiums of those who have had above average claims. There is also an excess per partner, a sum which must be paid by the insured before the liability takes effect. The insurers are advised by a panel of solicitors on the more difficult claims, for it is by the standards of the average competent solicitor that liability is established.

Inadequate professional services

There may be many instances of an unacceptable quality of service by a solicitor which fall short of negligence or are too minor to

50 See *The Laws of Scotland: Stair Memorial Encyclopaedia* vol 13, para 1189.
51 For the Rules, see *The Parliament House Book* section F, 307.

pursue as such; for example, not replying to letters or telephone calls. In such cases arising from conduct after 3 June 1991 the Law Society, on receiving a complaint from a solicitor's client, has powers to order its member to reduce or waive the fees and outlays charged, to refund payments already made by the complainer, to rectify errors and omissions and to pay the complainer up to £5,000 in compensation[52]. The Discipline Tribunal has similar powers in respect of cases prosecuted before it.

Excessive fees

Where fees charged by a solicitor are regarded by the Council of the Law Society as 'grossly excessive' it has power to order the excess, as established by the Auditor of the Court of Session, to be refunded and to suspend the solicitor from practice until this is done[53].

Advocates

By comparison with those against solicitors, the remedies of clients against advocates are less. In the case of *Batchelor v Pattison & Mackersy* (1876) 3 R 914, a celebrated judge of his day, Lord President Inglis, declared that because the advocate owed a duty to the court and must be independent of his client

'His legal right is to conduct the cause without any regard to the wishes of his client, so long as his mandate is unrecalled, and what he does *bona fide* according to his own judgment will bind his client, and will not expose him to any action for what he has done, even if the client's interests are thereby prejudiced'.

This pronouncement from over a century ago is subscribed to by advocates today and is quoted with the surrounding passages in full in the *Guide to the Professional Conduct of Advocates* of 1988. It was also followed by Lord Justice-Clerk Ross in *Brodt v King* 1991 SLT 272. So however negligent an advocate may be in conducting a case in court, his client has no legal redress against him.

However, in the English case of *Rondel v Worsley* [1969] 1 AC 191 the House of Lords upheld the immunity of barristers (and, by inference, of advocates) for actions done in court, on grounds ironically

---

52 Solicitors (Scotland) Act 1980, ss 42A–42C, 53A. *The Parliament House Book* F43.
53 Solicitors (Scotland) Act 1980, s 39A.

called 'public policy', but left open the possibility that they might be liable for negligent advice. In a later English case, *Saif Ali v Sydney Mitchell & Co* [1980] AC 198, a driver sued his solicitors for loss incurred through the latter's delay in pursuing an action. The solicitors sought to claim indemnification from a barrister who, they said, caused the delay. The House of Lords held that the immunity extended only to what was done in court and pre-trial work closely connected with it. By a majority it held that this third-party claim was not close enough and so should not be struck out. It is probable that the same distinction would be made in Scotland and since 1976 practicing advocates have collectively taken out insurance against actions against them for negligence out of court[54]. The cover amounts to at least £500,000 per member.

A further English case on this subject, on which the law in Scotland has arguably been developed, is *Arthur JS Hall & Co v Simons* [2002] 1 AC 615. In it, Lord Hope, a former Lord President, speaking *obiter*, opined that the 'core forensic immunity' (ie as to conduct in court) should remain in criminal cases in which the advocate might be harassed by a client who might well be 'devious, vindictive and unscrupulous'. However, in civil cases he regarded the core immunity as 'disproportionate', though it might be difficult to prove negligence. The same law, whatever it is, that applies to Scots advocates also applies to solicitor-advocates, on the authority of the Scottish case of *Anderson v HM Advocate* 1996 JC 29 at 35. In the same case Lord Hope could only say of solicitors that they were agents of their clients but could not be asked to follow the clients' instructions beyond what is 'lawful and proper'.

COMPLAINTS AND DISCIPLINE

Much of the cohesion of a profession derives from its ability to control the behaviour of its members, even to the extent of punishment. In this way the conduct of the offender is stigmatised and the correct norms of behaviour, which might be uncertain or taken for granted, are affirmed and reinforced.

---

54 On the likely scope of the immunity of advocates see *The Laws of Scotland: Stair Memorial Encyclopaedia* vol 13, para 1380, where the authors, then a judge and an advocate, attempt to extend the immunity affirmed in Rondel's case to settlements reached outside court, but immediately before or during a proof or jury trial. However see more recently Governed by Contract: the Advocate-Client Relationship 2006 SLT (News) 231, where John Carruthers, Advocate, argues that European Law imposes on an advocate and client a relationship of contract, not mandate.

Advocates

Until 1988 the disciplining of advocates was a matter for the discretion of the Dean alone. However, when most professions and occupations, including solicitors, had disciplinary procedures with ultimate recourse to the courts in some circumstances, it seemed anomalous that advocates should enjoy no such protection. Rules were published in that year and re-issued with amendments in 2002. They regulate the disciplining of advocates and reduce the role of the Dean, though he remains the key figure.

Anyone may make a complaint about the conduct of an advocate, in writing to the Dean of the Faculty. It will not be entertained more than six months after the date of the conduct complained about, unless there are exceptional circumstances. The complaint will be copied to the advocate complained about. He is asked to respond within 14 days. Further correspondence may ensue to clarify whether the material facts are in dispute or not. The Dean may also act without a complaint. The *Guide to the Professional Conduct of Advocates* gives information as to the conduct to be expected of advocates.

If the facts are not in dispute the complaint is sent to a Complaints Committee, composed of the Dean or Vice-Dean, a senior advocate and a lay person. If the complaint is upheld, the Committee can impose a penalty, including a financial one, or it may remit the matter to the Discipline Tribunal of four practising advocates and the same number of lay persons, whose powers of punishment are greater.

But if the facts are in dispute the Complaints Committee can remit the matter to an Investigating Committee who, after investigation, will submit a written report. Alternatively the complaint can be remitted directly to the Discipline Tribunal, chaired by a retired judge, to determine the facts and impose a penalty if appropriate. The standard of proof required is beyond reasonable doubt. Penalties which the Discipline Tribunal can impose include a fine not exceeding £15,000, suspension from practice for up to five years, and expulsion from the Faculty.

Solicitors

The machinery for disciplining solicitors is laid down in statute, with a right of appeal to the Court of Session. The first stage is that of complaint. The Law Society maintains a Client Relations Office which received 3623 complaints in 2006-07. About one in five of these are referred to one of ten Client Relations Committees which meet monthly. The rest are disposed of by some kind of administrative action, for example, where the complaint is of delay, by the delay being explained or the work resumed and/or by a cut in fees. The Society urges firms of solicitors to designate a complaints partner who will try to achieve a conciliated settlement.

The Client Relations Committees each have eight members: four solicitors and four lay members. They deal with the more serious or disputed complaints. They can censure the solicitor complained of or, if they find professional misconduct, reprimand the offender, make an order as for inadequate professional services[55], or recommend a prosecution before the Scottish Solicitors' Discipline Tribunal.

This body[56] is composed of ten to fourteen solicitors and eight lay persons. A quorum is four, of whom one must be a lay person. In most cases the Council of the Law Society acts as a prosecutor and appoints a solicitor to present the case against its member, who can be legally represented. But if a solicitor has been convicted of an offence involving dishonesty or sentenced to imprisonment for not less than two years, then the Tribunal can decide what action to take on that information alone. The Tribunal also acts as an appellate body against disciplinary decisions of the Council of the Law Society.

The Tribunal has the power to strike off, suspend from practice, censure and fine up to £10,000 a solicitor, or revoke the recognition of an incorporated practice. Its decisions must be published, unless to do so would harm the interests of persons other than the solicitor, partners and their families[57]. Its decisions may be appealed to the Court of Session.

The Ombudsman

Overseeing all these complaints and disciplinary procedures is the Scottish Legal Services Ombudsman. Formerly, as the Lay Observer, she investigated allegations about the Law Society's handling of complaints. Since 1 July 1991, with a new title, she has had a wider role[58]. Her remit covers complaints to the Faculty of Advocates and in respect of both solicitors and licensed

55 See p 420 above.
56 Solicitors (Scotland) Act 1980, ss 50–54 and Sch 4, Pt I. For Rules of 2002 see Parliament House Book F272.
57 Solicitors (Scotland) Act 1980, ss 50–54.
58 Law Reform (Miscellaneous Provisions) (Scotland) Act 1990, s 34.

conveyancers, as well as the Law Society. The Ombudsman cannot overrule the decisions of the professional body. She can only make recommendations to it. She may recommend a particular form of redress or further procedure in relation to an individual complaint, and she may make broader recommendations about the manner of dealing with such complaints or complaints in general. Under the Scottish Legal Services Ombudsman Etc Act 1997, s 2 she can recommend that the profession complained of should pay compensation of up to £1,200 to the complainer for loss, inconvenience and distress. If the Society ignores her recommendations she can publish notices recording that face. She also has power to refer cases directly to the Scottish Solicitors' Discipline Tribunal. In 2006–07 the Ombudsman received 405 complaints about the handling of complaints, all but 13 concerning the Law Society[59]; and prepared 539 Opinions. The Justice One Committee in its report on the handling of complaints by the legal profession urged that the Ombudsman's powers should be strengthened. However the Legal Profession and Legal Aid (Scotland) Act 2007 will when it comes into force replace the Ombudsman by a Scottish Legal Complaints Commission.

PRIVILEGES

Advocates have long enjoyed the monopoly of representing clients in the Court of Session, High Court of Justiciary, and equivalent courts. In addition they have the same rights as English barristers to appear before the House of Lords and Judicial Committee of the Privy Council. They now have to share representation in the Scottish superior courts with suitably qualified Scottish solicitors. Members of Bars of European Community member states may also appear in these courts, in conjunction with advocates and now qualified solicitors[60]. Members of the Bars of England and Wales and of Northern Ireland may also apply to practise before the superior courts[61]. Advocates have the right to appear in any court and tribunal within Scotland.

---

59 Scottish Legal Services Ombudsman, Annual Report. Her address is 17 Waterloo Place, Edinburgh. The office will be replaced by a Scottish Legal Complaints Commission under the Legal Profession and Legal Aid (Scotland) Bill. For a report on proceedings against an advocate, the complaint against whom was dismissed, see 2007 SLT (News) 76.
60 European Communities (Services by Lawyers) Order 1978, SI 1978/1910.
61 Law Reform (Miscellaneous Provisions) (Scotland) Act 1990, s 30.

Solicitors may appear in any sheriff or district court and tribunal in Scotland. Since 1993 certain of them have been granted the right of audience in the Court of Session, or the High Court or both[62]. For at least five years continuously before the application they must have had experience in advocacy or as solicitors instructing advocates. They must undergo an induction course in the rules and practice of the court to which they seek admission and undertake 'sitting-in' for a certain number of days in that court. Finally, they must sit and pass an examination in civil and/or criminal procedures. Training courses are also provided by the Law Society and must be attended by any applicant with less than ten years' experience as an instructing solicitor in the Court of Session or advocacy in solemn criminal procedure[63].

Solicitors have long enjoyed a monopoly in the preparation of deeds for reward, which in effect gave them a monopoly of conveyancing, the transfer of land and buildings, etc. For a few years those who were qualified in conveyancing, but not fully solicitors, were appointed licensed conveyancers and come now under the jurisdiction of the Law Society. They number just 21.

ALTERNATIVE WAYS OF DELIVERING LEGAL SERVICES

The legal profession is the most conspicuous provider of legal services. However, being motivated primarily by profitability, without which its members would not remain in business, it understandably concentrates on those services in which payment of fees is virtually assured, such as home ownership, financial services, and the distribution of the assets of the deceased. In recent years competition from estate agents, banks and accountants has led the legal profession to defend its stake in these areas vigorously. But there are many other needs for law. Those who are charged with crimes, or whose marriages break down, or who are dismissed from their jobs, are unwillingly caught up in the law. There are many other rarer events which lead people either to need to use the law or to find it being used against them. Yet the cost of legal services is such that most of these people will find them well beyond their means. Should they be enabled to get access to the law and, if so, how?

If people do not know of the laws that might benefit them, or lack

---

62 Law Reform (Miscellaneous Provisions) (Scotland) Act 1990, s 24.
63 Admission as a Solicitor with Extended Rights (Scotland) Rules 1992.

the means to utilise them, they are at a profound disadvantage compared with those who do have such knowledge and ability. Moreover, the purposes of the state in providing through legislation certain benefits are thwarted. In the period of the foundation of the welfare state, following the Second World War, an attempt was made to correct these defects. The principle was first established that people who had limited financial means and a genuine case should be enabled to raise and defend proceedings in court. They might well not have to do so, for their bargaining position would be greatly strengthened because the state would pay in whole or part for whatever services of lawyers were necessary. This principle was given effect to in the Legal Aid and Solicitors (Scotland) Act 1949. It is now repealed but the principle is still embodied in its main replacement, the Legal Aid (Scotland) Act 1986.

The legal aid schemes

The first form that legal aid took was in civil proceedings, for which it was made available from 1950. In its present form it enables people who pass means tests regarding their income and capital to be represented by solicitors or advocates in the House of Lords, Court of Session, sheriff courts, Scottish Land Court, Lands Valuation Appeal Court, Lands Tribunal for Scotland, Restrictive Practices Court and the Employment Appeal Tribunal[64].

In 1964 legal aid for criminal proceedings in the High Court and sheriff courts was introduced and extended in 1975 to district courts. In summary cases there is a financial condition that the accused must be unable to defend himself without undue hardship to himself or his dependants and have no other means, such as insurance, to cover court expenses. No financial contribution is required. In solemn cases there is no financial test other than undue hardship. In addition, everyone being brought before a court from custody is entitled to initial free advice and representation from a duty solicitor.

In 1972 a system of advice and assistance was introduced. Advice and assistance is oral or written advice on a matter of Scots law provided to a person by a solicitor. It does not include taking steps in connection with instituting, conducting or defending proceedings unless assistance by way of representation (ABWOR) is available.

---

64 An Act of the Scots Parliament of 1424 allowed courts to appoint an advocate in civil cases to 'onie pure creature, for fault of cunning, or expenses, that cannot nor may not follow his cause' (see APS II, 8). In 1535 two advocates for the poor were appointed and Fridays were set aside by the new Court of Session for the hearing of the cases of the poor (Acta Dominorum Concilii III, 434, 438).

There are financial tests of income and capital applied by the lawyer, who also collects any contribution due. Separate initial limits of expenditure apply depending on whether the matter is civil, criminal or relates to children's proceedings:

1. for civil advice and assistance
   - £35 for a "diagnostic interview" – that is, an initial meeting with the client about a matter that is not covered by "standard advice and assistance"
   - £95 or, in some cases, £180 for standard advice and assistance – that is, normally, cases included on an agreed list of categories.
2. for criminal advice and assistance, £80
3. for children's advice and assistance, £95

For most types of case, and provided certain criteria are met, lawyers can grant advice and assistance up to these limits without approval from the Scottish Legal Aid Board. To exceed these limits, they must apply to the Board.

The relative simplicity of the advice and assistance scheme and its administrative economy led to its being extended to cover certain forms of representation under the name of ABWOR (assistance by way of representation). So far ABWOR has been applied to certain summary criminal proceedings, such as changes of plea to guilty and proofs in mitigation of sentence, to applications and appeals to the sheriff by patients under the Mental Health (Scotland) Act 1984, to disciplinary proceedings before a prison governor, to applications for removal of a driving disqualification, and to unopposed petitions for the appointment of an executor, to those appearing from custody following breach of interdict and to life prisoners wishing to challenge their tariffs[65]. Subject to a few exceptions, the usual financial test for advice and assistance applies, and ABWOR is subject to the normal rules for limits on authorised expenditure. Solicitors may, in some cases, need the Board's prior approval to provide ABWOR.

There are special provisions for legal aid for children, who are assessed without regard to their parents' resources.

Administration of legal aid

Legal aid was administered from 1950 by committees of the Law Society of Scotland. The Hughes Royal Commission criticised this arrangement as 'wrong in principle' and by the Legal Aid (Scotland) Act of 1986 the Scottish Legal Aid Board was set up. It is classed

---

65 *The Parliament House Book* G 850.

officially as a 'non-departmental public body', sponsored by the Scottish Executive. It disburses on behalf of the Scottish Ministers to solicitors and advocates payments in respect of fees and outlays incurred in giving legal aid to people found eligible under the various schemes. The Board consisted in 2006 of a chairman, Iain Robertson, and ten members, of whom two are solicitors, two advocates and one a sheriff[66]. It operates from one office at 44 Drumsheugh Gardens, in the centre of Edinburgh.

Eligibility

The Board, through its staff, is responsible for most of the decisions that have to be taken on whether legal aid is to be granted or not. In a limited number of cases, judges still decide, but this is to end.

Civil legal aid. In civil legal aid the legal tests are (1) whether as pursuer or defender the applicant has a probable cause for litigating, that is, an arguable case in law backed up by sufficient evidence, and (2) whether it is reasonable in the circumstances that legal aid should be made available. Solicitors submit a sketch of the client's case in law and statements taken from potential witnesses. In straightforward cases staff of the Board take the decision, but it has also a panel of solicitors and advocates, to whom, as reporters, difficult cases can be referred. The opponent is given a chance to object to any proposed award of legal aid. Civil legal aid is not awarded if an organisation such as a trade union, insurance company or motoring organisation is available to pay. In actions of defamation or verbal injury it cannot be awarded.

There is also a financial test which is applied by the Board. Annual income and capital from all sources are separately assessed. Deductions are made in respect of dependants, housing costs, debts, National Insurance, tax etc. The applicant's home and its furnishings, clothing and tools are disregarded in assessing capital. If the applicant's annual disposable income does not exceed £2,995 or his disposable capital does not exceed £6,640 he is on income support or income-related job-seeker's allowance he is eligible with no contribution. If he has disposable capital over £11,070 he may be refused. If he has annual income over £9,871 he is ineligible. He may have to make a contribution out of disposable income or

---

66 On the Board's operations see its annual reports. For a comprehensive collection of legal aid legislation, see *The Parliament House Book* Division G. For the fullest commentary on the legislation, see Charles N Stoddart *Law and Practice of Legal Aid in Scotland* (4th edn, 1994 and supplement).

disposable capital or both between certain amounts. Those who fall in between these lower and upper financial limits are eligible, subject to having to make a fixed contribution, regardless of the length or complexity of the case. It may be paid by instalments from income, usually over ten months. In 2005-06 27% of those who received civil legal aid had to pay a contribution. In these calculations the income and capital of husband and wife (and of couples living together as such) is aggregated, unless they have opposed interests – as in divorce – or are separated.

To avoid financial hardship arising out of the award of civil legal aid, courts can modify the award of expenses in two ways. Normally the successful party is awarded the expenses of the action against the unsuccessful one. If an unassisted party wins, then the award of expenses against an assisted person is not to exceed a sum which in the opinion of the court it is reasonable for him to pay, having regard to the means of the parties and their conduct in the dispute (Legal Aid (Scotland) Act 1986, s 18). That might leave the successful unassisted party in a position of hardship. So the court may, secondly, award him all or part of his expenses out of the Legal Aid Fund, provided severe hardship would otherwise result and it is just and equitable to do so (1986 Act, s 19).

Criminal legal aid. In applications for criminal legal aid in summary prosecutions the legal test is that it is in the interests of justice that legal aid should be granted. Until 1986 no specification of this vague test was given and, as the award was granted by different sheriffs and justices, widespread differences occurred. Now the 1986 Act lists examples where legal aid should be provided, such as that a substantial question of law may arise or that the accused has difficulty in understanding the proceedings (s 24(3)). The financial test of undue hardship to the accused or his dependants is interpreted by the Board in a broad way, without the stringency of civil legal aid (s 24).

In solemn procedure it is assumed that the matter is grave enough to justify the award of legal aid, provided the test of undue hardship is met. It is the court that takes that decision, a function that is to be moved to the Board. Again, where a summary court is considering whether to impose a first sentence of imprisonment, it decides whether to award criminal legal aid on the hardship test (s 23). Applications for aid in criminal appeals are decided by the Board, which has to apply the hardship test and check that there are substantial grounds for making the appeal and that it is reasonable to do so (s 25).

Solicitors providing criminal legal aid have from 1 October 1998 had to be registered as such and agree to abide by a Code of Practice laying down their responsibilities towards the Board and clients in a manner consistent with the Law Society's Code of Conduct for Criminal Work, of 1996.

From the same date the Board began to provide criminal legal aid in summary proceedings in the Edinburgh sheriff and district courts and later in Glasgow and Inverness by means of salaried solicitors.

The fees of solicitors for work done under criminal legal aid have since April 1999 been fixed in accordance with the category of work done (known as block fees), on submission of detailed accounts[67].

Advice and assistance. Advice and Assistance (and its off-shoot ABWOR) is relatively simple and cheap to administer. The only test of eligibility is a financial one and it is applied by the solicitor giving the service (or an employee on his behalf). As with civil legal aid, there is a range of persons whose assets and those of partners entitle them to aid without and with a contribution. Those who receive income support or income-related job-seeker's allowance or have weekly disposable income under £88 can receive aid with no contribution. Those with disposable income between certain limits are liable to pay a contribution on a scale. Those with a weekly free income above £208 and free capital above £1,450 are ineligible. The scheme is a comprehensive one, covering advice, written or oral, on all aspects of the law of Scotland and assistance in making use of it, for example by letters and telephone calls. In 2005-06 411,290 grants of advice and assistance were made.

Costs of legal aid. Legal aid is not subject to cash limits (though its administration costing £12.3 million in 2005-06 is). The demand in any one year could not be predicted with accuracy. The soaring costs of legal aid have been a subject of concern to the Executive and UK Treasury. Great emphasis has been laid on efficiency at all stages of the award of legal aid, including the meeting of targets, and on value for money. In 2005-06 this contributed to a drop of 3% in all forms of legal aid bringing the cost to £147.9 million. However, the use of contracts and franchises with particular firms, as used in England and Wales, has not been adopted.

Deficiencies of legal aid

Such is the official provision of legal aid, as distinct from voluntary efforts, which we have still to mention. What are its defects? There

---

67 In 2006 it is intended to transfer the granting of Criminal Legal Aid from the courts to the Scottish Legal Aid Board, under the Legal Profession and Legal Aid (Scotland) Bill.

are problems with the legal aid schemes, with the lawyers who provide them and with the people who use them.

Unlike social security benefits, the entitlement conditions leading to the benefits of civil legal aid and advice and assistance are not linked to the cost of living. So, as all governments try to contain public expenditure where they can, legal aid entitlements tend not to be sufficiently updated.

Where the objective of an action is to recover compensation, then the sum recovered has to be paid into the Legal Aid Fund, pending decisions as to the expenses incurred by each side in the action. Normally the unsuccessful party has to pay the expenses of the successful party, but in matrimonial cases this is not always so. There can be disputes where each party succeeds to some extent. Settling the question may require another appearance before the court. Which expenditure is included is a matter for assessment by the Auditor of Court. There may also be decisions by the court under the Legal Aid (Scotland) Act 1986, ss 18 and 19[68].

Under what is often called the clawback, the Board takes from the sum paid to it all the outstanding expenses incurred by the Legal Aid Fund (s 17(2B)) (with certain exceptions in family and social security law). The successful litigant gets what is left. That can be little or literally nothing. For example, the sum may be reduced by contributory negligence, or the action may be settled out of court (sometimes without the knowledge of the pursuer) for a sum much less than the notional value of the claim or the sum sued for, because there would be difficulty in proving it. Of course, if the court expenses are all recovered from the unsuccessful side, then the Board may have been fully reimbursed. But the losing party may be unable to pay, or there may still be outstanding costs incurred in preparation for the action which are not covered by the court's award of expenses.

If the dispute is over property, whether heritable (such as land and buildings) or moveable, then, whether the assisted person has successfully made a claim to it or preserved it, the property becomes available to the Board to take unmet expenses out of its value. It has powers to sell moveable property and to require the owner to sell or grant a security over heritable property. This can be particularly hard in a divorce case, where the wife has successfully asserted or defended her rights in the matrimonial home, and no award of expenses is made or the husband is unable to pay them. Then, except for the first £2,500 of its value, the home is subject to the Board's

---

68 *The Parliament House Book* section G 47. See p 430 supra.

claims in respect of the aid it gave. From this power over property most social security and family law payments are exempt[69].

The same clawback principle applies to advice and assistance, but here there will be no payment of expenses by the other side, unless it has been agreed in an out-of-court settlement and paid. But the solicitor can apply to the Board, asking that the clawback be waived on the grounds of hardship. The majority of these applications are granted.

There is a second type of clawback which is not linked to legal aid, but as it affects those who receive most social security benefits, it does act as a second factor reducing any apparent victory in the courts. Where a person on benefit receives compensation for personal injuries or illness over £2,500, by court decree or through negotiation, then the person paying the compensation must first deduct the amount of benefits paid, arising out of the occurrence, up to the date when final payment is made or for five years, whichever comes first, and pay that sum to the Secretary of State for Social Security. That recoupment takes precedence over any reimbursement of the Legal Aid Fund[70].

To the successful legally aided litigant, it may look as if everyone – the government, the solicitors, the advocates – is paid, except him.

However, for most people, involvement with the civil courts is a rare and unwelcome experience. They are more likely to wish to use one of the busier tribunals. Yet, for them, no legal aid for representation is available. The only exceptions are the Employment Appeal Tribunal and the Lands Tribunal for Scotland, both of which are presided over by judges and almost the same as courts, apart from the participation of lay members along with the judge. For proceedings in these tribunals, civil legal aid is available. If one is financially qualified, it is possible to ask for advice under the Advice and Assistance scheme on how to present one's own case. But relatively little use is made of this possibility.

The government's attitude is that tribunals are supposed to be informal. The intervention of lawyers would tend to make them more formal. But, of course, lawyers are not actually debarred from attending. And in the Employment (formerly Industrial) Tribunals, where two private parties, the employee and the employer, are in dispute, much as in a civil court, the employers are usually represented by a solicitor or advocate and the employee will have to speak for himself. The involvement of lawyers and a legally qualified full-

69 *The Parliament House Book* G 605.
70 Social Security Administration Act 1992, Pt IV.

time chairman has led to the procedure of Employment Tribunals becoming quite formal and complex. Hundreds of appeals have been taken, usually by employers, to the courts and thus the brief statutory provisions are surrounded by case law. This creates a legal minefield for the applicant making his one and only appearance before an Employment Tribunal, and puts him at a serious disadvantage.

Another weakness of the legal aid provisions is that they accommodate individuals, not groups. It is one person who must show an interest and be financially assessed. But nowadays many cases arise which affect groups of people, for example, tenants in a block of damp flats or victims of harmful medication. Even by pooling their resources, they may be unable to afford to prepare a case against a powerful and well-informed adversary. The best they can hope for is to put forward one of their number who does qualify for legal aid, seek a decision on his case and hope that, if favourable, it will be applied to the others as a test case[71].

Then there are obstacles on the part of lawyers. The range of possible inquiries under advice and assistance can extend over the whole of the law operating in Scotland. But lawyers tend to know best the parts that they make a steady living from: mainly conveyancing, wills, trusts and succession, contracts and delict, divorce and other family disputes. Although they should be able to discover the answer to any legal question or problem, given time, the remuneration that they get from the Scottish Legal Aid Board, in the opinion of many of them, simply does not adequately cover the cost. Solicitors expect to earn at least £100 an hour, to cover their constant overheads, such as paying staff, rent of premises and equipment, etc and their own pay. Those with commercial clients would charge far more. But the legal aid scales often fall far short. For instance, under advice and assistance a solicitor can be paid £12.75 for 15 minutes for a meeting with the client and £2.90 for a short letter or framing a formal document[72]. Moreover, authorised outlays such as the cost of police and hospital reports or advertisements have

71 See, for example, *McColl v Strathclyde Regional Council* 1983 SLT 616, where a Glasgow pensioner, with legal aid, sought to interdict the council from fluoridation of the public water supply. Lord Jauncey commented 'it would be naive to assume that the petitioner alone has an interest in the outcome of this action'. His decision that the council lacked powers to fluoridise water held up the practice throughout Scotland for several years. See also *McInally v John Wyeth and Brother Ltd* 1992 SLT 344 where, in an action arising out of damage allegedly suffered by the user of a tranquilliser, the success of one pursuer in obtaining production of documents benefited other claimants co-ordinated by a tranquilliser addiction solicitors group.
72 *The Parliament House Book* G 592.

to be paid by the lawyer in the first place, in the expectation that they will eventually be recovered from the Board. The accounts have to be submitted in such minute detail and based on record-keeping of the length of each meeting, letter or phone call that many solicitors just refuse to have anything to do with advice and assistance, or in minor cases of pure advice they will opt for a standard fee of £25, regardless of the work involved, for that does not require the preparation of detailed accounts[73].

From the point of view of the person with a problem, there are barriers which are not so readily measurable, but are nevertheless real. Firstly, the person with a problem may not recognise that it has or might have a legal solution. For many people, the law means trouble and trouble equates with the police. Others with a wider view may not think of the law as having anything to do with social security. Even on learning, through advice and assistance, that a problem might be solved by raising a small claim action, a person may be put off by the idea of standing up in court (there being no civil legal aid for such cases) or put off by the risk of losing and having to meet the other side's expenses. These are restricted to £75, but that limitation does not apply if there is an appeal to the sheriff principal.

For people living in rural areas there may be no accessible solicitor or the only one may be acting for the opponent. Residents of peripheral city housing schemes for whom travel to a city centre is a costly matter may simply put up with a grievance that might have a legal resolution or they will pursue it through a councillor. But no doubt if recourse to a solicitor is unavoidable, they will make the effort and go to where one can be found. Recognising the difficulties, some firms have opened branch offices in housing schemes, but as the business is likely to be all legally aided, they have difficulty in making such offices pay.

Finally, there are matters of image. Among some sections of the population lawyers have the reputation of being aloof and grasping, and so best avoided, a reputation they have sought to dispel by advertising campaigns.

These obstacles are confirmed by the sharp decrease in some forms of legal aid. In the ten years before 2005–06 applications and grants of civil legal aid fell by over 40%. The Board suggest this may be due to a drop in fault-based divorces which with other family cases make up 70% of the civil law cases. Grants of advice and assistance have been falling for the last seven years and in 2005–06 were

---

73 Ibid G 593

9% down on the previous year. Criminal cases, combining advice and assistance and representation in court, as often happens, increased over the five years to 2005-06, but in that year fell by 5%, still £104 in monetary terms. This was in spite of automatic awards in the Glasgow Domestic Abuse Court and the Drug Courts in Glasgow, Kirkcaldy and Dunfermline.

The Board makes sure that people who seek information on any form of legal aid have access to it by phone on the Legal Aid Helpline (0845-122-8686 Monday to Friday 9 to 5). Fewer solicitors have been offering legal aid because of the low rates of pay, but an increase of 16% in their block fees in 2005–06 may serve to remedy this.

Dial-a-law

An attempt has been made to make the services of solicitors more accessible by the Law Society's Dial-a-law service. This is a list of over 40 recorded messages on common legal problems and how solicitors can help. It can be accessed 24 hours a day through the Society's website: http://www.lawscot.org.uk by clicking on Dial-a-law. In its first year Dial-a-law (then a much more accessible telephone service) received about 10,000 calls and referrals were made to 1,200 firms of solicitors.

Other sources of aid

However, there are other means by which people can obtain help with the law besides the legal profession and also ways to ease access to professional legal services.

Citizens Advice Bureaux

The Citizens Advice Bureaux network (CABx) is prominently involved in both these developments. Founded in 1939 on the outbreak of the Second World War, it operates in over 200 locations covering most of Scotland, including the islands. They are organised by full-time managers, but rely for their advisers almost entirely 2,273 trained, unpaid volunteers. No charge is made for help and the bureaux rely for their funding mainly on local authorities. The government sustains financially a supportive central organisation, Citizens Advice Scotland (or CAS), based in Edinburgh, which provides training and a continuously updated information system and ensures that standards are maintained in the local bureaux.

The CABx in Scotland dealt in 2005/06 with a total of 442,550 problems. CAS does not gather separate figures for inquiries on law, but most of its categories are based on legal rights and obligations. For example, in the same year there were 48,563 inquiries on employment matters, 43,085 on housing and 138,415 on social security benefits, much the largest number.

In all these areas advice is given and negotiations are conducted on the basis of a basic knowledge of the relevant law. This is supplied initially in training courses for volunteers and kept up to date by CAS. To deal with the more difficult questions a full-time legal adviser can be contacted at CAS by telephone or fax. Where a problem seems to need the services of a solicitor, for example, in marriage breakdown, the inquirer can be put in touch with one. Many firms provide, on a rota basis, services at CABx legal clinics in the evenings, often utilising the advice and assistance scheme.

As well as legal advice the Citizens Advice movement is increasingly becoming involved in representing clients at certain tribunals, among them Employment Tribunals and Disability Appeal Tribunals. In 2005–06, 3,011 clients had their cases presented to tribunals by trained volunteers.

The figure of 442,550 inquiries compares with 441,290 intimations of the giving of Advice and Assistance by lawyers in 2005–06. One may reasonably conclude, therefore, that the CABx are the largest providers of basic legal services in Scotland and the first port of call for a majority of people in need of them, albeit that a minority will have to be referred to solicitors.

Money advice centres

Overlapping with the Citizens Advice Bureaux are the specialised Money Advice Services, agencies which were set up in the 1980s in response to the increasing number of debt problems which followed the easier availability of credit through credit cards, store budget accounts, home mortgages etc. Some are adjuncts of Citizens Advice Bureaux, some are run by local authority consumer protection and trading standards departments and some are independent bodies started by local initiatives in deprived areas, some of them funded by Social Inclusion Partnerships. They specialise in negotiating payment arrangements on behalf of people faced with multiple debts and thus have to act within the constraints of the law on debt enforcement and bankruptcy.

Law centres

Law centres are non-profit-making charitable bodies, staffed by legally qualified staff and support staff. They exist to make up the lack of traditional legal services in deprived areas and concentrate on the branches of the law that could most benefit the residents of such areas, such as social security, housing, consumer protection and immigration. As well as advising individuals and groups, they give training to other users of the law, such as tenants' associations and disabled groups, and they raise awareness of the law and legal issues among residents generally. Some strive to change the law to the benefit of disadvantaged people by taking up test cases or campaigning for reforms in statutory law and law enforcement.

In England and Wales there are about 60 law centres, most of them funded by local authorities or the Lord Chancellor's Department. In Scotland they were later to develop and were denied central government funding. However, some were established with Urban Programme funding for limited periods. From April 1999 this has been replaced by the Social Inclusion Partnership, which is not confined to urban areas and not subject to time limits.

The longest-established law centre in Scotland is at Castlemilk, on the southern outskirts of Glasgow. It receives funding from the City of Glasgow Council. It holds conferences and produces publications, thus spreading knowledge of its more successful ventures, such as obtaining awards from the Criminal Injuries Compensation Agency for abused children and from landlords for illness attributable to dampness in defective houses.

For more than a decade Castlemilk was Scotland's only territorial law centre on the English model. However, in 1992 a similar law centre was set up in the Glasgow housing scheme of Drumchapel. Others followed in Glasgow East End, Clydebank, Dumbarton, Govan and Paisley. The Dundee North Law Centre was sponsored by the Dundee Legal Advice Association, which began in 1974. The Centre replaced it in 2002 and employs three solicitors.

A law centre based on the needs of a particular class of people, though still within a defined area, was set up in 1992 – the Ethnic Minorities Law Centre in the centre of Glasgow and now in Edinburgh also in association with the Citizens Advice Bureau there. It was created on the initiative of the Glasgow Community Relations Council and specialises in immigration, nationality, racial discrimination and housing matters. It is staffed by a solicitor and an advice and development officer and is funded by Glasgow Council. Shelter provides an advice service on housing law.

Another agency organised around the needs of a particular

interest-group is the Scottish Child Law Centre, based in Edinburgh. It was founded in 1988 to promote knowledge of and use of Scots law for the benefit of children and young people up to the age of 18. It offers them a Freephone telephone advice service (number 0800 328 8970). They can also use their mobile phones to send a text message. Key in 'SCLC', the question, and 80800 someone will then phone back. It also takes inquiries from social workers, teachers and others whose work is among children (number 0131 667 6333). It has a website at www.sclc.org.uk. It has played a prominent part in promoting reform of the law on children, especially as contained in the Children (Scotland) Act 1995, on which it has published an explanatory book. It is maintained by the Scottish Executive and local authorities.

Still another specialised venture in non-profit-making legal services is the Legal Services Agency, a limited company based in Glasgow, which undertakes case work, court and tribunal representation in cases likely to yield some clarification of the law. It also specialises in holding seminars and conferences in subjects of concern to disadvantaged groups. Prominent among these are the mentally ill. It runs a Mental Health Legal Representation Project which tackles not only mental health problems, but also those of dementia and brain injury.

Insurance companies

Certain insurance companies offer legal advice by telephone. The Automobile Association provides members with free legal advice and representation in relation to motoring matters.

Trade unions

Some of the major trade unions provide legal services for their members, either through their own staff or by standing arrangements with certain firms of solicitors to provide a free interview for members with any legal problem, whether or not related to employment, and, if there is a case to be pursued, how it can be financed, which in some cases might be through the union.

Qualified conveyancers and executry practitioners

To break the monopoly of solicitors in their most profitable areas of work and stimulate competition, the Conservative government in its

Law Reform (Miscellaneous Provisions)(Scotland) Act 1990 made provision for two new kinds of supplier of legal services – qualified conveyancers and executry practitioners. They were, respectively, to supply solely conveyancing services and executry services (ingathering and distributing the assets of deceased persons). A Scottish Conveyancing and Executry Services Board was set up by s 16 of the 1990 Act to keep registers of 'fit and proper persons' to fulfil these roles, set standards of education and training and exercise disciplinary functions akin to those of the Law Society. Financial institutions, such as banks and building societies and insurance companies, were to be permitted to provide executry services, under regulations as to the qualifications and training of those who provided the services. But that provision was not brought into effect. These opportunities did not prove attractive and in 2003 the Executive announced the abolition of the Board. However there are still 21 Licensed Conveyancers who are supervised by the Law Society.

15. Law reform

WHY LAW REFORM?

To be effective a law must be capable of being discovered and understood, so that people can know what is required of them. But there is no point in a law having these attributes if it is incapable of meeting changing human needs and wants or is plainly out of date. So an efficient law system must make provision for its own development. There has to be a mechanism for making brand-new laws, repealing outdated laws, and amending laws that are no longer able to achieve their goals.

Most changes in the law are of a minor character, adding to what is there already. A section in an Act turns out to be ambiguous and courts are interpreting it in different ways. Or it has left a loop-hole of which people, perhaps tax-payers or motorists, are taking advantage. The Misuse of Drugs Act 1971 has a provision enabling new drugs to be added to the list of controlled drugs by a resolution of both Houses of the UK Parliament. The highest court may resolve the problem by upholding one of the conflicting interpretations applied in lower courts. Or a department of government may secure an amendment of an unsatisfactory section by Parliament.

Apart from such deliberate changes, whenever existing law is applied by a court to new circumstances and a reasoned judgment is delivered and published, the law has been developed, even if only to a trivial extent. We can call this normal legal development. The law never stands still. It is always on the move, as it keeps being applied to new situations.

However, a law system should be capable of striking off in new directions or making a fresh start to some outmoded form of regulation. This is law reform and it is usually confined to the enacted law that Parliament produces, though occasionally judges can engage in law reform in what turns out to have been a dramatic way. Thus, in *Stallard(or s) v HM Advocate* 1989 SLT 469, 1989 SCCR 248 the judges decided that a wife could no longer be said to surrender herself to her husband's sexual demands. They were equal partners and he could be charged with raping her, as with any other person. Law reform is usually prompted by some assumptions as to what is right or good or necessary and thus to reflect a presumed social need. But sometimes, as in laws against racial and sexual discrimination, the law has an educative role and sets new standards that are in advance of social behaviour.

PRESSURES FOR LAW REFORM

Technological change

What are these cues that signal a need for law reform? Perhaps the most tangible is when some new technology or technique becomes available that has a potential for harm as well as good. The most obvious example is the advent and expansion of motor traffic, which revolutionised the transport of goods and people, but at the cost of killing and maiming many road users. A vast array of laws and regulations has been devised to try to contain these unwanted consequences. The introduction of a 30mph speed limit in built-up areas in 1934 was followed by a dramatic drop in road deaths. The advent of the breathalyser in the Road Safety Act 1967, now followed, under the Road Traffic Act 1988, ss 6 to 8, by a test of the alcoholic content of breath, blood or urine, avoided the difficulties of proving unfitness to drive through drink or drugs.

Sometimes the law's reaction is of a less coercive and punitive kind than road traffic law. Medical science has advanced rapidly in recent years in two ethically problematical areas: the transplanting of human organs and the use of embryos in assisting pregnancy and medical experiments. The general public has shown some concern at these developments and the medical profession itself looked for a clear statement of what is ethically permissible. The Human Tissue Act 2004 attempts to answer these questions.

Yet sometimes the new development appears out of the blue without human volition. The HIV virus, which is believed to cause the life-threatening condition of AIDS, has raised questions as to whether there is a role for law in charting its advance and impeding its transmission and whether tests for HIV should be performed, and if so, with or without consent. So far legislation is limited to the AIDS (Control) Act 1987, which requires health authorities to make reports on HIV and AIDS to the Secretary of State to facilitate the collection of statistics on their spread, and allows the detention of apparent sufferers.

Political pressure

Often the demand for law reform is put forward as part of the programme of a political party. Parties in a multi-party society such as ours exist to promote their vision of a better society (or, as some of them would say, to advance the interests of a class within it). So whatever they propose in and out of government is likely to meet with resistance from the other parties. But the SNP minority government, elected in 2007, requires consultation with and the support of other parties to enact any laws. Together they help through public debate to clarify the options for change. The reform, when it comes, will nearly always take the form of new law. Thus, throughout the 1980s industrial relations and the powers of trade unions were a highly contentious political topic. The prior law was transformed by six employment and trade union Acts between 1980 and 1990. Most were consolidated in the Employment Rights Act 1996 which was amended, in accordance with the policies of the Labour Government, in the Employment Act 2002.

A further form of pressure for law reform is created when a law system is expanded and the bounds of the territory in which it operates are redrawn. This has been one major consequence among many of the United Kingdom's membership of the European Community. As a member state the United Kingdom obliged itself to give effect to directives by the Commission. The implementation of the Single European Act by the end of 1992 with the object of equalising trading conditions throughout the Community impinges on innumerable areas of domestic law by setting uniform standards, such as on water quality and pollution.

Political and moral values

Behind many of these demands for change there lie tacit or explicit changes in values or conflict among rival value systems. Thus, the policies of the Labour Party, for example, in education and health, tend to exhibit a preference for equality and community action which translated into the public provision of services, show a tendency which became less distinct under the Blair administration. Those of the Conservative Party show a preference for individual choice and thus encourage a variety of services privately supplied. Sometimes, as on the suppression of dealings in dangerous drugs by the criminal law, the parties share a common stance. But some calls for law reform show straight clashes of values held by citizens, unmediated by political institutions. Thus, attempts to change the law on abortion, to make it either easier or more restrictive, reflect differing beliefs on the value of human life and the point from which it merits protection. The lowering to 16 of the age at which consensual male homosexual acts are permitted has cut across party political boundaries.

THE INSTRUMENTS OF LAW REFORM

How is this requirement that the law be kept up to date achieved? As shown above, the normal means is through legislation. But before examining how enacted law is used to revise the law, we should first examine what scope other sources of law play in this task.

Custom

Custom is so diffuse and uncoordinated that one would not expect it to be of use in the purposive enterprise which law reform requires. But on rare occasions concerted and sustained action may have the effect of changing the law. Thus, before the passing of the Abortion Act 1967, abortion was an offence at common law only. But most gynaecologists in Scotland did perform abortions in hospitals to save the life or avert serious risk to the health of pregnant women; and in so far as they did not incur prosecution, it could be said that a custom had emerged among leading gynaecologists and the Crown Office, tacitly amending the criminal law on abortion so as to exclude those performed by medical practitioners for therapeutic reasons. Under the guidance of a Scottish Office circular the medical profession until the Age of Legal Capacity (Scotland) Act 1991 had a firm practice of requiring the written consent of parents and guardians to treatment of children up to the age of 16, which ignored the common law of minority in Scots law[1].

Institutional writers

Institutional writers purported to declare and expound the law, including customary law, whether unwritten or evidenced in the decisions of courts. They did not therefore claim to be making law, though in gathering it, organising it and drawing inferences from it, they certainly developed it. But it would be misleading to describe this activity as an exercise in law reform.

Judges

Judges do from time to time have opportunities to reform the law in a deliberate way. Whether they seize the opportunity depends in part

1   See Scottish Law Commission, Report no 110, para 27.

on their temperament and in part on the scope that existing law affords them. It is mainly judges in the appellate courts who have the chance to reform the law. If the parties are able to pay for the full pleadings and exhaustive debate that civil appeals are given, it is likely that more is at stake than the outcome of the one case. An insurance company may want a ruling to settle some point concerning the assessment of damages. A local authority may want the legality of a financial practice followed by several others determined. (See eg *Morgan Guaranty Trust Co v Lothian Regional Council* 1995 SC151, 1995 SLT 299.) Judges will give a ruling arising out of the closest scrutiny of the facts of a genuine dispute. They are not considering the question, as Parliament does, in abstract terms. But if the matter is one in which the government of the day takes an interest, there is a risk that it will introduce a Bill to undo the change in the law, or even exceptionally to nullify the court's decision[2].

The response of the judiciary to the opportunity to reform the law can be expressed in some generalisations. Broadly speaking, Scottish judges in civil appeals are less willing to declare that they are changing the law than some English judges. This may be because they know there is the possibility of a further appeal to the House of Lords. Certainly some Scottish judges when sitting in the House of Lords have been at least as innovative as their English colleagues. Lord Kilbrandon, Lord Fraser and Lord Reid (though he was never a judge in Scotland) are examples. On the other hand, the criminal law of Scotland, which is not subject to appeal to the Lords and most of which is the creation of judges, not statute, is regularly developed by judges, though often without their declaring that they are doing so. Thus, in a few unpretentious cases the law of theft was expanded to embrace situations where there was only a temporary removal of another's property with no intention to appropriate it[3], or merely unlawful retention of it[4]. The conduct in question was denounced as 'nefarious' and that was enough to make it criminal by extension of the law of theft.

2   This occurred when the decision of the House of Lords in favour of the company in *Burmah Oil Co Ltd v Lord Advocate* 1964 SC(HL) 117 was overturned in the War Damage Act 1965. See Stott *Lord Advocate's Diary* p 145.
3   *Milne v Tudhope* 1981 JC 53.
4   *Kidston v Annan* 1984 SLT 279, 1984 SCCR 20. And see *Black v Carmichael* 1992 SLT 897, 1992 SCCR 709, where the wheel-clamping of a vehicle without removing it was held to be theft.

Signals to Parliament

The responses of judges to an invitation explicitly to develop the law may be arranged on a scale from timidity to boldness. Firstly, a judge may note a gap in the law or an unjust consequence of the law, but declare that it is for Parliament to remedy it. Thus, the Adoption Act 1930 required that a minor child consent to his or her own adoption. In B and B 1965 SC 44 the child was mentally retarded and unable to give consent. Although the adoption would be to the child's benefit, Lord Clyde declined to approve it as to do so would in effect be to amend an Act of Parliament. But the case did draw attention to the need for reform and by the Law Reform (Miscellaneous Provisions) (Scotland) Act 1966, s 4 the child's consent could be dispensed with (now Age of Legal Capacity (Scotland) Act 1991, s 2(3)). Since the creation of the Scottish Law Commission judges have been able to point to it as able to give more thorough consideration to the need for law reform than can judges adjudicating in a single dispute[5].

Overruling

Secondly, judges may overrule an unsatisfactory past decision. Thus, in *Dick v Burgh of Falkirk* 1976 SC(HL) 1 the question was whether a widow, as well as taking over as executor her late husband's action of reparation for injuries sustained at work, could also seek an award for herself for solatium and loss of support. The Court of Session judges felt constrained to follow a decision of the House of Lords in *Darling v Gray & Sons* (1892) 19 R(HL) 31 'despite the injustices which may follow from it' (per Lord Wheatley). But in the House of Lords the judges readily overruled the decision of their predecessors in Darling as 'wrongly decided', Lord Kilbrandon pointing out that 'your Lordships are here to do justice between the appellant and the respondents and should not leave it to Parliament to act on the recommendations of the Scottish Law Commission in Report 31 on the subject'. It was perhaps also significant that it was the Law Lords who created the injustice and it was therefore appropriate that they should remedy it at the first opportunity.

---

5   See Lord Reid in *McKendrick v Sinclair* 1972 SC(HL) 25; Lord Kissen in *Dick v Burgh of Falkirk* 1976 SC(HL) 1 at 7.

Reformulating case law

Thirdly, judges of the highest courts may reformulate case law in a new and broader manner and thus open up the way to a new line of cases. The best known and most dramatic example of this practice is the celebrated snail-in-the-gingerbeer-bottle case of *Donoghue v Stevenson* 1932 SC(HL) 31. In the case of *Mullen v Barr* 1929 SC 461 the Inner House of the Court of Session had held that the law did not require bottlers to maintain an infallible system to exclude mice from ginger beer bottles. But in Donoghue Lord Atkin in the House of Lords not only held that the manufacturer of a product not open to intermediate inspection owed a duty of care to the consumer of it; he also stated a general principle of negligence, to the effect that 'you must take reasonable care to avoid acts or omissions which you can reasonably foresee would be likely to injure your neighbour' (at 44). Though the majority in the Lords was only 3 to 2, *Donoghue v Stevenson* has been as significant a reform of consumer protection law in the United Kingdom and many Commonwealth countries as any statute, and has also been the springboard for the development of liability for several other forms of negligence.

In another House of Lords 'reformulating' case, *RHM Bakeries v Strathclyde Regional Council* 1985 SC(HL) 17, Lord Fraser showed himself to be anxious to dispel any suggestion that a person who creates a structure on land, such as a dam, is strictly liable for any consequential damage. Single-handed (the other Lords concurring), he re-interpreted an earlier case, *Kerr v Earl of Orkney* (1857) 20 D 298, described the suggestion that the English strict liability case of *Rylands v Fletcher* (1868) LR 3 HL 330 was part of Scots law as 'a heresy which ought to be extirpated', distinguished the House of Lords decision of *Caledonian Railway Co v Greenock Corporation* 1917 SC(HL) 56 as involving not a dam but a diverted stream, and thus reversed the decision of the Inner House.

Prospective change

Fourthly, judges can go beyond the factual bounds of the case before them and address those who they foresee may face similar but not identical questions in the future. To them they give an indication of the court's thinking on such prospective questions. This can be justified as making a lengthy and expensive recourse to the courts unnecessary. But it has the drawback that the judges deprive themselves of hearing the arguments of counsel on the issue. Lord Denning was an enthusiastic exponent of this practice. In *Jefford v Gee* [1970] 2 QB

130 the Court of Appeal had to interpret a new Act on the award of damages in personal injuries. But Lord Denning as Master of the Rolls said

> 'Parliament has quite understandably left it to the courts to decide the principles on which they should act. Up and down the country people want to know the answer. Trade unions, insurers, accountants, solicitors, barristers, all want to know .... Such is the confusion that we feel it our duty to set out the guide-lines.'

Such a practice comes close to judicial legislation and was almost unknown in Scotland. But in *Smith v M* 1982 SLT 421 Lord Wheatley, who as Lord Justice-Clerk considered nearly all Scottish bail appeals, set out guidelines for all lower judges in saying that where 'the accused was in a position of trust to behave as a good citizen and not to break the law he should be refused bail unless there were cogent reasons for deciding otherwise'. But that the police were making further inquiries was not a sufficient reason for refusing bail. This guidance was not, however, well received by defence lawyers and social workers. In a case which carries the authority of a bench of seven judges, *Morrison v HM Advocate* 1991 SLT 57, 1990 SCCR 235, where the admissibility of a statement by an accused which was both incriminating and exculpating was in issue, Lord Justice-Clerk Ross, giving the opinion of the court, said 'The following is a statement of the law which applies to all such statements', that is, statements made by an accused after the offence and prior to trial, if accurately recorded and fairly obtained. However this clarification of the law in advance in the broadest of terms was not wholly successful. In *McCutcheon v HM Advocate* 2002 SLT 7 a court of nine judges was formed which disapproved of *Morrison* in part as being capable of creating injustice. And in the civil case of *West v Secretary of State for Scotland* 1992 SC 385 at 392 Lord President Hope, noting that guidance should be given as to the scope of judicial review, said he would 'set out what we consider to be the principles which may be used to define the limits of the supervisory jurisdiction of this court'.

Procedural legislation

In the last of these practices judges come close to legislating. Through their power to control the procedure of the courts, they can widen remedies and thus give new access to the law. Through Acts of Sederunt in civil matters and Acts of Adjournal in criminal matters judges do engage in a specialised form of legislation and from their creation until 1756 the Court of Session and High Court produced a mass of law, much of it changing the substantive law[6]. Nowadays such Acts usually merely spell out the consequences for Scottish court procedure of some innovation in the law elsewhere. For example, the power of a court of a member state of the European Community to seek a ruling on a point of Community law from the Court of Justice (under article 177 of the Treaty of Rome) led to the Court of Session amending its Rules of Court by Act of Sederunt. But occasionally the court will be bolder. Thus, the lack of effective remedies against unlawful administrative action had been the subject of criticism in Scotland for many years without response. Lord Fraser (obiter in the House of Lords) in the case of *Brown v Hamilton District Council* 1983 SC(HL) 1, a case on the Housing (Homeless Persons) Act 1977, observed 'It is for consideration whether there might not be advantages in developing special procedures in Scotland for dealing with questions in the public law area'. Lord President Emslie leapt into action and set up a working party under Lord Dunpark which quickly produced a simple scheme for judicial review of administrative decisions, that came into effect as Rule of Court 260B in 1985. A similar rapid reform was the provision of simplified commercial procedure in 1994 by amendment of the Rules of Court, following the recommendations of a Committee under Lord Coulsfield.

The UK and Scottish Parliaments

The UK Parliament

On the surface the most suitable vehicles for changing the law are the legislatures. The individual members that constitute the UK Parliament and the government which controls much of its activity are in touch with most aspects of public life and receptive to complaints of things that are wrong and which the law might remedy. Through select committees MPs who are not in the government can inform themselves on the current state of affairs in most government departments. The law that emerges from Parliament is general in its terms and seeks to determine some form of human conduct for the future. The manner in which it is expressed can be thoroughly considered through the legislative process. Its links with adjacent law can be checked. Finally, the ideology which holds that

---

6   According to the House of Lords, in later condemning this tendency. See *An Introduction to Scottish Legal History* (Stair Society, vol 20, 1958) pp 27, 53.

Parliament expresses the will of the majority of the people who have elected it, gives to measures of law reform approved by it a legitimacy lacking in changes made to law by other means, such as the judgments of judges.

However, most of these points are subject to some qualification. Governments are in fact usually elected by a minority of the electorate and obtain power through their ability to command a majority in the House of Commons. The exigencies of the parliamentary timetable and in particular the crude device of the guillotine by which parts of a Bill may receive no scrutiny at all mean that statutes can turn out to be unworkable in some respect. Sometimes too much activity at the committee or report stages can mean that late amendments are inserted without the draftsmen having a chance to consider fully their impact on other parts of the Bill. The conventions of legislative drafting make the resultant law often incomprehensible to the people who are supposed to comply with it. Nevertheless, the parliamentary process does provide a semblance of popular participation through representatives and an opportunity for careful forethought. It is thus better than any alternative method of law reform. And as we shall see shortly, in some areas of the law Parliament is assisted by the careful preparatory work of the Law Commissions.

Most UK parliamentary time is controlled by the government and in so far as it is used for drafting legislation is taken up with the enactment of the government's own programme as announced in the annual Queen's Speech. Much of that will take the form of new areas of legal coverage. But some kinds of government activity are constantly being monitored by the department concerned and new legislative proposals are frequently brought forward in the hope of improving the existing law and keeping it in line with the government's objectives. Thus, between 1980 and 1989 ten social security Acts were passed (including ones on contributions), an average of one a year. In the same period there were seven Acts on aspects of road traffic.

The Scottish Parliament has no Queen's speech and the Executive has simply issued a statement of its legislation intentions. It is likely that the SNP minority government of 2007 will try to achieve its goals through administrative action.

Law reform Acts

One kind of statute promoted by the government declares itself to be a law reform measure. This is the law reform act. The low priority given to Scottish legislation led to many matters of Scots law being changed by this device. An example of this genre, which aroused much criticism from the legal profession and other quarters, is the

Law Reform (Miscellaneous Provisions) (Scotland) Act 1990, which has 75 sections and 9 Schedules. It includes what amount to whole statutes on charities, on arbitration, and on legal services, including the restructuring of the legal profession, substantial amendments to the law on liquor licensing, provisions on the giving of blood samples in civil proceedings, on the giving of evidence by children and many other lesser matters. Given the heterogeneous character of such Bills, it is difficult to ensure that the standing committee which will scrutinise it in detail is staffed with members who will have an interest in or knowledge of its coverage or to avoid excluding members who are strongly concerned about one of its ingredients.

The Scottish Parliament

The limited opportunities for the examination of legislation affecting Scotland in the Westminster Parliament and the problems Scots people and organisations had in lobbying MPs and attending proceedings there were among the reasons why a devolved form of government for Scotland was created in the Scotland Act 1998. The Consultative Steering Group on the Scottish Parliament in its Report entitled Shaping Scotland's Parliament laid down as a key principle that 'the Scottish Parliament should be accessible, open, responsive and develop procedures which make possible a participative approach to the development, consideration and scrutiny of policy and legislation'. To promote these objectives it recommended that a structure of specialist Committees of MSPs should be set up. They should be able to influence the formulation of policy emanating from the Executive even before a Bill is drafted. In this role they should be accessible to interested organisations and individuals. If authorised to do so under s 23(8) of the Scotland Act 1998 a Committee might require 'any person' to attend its proceedings to give evidence and to produce relevant documents. The Steering Group recommends that these specialised committees should also have the power to initiate legislation. Under the Scotland Act, 1998, Sch 3, para 6, the Parliament has created 16 committees.

The Scotland Act 1998 envisages modification of existing Scots private law or Scots criminal law which bears upon reserved matters as described in s 29(4). A simplified procedure can be created by standing orders under s 36(3) for Bills which merely restate the law and ones which repeal spent laws and for private bills.

The procedures of the Scottish Parliament have on the whole fulfilled these objectives. It is possible for any individual or organisation to petition the Procedures Committee with some grievance which may result in a new or amended law. All Bills promoted by the

Executive are examined in detail by one or more relevant committees who under the Scotland Act 1998, s 23 have been given the
power to summon witnesses including, with certain qualifications,
ministers and civil servants and to call for documents to be
produced. The resultant output of legislation produced during the
Parliament's first four years ranges from the Dog Fouling (Scotland)
Act 2003, introduced by Mr Keith Harding, to two large Executive
Acts on mental health and others making extensive changes to land
law to the extent of the abolition of the feudal system, as one Act
claims. In one of the earliest Bills the then Justice and Home Affairs
Committee took evidence from various women's organisations and
individuals who pointed to the need to have interdicts not only
under the Matrimonial Homes (Family Protection) (Scotland) Act
1981 but where any abuse was claimed to be supported by a power
of police arrest. This resulted in the Protection from Abuse
(Scotland) Act 2001. The Law Society used its experience of operating the main Act of 1980, the Solicitors (Scotland) Act, to enable
any power given to its Council to be exercised with some exceptions
by a sub-committee or individual in the Council of the Law Society
of Scotland Act 2003.

Commissions and committees

Governments were formerly often prompted to introduce legislation
by the reports of Royal Commissions and departmental committees,
composed of people from various walks of life, which they set up to
inquire into some particular problem. Major inquiries included the
Crowther Committee on Consumer Credit, which led to the massive
Consumer Credit Act of 1974, and the Clayson Committee on
Scottish Licensing Law on whose report the Licensing (Scotland)
Act of 1976 is based. Under the administrations of Margaret
Thatcher this method of law reform fell out of favour as being too
slow and liable to produce proposals unacceptable to the government. The major reform of social security in the Social Security Act
1986 was based on the work of small review teams chaired by ministers. Where, exceptionally, external bodies are created to recommend
changes in public policy they are now given a clear indication of the
direction of the reform expected of them and set a time limit within
which to report[7]. The Scottish Executive has made little use of ad

7   Eg the Sheehy Inquiry into Police Responsibilities and Rewards (1993) (Cm
    2280); the Maclean Committee on Serious Violent and Sexual Offenders
    (1999). A Royal Commission on reform of the House of Lords was set up in
    December 1998 to report by 31 December 1999.

hoc committees, perhaps because of the accessibility of the Committees of the Parliament. Thus the Justice I Committee in 2001 began an investigation of the regulation of the legal profession, including under that term judges, sheriff officers and prosecutors. It soon decided that this was a burdensome task and confined itself to the treatment of complaints against solicitors, advocates and conveyancing and executry practitioners. The typical mode of paving the way for law reform practised by the Executive has been the issue of consultation papers, to which any interested party can respond.

Private members' Bills

At Westminster individual MPs who have limited access to the legislative process through the annual ballot for the chance to introduce a Bill can bring about law reform. Usually it takes the form of a limited amendment to existing law, which has been shown to be defective[8]. Large-scale innovations requiring new administrative structures and increasing public expenditure are unlikely to be supported by the government. But the Housing (Homeless Persons) Act 1977 is an example of an important social reform introduced by a Liberal MP, Stephen Ross, although in its early years it suffered from a lack of government funding and local government support[9]. Sometimes major matters on which the government does not wish to take up a position are left to the initiative of individual MPs. Thus, the Abortion Act 1967 was steered through the Commons by David Steel MP (now Lord Steel).

The Scottish Parliament also makes provision for members' legislation; of which the Dog Fouling (Scotland) Act 2003 is an example of general application. Legislation may also be introduced for the benefit of particular organisations within the devolved matters. Thus St Andrews University wished to be able to award degrees for research in medicine, despite losing the power to award any degrees in medicine in the Universities (Scotland) Act 1966. The local MSP, Mr. Iain Smith, introduced a Bill which became the University of St Andrews (Postgraduate Medical Degrees) Act 2002.

THE LAW COMMISSIONS

In preparing comprehensive schemes of law reform on subjects which are neither of concern to political parties, nor likely to attract

---

8   Eg the Badgers Act 1991.
9   See now Homelessness etc. (Scotland) Act 2003.

the interest of individual MPs, the United Kingdom and Scottish Parliaments have the benefit of the Scottish Law Commission. There is also a Law Commission for England and Wales. A wide area of law exists, covering, for example, contract, delict, succession and property, which is the everyday concern of members of the legal professions, but impinges only rarely on the lives of ordinary people. As such it is often called 'lawyers' law', misleadingly so, for of course it would not exist without the problems of the general public and its rules can dramatically affect their lives. If for instance a person is rendered paraplegic in the course of an operation, legal definitions of what constitutes medical negligence and how it can be proved will have a vital impact on his future standard of living. But such questions are not the everyday concern of the general public. The Law Commissions provide a process by which what the law ought to be on these matters can be exhaustively considered.

The genesis of the Law Commissions is to be found in a book entitled *Law Reform Now*, written by a barrister, Gerald Gardiner, and an academic lawyer, Andrew Martin, in 1964. In it they argued that the Lord Chancellor's Office (for England and Wales) should have attached to it a unit composed of five highly qualified lawyers, independent of government and civil service, to be called Law Commissioners. Their main task would be 'to review, bring up to date and keep up to date what may be called the "general law"'. In the same year Gerald Gardiner gained the opportunity to turn his vision into reality, for he was appointed Lord Chancellor in the Labour government which took office in October 1964. The Law Commissions Act 1965 was one of its first pieces of legislation.

Because of the wide differences between English and Scots law in the areas to be the concern of the Commissioners it was decided that there should be a separate Law Commission for Scotland. But the two Commissions should act in consultation. Scotland had had since 1954 a Law Reform Committee, but it was a part-time body with no permanent secretariat. It had no power to take an overview of the law but could act only on references from the Lord Advocate. Like its English counterpart its output was small. Its main achievement was the important Occupiers' Liability (Scotland) Act 1960, which followed its first report.

In 1965 the Scottish Law Commission was created, with, as its first Chairman, a judge, Lord Kilbrandon, best remembered for leading the committee whose report on children and young persons led to the setting up of children's panels. The numbers of the two Commissions are the same, at five. But the Scottish Commission has usually included two part-time members. Academic lawyers, seconded from the universities or combining work for the

Commission with their university duties, have been prominent in the work of the Commission. There has also usually been one advocate and one solicitor.

Powers of the Commissions

The powers of the two Commissions are laid down in s 3 of the Law Commissions Act 1965. They have a general duty:

> 'to take and keep under review all the law with which they are respectively concerned with a view to its systematic development and reform, including in particular, the codification of such law, the elimination of anomalies, the repeal of obsolete and unnecessary enactments, the reduction of the number of separate enactments and generally the simplification and modernisation of the law'.

In fulfilment of that duty, they have the positive function of submitting programmes of law reform to the Lord Advocate and Secretary of State. Otherwise their functions are of a reactive nature. When requested by these ministers they are to examine specified branches of the law and make proposals for reform by draft Bills or otherwise, and to prepare schemes for the consolidation and revision of statute law. They are also to respond to requests for advice and information from government departments on law reform. They are to receive proposals for law reform from anyone. To facilitate their work they may seek information on the law systems of other countries.

The Scottish Law Commission

The Scottish Law Commission consists in 2007 of five commissioners appointed by the Scottish Ministers. The part-time Chairman is Lord Drummond Young, a judge seconded from the Court of Session. There are three full-time Commissioners, Professor George Gretton, Professor Gerard Maher and Professor Joseph Thomson, and one part-time Commissioner, Mr Colin Tyre QC. Thus within its small number the Commission has representation from the judiciary, the legal profession, and academic lawyers. There are no members who do not have some professional involvement with law. Section 2(2) of the Law Commissions Act 1965 so limits the appointments. However, the Commission has been scrupulous in seeking responses to its proposals from all interested bodies and persons and on some subjects commissioning social research. The Commission has a core staff of five full-time lawyers, drawn from the Government Legal Service for Scotland, and legal assistants appointed for a year at a time, several trainee solicitors and access to draftsmen, though this last has not always proved sufficient.

Its method of working

Each law reform project is assigned by the Commission to a Commissioner (occasionally more than one), who leads a team drawn from the Commission's staff. Their first task is to ascertain exhaustively the existing state of the law and uncover its deficiencies. Some, but not necessarily all, of these may have led to the reference to the Commission. Occasionally this research on the relevant law is entrusted to outside experts. Thus, Sheriff (now Lord) ID Macphail, later a member of the Commission, produced an extensive research paper on the law of evidence, which was revised and published as a book on the subject. Social surveys are sometimes commissioned on the way the existing law is used and perceived by users. The most extensive use of this technique was in preparation for consultative memoranda on debt recovery and diligence. Eight studies were conducted by or for the Central Research Unit of the then Scottish Office. Since then there have been surveys on public attitudes to succession law, on the financial arrangements made on divorce, as shown in a sample of 1,104 divorce actions, on the legal powers of young people and on attitudes to corporal punishment. Commissioners meet fortnightly to debate and approve the work in progress and individual teams meet more frequently to advance their projects.

Once the Commissioners have formed provisional views on the options for change, they issue a discussion paper (formerly called a memorandum) to all organisations and persons likely to be knowledgeable and interested in the subject. Summaries are issued to legal periodicals and the press. More popular pamphlets aimed at the general public have occasionally been issued. Examples are the law regarding young people and that on inheritance. Any member of the public is entitled to a copy of a discussion paper on application to the Commission. Responses, often in the form of answers to specific questions, are invited by a certain date. Sometimes, on very specialised topics, for example the recognition of foreign nullity decrees, consultation is by means of consultation papers issued to a few selected experts.

When the Commissioners have considered the replies and come to a final view on the nature of the reforms, the team produce a draft report for consideration by the Commission, often mentioning the views of respondents. If a Commissioner disagrees with the final recommendations he is entitled to dissent and add a note of dissent to the report, but this has not so far been necessary in a report pertaining to Scotland only. Where legislation is recommended, the report will be accompanied by a draft Bill. Thus, the Commission has addressed itself not only to what reforms are desirable, but also to how they can be achieved. Finally, the government, as the recipient of the report, may choose to issue its own consultative document on how it should respond to the report.

This is the most visible part of the Commission's work and arguably the most important. But it also engages in some painstaking and less dramatic tasks. In its interpretation of its remit in the Law Commissions Act 1965, s 3 (see above) it examines old Acts to see which are ripe for repeal in a Statute Law Repeals Act. There have been 17 of these emanating from the two Commissions and enacted by the UK Parliament. The consolidation of laws covering a certain subject but still needed is another form of 'tidying up' in which the Commission engages. The process allows for obsolete words to be replaced by contemporary ones to make the enactment more comprehensible. For example, the law on criminal procedure in Scotland was consolidated in the Criminal Procedure (Scotland) Act 1995. But one cannot be certain that all the law relating to the topic in the title of the Act is there. That Act by 2006 had been amended nearly thirty times, as well as being interpreted in 35 reported cases. The Court of Session Act 1988 consolidates only certain enactments relating to the Court of Session and repeals only some. A statute law revision report is planned for 2008.

Its achievements

In its early days the Commission issued ambitious Programmes of Reform for the approval of the Lord Advocate, as it might be required to do under the 1965 Act, s 3(1)(b), undertaking to reform areas of law as extensive as obligations and succession. Some foresaw in this power the possibilities of codification on the scale of European systems of law, such as the French and German. But difficulties of achieving agreement on such complex areas, where continental and English models were at odds, doubts about the desirability of such a comprehensive reform, with its implications of permanence, and the number of small-scale referrals to the Commission combined to make progress on Programmes very slow.

A major report on the law of succession, testate and intestate, was issued in 1990, as part fulfilment of the Second Programme of 1968 and has still to be implemented in legislation. A series of innovative Acts has brought a comprehensive restatement of family law in a single consolidating Act closer to achievement, as promised in the Second Programme. Diligence (debt enforcement), also in the Second Programme, was in part codified in the Debtors (Scotland) Act 1987, but now heavily amended in the Debt Arrangement and Attachment (Scotland) Act 2002.

In its 32nd Annual Report in 1997 the Commission announced a new mode of operation. Its Fifth Programme is a rolling one, gathering up whatever has not been completed from previous ones. The projects are arranged under most of the main branches of law. Timetables have been set for each. A short-term project should take just one year; a medium one, two or more years; a long-term one is not time-limited. The 37th Report highlights what progress has been made with each project in these three categories under the Sixth Programme of Law Reform of 2000.

Another factor which can determine the allocation of the resources of the Commission is the collaboration in which it is bound to engage with the other Law Commission. Certain topics are referred by the Lord Chancellor and the Lord Advocate jointly to the two Commissions and result in joint reports; for example, on commercial law topics, such as partnership and the sale of goods, and on questions of private international law. Legislative change may go forward in a single Bill or parallel Bills. Then there are draft English measures which may impinge upon the law of Scotland and which have to be considered within the English Commission's timetable. Requests for informal advice from government departments, often at short notice, add to the Commission's workload and can alter its timetable.

The recommendations and draft Bills of the Law Commissions remain no more than aspirations until they are turned into law by Parliament. Except for consolidation (under the Consolidation of Enactments (Procedure) Act 1949), Bills have to go through the normal legislative process with the possibility of amendment. They have to compete for space in the government's legislative programme, but usually lack any political glamour. But sometimes a sympathetic MP, often a lawyer, who has been fortunate in the private members' ballot, or a member of the House of Lords, will take up a ready-made Commission Bill. For example, the Age of Legal Capacity (Scotland) Bill was introduced in the Commons by Sir Nicholas Fairbairn MP and piloted through the Lords by Lord Macauley QC in 1991. The Scottish Parliament may be expected to be a forum in which there will be more understanding of the objectives of the Scottish Law Commission's proposals and the means of accomplishing them. No special procedure is laid down in the Scotland Act for enacting its Bills, except, under s 36(3), those that restate the law or repeal obsolete laws. The abolition of the feudal system of land tenure, as proposed by the Commission in its Report No 168[10], is one recommendation of the Commission which received a strong ground-swell of support from most interested bodies and most political parties. It was given effect in the Abolition of Feudal Tenure etc (Scotland) Act 2000, s 1 and consequential legislation. In its Annual Reports the Commission lists the Reports that have been implemented, sometimes with their assistance.

Once a report has been enacted it may be referred to in court to help to clear up an ambiguity in the statute or to discover what mischief it was designed to remedy. For example in *MacDonald v H.M.Adv.* 1999 SLT 533 the court, in considering whether a prior statement should be admitted in evidence when a witness refused or was unable to give testimony in court, quoted extensively from a Commission report which had led to this being permitted in the Criminal Procedure (Scotland) Act 1995, s 259.

The Scottish Law Commission has firmly established itself as the paramount means of keeping Scots law in line with changing social needs. With the coming of a Parliament wholly dedicated to Scottish affairs, the rate and speed of implementation of its reports may, it is to be hoped, improve.

---

10 See Rennie 'Abolition of the Feudal System' 1999 SLT (News) 85.

Appendix 1

A NOTE ON THE NATURE OF RULES[1]

Two models of rules

Law is generally thought of as comprising rules. Rules can, however, be usefully divided into more than one type.

Rules in fixed verbal form and rules not in fixed verbal form

Some rules are written, usually in formal, even stilted, language. They are usually written to encapsulate, as exactly as may be, the intentions of those drafting them, and they attempt to cover all likely eventualities. Often they are broken down into sections, subsections, and the like, and these may be indicated by arabic or roman numerals, or letters, and indented. These are draftsman's devices to express the rule logically and unequivocally. Rules of golf clubs and other societies are generally of this nature, as are the rules within a university on who may be awarded an LLB degree. They are what we usually expect rules to look like. They have been referred to as 'rules in fixed verbal form'.

Some rules are not of this nature, however, and we are familiar with the idea of unwritten rules. One of the commonest ways of making a rule is by saying 'don't do that!' (or 'do it this way!', or 'watch me!'). Rules within families and workplaces are commonly of this kind. Here there is no written form of the rule, indeed quite possibly no attempt to articulate at all closely what the rule is. Nevertheless, a rule may be inferred, by observing the prohibition (or requirement) made and the behaviour which precipitated it, against a general knowledge of the relationship between the parties involved. It may be that no clear inference is possible from a single instance, and impartial observers might differ as to what inference is correct. Clarification might be sought by asking for a 'fixed verbal

1 See W Twining and D Miers *How To Do Things with Rules* (4th edn, 1999). The debt owed to them in what follows will be obvious to those who read that book.

461

form' of it; in other words, for this unwritten rule to be written down. However, this may not be possible or reasonable in practice. In this case, only further examples are likely to specify more closely what the rule is. These have been called 'rules not in fixed verbal form'.

The significance of the two types of rule

Both types of rule exist within the legal system. Legislation is generally speaking in fixed verbal form. It is laid down in advance, with reasonably precise instructions to cover foreseeable cases. Common law is not in fixed verbal form. It is inferred from a series of decisions by judges on more or less similar facts, and a clear view may emerge only after quite a number of decisions. These two types of rule require different handling.

With those in fixed verbal form, there is a text which has a single authoritative version. A person applying it cannot alter this text, but only apply what it requires. This may be straightforward, but where it is not, the interpretation applied must be one the text can reasonably bear. It follows that it is all-important to have an accurate version of the text, and that any text departing from the original is not authentic, and cannot be relied upon.

With those not in fixed verbal form, there is no authoritative text in the same sense, although there are decisions, expressed in words. It is important to have an accurate report of what the judge said, but the rule lies not in his precise words. It must be inferred from those words, for he is not constructing a rule in fixed verbal form. The inference can only be made in the light of the dispute which gave rise to the judgment, against the background of the already known rules of the system. Indeed, a clear view of the rule may often emerge only when a series of decisions has been made[2]. In any case, such rules are never in final form, for they can always develop through further precedents, and there can be reasonable argument as to the precise applicaton of the inferred rule to a new set of facts. Each case can indeed be seen as a 'rule-fragment'.

Dealing with rules in fixed verbal form is akin to dealing with a fixed standard like Greenwich Mean Time. There is a correct version which is to be applied, and all other calculations of time of day are

---

2 Jeremy Bentham, a great legal philosopher of two centuries ago, observed (in relation to English law), that common law, working through precedent, operates in the same way as you train a dog. You do not draft precise rules for it in advance. You wait till it does something you regard as wrong, and then punish it. Bentham's mummified body can be viewed in University College, London.

accurate only in so far as they accurately reflect it. Dealing with rules not in fixed verbal form is more like building a dry-stone dyke. Rules of thumb, born of long experience, must be applied to the materials to hand, which are less than ideal, in order to produce a structure which will stand up to the weather and keep the sheep in.

The structure of rules

Rules, whether in fixed verbal form or not, can be said to have a certain structure. They are one class of 'if ... then' statements. In other words, they appear, or can always be redrafted to appear, as statements which say 'if a certain thing or things happen, then there will be a certain result'. In the case of legal rules the result is a legal result, for example a permission or a penalty[3].

Protasis and apodosis

The 'if' part of the statement is sometimes called the *protasis*, and is descriptive. That is, it describes those facts or conditions which have to be fulfilled if the result is to occur. The 'then' part can be called the *apodosis* and, in a legal rule, it is prescriptive. That is, it prescribes the legal result of the fulfilment of the facts or conditions in the *protasis*.

This structure may be obvious, for rules in fixed verbal form, particularly offences, are sometimes actually drafted in something close to this mould. For instance, s 3(1) of the Prevention of Terrorism (Temporary Provisions) Act 1989 read:

> 'Any person who in a public place –
> (a) wears any item of dress; or
> (b) wears, carries or displays any article,
> in such a way or in such circumstances as to arouse reasonable apprehension that he is a member or supporter of a proscribed organisation is guilty of an offence and liable on summary conviction to imprisonment for a term not exceeding six months or a fine not exceeding level 5 on the standard scale or both.'

Commonly, however, the structure is less than obvious[4], particularly so with rules not in fixed verbal form. Thus the rule laid down in

---

3 Not all 'if ... then' statements are rules, let alone legal rules. 'If you hit a person without legal excuse, then you commit an offence' is a simplified legal rule. 'If you hit him, then you will be sorry' is a prediction.
4 'No entry', 'Keep out' and 'Trespassers will be prosecuted' can all be redrafted into something like 'If a person enters, then he will be punished'.

Donoghue v Stevenson 1932 SC(HL) 32 could be rendered as something like: If you act in such a way as to make it reasonably foreseeable that you will injure someone, if that person ought reasonably to be in your contemplation, and if such a person is in fact injured as a result of your act, then you are liable to compensate that person for the injury suffered[5].

It is often useful to analyse rules in terms of this structure in order to understand them. Firstly, it may be useful in specifying what the facts in the *protasis* actually are[6]. Secondly, it may be useful in specifying the relationship between the various facts[7]. The relationship between the facts in a *protasis* is either cumulative (all must be true) or alternative (either must be true). Thirdly, it draws attention to, and requires specification of, the *apodosis*[8].

This form of analysis can usefully be done by constructing algorithms, although these are rarely found in legislation[9].

5 But see Ch 12.
6 The prevention of terrorism offence includes 'wears ... any article' as well as 'wears any item of dress', so badges are included as well as uniforms.
7 Thus 'wears' or 'carries' or 'displays' are alternatives, so any one of them suffices. On the other hand, the requirement that it be 'in such a way or in such circumstances as to arouse reasonable apprehension ...' of certain things is cumulative, and must be fulfilled in all cases, or no offence is committed. The important words (expressed or implicit) are 'and' and 'or'.
8 The penalty is imprisonment, or a fine, or both, subject to certain maxima.
9 One example found in quasi-legislation is Chart I in Annex 2 (NHS Charges to Overseas Visitors: Manual for Hospital Staff) to Scottish Home and Health Department Circular 1982 (GEN) 29 (NHS Treatment of Overseas Visitors: Summary) (reference NFE/4/2) dated 15 December 1982 to health board secretaries. These attempted to explain the effect of the National Health Service (Charges to Overseas Visitors) (No 2) (Scotland) Regulations 1982, SI 1982/898.

Appendix 2

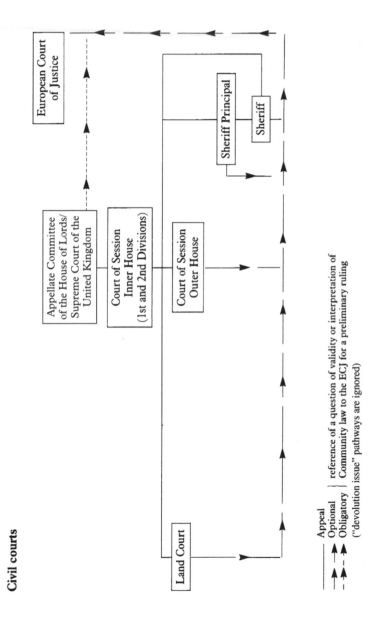

SCOTTISH COURTS (SIMPLIFIED)

Civil courts

- European Court of Justice
- Appellate Committee of the House of Lords/ Supreme Court of the United Kingdom
- Court of Session Inner House (1st and 2nd Divisions)
- Court of Session Outer House
- Sheriff Principal
- Sheriff
- Land Court

Appeal

Optional — reference of a question of validity or interpretation of
Obligatory — Community law to the ECJ for a preliminary ruling
("devolution issue" pathways are ignored)

Criminal courts

Solemn procedure (with jury)

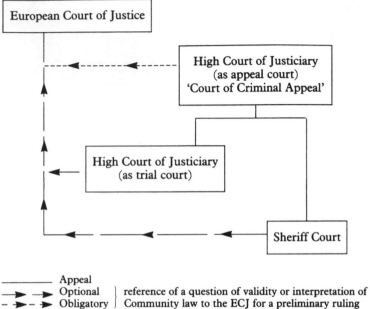

_____ Appeal

⟶ ⟶ Optional ⎫ reference of a question of validity or interpretation of

- ▶- ▶ Obligatory ⎭ Community law to the ECJ for a preliminary ruling

("devolution issue" pathways are ignored)

Summary procedure (without jury)

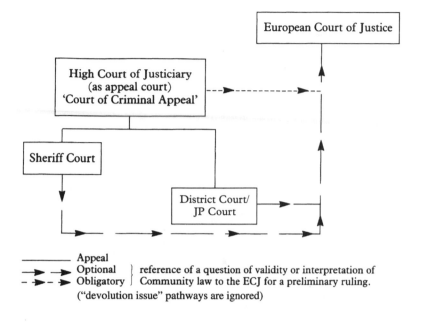

─────── Appeal
───➤ ──➤ Optional   } reference of a question of validity or interpretation of
─ ➤─ ➤ Obligatory   } Community law to the ECJ for a preliminary ruling.
            ("devolution issue" pathways are ignored)

ENGLISH AND WELSH COURTS (SIMPLIFIED)

Civil courts

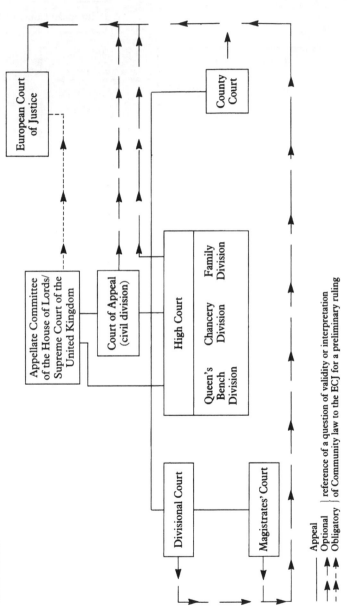

Criminal courts

Indictable procedure (with jury)

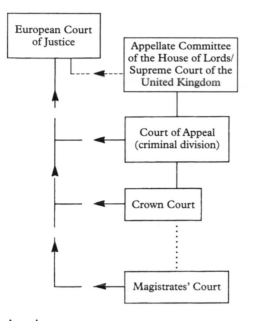

_____ Appeal
◄— ◄— Optional ⎫ reference of a question of validity or interpretation of
◄ - ◄ - Obligatory ⎭ Community law to the ECJ for a preliminary ruling
. . . . Committal for trial ie preliminary sieving process

Summary procedure (without jury)

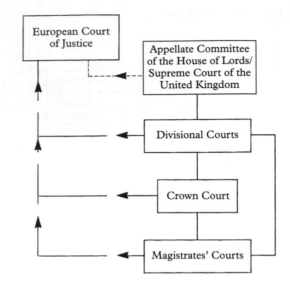

_____ Appeal
 Optional } reference of a question of validity or interpretation of
Obligatory } Community law to the ECJ for a preliminary ruling.

NORTHERN IRELAND COURTS (SIMPLIFIED)

Civil Courts

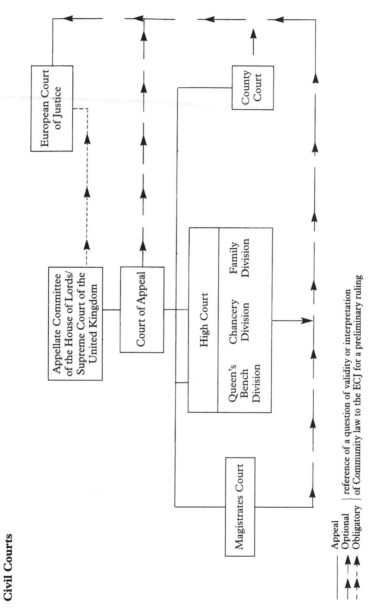

Criminal courts

Indictable procedure (with jury)

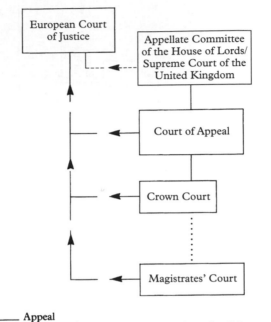

_____ Appeal
◄— ◄— Optional ⎫ reference of a question of validity or interpretation of
◄ – ◄ – Obligatory ⎭ Community law to the ECJ for a preliminary ruling
. . . . Committal for trial i e preliminary sieving process

Summary procedure (without jury)

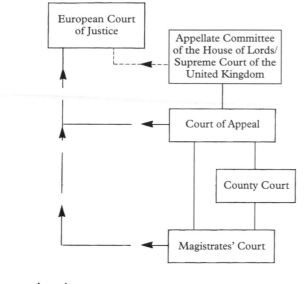

————— Appeal

————▶ Optional } reference of a question of validity or interpretation of

- ▶- ▶ Obligatory } Community law to the ECJ for a preliminary ruling.

SOME UNITED KINGDOM TRIBUNALS

References to the European Court of Justice omitted and otherwise slightly simplified.

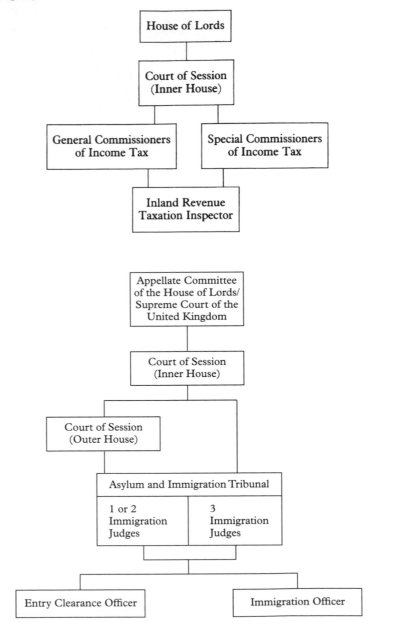

House of Lords

Court of Session
(Inner House)

Employment
Appeal Tribunal

Employment
Tribunal

Appellate Committee
of the House of Lords/
Supreme Court of the
United Kingdom

Court of Session
(Inner House)

Court of Session
(Outer House)

Commissioner

Appeal Tribunal

Secretary of State

Appendix 3

'EUROPE'

COUNCIL OF EUROPE	EUROPEAN UNION (including 'three pillars' of: – **European Community** – **Common Foreign and Security Policy** – **Police and Judicial Co-operation on Criminal Matters** – formerly Justice and Home Affairs)
47 Members (2007) (founded 1948, UK founder member)	**27 Member States (2007)** (founded 1950s, UK joined in 1972)
Strasbourg	**Brussels** European Commission Council of the Union COREPER European Parliament (committees) **Strasbourg** European Parliament (plenary sessions) **Luxembourg** European Parliament (secretariat) European Court of Justice and Court of First Instance (and 'judicial panels')
(**European Commission on Human Rights** – merged with European Court of Human Rights in 1998)	**European Commission**
Committee of Ministers	**Council of the Union** (*alias* 'Council of the European Union' and formerly 'Council of Ministers') **European Council**
Parliamentary Assembly	**European Parliament**
European Court of Human Rights	**European Court of Justice** and **Court of First Instance (and 'judicial panels')**

Nearly 200 treaties between various members including principally:
 	
– **European Convention on Human Rights and Fundamental Freedoms** ('ECHR')
 	
– but also a variety of matters from social security to cybercrime, via patents, extradition, travel by young persons on collective passports, exchange of blood grouping reagents, liability of hotelkeepers for property of guests, protection of the archaeological heritage, protection of pet animals, cinematographic co-production, etc.
	Various treaties, including:
	
	– **Treaty Establishing the European Community** ('TEC', alias EC Treaty, and formerly EEC Treaty, aka, Treaty of Rome')
	– **Treaty on European Union** ('TEU', alias, Maastricht Treaty')
	– **Treaty of Amsterdam** ('ToA')
	– **Treaty of Nice** ('ToN')
	
	Also 'secondary legislation' under TEC (main means of legislating):
	– **Regulations**
	  (thousands every year)
	– **Directives**
	  (hundreds every year)
	– **Decisions**
	  (hundreds every year)
	
	TEC + secondary legislation = 'Community law' (alias 'EC law' or possibly 'European Union law')

No **'direct effect'** of human rights or other law (i e no direct incorporation into UK law), but: – **most of rights under ECHR transferred into UK law by Human Rights Act 1998** and contents of various other treaties similarly taken into account in UK legislation – **right of individual petition** to European Court of Human Rights, which may produce a favourable decision (including compensation), which the state is obliged by the ECHR to effect, but which is unenforceable in domestic law.	**'Direct effect'** (i e direct incorporation into UK law) of some Community law, i e: – **parts of Treaties** – **all Regulations** – **Directives under some circumstances** – **Decisions** Community law **without 'direct effect'** transferred into UK law by: – **statutory instruments under European Community Act 1972, s 2,** or – **Act of Parliament.**

Index

[references are to page numbers]

A

Act of Parliament, *see also*
LEGISLATION
Scotland, *see* SCOTTISH PARLIAMENT
UK, *see* UNITED KINGDOM
Acts of Adjournal, 270–1, *see also*
DELEGATED LEGISLATION
Acts of Sederunt, 270–1, *see also*
DELEGATED LEGISLATION
Administrative quasi-legislation,
173–7
Advocate, *see* LEGAL SERVICES
Advocate-depute, 132
Advocate General (ECJ), 124
Advocate-General for Scotland, 42,
64, 118
Draft Bills sent to, 223
Agency, regulatory
quasi-legislation, 173–7
Alternative dispute resolution, 129,
148–9
Amendments to Acts, *see also*
REFORM OF LAW
SI, by, 265–7
Scottish Acts, 250–1
UK Acts, 215–16, 219, 234, 265
Apodosis, **344**
Appeal, 86
civil, 116–17, 130–1
criminal, 116–17, 137–9
decisions, *ratio decidendi* in, 348–51
final, 116–19
Appellate Committee of the House
of Lords (ACHL), 37, 86, 89,
111–17
appeal to, 101, 105, 110, 116–17
criminal (English courts), 116–17
English Court of Appeal, from,
153, 154
final civil appeal for both Scotland
and England, effect, 301–2
NI Court of Appeal, from, 156
chair, 114

Appellate Committee of the House
of Lords (ACHL)—*contd*
composition, 114
judges, 113–16
eligibility and selection, 115–16
origins of, 113
replacement proposal, 111–12, 113
Scottish courts, appeals from,
112–13
stare decisis in, 361–4
work of, 116–17
Arbitration, 147–8, 149, 410
Assistance by way of representation
(ABWOR), 427, 428, 431

B

Bills
Scottish Law Commission, 458–9
Scottish Parliament, 251–4,
451–2
Committee legislation, 253
Private, 447, 449
UK Parliament, 219–26
guillotine, effect of, 450
Private, 235–6, 453
Burgh courts, 18, 92–3
By-laws
Scottish, 288, 291
UK, 271, 275–6

C

Cases, *see* JUDICIAL PRECEDENT; LAW
REPORTS
Circulars, government, 175–7
Citation of law
cases, *see* LAW REPORTS
Community law, 201–6
cases, 377, 378
Scotland, 258, 259
SSIs, 291–2
UK, 240
Statutory Instruments, 276–8
Citizens advice bureaux, 436–7

Citizen's Charters, 174, 177
Civil law systems, 161–2, 181, 340
Civil legal aid, *see* LEGAL AID
Civil procedure, 126–31
    adversarial proceedings, 126, 127
    appeal, 130–1
    commercial, informal, 129
    debate, 127–8
    diligence, 131
    dispute resolution, 129, 147
    expenses, 131
    inquisitorial, 126, 129
    interlocutors, 128
    judge's decision, 128
        enforcement, 131
    non-contentious petitions, 129–30
    ordinary procedure, *see* SHERIFF
        COURT
    parties, 127
    pleas, 128
    proof, 127
    remedies, 130
    review of, 129
    small claim, 128
    summary cause, *see* SUMMARY
        PROCEDURE
    summons or initial writ, 127
    witnesses, 127
    written pleadings, 127
Codes of Practice, 174–5
    Highway Code, 174–5
    professional, 175
Committees
    ad hoc, 452–3
    Committee of Inquiry, 222
    Committee legislation, 255
    departmental, 452
    Judicial Studies, 91–2, 100, 104,
        109
    Law Reform Committee, 454
    select, 449
        European Law, on, 200
    Subordinate legislation, 290–91
Common law
    countries with system of, 162, 339
        precedents cited in Scottish courts,
            366
    law reporting, *see* LAW REPORTS
    meanings, 10–11, 340
    precedent as part of, *see* JUDICIAL
        PRECEDENT
Community law, *see* EUROPEAN
    UNION

Computerised retrieval systems,
    396–7
    commercial databases, 397
    Community law, 202–6, 396, 398
    human rights, 396, 398
    Scotland, 259
        delegated legislation, 293
        pre-1707 Acts, 258
    UK, 239–40, 396–7
        delegated legislation, 281–2
Constitutional background, 37–8
    Scottish Parliament, *see* DEVOLUTION;
        SCOTTISH PARLIAMENT
    UK, *see* UNITED KINGDOM
Constitutional conventions
    quasi-source of law, 172–3
Construction, *see* STATUTORY
    INTERPRETATION
Conveyancer, *see* LEGAL SERVICES
Court(s), 85 *et seq*
    adversarial proceedings, 126, 127
    appeal, 86, 116–17
    application of legislation by judges,
        see STATUTORY INTERPRETATION
    civil, 86, 87, 97, 100–1, 104
        English and Welsh, 152
        hierarchy, 356–8
        precedent in, 360–66
        special jurisdiction courts, 365–6
    criminal, 86, 87, 93, 96–7, 101, 102
        development of law by, 445
        hierarchy, 356–8
        precedent in, 367–71
    delegated legislation, striking down
        of, 278–80
    delegation to, 270–1
    devolution issue, decision on, 63–4
    ECJ, reference to, *see* EUROPEAN
        UNION
    First Minister responsibility, 97–8,
        100, 108
    hierarchy, 85–6, 161, 354, 356–8
    High Court of Justiciary, *see* HIGH
        COURT OF JUSTICIARY
    historical
        decisions of, law from (judicial
            precedent), 4, 19, 31–2, 158,
            see also JUDICIAL PRECEDENT
        development of, 16–18
        restructuring, 31
    House of Lords (ACHL), *see*
        APPELLATE COMMITTEE OF THE
        HOUSE OF LORDS (ACHL)

Court(s)—*contd*
legislative power
exceptional exercises of, 337–9
judges coming close to, procedural
legislating, 447–9
Northern Ireland, 155–6
precedent system, *see* JUDICIAL
PRECEDENT
procedure, 126 *et seq, see also* CIVIL
PROCEDURE; CRIMINAL
PROCEDURE
public nature of, 126
Scottish, 92–121
meaning, 87
Sheriff, *see* SHERIFF COURT
Supreme Court of the UK, proposal,
see SUPREME COURT OF THE UK
tribunals, *see* TRIBUNAL
**Court of Criminal Appeal, 102,
104**
Court of the Lord Lyon, 121
Court of Session, 103, 104–11
appeal from, 105, 110
delegation to, 270–1
historical, 105–6
Inner House, 104, 106, 107, 109,
110
appeal to, 110, 120, 360
judges, 103, 104–5, 106–9
appointment of, 88–90, 107–9
payment, 109
removal, 109
'Senators of the College of Justice',
107
titles, 108–9
judicial review, 111, 130
jurisdiction, 104–5, 110
Lords Ordinary, 104–5, 106, 360–1
Lord President, 103, 106, 107, 109
nobile officium, 111, 337–9
Outer House, 104, 106, 110
appeal from, 110
precedent in, 360–1
procedure, 128–9
summons, 129
reclaiming motion, 360
sittings, 104
Temporary, 106, 108
training, 109
work of, 104, 110–11
Court of Teinds, 120
**Criminal Case Review
Commission, 138–9**

Criminal cases
citation, 379–80
Law Reports, 388
Legal aid, 430–1
Criminal courts, *see* COURT(S)
**Criminal Injuries Compensation
Scheme, 144, 151, 166**
Criminal offence
court exceptional legislative powers,
338–9
Criminal procedure, 126, 131–9
acquittal, 134
adversarial nature, 132
appeal, 137–9
conviction, 134, 136, 137–8
diversion schemes, 136–7
evidence, 134
exclusion of public, 131
expenses, 139
guilty plea, 134, 136
jury, *see* JURY
non-guilty plea, 134
public nature, 131
public prosecution system, 132–3, *see
also* PROCURATOR FISCAL
reference procedures, 138–9
sentence and penalties, 134, 136, 137
solemn, 134, 135
summary, 134–5
trial, 134–5
verdict, 134
Crown, *see* UNITED KINGDOM
Crown counsel, 132
**Crown Office and Procurator
Fiscal Service (COPFS), 132**
Custom, 3, 10–11, 158, 170–1
delegation by legislation to, 171
enforceability, 170–1
precedent, becoming, 339

D
Databases, *see* COMPUTERISED
RETRIEVAL SYSTEMS; ONLINE LAW;
WESTLAW
Declaratory power
High Court of Justiciary, 338–9
Defender, 127, 129
Law Reports, in, 382
case citation, position in, 377–9
Delegated legislation, 160, 216
interpretation, 302
Scotland, 268–9, 283 *et seq*
by-laws, 288, 291

Delegated legislation—*contd*
  Scotland—*contd*
    citation, 291–2
    controls, 284–91
    devolution, and, 284–88, 291, 292
    existing SIs, 285–6
    form of, 291–2
    judicial control and ultra vires
        doctrine, 292
    non-statutory instrument form,
        288, 291
    principles applying, 284
    procedure, 290
    publication, 292
    replacement of existing SIs,
        286–7
    reserved matters, 284–5
    SSIs, 283, 284, 289, 290–1
    sub-delegated legislation, 283,
        287, 291
    UK delegated legislation applying
        to, 283, 289
    use and range, 288–9
  UK, 261 *et seq*
    amendment of Acts ('Henry VIII
        clauses'), 265, 266
    amendment of legislation to
        remove 'burden', 234, 266–7,
        274
    benefits and purposes, 261–2
    body delegated to, 263, 269–71
    by-laws, *see* BY-LAWS
    citation, 276–8
    control of use, 267–8
    degree of control, classification by,
        268, 272–6
    delegate and name, classification
        by, 268, 269–71
    extraordinary use, 265–7
    form of, 268, 276–7
    framework Acts, controversial use
        for, 265
    judicial control and ultra vires
        doctrine, 278–80
    meaning, 261
    nature of, 263–8
    non-statutory instrument form,
        272, 275–6, 282
    orders, regulations and rules,
        269–71
    publication, 280–2
    standard use for detail, etc, 264
    statistics, 268

Delegated legislation—*contd*
  UK—*contd*
    Statutory Instruments, 159, 268,
        272–5, 276
    types, 264–7
    uses, 264–7
    wide delegation, 265–7
Devolution, 38, 40–1, 47 *et seq*
  'agency arrangement', 58, 285
  delegation central to, 283–4
  devolution issues, procedures for,
      62–3, 254
    Judicial Committee of the Privy
        Council role, 86, 118, 119,
        365, 370–1
  devolved powers and reservations,
      48–51, 52–3, 57–9
    complexity, 58–9
    delegated legislation, and, 284–8,
        291, 292
    effect of, 209
    general reservations, 48
    specific reservations, 48–50
    transfer power of UK government,
        58
  'executive devolution', 58, 285
  institutions, *see* SCOTTISH
      PARLIAMENT
  legal system, responsibility for, 50
  legislative competence of Scottish
      Parliament, *see* LEGISLATIVE
      COMPETENCE
  Memorandum of Understanding, 59,
      61–2
  progress of, 47–8
  UK Parliament power and role after,
      51, 57–8, 243–4
    Advocate-General for Scotland,
        42, 64, 118
    delegated legislation, as to, 284–5,
        289
    Secretary of State for Scotland, 41
***Dial-a-law*, 436**
Diligence, 131
District Court, 92–4, 96–7
  justices, *see* JUSTICES OF THE PEACE
  Justices Committee, 93
  precedent in, 368
  prosecution system, 132, 134
  replacement of, 92
  work of, 96–7
Document of title
  origins, 13

E

Election Petition Court, 120–1

Electronic legal database, *see*
ONLINE LAW

Employment tribunal, 87,
141–145
Appeal Tribunal, 142
appeal from, 110
chairman, 143
expenses, 142
lay members, 143
legal aid for representation, 433
precedent, 367

English and Welsh courts, 152–5
civil courts, 152–3
County Courts, 152
Court of Appeal, 153, 154
Lords Justices of Appeal, 153
criminal courts, 153–4
Crown Court, 153–4
High Court of Justice and Divisions,
152–3, 155
House of Lords, *see* APPELLATE
COMMITTEE OF THE HOUSE OF
LORDS (ACHL)
judges, 152–3, 154–5
magistrates' courts, 152, 153–4
precedent from, 366

English law
influence of, 21

Equity, 340

Europe, Council of, *see* HUMAN
RIGHTS

European Court of Human Rights,
see HUMAN RIGHTS

European Court of Justice, *see*
EUROPEAN UNION

European Union, 179 *et seq*
COREPER, 82–3, 188
Commission, *see* 'European
Commission' *below*
Committee of the Regions, 84
'Community law'
assent procedure, 189
characteristics of, 322
co-operation procedure, 188
co-decision procedure, 189
construction of legislation under
influence of, *see* STATUTORY
INTERPRETATION
law reports, 390–3
meaning, 179–81
powers, 187–8

European Union—*contd*
'Community law'—*contd*
precedent system, and civil courts,
360–1, 364, 367
precedent system, and criminal
courts, 368, 370, 371
procedures, 188–9
publication and citation, 201–6
status, 3, 34, 38, 47, 80, 125, 160
types, 182–7
Council of Europe distinguished, 65,
75, 82
Council of the Union (Council of
Ministers), 81–2, 182, 186–7
legislative powers, 187
Court of Auditors, 84
Court of First Instance, 84, 123,
124–6
Decisions, 186, 190
binding nature, 195
publication and citation, 205–6
'democratic deficit', 189
direct applicability, 190–1
'direct effect' of law, 80, 125, 184,
190–5
conditions for, 192–3
delegated legislation, use for, 264–5
effect on Member States'
legislative powers, 208
horizontal, 192
types of legislation considered,
193–5
UK court interpretation of, 326–7
vertical, 192
Directives, 185–6, 190
binding nature, 193–5
implementation in Member States,
193, 198
publication and citation, 205–6
ECJ, 65, 75, 84, 123–6
application of legislation by,
321–25
citation of cases, 377, 378
court hierarchy, position in, 357,
372
decisions of, and national courts,
372
direct applicability, decisions build
on, 190–1, 192
judges and composition, 123–4
languages, 126
literal technique, 324
location of, 123

European Union—*contd*
  ECJ—*contd*
    precedent, and, 372–3
    procedure in, 124–6
    reference to, 86–7, 197
    role, 189–90
    schematic technique, 324
    teleological technique, 324
  ECOSOC, 84
  EUR-lex, 202, 203, 205, 206
  EUR-OP, 201, 203, 205
  European Commission, 81, 182, 186
    COM documents, 206
    legislative powers, 187–8
  European Community, 76, 179–81
  European Parliament, 83–4
    powers, 187–8
    publication of documents, 206
  'European Union law', 181
  'pillars' of, 180–1
  evolution of, 76–9, 180
    current EU membership, 80
    original membership of EEC, 80
  human rights enforcement through,
      181–2, 330–1
  institutions and bodies, 81–4
  interpretation issues, 125–6, 197,
      321–9, 372
  national law, relationship with, 190–5
    case showing, 191
    direct effect, 191–5
    invocation by national court, 191
    primacy of Community law, 190–1
  Official Journal, 201–2, 203, 205
  Opinions, 186
  primacy, 190–1
  publication of material, 201–6
  Recommendations, 186
  Regulations, 182, 184–5
    binding nature, 193
    publication and citation, 205–6
  restriction on Scottish legislative
      competence, 54
  Treaties, 182–4, 187–8, 317
    binding nature, 193
    interpretation of, 322–7
    languages, 183
    principal, list of, 182–3
    principles stated in, 208
    publication and citation, 203–4
  UK law, relationship with, *see* UNITED
      KINGDOM
  website, 203

Executive, *see* SCOTTISH PARLIAMENT
Executry services, 440

F
Feudalism, 11–15
  land law ill-suited to Industrial
      Revolution, 30
  legal institutions emanating from,
      16–17
  procedural law, 19
  tenure, 11–14

G
Government
  delegation control, 272–3
  delegation to, 269–70
  UK, *see* UNITED KINGDOM
Governmental guidance, 173–7
  circulars, 175–7

H
Hansard, **309–13**
Heritable property
  diligence, 131
  origins, 13
High Court of Justiciary, 102–4
  administrative responsibility for, 103
  appeal from, 104
  appeal to, 97, 102–3, 104
  court of appeal, sitting as, 104
  declaratory power, 338–9
  historical, 103
  judges, 103
  jurisdiction, 102
  Lord Justice General, 103
  nobile officium, 337–8
  precedent in, 369–70
  prosecution system, 132, 134, 135
  work of, 102, 104
Historical background, 9 *et seq*
  Enlightenment, 29–30
  independence, 14–15
  Industrial Revolution/nineteenth
      century, 30–1
  medieval period
    early period, 11–15
    feudal system, *see* FEUDALISM
    later middle ages, 15–21
  'nation', Scotland as, 9–10, 14–15,
      16, 22, 23–4
  recent times, 32–5
  Reformation, 21–2
  religious issues, 21, 24–6, 27

Historical background—*contd*
Scottish Assembly Campaign, 33
statehood
    early signs, 12
    emergence, 16, 21
Treaty of Union, 27–8
Union of the Crowns, 23–4
Home Secretary (UK), 44
House of Lords, 108, 110
appellate committee (court), *see*
    APPELLATE COMMITTEE OF THE
    HOUSE OF LORDS (ACHL)
Bills, role as to, 224, 225, 226
Select Committee on European
    Union, 200
UK Parliament, 44, 45–6, 52
Human rights, 3–4, 37, 64, 65 *et seq*
Community law, enforcement
    through, 181–2
'Convention rights', 159, 228
    compatibility of UK law with, 229,
        330–2, 333
Council of Europe, 65–7, 122
devolution, issues relating to, 54, 64
European Convention on Human
    Rights, 67 *et seq*, 121, 159, 228
    declaration of incompatibility,
        effect of, 331–2
    enforceability, 70–3
    interpretation of UK legislation,
        effect on, 330–2
    rights and freedoms under, 67–70
    significance, 159, 208
European Court of Human Rights,
    121–3
    application procedure, 122–3
    court hierarchy, position in, 357
    enforcement of judgments, 123
    judges, 122
    law reports, 393–4
    location of, 122
    official languages, 122
    petition to, 70–1, 87, 121–3
    precedent system, and, 360, 361,
        364, 368–9, 370, 371, 373
interpretation issues, 329–32
legislation (Human Rights Act),
    228–9
    court account of ECJ
        jurisprudence, 330, 373
    embeds human rights, 228
    interpretation to give effect to
        Convention Rights, 331

Human rights—*contd*
national (UK) remedies, use of, 71,
    72–3
public authority incompatible act,
    73, 229
restriction on Scottish legislative
    competence, 54, 64
Scottish cases, 73–4
Scottish Commission, 74–5

I
Indictment, 135
English, 153
**'Institutional Works', 158, 162,
    166–9, 444**
Institutions, 47 *et seq*, *see also*
    SCOTTISH PARLIAMENT
courts, *see* COURT(S)
EU, *see* EUROPEAN UNION
UK Parliament, *see* UNITED KINGDOM
Insurance company
legal advice from, 439, 440
Interlocutors, 128
Interpretation
Community law, *see* EUROPEAN
    UNION
statutory, *see* STATUTORY
    INTERPRETATION

J
**Judge, *see also* COURT(S); JUSTICES
    OF THE PEACE**
ACHL, 113–16
application of legislation by, 296–300
appointment, 87–91, 115–16
    Judicial Appointments Board for
        Scotland (JABS), 89–90,
        116
    methods in Scotland, 89–91
'commercial court', 129
Court of Session, 106
English, 152–3, 154–5
    Lord Chief Justice, 154
High Court, 103, 106
    Temporary, 103
independence issues, 88–9
precedent, creating, *see* JUDICIAL
    PRECEDENT
promotion, 88
reform of law by, 441, 444–9, *see also*
    DECLARATORY POWER; NOBILE
    OFFICIUM
    appellate courts, 445

Judge—*contd*
  reform of law by—*contd*
    criminal law, regular development
      of, 445
    example, 441
    invitation to Parliament to amend,
      446
    overruling unsatisfactory decision,
      446
    procedural, specialised form of
      legislation, 448–9
    prospective, 447–8
    'reformulating' cases, 447
  training, 91–2, 104
**Judicial Committee of the Privy
  Council, 117–19**
  appeal court, as, 117–18
  devolution issues, role, 86, 118, 119,
    253, 365
  jurisdiction, 117–18
    devolution, 86, 118, 119
  members and composition, 118–19
  precedent system, and
    civil matters, 365
    criminal matters, 370–1
    devolution issues, 365
    relationship with ACHL, 364
  reference of Bill to (legislative
    competence), 253
  removal of Senator, role in, 109
  work of, 119
Judicial precedent, 335 *et seq*
  Appellate Committee of House of
    Lords, 361–4
    binding itself, 363–4
    Judicial Committee of Privy
      Council decisions, 364
    precedents from other UK
      hierarchies, 362–3
  approving, 355
  binding nature, 354–6, 358–9
  citation, *see* LAW REPORTS
  civil courts, 360–6
  common law systems, in, 163,
    336–7, 339–40
  Court of Session, in, 361
  criminal courts, 367–71
  District Court, 368
  earlier and later precedents, 161
  English courts/other common law
    systems, 365, 371
  European Court of Human Rights
    position of, 373

Judicial precedent—*contd*
  European Court of Human Rights—
    contd
    Scottish civil courts, and, 360,
      361, 364
    Scottish criminal courts, and, 368,
      370, 371
  European Court of Justice
    position of, 372–3
    Scottish civil courts, and, 360,
      361, 364, 367
    Scottish criminal courts, and, 368,
      370, 371
  following, 355
  High Court of Justiciary, 369–70
  higher and lower courts, 161, 354,
    356–8
  historical, 4, 19, 31–2
  Law Reports, *see* LAW REPORTS
  obiter dicta, 335, 353, 359
    definition, 353
  per incuriam, 358
  persuasive, 354–5, 359
  Privy Council, Judicial Committee
    of, 365, 370–1
  ranking of, 161
  ratio decidendi, 335, 343, 344–53
    definition, 344–5
    distinguishing contrasted, 355,
      356, 357
    example case (*Donoghue v
      Stevenson*), 352–3
    facts of case, 347–8
    generality, level of, 348
    identification of, 346–51
    'in point', 354, 355, 357
    leading judgment, 349, 350
    majority decisions, 349
    multiple, 348–51
    riders to definition, 345–6
    separate judgments, 348–9, 350–1
    single judgment, 348, 351
    wide or narrow, 351–3
  Scots law acceptance of, 162, 340–2
  Sheriff Court, in, 360, 368
  single precedent, 358
  source of law, 158, 161, 163–4,
    335–44
    adjudication system, and, 343, 346
    authority as, 336–7
    emergence of rules from cases,
      342–44
    nobile officium, 111, 337–9

Judicial precedent—*contd*
source of law—*contd*
rules not in 'in fixed verbal form',
335–6
special jurisdiction civil courts, 365–6
stare decisis, 335, 354–9
court hierarchy for, 356–8
exceptions where does not bind,
358–9
factors, 354–5
meaning, 354
reason for, 354
terminology, 355–6
statutory interpretation, use for,
306–7
tribunals, 367
Judicial review, 111, 130
Judicial Studies Committee, 91–2,
100, 104, 109
Judiciary, *see* COURT(S); JUDGE
Jury, 102, 103, 134, 135
appeal from jury trial, 131
civil trial, 127
Justice of the Peace courts, 92, 95,
97
Justices Committee, 93
Justices of the Peace, 92, 94–6
appointment, 89, 90–1
new regime, 95–6
clerk of court, 93, 96
JP courts, 92, 95, 97
lay justices, 88, 92, 95
stipendary magistrates, 92, 95
training, 96
work, 96–7

L
Land Court, 365
Lands Tribunal for Scotland, 120,
142
legal aid for representation, 433
Lands Valuation Appeal Court, 120
Law, introductory
bodies and organisations, 4
changes and amendments, 5–7, 8
hybrid system, Scots law as, 162, 340
judge-made, 4, 19, 31–2
meaning, 2–3
power, link with, 7
reasons for, in society, 1–2, 5, 7–8
Roman law, influence of, 21, 162,
340
statutes, 3–4, 20, 32–3

Law, introductory—*contd*
study of law at Universities, 34
historical, 20–1
written law, 34–5
historical, 19, 20, 28–30
'Institutional Works', 158, 162,
166–9
use of textbooks for interpretation
of legislation, 304
Law, sources, 157 *et seq*
custom, *see* CUSTOM
formal, 157–8
major, 157–8, 161–4, 331
minor, 158, 161, 164
historical, 157
'in fixed verbal form', 302, 318
rules not in, 298, 335
legislation, *see* LEGISLATION
meaning, 157–9
precedent, *see* JUDICIAL PRECEDENT
quasi-sources, 159, 171–7
administrative quasi-legislation,
173–7
constitutional convention, 172–3
ranking of, 159–61
reform of law, role in, 444–9
Law centres, 438–9
Law Commission for England and
Wales, 222, 453–5
genesis of, 454
membership, 454–5
powers, 455
recommendations of, 458
Law Commission, Scottish, *see*
SCOTTISH LAW COMMISSION
Law Officers of the Crown
Scotland, 59–60
UK, 42–3
Law Reform Committee, 454
Law Reports, 375–98
citation of cases, 377–82
Community law, 377, 378
criminal cases, 379–80
English civil cases, 395
English criminal cases, 380
location of case (year, judge etc),
380, 381–2
names, 377–9
'neutral', 381–2
'official', 377, 386–7
reporting restrictions, confusion
from, 379
traditional, 377

Law Reports—*contd*
Community law reports, 390–3
All England Law Reports
European Cases, 392–3
Common Market Law Reports,
392–3
Official, 390–2
databases, *see* ONLINE LAW
English law reports, 394–6
All England Law Reports, 396
Official, 394–5
The Law Reports, 395
form of, 382–6
catch words and Headnote, 383–4
commentary, 385
counsel and solicitors, 380, 385
decision (disposal), 385
facts, recital of, 384
judges, 383
law cited, 384
names, 382–3
number and date, 383
opinions, 385
reporter's name, 386
human rights reports, 393–4
commercial, 394
European Human Rights Reports,
393
Official, 393
Journals and newspapers, 394
overview, 375–7
Scotland, 376–7
Scottish Council of Law Reporting,
376, 387
Scottish Court Service website, 386
Scottish law reports, 386
commercial, 387
early reports, 390
Greens Weekly Digest, 389–90
House of Lords, 387, 388
Justiciary Cases, 387–8
nominate reports, 387
official, 386–7
Practicks, 376, 390
Scots Law Times, 389
Scottish Civil Law Reports, 388
Scottish Criminal Case Reports,
388
Session Cases, 387–8
specialised, 394
**Law Society of Scotland, 414–15,
421**
accounts inspection, 417

Law Society of Scotland—*contd*
admission as solicitor controlled by,
413
Client Relations Office and
Committees, 423–4
complaints against, 425
complaint to, 421, 423–4
appeal, 424
Dial-a-law, 436
Guarantee Fund, 419
professional indemnity insurance,
Master Policy, 420
solicitor-mediators, sponsorship of,
412
roll of solicitors, 408
website, 436
Legal advice, *see* LEGAL SERVICES
Legal aid, 132, 139, 427–36
administration, 428–9
advice and assistance, 427–8, 432–3,
435–6
expenditure limits, 428, 434
assistance by way of representation
(ABWOR), 427, 428, 431
background to, 427
civil, 429–30
statistics, 435
clawback, 432–3
costs, 431
criminal, 430–1
defects and weaknesses, 431–36
eligibility, 429–31, 432
group actions, 434
heritable property, Board expenses
from, 432
social security benefit recoupment,
433
tribunals, 433–4
Legal database, *see* ONLINE LAW
Legal representatives, 126
Legal services, 399 *et seq*
advocates, 196, 406–8
Complaints and Investigating
Committees, 423
'core forensic immunity', extent
of, 409, 421–2
Discipline Tribunal, 423
duty to court, 421
Guide to Professional Conduct, 415
historical, 400–2
legal expertise, 408–10
professional negligence, 409,
421–2

Legal services—*contd*
advocates—*contd*
rights of audience, 425
training and admission, 413–4
alternative delivery methods, 426–40
background, 399–400
citizens advice bureaux, 436–7
conveyancers
licensed, 426, 440
qualified, 439–40
executry practitioners, 440
Faculty of Advocates, 406–7, 413
complaints to, 424–5
Dean's role, 423
law centres, 438–9
legal aid schemes, *see* LEGAL AID
'legal profession', 405–6, 426
money advice centres, 437
notary public, 412
Ombudsman, 424–5
replacement proposed, 425
solicitor-advocates, 412–3, 422
solicitors, 126, 408
accounts, 417
advertising, 416
Client Relations Office and
Committees, 423–4
Codes of Conduct, 415–6
complaints against, 419–21, 423–5
Discipline Tribunal, 415, 421, 424,
425
fees, remedy for excessive, 421
Guarantee Fund, 419
historical, 402–5
inadequate services, 420–21
incorporated practices, 417
Law Society of Scotland role, *see*
LAW SOCIETY OF SCOTLAND
legal expertise, 408–9, 410–12
limited partnerships, 417
multi-disciplinary practices
(MDPs), 417–8
multi-national practices, 418–9
partnerships, 417
Practice Guidelines, 417
professional negligence insurance,
419, 420
rights of audience and
representation, 425–6
specialists, 411–12
training and admission, 413–4
standards and supervision, 414–6,
419, 422–24

Legislation
application of, by judges, 296–300,
see also STATUTORY
INTERPRETATION
'Community legislation', 181, *see also*
EUROPEAN UNION
delegated, *see* DELEGATED
LEGISLATION
drafting methods, 297, 298–9
earlier and later, principle for, 160
financial, 229–30
interpretation issues, *see* STATUTORY
INTERPRETATION
Scottish, *see* SCOTTISH LEGISLATION
source of law, 157–8, 163
prerogative legislation, 158,
164–6
special cases, 228–36
status of, 160
subordinate or secondary, *see*
DELEGATED LEGISLATION
UK Parliamentary, *see* UNITED
KINGDOM
Legislative competence, *see also*
DEVOLUTION
Act outside, 62, 64
breadth and concept of, 50–1, 52–4,
57–65, 244
checks for, during progress of Bills,
251, 253
provisions outside, 52–4, 64–5
'Sewel Convention' and 'Sewel
Motions', 226–7, 245, 248, 287
status of Scottish legislation, 160
Literal interpretation
Rule. Literal, 318, 319
technique of ECJ, 324
Local Act
Scottish, 256
UK, 235, 240
Local government
delegation to, 270, 275–6
'public authority', *see* HUMAN RIGHTS
Lord Advocate (Scotland), 59–60,
61, 64, 118, 132
reference in criminal case, 138
Lord Chancellor, 43–4, 89, 113–14,
154
change in status, 43
Secretary of State for Justice, role as,
43
**Lords of Appeal in Ordinary (Law
Lords),** 113, 119, 153

M
MPs (UK Parliament), 9, 46
  select committees, 449
MSPs (Scottish Parliament), 51–2,
  56
Mediation, 148–9, 408
  solicitor-mediators (ACCORD and
    CALM), 412
Minister for Justice (Scotland),
  60–1
Ministry of Justice (UK), 43–4
Mischief Rule, 317–8, 319
Money advice centres, 437
Moveable property
  origins, 13

N
Negligence, professional
  advocates, 409, 422
  solicitors, 419, 420
Nobile officium, **111, 337–8**
  citation, 379
  invoking of, 337–8
    criminal cases, 338
  nature of, 337
Northern Ireland courts, 155–6

O
Obiter dicta, *see* JUDICIAL
  PRECEDENT
Office of Public Sector Information
  website, 293
Ombudsman
  Legal Services, *see* SCOTTISH LEGAL
    SERVICES OMBUDSMAN
  Parliamentary Commissioner for
    Administration (PCA), 149–51
Online law, 396–8
  cases, 381–2, 386–7, 397
  legislation, 202–6, 239–40
  Lexis-Nexis Butterworths, 397, 398
Orders, 269–70, *see also* STATUTORY
  INSTRUMENT
Ordinary procedure, 128–9
  summons, 129

P
Parliament
  European, *see* EUROPEAN UNION
  Scottish, *see* SCOTTISH PARLIAMENT
  UK, *see* UNITED KINGDOM
Parliamentary Commissioner for
  Administration, 150–1

Police
  conditional fixed penalty offer in
    road traffic case, 136
Precedent, see JUDICIAL PRECEDENT
Prerogative legislation, 158, 164–6
  names and citations, 166
Prescription, 171
Presumptions, 313, 314–17
  legal, 314–5
  linguistic, 315–17
Privy Council, 117
Procurator fiscal, 93, 94, 96, 102,
  132
  appeal by, 138
  COPFS, 132
  decision not to prosecute, 137
  depute, 132
  diversion schemes, 136–7
  solemn procedure, role in, 135
  summary procedure, role in, 134
  warning, 137
Protasis, **344**
Public authority, *see* HUMAN
  RIGHTS
  delegation to, 271, 275–6
Public Defence Solicitors' Office,
  133
  criminal legal aid system, 430–1
Public prosecution system, 132
Publication of legislation
  Community law, 201–6
  computerised, *see* COMPUTERISED
    RETRIEVAL SYSTEMS
  Scotland, 257–9
    chronological, 258
    commercial reprints, 258
    encyclopaedic series, 258
    indexes, etc, 258
    pre-1707 Acts, 257
  Scottish delegated legislation, 292–3
    chronological, 292–3
    indexes, 293
  UK delegated legislation, 280–1
    chronological series, 280
    commercial reprints, 281
    encyclopaedic series, 280
    indexes, 281
  UK Statutes, 237–41
    chronological, 237
    commercial reprints, 238
    encyclopaedic series, 238
    indexes, etc, 239
    Is It In Force?, 239

Pursuer, 127, 129
Law Reports, in, 382
case citation, position in, 377–9

Q
Quasi-legislation
administrative, 173–7

R
Ratio decidendi, *see* JUDICIAL
PRECEDENT
Reform of law, 441–59
Law Commissions
England and Wales, *see* LAW
COMMISSION FOR ENGLAND
AND WALES
Scottish, *see* SCOTTISH LAW
COMMISSION
Law Reform Acts, 450–1
reasons for
expansion of law system, 443
political pressure, 442–3
social or moral change, 441–2,
442
technological development
prompting, 442
vehicles for, 444–53
custom, 444
institutional writers, 444
judges, *see* JUDGE
Scottish Parliament, 451–3
UK Parliament, 449–51
**Registration of Voters Appeal
Court, 120**
Regulations, 269–70, *see also*
DELEGATED LEGISLATION
Remedies (civil), 130
Repeal
Scottish Parliament Acts, 248–9
UK Parliament Acts, 215–16, 219
Restrictive Practices Court, 365
Roman law, 21, 162, 340
Royal Commissions, 222, 452
Royal prerogative, *see* PREROGATIVE
LEGISLATION
Rules, 269–70, *see also* DELEGATED
LEGISLATION
**Rules of interpretation, 313,
317–19**
Golden Rule, 318–19
Literal Rule, 318, 319
Mischief Rule, 317–18, 319
Rules of law, *see* LAW, SOURCES

S
Scotland, historical background,
see HISTORICAL BACKGROUND
**Scottish Council of Law Reporting,
376**
**Scottish Criminal Case Review
Commission, 138–9**
Scottish delegated legislation, *see*
DELEGATED LEGISLATION
Scottish Executive, 9
Scottish Land Court, 120
**Scottish Law Commission, 34, 231,
454–9**
Bill, ready-made, 458–9
creation, 454
membership, 454–6
powers, 455
Programmes of Reform, 427–8
recommendations of, 458–9
reform, consideration of need for,
446
Reports of, use for statutory
interpretation, 313, 459
working methods, 456–7
**Scottish Legal Aid Board, 133,
428–9, 432–3, 435–6,** *see also*
LEGAL AID
**Scottish Legal Services
Ombudsman, 424–5**
Scottish legislation, 243 *et seq*
Acts of Scottish Parliament, 47, 54,
62, 243–50, 284
amendments, 248–9
citation, 258, 259
Commencement Provisions, 249
Committee legislation, 255
Contents, 246
Explanatory Notes, 249–50, 252,
311–12
Extent Provisions, 249
Headings, 247
hybrid, 256
Interpretation Sections, 248
Local Acts, 256
Long Title, 247
Marginal Notes, 247
Members', 255
Number, 246
Parliamentary Stages for Bills,
251–4
Personal, 256
post-enactment checks, 86, 118,
119, 253

Scottish legislation—*contd*
　Acts of Scottish Parliament—*contd*
　　Preamble, 247
　　pre-enactment legislative
　　　competence checks, 251, 253
　　pre-Parliamentary Stages for Bills,
　　　251
　　pre-1707 Acts, 257
　　procedure, 250–56
　　'public' and 'general', 245–6
　　public/private distinction, 256
　　repeals, 248–9
　　Royal Assent, 252, 253
　　Schedules, 219
　　Secretary of State forbidding,
　　　253–4
　　Sections, 249
　　Short Title, 246, 249
　　Standing Orders, 251–2
　　Statement of Enactment, 246
　　transitional provisions, 249
　　background to, 243–5, *see also*
　　　DEVOLUTION; LEGISLATIVE
　　　COMPETENCE
　delegated legislation, *see* DELEGATED
　　LEGISLATION
　initiation of, 250–1
　interpretation issues, 332–3
　publication, 257–9
　subordinate nature, 244
　types and form, 245–50
Scottish Parliament, 47, 51–5
　Acts of, *see* SCOTTISH LEGISLATION
　activities, 54–5
　Administration, 47, 56, 61
　Committee structure, 55
　Community law, relationship with,
　　see also UNITED KINGDOM
　　Committee concerned with EC
　　　legislation, 200
　　direct effect, 199
　　implementation, 198
　composition, 51
　constituencies, 46, 51–2
　constitution and role, 51–5
　devolution to, *see* DEVOLUTION
　election of, 51
　　first (1999), 9, 33
　　period, 52
　　third (2007), 48, 55
　Executive, 47, 55 *et seq*
　　appointment, 55–7
　　civil servants, 56–7

Scottish Parliament—*contd*
　Executive—*contd*
　　'devolved competence', 50–1, 57,
　　　62
　　functions, and extension of, 57–9
　　shared powers, 57
　financial arrangements, 61
　First Minister, 56
　historical background
　　law from, middle ages, 20
　　origins, 13
　　post-English Restoration, 25
　　union of English and Scots
　　　Parliaments, 26–8
　Law Officers of the Crown, 56,
　　59–60
　legislation, *see* SCOTTISH LEGISLATION
　legislative competence, *see*
　　LEGISLATIVE COMPETENCE
　legislative use of, 226–7
　members (MSPs), 56
　　member of UK House of
　　　Commons/Lords as well, 52
　　voting for, 51–2
　Minister for Justice, 60–1
　Parliament House Book, 238
　'public authority', 73, 229
　reform of law by, 447–9
　Sewel Motions, 226–7, 245, 248,
　　287
Scottish Public Service
　Ombudsman, 151
Scottish Solicitors' Discipline
　Tribunal, 415, 421, 424
　powers, 424
　reference from Ombudsman to, 425
Sentence, 134, 136, 137
Sewel Convention and Motions,
　226–7, 245, 248, 287
Sheriff, 98–100, 107–8
　appointment, 88–90, 99
　Deputes, 98–9
　historical background, 17–18, 31,
　　98
　　hereditary office, 18
　honorary, 100
　part-time, 74, 99, 100
　Principal, 98, 101
　removal and fitness, 100
　salaried, 99–100
　substitute, 98–9
　temporary, human rights case, 74
　training, 91–2, 100

Sheriff Court, 86, 96, 97–8
appeal from, 104, 110
civil, 101
criminal, 102, 368
appeal to, 101
jurisdiction, 97, 100–2, 368
ordinary procedure, 128–9
precedent in, 360, 368
prosecution system, 132, 134
work of, 100–2
Sheriffdom, 95–6, 97–8
regional clerk, 98
Sheriff Principal, 98, 101
Small claim, 128, 435
Solemn procedure, 134, 135–6, *see
also* JURY
Solicitor, *see* LEGAL SERVICES
Solicitor-advocate, 126
**Solicitor-General (Scotland),
59–60, 132**
Stare decisis, *see* JUDICIAL
PRECEDENT
Statutes, *see* LEGISLATION
**Statutory instruments, 160, 268,
272–5,** *see* DELEGATED
LEGISLATION
amendment of legislation by, 265–7
approval, 274
citation, 276–8
classification of delegated legislation
as, 272
controls, 274–5
dating and numbering, 273, 277
definition, 273
procedure for, 273–4
Scottish (SSI), 283, 284, 289
controls over, 290–1
Statutory interpretation, 295 *et seq*
Community law mode, 301, 321–9
direct effect, law with, 325–7
ECJ methods of construing
Community law, 321–4
ECJ techniques of construing
Community law, 324–6
European Convention on Human
Rights, modifying effect of,
329–30
Human Rights Act 1998,
interpretation under, 330–32
law without direct effect, after
implementation, 327–9
'purposive' interpretation of
implementing legislation, 329

Statutory interpretation—*contd*
Community law mode—*contd*
UK court approach when
Community law element,
326–9
'construction', 298–300
delegated legislation, 302
Act of Scottish Parliament, 332–3
drafting methods, 297, 298–9
issues involved, 295–6, 300–1
judges' application of legislation,
296–300, 302–3
traditional mode in UK, 301–321
basic rule synthesised, 320–1
earlier judicial decisions, 306–8
earlier legislation, 306–8
Explanatory Notes, 311–12
Golden Rule, 318–19
Hansard, 309–11
'intention of Parliament', 302–3
International Treaties, 308–9
Interpretation Act 1978, 308
legislative text, first consideration
of, 303–6
Literal Rule, 318, 319
Mischief Rule, 317–18, 319
other documents for consideration,
306, 311
presumptions, legal and linguistic,
313, 314–17
Reports of Scottish Law
Commission, 313
Rules, 313, 317–20
Scottish same as, 301–2, 320
**Subordinate Legislation
Committee, 290–1**
**Subordinate or secondary
legislation,** *see* DELEGATED
LEGISLATION
Summary procedure
appeal, 104
criminal, 134–5, 136
complaint, 134
District Court cases prosecuted by, 96
procedure and financial limits, 128–9
Sheriff Court, 101–2
Summons, 127, 129
**Supreme Court of the UK, 37, 46,
86, 105, 111–17**
appeal from Scotland to, 117
devolution issues, future role, 118
judges, 115
proposal for, 111–12, 113

T

Textbooks
written law, *see* LAW, INTRODUCTORY
Trade union
legal advice from, 439
Tribunal, 87, 106, 140–7
areas covered, 140
case statistics, 145
Council on Tribunals supervision,
144–5
decisions and enforceability, 143
employment, *see* EMPLOYMENT
TRIBUNAL
examples of, 140, 141
free, 142
informal procedure, 141–2, 145–6
legal aid position, 433–4
legal powers, 143
members, 140–1, 143
precedent in, 367–8
rapid settlement, 142
representation, 142, 146
review of tribunals,
recommendations, 146
Scottish, 144
Social Security, 87, 146
Solicitors' Discipline Tribunal, 415,
421, 424, 425
specialisation, 142–3
Tribunal Service, 146–7

U

Ultra vires doctrine
judicial control of delegated
legislation through, **278–80, 292**
review of ultra vires decision, *see*
JUDICIAL REVIEW
United Kingdom
commencement of, historical, 27
Community law, relationship with,
195–200
case showing, 191
committees concerned with
Community matters,
199–200
direct effect examined, 191–5,
199–200
implementation where no direct
effect, 198
invocation of Community law by
national court, 191
legislation to ensure direct effect
(ECA 1972), 195–6, 199

United Kingdom—*contd*
Community law, relationship with—
contd
primacy of Community law,
190–1, 199
reference to ECJ, 197
constitution, 38–65
background, 38–9
changes, 37, 45
conventions of, 172
principle of parliamentary
supremacy, 47
courts and tribunals, 85 *et seq, see also*
COURT(S)
Crown, 39–40
meaning, 39
prerogative legislation, 158, 164–6
delegated legislation, *see* DELEGATED
LEGISLATION
EC legislation, official and
commercial publication
Regulations, Directives and
Decisions, 205–6
Treaties, 204
Government, 39 *et seq*
Advocate-General for Scotland,
42, 64, 118
Cabinet, 40
composition, 40
Home Secretary, 44
legislation, 40, 46
Ministry of State for Justice/Lord
Chancellor, 43–4, 89
Scotland (formerly Scottish)
Office, 40–1, 47
Secretary of State for Scotland, 41
Law Officers of the Crown, 42–3, 64
legislation, 207–40
amendments, 215–16, 219, 234,
265
Arrangement of Sections, 211, 213
Bills and stages of, 219–26
Chapter Number, 211, 217
citation, 241
codification, 233
Commencement Provisions, 217
Committee Stage, 224, 225–6
Committees and consultation on
Bills, 222, 225–6
consolidation, 231–3
Drafting by Parliamentary
Counsel, 223–4
Enacting Formula, 212, 224

United Kingdom—*contd*
legislation—*contd*
  enactment procedure, 226–7
  Explanatory Notes, 219, 223, 311
  Extent Provisions, 218
  financial, 230
  First Reading, 224, 225
  Headings, 214, 305
  House of Lords' role, 224, 225, 226
  human rights compatibility, scrutiny for, 229
  hybrid, 236
  initiation of, 220–1
  Interpretation Sections, 215, 300
  introduction of Bill to Parliament, 224
  Local Acts, 235, 240
  Long Title, 211–12
  Marginal Notes, 213–14, 301–2
  Marginal References, 214
  Members', 234
  overview, 209–10
  Parliament Acts 1911 and 1949, under, 230
  Parliamentary stages for Bills, 224–6
  Personal, 235–6, 240
  Preamble, 212, 305
  pre-Parliamentary stages for Bills, 221–4
  Private Bill, 235–6
  public/private distinction, 235
  publication, 237–41
  repeals, 215–16, 219
  Report Stage, 224, 226
  Royal Assent, 212, 226
  Schedules, 219
  Second Reading, 224, 225
  Sections, 212–13, 214
  Sewel Convention and Motions, 226–7, 245, 248, 287
  Short Title, 210–11, 217
  Statute Law Revision and Repeal legislation, 230–1
  Third Reading, 224, 226
  transitional provisions, 216

United Kingdom—*contd*
legislation—*contd*
  'Westminster stage', 224–6
  'Whitehall stage', 221–4
Parliament, 44–7
  Acts of, *see* 'legislation' *above*
  control over delegated legislation, 272–3, 278–80
  House of Commons, 44, 46, 52
  House of Lords, 44, 45–6, 52
  legislation status, 160, 207
  legislative power, 46, 208
  legislative procedure, 219–27
  MPs, 9, 46
  reform of law by, 451–2
  Scottish constitutencies, 46
  Scottish Committees, 47
  select committees, 449
  Sovereign, 44, 45
  'supremacy', 46, 199, 208
  status of Scotland within, 9, 33
Utilities by-laws, 271

W
Website
  European Community, 203
  Law Society of Scotland, 436
  Office of Public Sector Information, 293
  Scottish Court Service, 386
  UK Parliament, 310
Witnesses
  civil proceedings, 127
  criminal proceedings, 134
Westlaw
  cases reported on, 388, 389, 392, 395
    Common Market Law Reports, 392
    Westlaw Scots Law, 397
  EC Treaties, 204
  SIs, 281
  Scottish Acts, 259
  UK Acts, 240
Writ, initial, 127
Written law, *see* LAW, INTRODUCTORY